KEYSTONE CANOEING

BY EDWARD GERTLER
A GUIDE TO CANOEABLE WATERS
OF EASTERN PENNSYLVANIA
THIRD EDITION
SENECA PRESS
1993

The Seneca Press
530 Ashford Road
Silver Spring, Maryland 20910
Printed in the United States of America
By BookCrafters, Inc.
ISBN 0-9605908-6-2

Foreword

I began canoeing in 1962, in the Washington, D.C. area, under the tutelage of the Canoe Cruisers Association (CCA). The CCA has long been a large and energetic club with a strong tradition of education, safety and trip organization. Taking advantage of this, for many years I joined club outings, eager to expand my horizons and to explore new streams. But after a while I noticed that most of our paddlers did most of their cruising on streams of northern Virginia and West Virginia. I asked veteran after veteran why this was so, and they did not know. They just assumed that there was little worth doing north of the Potomac. Also there was only one popular guidebook back in those days, and it was on northern Virginia and eastern West Virginia. So it being clear that I would have to find the answer for myself, I struck out, often alone, to find the truth. In 1979 I reported my findings to the paddling community by publishing *Maryland and Delaware Canoe Trails*.

Pennsylvania, though it was just as close to us as West Virgina, was even more of a mystery. Washington paddlers visited the Yough and Lehigh, but little more. As the years went by, however, I befriended many Pennsylvania paddlers and discovered that they had plenty of local favorite streams. But still, nobody had much of an overview, and no guidebooks filled that void. The Pittsburgh AYH was attempting to inventory the western third of the state, but only some local guides or outdated literature incompletely covered the east. So once again I saw the need and decided that I would write the guidebook.

My guiding principle (no pun intended) has been to only describe those streams which I have personally canoed. But because so many of Pennsylvania's streams are small and ephemeral, sticking to this ideal presented a big challenge. It was clearly a task for someone of sound body and unsound mind. It meant commuting from D.C. to Pennsylvania weekend after weekend, taking weeks off during spring melt, and becoming mysteriously ill when heavy rains inconveniently struck during the work week (I hope my boss does not see this). It meant paddling in rain, snow, and, when I misread the map mileages, even in the dark. It meant tricking whitewater boating friends into helping me explore flatwater, swamps, and sewers. It meant begging, borrowing, and anything but stealing shuttles. Anything to catch a creek while it was up. And I enjoyed every minute of it.

Why did I cover what I covered? I wrote about eastern Pennsylvania because that was where there was the greatest need for a comprehensive and dependable guidebook. But I included a special selection of western streams because these were some of my favorites, and I wanted you to know about them. Since *Keystone Canoeing* would, for many people, be their only Pennsylvania guidebook, it seemed to me that if they did not read about them here, they would never know about these beauties. I also admit that I missed a few of the eastern streams. My only excuse is that I have yet to paddle them. Finally, I confined my coverage to streams, lakes formed by damming of those streams, and tidewater. I omitted most other lakes and ponds because of their sheer number and my aversion to paddling still water.

In exploring for this book I met many friendly people living along these streams and added many of these streams to my list of favorites. I hope that as you follow in my wake you will keep the goodwill going and that some of these streams will become your favorites too. I hope also that you will become the protector of these streams if they are ever threatened by dams, channelization, or unwise development. They are your streams. Enjoy them and please see to it that others can do the same.

Acknowledgements

While my name goes on the cover, there is a whole army of friends, family, business associates, acquaintances, and good Samaritans whose contributions have made this book (my dream) possible.

My thanks to Roger Corbett, author of *Virginia Whitewater* and others, who started me on all this book writing nonsense several years ago, coaching me, encouraging me, lending me materials, and altogether donating mounds of his time. Also, twenty years ago, when I was a weak, inept, and unpromising novice, Roger played a similar role in developing my canoeing skills (did he create a monster?). I wish to thank my good friends Tom and Paulette Irwin, who helped me explore many of these streams, ran shuttles, lent me maps, and gathered valuable field data. Thanks to Don Rau and Bert Hauser of Word Design, who set the galleys, contributed to the cover and interior design, and generally assumed responsiblity for turning my manuscript and maps into a slick publication. Thanks to Charlie Walbridge, who modelled for the front cover and who provided shuttles and shelter on my explorations around the Philadelphia area. Thanks to Barb Brown for the back cover portrait. Thanks to the staff of the Library of Congress Geography and Map Room for attending to my map research needs, to my parents for providing me with valuable office space and other logistical support, to Bob Helm of the U.S. Geological Survey, Harrisburg, for supplying me with flow records and gauge rating tables, to the staff of the U.S. Weather Service River Forecast Center, Harrisburg, for answering questions and hundreds of calls for gauge readings (often for weird and obscure gauges that they thought no canoeists ever cared about), to Megan Kealy for her expert cartographic advice, to Rich Olin and various damkeepers of the Corps of Engineers, to the public relations people of Penelec, P.P. & L., Bethlehem Steel, New Jersey Zinc, Pennsylvania Fish Commission, and Pennsylvania Bureau of State Parks, to Peter Wilshusen of the Geological Survey, a chance acquaintance from an Appalachian Trail hike, who directed me to a wealth of geological references, and to the various paddlers who accepted my invitation to go up to Pennsylvania and explore streams that they had never heard of (often for good reason).

Finally this page would not be complete without a warm thanks to all the citizens of the Keystone State, especially those people who live along the rivers, who stopped and picked me up when I was hitch-hiking my shuttles, who watched over my boat while I was off on those shuttles, who fed me, who entertained me, and who, time after time, made me feel like a guest, not a tourist. They made Pennsylvania's tourism promotion slogan, "You've Got A Friend In Pennsylvania," really come true.

Contents

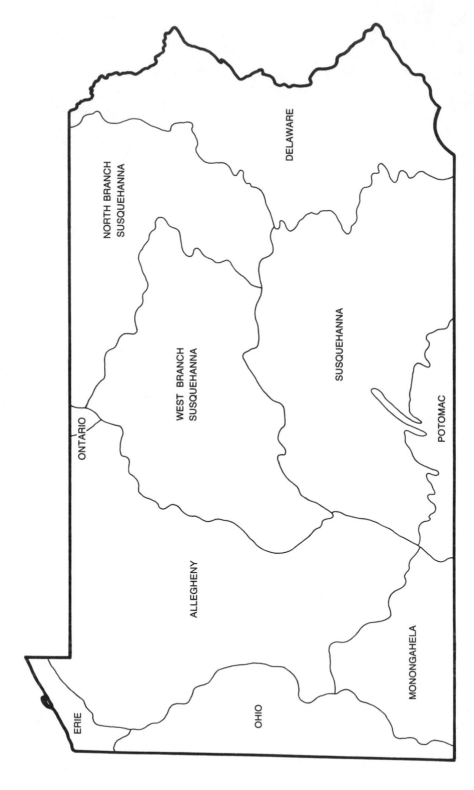

Pennsylvania by Watershed

ERIE

ONTARIO

NORTH BRANCH
SUSQUEHANNA

DELAWARE

WEST BRANCH
SUSQUEHANNA

ALLEGHENY

SUSQUEHANNA

OHIO

MONONGAHELA

POTOMAC

Chapter 1
Introduction

My idea of a good canoeing guidebook is that it should be exactly that—an inventory and description of boatable streams. It should provide all the hard data necessary to plan a trip, yet it should be pleasant and interesting to read, so as to provide some good armchair canoeing on some frozen winter evening. In addition, I believe that good maps are necessary to tie together all the strange names and to explain the shuttle far better than words can. Such a package, hopefully, will answer the question of where to go canoeing, whether the inquirer is a thrill-seeking expert or the most casual or timid beginner.

Recognizing that a lot of beginners and novices might be using this book, there was a temptation to dedicate much of this chapter to how to canoe. While I have included a few basic tips, I refrained from adding any more because the wealth of literature and club, Red Cross, and commercial boating intruction available in this area can do a much better job. I urge you to use these resources.

So let us now get down to what is important.

How To Use This Book

I have organized this book by major watersheds, starting in the east. Each chapter has been ordered from the downstream end to headwaters. When the branches have branches, they have been ordered in the same manner. In addition, I have included a watershed map with each chapter's introduction. If you are searching for streams in a specific area, this order will be convenient. If you are alphabetically oriented, there is an alphabetical index at the end of the book. This index also specially identifies all streams with advanced whitewater sections, to help serious whitewater paddlers to get to the meat of the state.

Each river report starts with a (usually) brief **Introduction**. This may locate the stream, identify its outstanding qualities or deficiencies, or inject some historical or contemporary color.

Next the **Section** is identified. I have selected sections most often because there was some unifying characteristic to that stretch—either aesthetic, the nature of the whitewater, or duration of its boatable season. Sometimes the section is just what comprises a good day's run. And on many small streams, it is simply the whole stream.

Each section begins with a table of vital statistics: gradient, difficulty, distance, time, scenery, and map.

Gradient describes how steeply the stream drops. It is expressed as feet per mile and comes from dividing the total drop of the segment by its length. Runnable gradients range from zero on lakes and tidewater to as much as 160 feet per mile on little torrents like Jacobs Creek in western Pennsylvania. If the gradient is sufficiently unevenly distributed, I have also included the gradient of the steepest stretch (example 10 @ 50 means ten miles at 50 feet per mile).

The gradient is a general indication of the likelihood of rapids. The higher the gradient, the more rapids or riffles likely to be present. Uneven distribution of drop or high water levels, however, can produce difficult whitewater with relatively low gradients. For example, look at the pool and drop nature of the 27 fpm Lower Yough or the Susquehanna below Holtwood Dam, at 80,000 cfs, which only drops a few fpm. Conversely, an evenly distributed steep gradient on a small stream can result in surprisingly easy whitewater, as on Big Cove Creek in Fulton County.

Difficulty is based on the international whitewater rating scale that runs from 1 to 6 and a smooth water scale that goes from A to C. I have expanded the whitewater numbers to include + and − to improve its precision. I have expressed difficulty as a range (example 1 to 3 +) because few rivers stay the same difficulty for very far. If a stream includes a markedly different stretch or one bad rapid, I have set that difficulty off with a comma (example 1, 4 −). The inventors of the rating scale intended it to be quite descriptive and objectively applied. It can be interpreted as follows:

A. **Smooth Water.** This is a condensation of the A to C scale which describes if there is current, and how much. Since current velocity varies according to both flow and cross sectional area of the stream, it is meaningless to describe typical current velocity. If a stream is flat, that is all that matters.

1. **Easy.** Short straightforward riffles usually formed by gravel or sand bars, low ledges, or constrictions of the river. Waves are less than one foot high and little maneuvering is required. Routes are easy to determine and all riffles are followed by adequate rescue opportunity.

2. **Medium Difficulty.** Rapids are more frequent, composed of waves less than two feet high and in regular patterns with easy eddies. There are more rocks and obstructions, but maneuvering is still easy and rescue spots are still plentiful.

3. **Difficult.** Rapids are long and require extensive maneuvering. Both ledges and waves are up to three feet high, and waves are often irregular. Course is not always easily recognizable. Rescue opportunities are spaced farther apart.

4. **Very Difficult.** Long, pushy extended sets of rapids with high, irregular waves. Boulders and ledges block the course and along with powerful crosscurrents require abrupt and intricate turns. Course is often difficult to recognize and scouting is often necessary. Rescue is difficult.

5. **Exceedingly Difficult.** Long, heavy rapids with high, irregular waves and powerful crosscurrents, or steep, complex, boulder-clogged rapids with poor visibility. Big drops and powerful hydraulics are unavoidable, and ability to catch small, fast eddies is essential for control. Rescue is very difficult and scouting is often unavoidable.

6. **Utmost Difficulty.** All the difficulties stated in Class 5 carried to the extreme. Running such water involves an unusual risk of life.

The objective classification system, unfortunately, can be influenced by subjective assessments, including such variables as experience of the rater, size of his or her ego, effect of adverse weather, and the number of wipe-outs, swims, and rolls associated with a particular trip. There has been a trend in recent years, as paddle skills and equipment improves, to downgrade river ratings. The Lower Yough, for example, was regarded an expert's-only run in the 50's and early 60's. Now, some people begin their whitewater paddling on that section. Of course, the river has not changed any. What is particularly important to recognize is that Class 6 does not hold a monopoly on risk of life. If you are improperly prepared, almost any grade of whitewater can hurt you. In fact, most whitewater casualties that have happened in recent years to competent whitewater paddlers have occurred on only Class 3 and 4 water.

To standardize my ratings in this book, I have intended them to describe the given river at a level of about six inches of runnable water. If you encounter higher or lower water, be prepared for a different difficulty. Since there is no standardization of ratings between various guidebooks, do not count on my application of the rating scale to necessarily match those of other authors. Though I have tried to take the middle of the road, the best way for you to get a feel for my ratings is to first try a stream well within your ability and then take it from there. Finally, please note that this is a whitewater rating system only and thus only addresses conditions encountered on an ideal unobstructed stream. In reality, many of Pennsylvania's small streams are complicated by fallen trees, fences, and other strainers that greatly increase the difficulty and risk involved in paddling these streams. To this, add factors of coldness of water, coldness of weather, and your physical condition to determine if you can handle a given class of difficulty.

Distance is expressed in statute miles and is rounded off to the nearest tenth mile. The number describes the distance from one end of the stream segment to the other, even if there is no convenient access to one of those points. This is all pretty straightforward until one must describe big lakes, such as Raystown, or wide rivers, such as the Susquehanna. Here distances are measured down the centerline of the stream. Remember that on the Susquehanna you can add an extra mile to the trip by just having to paddle to a take-out on the opposite bank.

Sometimes distance does not tell the whole story. For example, a battle through a mile of the strainer-choked upper Yellow Breeches Creek will consume about as much time and effort as ten miles on the upper Delaware at highwater. And battling a mile of headwinds on Raystown Lake is far different from a mile of sprightly Cedar Run. So you must allow for this with time.

Time is also included, expressed in hours and rounded off to the nearest half hour. This represents paddling and portaging time only. Be sure to allocate extra time for lunch, scouting, and rescue.

Scenery is self explanatory. I can sometimes be hard to please, especially since I explore many streams in the cold months when there is no foliage to hide the trash, summer homes, industry, etc.

Maps listed are those applicable to that section. The numbers correspond to those on the lower right hand corner of the map.

Next **Hazards** are listed. This inclusion is usually redundant, but better safe than sorry. You will note that I have often indicated which dams and falls are runnable. Unless otherwise stated, if I have declared a drop runnable, it is because I have tried it successfully. As a rule, I discourage beginners and novices from following my lead, because the consequences to the unprepared can be as serious as death in a keeper hydraulic. On the other hand, experienced paddlers who understand these hazards might as well enjoy as much drop as the stream has to offer. But do so at your own risk.

Water Conditions describe the best time of year and under what hydrological and meteorological conditions one can expect to find adequate water in the stream. Since I detest driving long miles and endless hours, while wasting gallons of precious gasoline, to find an empty river, the time spans recommended for catching a stream are slightly conservative. The creeks may retain water longer than indicated, but do not count on it.

Most streams in this book are small and convey a rapid runoff. Some general rules describe when you should most likely find water in them. First, best flow conditions occur between November 1 and April 30. One reason is that this is the time that large frontal storms, that drop large amounts of rain over a wide area, roll through the state. Summer showers, in contrast, can be incredibly heavy, but they often only dump on a few square miles. Also, in the cold months vegetation, which in summer consumes a tremendous amount of moisture, is dormant. Second, Pennsylvania, being a northern state, often accumulates snow for a few months and then, over three or four weeks in spring, this melts, assuring weeks of wonderful and consistent raised water levels.

As mentioned earlier, the volume of flow can determine the difficulty, not to mention the floatability, of a stream. Since paddlers can seldom measure streamflow, they attempt to establish on each stream a point of reference, called a **Gauge**, to relate stream height at a given point to flow and canoeability. Sometimes the point of reference is just a joint on a bridge pier, or the depth of an indicative riffle. A great number of Pennsylvania streams, however, are graced by some sort of numbered staff gauge.

The best of these gauges are United State Geological Survey (USGS) streamflow gauging stations. You can usually identify a USGS gauge as a tall, rectangular, concrete tower, often located near a bridge. Some others are constructed of a vertical corrugated pipe with a green wooden or metal box on top. These stations have flow measuring and recording instruments inside and often have a readable staff gauge outside. The gauge scale is usually set so that the stations will never report a negative level. Hence, the zero canoeing level on a stream may read, for example, 2.0 feet on the USGS gauge. Generally paddlers must personally inspect a gauge for a reading. But in a few dozen lucky instances, daily readings are available from National Weather Service River Forecast offices. For Delaware Basin readings call the former Philadelphia Forecast Office at 800-431-4721. For Susquehanna Basin readings call the State College Forecast Office (referred to in text as Central PA) at 814-234-9861 or 800-362-0335. Call the Washington, D.C. Forecast Office at 703-260-0305 for Potomac Basin and Monongahela Basin readings. Call the Pittsburgh Forecast Office at 412-262-5290 for Ohio Basin readings or, for Ohio Basin gauges not reported by the River Forecast Center, call the Reservoir Control Center, Corps of Engineers, Pittsburgh District at 412-644-6847. In many cases, the outside staff of the USGS gauge has washed away. So for the call-in gauges I have also noted if they are readable on site. There are also many USGS gauges that would be very useful, but they neither have outside staffs nor are they reported to the Weather Service. But I sometimes have included references to these gauges in hope that the staffs will some day be replaced.

One final word about USGS gauges. The National Weather Service performs a tremendous favor to the paddling community by making these readings available to us. Washington, for example, maintains a multiple-line recording, changed twice a day, just for recreational users. In these budget-trimming times we cannot take these services for granted. So if you use these phone numbers, please take the time to write the Director of the National Weather Service, 8060 13th Street, Silver Spring, Maryland, 20910, and let him or her know how much you appreciate the service. It helps at budget time.

Other gauges include a wonderful system of painted or wooden staff gauges, put on bridge piers and abutments for further flood monitoring. On some popular streams, canoeists have painted simple gauges, usually marked at foot or half-foot increments, usually on bridge piers and abutments. This system, developed and refined by the late Randy Carter, a renown and widely travelled whitewater canoeist and guidebook author, usually establishes the zero mark to represent the minimum possible level of navigation. However, you must realize that paddlers possess varying ideas of what constitutes "too low," depending on such variables as the gauge painter's boating prowess, boat materials and durability of construction, and degree of aversion to boat repair and maintenance. So the boater who runs a river by an unfamiliar canoe gauge that reads zero may be a real gambler. As for my definition of zero, it is the level at which you unavoidably start scraping in more than a few shallows, unless I have specified otherwise.

For each river I have tried to include a gauge that you can inspect on site and, if possible, a call-in gauge. Where there is a call-in gauge on a nearby stream, I have included readings that must only be regarded as rough correlations.

Understand that gauges have their limits of usefulness. Unless otherwise stated, the recommended gauge level reflects the stretch adjacent to the gauge. Since high water moves like a big wave, especially on small and flashy streams, an adequate level at the gauge may be already too low ten miles upstream. So it helps to know if the stream is rising or falling. You may, for example, call Central PA on Friday and find that Hogestown is reading 2.0 feet, but when you arrive on Saturday, it has already dropped to 1.5 feet. So it often wise to start calling two days before you go paddling. Also, when using the roughly correlated gauges mentioned above, remember that the correlation holds best if there is snowmelt or a uniform rainfall. So do not count on these gauges in the showery summer months.

Maps accompany each river description most importantly to answer shuttle and access questions. Except for the usually exaggerated river widths, the maps are spatially accurate. To help you break the stream into a trip of suitable length, I have included as many river mileages as possible. These are the little numbers hugging the rivers, and they denote the distances between the little arrowheads. These arrowheads do not necessarily denote access points. Sometimes I have simply located them at landmarks, such as high bridges and mouths of major tributaries, just so you can mark your progress on your trip. In general, though, you can assume that most bridges afford some degree of access and that those dead-ending roads that I have included will also get you to a public, or friendly private, access point. Pennsylvania also has, at least on its big streams, an excellent system of public access areas, usually boat ramps, provided by the Pennsylvania Fish and Boat Commission (PFC). In addition, the Pennsylvania Game Commission (PGC), power companies, towns, and service clubs often provide boating access areas, or at least conveniently located streamside parks. Where space allowed, I have also included these access points. As for gauges, I have included most gauges that you must inspect on site and some call-in gauges.

Finding Your Way Around The Backwoods

If Pennsylvania ever goes bankrupt, it will not be because they spent too much money on road signs. Many counties and townships have been horribly remiss in labelling their secondary roads. This, combined with sign vandalism, can make navigating your shuttle an adventure.

Pennsylvania now identifies its state-maintained secondary roads, called State Routes (SR) by four-digit numbers. They are posted on small white signs, about 12 inches by 18 inches, set on corners at eye level. Some localities, in addition, give regular names to these roads, and post them on street signs. Township-maintained secondary roads are usually identified by a three-digit number prefixed by the letter T (T354 for example). They are usually posted on street signs, if they are posted at all. Some townships also assign and post the regular names for these roads, and others post both (T354, Maple Road for example). On my maps I have tried to identify all roads by at least their number, even if there are currently no signs so identifying them. I have done this in hope that the county or township will some day come along and post these roads. In addition, I have tried to include the regular name, as posted (and spelled) on the street signs. On the maps, if a road bears both a name and a number, I have put the number in parentheses.

As for which routes to take for shuttling, most federal and state highways are at least hard-topped (hardtop in Pennsylvania should be interpreted to include a liberal dose of hard-on-your-alignment potholes). The secondary state routes are also hardtopped or at least well-graded gravel. Township roads are variable, so use them at your own vehicle's risk. I have driven almost all of the roads shown on the shuttle maps in my conventional, low-clearance, rear-wheel-drive automobile. Some were terrible, but all were passable.

Access, Rights, And Regulation

There is no final answer to whether you have a right to float any stream in Pennsylvania. Unlike some other states, neither the lawmakers nor the courts have ever established a uniform determination of what is navigable. While the Federal Rivers and Harbors Act of 1899 declared all waters of this country as a public resource, this apparently did not carry over to include navigation.

Probably nobody will ever challenge your right to float any of the state's rivers or larger creeks, especially if they have a history of commercial navigation, including logging drives. On small streams, however, even if you do have the right to float the waters, strainers and falls often force you into setting foot on adjacent land and thus trespassing. Furthermore, as noted in the text, there are some streams where adjacent landowners are likely to challenge your presence, even if you do not touch the banks or bottom.

On most small streams you will probably have no problems with rights of passage. And if you do, tact and good manners can usually cool down the upset landowner. Most exceptions to this rule occur in the Poconos, where private clubs often exercise little flexibility. I advise you to simply avoid these streams. More litigious individuals or groups, with the time and resources to sustain a lengthy court battle, have contested such situations in other states, most recently in Montana, and won, thereby establishing some clearly defined and favorable recreational navigation rights. But courts are a two-edged sword. If you are not prepared to competently fight to the highest court, you may not only lose, but you would set an unfavorable legal precedent that could haunt paddlers on many more streams about the state. So think it out carefully before you leap into battle.

Some waters of the Commonwealth will cost you to paddle. You must obtain a launch permit to paddle on most lakes in the Pennsylvania State Park System. You can secure this permit for $6.00 at park offices or from the Pennsylvania Department of Conservation and Natural Resources, Bureau of State Parks, P.O. Box 8551, Harrisburg, Pa. 17105. Also costing you now is a $5.00 (per boat) registration fee to use any access operated by the Pennsylvania Fish and Boat Commission. For details, write the Commission, Bureau of Boating, P.O. Box 1673, Harrisburg, PA 17105-1673.

River Manners

In spite of all the posted lands in Pennsylvania, most streams in the state suffer no access problems. But with the increasing popularity of river running, this situation could change, if we do not abide by some basic principles of river etiquette. The following suggestions address most of the sort of actions that have made us unwelcome. Please remember these so you never spoil the fun for others who follow.

1. When possible, always ask permission to cross, park on, or camp on private land. Most people are glad to share a corner of their land if you just grant them this formality of respect.
2. Find a secluded spot for changing your clothes. Public nudity is incredibly offensive to many people, both in backwoods and "enlightened" urban areas, especially when you bare yourself right in front of their house, family, etc.
3. Do not block roads or driveways, even just to slow down for a brief chat. If you cannot find a decent shoulder, keep moving until you do. Otherwise not only do you create a safety hazard, but you might get a ticket. Too many times paddlers have been known to park in and block private driveways, without permission. Besides being a serious breach of etiquette, you could be responsible for blocking a fire truck or ambulance from its destination. How would you feel then?
4. If you are floating down a creek and a landowner tells you to "git," then git. Arguing or obscenely gesturing will get you nowhere, will only exacerbate his grudge against paddlers, and besides, you were headed in that direction anyhow. A humble demeanor or apology can often shame a hothead into a more mellow stance.
5. Do not damage those horrible barbed wire, electric, and other fences. They are there to keep the farmer's livestock in during the 99% of the year when the creek you are floating is only ankle deep. They are not there to intentionally hurt you.
6. Litter leaves hard feelings, so do not litter, even if the stream is already trashy (usually from locals).

7. Be discreet about where you start fires, ask permission where possible, use other people's fire rings at popular campsites, leave as little evidence of your fire as possible, and of course, thoroughly douse your fire when you are done.
8. Be nice to the fishermen, even if a few are not nice to you. Give them a wide berth, do not run over their lines, keep the noise down when passing by, and avoid the popular fishing streams during the first week of trout season. Remember, they enjoy the river as much as you do. And if that does not sway you, remember, there are far more fishermen than canoeists in Pennsylvania, they are better organized, they have more economic clout, and have more friends in the State Legislature.

No Paddler Is An Island

The growing popularity of paddling has resulted in the appearance of paddling communities and clubs in about every sizable town. A membership in a canoe club will be the best buy for your boating dollar that you will ever find. Besides affording you the chance to meet other people of similar interests, many clubs conduct excellent educational programs. Here is a chance to acquire techniques that might take you years to learn on your own, and it is free. Clubs serve as a marketplace to buy and sell the highly specialized equipment that newspaper adds could never serve. This is the place to keep up with the latest techniques, materials, and other consumer information. If a new safety hazard appears on a nearby stream, this will be your first opportunity to learn about it, other than the hard way. If an access problem arises, this is where you learn about it first. Essentially a club is your contact with the world of paddling, and no matter if you go boating once a year or every week, or if you are a rugged loner or a group person, you will get the most out of the sport if you keep in touch.

Clubs have another important function. They give you the strength of numbers needed to get your way in this world. It has been clubs that have succeeded in getting special recreational water releases from reservoirs on Tohickon Creek, the Lehigh, Slippery Rock Creek, and the nearby Savage River and North Branch Potomac River. Club input and cooperation has helped guide management decisions on publicly owned rivers such as the Yough at Ohiopyle or the upper Delaware. Clubs have helped local rescue squads to improve their river rescue capability. Clubs have spearheaded river conservation movements. Essentially, clubs are your canoe lobby. They are your paddler's union. Your support of a club, if only by adding your name to its roster, increases its clout to protect your favorite streams and your right to enjoy them with a minimum of interference.

The following are some clubs that serve the area described in this guidebook. Since most club contacts change from year to year, an inquiry at the nearest outing store should produce an address for those clubs without a perennial address.

Chester County: Buck Ridge Ski Club (P.O. Box 179, Bala Cynwyd, Pa. 19004)
Easton/Allentown/Bethlehem: Lehigh Valley Canoe Club (P.O. Box 877, Easton, Pa. 18042)
Hagerstown, Md.: Mason Dixon Canoe Cruisers
Harrisburg: Canoe Club of Greater Harrisburg
Indiana: Keystone River Runners
Lancaster: Lancaster Canoe Club
Oil City: Allegheny Canoe Club
Philadelphia: Philadelphia Canoe Club (4900 Ridge Ave., Philadelphia, Pa. 19128)
　　　　　Appalachian Mountain Club, Delaware Valley Chapter
Pittsburgh: Pittsburgh AYH (6300 5th Ave., Pittsburgh, Pa. 15232)
　　　　　Three Rivers Paddling Club
Reading: Keystone Canoe Club
Scranton: Scranton Kayak Club

State College: Penn State Outing Club, Canoe Division (8 1.M. Bldg., University
   Park, Pa. 16802)
Wilmington, De.: Wilmington Trail Club (P.O. Box 1184, Wilmington, De. 19899)
York: Conewago Canoe Club

One More Plug (Conservation)

We river lovers are fortunate to actually have an official lobbying organization representing us in the big seat of power, Washington, D.C. They go by the name American Rivers. They are a small and dedicated band who fight for the preservation of free-flowing streams and fight against needlessly destructive projects such as dams, river channelization, etc. They are our David fighting our numerous river-eating Goliaths. Please support them (and help yourself) by joining. Individual memberships are $20 per year, sent to American Rivers, 801 Pennsylvania Ave., S.E., Washington, D.C. 20003. Keep a river friend in high places.

Further River Reading

Good river running does not end at the state line. So here is a list of the fine guidebooks that cover the surrounding neighborhoods.

Maryland and Delaware Canoe Trails by Edward Gertler (Seneca Press, 530 Ashford Road, Silver
   Spring, Md. 20910)
Virginia Whitewater by H. Roger Corbett (Seneca Press, 512 Monet Dr., Rockville, Md. 20850)
Wildwater West Virginia, Vol. 1 and 2 by Paul Davidson, Ward Eister, and Dirk Davidson
   (Menasha Ridge Press, P.O. Box 59257, Birmingham, AL 35259)
Canoeing Guide to Western Pennsylvania and Northern West Virginia by American Youth Hostels,
   Pittsburgh Council (AYH, Inc. 6300 Fifth Ave., Pittsburgh, Pa. 15232)
A Canoeing and Kayaking Guide to Streams of Ohio, Vol. 1 and 2 by Richard Combs and Stephen
   E. Gillen (Menasha Ridge Press, P.O. Box 59257, Birmingham, AL 35259)
Canoeing Central New York by William P. Ehling (Backcountry Publications, Inc., P.0. Box 175,
   Woodstock, VT 05091)
Garden State Canoeing by Edward Gertler (Seneca Press, 530 Ashford Road, Silver Spring, MD
   20910)

Help Set The Author Straight

Writing a canoeing guidebook is frustrating. I just know that right this moment, as I write this page, somewhere in Pennsylvania some flash flood is moving some rock in a stream bed to somewhere different than where I said it was. And some farmer is stringing a barbed wire fence across, some tree is falling across, and some beaver is damming up some stream that I called "unobstructed." Penn D.O.T. is probably changing Rte. 66 to 99, and some bored delinquents are probably shooting holes in the street sign that marks the crucial turn on one of the shuttles. And shifting gravel probably has caused some gauge to now read two feet off what I said it should.

It is hard to nail a moving target. So help me out. Do not be shy. If you find any mistakes or changes, I welcome your comments. Just write Seneca Press, 530 Ashford Road, Silver Spring, Md. 20910 and help build a better guidebook.

Glossary

In order to reach as many people as possible, I have tried to limit the amount of canoe jargon in my descriptions. The newcomer may, nevertheless, still be baffled by a few commonly used river terms. So I have included this brief glossary.

Advanced: Paddler who is competent at maneuvering his or her boat, reading the water, and staying out of trouble in Class 4 or greater whitewater.

Beginner: A person who knows little or nothing concerning basic strokes, canoe handling and how a river works. Seldom gets out more than once or twice a year.

Braiding: Situation where a stream channel splits, and then the split splits, and then the split splits split, ad nauseum, to form a pattern resembling a braided rope. Such areas can often spell trouble because narrow and shifting channels are prone to strainers.

Camps: A local term, especially in northern part of the state, for vacation homes and cabins. These often also take the form of old school buses, tarpaper shacks, and trailers. A string of these along an otherwise pretty river is called a river slum.

Hole (a.k.a. hydraulic, keeper, stopper, souse hole, reversal, roller): A foam-filled depression in the water caused by water flowing over a rock, weir, or ledge to displace the water at the bottom of the drop. This results in a recirculating surface current that can slow down or trap boats that enter it. Potentially dangerous.

Intermediate: Paddler who understands the principles of boat handling and the river, and can roughly move their boat to where they desire on up to Class 3 water.

Left (or Right): One side as distinguished from the other, when one is facing downstream.

Low-water Bridge: A low concrete slab or culvert bridge designed to function at only low water levels, and to accept inundation without damage at high water. A poor man's special but a paddler's headache.

Novice: Paddler who has learned the basic canoe strokes, simple fast water maneuvers, such as eddy turns and ferrying, and understands the nature of currents, eddies, holes, etc., but has not become proficient at using all that knowledge.

Playing: Activity where skilled whitewater paddlers practice precise boat maneuvers by using the current. This includes surfing, hole sitting, and catching eddies for fun. If this still makes little sense, a brief whitewater canoeing lesson would be worth a thousand words.

Shuttle: Complex car positioning exchange undertaken by groups of paddlers to make sure that when they reach the take-out they have a way to get back to the put-in.

Strainer: Any obstacle across the current that allows water to flow through while trapping any floating scum or debris, including boats and boaters. Very dangerous. In this book I have usually used this term to denote fallen trees, logjams, and brush. I have usually separately described the man-made strainers.

Weir: A little dam, but often just as dangerous as a big dam, because of its hole.

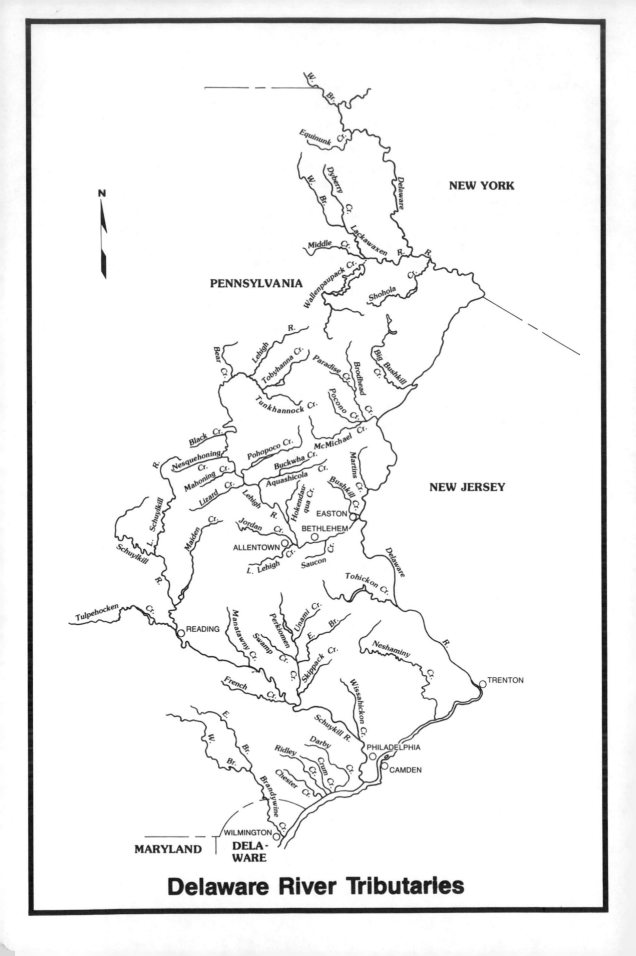

Delaware River Tributaries

Chapter 2
The Delaware Basin

   The Delaware Basin encompasses 6325 square miles of the eastern edge of Pennsylvania. Its elongated form spans five major geological provinces, from the Allegheny Plateau to the Atlantic Coastal Plain. No other basin in the state possesses such diversity. Needless to say, this has resulted in a varied landscape, both cultural and natural. The relatively low and gentle lower basin is heavily populated and heavily industrialized, yet still also includes acres of open space, partly in the form of excellent farmlands. This is Pennsylvania's oldest neighborhood, and it is rich in old houses, bridges, mills, canals, and other historical memorabilia. The more rugged upper basin is an emptier area that is vacationland for the throngs that stream out of the Philadelphia and New York metropolitan areas. It is also, unfortunately, close enough that it is becoming an outer suburb of each. Throughout its length, the basin is endowed with a wealth of fine canoe routes. Some like the Delaware or Lehigh are well established. Others are just waiting for you to wake up and discover them.
   The following streams are described in this chapter:

Delaware River
Brandywine Creek
East Branch Brandywine Creek
West Branch Brandywine Creek
Chester Creek
Ridley Creek
Crum Creek
Darby Creek
Schuylkill River
Wissahickon Creek
Perkiomen Creek
Skippack Creek
East Branch Perkiomen Creek
Swamp Creek
Unami Creek
French Creek
Manatawny Creek
Tulpehocken Creek
Maiden Creek
Little Schuylkill River
Neshaminy Creek
Tohickon Creek
Lehigh River
Saucon Creek
Jordan Creek
Little Lehigh Creek
Hokendauqua Creek
Aquashicola Creek

Buckwha Creek
Lizard Creek
Pohopoco Creek
Mahoning Creek
Nesquehoning Creek
Black Creek
Quakake Creek
Bear Creek
Tobyhanna Creek
Tunkhannock Creek
Bushkill Creek
Martins Creek
Brodhead Creek
Pocono Creek
McMichael Creek
Paradise Creek
Big Bushkill Creek
Shohola Creek
Lackawaxen River
Wallenpaupack Creek
East Branch Wallenpaupack Creek
Middle Creek
Dyberry Creek
West Branch Lackawaxen River
Equinunk Creek
West Branch Delaware River
The Canals

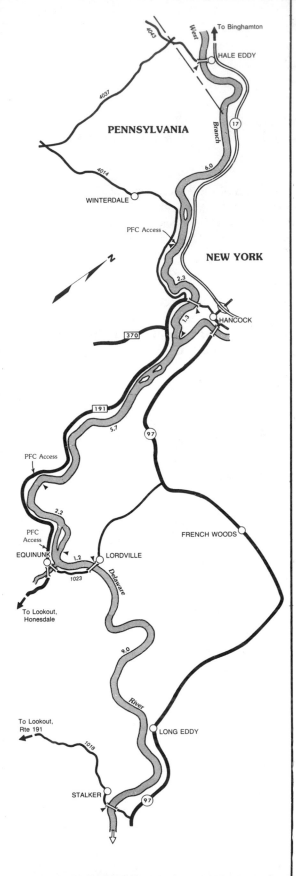
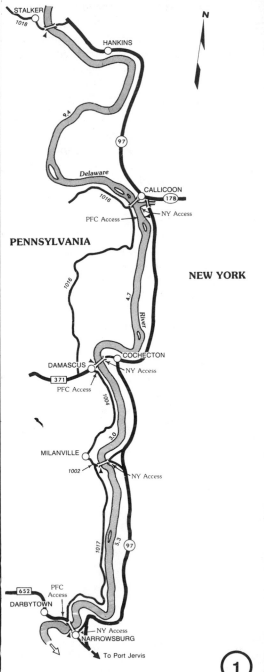

Delaware River
West Branch
Delaware River

①

Delaware River

INTRODUCTION: The Delaware River defines Pennsylvania's eastern border, molding the state's distinctive and craggy profile. Pennsylvania owns half of the river. New Jersey and New York divide up what is left. Its headwaters drain the magnificent 3,000- and 4,000-foot-high peaks of the Catskill Mountains, feeding the Delaware by such tributaries as the East and West branches, Neversink, Beaverkill, Willowemoc, and Mongaup. The Delaware is officially born at the confluence of the East and West branches, about a mile south of Hancock, N.Y. From there it flows 197 miles to tidewater, at Trenton, and then sloshes back and forth for another 85 miles to a point south of New Castle, Delaware, where it arbitrarily becomes Delaware Bay.

The Delaware is an anomaly. It is the only major river on the Eastern Seaboard that is unshackled by dams. Major highways seldom follow it very far. Neither do the railroads. Above tidewater, there is only one city on its banks and only a few large towns. There are few big factories along it either, and only four power plants. Not surprisingly, with this absence of development, the water in the free-flowing Delaware is clean and often clear.

With all this clean water, the Delaware just had to become somebody's water supply. New York City, to slake its voracious thirst, has constructed Cannonsville Reservoir, on the West Branch, Pepacton Reservoir, on the East Branch, and Neversink, on the Neversink, tapping as much water as it legally can. It grudgingly releases water for downstream users. One of the downstream users is Philadelphia. It draws part of its water from (yuk) tidewater, at the north end of the city. This is usually just fine, as the mass of fresh water coming from upstream keeps at bay the brackish water from the lower estuary and pollution from Philadelphia. But back in the mid-60's, a period of record drought, New York was hard pressed to spare the water from the shrinking reservoirs. Meanwhile, a tide of foul and brackish waters was ominously advancing upstream toward Philadelphia's intakes. The cities almost went to war over that remaining reservoir water before a United States Supreme Court decision and timely rains laid the dispute to rest.

Of course, rather than decrease the water demand by such logical measures as metering all water users, fixing leaks, and offering water rate conservation incentives, the attitude towards drought busting has long been to build another dam. The planners have dreamed of plugging the Delaware River at Tocks Island, above the Water Gap, to form a huge reservoir that would back up almost to Port Jervis. The plan lies dormant now — a victim of questionable benefit cost ratios, environmental awareness, and recent abundance of water. When the dry years return, however, canoeists can count on this project again rearing its ugly head.

Wedged between two of the nation's biggest metropolitan areas, the relatively empty Delaware Valley has long been a prime recreational refuge. The hills surrounding the river's upper reaches are filled with plush resorts, camps, second home developments, private hunting and fishing preserves, and great estates. The immediate river, however, is now partially protected from further unchecked development by the Upper Delaware National Scenic and Recreational River, from Hancock to Port Jervis, the Delaware Water Gap National Recreation Area, from Port Jervis to the Water Gap, Roosevelt State Park, from Easton to Morrisville and D & R State Park, from Raven Rock to Trenton. This quality has not gone unnoticed by boaters. For streams just do not come much more popular. Between Hancock and Trenton, there are at least 20 major liveries supplying over 4,000 canoes to eager refugees from the sweltering city. On a hot summer weekend, the boats are often all used. Over 2,000 boats a day ply just the section between Hancock and Port Jervis. Add to this population thousands of rental inner tubes, rafts, and kayaks, then a wave of private canoeists, tubers, and kayakers, and finally an untold number of calloused fishermen on shore, and you have the American version of the River Ganges. So if you want the Delaware for yourself, it is best to visit during the week, after the season, in rotten weather, or after a nuclear war.

Delaware River
Lackawaxen River
Shohola Creek

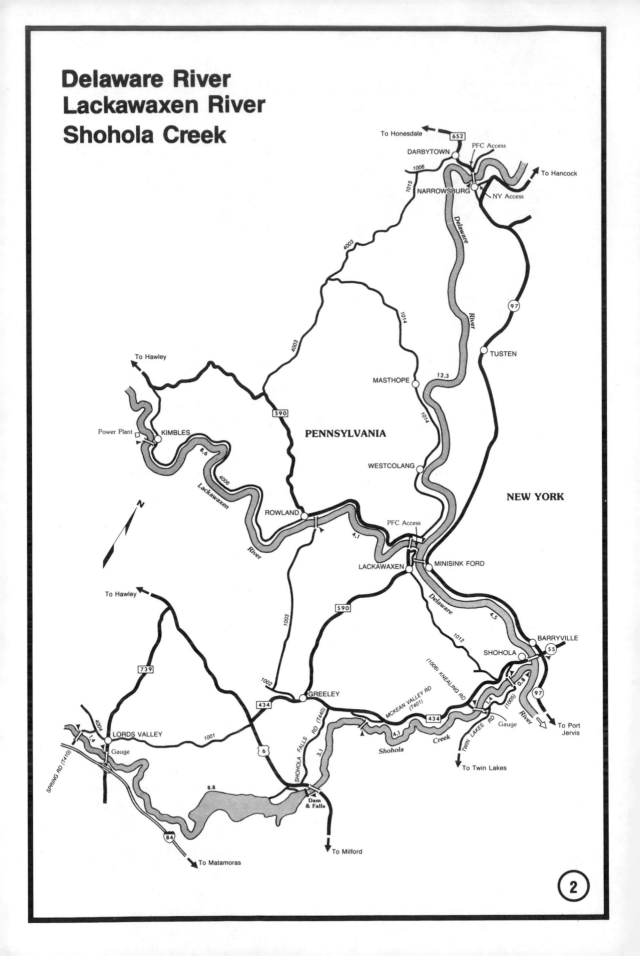

If you are a serious river runner, then a trip to the upper Delaware on a crowded summer weekend offers a unique sociological experience. You will observe hundreds of boaters floating the river, in all stages of ineptness, with no concept of river currents, canoemanship, or even that a life vest is not just a funny-shaped seat cushion. Many do not really care, their minds pickled by drugs or alcohol. They drown and injure themselves on this simple river with amazing frequency. They do not just break canoes here, but manage to perform incredible five-canoe pile-ups. There are even river pirates on the Delaware. Enterprising locals wait on shore at some of the more difficult rapids and direct neophytes into rough sections of those rapids, where the unsuspecting victims would hopefully capsize, with inevitably unsecured equipment spilling into the river. As this happens, teams of SCUBA-outfitted cohorts slither into the water like crocodiles, gleaning wallets, cameras, coolers, and other salvage, before the misled victims ever slog onto the banks, far below. Yet, in spite of all these horror stories, most people who visit the Delaware have a first class time.

Section 1. Hancock, N.Y. to Matamoras PFC Access					
Gradient	Difficulty	Distance	Time	Scenery	Map
6	1 to 2 +	75.9	24.0	Good to Excellent	1,2,3

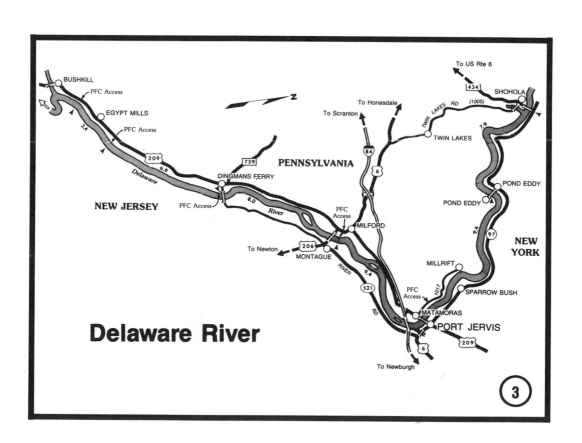

15

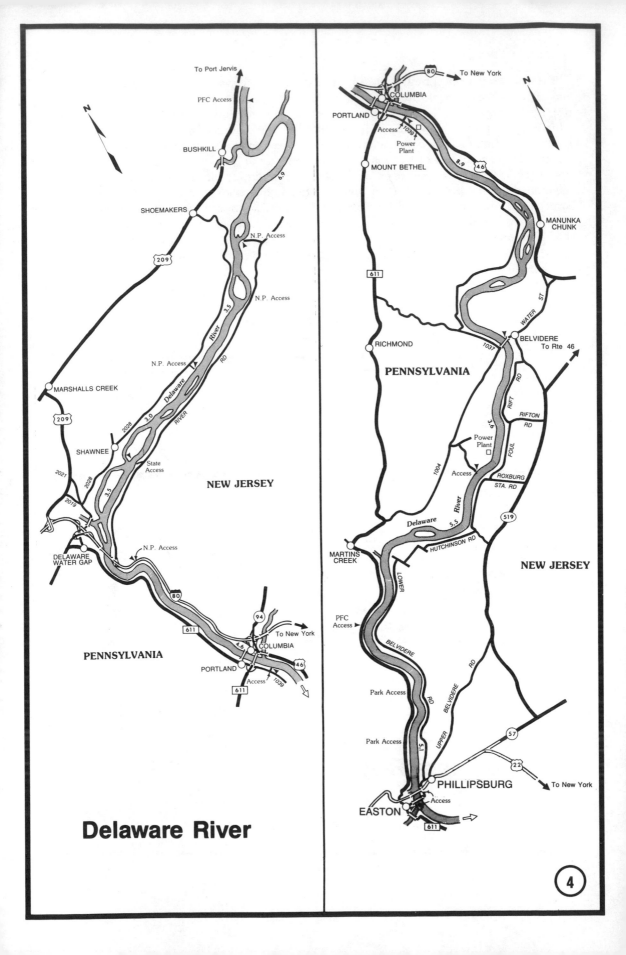

Delaware River

TRIP DESCRIPTION: You can start your trip at Pa. Rte. 191, on the West Branch, or at N.Y. Rte. 97, on the East Branch, depending upon the water levels in the branches. During the summer busy season, it is best to avoid Hancock and start seven miles downstream at the Buckingham PFC Access.

The upper Delaware offers a grand tour through this mountainous region. For its first half, it flows down a narrow valley, bordered by high, rounded, and forested hills. In places the hillsides harden to tiers of cliffs over which plummet a delicate selection of wet-weather waterfalls. Grassy banks line the river, which frequently splits around flat and grassy islands. The bottomlands are often undeveloped, especially on the isolated reach from Lordville to Long Eddy. Below Narrowsburg, the hillsides now grow to the stature of mountainsides and converge, creating more of a canyon. Clusters of vacation homes continue to alternate with undeveloped banks. The river is often rimmed by shelves of sandstone and siltstone. This is particularly striking at the Narrows, at Narrowsburg, and at the aptly named "Elephant's Feet," on the right, below the railroad bridge at Millrift. This same rock also rises high above the river as cliffs. Combined with wet-weather waterfalls, they are at their best between Mongaup and Matamoras. Finally, rounding out the scenery are the first of the Delaware's many swinging bridges. The most interesting is a former aqueduct, now a footbridge, that was built to carry the Delaware and Hudson Canal over the river at Lackawaxen. This was an engineering milestone, the first of many, by John Roebling, a German immigrant and suspension bridge pioneer who would later reach his zenith with the design of the Brooklyn Bridge.

At moderate levels, the Delaware is suitable for beginners. Its clear waters are mostly smooth. Its well-spaced rapids and riffles are usually wide open and sluice gently over a cobble bottom. Two notable exceptions are Skinners Falls and Shohola Rapids. Located at Milanville, 100-yard-long Skinners Falls, a rapid, drops comparatively steeply over a bouldery and ledgy bottom, throwing up some big waves and holes. You can avoid both rocks and the biggest waves by sneaking slowly down the right side. The rapid's fearsome reputation stems purely from the ineptitude of so many of its challengers, not its inherent difficulty. Shohola Rapids, below Shohola, is a long and heavy, but uncomplicated rapid, which when the water is up, can easily swamp a mismanaged open canoe.

One final note. During the summer busy season, on this section as all others, you should put in and take out only at public launch areas. The normally accepted access spots, as at bridges and by roadsides, just cannot accomodate the throngs that converge on this popular river. Some river towns even have ordinances that prohibit access at bridge right-of-ways.

HAZARDS: None.

WATER CONDITIONS: Always canoeable (except when frozen or flooding), although it can get pretty shallow in spots at low water. The river is partly dam controlled, with water often held back in June, but increased in late July and in August.

GAUGE: USGS gauge at Barryville (call Philadelphia, or the National Park Headquarters at 914-252-3847). Summer levels drop down around 2.9 feet (low, but adequate). At levels above 5.0 feet, beginners should avoid Skinners Falls or Shohola Rapids.

Section 2. Matamoras, Pa. (Matamoras Access) to Delaware Water Gap (Kittatinny Access)					
Gradient	Difficulty	Distance	Time	Scenery	Map
3	1 –	44.6	15.0	Good	4

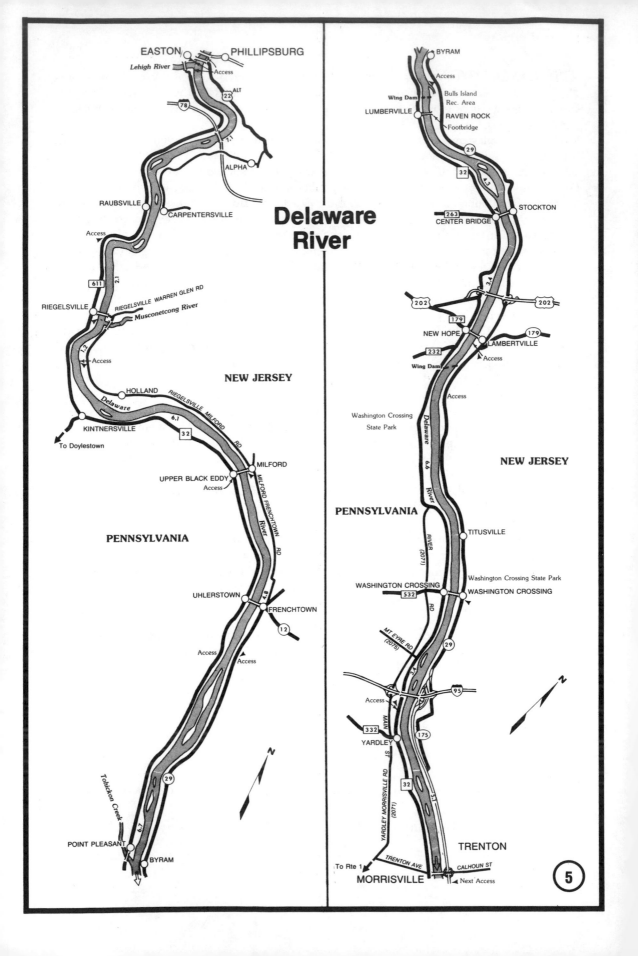

Delaware River

EASTON · **PHILLIPSBURG**

Lehigh River

Access

22 ALT

78

7.1

ALPHA

RAUBSVILLE

CARPENTERSVILLE

Access

611

2.1

RIEGELSVILLE

RIEGELSVILLE WARREN GLEN RD

Musconetcong River

1.2

Access

NEW JERSEY

HOLLAND

Delaware

RIEGELSVILLE MILFORD RD

6.1

KINTNERSVILLE

32

To Doylestown

MILFORD

UPPER BLACK EDDY

Access

MILFORD FRENCHTOWN River RD

PENNSYLVANIA

UHLERSTOWN

4.8

FRENCHTOWN

12

Access

Access

29

Tohickon Creek

6.7

POINT PLEASANT

BYRAM

BYRAM

Access

Wing Dam

Bulls Island Rec. Area

LUMBERVILLE

RAVEN ROCK

Footbridge

29

32

4.3

263

CENTER BRIDGE

STOCKTON

3.4

202

202

179

NEW HOPE

179

232

LAMBERTVILLE

Access

Wing Dam

Access

Washington Crossing State Park

Delaware River

6.6

NEW JERSEY

PENNSYLVANIA

RIVER (2071)

TITUSVILLE

Washington Crossing State Park

WASHINGTON CROSSING

532

RD

WASHINGTON CROSSING

MT EYRE RD (2075)

29

3.4

95

Access

MAIN ST

332

175

YARDLEY

YARDLEY MORRISVILLE RD (2071)

32

51

TRENTON

TRENTON AVE

CALHOUN ST

To Rte 1

Next Access

MORRISVILLE

⑤

TRIP DESCRIPTION: At Port Jervis, the Neversink joins and the Delaware turns 90 degrees to the southwest. On the right lies the low and uniform escarpment of the Pocono Plateau. On the left runs the high ridge of Kittatinny Mountain, which peaks at 1,803 feet at High Point, near Port Jervis. The Delaware remains so sandwiched until it escapes through the famous Water Gap.

This section, part of which may some day be the bottom of Tocks Island Reservoir, is surrounded by the holdings of the National Park Service. The clumsy condemnation and acquisition practices of the Corps of Engineers, and then subsequent regulation by the National Park Service, have left a trail of bitterness amongst some of the valley's inhabitants. This is not a neighborhood in which to walk around bragging that you are a preservationist.

However unfair that the acquisition episode was, the river scenery and we users have benefitted. The subsequent leveling of many riverside houses has restored the banks to a primitive condition that they have not enjoyed for years. Many places where you may now camp (and this is certainly a good stretch for an overnight canoe trip) would have been posted and developed in the past. All this, combined with fine mountain views and mostly glass-smooth water, makes this an excellent trip for the most cautious of beginners.

HAZARDS: None.

WATER CONDITIONS: Always canoeable.

GAUGE: USGS gauges at Port Jervis and Montague (call Philadelphia, or National Park Service at 717-588-2435). Levels of 2.3 feet at Port Jervis and 4.9 feet at Montague represent summer low-flow conditions.

Section 3. Delaware Water Gap (Kittatinny Access) to Easton (Front Street Access)					
Gradient	Difficulty	Distance	Time	Scenery	Map
4	1,2	27.7	9.0	Fair to Good	4

TRIP DESCRIPTION: This is the least scenic portion of the Delaware this side of Trenton. The Water Gap, of course, is magnificent, but the interstate highway that passes through it is not. There are three power plants on this reach, and there are long lines of houses on its banks. This section ends in the heart of Easton and Phillipsburg, whose hillside facade is reminicent of an Old World town.

This is a smooth-flowing section, with the notable exception of Foul Rift. Located a mile below Belvidere, Foul Rift is a long rapid through a staircase of jagged and diagonal limestone ledges. For a beginner it can be a nasty place to be, at any levels.

HAZARDS: None.

WATER CONDITIONS: Always canoeable, except when frozen or flooding.

GAUGE: USGS gauges at Belvidere and Easton (call Philadelphia). Levels of 3.4 feet at Belvidere and 0.8 feet at Easton represent summer and fall low-flow conditions.

Section 4. Easton (Front Street Access) to Trenton (Old Wharf Access)					
Gradient	Difficulty	Distance	Time	Scenery	Map
3	1,2	50.8	16.5	Fair to Good	5

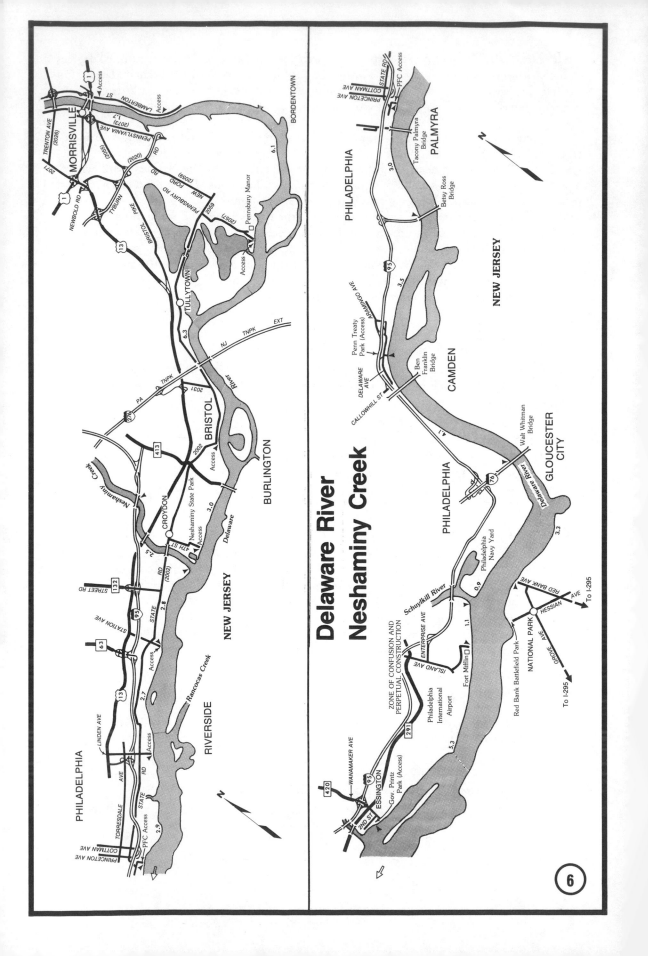

Delaware River
Neshaminy Creek

6

TRIP DESCRIPTION: Fortified with Lehigh River water, the Delaware now cuts through the last of the Appalachian ridges and heads off across the Piedmont to tidewater at Trenton. This is a surprisingly beautiful section, often lined by wooded bluffs and high rock cliffs. There are a few too many houses on its banks, but many are old and attractive, as are the many small towns along the way. Approaching Trenton, Morrisville, and Yardley, the area becomes increasingly suburban, then urban. But the neighborhood might have ended up far more crowded had Morrisville been successful, back in 1783, in its bid for the site of the new nation's capital.

This is also a section of smooth waters and simple and well-spaced riffles. But there are a few splashy surprises. The first, at Lumberville, is the two-foot wing dam (used to divert water into the Delaware and Raritan Canal) with its wide and wavy chute in the center. Next comes another wing dam, this one below New Hope, with an interesting boulder-and-ledge-formed rapid at its foot. Finally, there is Scudders Falls—a low, diagonal reef, above I-95, with a variety of easy chutes. Only a few easy and rocky riffles mark the fall line and the Delaware's entry into tidewater, above the U.S. Rte. 1 Bridge in Trenton.

HAZARDS: Avoid blundering over the edges of the wing dams at Lumberville and New Hope. At moderate to high levels the resultant hydraulics could trap a boat (and boater), so stick to the center.

WATER CONDITIONS: Always canoeable, except when frozen or flooding.

GAUGE: USGS gauges at Easton, Reigelsville, and Trenton (call Philadelphia). Levels of 0.8 feet, 2.8 feet, and 8.1 feet, respectively, represent late summer and fall low-flow conditions.

Section 5. Trenton (Old Wharf Access) to Essington (Gov. Printz Park)					
Gradient	Difficulty	Distance	Time	Scenery	Map
0	A	46.7	21.0	Fair to Different	6

TRIP DESCRIPTION: This section will appeal to few. It is tidal, meaning that getting in and out at low tide is a muddy mess and, for two quarters of the day, the current is going the wrong direction. And to make matters worse, as the river approaches Philadelphia, the water becomes filthy and the air often smelly.

But this section has its virtues too. The reach from Trenton to Bristol is still partially undeveloped and pretty. William Penn's Pennsbury Manor and the riverfront of Bristol are also a pleasure to behold. Getting on into the city, aesthetics are displaced by an interesting array of the technological complexities of the human anthill: the great bridges, a steel mill, loading docks, cranes, shipyards, and ships. There are huge and intimidating warships at anchor at the Navy Yard and great jet planes zooming in and out of the International Airport. And there is the skyline of the great city, looming behind it all, like the castle of a medieval town. True, it is not as pretty as a rose. But it is an opportunity to view, at a leisurely pace and in a simple and detached way, the high-speed and complex world of which you and I are party. It is fascinating.

If you prepare for this section's peculiarities, you should have a pleasant trip. When you embark on these waters, use the tides, do not fight them. Remember that access points are few and far between. Remember that the shipping channels are for ships, not canoes. Finally, once in Philadelphia, the shores are often bulkheaded; so you are limited to where you can even get out and stretch. Plan accordingly.

HAZARDS: Give commercial shipping a wide berth. Beware of disgusting water quality.

WATER CONDITIONS: Always canoeable.

GAUGE: None necessary.

Brandywine Creek

INTRODUCTION: The Brandywine flows down one of the earliest-settled valleys in Pennsylvania. Yet, the years have been kind to Brandywine Creek. Industrialization came to its banks early, but, except in its headwater towns of Coatesville and Downingtown, has long since yielded to floods and obsolescence. Only a few crumbling dams and millraces remain today as evidence. Filling the vacuum, expensive, low-density suburbia now occupies the area. It is a land graced by rambling estates, horse farms, and museums, all of which mold the personality of the creek.

Brandywine Creek is, in itself, only a mediocre canoe stream. But easy water, a relatively long season, a lively livery trade, and proximity to Wilmington and Philadelphia have made it one of the most popular streams in the state. On a typical, warm, late spring weekend, you will witness a continuous tide of canoes and tubes drifting downstream, while picnickers and fishermen vie for room along its banks. Solitude seekers need not apply.

Section 1. Confluence East and West branches to Thompson Bridge					
Gradient	Difficulty	Distance	Time	Scenery	Map
4	A to 1	11.2	4.0	Fair	7

TRIP DESCRIPTION: You can put in at the Pa. Rte. 842 Bridge over either the West or East Branch, the latter being preferable at low water levels. This is mostly a smooth water run, partly the backwaters of three old milldams, with easy riffles in between. The first two dams, one just above the amusement park at Lenape, the next about a mile above U.S. Rte. 1, are three to four feet high, built of rubble, and are canoeable at fairly high levels, though beginners should carry each on the left. The little two-foot dam, just above Rte. 1, has an easily-shot breach on the right.

Above Chadds Ford the valley is open, attractive, and fairly visible from the creek. Unfortunately, a persistent high voltage power line sullies the view. Below Chadds Ford and its Brandywine Museum attractive wooded hills hem the creek. Both sections are nicest after summer foliage softens the scenery.

The take-out at Thompson Bridge is on the left, in Brandywine Creek State Park. The park is quite strict about closing (and towing away vehicles) at sundown, so make sure that you allow enough time for your trip.

HAZARDS: Three small dams.

WATER CONDITIONS: Canoeable winter, spring, and usually into mid-summer. In wet years it stays up all summer.

GAUGE: USGS gauge at Chadds Ford (call Philadelphia) should read at least 1.4 feet for the discriminating boater, though livery canoes keep grinding down all summer, regardless of level. There is also a staff gauge on the right abutment of the U.S. Rte. 1 Bridge. Zero on this gauge is approximately zero canoeing level.

East Branch Brandywine Creek

INTRODUCTION: Chester County is a beautiful parcel of land, both to live on, or to visit. Just look at the real estate prices, and you will find that many others are of a similar opinion. Chester is an old neighborhood, some of the first land to be settled in Pennsylvania. This is evident in the scores of solid old houses, mills, ivy-covered barns, old towns, and creeper-covered stone walls that run through woods that once were farms. You can enjoy a slice of all this from your canoe, for the East Branch ambles right down the middle of Chester County. Wait for a good rain and see.

Section 1. Pa. Rte. 82 to mouth					
Gradient	Difficulty	Distance	Time	Scenery	Map
14	A to 2	21.1	8.0	Fair to Good	8
2.3 @ 37					

TRIP DESCRIPTION: The headwaters of the East Branch lie right beside those of the West Branch. And only a few miles downstream, tiny as it may be at Pa. Rte. 82, the East Branch is canoeable, and nicely so. The first few miles down to Lyndell are a delight as the water takes a hide and seek path through patches of boulders. Unfortunately, this stretch is now interrupted

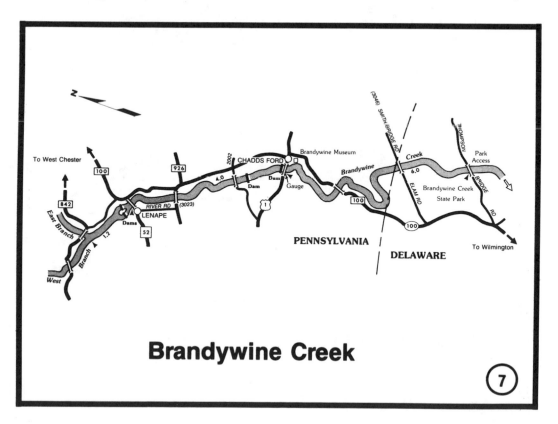

Brandywine Creek

⑦

23

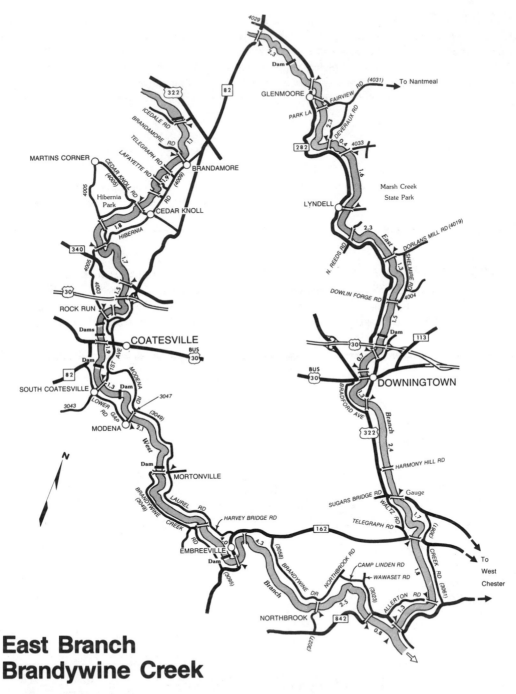

East Branch
Brandywine Creek

West Branch
Brandywine Creek

by a 30-foot-high flood control dam which creates an unwelcome portage. The boulders disappear, but ample drop through open riffles carries you on to Downingtown. Below Downingtown you find mostly just a fast current. Amazingly, there is only one more dam (yes, only one), just a two-foot bump located about a quarter mile above the U.S. Rte. 30 Bypass. The dam has a canoeable ramp on the right.

The East Branch weaves in and out of farms, woods, and one big town. The banks are usually low, so you get to see a lot. The surrounding woods include shady groves of hemlock on cool northern exposures and some extraordinarily big hardwoods. Occasionally the creek nudges some attractive rock formations. Downstream of Pa. Rte. 162 one such little cliff, called Deborah Rock, commemorates the legend of a love-smitten Indian maiden who lept to her death in the East Branch's murky waters. You see few Indian maidens anymore along the Brandywine. But you do see many attractive houses and farms by the creek, some obviously quite ancient. And you see a slice of Downingtown, which at least for its first half, is also pretty. Finish your East Branch tour at Pa. Rte. 842, unless you intend to continue on down the Brandywine.

HAZARDS: Two dams and some fallen trees.

WATER CONDITIONS: Most of this creek is only canoeable winter and spring within two days of hard rain. However, the last six miles are usually passable all spring and sometimes into early summer.

GAUGE: USGS gauge at east end of U.S. Rte. 322 Bridge, three miles below Downingtown (call Philadelphia or read on the spot), must read over 3.6 feet for the upper creek, but 2.4 feet is adequate for the last six miles.

West Branch Brandywine Creek

INTRODUCTION: The West Branch is a town and country stream with at least a little something to please, or offend, almost every paddler. It rises right on the Lancaster-Chester Line near Honey Brook, and in only several miles becomes a wet weather canoe stream.

Section 1. Icedale Road, T443 to Pa. Rte. 340					
Gradient	Difficulty	Distance	Time	Scenery	Map
34	A to 3 +	6.6	2.5	Good	8
1.1 @ 80					

TRIP DESCRIPTION: When your party disembarks at the Fish and Boat Commission parking area at Brandamore Dam, beginners can head upstream and enjoy the attractive, mile-long Icedale Lake, while intermediate to advanced paddlers can head downstream to frolic in the best whitewater in Chester County (some might say, the only whitewater). You can first relax on about two and a half miles of easy cruising as the creek steals through quiet woods that only occasionally are interrupted by a house or farm. The rapids begin below Cedar Knoll Road. They remain easy until the creek rounds the bend below Martins Corner Road, where it begins crashing, tumbling, and tossing tightly through a slalom of boulders and ledges. This stretch is located in lovely Hibernia

Park, so that on a nice spring day picnickers can munch on fried chicken while watching some boulder munch on your pinned canoe. Unfortunately, the good stuff only lasts for three quarters of a mile. But rapids of some sort continue to carry you all the way to Pa. Rte. 340.

HAZARDS: Possible fallen trees.

WATER CONDITIONS: Canoeable winter and spring within 24 hours of hard rain.

GAUGE: None on stream. For rough correlation, both USGS gauge below Downingtown, on the East Branch (call Philadelphia), and USGS gauge at Chadds Ford (call same) should be over 4.0 feet. But there is no substitute for an on-the-spot inspection at Hibernia Park.

Section 2. Pa. Rte. 340 to Modena (SR3047)					
Gradient	Difficulty	Distance	Time	Scenery	Map
20	A to 1 +	4.6	1.5	Poor	8

TRIP DESCRIPTION: Most people will choose to bypass this section, as it is mainly a tour of the grimy side of Coatesville. Coatesville is dominated by a huge steel mill, once the largest steel plate rolling mill in the world. Steel and iron go back a long way here. In fact, back during the Civil War it was nearby Laurel Forge that produced the armor plates for the ironclad *Monitor*. If the steel mill's historic and economic significance does not impress you, then neither will the miscellaneous industry, railroad yards, shabby houses, dumps, and scattered trash that comprise the rest of the scenery.

There are at least some easy rapids on this stretch, including an exciting chute through a crumbling dam above Coatesville. But dams that are still intact also plague you. You will need to carry a sloping, six-foot dam about a quarter mile below Rock Run Road. You can run the center notch in a sharp, three-foot dam above the main Conrail bridge in town, but you will clunk. Then, where the creek is confined within a forbidding, stone-walled corridor in the heart of the steel mill, you can run a two-foot weir at low levels. Stay away from here at high water, for without any way to portage, this could be a death trap. Farther down in the mill a vertical, eight-foot dam (with a bad roller at bottom) must be carried on the right.

HAZARDS: Three dams.

WATER CONDITIONS: Canoeable winter and spring within two days of hard rain.

GAUGE: None. For rough correlation, USGS gauge below Downingtown should be over 3.5 feet and Chadds Ford over 3.2 feet.

Section 3. Modena (SR3047) to mouth					
Gradient	Difficulty	Distance	Time	Scenery	Map
7	A to 1 −	13.7	4.0	Fair to Good	8

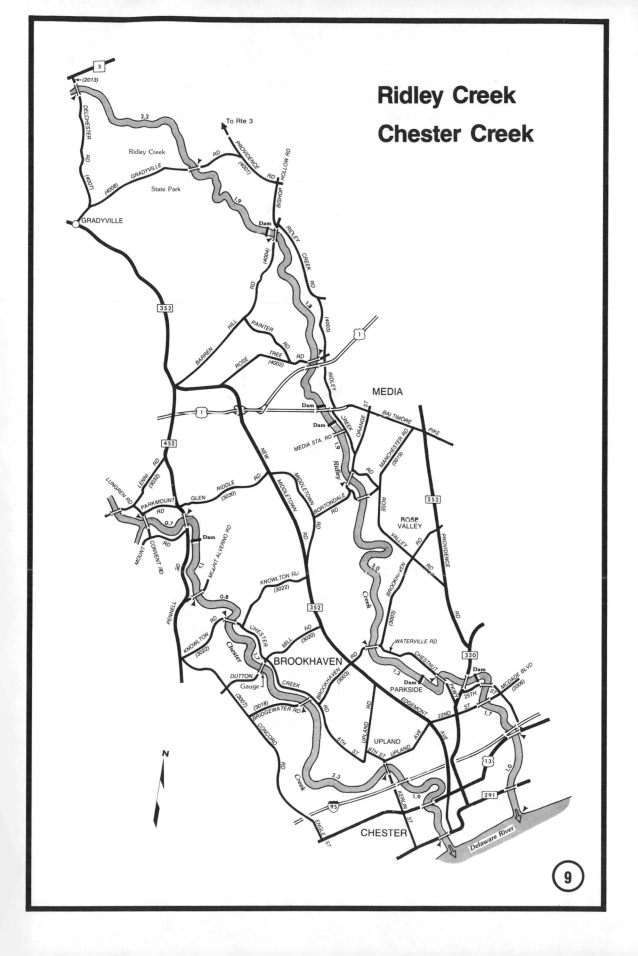

Ridley Creek
Chester Creek

9

TRIP DESCRIPTION: The creek's personality returns to what you would expect of a fork of the Brandywine. Though partly hidden behind high mud banks, the surroundings revert to an orderly, peaceful, rolling, and rural landscape that is graced with some beautiful, old houses. Only the residual trash that is lodged on the banks and bushes reminds you of what you have left behind upstream.

The water moves along nicely, with lots of riffles all along. You will have to carry an eight-foot, sloping rock mill dam just above Strasburg Road, but you can shoot the three-foot weir about three quarters of a mile above Pa. Rte. 162. Pa. Rte. 842 is your last take-out on the West Branch, the confluence with the East Branch being a mile below.

HAZARDS: Two dams.

WATER CONDITIONS: Canoeable winter and most of the spring. Below Embreeville, it is often canoeable into early summer.

GAUGE: None. Roughly, USGS gauge below Downingtown, on the East Branch, should be over 2.4 feet and Chadds Ford should be over 1.7 feet.

Chester Creek

INTRODUCTION: Chester Creek is the southernmost of Delaware County's flash-flowing ministreams. It is not particularly interesting, and not worth driving far for to paddle.

Section 1. Convent Road to Pa. Rte. 291					
Gradient	Difficulty	Distance	Time	Scenery	Map
15	A to 2	8.5	2.5	Poor	9
.75 @ 31					

TRIP DESCRIPTION: The put-in is below the confluence of the West Branch Chester Creek. It probably would be even nicer to start upstream of here, but it is extra difficult to find acceptable levels that far upstream. This is a shame, for that is where the steepest gradient lies. Whitewater boaters will probably find a worthwhile exploratory trip by starting about four miles above Convent Road at Glen Mills.

Chester Creek is generally a trashy run, rolling past a densely populated and built-up neighborhood, though sometimes a thin strip of woods buffers the paddler from the harsher scenery beyond. As far down as Chester, the stream runs swiftly, with riffles and a few Class 2 rapids through boulder patches and old dam remains. Portage a seven-foot dam located by the factory below Pa. Rte. 452. The final miles through Chester are tidal and flat. Take out at the town park on the left, just above Pa. Rte. 291.

HAZARDS: Seven-foot dam below Pa. Rte. 452 (carry left).

WATER CONDITIONS: Canoeable only within 24 hours of heavy and intense rain.

GAUGE: USGS gauge at Dutton Mill Road, downstream right (call Philadelphia or inspect on site). Zero canoeing level is around 3.2 feet.

Ridley Creek

INTRODUCTION: Ridley Creek introduces you to an attractive side of suburbia, in the heart of Delaware County. Actually the creek spans a variety of settings, ranging from woods and open countryside to the grimy industrial flats of Eddystone. Suburbia is just the average of it all. This creek is a good rainy weather selection if you live nearby.

Section 1. Delchester Road to U.S. Rte. 13					
Gradient	Difficulty	Distance	Time	Scenery	Map
16	A to 2	13.8	4.5	Poor to Good	9

TRIP DESCRIPTION: The muddy brook below Delchester Road will challenge you right at the start, not with roaring rapids and thundering cataracts, but with fallen trees and woven wire fences. Conditions soon become more forgiving though as the stream burrows into the beech-filled woods of Ridley Creek State Park. But the paddler gets only a taste of this pretty preserve. There are almost 2,600 acres beyond the creek, to be explored on foot. In addition to open space, this park includes a restored 18th-century mill village where an enthusiastic staff brings those days back alive with demonstrations of various everyday skills and routines of colonial life. And when you run out of park to explore, neighboring Tyler Arboretum offers a green adventure also worthy of your time

Below the park, wooded floodplain and hillsides generally accompany the creek, with many beautiful houses on neatly landscaped grounds set just beyond. The surroundings remain that way almost to the end where the creek breaks out onto the more crowded, run-down, and industrial coastal plain. You finish at the head of tidewater, which means a slippery, mucky exit if you arrive at low tide. Undoubtedly, the most memorable scenic wonder of this journey is the railroad trestle below Baltimore Pike, on which some midnight Michelangelo has painted in giant letters, "LIONEL."

Most of Ridley Creek is simple. The best sustained whitewater consists of some long rock gardens and boulder patches within the state park. Below the park there are occasional Class 2 rapids, often the remains of past dams, but mostly you will find just swift water and riffles. You will also find five little dams, three to seven feet high, spread throughout the trip, and all requiring carries.

HAZARDS: Fences above Ridley Creek State Park and five dams between the park and 25th Street, Chester.

WATER CONDITIONS: Catch within 24 hours of hard rain.

GAUGE: Judge level by scouting rock garden between dam at Sycamore Mills and Barren Road in the state park.

Crum Creek

INTRODUCTION: Crum Creek is about the prettiest of Delaware County's ephemeral canoe streams. Sequestered down in Smedley Park, the Swarthmore College Campus, and various parcels of undeveloped real estate, it provides a novice cruise that often could easily pass for some place far more remote.

Section 1. Beatty Road to U.S. Rte. 13					
Gradient	Difficulty	Distance	Time	Scenery	Map
13	A to 1	6.4	2.0	Fair to Good	10

TRIP DESCRIPTION: Much of this run is set in a shallow, wooded gorge. Vegetation down there is lush and tangled, and in the summer great, green draperies of vines hang from the trees, creating a jungle-like atmosphere about the narrow creek. Towards the end of this section the paddler sees more of the suburbia that this area really is.

The first few miles are mostly smooth, partly because of three small dams, all of which should be carried. The remainder of the run is fast and riffly.

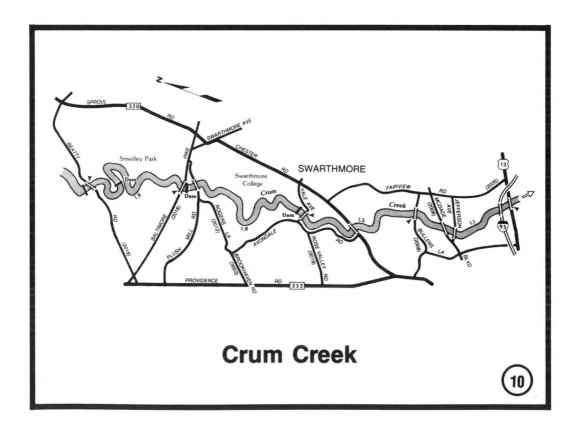

Crum Creek

10

You can end your trip on a good aesthetic note if you take out at McDade Boulevard or Jefferson Avenue, rather than grimy, old Rte. 13. Definitely do not go below Rte. 13. The creek files into a walled channel and about a quarter mile downstream drops over a three-foot weir with an ugly roller at its foot. But the real problem comes shortly below, where Crum Creek goes underground for a quarter mile. At levels that are suitable for boating the upper creek, this tunnel has inadequate clearance for a canoe. Needless to say, this would result in a long, dark, cold, and raunchy swim. You might even discover just what ever became of Cousin Fred's pet alligator, the one that he flushed down the toilet ten years ago.

HAZARDS: Dams below the water treatment plant, below Baltimore Pike, above Yale Avenue, and below Rte. 13. Assorted fallen trees. The subsurface channel of doom below Rte.13.

WATER CONDITIONS: Canoeable only within 24 hours of hard rain.

GAUGE: None.

Darby Creek

INTRODUCTION: Darby Creek is a thoroughly suburban waterway that brushes against the southwest side of Philadelphia. In its upper part, it is a radically intermittent storm drain, as are most other Delaware County streams, while its lower section is a tidal estuary. The later is unique in that it affords the only small stream tidal trip in Pennsylvania, passes through the only significant tidal wetlands remaining in the state, and it takes you through a national wildlife refuge.

Section 1. Pa. Rte. 320 to Darby (Pine Street)					
Gradient	Difficulty	Distance	Time	Scenery	Map
17	A to 2 –	10.8	3.0	Poor to Fair	11
2 @ 33					

TRIP DESCRIPTION: This is truly an urban and suburban tour, with practically no parkland to buffer you from the real world around. Nevertheless, enough woodlands, rolling estates, and generally nice neighborhoods counterbalance the apartment houses, industry, and commercial structures to create a pleasant trip.

The water is always fast and spiced with riffles. The descent of the fall line begins around Rosemont Avenue. It is not difficult, but the whitewater can be bouncy at times and is fairly continuous for about a mile. The gradient then gradually levels off, becoming smooth again by Providence Road. Complicating this section are an eight-foot dam above and a six-foot dam below Bridge Street, and a four-foot dam, with a nasty roller, beneath the railroad bridge below Baltimore Avenue. Carry all three. The take-out at Pine Street is steep and slippery, but if you proceed farther, you must paddle tidewater.

31

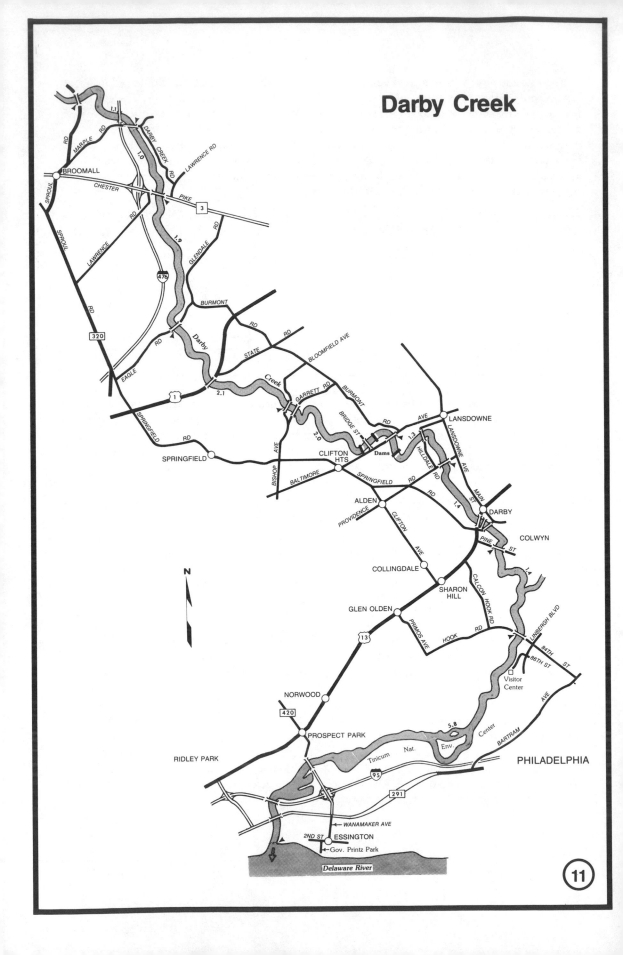

Darby Creek

11

HAZARDS: Three small dams and maybe some fallen trees.

WATER CONDITIONS: Only canoeable within 24 hours of hard rain.

GAUGE: Judge conditions at Rte. 320.

Section 2. Darby (Pine Street) to mouth					
Gradient	Difficulty	Distance	Time	Scenery	Map
0	A	7.2	3.0	Poor to Good	11

TRIP DESCRIPTION: The first 300 yards below Pine Street are still nontidal, so except after a rain, you will have to walk your canoe this distance. Only put in here at high tide, or your walk (slog) will be at least twice as far.

This section is initially drab. But below Hook Road, Darby Creek enters the Tinicum National Environmental Center. Initially high banks soon diverge, and the creek loses itself in a broad marsh. Your odds of spotting flocks of waterfowl here are good. In addition, you can always count on seeing plenty of big, silver birds, soaring in and out of nearby Philadelphia International Airport.

There is no access at the mouth, so paddle a half mile up the Delaware to Governor Printz Park in Essington. Better yet, just plan this as a circuit tour, putting in at the Tinicum Visitor's Center (off 86th Street and Lindbergh Boulevard).

HAZARDS: Bloodsucking insects during summer.

WATER CONDITIONS: Canoeable any time.

GAUGE: None.

Schuylkill River

INTRODUCTION: The Schuylkill is the largest and probably the most important tributary to the Delaware River. The name Schuylkill is Dutch for "hidden creek," apparently so chosen because its reedy mouth was so easy to miss by a ship passing up the Delaware. But once they discovered the Schuylkill, the founding fathers (and mothers) wasted no time in developing it. They cleared its valley's forests, farmed its valley's soils, and founded the "City of Brotherly Love" near its mouth. When they discovered iron ore in those soils, they smelted the ore in dozens of stone furnaces, fueled by charcoal made from the wood of the inexhaustable surrounding forests. Then when they exhausted the wood supply, and someone figured out how to properly burn anthracite, coal mines sprung up like mushrooms among the headwater hills around Pottsville. And when all this new industry, agriculture, and population created a demand for good, dependable transportation, the Schuylkill was elected to carry the load.

People have navigated the Schuylkill for a long time, but the river had its limitations. Except during high water periods, the shallow river was suitable only for canoe travel. While the canoe was adequate to carry the Indians, and was even used by William Penn to explore the river, this means was insufficient to move bulk commodities like coal, iron, and grain. So Pennsylvania chartered the "Schuylkill Navigation Company," which by 1828 had dug a canal along the river all

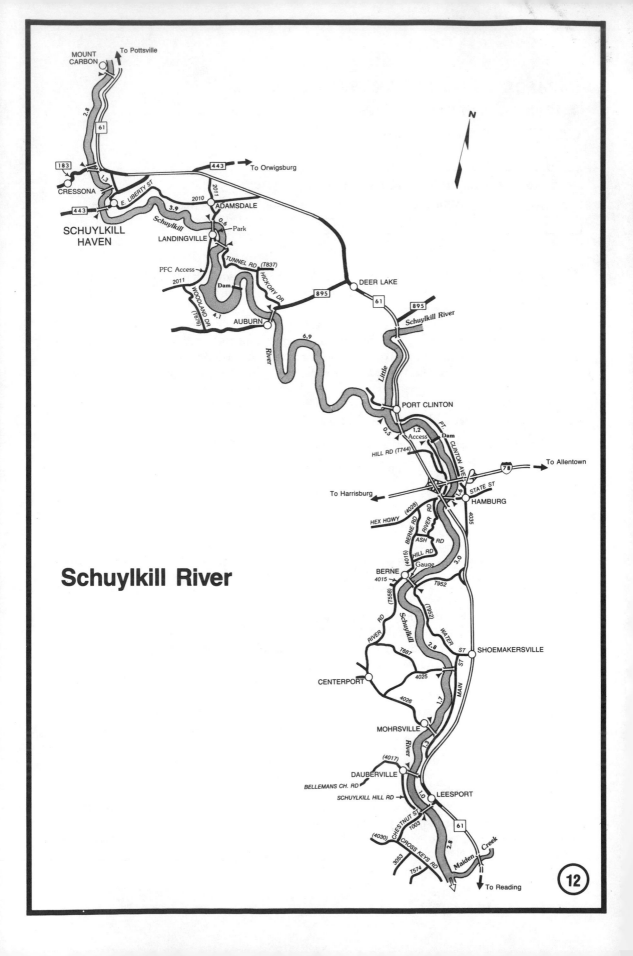

Schuylkill River

the way up to Port Carbon, above Pottstown, almost to the head of the river. But repeated clogging by silt spelled ruin for the upper section by 1853. Meanwhile, another branch of the canal system, the Union Canal between Reading and Middletown, also found unsuspected difficulties. Built through a belt of limestone, the canal leaked like a sieve. Part of the system, nevertheless, muddled through floods, siltation, and competition by the railroads, to survive all the way to the 1930's.

River commerce had its problems too. Back in the 18th century commercial boatmen (canoeists) found navigation repeatedly hindered by fishtrap weirs constructed by commercial fishermen. War broke out in the summer of 1738 when the boatmen organized and attempted to destroy some weirs above Phoenixville. The fishermen were better organized, however, and got the upper hand, destroying all the boatmen's canoes instead. Then there was the never resolved problem of sailors versus the ferry boaters. It seems that the sailors kept catching their masts in the ferry ropes. So the next time fishermen, rafters, or other boaters give you claustrophobia on your favorite stream, look to the past and count your blessings.

Industrialization and commerce had a predictable effect on the Schuylkill—pollution. Much of this problem, fortunately, is now a thing of the past. One of the first pollution abatement programs on the Schuylkill was the attempt to control the enormous sediment load in the stream, largely contributed by the coal mines. The unique approach was to construct a series of dams on the river (not at the mines as would be done today) to act as silt traps. Dredges would then ply these pools, depositing their loads in special disposal basins set back on the floodplain or in old mine pits. Some individuals even found a profit in dredging the substantial load of coal dust that also collected behind the dams. But most of the dredges are dormant now, and the dams are just that many more obstacles for the canoeist.

The Schuylkill is a handy recreational resource for southeast Pennsylvania. Being a generally placid waterway and having a relatively long boatable season, it is especially suitable for beginners to enjoy. In spite of the crowded and industrialized nature of the valley, the riverscape, especially after the foliage greens up, offers a nice escape from it all. It is nearby to so many, yet still uncrowded. Why drive all the way to the upper Delaware to go canoeing?

Section 1. Mt. Carbon to Port Clinton					
Gradient	Difficulty	Distance	Time	Scenery	Map
10	A to 2	19.6	6.0	Poor to Good	12

TRIP DESCRIPTION: It is unlikely that you will be enamored by the steep, slippery, and trash-strewn put-in at the bridge in Mt. Carbon, or by the essence of sewage wafting up from the cloudy waters, or by the crumbling, rubble banks covered by trash and topped by dismal buildings, rundown houses, more garbage, etc., that extends down to Schuylkill Haven. Indeed, some of the raunchy, old-time Schuylkill lives on. In fact, the only redeeming value of this first three miles is the swift, almost continuous whitewater ride down through rock gardens and gravel bars.

As it passes from Schuylkill Haven to Landingville, the river becomes more isolated and can even be pretty at times. But it has still not escaped from some lingering trash, coal refuse heaps, and mine drainage stains. The water is mostly calm now, but whitewater boaters can look forward to one nice playing hole churning in a chute below the first railroad bridge below Schuylkill Haven. Then things get really calm. Landingville, so named because it was once the river port for nearby, once-bustling Orwigsville, marks the head of the first sediment basin on the river. The

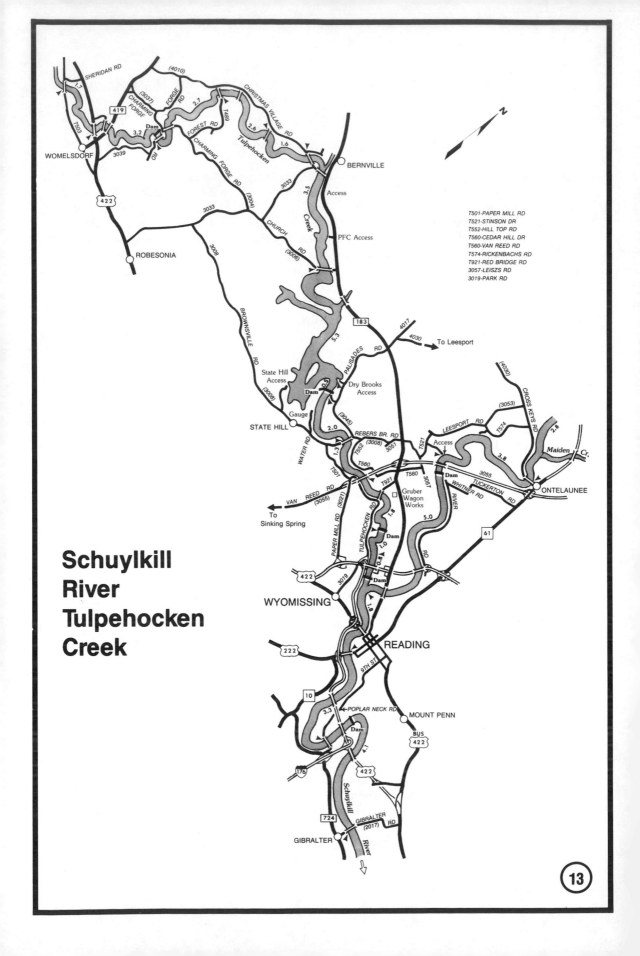

Schuylkill
River
Tulpehocken
Creek

SHERIDAN RD
(4010)
CHARMING FORGE RD
FORGE RD
(3037)
2.7
CHRISTMAS VILLAGE RD
T489
2.6
419
FOREST RD
Dam
3.2
1.6
Tulpehocken
WOMELSDORF
T503
3039
CHARMING FORGE RD
DB
1.7
422
(3004)
3033
CHURCH RD
3.5
Creek
3033
(3006)
BERNVILLE
Access
ROBESONIA
3008
PFC Access
BROWNSVILLE RD

T501-PAPER MILL RD
T521-STINSON DR
T552-HILL TOP RD
T560-CEDAR HILL DR
T560-VAN REED RD
T574-RICKENBACHS RD
T921-RED BRIDGE RD
3057-LEISZS RD
3019-PARK RD

183
4017
4030
To Leesport
(4030)
5.3
PALISADES RD
State Hill Access
(3008)
Dry Brooks Access
Dam
(3053)
CROSS KEYS RD
2.8
T574
Gauge
STATE HILL
WATER RD
2.0
(3045)
LEESPORT RD
Maiden Cr.
3.8
Access
T552
REBERS BR. RD
(3008)
3051
T521
ONTELAUNEE
1.3
T560
3055
TUCKERTON RD
Dam
VAN REED RD
T501
(3055)
(3021)
T921
T560
3057
WHITNER RD
To Sinking Spring
Gruber Wagon Works
RIVER
1.8
5.0
61
PAPER MILL RD
TULPEHOCKEN RD
Dam
1.0
422
3019
0.8
RD
Dam
WYOMISSING
1.8
222
READING
9TH ST
10
3.3
Poplar Neck Rd
MOUNT PENN
Dam
BUS 422
176
4.1
422
Schuylkill
724
GIBRALTER RD
(2017)
GIBRALTER
River

(13)

three-mile-long, mountain rimmed pool is attractive, and before you know it, you are finishing the easy carry (on right) around the 25-foot dam that pools the river.

The scenery continues to improve as the Schuylkill becomes mostly a remote, woodsy passage at the base of high mountain ridges. The still slow river finally picks up its pace to offer some long, even bouncy rapids in the last few miles down to Port Clinton. It also treats you to a sudden, splashy plunge beneath the shadowy, multiple spans of the double railroad bridge below Auburn (best chutes are to the right of center). If canal history interests you, watch for a well-preserved lock on the left a few miles below Auburn. Take out at the ball field on the left, just above the railroad bridge in Port Clinton.

HAZARDS: A 25-foot dam three miles below Landingville. Debris lodged in bridge piers.

WATER CONDITIONS: Canoeable in spring within week of hard rain. Sometimes up all spring.

GAUGE: Nearest usable gauge is USGS gauge at Berne (call Philadelphia) which should read over 5.5 feet. If the USGS ever restores the outside staff, the gauge at Landingville bridge should read 4.1 feet for above Schuylkill Haven and 3.6 feet for below. This reading is sporadically available from Philadelphia forecast office.

Section 2. Port Clinton to Reading (Poplar Neck Road)					
Gradient	Difficulty	Distance	Time	Scenery	Map
7	A to 1	29.8	10.0	Fair to Good	12,13

TRIP DESCRIPTION: With the addition of the Little Schuylkill, the Schuylkill starts looking like a river, though it is still pleasingly small. The passage starts with a pretty trip around Blue Mountain before heading off across the lowlands. Towns pass by quickly, while in between stretch miles of lonely, wooded banks. It is difficult, unfortunately, to escape the drone of distant highway noise. Even the passage through dingy old Reading is for the most part pleasant. There are some busy highways and big factories nearby, but there are also a lot of public parklands, old canal locks, and even some interesting vistas of the city.

The river generally moves along nicely, spiced by plenty of riffles. A few easy rapids race over the ruins of old canal dams. Two dams that are not in ruins are the 20-foot Kernsville Dam about 1.5 miles below the start (carry right) and the 17-foot Felix Dam a few miles below Maiden Creek (carry left). This section ends with an easy exit via a local park on the left.

HAZARDS: Two big dams.

WATER CONDITIONS: Above Maiden Creek it is usually canoeable until mid-May while below Maiden Creek it often lasts until mid-July.

GAUGE: USGS gauge at Berne (call Philadelphia) should read at least 5.1 feet to start at Port Clinton and 4.9 feet to run below Maiden Creek.

Section 3. Reading (Poplar Neck Road) to Philadelphia (The Waterworks)					
Gradient	Difficulty	Distance	Time	Scenery	Map
3	A to 1	62.1	22.0	Fair to Good	13,14,15

Schuylkill River

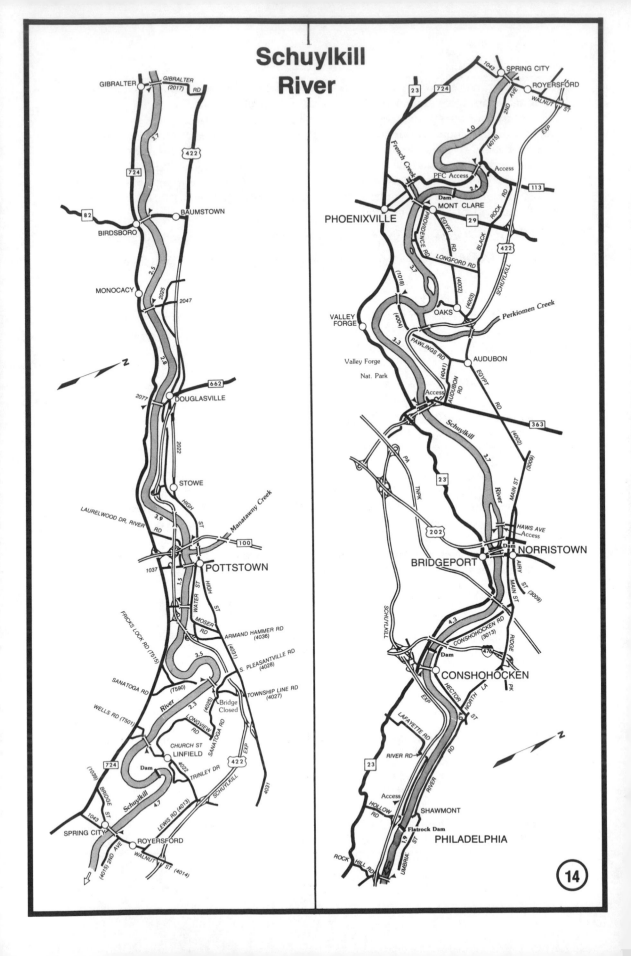

GIBRALTER   GIBRALTER (2017) RD

724   422   3.7

82   BAUMSTOWN
BIRDSBORO

2.5   MONOCACY   2025   2047

2.8   662

2077   DOUGLASVILLE

2022

STOWE

LAURELWOOD DR. RIVER RD   3.9   HIGH ST   Manatawny Creek   100

1037   POTTSTOWN   HIGH ST   WATER ST   MOSER RD

1.5   ARMAND HAMMER RD (4036)

FRICKS LOCK RD (T515)   3.5   (4031)   S. PLEASANTVILLE RD (4028)

SANATOGA RD   (T590)   TOWNSHIP LINE RD (4027)

WELLS RD (T501)   River   (4029)   2.3   Bridge Closed   SANATOGA RD

LONGVIEW RD   CHURCH ST   LINFIELD   4023   TRINLEY DR   422 EXP

724   (1039)   Dam   Schuylkill   4.7   LEWIS RD (4013)   SCHUYLKILL   4031

BRIDGE ST   1043   SPRING CITY   (4015) 2ND AVE   ROYERSFORD   WALNUT ST (4014)

1043   SPRING CITY   ROYERSFORD
23   724   4.0   (4015) 2ND AVE   WALNUT ST EXP

French Creek   Access   113

PFC Access   2.4

PHOENIXVILLE   Dam   MONT CLARE   29   EGYPT RD   BLACK ROCK RD   422

PROVIDENCE RD   LONGFORD RD   (4002)   SCHUYLKILL

(1018)   3.7   (4003)

VALLEY FORGE   (4004)   OAKS   Perkiomen Creek

3.3   PAWLINGS RD   AUDUBON

Valley Forge Nat. Park   (4041)   AUDUBON RD   EGYPT RD   363   (4002)

Access   Schuylkill   3.7   River   (3009)

PA TNPK   23   MAIN ST

202   HAWS AVE   Access

BRIDGEPORT   Dam   NORRISTOWN   AIRY ST   MAIN ST (3009)

SCHUYLKILL   4.3   CONSHOHOCKEN RD (3013)   RIDGE PK   476

Dam   CONSHOHOCKEN

HECTOR ST   NORTH LA

EXP   LAFAYETTE RD   RIVER RD

23   River RD   SHAWMONT

Access   HOLLOW RD   Flatrock Dam   1.9   UMBRIA ST   PHILADELPHIA

ROCK HILL RD

(14)

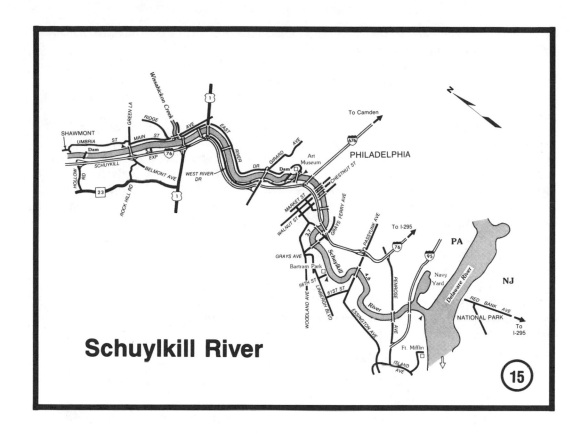

Schuylkill River

(15)

TRIP DESCRIPTION: The lower Schuylkill moves at a leisurely pace. This is a section where one long pool drops over a simple riffle or old dam to the next long pool. It is a fine place for beginners to wet their paddles.

The valley is filled with towns, industry, and power plants, yet this is not always apparent to the paddler. Much of the riverbank, as far down as Valley Forge, is quite undeveloped. There are occasional summer homes, but they are compensated for by many fine, traditional houses of native stone. History is everywhere along here, but it is seldom obvious. Did you know that it was back in these very woods, near Baumstown, that famed frontiersman, Daniel Boone, was born and raised over 200 years ago? Even Abe Lincoln had ancestral roots in this neighborhood. And of course, George Washington slept here, for one long, cold winter at Valley Forge.

Below Valley Forge civilization prevails. Strings of summer homes crowd the banks below Pa. Rte. 363 and around Flat Rock, while installations of heavy industry loom like sooty castles on the bluffs and bottoms around Norristown and Conshohocken (which ironically means "beautiful valley"). Entering Philadelphia, the river is confined by a steep gorge, with factories on its narrow bottoms, railroads and the expressway clinging to its sides, and houses of the city crowning the top. The river swirls through some jagged fall line reefs (there is even a small rapid here) and then slows in a final pool for its entry into elegant Fairmount Park.

Fairmount Park is a strip of manicured parkland, complete with ornate mansions, riverside sculptures, and even stands for viewing rowing regattas. It swarms with joggers, walkers, picnickers, and bicyclers—all sorts of city dwellers searching for elbow room. There is even wildlife here. On a winter's day you may find more Canada geese in the park than in nearby Tinicum National Wildlife Refuge. You will inevitably share the river with rowers, afloat in racing shells and sculls, all operating out of "Boathouse Row," a unique chain of ancient boat clubs. Paddle by at night

39

to enjoy their year-round Christmas light display. Even the roadbridges over this section are fancy, being decorated in ornate ironwork.

A few neo-classic structures on the left, set at the foot of the huge, temple-like Philadelphia Museum of Art, mark the site of the old city waterworks and the end of this section. There is no good take-out here, so you must double back to Columbia Bridge where there is parking by the river.

Dams, seven of them, are the only problems on this section. The tiny weir at the power plant below Poplar Neck Road is easily shot on the far left. At moderate levels, the sloping eight-foot dam above Spring City is canoeable, while the eight-foot dam above Pa. Rte. 23 should be carried. A sloping seven-footer at Norristown can be run on the left at low levels. Definitely avoid the dams at Conshohocken and The Waterworks. Portage 20-foot Flat Rock Dam, even though some eccentric sorts have actually run it. A safer sport at Flat Rock is to stand on shore and watch the flocks of seagulls play a game of chicken on its brink. These birds will play a game where they face upstream and drift down to the curving crest of the dam. The bravest will actually begin arcing over the brink before it flaps its wings and takes off upstream for another try. If only we paddlers could do that too.

Finally, much of this section and the next is conveniently shuttled via freeway, the infamous Schuylkill Expressway, known locally as the "Surekill Distressway." A ride on this high-speed, potholed wonder, filled with wild, weaving, kamikaze local drivers will more than compensate for the tranquility of the river trip.

HAZARDS: Seven weirs and dams ranging from two to 20 feet high.

WATER CONDITIONS: Canoeable from spring thaw to winter freeze-up, though in late summer or early fall it can get scratchy in some riffles.

GAUGE: USGS gauges at Berne and Pottstown (call Philadelphia). Levels below 4.8 feet at Berne and 1.4 feet at Pottstown may mean scraping in some riffles.

Section 4. The Waterworks to mouth					
Gradient	Difficulty	Distance	Time	Scenery	Map
0	A	8.4	4.0	Different	15

TRIP DESCRIPTION: Tidewater starts immediately below The Waterworks Dam. Most people do not think of this as canoeing waters. And admittedly, these waters are rather rank. But the tidal Schuylkill makes an interesting tour, and if you pick your tides correctly, it can offer easy paddling too.

Start by parking at the Art Museum and carrying behind The Waterworks, down a bicycle path, to an easy put-in beneath the West Drive Bridge. From here the narrow channel carries you by the edge of hustling, bustling downtown, past the great, gray walls of the Main Post Office and the 30th Street Train Station, and beneath a grillwork of busy bridges. The next few miles are drab—a world of rotting bulkheads, rusting corrugated buildings, abandoned factories, and junked vehicles. On the other hand, you will not be bothered by obnoxious water skiers, screaming idiots in rafts, cranky fly fisherman, and various other annoying patrons of more attractive waters. It is sort of an urban wilderness. You will be surprised to find that at its heart is a contrasting little patch of tattered green called Bartram Park. Located on the right, this was once the home of colonial botanist, John Gartram, who lived back in the days when plants grew in south Philly. It is also the last reasonable take-out. Below here, the Schuylkill files through a huge, fascinating complex of oil refineries, a pipefitter's dream world, that is most impressive after dark when it is lit up like a Christmas tree. When the refineries give way to the intimidating gray hulks of aircraft carriers and destroyers, you have reached the Philadelphia Navy Yard and the mouth. There is, unfortunately, no public access here, so your best choice of take-outs is across the wide Delaware River (allow for swift tidal current) at National Park, New Jersey.

HAZARDS: Wretched water quality, so avoid contact, especially after a rain. Also, give commercial shipping a wide berth.

WATER CONDITIONS: Always canoeable.

GAUGE: Not necessary.

Wissahickon Creek

INTRODUCTION: The "City of Brotherly Love" loves its little Wissahickon Creek. That is why, long ago, it swaddled Wissahickon's wooded gorge in a protective park called Fairmount, one of the largest and prettiest city parks in the nation. Preserved are the trees, old mills, and many a graceful bridge, banished are the vile automobiles, and welcome are the joggers, fishermen, strollers, bikers, and picnickers. And when it rains hard enough, a few smart canoeists sneak in and join the fun, discovering Philadelphia's amazing downtown wilderness.

Section 1. Penllyn Pike to Ridge Avenue					
Gradient	Difficulty	Distance	Time	Scenery	Map
12	A to 2 –	15.8	5.0	Fair to Very Good	16

TRIP DESCRIPTION: Wissahickon starts in a checkerboard of suburbs and remnant countryside north of Center Square, Montgomery County. With enough water, one can squeeze in as far upstream as Horseford Road, but it is a much easier target to hit by Penllyn Pike. The initial miles past Ambler are uninspiring—a tour of suburbia, complete with trashy banks, a big sewage treatment plant, and assorted drab buildings. But these features are soon enough displaced by stately private schools, country clubs, and parklands. By Stenton Avenue (good put-in upstream on right, in Fort Washington State Park) you will be paddling through a very posh neighborhood. Up here they feed croissants to the park squirrels and pigeons. The creek gushes onward, first through the elegant White Marsh Valley Golf Course, then past chateau-like Mount Saint Joseph's College, and finally into Philly and Fairmount Park. From here on to the Schuylkill the Wissahickon is entrenched within a shallow, wooded gorge. Pretty bridges, including a covered bridge, many dark stone arches, and the dizzying concrete arches of the Walnut Lane Bridge, regularly span the murky waters. Yet, with many of these bridges and the parallel park drive closed to motor vehicles, an atmosphere of remoteness prevails.

41

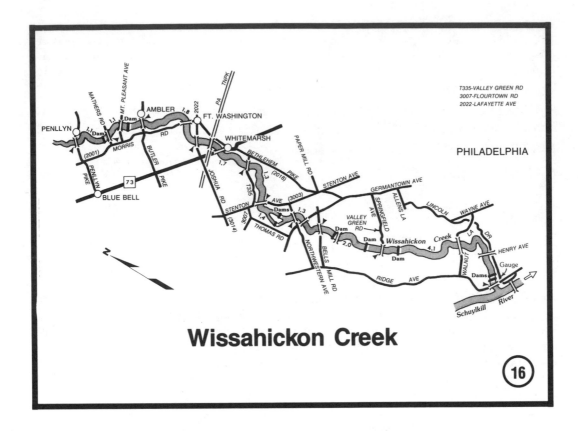

Wissahickon Creek

16

All of Wissahickon is fairly easy to paddle. There are many short riffles and, down in Fairmount Park, there are some short, rocky rapids. Fallen trees are always a potential but never a pervasive problem. Dams are. There are eight of them, ranging from two to eight feet high (shown on shuttle map). Carry all but the broken three-footer below Mount Pleasant Avenue and the two-foot weir that blocks the right channel of the island below Stenton Avenue (left channel requires a carry around a three-foot weir). A long, tiring carry on the right around the final two dams delivers you to the take-out at Ridge Avenue, 200 yards above the Schuylkill River.

HAZARDS: Possible trees and eight dams.

WATER CONDITIONS: Canoeable only within 24 to 48 hours of hard rain.

GAUGE: USGS gauge about 100 feet above Ridge Avenue on river left should read over 2.7 feet. Also, enough water to cleanly negotiate the riffles below Penllyn Pike indicates adequate water below.

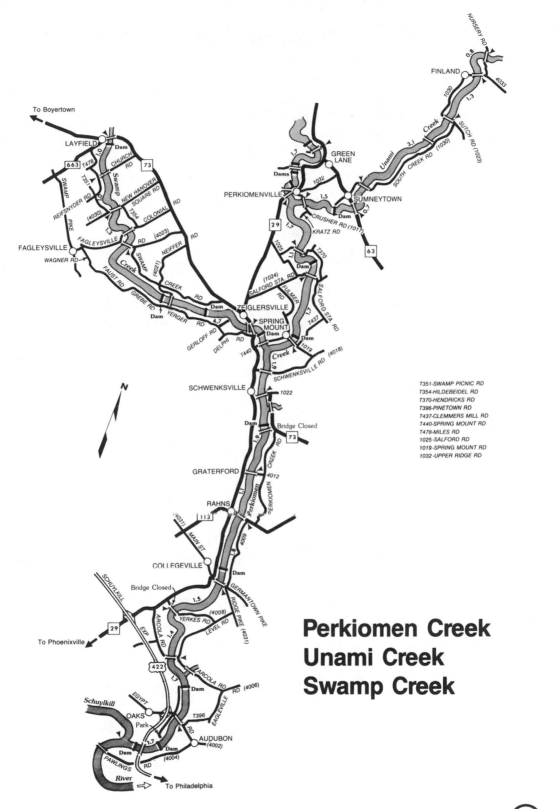

To Boyertown

LAYFIELD
Dam
663 T478 1.0 CHURCH RD
73
T351
Swamp
NEW HANOVER SQUARE RD
COLONIAL RD
T354
(4030)
FAGLEYSVILLE
WAGNER RD
SWAMP PIKE
REIFSNYDER RD
1.3
FAGLEYSVILLE RD
NEIFFER RD
(4023)

Creek
Swamp
FAUST RD
GREBE RD
YERGER RD
CREEK RD
(4020)
Dam
Dam 4.7
GERLOFF RD
DELPHI RD
T440
ZEIGLERSVILLE
SPRING MOUNT
Dam

0.8 NURSERY RD
FINLAND
1030
4033
1.3
SUTCH RD (1023)
Unami Creek 3.1
SOUTH CREEK RD (1030)
1.7
GREEN LANE
Dams
1032
PERKIOMENVILLE
SUMNEYTOWN
Dam 0.7
1.5
UPPER RIDGE RD (1017)
CRUSHER RD (1017)
KRATZ RD
29 1.3
1025
T370
1.1
Dam
63
(1024)
SALFORD STA. RD
FULMER RD
SALFORD STA. RD
1.7
T437
1019
Creek 1.9
SCHWENKSVILLE RD (4018)

SCHWENKSVILLE
1022
Dam
Bridge Closed
73
1.8

GRATERFORD
4012
RAHNS
113
(4031)
MAIN ST
PERKIOMEN CREEK RD
1.3

COLLEGEVILLE
Dam
Bridge Closed
GERMANTOWN PIKE
1.5
YERKES RD
(4008)
LEVEL RD
RIDGE PIKE (4031)
SCHUYLKILL EXP
ARCOLA RD
To Phoenixville
29
422
ARCOLA RD
EAGLEVILLE RD (4006)
1.7
Dam
Schuylkill
EGYPT
OAKS Park
T396
EAGLEVILLE RD
AUDUBON (4002)
Dam (4004)
1.7
RD
Dam
PAWLINGS
River
To Philadelphia

T351-SWAMP PICNIC RD
T354-HILDEBEIDEL RD
T370-HENDRICKS RD
T396-PINETOWN RD
T437-CLEMMERS MILL RD
T440-SPRING MOUNT RD
T478-MILES RD
1025-SALFORD RD
1019-SPRING MOUNT RD
1032-UPPER RIDGE RD

N

Perkiomen Creek
Unami Creek
Swamp Creek

17

Perkiomen Creek

INTRODUCTION: Perkiomen Creek (pronounced perky·omen and meaning "cranberry place") is a large, sleepy tributary to the Schuylkill, draining much of upper, slowly suburbanizing Montgomery County. Shackled by a host of old milldams and extensively lived upon, this is a disappointing canoe stream. It is, nevertheless, conveniently near to the big city, and beginners are likely to enjoy its leisurely miles. Small stream connoisseurs should wait for a hard rain and tackle its four lovely tributaries.

Section 1. Green Lane (Pa. Rte. 29) to mouth					
Gradient	Difficulty	Distance	Time	Scenery	Map
6	A to 1	17.5	6.0	Fair	17

TRIP DESCRIPTION: You can put in 1.75 miles upstream, at the bridge above Green Lane, and enjoy some pretty park scenery and a few short and exciting boulder rapids. But there are also three dams to carry in this short distance. It is a questionable trade-off.

Perhaps half of Perkiomen Creek is pooled behind little dams. The rest is swift and riffly, with many easy rapids formed by the rubble of past dams. Nine dams still stand between Pa. Rte. 29 and the mouth. Beginners should portage all but two of these. The exceptions are a two-foot weir between Rte. 29 and Hendricks Station Road (run right) and a broken three-foot rock dam above Salford Station Road (passable in several spots). Take special care to avoid the sloping three-foot dam at the county park below Egypt Road and the rounded three-foot weir just above the mouth. Both have deceptively powerful and potentially lethal rollers.

The riverscape of Perkiomen is often mediocre. Both summer and permanent dwellings dot the banks, especially between Collegeville and Schwenksville, where busy and noisy Pa. Rte. 29 follows closely. In between remain stretches of wooded banks and bluffs, here and there preserved in parcels of county park land. An Audubon wildlife sanctuary accompanies a mile of the left bank below Egypt Road. This sanctuary, called Mill Grove Farm, was once the estate of famed 19th-century ornithologist John James Audubon. If you follow the Perkiomen to its mouth, continue on down the Schuylkill for .75 miles to an easy take-out beneath the left end of SR4004, Pawlings Road.

HAZARDS: Nine dams and weirs, particularly the two below Egypt Road.

WATER CONDITIONS: Canoeable winter and spring within four days of hard rain.

GAUGE: USGS gauge at Graterford (call Philadelphia) should be at least 2.2 feet to float over all the riffles.

Skippack Creek

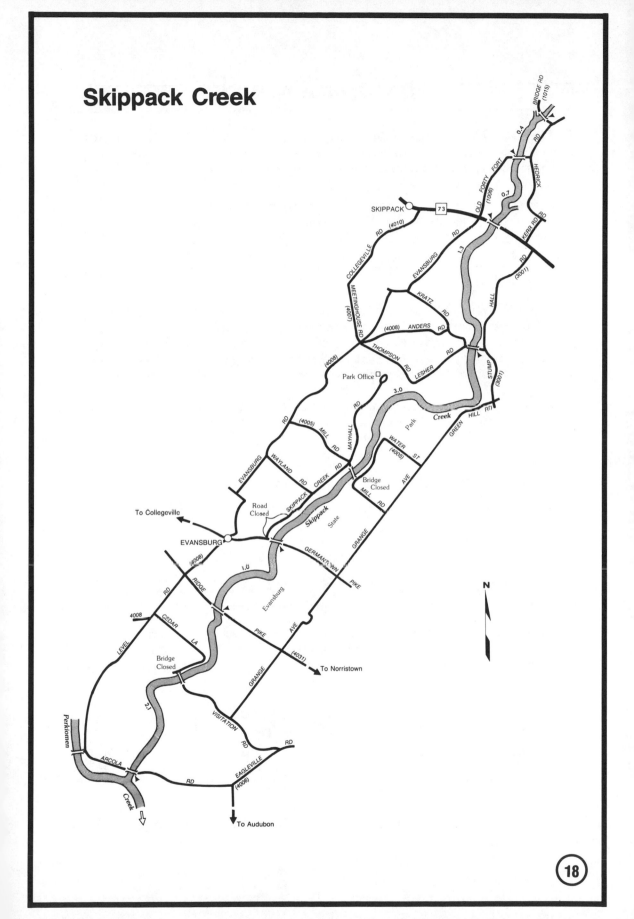

Skippack Creek

INTRODUCTION: Skippack Creek is a quick rising and quick falling little tributary to the Perkiomen that enters a few miles below Collegeville. It offers a pleasant and conveniently situated novice outing, largely within the confines of obscure Evansburg State Park.

Section 1. Bridge Road, SR1015 to mouth					
Gradient	Difficulty	Distance	Time	Scenery	Map
10	A to 1	8.5	3.0	Good	18

TRIP DESCRIPTION: Skippack Creek flows mostly down through dense and tangled what seems like tenth-growth forest. Though inside a park, it still passes under a few power lines, and a moderate number of farms and houses are visible through the trees. But the atmosphere grows increasingly remote with each mile. By the end, Skippack is fringed by little rock ledges and even a few cliffs. Typical of a Perkiomen tributary, Skippack is crossed by a number of graceful, stone arch road bridges.

The creek is easy. It flows over a sand and gravel bottom, and the gravel-formed riffles come frequently. A few fallen trees are inevitable, but surprisingly few block this tiny waterway. Take out at Arcola Road, just above the mouth.

HAZARDS: Watch for strainers.

WATER CONDITIONS: Canoeable winter and spring within two days of hard rain.

GAUGE: Judge riffle below Skippack Pike.

East Branch Perkiomen Creek

INTRODUCTION: The East Branch is a lovely little canoe trail, precariously perched on the outer edge of creeping suburbia. Born in rural Bucks County, northwest of Doylestown, it meanders many miles to meet the Perkiomen at Schwenksville, always moving at a gentle pace that can be managed by novices.

Section 1. Allentown Road, SR1001 to Skippack Pike, Pa. Rte. 73					
Gradient	Difficulty	Distance	Time	Scenery	Map
10	A to 1	11.2	4.0	Good	19

TRIP DESCRIPTION: Do not be confused by the road signs when you search for this creek. The signs label it "Branch Creek."

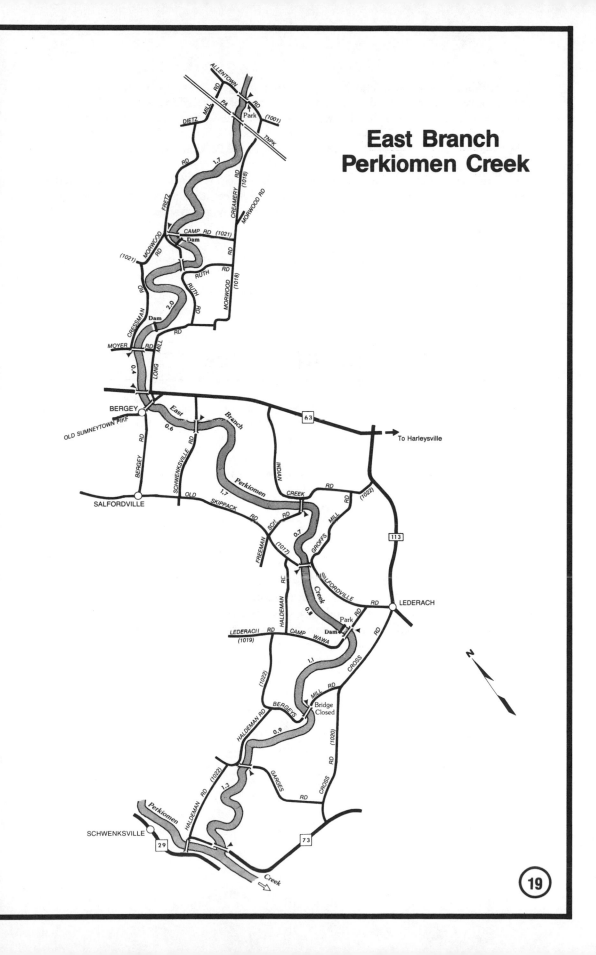

East Branch
Perkiomen Creek

ALLENTOWN RD

PA

RD

Park

(1001)

DIETZ

MILL

TNPK

RD

1.7

CREAMERY (1018)

MORWOOD RD

MORWOD RD

FRETZ

CAMP RD (1021)

Dam

RD

(1021)

RUTH

RD

MORWOOD (1018)

CRESSMAN RD

2.0

RUTH RD

Dam

MOYER RD

0.4

LONG MILL RD

BERGEY

East

Branch

63

0.6

To Harleysville

OLD SUMNEYTOWN PIKE

BERGEY RD

SCHWENKSVILLE RD

Perkiomen

INDIAN

RD

(1022)

SALFORDVILLE

OLD

SKIPPACK

Creek

RD

1.7

RD

113

FREEMAN SCH. RD.

(1017)

0.7

GROFFS MILL RD

SALFORDVILLE

Creek

LEDERACH

RD

LEDERACH

0.8

Park

RD

Dam

HALDEMAN RD

CAMP

WAWA

Dam

LEDERACH RD

(1019)

(1022)

1.1

CROSS

N

BERGEYS MILL RD

Bridge
Closed

HALDEMAN RD

0.9

CROSS RD (1020)

HALDEMAN RD (1022)

1.3

GARGES

RD

CROSS RD

Perkiomen

SCHWENKSVILLE

29

73

Creek

19

The East Branch is nice enough at its start and then just gets better and better. The first miles pass mainly through a quiet, rural setting, with some glimpses of scattered housing developments lurking in the distance. The creek then works its way back into the woods. Sloping rock shelves begin to line the banks—shelves which eventually grow to the stature of cliffs. The journey finishes in a shallow, wooded gorge that suddenly opens to the Perkiomen Valley. Throughout this trip the creek glides beneath moldy, old, stone arch bridges.

A mild gradient is expended over broad gravel riffles and a few ledges. The pools in between are swift and often shallow. Three weirs, from three to five feet high, all require carries. But with riverwide strainers infrequent, these dams may be your only annoyance.

HAZARDS: Three weirs.

WATER CONDITIONS: Canoeable winter and spring within two days of hard rain.

GAUGE: Judge riffle below Allentown Road.

Swamp Creek

INTRODUCTION: Swamp Creek runs down from the Berks County Line to join the Perkiomen above Schwenksville. The creek is neither swampy nor sluggish and makes an enjoyable, but not demanding, trip for the novice whitewater canoeist.

Section 1. Layfield (Pa. Rte. 73) to mouth					
Gradient	Difficulty	Distance	Time	Scenery	Map
14	A to 1+	8.4	3.0	Good	17

TRIP DESCRIPTION: This run is mostly set back in quiet woodlands, interrupted now and then by a summer home or roadbridge (often including some ancient stone arches). The creek yields a bountiful supply of riffles, including a tortuous shot through some old dam remains and an easy rock garden slalom through a short diabase gorge approaching Pa. Rte. 29. You will need to carry four small dams (shown on map), but you can avoid the last one by taking out above Pa. Rte. 29.

HAZARDS: Four small dams.

WATER CONDITIONS: Canoeable winter and spring within two days of hard rain.

GAUGE: Use New Hanover Square Road Bridge. Zero canoeing level is three joints and two inches down from the top of the left abutment. You can also judge by looking at the wide riffles above Spring Mount Road.

Unami Creek

INTRODUCTION: Unami is a weird creek. Who would expect to find this piece of wild West Virginia-like whitewater set in the gently rolling countryside of civilized Montgomery County? But there it is; running into the tired old Perkiomen no less. Advanced paddlers who like an expeditionary flavor to their outings should pay the Unami a visit after the next hard rainfall.

Section 1. Nursery Road, T334 to mouth					
Gradient	Difficulty	Distance	Time	Scenery	Map
33	A to 4,6	7.7	4.5	Good	17
1.3 @ 69					

TRIP DESCRIPTION: From its whitewater start near Finland, to Sumneytown, Unami is characterized by an erratic descent through clogged patches of rounded diabase boulders. Two of the rapids are so frighteningly steep, clogged, and undercut that they are impassable at any level. To complicate matters even more, dense growths of living trees and brush often sprout from the stream bed, similar to what occurs on the intermittent limestone streams of central Pennsylvania. So you find a slalom within a slalom. Then to further complicate matters, there are no fewer than six small dams, in various states of repair, many of which will invite a carry (usually on heavily posted lands).

The creek runs down a shallow, narrow, and v-shaped valley, where the adjacent wooded slopes are as bouldery as the stream bed. In spite of its ruggedness, too many people have planted their houses in this otherwise wild setting.

The lower creek leaves the diabase belt, and as a result, is much more reasonable to attempt. There are still lots of riffles, but no rapids, and only one dam to carry. Best of all, this section suffers little development. Take out on the Perkiomen where Kratz Road approaches the creek.

HAZARDS: Dams, the rapids, and living trees and brush.

WATER CONDITIONS: Canoeable winter and spring within day of hard rain.

GAUGE: None. Inspect from Creek Road, SR1030.

French Creek

INTRODUCTION: French Creek is an enjoyable, novice, but ephemeral canoe stream that rushes into the Schuylkill at Phoenixville. It sneaks in beneath the Pa. Rte. 29 Bridge, at first glance appearing to gush right from the innards of the big steel mill upstream. Do not be deceived.

When most people think of steel and Pennsylvania, they think of Pittsburgh. But just go by Fairless Hills, Steelton, Lebanon, Bethlehem, or Coatesville, and you will conclude that the industry has been very much present in the east too. And it has been iron and steel, not canoeing, that has long put French Creek on the map. Of course the importance of the big mill in Phoenixville is obvious. But did you know that long before it was there, they were making metal in this valley? The first attempt at steel making in Pennsylvania commenced in 1732 at Coventry Forge, right along French Creek. And it is along the headwaters of French Creek today that one can find one of the best opportunities to study the art of iron making as was practiced in the late 18th and early 19th centuries. The place is Hopewell Village National Historical Site, in French Creek State Park. There you will find a superbly restored iron making village, a partially working iron furnace, and an excellent interpretive program to breathe life into it.

Studying history and industrial arts are not the only added attractions to a visit to French Creek. Geology becomes the attraction just three miles west of the Coventryville put-in, at the Village of Saint Peters. Here the tiny headwaters take a wild tumble through a jumble of diabase boulders. Called the Falls of French Creek, this stretch is not only interesting, but certain to inspire some wild whitewater fantasies.

Section 1. Coventryville (T517) to mouth					
Gradient	Difficulty	Distance	Time	Scenery	Map
14	A to 2 –	14.0	4.5	Poor to Good	20

TRIP DESCRIPTION: The most appealing run extends from T517 to Pa. Rte. 23. Up here French Creek forges an attractive path through a combination of woods and farmlands. This is still a pretty densely populated area, so one does not travel far without encountering a house or two. On the bright side, many of these houses are old, beautiful, and well maintained.

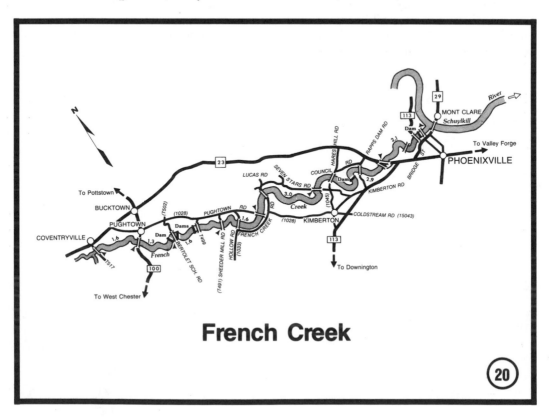

French Creek

⑳

This is a shallow and rocky stream. Riffles and easy rapids are frequent, often even continuous. Interrupting the fun are four weirs, from two to five feet high, all located on the shuttle map. You will probably want to carry at least three of these, the two-foot weir above T499 being canoeable.

The streamscape turns ugly below Pa. Rte. 23. Banks become big slag piles as the creek begins an intimate tour of the steel mill. A seven-foot dam requires a carry and potential trespass on mill property. If you continue to the mouth, take out across the Schuylkill in Mont Clare, just below the Rte. 29 Bridge, in Schuylkill Canal Park.

HAZARDS: Five weirs and dams.

WATER CONDITIONS: Canoeable winter and spring within two days of hard rain.

GAUGE: If you can cleanly run the rock riffle just downstream of T517, that should be adequate. For rough correlation, both USGS gauges at Chadds Ford, on Brandywine, and Graterford, on Perkiomen (call Philadelphia for both), should read at least 3.2 feet.

Manatawny Creek

INTRODUCTION: Manatawny Creek is an exceptionally attractive country brook that flows into the Schuylkill River at Pottstown. Its pretty name is Indian for "place where we drink." But the good old days are long gone, for a quick glance at the cows milling about the put-in will convince you that you had better bring your own bottle.

Section 1. Pleasantville (SR1030, Covered Bridge Road) to mouth					
Gradient	Difficulty	Distance	Time	Scenery	Map
11	A to 1	15.8	5.0	Good to Very Good	21

TRIP DESCRIPTION: The start is so appropriate—at a calendar-perfect covered bridge. The quiet brook rambles off across a roomy valley bordered by some wooded hills that, in this neighborhood, look like mountains. The winding route carries you past farms and big, cow-filled pastures, past old mills, stone houses and barns, quiet woods, rock cliffs and outcrops, and another covered bridge. The surroundings are built up only around Earleville and Pottstown, while the section below Earleville down to Pine Forge is particularly pretty and remote. You will find this creek is more a home to ducks and geese than people.

This is a gentle stream, but it is by no means flat. Countless riffles break over a bottom of fine gravel, a few ledges, and old dam remains. You will need to carry a three-foot dam above Fisher Mill Road, T575 and a six-foot dam by a picturesque, old mill below Earleville.

The easiest take-out is at the town park in Pottstown. If you paddle to the mouth, you must add a short, slippery portage (on right) around a diagonal, five-foot dam located above the railroad bridge in Pottstown. The best take-out at the mouth is directly across the Schuylkill, beneath the Pa. Rte. 100 Bridge.

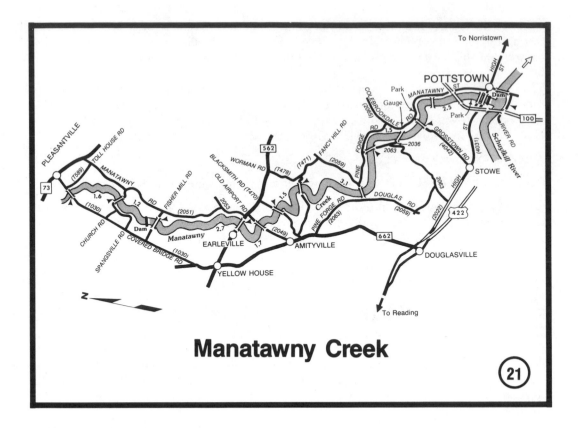

Manatawny Creek

㉑

HAZARDS: Three small dams to carry.

WATER CONDITIONS: Canoeable winter and spring within three days of hard rain.

GAUGE: USGS gauge upstream left of SR2036 should roughly be over 3.5 feet. Riffle upstream of SR1030 must be cleanly passable. For rough estimate, USGS gauge at Graterford, on the Perkiomen (call Philadelphia), should read over 2.3 feet.

Tulpehocken Creek

INTRODUCTION: Tulpehocken (Indian for "stream of the turtles") is the creek next door for Reading area paddlers. For these people, its swift, winding waters are the ideal place to dust off the old boat and start the season, when the ice clears out. And for boaters oriented only towards placid waters, there is plenty available, thanks to a Corps of Engineers-built lake that now floods the middle section.

Section 1. Sheridan Road, SR3061 to mouth					
Gradient	Difficulty	Distance	Time	Scenery	Map
6	A to 1	28.0	10.5	Good	13

TRIP DESCRIPTION: A reasonable head of navigation is SR3061, near Stouchburg. It is possible to put in even higher, when the water is really up, but a five-foot dam at Scharff Road and numerous electric fences complicate this pastoral passage. To Pa. Rte. 419, the creek winds by a few summer homes, some pretty, old farms, and a picturesque, old mill at U.S. Rte. 422. After that, it runs through sparsely populated countryside, past wooded bluffs and bottoms and old, weed-choked fields. Carry the six-foot dam that hides beneath SR3037, Charming Forge Road, on the left, while farther downstream you will find a two-foot weir canoeable. In general, the water is swift and smooth, but often broken by gentle, gravel-formed riffles.

At normal pool, Blue Marsh Reservoir begins about a mile above Bernville. The view surrounding this mostly narrow lake is largely preserved by state game lands and Blue Marsh State Park. Thus, except where busy Pa. Rte. 183 crowds the north bank near Bernville, the paddler sees few houses and enjoys a quiet lake (assuming that he visits out of motorboat season) surrounded by forested hillsides and both cultivated and abandoned fields. There are boat launch areas at Church Road, T489, State Hill (right), and Dry Brooks (left), the latter two just above the dam. If your itinerary includes portaging the dam, which rises less than a hundred feet above the stream bed, the most expedient route (also illegal) is straight up the dam face, at the intake structure, and then straight down the other side.

The lower creek is a pleasant run, with easy access via the road to the stilling basin, at the foot of Blue Marsh Dam. This section is often relatively wide, shallow, and sprinkled with frequent, rocky riffles. Wooded bluffs and tangled bottomlands make Reading seem as if it were much more than six miles away.

About four miles below the dam, Tulpehocken passes beneath an extraordinarily long, single span covered bridge. Up on the hill, to the left, rises an imposing wooden building, freshly painted in yellow with black trim, that is clearly neither a barn nor a house. This is the Gruber Wagon Works. Built in 1882, at a site now inundated by Blue Marsh Lake, this ancient factory produced farm wagons, work sleighs, wheelbarrows, and later, wooden truck bodies. It operated until 1972, and in 1976 it was moved to this spot and restored. If you have any love of gadgetry and history, you will want to stop and tour this rare landmark.

Tulpehocken drifts onward, past an immaculate, gray, stone mill, whose pond is likely to be filled with noisy flocks of mallards and Canada geese. The millpond is formed by a six-foot dam, which can be carried on the right. Finish your cruise at the Berks County Leisure Area, on the right bank upstream of the U.S. Rte. 422 Bypass, or downstream left of that bridge, at the Stonecliff Recreation Area, at the foot of Columbia Street, Reading. Those desiring to continue on to the Schuylkill will find a 12-foot dam to carry (steep walk on right). Finally, if this last section is too low to canoe, you can still enjoy it on foot or bicycle, via the Union Canal Towpath, extending from Rebers Bridge down to Stonecliff.

HAZARDS: Three small dams. Blue Marsh Dam is an obstacle, not a hazard.

WATER CONDITIONS: Canoeable late fall, winter, and spring within three days of hard rain, above Bernville, and for week after rain, below Blue Marsh Dam. Lake canoeable from ice-out to freeze-up.

GAUGE: USGS gauge on right bank, a mile above Rebers Bridge Road, upstream of water treatment plant (drive past treatment plant on Water Road and bear right at first turn). You need 3.3 feet to start at Stouchburg, 2.6 feet to start at Blue Marsh Dam. For rough estimate, USGS gauge at Berne, on Schuylkill (call Philadelphia), should read over 5.5 feet to start at top.

Maiden Creek

INTRODUCTION: Maiden Creek is a tranquil tributary to the Schuylkill, joining northeast of Reading. It is the source of most of that city's water supply, and it can be the source of fun for novices and beginners seeking a scenic and easy float.

Section 1. Kempton (Pa. Rte. 737) to Moselem (Pa. Rte. 662)					
Gradient	Difficulty	Distance	Time	Scenery	Map
8	A to 1	11.6	3.5	Good	22

TRIP DESCRIPTION: If there is enough water, you can tag on an extra 2.75 miles by starting at SR4036, Steinsville, on Ontelaunee Creek. The entire passage down to Lenhartsville is quite scenic. The little creek picks its way through the rugged to rolling foothills of Blue Mountain.

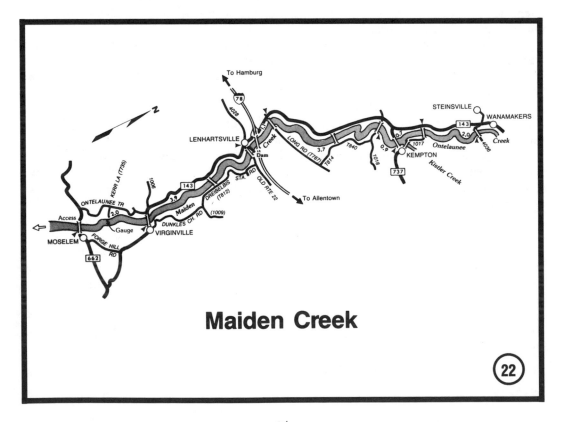

Maiden Creek

22

Little Schuylkill River

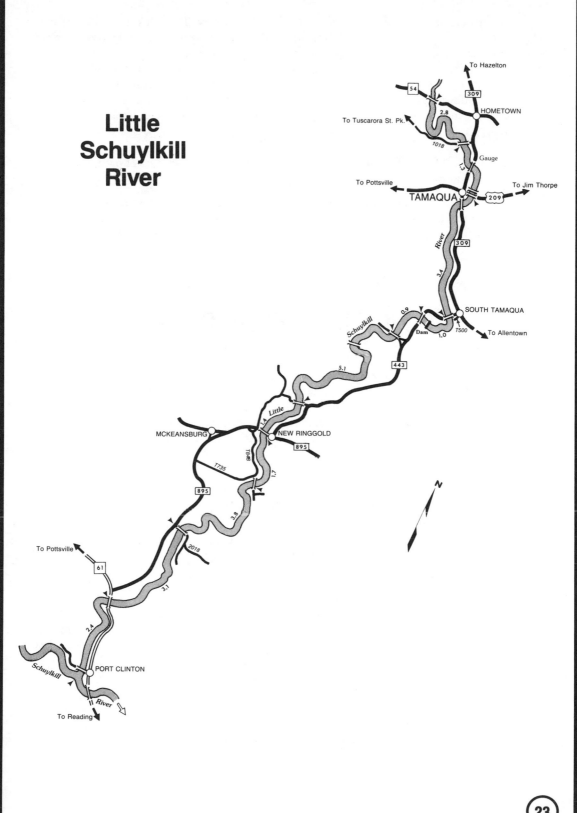

To Hazelton

54

309

2.8

HOMETOWN

To Tuscarora St. Pk.

1018

Gauge

1.3

To Pottsville

TAMAQUA

209

To Jim Thorpe

River

309

3.4

SOUTH TAMAQUA

0.9

Schuylkill

Dam

7500

To Allentown

1.0

5.1

443

Little

1.4

MCKEANSBURG

NEW RINGGOLD

895

T735

T788

1.7

895

3.8

To Pottsville

2018

61

3.1

2.4

Schuylkill

PORT CLINTON

River

To Reading

N

Amazingly, rugged as the terrain may be, this is still farm country. The creek though is not rugged, offering a swift, smooth float spiced by simple riffles. A few trees are the only hazards, until you come upon the five-foot dam at Lenhartsville. Carry on the right.

Below Lenhartsville, the creek passes through a short, wooded, gorge-like section, before breaking out into a more open valley. Bottomland woods and weedy fields mix with houses and a bit of litter, but it is still pleasant. The trip ends at the head of Reading's beautiful Lake Ontelaunee. Because Reading forbids boating on its reservoir, take out at the public access area at Pa. Rte. 662.

HAZARDS: Dam at Lenhartsville and possible fallen trees.

WATER CONDITIONS: Canoeable winter and spring within three days of hard rain, above I-78, for a week after rain, below.

GAUGE: USGS gauge at end of Kerr Lane, T735. You need 3.0 feet to start at SR4036 and 2.8 feet to start at Lenhartsville. For rough estimate, USGS gauge at Berne, on Schuylkill River (call Philadelphia), should read over 5.8 feet.

Little Schuylkill River

INTRODUCTION: The Little Schuylkill River is altogether probably the nicest canoe stream in the Schuylkill Basin. Born in the slimy, grimy, mine-scarred hills that surround Tamaqua, and then flowing through the tidy, well-tended, ridge and valley farm country, between Blue and Sharp mountains, the stream actually reflects little of either. It is a loner. It keeps to itself, bearing its own personality. Mostly suitable for novices, it is a convenient and recommended springtime tour.

Section 1. Pa. Rte. 54 to South Tamaqua (Pa. Rte. 443)					
Gradient	Difficulty	Distance	Time	Scenery	Map
35	1 to 2 +	7.5	2.0	Poor to Very Good	23

TRIP DESCRIPTION: This is by far the most interesting whitewater portion of the Little Schuylkill. The diminutive brook at Pa. Rte. 54 hurries off into remote woodlands whose facade of hemlock, alders, rhododendron, and even a towering cliff crowd the clear waters. Its rapids, which are frequent, rocky, but of mild pitch, are formed by boulders, ledges, and cobbles. They hurry you past the fascinating stone ruins of old millworks, now being repossessed by saplings and rhododendron. Then suddenly the creek rounds a bend, a tank farm looms on the right, and Tamaqua envelopes the Little Schuylkill. Following a few steep, rocky rapids, the creek evens out in a dredged channel, through densely packed urban surroundings. Tamaqua ends almost as suddenly as it begins, and the remaining distance to South Tamaqua follows a uniform, riffly descent through a fairly attractive mountain gap. Take out just below Pa. Rte. 443, at dead ending T500.

HAZARDS: Strainers above Tamaqua.

WATER CONDITIONS: Canoeable in spring within two days of hard rain, or during good snowmelt.

GAUGE: USGS gauge located on north side of Tamaqua, 100 yards north of Pa. Rte. 309 Bridge, left bank, by Fire Dept. Training Area. Zero canoeing level for upper creek is 2.5 feet. For below Tamaqua, you need 2.4 feet. If staff gauge is washed away, there must be at least 0.6 feet of water flowing over the concrete weir at gauge. Roughly, USGS gauge at Berne, on Schuylkill River (call Philadelphia), should be over 6.5 feet.

Section 2. South Tamaqua to Port Clinton					
Gradient	Difficulty	Distance	Time	Scenery	Map
15	A to 1+	19.4	6.0	Fair to Very Good	23

TRIP DESCRIPTION: The Little Schuylkill now leaves the coal country. But it does not go very far before pausing in a short lake—another Schuylkill silt basin, complete with floating dredge. The lake is formed by a seven-foot dam, easily portaged on the right. The next point of interest appears about a mile farther, in the form of a complex of mysterious, sinister-looking buildings and many warning posters. This is the Atlas Powder Company. The name refers to GUNpowder, not baby powder, face powder, etc. So please refrain from smoking or trespassing.

Below the explosives plant, the Little Schuylkill enters a remote, wooded, canyon-like stretch that is by far the prettiest reach of the river. The gray waters (from coal dust) rush over almost continuous riffles, but this remains a novice trip.

After hurrying past New Ringgold, the Little Schuylkill regains its remoteness, as it passes through woodlands thick with rhododendron and dotted with beech. There are also expansive views of big Blue Mountain, which now assumes the name Hawk Mountain. For here, each fall and spring, great numbers of migrating hawks, and even greater numbers of migrating hawk watchers, converge on this drafty ridge. Paddlers get to share a piece of the show, without having to trudge up the lousy mountain. Numerous gravel and cobble riffles make progress easy, soon delivering the paddler to Port Clinton. Take out at the church park on the left, along Penn Street, or on private land (after asking permission) on the left, at the mouth.

HAZARDS: Silt basin dam 0.75 miles below T500.

WATER CONDITIONS: Canoeable in spring during snowmelt or within five days of hard rain, above New Ringgold, and within two weeks of hard rain below.

GAUGE: USGS gauge at Berne should be over 6.1 feet for above New Ringgold, over 5.5 feet for below.

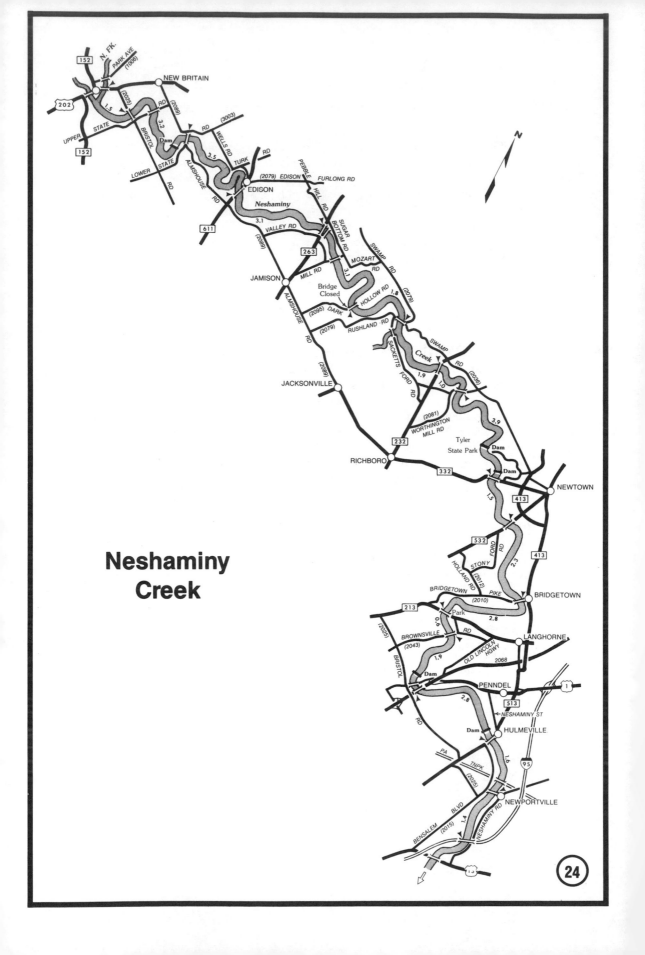

Neshaminy Creek

24

Neshaminy Creek

INTRODUCTION: Neshaminy Creek (Indian for "double stream") meanders down the center of Bucks County to a tidal rendezvous with the Delaware River, below Bristol. It presents many miles of beginner grade, small stream paddling, through a rolling, Piedmont countryside, not yet engulfed by that creeping, bland blob called suburbia. So hurry. Get there while it is still nice.

Section 1. *Chalfont (U.S. Rte. 202) to mouth*					
Gradient	Difficulty	Distance	Time	Scenery	Map
7	A to 1	40.4	13.5	Poor to Good	24,6

TRIP DESCRIPTION: The put-in is on the North Fork Neshaminy Creek. Because U.S. Rte. 202 is such a busy road, you might consider starting either a quarter mile upstream, on the North Fork, at Park Avenue, SR1006, or a mile below, on the main stem, at Bristol Road, SR2025.

Upper Neshaminy is particularly appealing in that while many roads cross the creek, few follow close by. Wooded banks and bluffs hide much of Neshaminy from the outside world. There are occasional views of farms, houses, and even great, landscaped estates, but generally the scenery is pleasantly closed in. Many jutting, rock outcrops and low ledges decorate the creekside, and there is even a beautiful, old restored mill, at Castle Valley, that dates back to 1730. All this is at its best in late spring, when the banks are draped in a great bouquet of dames rockets, while the waters blossom as noisy nurseries for scores of Canada geese and mallards.

Neshaminy finally blunders into suburbia below Pa. Rte. 213, Langhorne. Few will care to paddle these final miles through heavily residential and commercial surroundings, highways, railroads, power lines, and, on tidewater, marinas. If you do go the whole way, turn left at the mouth, and take out in Neshaminy State Park, approached on land via 4th Street, Croydon.

Neshaminy's muddy waters usually flow smooth, though in between there are lots of riffles rushing over gravel, broken ledges, and the rubble of old mill dams. But there is nothing that a beginner cannot figure out. Only a Class 1 rock garden hints that this stream crosses the fall line. At Newportville, Neshaminy finally sinks into tidewater.

There are five dams on this creek, all shown on the shuttle map. Take great care to avoid the deceptive three-foot dam, with its lethal hydraulic, in Tyler State Park (there will be a warning sign). Just below the park, a seven-foot, sloping, crescent-shaped dam is runnable at moderate levels. Carry all the rest of the dams.

HAZARDS: Five dams.

WATER CONDITIONS: Canoeable winter and spring within four days of hard rain above Newportville. Below there, it is always boatable, unless frozen.

GAUGE: USGS gauge at Langhorne, at Pa. Rte. 213 (call Philadelphia), should read at least 2.0 feet.

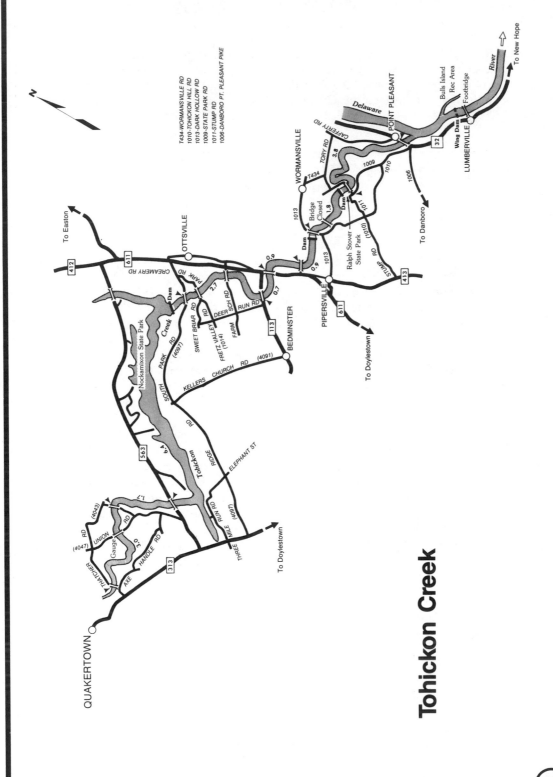

Tohickon Creek

T434-WORMANSVILLE RD
1010-TOHICKON HILL RD
1013-DARK HOLLOW RD
1009-STATE PARK RD
1011-STUMP RD
1006-DANBORO PT. PLEASANT PIKE

Tohickon Creek

INTRODUCTION: Tohickon Creek is a small, should-be-obscure tributary to the mighty Delaware, cutting a secret gorge down through the big river's bluffs, above New Hope. But it is no longer a secret to paddlers. Thanks to an annual fall and spring water release from Lake Nockamixon, this has become one of the most dearly beloved intermediate to advanced whitewater runs in the mid-Atlantic megalopolis. For example, when the annual release was staged on the first weekend of November, 1984, about 1,200 boaters crowded onto the prime 3.75 miles of creek at Stover State Park. You will like Tohickon too. Just do not plan on having it all to yourself.

Section 1. Quakertown (Thatcher Road, SR4043) to Pa. Rte. 563					
Gradient	Difficulty	Distance	Time	Scenery	Map
20	A to 3	4.7	1.5	Fair	25
1.2 @ 50					

TRIP DESCRIPTION: This is a yet little-known reach of Tohickon, only found up after a whole lot of rain. At such times, it provides a short, exhilarating, intermediate race down to Lake Nockamixon. You warm up on flatwater, as the creek flows through quiet tenth growth woods. Below Union Road, SR4047, short, well-spaced rapids appear, climaxing with a few long, bouldery, sometimes powerful rapids, and ending in the lake, beneath the Pa. Rte. 563 Bridge. With scores of second homes sprouting in the surrounding boulder-strewn woods, the scenery does not complement the wild whitewater.

HAZARDS: Logjams and living trees in the rapids.

WATER CONDITIONS: Canoeable winter and spring within two days of hard rain.

GAUGE: USGS gauge on left abutment of Union Road Bridge must read over 3.0 feet. The rapid beneath Pa. Rte. 563 also indicates the water conditions.

Section 2. Pa. Rte. 563 to Nockamixon Dam					
Gradient	Difficulty	Distance	Time	Scenery	Map
0	A	6.1	3.0	Good	25

TRIP DESCRIPTION: All of this section is on Lake Nockamixon. This is an attractive man-made lake that is completely surrounded by a state park. Its wooded shores are interrupted only by a few old farm houses and state park recreation areas. Access is plentiful all around the lake.

HAZARDS: None.

WATER CONDITIONS: Canoeable from spring thaw until winter freeze-up.

GAUGE: None.

Section 3. South Park Road to Ralph Stover State Park (State Park Road, SR1009)					
Gradient	Difficulty	Distance	Time	Scenery	Map
9	A to 1 +	7.0	2.0	Good	25

TRIP DESCRIPTION: This is a nice, leisurely, novice run. There are enough riffles and, towards the end, easy rapids to add interest to this otherwise sedate stretch. The creek glides past north-exposed rock outcrops, capped by thick, green mops of ferns. It passes through a rural landscape, partly screened by tangled bottomland woods. Near Pipersville, be sure to stop and explore the beautifully restored Stover Mill, with its water-powered sawmill. You must stop near there anyway to carry the four-foot milldam. A second four-foot dam signals the end of the easy water, at Stover State Park.

HAZARDS: Two dams.

WATER CONDITIONS: Canoeable winter and spring within three days of hard rain. Also, special water releases are usually scheduled on the last weekend of March and the first weekend of November.

GAUGE: Painted gauge on SR1009 Bridge in Stover Park. Zero is zero canoeable level. Check your local canoe clubs for dates of releases.

Section 4. SR1009 to Point Pleasant (Pa. Rte. 32)					
Gradient	Difficulty	Distance	Time	Scenery	Map
40	1 to 3 +	3.8	1.5	Excellent	25

TRIP DESCRIPTION: The state park marks the beginning of what grows into a deep, narrow, and shadowy gorge, hugged at times by great, black, gothic cliffs. To totally appreciate this gorge, drive up to High Rocks, off Tory Road, and see it from the top also. The whitewater, interesting at the start, steadily improves as it speeds toward the Delaware, rounding out with a thrilling series of jagged, ledge rapids. Take out at Pa. Rte. 32, but take special care to park your car where it will not block any locals or the nearby fire house. The residents of Point Pleasant have been very tolerant of boaters' invasions so far. Let us keep the relations cordial.

HAZARDS: Being speared by another boat.

WATER CONDITIONS: Canoeable winter and spring within three days of hard rain, or during March and November releases.

GAUGE: Same as Section 3.

Tunkhannock Creek
Tobyhanna Creek
Lehigh River
Bear Creek

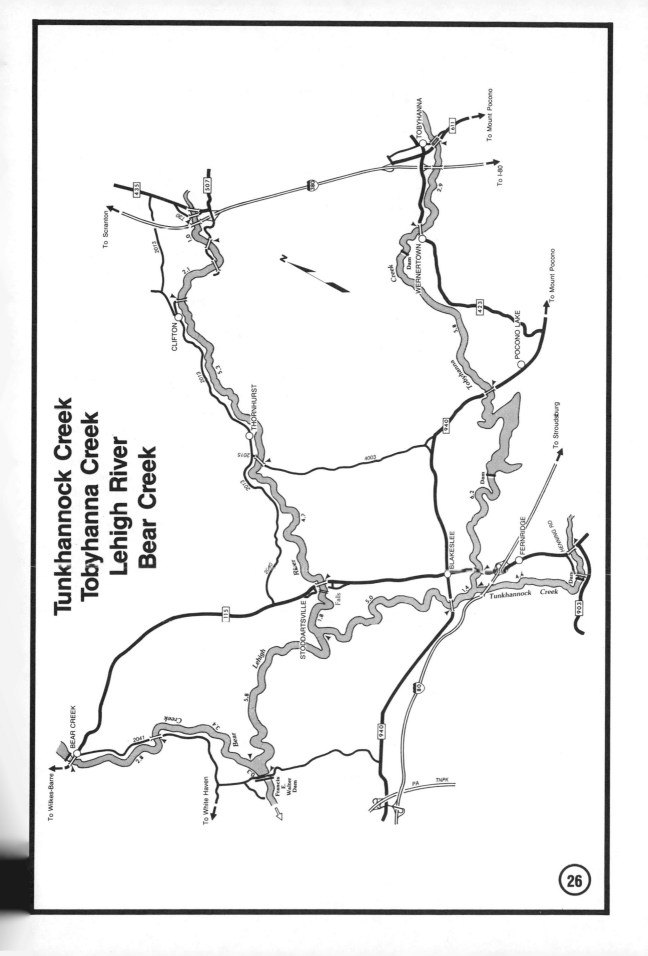

26

Lehigh River

INTRODUCTION: There are few waterways in Pennsylvania more near and dear to the hearts of those who paddle whitewater than the Lehigh. Ideally situated right in the middle of eastern Pennsylvania, just off I-80 and the Pennsylvania Turnpike, it has attracted thousands of boaters, both private and commercial, for many years. And while most visitors limit themselves to the 26-mile reach between White Haven and Jim Thorpe, the entire river offers rewarding canoeing.

While the Lehigh may be famous among middle-Atlantic boaters, the Lehigh Valley enjoys a national reputation for its industrial might. Foremost, the Lehigh Valley is the home of the Portland cement industry in the United States. This came to be when industrial pioneers found the native limestone specially suited for cement, back in the days before anyone had the chemical understanding to synthesize cements from just any type of limestone. So at one time, in the 1890's, three quarters of this country's cement was produced here. Today, if you climb any high hill in southwest Northampton County, you can spot the stacks of at least a half dozen cement plants. The Lehigh Valley has long been active in steelmaking. The furnaces and mills of Bethlehem Steel line the river at (where else?) Bethlehem. Upstream at Palmerton, New Jersey Zinc Company's East Plant churns out tons of zinc and zinc compounds for the nation. And until recently, they mined it all here too, at Friedensville, near Bethlehem. Speaking of mines, the extraction of anthracite and slate are originally what put this valley on the map. Finally, on a more delicate scale, the Lehigh Valley has been a silk milling center since the 1880's.

As with most other Pennsylvania rivers, the Lehigh's first important role was as a means of transportation. This originally meant the floating of barges, filled with coal, grain, and lumber, down to Easton and beyond on spring freshets. Downriver navigation was then improved by a series of dams and one-way locks. Finally, in 1829, the Lehigh Coal and Navigation Company completed a two-way canal between Easton and Mauch Chunk (now Jim Thorpe). Later they extended the canal up the rugged gorge to White Haven and improved one-way navigation all the way to the falls at Stoddartsville. Connected to the Carbon County coal fields by an ingenious system of railways, this busy canal system was one of the only in Pennsylvania to turn a profit. At least a bit of the canal remained in commercial use as late as 1942. Today, the canal is being revived for its recreational values. You can hike and bike sections of its towpath, and even paddle some rewatered sections in Allentown and Easton.

Section 1. Pa. Rte. 435 to Stoddartsville (Pa. Rte. 115)					
Gradient	Difficulty	Distance	Time	Scenery	Map
23	A to 2	13.1	4.0	Good	26

TRIP DESCRIPTION: Put in just downstream of Pa. Rte. 435, on T30. Clear water, the color of strong tea, hurries off under I-380 and into the forest. It is a busy descent over gravel and little boulders, sometimes blocked by fallen trees. From Clifton to Thornhurst, houses frequently appear along the riverside. The land here is flat, as a plateau should be, and the river smooths out accordingly. The Lehigh returns to the quiet of the forest below Thornhurst.

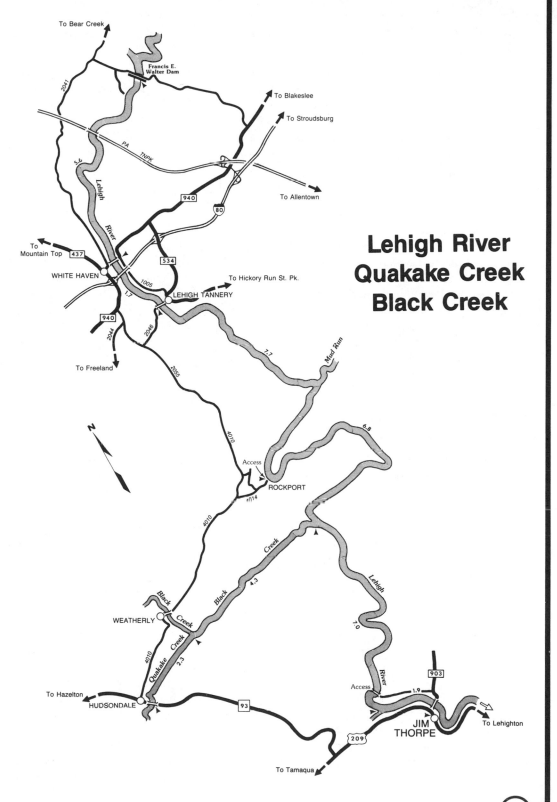

Lehigh River
Quakake Creek
Black Creek

To Bear Creek

Francis E. Walter Dam

2041

To Blakeslee

To Stroudsburg

PA TNPK

5.6

Lehigh

To Allentown

940

80

To Mountain Top

437

534

WHITE HAVEN

To Hickory Run St. Pk.

River

1005

1.7

LEHIGH TANNERY

940

2044

2046

Mud Run

7.7

To Freeland

2065

6.8

4010

Access

ROCKPORT

4014

4010

Creek

Lehigh

Black Creek

4.3

7.0

Black Creek

WEATHERLY

4010

Quakake Creek

2.3

River

Access

903

1.9

To Hazelton

HUDSONDALE

93

JIM THORPE

To Lehighton

209

To Tamaqua

N

27

HAZARDS: Strainers above Clifton.

WATER CONDITIONS: Canoeable two to three weeks in spring, during snowmelt, or within three days of hard rain.

GAUGE: Roughly, USGS White Haven gauge, below Walter Dam (call Philadelphia), should read over 4.4 feet (approximately 1,000 cfs). If the outside staff is ever restored on the USGS gauge at Rte. 115, minimum level is 1.65 feet.

Section 2. Stoddartsville (Pa. Rte. 115) to Francis E. Walter Dam					
Gradient	Difficulty	Distance	Time	Scenery	Map
28 above lake	A to 1 +	8.0	3.0	Good to Very Good	26

TRIP DESCRIPTION: Just below Pa. Rte. 115, on a blind bend, the Lehigh slips over a rugged and picturesque falls. It is a joy to behold, from every angle, except from a canoe being drawn over its lip. So scout early, carry on the right, and be sure to inspect the old mill ruins as you pass by. Two miles into this section, the Tobyhanna joins, doubling the volume, and a shallow gorge begins to form. If you come here at flood, man-made Francis E. Walter Lake may start just below. Otherwise you can look forward to at least four miles of easy, wavy rapids, clear pools, stone cliffs, and an isolated setting. With absolutely no development, the lake is also pretty. A steep band of exposed mud, dead trees, and bleached stumps, unfortunately, ring the shore. Take out at the dam, where a convenient road comes down to the water from both sides.

HAZARDS: Falls at Stoddartsville.

WATER CONDITIONS: Above reservoir, same as Section 1. Reservoir canoeable from late April (thaw) to late November (freeze).

GAUGE: Same as Section 1 for above the lake. The lake gauge is on the intake tower at the dam. Normal pool is about 1,300 feet. At the maximum pool of 1,396 feet, the lake backs up almost to the Tobyhanna.

Section 3. Francis E. Walter Dam to Jim Thorpe					
Gradient	Difficulty	Distance	Time	Scenery	Map
23	1 to 3 +	30.6	9.0	Good to Excellent	27

TRIP DESCRIPTION: The only trouble with putting in here is the long carry down a dirt road (on right) to the base of the dam. The steep rapid at the start may be of some consolation. If it is not, from May 1 to September 1, the gate is open on a primitive road that leads from the picnic area at the top to a small picnic area (with plenty of parking) by the riverside, 0.7 miles downstream of the dam. The reborn river proceeds down a shallow, wooded gorge. Rapids, sometimes long, but usually mild, work down a bed of large cobbles and little ledges. This makes an interesting novice to intermediate trip down to White Haven.

Most people, both private boaters and patrons of commercial, guided raft trips, start at White Haven (the recommended access is river right beneathI-80) or ten miles downstream at Rockport. This section is all protected now by a new state park. It flows through a narrow, ever deepening

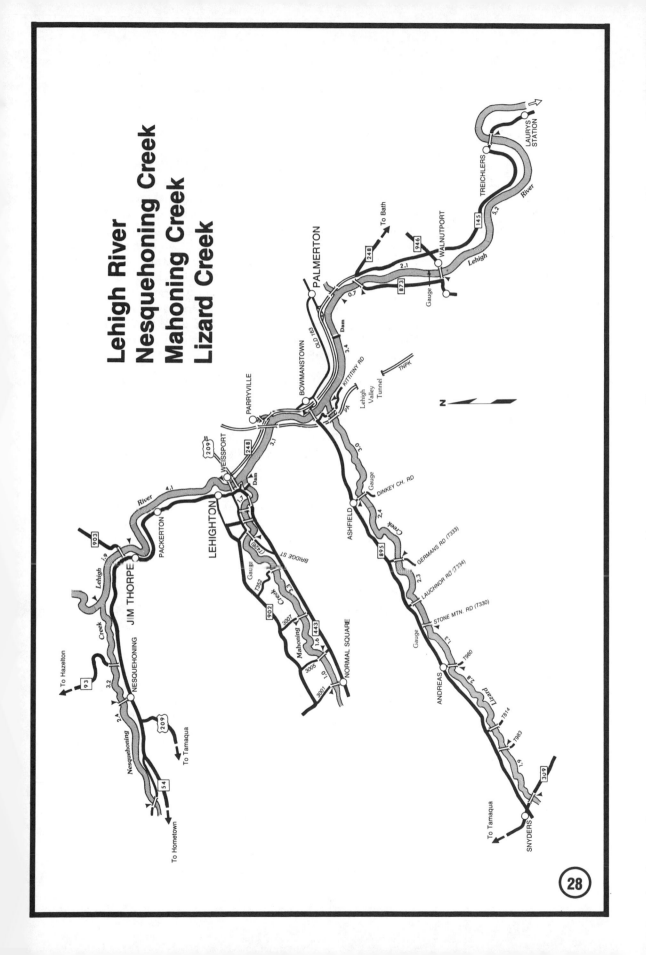

Lehigh River
Nesquehoning Creek
Mahoning Creek
Lizard Creek

LAURYS STATION

TREICHLERS

5.2

Lehigh River

145

WALNUTPORT

946

To Bath

248

PALMERTON

2.1

Gauge

873

0.7

Dam

OLD 163

3.4

KITTITINY RD

Lehigh Valley Tunnel

TNPK

PA

3.0

BOWMANSTOWN

PARRYVILLE

3.1

248

209

WEISSPORT

Dam

1.7

Gauge

DINKEY CH. RD

ASHFIELD

Gauge

2.4

Creek

GERMANS RD (T333)

895

2.3

LAUCHNOR RD (T334)

Creek

4.1

River

PACKERTON

LEHIGHTON

903

Lehigh

1.9

JIM THORPE

STONE MTN. RD (T330)

Gauge

1.3

ANDREAS

T960

2.8

Lizard

To Hazelton

Creek

93

3.2

NESQUEHONING

2.4

209

To Tamaqua

Nesquehoning

54

To Hometown

BRIDGE ST

T252

Gauge

(T228)

Creek

3.3

902

3007

Mahoning

1.6

443

3005

1.0

3001

NORMAL SQUARE

T814

T983

1.9

309

To Tamaqua

SNYDERS

N

(28)

gorge, whose rims are eventually crowned by a spectacular array of jagged cliffs. Vying with the scenery for your attention are a succession of cobble and boulder patch rapids. They can be quite long at times, but generally the rate of descent is mild and the visibility is good. Especially down between Black Creek and Nesquehoning Creek, the path through the rocks and holes can be reasonably complex. At levels of less than 1,500 cfs, this measures up to a challenging intermediate or easy advanced run. Perhaps the prettiest spot in the gorge is on the right, a few miles above Jim Thorpe—a place called Glen Onoko. Waterfalls tumbling down this short, hemlock-shaded side canyon have charmed visitors since back in the 19th century, when special excursion trains chugged in from cities downstream. And today, once again, you can visit this spot by a colorful, smoke-belching, steam-powered tourist train, conveniently operating out of Jim Thorpe.

Boaters have traditionally taken out on the right bank at Jim Thorpe, behind the old railroad station. Unmetered parking here is available on weekends only. Now the preferred spot, however, is the state park access about two and a half miles upstream at the old railroad bridge and tunnel. To get there, cross the Lehigh (north) on Rte. 903 and turn left (upstream). Follow Front Street and Coalport Road a bit over a half mile and turn left onto a gated gravel road that runs to the new access. If you need a place to camp, try nearby Hickory Run State Park. And while you are there, be sure to visit the Boulder Field, a curious glacial remnant that resembles the Lehigh when the Corps of Engineers renege on their "promised" summer releases.

HAZARDS: Sustaining a hernia when carrying in at the dam. Being run over by a rubber raft during the April or May busy season.

WATER CONDITIONS: Usually canoeable from late March until the end of May. In wet years, November, early December, and June are also often good. Also special one-day recreational releases of 500 to 700cfs are usually scheduled monthly, during summer and early fall. For release schedule and volume, call 215-656-6500.

GAUGE: USGS White Haven gauge, below Walter Dam (call Philadelphia for gauge height, or 215-656-6500 for discharge in cfs), should be over 3.7 feet (500 cfs) for clean run from dam. Below White Haven, 3.4 feet (300 cfs) is minimal. A fine open boat level is 4.4 feet (1,000 cfs). Roughly, 2.6 feet on USGS gauge at Walnutport (call same) means about 3.4 feet at White Haven.

Section 4. Jim Thorpe to Canal Park Access, Allentown					
Gradient	Difficulty	Distance	Time	Scenery	Map
9	A to 2	30.4	10.0	Poor to Good	28,29

TRIP DESCRIPTION: The Lehigh now begins its exit from the wild Poconos and entry into the settled lowlands. For novices and beginners, the river begins here. The Lehigh starts by punching through a pair of impressive gaps in Mauch Chunk Mountain, at Jim Thorpe, and then Blue Mountain, at Palmerton. You can really best appreciate the former from the spectacular vantage atop Flagstaff Park (private, you pay, it is worth it). The view from the river is less appealing, especially down towards Palmerton, where industry, highways, and denuded mountainsides fill out the panorama. You certainly will not mistake the valley for Yosemite. But the river is still a pleasure to paddle, its waters accelerating down lots of easy rapids, formed by cobble bars and old dam remains. As you approach Palmerton, BEWARE of an almost invisible, two-foot weir, marked by a pumphouse on the left bank. The weir's hydraulic is a death trap, so play it safe and carry.

The river leaves the mountains below Palmerton. To Allentown, it spends most of its time passing through towns. But there still remain some relatively natural segments, especially in a

Lehigh River

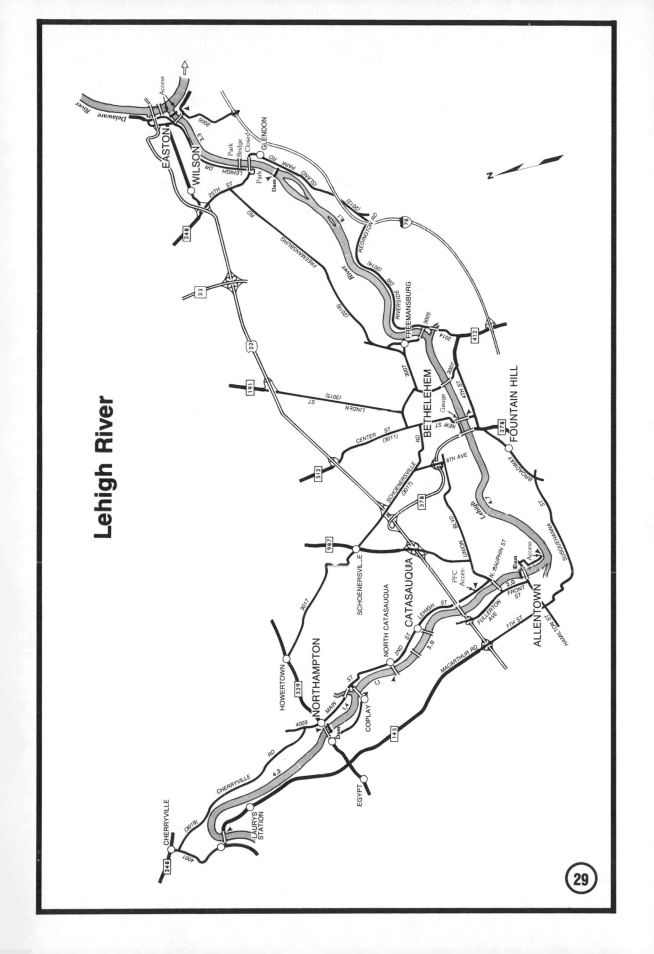

29

bluff-lined stretch below Treichlers. On the other hand, the appearance of dusty cement plants, at places like Cementon, remind one that this is uniquely the Lehigh Valley. But nothing there is so unique as the profile of several strange towers, resembling pieces from a Brobdingnagian chess set, rising above the right bank at Coplay. These are the vertical kilns from one of the first cement plants in the valley (now a museum).

The path continues to be graced with many easy rapids, still the product of cobble bars and old, broken-out, canal feeder dams. A strong chute through such a breached dam, at North Catasauqua, forms a good, wavy play spot. There are also occasional series of ledges on this section. The best, located just above Walnutport, forms several delightful surfing holes. As for hazards, carry a five-foot dam located below the bridge in Cementon (easy carry on right), and be sure to see a new eight-foot dam above Hamilton Street, in Allentown. This has a hydraulic and barricade of energy dissipators that form a lethal trap, so carry on the left. A final, good rapid runs just below. The Canal Park Access is reached by turning south, one block past the east end of the Hamilton Street Bridge, onto Bradford Street, then right, onto Walnut Street, and finally, left, along the canal, to the end of the road.

HAZARDS: Dangerous weir above Palmerton, at Cementon, and at Hamilton Street, Allentown.

WATER CONDITIONS: Usually canoeable until August, and even longer in wet summers.

GAUGE: USGS gauges at Walnutport and Bethlehem (call Philadelphia, or inspect on spot). Zero corresponds to about 2.0 feet at Walnutport and 1.5 feet at Bethlehem.

Section 5. Canal Park Access, Allentown to mouth					
Gradient	Difficulty	Distance	Time	Scenery	Map
5	A to 1 –	16.1	5.0	Poor to Good	29

TRIP DESCRIPTION: The remainder of the Lehigh is a good beginner's run. This section is mostly smooth, partly the pools behind two dams. Carry the 13-foot dam at Glendon (a warning sign hangs from a cable between the old bridge piers upstream) and a sloping 12-foot dam, at the mouth. There is easy egress at the second dam, on the right, or via a park boat ramp, at the mouth, on the left.

The scenery is poor down to Freemansburg, though the passage by Bethlehem Steel is fascinating. High banks screen much of the city of Bethlehem from view, which is unfortunate. Bethlehem is a pretty city with a beautiful, historic section by its downtown. It is worth a side trip to explore. Below Freemansburg, to Glendon, the riverside is fairly undeveloped and attractive.

HAZARDS: Dams at Glendon and mouth.

WATER CONDITIONS: Usually canoeable from spring thaw until December, except during dry autumns.

GAUGE: USGS gauge at Bethlehem should preferably read over 1.2 feet.

Saucon Creek

INTRODUCTION: Saucon Creek is a popular local gem that meanders through the southern suburbs of Bethlehem. It bears the unique notoriety of being the only creek around that was put out of business by the recession. The story goes that New Jersey Zinc Company worked a huge system of deep mines at the head of the Saucon Valley, near Friedensville. In order to keep the copious volume of ground water, that underlies this limy region, from flooding these mines, huge pumps ran 24 hours a day, seven days a week, withdrawing that ground water and discharging about 30 million gallons a day of that clear, cool bounty into Saucon Creek. Local paddlers and tubers could, hence, always delight in a flowing Saucon when other comparable-sized brooks would not even float a stick. But when the economic recession of the early 1980's hit the zinc market, the mines no longer drew a profit and were closed. A short time later the pumps were shut off, and the creek returned to dribbling reality. So now the rest of us must just sit and wait for the next heavy rain, if we want to enjoy this fine little creek.

Section 1. Pa. Rte. 378 to Pa. Rte. 412					
Gradient	Difficulty	Distance	Time	Scenery	Map
16	1 +	8.0	3.0	Good	30

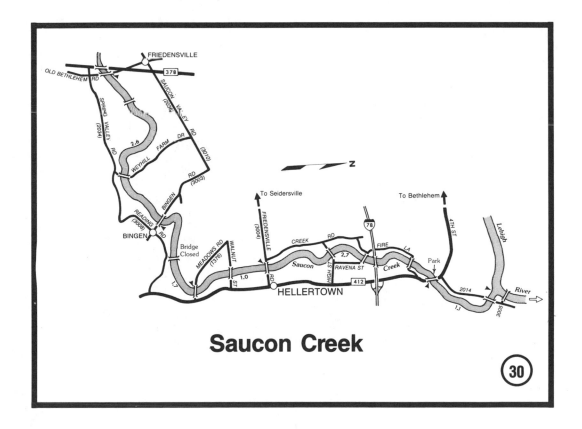

Saucon Creek

30

Jordan Creek

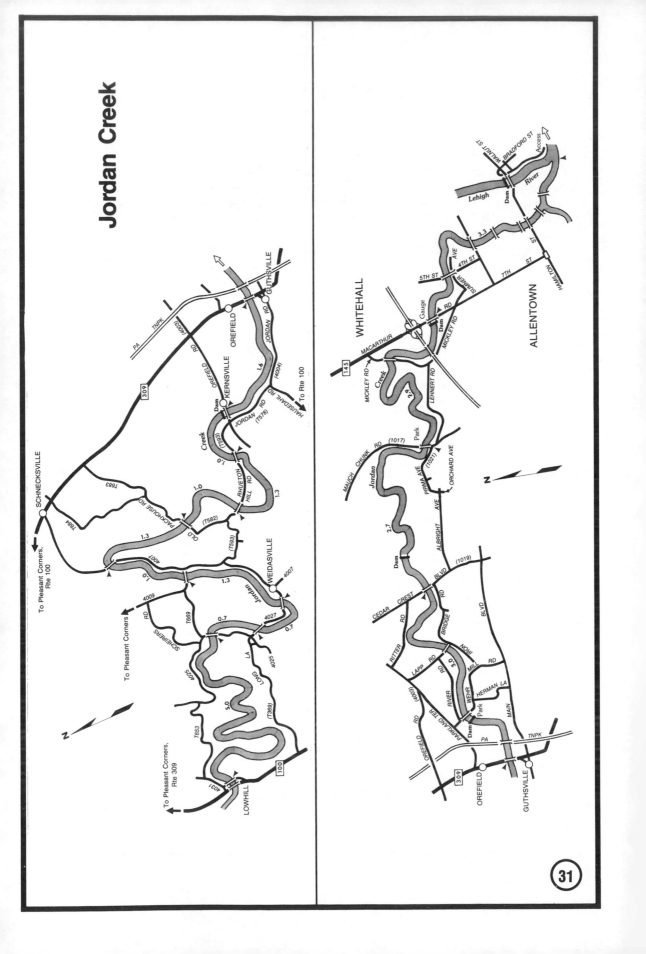

TRIP DESCRIPTION: Tiny as it may be, Saucon is floatable beginning at Pa. Rte. 378. For starters, it carries you on an all-pro tour of a chain of beautiful, rolling, and green golf courses. Helmets are useful here, not only for little round, white missiles, but also for the numerous, low footbridges. On past the golf courses, the creek wanders through a variety of open space — patches of woods, weedlots, or developed parklands. Many of the houses that you pass are attractive, old structures, constructed of the native limestone. Most paddlers prefer to finish their Saucon cruise at the ballfield at Pa. Rte. 412, if not sooner. Once below this point, the creek immerses itself in industry, slag heaps, and other less-than-postcard-grade scenery. Also, there is no good take-out at the mouth.

The creek heads for the Lehigh in a hurry. Riffles are seldom far apart. They are usually short and moderately steep, sometimes dropping over simple gravel bars and sometimes rattling through challenging little rock gardens. There are also three little weirs, between Bingen and Hellertown, but they are all easy and reasonably safe to attempt. Finally, strainers are seldom a problem on Saucon Creek. So it is a delightful novice run.

HAZARDS: Low bridges are a problem at extra high levels.

WATER CONDITIONS: Canoeable in spring, only within 24 hours of hard rain.

GAUGE: None. Enough water to cleanly run riffles just above and below Rte. 378 is enough for the whole trip.

Jordan Creek

INTRODUCTION: Jordan Creek is an exceptionally pleasant canoe stream that flows into Allentown and the Lehigh River from the northwest. Scenic novice runs seldom come more conveniently located to an urban area.

Section 1. Lowhill (Pa. Rte. 309) to mouth					
Gradient	Difficulty	Distance	Time	Scenery	Map
9	A to 1	26.8	9.0	Poor to Good	31

TRIP DESCRIPTION: Jordan is relatively long for such a little creek. It packs those extra miles in on its upper reaches by carving great, fitful loops in the rugged to rolling countryside. Protected by state game lands, large farms, and the Trexler-Lehigh County Game Preserve, these first miles of the creek present to the floater an amazingly unpopulated, pastoral, and wooded landscape, as far as Kernsville. Also gracing this stretch are the first of Jordan's five lovely covered bridges.

The Game Preserve envelopes about three miles of creek, from SR4009 to the first Rhueton Hill Road bridge. To pass through, one must scale a substantial woven wire fence (there to contain a large and varied herd of untethered wildlife) at SR4009 and again at Old Packhouse Road,

Little Lehigh Creek

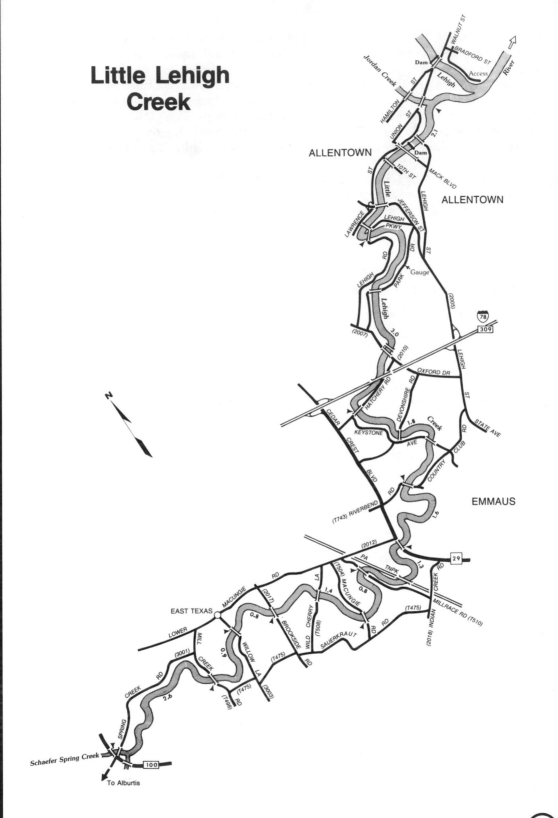

though a good spring ice break-up often opens up these barriers. Since the county frowns on people floating through their preserve, paddlers should at least avoid this stretch during the season, which extends from mid-April to the end of October, when one is most likely to be noticed.

Below Kernsville, a little of suburbia begins to show, although much of the nearby floodplain is protected as parkland. The parks continue on into Allentown, leaving only the last few miles to creep through an interesting, but unsightly, urban setting. If the backside of Allentown does not appeal to you, take out by Sumner Avenue, beneath the high 5th Street Bridge. If you float to the Lehigh, take out across the river, at the Canal Park Access.

Jordan Creek has a healthy gradient for its entire length. The same tilting, slate shelves that often decorate its banks, also form little ledges, on the upper creek. Otherwise, gravel forms the numerous riffles. Dams at Kernsville, Wehr Mill Road, and by the big, mysterious chemical plant, below Cedar Crest Boulevard, require carries. A three-foot gauging station weir, above Pa. Rte. 145, is runnable, as is a sharp, two-foot ford, in the city park downstream.

HAZARDS: Four dams and weirs. Woven wire fences and caretakers at the Game Preserve. Cute little cherubs, in Allentown, who delight in tossing rocks at canoes and canoeists.

WATER CONDITIONS: Canoeable late fall and spring within four days of hard rain.

GAUGE: USGS gauge above Pa. Rte. 145, on right, should read at least 3.4 feet. Very roughly, USGS gauges at Berne on the Schuylkill and Graterford on the Perkiomen (call Philadelphia) should be over 6.0 feet and 2.1 feet respectively.

Little Lehigh Creek

INTRODUCTION: The Little Lehigh gurgles out of the rolling farmlands along the Berks–Lehigh County Line to join Jordan Creek in Allentown, just above the Lehigh River. Most people would not even think of canoeing anything so miniscule. But it is indeed big enough for a canoe, is easy enough for a novice, and offers one of the most pleasant means to see the nicest side of Greater Allentown.

Section 1. Pa. Rte. 100 to mouth					
Gradient	Difficulty	Distance	Time	Scenery	Map
8	1	16.3	5.0	Good	32

TRIP DESCRIPTION: The put-in and first quarter mile are on Schaefer Spring Creek. Schaefer combines with the Little Lehigh to form a two- to three-foot-deep, 15- to 20-foot-wide brook, that never gets much bigger. Its winding course is typified by unusually low, grassy banks that offer sumptious views of the pretty valley.

The trip starts beside a housing development, but progresses through dairy farms, woods, and fields. Some fallen trees and a few fences are a problem up here. Entering Emmaus, the Little Lehigh flows through an attractive residential neighborhood, with houses getting bigger and prettier with each mile. Once inside the Allentown limits, the creek is enveloped by a beautiful city park, graced not only with lots of tidy, green, open space, but also pretty bridges, old industrial ruins,

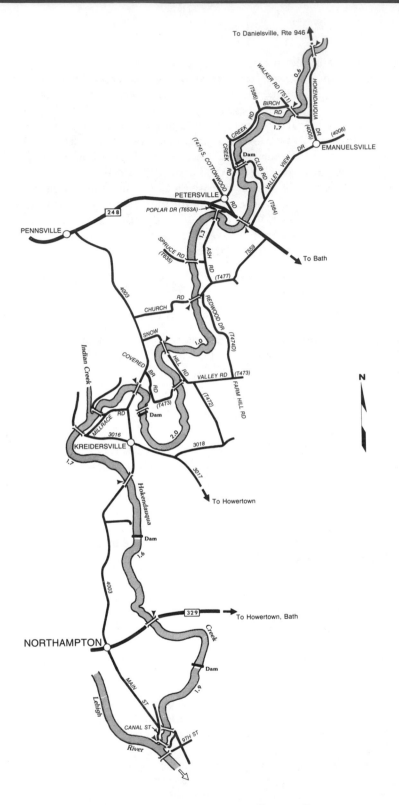

Hokendauqua Creek

and well-preserved native stone buildings. This section of creek is always well-populated by fisher-men, as it is designated as a "fish for fun" section, where the fishermen must use only barbless hooks and release their catch. So travel in small, quiet groups and watch for lines. Of even more concern, the city has posted this section, below Hatchery Road, against floating. The city's right to ban boating on this clearly navigable waterway is questionable. However, until someone steps forth with a proper legal challenge, be advised that you might be fined for paddling through this part of Allentown. The final mile of the Little Lehigh leaves the park for a pass through industrial scenery and trash-strewn woods. If you follow the creek to the end, continue down Jordan Creek to the Lehigh, and take out across the river at Canal Park.

The creek offers an enjoyable mix of swift smooth water, short, rocky riffles, and countless runnable one to two-foot weirs. You must carry a six-foot dam at Mack Trucks, below 10th Street, and you may need to carry a crumbling two-foot weir, in the woods above Millrace Road.

HAZARDS: Some strainers and two dams. Also, possible run-ins with policemen or fishermen.

WATER CONDITIONS: Canoeable in spring within two days of hard rain.

GAUGE: USGS gauge along Park Drive, in Allentown, 0.6 miles below where Park Drive crosses the Little Lehigh. Minimum is about 2.6 feet. Roughly, USGS gauge at Graterford, on the Perki-omen (call Philadelphia), should read over 2.0 feet.

Hokendauqua Creek

INTRODUCTION: Hokendauqua Creek is a tiny, splashing, and dashing whitewater delight, spilling out of the slate belt of Northampton County, into the Lehigh, at the town of Northamp-ton. This ephemeral brook provides a remarkable run through sustained, easy intermediate whitewater, unbelievably near to the heart of Allentown-Bethlehem. Creeks like this explain why whitewater boaters go into a frenzy when it starts to rain.

Section 1. SR4005 to mouth					
Gradient	Difficulty	Distance	Time	Scenery	Map
26	1 to 2 +	11.8	3.5	Fair to Good	33
2.2 @ 43					

TRIP DESCRIPTION: SR4005 crosses Hokendauqua north of Emanuelsville. The tempo is established right at the put-in, where your boat explodes from the eddy, like a racehorse from a starting gate. The creek screams down a busy combination of rock gardens and cobble bars, spaced by an occasional strainer. The whitewater becomes simpler and more straightforward be-low Pa. Rte. 248, but remains just as continuous as above. Two two-foot weirs (shown on map) are no problem to run. Then, around the confluence with Indian Creek, just when you are figur-ing that the best has passed, the Hokendauqua rambles down a delightful series of ledges that provide some extra bounce and an assortment of juicy playing holes. The whitewater usually oc-cupies much of your attention, but if you let your eyes wander, much of this run introduces you to an attractive wooded or rural landscape. There is even one pretty rock cliff on the itinerary.

Aquashicola Creek
Pohopoco Creek
Buckwha Creek

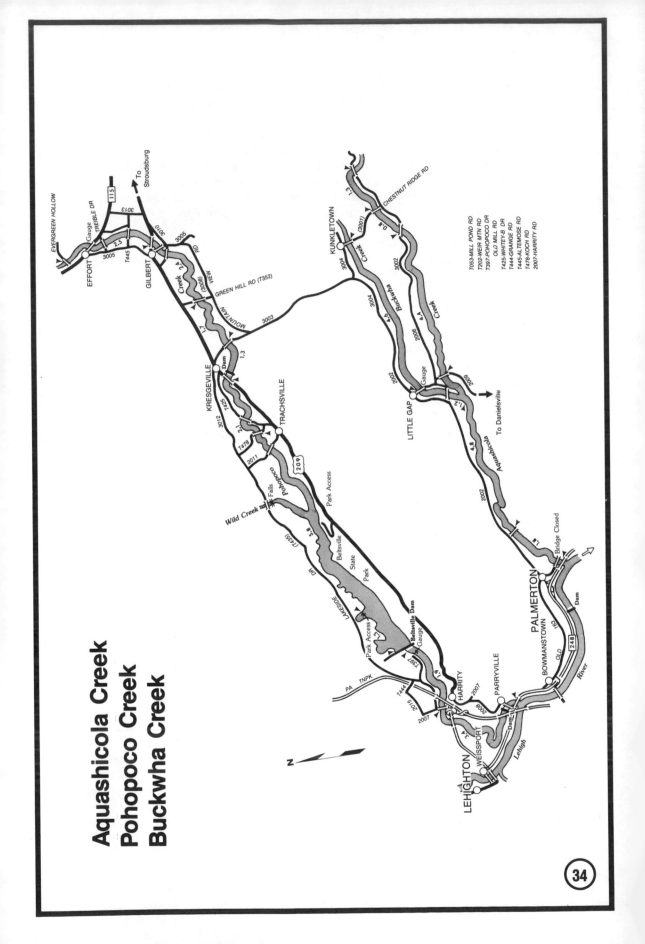

T053-MILL POND RD
T202-WEIR MTN RD
T397-POHOPOCO DR
OLD MILL RD
T425-WHITEY-B DR
T444-GRANGE RD
T445-ALTEMOSE RD
T478-KOCH RD
2007-HARRITY RD

EVERGREEN HOLLOW

EFFORT
3005
2.5
T445
GILBERT
3010
3005
Creek
(3008)
MOUNTAIN VIEW RD
GREEN HILL RD (T352)
3003
1.7
1.3
Dam
KRESGEVILLE
3012
T425
T478
2011
209
TRACHSVILLE
LAKESIDE DR (T439)
5.8
Pohopoco
Falls
Wild Creek
Park Access
Beltsville
State
Park
Park Access
1.3
Beltsville Dam
Gauge
T397
1.9
PA TNPK
T444
2015
2007
2008
LEHIGHTON
WEISSPORT
3.4
Dam
HARRITY
2007
PARRYVILLE
BOWMANSTOWN
OLD 163
248
Dam
Lehigh
River
PALMERTON
Bridge Closed
.8
2002
4.8
Aquashicola
To Danielsville
1.1
1.2
2009
Gauge
2002
LITTLE GAP
3004
4.9
2006
Buckwha
4.4
Creek
3002
0.8
CHESTNUT RIDGE RD
1.3
KUNKLETOWN
3004
(3001)
Creek
115
To Stroudsburg
3013
TREBLE DR
Gauge

N

34

SR4003, south of Kreidersville, is a nice place to end this trip. The remaining few miles are disappointing. There is some good, splashy whitewater in the last half mile, but this is offset by some long pools, including an old flooded quarry and some carries around a four-foot dam, just below SR4003, and a 15-foot dam, by the old cement plant. If you stick with the creek to Northampton, take out at the mouth, at Canal Street.

HAZARDS: Some strainers and two dams.

WATER CONDITIONS: Canoeable in late fall and spring within 24 hours of hard rain.

GAUGE: Check drainholes on left abutment of Pa. Rte. 248 Bridge. Water level must be within two inches of the bottom of the lowest hole.

Aquashicola and Buckwha Creeks

INTRODUCTION: Aquashicola Creek is a really rotten canoe stream that flows in the shadow of Blue Mountain, entering the Lehigh at Palmerton. Pronounced A'·qua·shi'·co·la, the name is Indian for "where we fish with the bushnet." But survivors of this wicked stream will stumble away wondering if Aquashicola is, in itself, a bushnet of nature, devised to catch paddlers.

Buckwha Creek is a tiny fork of the Aquashicola. It is a preferable way to start a trip on that tangled creek.

Section 1. SR3002 to SR2009					
Gradient	Difficulty	Distance	Time	Scenery	Map
15	2 –	6.5	3.0	Good	34

TRIP DESCRIPTION: The put-in most recommended for people that we do not like is located six miles up SR3002 from the intersection with the road to Little Gap. Tiny Aquashicola commences to run the gauntlet through a nightmarish sequence of trees, fences, low bridges, and worst of all, overhanging and often interlocking alders and assorted shrubbery. One can only think of bushnets as one's boat catches, broaches, and capsizes in these diabolical sieves. The water is often smooth, but is very fast, often making it a challenge to stop. There are also many riffles and trout weirs to push one even faster. After a few miles, the creek slows and meanders through a swamp, choked with even more alders. The scenery up here, dominated by the sweeping face of Blue Mountain, is pleasant, when one has an opportunity to look.

HAZARDS: Strainers, strainers, and more strainers.

WATER CONDITIONS: Canoeable in spring during fast snowmelt or within two days of hard rain.

GAUGE: None on creek. Staff gauge on left abutment of covered bridge over Buckwha Creek at village of Little Gap should read at least 1.8 feet.

Section 2. SR2009 to mouth					
Gradient	Difficulty	Distance	Time	Scenery	Map
11	A to 1+	6.6	2.0	Fair to Ugly	34

TRIP DESCRIPTION: After Buckwha Creek swells the volume, Aquashicola is no longer an obstacle course. There are still plenty of riffles, but otherwise smooth water rushes through the woods and, all too soon, into possibly the most ravaged landscape in the state. An ancient giant of a zinc mill sprawls along the banks for almost a mile. Behind it looms an immense, black, and terribly unstable-looking mountain of slag, only overshadowed by high Blue Mountain. But Blue Mountain is now gray. Toxic fumes, from back before pollution control became a part of doing business, annihilated all vegetation up there, long ago. Now it is a mass of bare rock covered by a spider web of bleached, dead trees. The unvegetated soil has all washed away. On past the mill, more moonscape, the backside of Palmerton, and trashy banks complete the less than pretty picture. Take out at the condemned road bridge, just above Pa. Rte. 248.

HAZARDS: None.

WATER CONDITIONS: Canoeable in spring during snowmelt or within four days of hard rain.

GAUGE: None.

Section 3. Buckwha Creek, Kunkletown (SR3001) to mouth					
Gradient	Difficulty	Distance	Time	Scenery	Map
15	1	5.8	2.0	Fair	34

TRIP DESCRIPTION: Though as small as upper Aquashicola, Buckwha is much easier to negotiate. Swift water and lots of riffles are only occasionally blocked by strainers. The scenery, unfortunately, is only fair. Though the valley is quite pretty, the creek offers a poor and too closed-in perspective from which to appreciate it. Take out at SR2006 unless you want to drift into the ugliness of lower Aquashicola.

HAZARDS: Occasional strainers.

WATER CONDITIONS: Canoeable in spring during snowmelt or within two days of hard rain.

GAUGE: Staff gauge on left abutment of covered bridge at Little Gap should read at least 1.9 feet.

Lizard Creek

INTRODUCTION: Lizard Creek is a small and obscure tributary to the Lehigh, joining just across the river from Bowmanstown. If the Lizard ever does become well-known amongst paddlers, it will owe it all to the short, sweet stretch of whitewater formed as it cuts down to the level of the Lehigh.

Section 1. Pa. Rte. 309 to Ashfield (Dinkey Church Road)					
Gradient	Difficulty	Distance	Time	Scenery	Map
11	1	10.8	3.5	Fair	28

TRIP DESCRIPTION: You can run this creek as far up as Pa. Rte. 309, if whitewater is not your passion. The tiny, cloudy brook winds about woodlands interrupted by views of fields, farms, houses, mountainsides, and a big rock mining operation. It is a nice but unspectacular place to float the day away. Lizard's generally smooth water drops over many gravel bars as it heads for Ashfield. Though the creek is easy, anticipate carrying a few trees, including one huge logjam that seems to be anchored on some old dam remains.

HAZARDS: Strainers.

WATER CONDITIONS: Catch this within two days of hard rain in late fall or spring.

GAUGE: Staff gauge on the right abutment of Dinkey Church Road Bridge (T336), at Ashfield, should read at least 2.8 feet to do the whole run.

Section 2. Ashfield (Dinkey Church Road) to mouth					
Gradient	Difficulty	Distance	Time	Scenery	Map
28	3 –	3.0	1.0	Good	28

TRIP DESCRIPTION: Paddlers primarily interested in whitewater will want to start at Ashfield. After a short, smooth warm-up, the creek begins its two-mile tumble down increasingly long, complex, boulder patch rapids. The gradient is moderate, and together with a million eddies and quick decisions, this is an ideal run for intermediates. Take out at Kittitiny Road, T354, as the only egress at the mouth is either by a quarter-mile paddle up the Lehigh to West Bowmanstown (not all that difficult) or by a hike up the railroad grade.

HAZARDS: None.

WATER CONDITIONS: See above.

GAUGE: See above.

Pohopoco Creek

INTRODUCTION: Pohopoco Creek is easier to paddle than pronounce. Much of it is flat-water, both man-made and natural, and that which is not flat is not difficult.

Section 1. Gilbert (U.S. Rte. 209) to mouth					
Gradient	Difficulty	Distance	Time	Scenery	Map
14	A to 1	20.2	8.0	Fair to Good	34

TRIP DESCRIPTION: If the water is high, and you are a competent boater, you can squeeze in 2.5 extra miles by putting in above Effort, at Evergreen Hollow. Here Pohopoco is a tiny, busy brook that hurries off of the base of the Pocono Plateau to the long, straight valley below. The whitewater is relatively easy, but a sharp two-foot weir, some fences, and brush demand some boat control.

Conditions change at U.S. Rte. 209. The creek turns right, turns flat, and then disappears into a dense and tangled bottomland swamp. Though far longer than it is wide, the swamp forms an effective screen between you and the open, cultivated, and populated valley beyond. Fallen trees can be an annoyance on this section. When the swamp ends below T560, the banks rise, and a continuous series of riffles begins above Rte. 209, at the foot of a runnable (on right) two-foot weir. But the fun ends too soon in the backwater of Beltzville Lake, near Trachsville.

The upper half of Beltzville Lake, which here is narrow and hemmed by steep, wooded slopes, is nicest. If time allows, paddle up to the head of Wild Creek Cove, opposite Preachers Camp Boat Launch, and then hike up to the tiny, hemlock-shaded Wild Creek Falls. The second half of the lake is wide, and the surrounding mountains and farms uninspiring. If you only plan to paddle on the lake, Beltzville State Park requires that you use their two designated launch areas (where they can charge you). If you are just passing through, the charge is in sweat, when you portage the 170-foot Beltzville Dam. The easiest carry is straight up and down the left face.

The lower creek is generally unappealing, flowing past houses and turnpike. As for navigation, the current is fair and there are riffles. You should carry the skeleton of a wooden weir at Herrity, but you can shoot the sloping, eight-foot dam (on left) at Parryville, at moderate levels. A short rush through the best riffles on the creek carries you from the dam to the Lehigh.

HAZARDS: Strainers above the suggested put-in. Dam and dam ruins on lower creek.

WATER CONDITIONS: Up in spring, during snowmelt or for week after hard rain. Swamp section below Gilbert is probably passable even longer. Lake is canoeable from April thaw until December freeze-up.

GAUGE: For above the lake, a staff gauge on Pa. Rte. 115 Bridge, Effort, should read over 1.6 feet. For below the lake, a USGS gauge a quarter mile below Beltzville Dam, along Old Mill Road, must read over 3.0 feet.

Mahoning Creek

INTRODUCTION: Mahoning Creek is a lackluster run that will be most enjoyed by people who are easily satisfied. Dribbling into the Lehigh at Lehighton, this is a good stream to cross over while driving on to at least a half dozen nicer creeks within a fifteen-mile radius.

Section 1. Normal Square (SR3001) to mouth					
Gradient	Difficulty	Distance	Time	Scenery	Map
15	A to 1	7.6	2.5	Fair to Poor	28

TRIP DESCRIPTION: Those resolved to paddle this creek anyway can start as far up as Normal Square (there really is such a place). At times, the twisting creek will serve you up pretty views of smooth mountain ridges, neat farms, hemlock-shaded bends, and little, rocky cliffs. But at more times, it will take you past too many houses, too much streambank trash, and finally, the ugly backside of Lehighton. If the creek is high enough to float, it will be swift, with many little riffles. There will also be some trees to carry on the first few miles and a six-foot dam to carry (easiest on left) at Lehighton. Take out at this dam or at the town sewage treatment plant just downstream. The road into the plant is labelled "Carbon Canine."

HAZARDS: A dam and several strainers.

WATER CONDITIONS: Canoeable in spring within three days of hard rain.

GAUGE: Staff gauge on T352 Bridge should read over 1.65 feet.

Nesquehoning Creek

INTRODUCTION: If you have paddled the Lehigh Gorge, then you have been exposed to the elusive Nesquehoning. You have floated by its mouth, two miles above the Jim Thorpe take-out, and you have crossed over high above it, on your shuttle, when you turned off of U.S. Rte. 209 onto Pa. Rte. 93. Do not feel bad, as few people notice that there is a rushing, rocky brook down in that yawning side canyon. So what everyone has been missing is a delightful, challenging, micro-stream cruise of intermediate difficulty. Next time the water is high, see for yourself.

Section 1. Confluence Broad Run to mouth					
Gradient	Difficulty	Distance	Time	Scenery	Map
66	2 to 3	5.6	2.0	Poor to Good	28

TRIP DESCRIPTION: To reach the put-in, turn off of Pa. Rte. 54, 1.5 miles west of Nesquehoning, onto the road marked "Green Acres Industrial Park West," and follow 0.7 miles to the first road bridge. The tiny brook takes off downhill at a steady gradient, over a mostly uniform cobble bottom; so uniform, in fact, that locals get their summertime kicks by racing up the now dry creek bed in four-wheel-drive vehicles. Running fairly straight, between high cobble banks, the creek almost seems like a whitewater ditch. This coupled with some factories, gob piles, acid tributaries, and assorted trash, makes this initially less than scenic.

Because of man's incursions, treat this section with caution. There is a big, tilting culvert that can be safely run for thrills, but the tempting-looking broken dam, shortly downstream, can send you to the promised land. Carry this dam, as directly in the outflow jet is a submerged, jagged piling that can cause a serious pinning. The author advises you from hard experience.

The creek changes character below the Town of Nesquehoning as it plunges into deep woods. Lined now by hemlock and rhododendron, and filled with boulders, it is a world apart from the abused creek upstream. You will find a slalom awaiting you as the now steepening waters weave through the patches of sandstone boulders, while being further complicated by overhanging vegetation. This section's only fault is that it is too short. There is no take-out at the mouth, so keep floating down the swollen Lehigh two miles to Jim Thorpe.

HAZARDS: Broken dam above Nesquehoning and strainers.

WATER CONDITIONS: Canoeable in spring during snowmelt or within two days of hard rain.

GAUGE: None. Judge riffles below Rte. 93 Bridge, or at put in.

Black and Quakake Creeks

INTRODUCTION: Black Creek is that intriguing little torrent that gushes into the Lehigh Gorge, on the right, at the railroad bridge, several miles below Rockport. Quakake Creek is the best fork on which to start a Black Creek trip. Together they present an excellent, tumbling, and tortuous secret entry into the regular old Lehigh run.

Section 1. Hudsondale (Pa. Rte. 93) to mouth					
Gradient	Difficulty	Distance	Time	Scenery	Map
58	2 to 4	6.6	2.0	Very Good to Excellent	27

TRIP DESCRIPTION: Quakake is Indian for "pine woods." That is almost correct. For the clear brook at Pa. Rte. 93 hurries off into a tunnel of hemlock, which along with the prolific rhododendron undergrowth, are equally as green and fragrant as any pine woods. The crumbling ruins of an old factory are the only reminders that this is not a wilderness. Boating Quakake is a delight, as its waters spill over and through small sandstone boulders, requiring tight manuevering. You may find a strainer to carry, but a small wooden dam at the factory is runnable.

Black Creek joins Quakake in the middle of nowhere, adding welcome flow and some unwelcome pollution. A real canyon begins to form now, climaxing in high tiers of cliffs and talus slopes. The stream continues its wonderful rush down through boulder patches and rock gardens, climaxing about halfway (below the railroad bridge) with some exciting, blocked, diagonal ledges and boulder rapids. But more importantly, be alert for two low-slung steel cables, each strung across the fastest parts of some steep rapids on the first half of Black Creek.

There is no take-out at the mouth, but if there is enough water to float Black Creek, the Lehigh will be a fast, swollen flush down to Jim Thorpe.

HAZARDS: Two barely visible, low cables in whitewater.

WATER CONDITIONS: Canoeable in spring during snowmelt or within two days of hard rain.

GAUGE: None on stream. Roughly, USGS gauges at White Haven on the Lehigh and Berne on the Schuylkill (call Philadelphia) should be over 4.0 feet and 6.5 feet respectively.

Bear Creek

INTRODUCTION: Bear Creek is only eight miles, as the crow flies, from downtown Wilkes-Barre, but it could be 800 miles. Located up on the Pocono Plateau, on land that drains to the Lehigh, this clear, clean, evergreen bound brook resembles a little piece of the wild north woods that somehow slipped down from Canada when nobody was looking.

Section 1. Pa. Rte. 115 to Walters Dam (on Lehigh)					
Gradient	Difficulty	Distance	Time	Scenery	Map
42	A to 3 –	6.6	2.5	Very Good	26

TRIP DESCRIPTION: At Pa. Rte. 115, a shallow, clear, amber-colored trout stream, flecked with tan foam from its plunge over the dam upstream, rushes off past a few summer homes and into the forest. Though a fine road is never far from the stream, that road is little-travelled and seldom seen or heard. In the shade of hemlock, the creek hurries fairly evenly over a cobbly and rocky bottom, periodically leaping over sharp little two- and three-foot ledges that have a way of sneaking up on you. About three miles down, above the highway bridge, an irregular seven-foot ledge sneaks up, then followed by some lesser but still challenging ledges. Most paddlers should carry the first drop. Below the bridge, the gradient increases, with some bouncy, bouldery rapids near the end, i.e. assuming that Francis E. Walter Lake is at normal pool. Also, at normal pool, you have only about a mile and a half of flatwater to reach the take-out at the right end of Francis E. Walter Dam. But if the water is high everywhere, and flooding threatens the lower Lehigh Valley, the Corps may let the reservoir fill, backing the slackwater all the way up to the highway bridge. So check the level of the reservoir, at the dam, before starting.

HAZARDS: Unfriendly ledge (small falls) above highway bridge.

WATER CONDITIONS: Canoeable in spring during snowmelt or within three days of hard rain.

GAUGE: None on stream. Roughly, White Haven gauge on Lehigh (call Philadelphia) should be over 4.4 feet. For maximum miles of whitewater, lake level (gauge on intake tower of dam) should be 1,300 feet. At 1,396 feet (maximum pool), the lake reaches up almost to the highway bridge.

Tobyhanna Creek

INTRODUCTION: Tobyhanna Creek is a major tributary of the upper Lehigh. Its name means "alder stream," which may conjure up images of a tangled and tough swamp expedition. But the significant challenges on the Tobyhanna are legalistic, not natural. Some closely guarded private property along the Tobyhanna, unfortunately, makes cruising this stream an uncertain proposition. The truly prepared paddler will bring first aid, throw line, lifejacket, and a lawyer.

Section 1. Tobyhanna (Pa. Rte. 611) to Pa. Rte. 940					
Gradient	Difficulty	Distance	Time	Scenery	Map
29	A to 2 +	8.7	3.0	Very Good	26

TRIP DESCRIPTION: You should not have any people problems up here. The upper Tobyhanna is a beautiful and isolated run, flowing mostly through state game lands. Put in on Main Street in Tobyhanna. After the last few houses of Tobyhanna and except for a few more at Warnertown, this is pretty much a wilderness experience down to Pocono Lake. The creek passes through a hardwood forest, with patches of hemlock and rhododendron clinging to the stream banks. Its waters are clear, clean, and tea-colored.

Up here the Tobyhanna is always swift and breaks over long riffles and easy rapids. Some of those rapids can be extremely rocky or bouldery and quite tortuous. The shallowest stretches lie where the channel braids. About three miles into the trip, the creek wanders into a large, reedy glade, that was once the bottom of Ice Pond. Carry the old dam at the outlet (on the left) and continue walking around a long, sloping falls, just below.

HAZARDS: Falls and old dam about a mile below Warnertown. Possible strainers.

WATER CONDITIONS: Canoeable in spring during the height of the thaw or within two days of hard rain.

GAUGE: None on stream. If USGS ever replaces outside staff on its gauging station at Pa. Rte. 940, Blakeslee, 5.6 feet is minimal.

Gradient	Difficulty	Distance	Time	Scenery	Map
20	A to 2	12.6	4.5	Very Good	26

TRIP DESCRIPTION: Pa. Rte. 940 crosses the upper reach of Pocono Lake, which is dammed and surrounded by a large private development called Pocono Lake Preserve. The preserve includes possibly the most attractive and tastefully arranged second home development that you will ever see. The owners have seen to it that all homes are set far enough back from the lake that the lake shore appears essentially wild. The preserve, unfortunately, only permits visitors to enter if they are guests of the individual members. So if you have no friends in the club to grant you a visitor's pass, remember that portaging around the dam (on left is best) will put you in a trespassing situation. Proceed only at your own risk.

A shallow gorge starts to shape up below the dam. This is a particularly pretty segment, where dense stands of hemlock and rhododendron green the slopes and banks, while reddish, siltstone ledges, mottled with white lichen, rim the water. The long and easy rapids through here are bouncy and straightforward, until a short way below Pa. Rte. 115, where the creek thunders over a steeply sloping eight-foot ledge. This looks runnable, but you will have to go first.

The gorge just gets prettier below Pa. Rte. 940. Grassy bottomlands are backed by gentle slopes covered by birch woods that look like the sort of woods that Robert Frost would have lingered in on a snowy evening. But if he did, he would have been arrested. A rod and gun club owns much of the surrounding lands and claims to own the stream too. Since their low-water bridge requires a portage, chances are excellent that you would get to meet the caretaker. Proceed at your own risk.

Since there is no access to the mouth, plan on paddling an additional six miles of Lehigh and lake, to the first road, which is at Francis E. Walter Dam.

HAZARDS: Dam at Pocono Lake, small falls below Pa. Rte. 115, low-water bridge below second Pa. Rte. 940 crossing, and hostile landowners.

WATER CONDITIONS: Canoeable in spring during snowmelt and within week of hard rain. Stay away in trout season.

GAUGE: None. If USGS ever replaces the outside staff on its gauging station at Pa. Rte. 940, Blakeslee, 3.5 feet is about minimal. Roughly, USGS gauge at White Haven (call Philadelphia) should be over 4.4 feet.

Tunkhannock Creek

INTRODUCTION: This Tunkhannock Creek is a sparkling brook that dashes into the Tobyhanna near Blakeslee. It is a typical Pocono trout stream — beautiful, remote, and posted. Consider the Tunkhannock as a short and sweet selection for some time when every creek in northeast Pennsylvania is gushing.

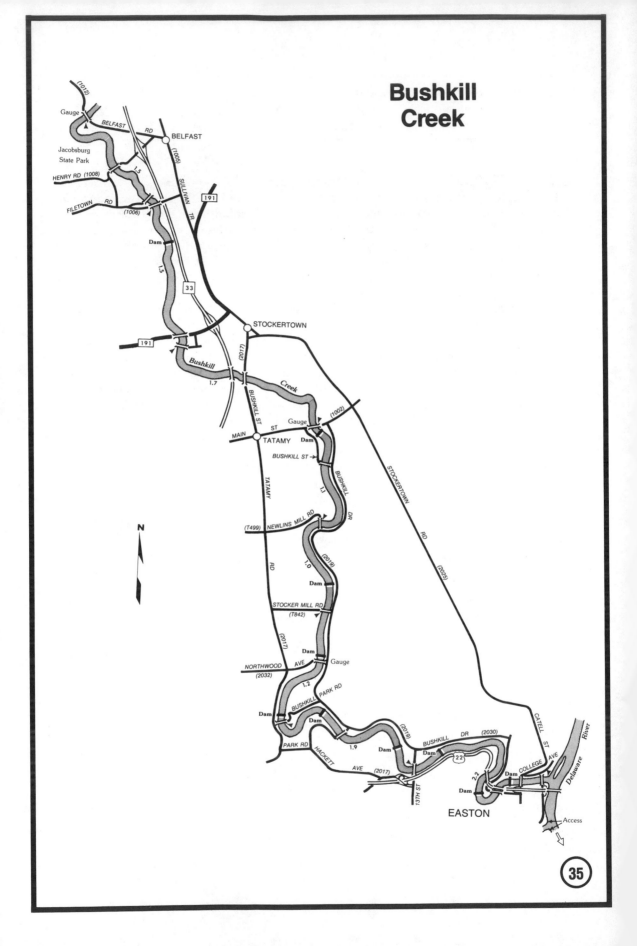

Bushkill Creek

(1072)

Gauge

BELFAST RD   BELFAST

(1005)

Jacobsburg
State Park

HENRY RD (1008)   1.5

FILETOWN RD
(1006)

SULLIVAN TR

191

Dam

1.5

33

191

Bushkill

1.7

(2017)

STOCKERTOWN

BUSHKILL ST

Creek

Gauge   (1002)

MAIN   ST

TATAMY   Dam

BUSHKILL ST →

TATAMY

1.1

BUSHKILL DR

(T499) NEWLINS MILL RD

N

1.0   (2019)

STOCKERTOWN RD

(2025)

RD

Dam

STOCKER MILL RD.
(T842)

(2017)

Dam

NORTHWOOD   AVE   Gauge
(2032)

1.2

Dam   BUSHKILL PARK RD

Dam

PARK RD   1.9   Dam   (2019)   BUSHKILL   DR   (2030)

HACKETT   Dam

AVE   (2017)   22   2.2   Dam

CATELL ST

COLLEGE AVE

Delaware River

13TH ST   Dam

EASTON   Access

35

Section 1. Pa. Rte. 115 to mouth					
Gradient	Difficulty	Distance	Time	Scenery	Map
52	1 to 3	4.4	1.5	Very Good	26

TRIP DESCRIPTION: This is a busy run, typically pouring over a gravel bed. But periodic, surprise ledges of up to five feet high make it a thrill. Watch for a small, unrunnable dam that caps a sharp ledge, just below T629, and strainers at the mouth. The take-out is 0.7 miles down the Tobyhanna at Pa. Rte. 940.

This is one of those streams that, in places, is so enveloped by the hemlock, pine, and rhododendron, that it looks as if it were summer even in March. But behind this evergreen facade is a more seasonally hued, park-like forest of birch and maple. The Tunkhannock is one of the most heavily posted streams that you may ever travel. The first mile of both banks is owned by a fishing club that, besides tacking up "No Trespassing" signs, has also hung a collection of neat, little, blue signs that attach a name to practically every pool and riffle on that section. This, combined with the small, green park benches that are spaced about every hundred yards, gives one the impression of paddling through a formal garden. It is clear that one should avoid this section during trout season. In contrast, the lower reach of the Tunkhannock is totally primitive, where you must sit on stumps, not benches.

HAZARDS: Nasty drop just below T629. Hostile landowners.

WATER CONDITIONS: Canoeable in spring at height of snowmelt or within two days of hard rain.

GAUGE: None. Judge riffles at Rte. 115.

Bushkill Creek

INTRODUCTION: Do not confuse Bushkill Creek with Big Bushkill Creek, that sparkling jewel that tumbles out of the clean and green Poconos. This Bushkill is a disappointing ditch that exposes the paddler to too much of the bland and ugly side of Easton. Surrounded by noise and congestion, and cursed by a plethora of dams, this will not be your dream stream.

Section 1. Belfast Road, SR1012 to mouth					
Gradient	Difficulty	Distance	Time	Scenery	Map
23	A to 2 –	12.1	5.0	Good to Poor	35

TRIP DESCRIPTION: The put-in is at Jacobsburg State Park, 1,166 acres of prime open space. But back in the early 19th century, when there really was a Jacobsburg at this site, this narrow valley hummed with industry: an iron furnace, two gun factories, a tannery, a sawmill, and a gristmill. Now there are only a few restored houses, some foundations, and memories. Nature has wasted no time in reclaiming its territory.

The creek starts out with such promise. The quiet passage through Jacobsburg State Park winds past wooded hillsides, big hemlocks, and platy, little shale cliffs and ledges. Here Bushkill lives up to its name, which is Dutch for "forest creek." But as it approaches Pa. Rte. 33, there goes the neighborhood. Much of the remaining creek is paralleled by roads, and these are busy and noisy roads. Houses, trash, and junk are commonplace. Industry also appears, including the huge cement plant at Pa. Rte. 191. Surprisingly, in spite of all the development, the water quality remains relatively good.

Bushkill has a healthy gradient that at least provides the paddler with an enjoyable assortment of easy rapids and riffles. But there would be even more rapids if there were not ten dams on this stretch (that is almost one dam per mile). All but one, a three-footer at the park below SR1002, should be carried. Some of the carries on the last few dams, down in Easton, can be quite nasty, with slippery footing, broken glass, sharp concrete, and even some vicious guard dogs. Take out down the Delaware at the park at the mouth of the Lehigh.

HAZARDS: Ten dams and weirs.

WATER CONDITIONS: Canoeable in spring within two days of hard rain.

GAUGE: Staff gauge on left abutment of SR1012 Bridge: 0.0 feet is zero. Staff gauge on right pier of Main Street, SR1002: 0.7 feet is approximately zero. Staff gauge on left abutment of Northwood Avenue: 1.3 feet is enough.

Martins Creek

INTRODUCTION: Slipping into the Delaware behind a dusty, old cement plant at the town of Martins Creek, this creek of the same name hardly seems worthy of further attention. But come a hard rain, you will find six delightful miles of novice to intermediate whitewater boating waiting for you.

When you drive to Martins Creek, you may notice that the countryside, especially near the base of Blue Mountain, is dotted with great mounds of shiny shards of gray rock — refuse from the quarrying of slate. A 200-square-mile belt of slate spans the north of Northampton and Lehigh counties. That is why you may pass through Slatington, Slatedale, Slateford, or Martins Creek's headwater town of Bangor, which was named for a slate mining town in Wales.

Section 1. Flicksville (T170) to mouth					
Gradient	Difficulty	Distance	Time	Scenery	Map
37	2, 3 +	6.0	2.0	Fair	36

TRIP DESCRIPTION: This is a well-designed stream. The rapids and riffles are long enough to exercise your mind and muscles, while the pools are just long enough for you to relax. Cobble bars, a smattering of boulders, and some ledges form the rapids. One particularly good rapid, formed by a set of sloping ledges that are spotted with cozy surfing holes, dashes through the village of Martins Creek. But the most exciting spot comes shortly downstream, located behind the big cement plant. The excitement takes the form of a man-made drop — an ugly pile of angu-

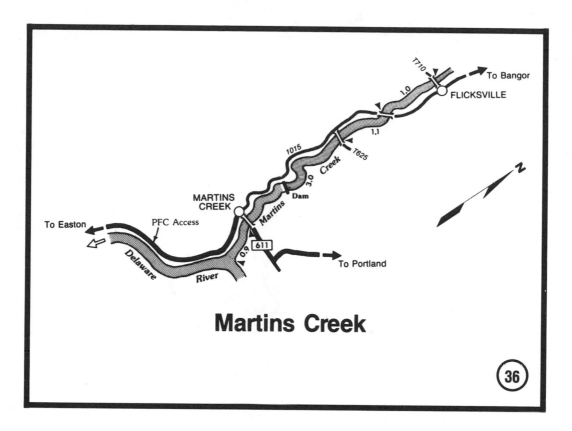

Martins Creek

(36)

lar rubble whose twisting chute is runnable. But there is also enough twisted, protruding steel and jagged concrete to persuade you to carry it anyway. Other hazards on this creek include a vertical, five-foot dam (carry), about four miles below the start, and maybe a fallen tree.

The scenery along Martins Creek is generally fair, though it can shine in spots. The water quality takes a beating when sewage-laden Waltz Creek joins. You can take out at the mouth, on the right, at a spot approached from land (Pa. Rte. 611) via a gate at the south end of the old cement plant. If the gate is closed, continue 1.5 miles down the Delaware to Sandts Eddy Access.

HAZARDS: Possible strainers, a small dam, and the man-made drop behind the cement plant.

WATER CONDITIONS: Canoeable in spring within two days of hard rain.

GAUGE: None.

Brodhead Creek

INTRODUCTION: The best way to describe Brodhead Creek is that it is consistantly inconsistant. Brodhead takes a temperamental tumble from the Pocono Plateau to join the Delaware River at the head of the Delaware Water Gap. It is exciting for a bit, then mellow, then exciting, and so on. The aesthetics vary similarly. But altogether it is worthy of any whitewater boater's attention.

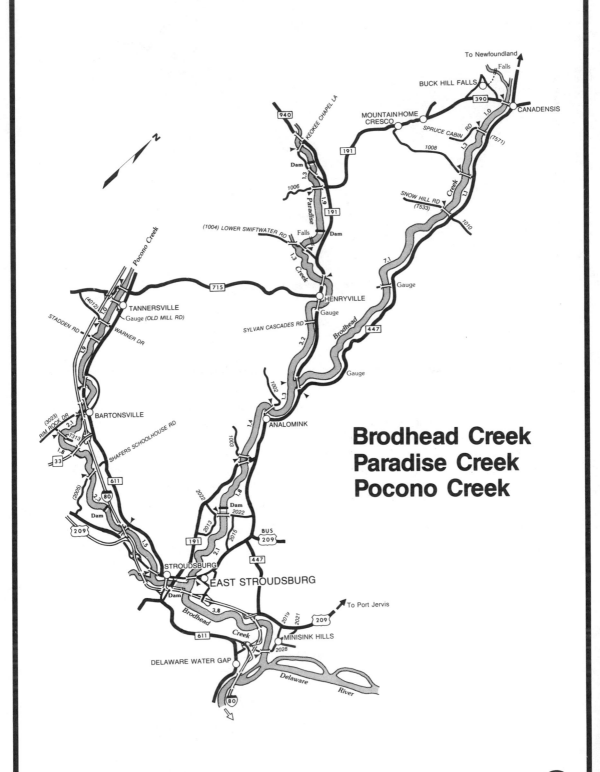

Brodhead Creek
Paradise Creek
Pocono Creek

37

Section 1. Canadensis (Pa. Rte. 390) to mouth					
Gradient	Difficulty	Distance	Time	Scenery	Map
33	A to 4 –	21.2	7.5	Fair to Poor	37
1 @ 78					

TRIP DESCRIPTION: Before starting at Canadensis, zip up the hill to the right, following the signs, and see beautiful Buck Hill Falls. While certainly no Niagara, its rare setting in a green, natural amphitheater is bound to charm you.

Brodhead starts off on the right foot as it tumbles out of Canadensis over an abrupt series of ledges and boulder patches. It moderates for about three miles until it again crashes through a similarly exciting stretch. The ledges form both sharp drops and slides. Since the upper creek is narrow, these rapids may be further complicated by an occasional fallen tree. Generally, in between the steep sections, Brodhead provides a lively pool and rapid run that does not exceed Class 2 in difficulty. The next point of interest lies below Analomink and is signaled by a small milldam (carry) above Stokes Avenue, SR2022. There are some fun ledges right below and then, about a half mile downstream, comes the whopper—a tilting, eight-foot ledge with a nasty, curving chute on the right. There is a friendly pool below.

The scenery along most of the Brodhead above Stroudsburg is adequately attractive. Development is spotty and usually confined to along the highway. The streambanks are usually wooded, often densely so.

The creek muddles through Stroudsburg and East Stroudsburg via a leveed flood channel, where it is wide and shallow. But below town, it escapes to a wooded gorge. In that gorge, just past an old paper mill, the creek breaks over the still formidable remains of an old dam, with a good, swift chute on the far left. Take out at SR2028, south of Minisink Hills, unless you plan on continuing down the Delaware.

HAZARDS: Small dam above Stokes Avenue. Possible strainers.

WATER CONDITIONS: Canoeable in spring during snowmelt and within four days of hard rain.

GAUGE: USGS gauge above Analomink is located 1.4 miles above Paradise Creek, on left. This should read at least 2.6 feet to start at Canadensis (call Philadelphia or inspect on site). Staff gauge on center pier of bridge to Alpine Mountain Ski Area (2.4 miles below Snow Hill Road) must read at least 1.6 feet.

Pocono Creek

INTRODUCTION: Hidden in the shadow of busy highways, little Pocono Creek slips into Stroudsburg and Brodhead Creek almost unnoticed. But given enough heavy rain to raise a foot of canoeable water, there lurks a raging, rampaging, whitewater wonder.

Gradient	Difficulty	Distance	Time	Scenery	Map
46	2 to 4 +	10.6	4.5	Good to Poor	37

TRIP DESCRIPTION: Pocono Creek can be nasty at times. This is first evident at the put-in, when you attempt to penetrate the impenetrable sapling curtain that brackets the bulldozed channel in Tannersville. After a fast start, the creek carries you through a long mellow stretch of just swift water, many long, easy rapids, and a few bouncy surprises. The soothing streambank scenery of hemlock and rhododendron lulls you into complacency. Then just when you are really off guard, there comes the shock. The creek rounds a blind curve, above Martz Road, T313, and plunges into a short chasm. Scout the long, complex rapid within, and set up some safety lines if you choose to run it, as the creek then spills over a 15-foot waterfalls only 200 short yards below. Please be discreet on your portage around the falls and the five-foot dam below it, as this is through somebody's backyard. Next begins three miles of heaving, crashing, hole- and boulder-studded rapids, with problems. The first problem lies around a blind, right-hand bend below Pa. Rte. 33 Bridge. Get out and scout this long, sloping ledge, a huge eyetooth boulder at the foot of this ledge, the incredible exploding pillow that hurls back upstream from this boulder, and the undercut boulder on the right, where you might have otherwise snuck that pillow. Next, well below Shafers School House Road, SR2005, where the creek hits I-81, a ten-foot dam sneaks up; so carry on the right. Shortly below, a series of ledges throw up some deceptively strong hydraulics. Then, all too soon, the gradient eases off, the scenery goes to the dogs, and you drift into downtown Stroudsburg. Take out on the downstream right, behind some garden apartments.

You will not regret skipping the final 1.2 miles of creek, from Main Street to the mouth. The surroundings are the ugly backsides of buildings, as far as Rte. 191, and leveed channel below. There is also a nasty dam and falls to carry, beneath Rte. 191. If you paddle it all anyway, you can almost get your vehicle to the mouth via Storm Street, on river right, below Rte. 191.

HAZARDS: Two dams, a falls, and two particularly nasty rapids.

WATER CONDITIONS: Canoeable in spring, within two days of hard rain, or during rapid snowmelt.

GAUGE: Painted canoe gauge on the left abutment of Old Mill Road Bridge, Tannersville. Roughly, USGS gauge above Analomink, on Brodhead Creek (call Philadelphia or inspect on spot), should be over 3.5 feet.

McMichael Creek

INTRODUCTION: McMichael Creek is a pleasant country brook that wanders into Pocono Creek and Stroudsburg, from the southwest. After it calms down from its swift, tangled start, it provides some good small stream boating that can be easily managed by beginners.

Section 1. Effort–Neola Road, SR3018 to Sciota (Bus. Rte. 209)					
Gradient	Difficulty	Distance	Time	Scenery	Map
37	1 to 2 +	5.8	2.0	Good	38

TRIP DESCRIPTION: McMichael Creek becomes canoeable near the conclusion of its descent off the Pocono Plateau. From SR3018 it runs steeply for a half mile, but then quickly settles into a steady, moderate gradient, rushing over continuous gravel riffles and lots of little fish weirs. This is not to say that it is easy. There is a four-foot dam, with a fast approach, to carry, about a half mile below the start, a runnable three-foot wooden weir below Kennel Road, T434, some low foot and road bridges, strainers, two dangerously low-slung wires that span the creek on a braided section below Kennel Road, and devious dead-end channels on braided sections. Just below Pa. Rte. 715, where the creek forks, be sure to stay to the right to avoid a dead-end passage. Finally, note that a fishing club owns and has heavily posted both banks from the put-in to Deer Lane, T432; so stay away during trout season.

This section of McMichael Creek flows through a variety of pleasant, uncrowded scenery. It takes in rhododendron thickets, woodlands (including a stretch of floodplain swamp), and a little farmland. Houses and people are few and far between.

HAZARDS: Dams, strainers, low bridges, and cables.

WATER CONDITIONS: Canoeable in spring during snowmelt and within two days of hard rain.

GAUGE: None on this section. Staff gauge on Hickory Valley Road, SR2010, should be over 2.0 feet.

Section 2. Sciota (Bus. Rte. 209) to mouth					
Gradient	Difficulty	Distance	Time	Scenery	Map
13	1	11.4	4.0	Good	38

TRIP DESCRIPTION: The remainder of McMichael Creek can be as gentle as a lamb. A small falls drops beside a rustic mill and beneath Old Mill Road, T219, demanding a short, slippery carry on the right. But that should be your only hazard. Otherwise the creek flows calmly or over simple riffles. The setting is mostly rural, complete with well-kept barns, old houses, and stone bridges. More people live near this section of creek, but it is still uncrowded. Take out on Pocono Creek at the little park on the left, at Pa. Rte. 191, taking care not to wash over the dam immediately below.

HAZARDS: Dam and falls beneath Old Mill Road and again at Rte. 191.

WATER CONDITIONS: Canoeable in spring during snowmelt or within four days of hard rain.

GAUGE: Staff gauge on right abutment of Hickory Valley Road, SR2010, should read at least 1.3 feet. Roughly, USGS gauge above Analomink, on Brodhead Creek (call Philadelphia or inspect on spot), should read over 2.6 feet.

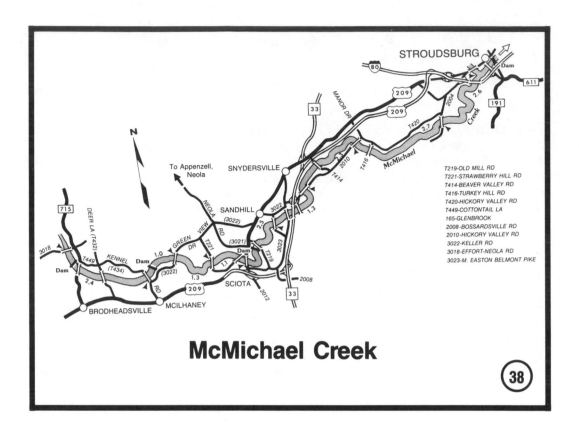

McMichael Creek

T219-OLD MILL RD
T221-STRAWBERRY HILL RD
T414-BEAVER VALLEY RD
T416-TURKEY HILL RD
T420-HICKORY VALLEY RD
T449-COTTONTAIL LA
165-GLENBROOK
2008-BOSSARDSVILLE RD
2010-HICKORY VALLEY RD
3022-KELLER RD
3018-EFFORT-NEOLA RD
3023-M. EASTON BELMONT PIKE

38

Paradise Creek

INTRODUCTION: Paradise Creek drops precipitously into the Brodhead at Analomink. Bristling with hazards and complications, this whitewater terror should provide adequate amusement for the bored whitewater boater looking for something unusual to do with two inches of rain on Monroe County.

Section 1. Keokee Chapel Lane to mouth					
Gradient	Difficulty	Distance	Time	Scenery	Map
66	3 to 4 –	7.7	3.0	Good to Very Good	37

TRIP DESCRIPTION: Put in at the upper Keokee Chapel Lane bridge. The tiny creek hurries off downhill with great promise. But before you can get comfortable, you must get out for a seven-foot dam (carry left) hidden behind a big, garish resort complex. The creek then dashes onward without complication, except for a possible strainer, for about two and a half miles. Then at the end of a short pond, you must carry a twenty-foot dam. A few hundred yards below this dam, the creek tears around a blind, right hand bend and pours over a nasty ledge rapid that piles into an undercut rock. A carry here would also be wise. Shortly downstream, Paradise Creek plunges over beautiful, but unrunnable, Paradise Falls. Carry left. Your troubles are still not over as next the creek runs the gauntlet through a stretch of fallen hemlock trees. Lower Swiftwater Road, SR1004, soon appears, and Swiftwater Creek injects new volume and power into friendly(?) Paradise Creek. This flushes you into the maw of Redrock Glen, a lovely and aptly-named, short chasm, with an irregular small falls at its entrance and a series of complex diagonal ledges near its exit. As you bushwack and stumble around this chasm via the steep, slippery woods on the left, you will no doubt be wondering by now why someone named this place "paradise." Then, finally, the creek settles down to just plain old boatable whitewater. The final 3.5 miles of long, sometimes heavy rapids, over cobbles, boulders, ledges, and trout weirs are sheer delight.

Generally this is a beautiful stream. Set in a bit of a gorge, the surroundings are usually wooded and the streambanks are often lined by pretty rock ledges and feathery, green hemlocks. This, unfortunately, is another creek to avoid during trout season.

HAZARDS: Two dams, trees, a falls, a difficult (maybe impossible) chasm, and an undercut rock rapid.

WATER CONDITIONS: Canoeable in spring only within 24 hours of hard rain.

GAUGE: Staff gauge on right abutment of Pa. Rte. 191 Bridge, below Henryville, should read at least 3.0 feet to start at Keokee Chapel Road.

Big Bushkill Creek

INTRODUCTION: The southeast flank of the Pocono Plateau plunges abruptly to the level of the Delaware River. Of the roughly dozen creeks that cross this escarpment, only one, Big Bushkill, is large enough and steady enough to reasonably consider canoeing. Skilled paddlers might want to consider doing just that.

Big Bushkill's biggest flaw is that it is so nice. As a result, much of the riparian land has been snapped up as carefully guarded private property. At least two private clubs, on the upper creek, and a Boy Scouts of America camp, on the lower, do not like you to be on their stream. Whether this is indeed their stream or not is really moot, for you must trespass on at least two of these properties to portage unrunnable waterfalls. So the potential cruiser of Big Bushkill must consider this to be a forbidden fruit expedition, legally risky at best.

Section 1. Roadbridge below Pickeral Lake to T317					
Gradient	Difficulty	Distance	Time	Scenery	Map
25	A to 2 +	11.2	4.0	Very Good	39

TRIP DESCRIPTION: Much of this section runs through private clubs (but not the put-in). From the put-in, the narrow, clear, and tea-colored waters gush past a string of summer camps and then on into the wilderness. About a mile farther, the water pauses in a wide, attractive, man-made pond. Two sharp, but runnable, dams and probably an angry caretaker will greet you at the pond's outlet. The following miles are quite variable—sometimes rushing, then smooth, then dropping over many little trout weirs and some natural ledges, and finally cascading over a beautiful pair of waterfalls (carry on left). Below the falls, Big Bushkill slips into a long and dreamy, pond-like pool that extends to the take-out and possibly the waiting sheriff.

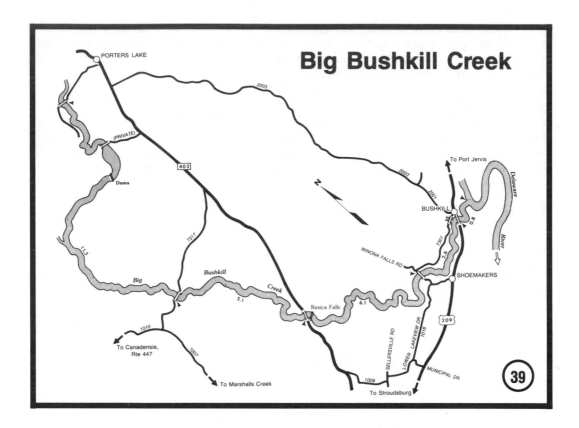

HAZARDS: Two sharp weirs at the end of Beaver Run Lake, a pair of waterfalls, and enraged caretakers (be polite).

WATER CONDITIONS: Canoeable in spring during hard snowmelt or within two days of hard rain.

GAUGE: USGS gauge near Shoemakers, at Winona Falls Road (call Philadelphia), should read over 3.0 feet.

Section 2. T317 to Bushkill (U.S. Rte. 209)					
Gradient	Difficulty	Distance	Time	Scenery	Map
46	2 to 4 –	13.8	5.0	Good to Excellent	39

TRIP DESCRIPTION: Do not put in at the bridge. An inspiring, but unboatable, double falls lies just downstream. The run down to Resica, Pa. Rte. 402, is beautiful and thrilling, hidden away in a remote gorge. The creek churns down some interesting ledge rapids, including another unrunnable double falls that is lodged in a short chasm about 1.5 miles below T317. Take out just below Pa. Rte. 402, on the left, to portage the magnificent Resica Falls and possibly meet the angry caretaker of the Boy Scout camp.

The creek now runs deep within a wild, sometimes partially rock-walled gorge. A steady gradient carries you down mostly straightforward and sometimes relatively heavy rapids. A few fairly

98

steep boulder rapids with mushy holes spice the run. After about four miles, the gorge opens up a bit, and houses begin to line the banks. The best of this run is now past, but the remaining distance is still fun, being a fast and easy flush. Take out at the Village of Bushkill, where the people are still friendly.

HAZARDS: Two pairs of small falls between T317 and Rte. 402, and Resica Falls, just below Rte. 402. Boaters wishing to avoid caretaker confrontations at the Boy Scout camp can write for permission (well in advance) from the Camping Director, Valley Forge Council, BSA, P.O. Box 806, Valley Forge, PA 19482.

WATER CONDITIONS: Canoeable in spring during snowmelt or within five days of hard rain.

GAUGE: USGS gauge near Shoemakers should read at least 2.3 feet.

Shohola Creek

INTRODUCTION: Streams associated with plateaus usually have split personalities. Where they gather their waters, up on the plateau, they are usually smooth and winding, good places for novices and for concentrating on scenery and wildlife. Where they reach the edge, they plummet and crash in cool, shady, often rock-bound canyons and chasms. These are places for whitewater boaters only—places to see the stuff of which the plateau is made. You will find this true of tiny Shohola Creek.

Shohola Creek gushes into the Delaware River about 17 miles upstream of Port Jervis, after dropping off of the Pocono Plateau. It is certainly easy to miss when you pass by its mouth, bouncing down the long Shohola Rapids of the Delaware. Perhaps that is why the Indians called the creek Shohola, which means "meek" or "faint." Though it is never more than a diminutive stream, its beauty and select fillets of whitewater will make it loom big in your memory.

Section 1. Lords Valley (Spring Road) to State Rec. Area (U.S. Rte. 6)					
Gradient	Difficulty	Distance	Time	Scenery	Map
21	A to 3 −	10.2	4.0	Very Good	2
0.6 @ 40					

TRIP DESCRIPTION: This is a pretty stretch, marred only by a few, brief brushes with I-80. The creek passes a few houses in Lords Valley, but from there on down it is all wild. Its clear, brown waters follow a writhing channel between sandy banks, through meadows, and past forests of silvery hued hardwoods, integrated by a few pines. Most of this reach is smooth flowing, but there is a taste of rapids just above Pa. Rte. 739 and a long, interesting chain of boulder-formed Class 3 rapids just above the lake.

Above U.S. Rte. 6, a small dam caps Shohola Falls to form a four-mile-long lake. Wide glades followed by a swamp forest of dead, drowned trees mark the head of the lake. The twisting and sometimes dividing channel in this woody maze can be confusing. But if you keep to the right at the first and most pronounced fork, you should not get lost.

The lake is lovely. It has an undeveloped shoreline because all of the surrounding territory, here and upstream almost to Rte. 739, is state game land. So enjoy one of the few riparian stretches in the Poconos that is devoid of "no trespassing" signs. Take out at the ramp, on the left shore, behind the state picnic area. Game land roads touch the lake at other points, but they are not always open to public vehicle use.

HAZARDS: None.

WATER CONDITIONS: Canoeable in spring during good snowmelt or within three days of hard rain.

GAUGE: Staff gauge on left downstream abutment of Pa. Rte.739. Zero is about 17.5 feet.

Section 2. U.S. Rte. 6 to mouth					
Gradient	Difficulty	Distance	Time	Scenery	Map
51	1 to 4	9.2	3.0	Good to Excellent	2
.85 @ 118					

TRIP DESCRIPTION: You only park your car at Rte. 6. The put-in, unfortunately, is a quarter mile downstream, at the end of a fearsome chasm. Rumor has it that some paddlers, putting in at the base of Shohola Falls, run this flume, which is sheer-walled and bristling with undercut edges. The author recommends, instead, a hike along the right rim via primitive trails and easy bushwacking. This brings you to the chasm's abrupt outlet into a round, dark pool. The pool spills into a wild, wonderful mile of unevenly distributed, yet continuous, whitewater, formed by sharp boulders and ledges. Sadly, it is only a mile. The creek then turns absolutely flat for awhile, but upon reaching Greeley, it begins a long, moderate descent over Class 1 and 2 rapids.

Incidently, Greeley was named after none other than Horace "Go West Young Man" Greeley. In 1842, idealistic Mr. Greeley established a commune at this site called Sylvania, for those who stayed east. This social experiment failed; so do not expect to find sixth generation hippies wandering about the surrounding woods.

The following miles run mostly through woodlands affected by only moderate development. After passing Knealing Road, the creek starts dropping over a series of shallow, sloping ledges. This is the warm-up for the passage through a short, shadowy rock chasm. The chasm is the most beautiful spot on the creek, but your eyes will be glued on the whitewater. Most notable are the entrance drop and the exit rapid. The entrance drop is verticle and mean, with a deep churning hole, best negotiated to the left of center. The exit rapid is intimidating but easy, run diagonally from left to right.

Twin Lakes Road, immediately below the chasm, is the last road bridge on Shohola Creek. But the adjacent land is heavily posted, by an owner that is reputed to object to paddlers. So consider either hiking out via the railroad, at the mouth, or continuing on down the Delaware. Since the rapids on Shohola are exhilarating to the very end, it is worth the extra effort.

HAZARDS: Possible strainers on the first mile.

WATER CONDITIONS: Canoeable in spring during snowmelt or within four days of hard rain.

GAUGE: Fading canoe gauge on right, upstream face of abutment, Knealing Road. Zero is about 2.0 feet. For rough correlation, USGS gauge at Shoemakers, on Big Bushkill Creek (call Philadelphia), should read over 2.3 feet.

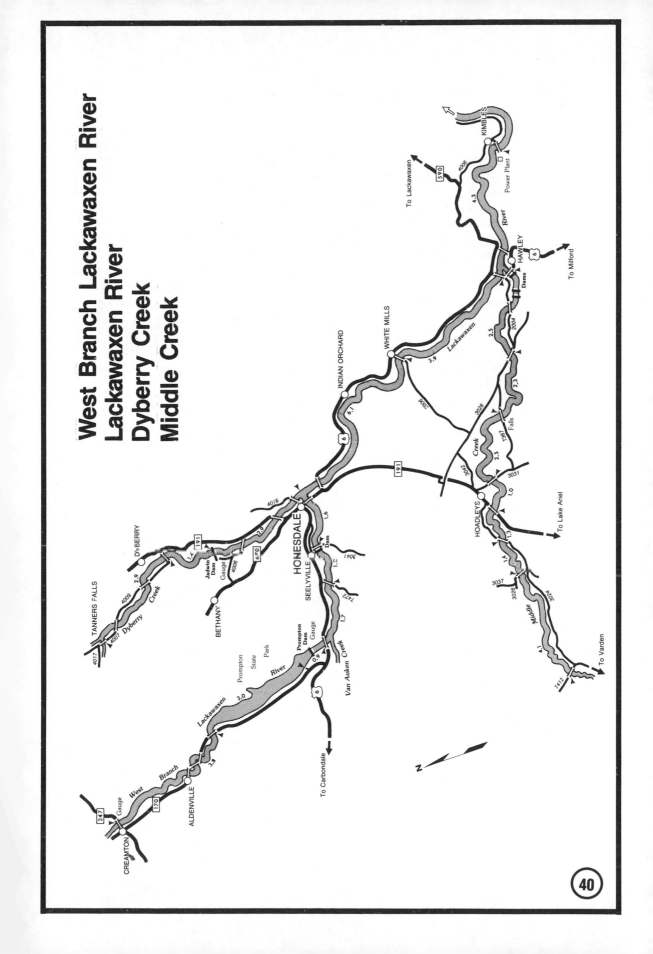

West Branch Lackawaxen River
Lackawaxen River
Dyberry Creek
Middle Creek

KIMBLES

To Lackawaxen

590

4006

4.3

River

Power Plant

HAWLEY

To Milford

6

Dams

2004

2.5

Lackawaxen

3.9

2.3

2008

3028

1967

Falls

INDIAN ORCHARD

WHITE MILLS

Creek

2.5

6.1

3042

3031

6

1.0

191

HOADLEYS

To Lake Ariel

1.3

4016

2.5

1.6

DYBERRY

191

Dam

1.4

4006

Jadwin Dam

Gauge

3041

1.1

3037

3028

1.4

1.7

T412

T472

Middle

3024

2.9

SEELYVILLE

HONESDALE

4009

Creek

BETHANY

4.1

Dyberry

0.9

Prompton Dam

Gauge

To Varden

TANNERS FALLS

4007

Prompton State Park

Van Auken Creek

4017

River

3.0

6

Lackawaxen

To Carbondale

Branch

3.8

N

West

Gauge

247

170

ALDENVILLE

CREAMTON

40

Lackawaxen River

INTRODUCTION: The Lackawaxen is the first major tributary to the Delaware, draining about 600 square miles of Wayne and Pike counties. Its whitewater descent into the Delaware Gorge has made it a favorite for novice and intermediate paddlers. And thanks to Pennsylvania Power and Light's power generation releases on weekdays, it is frequently available when all other little streams in the area have dwindled to mere trickles.

In spite of the Lackawaxen's steep gradient, the canal builders of the 19th century chose the Lackawaxen and Delaware rivers as the best route to transport coal from the anthracite fields near Carbondale to New York City. So they dug the Delaware and Hudson Canal. Completed in 1829, the canal ran 108 miles from Eddyville, on the Hudson River, to Honesdale, Pennsylvania. It took 34 locks just to lift the boats from the aqueduct, spanning the Delaware, to Honesdale. A series of inclined planes and railroads delivered the coal from Carbondale to Honesdale. The effort must have been worthwhile, for the canal continued to operate almost to the turn of the century.

Section 1. Prompton to Honesdale					
Gradient	Difficulty	Distance	Time	Scenery	Map
27	A to 2 –	4.3	1.5	Fair to Poor	40

TRIP DESCRIPTION: The Lackawaxen is born at the confluence of the West Branch and Van Auken Creek. Put in at U.S. Rte. 6 on the West Branch. You will probably find this to be a disappointing stretch of river. The surroundings are mostly developed, both residentially and commercially, and the banks are often strewn with trash. The water is clear and dark, but that only allows you to better see the beer cans and old tires on the creek bed.

On the bright side, the paddling is fun. Cobbles and patches of small boulders create numerous Class 1 and 2 rapids. You have only one carry to make, around a 15-foot dam and natural falls, at the bridge at Seelyville (carry left, under bridge). Take out from this section on the left, at the mouth of Dyberry Creek, following a path up to the YWCA on Park Street.

HAZARDS: Dam and falls beneath SR3041, Seelyville.

WATER CONDITIONS: Canoeable in spring during snowmelt and within four days of hard rain.

GAUGE: USGS gauge on West Branch, 1,500 feet upstream of U.S. Rte. 6, on right bank. Zero canoeable level is 1.9 feet. USGS gauge at Hawley (call Philadelphia) should be over 3.3 feet.

Section 2. Honesdale to Hawley (Church Street)					
Gradient	Difficulty	Distance	Time	Scenery	Map
9	1	10.7	3.5	Poor to Good	40

TRIP DESCRIPTION: This is the quiet section of the Lackawaxen. After an ugly passage through the Honesdale area, the growing creek flows mostly out of sight of the highway and other development. Except for one huge junkyard, you mostly see only floodplain woods, high grassy banks, low wooded hillsides, and, on the left bank, ruins of the old canal. The water flows mostly smooth, but swift, broken occasionally by a short rapid or riffle. Hawley, as seen from the river, is a mix of grand, old frame houses, drab mobile homes, and a high grassy levee.

HAZARDS: None.

WATER CONDITIONS: Same as Section 1.

GAUGE: Same as Section 1.

Section 3. Hawley (Church Street) to mouth					
Gradient	Difficulty	Distance	Time	Scenery	Map
16	1 to 2 +	16.3	4.5	Good	40,2

TRIP DESCRIPTION: The Lackawaxen now begins cutting a gorge-like, narrow valley. The wide river tilts over increasingly frequent, and often long, bouldery rapids. Even the pools are swift. If it is a weekday, the powerhouse may be kicking in lots of water, above the bridge at Kimbles. During low natural flow, Kimbles should be your put-in. A brief rocky chasm beneath the Kimbles Bridge creates some big river turbulence when the Lackawaxen is high. This and a stretch below Rowland create the most exciting moments of your run. Take out at the public access area at the mouth.

HAZARDS: Beware of the sudden rise in river level when the power station kicks on.

WATER CONDITIONS: Canoeable on natural flow in spring during snowmelt and within two days of hard rain. Hydro station at Kimbles usually operates winter, spring, and summer, on weekdays, usually starting at 8:00 AM and lasting a minimum of four hours. Their normal release rate of 1400 cfs is a fine level. Hot summer days with high power demand usually means reliable water.

Wallenpaupack Creek

INTRODUCTION: Most of Wallenpaupack Creek lies either buried beneath Pennsylvania Power and Light's Lake Wallenpaupack, or flows through a penstock to their powerhouse. But a bit of its headwaters remain, offering some short, fast, whitewater runs.

Section 1. Wallenpaupack Creek: Mountainview Road to Ledgedale Road, SR4001					
Gradient	Difficulty	Distance	Time	Scenery	Map
16	A to 3	10.3	3.5	Fair to Good	41

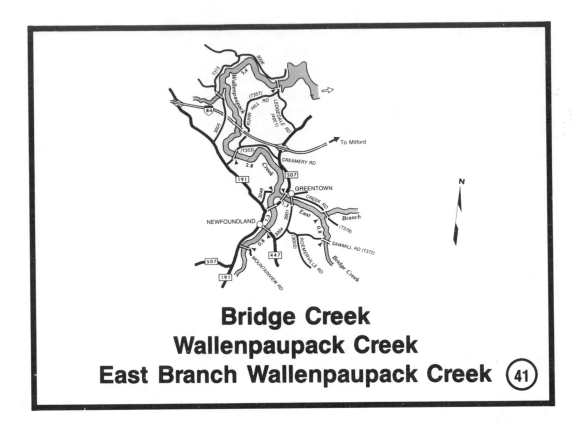

Bridge Creek
Wallenpaupack Creek
East Branch Wallenpaupack Creek (41)

TRIP DESCRIPTION: This tiny creek starts with a drab, channelized dash over a respectable but uniform gradient through Newfoundland. It then transforms to a deep and sluggish ribbon that meanders between high, grassy banks, through an attractive mix of farms and woods. Only a few houses are hidden back there. Whitewater returns in the form of well-spaced boulder and cobble rapids that do not exceed Class 2 difficulty until just above the confluence with the West Branch. Here the creek squeezes through a rocky narrows and careens through a strong, tight, and twisting flume followed, a little farther, by a strong boulder patch rapid. Partly the backwater of Lake Wallenpaupack, the remainder of the way is dead flat.

Lake Wallenpaupack stretches for another 11 miles beyond Ledgedale Road. It is wide, often windy, filled with power boats, and lined with summer homes. In fact, the name Wallenpaupack is Indian for "deep, dead water." The lake has little that will appeal to the tastes of any river rat.

HAZARDS: Narrow chute in rapid above West Branch

WATER CONDITIONS: In spring, during snowmelt or within two days of hard rain.

GAUGE: None. Look for enough water to float the wide, shallow reach at Rte. 447 Bridge, Newfoundland. Roughly, USGS gauge at Hawley, on the Lackawaxen (call Philadelphia), should be at least 3.4 feet.

Section 2. Bridge Creek and East Branch Wallenpaupack Creek: Sawmill Road, T372 to mouth					
Gradient	**Difficulty**	**Distance**	**Time**	**Scenery**	**Map**
48	3 –	2.4	0.5	Good	41

TRIP DESCRIPTION: This is an exhilarating, short, and fast run, with which to top off your day. Bridge Creek is microscopic, but still big enough for you to squeeze in a canoe. It offers an evenly dropping dash over cobbles and a few ledges, while lingering in only a few short pools. The East Branch is only a wider version of Bridge Creek. Since the adjacent lands are heavily posted, you should definitely avoid this run during trout season.

HAZARDS: Some strainers.

WATER CONDITIONS: Same as Section 1.

GAUGE: None. Judge at Pa. Rte. 507.

Middle Creek

INTRODUCTION: Middle Creek runs into the Lackawaxen at Hawley. Though it is mostly a scenic, novice route, it ends with a contrastingly challenging stretch of intermediate whitewater.

Section 1. T412 to SR3028					
Gradient	Difficulty	Distance	Time	Scenery	Map
9	A to 1 +	12.6	4.5	Good to Very Good	40

TRIP DESCRIPTION: Upper Middle Creek is generally narrow, deep, and sluggish. At T412 it is just a rivulet, confined by nodding alder bushes or high, grassy banks. The atmosphere is generally woodsy, remote, and correspondingly pleasant. The gentle creek occasionally breaks over a riffle or short stretch of rapids, and there is a runnable two-foot wooden weir below Pa. Rte. 191. But the stream then compensates for this docile start with a vengeance when, a few miles below Pa. Rte.191, it suddenly plunges over beautiful Wangum Falls. A road bridge directly above the falls should be your landmark. Portage on the left. The creek then resumes its mild pace, remaining that way to SR3028.

HAZARDS: Wangum Falls at T367. Get out well above and carry on the left.

WATER CONDITIONS: Canoeable in spring during fast snowmelt or within two days of hard rain.

GAUGE: None on creek. USGS gauge on the Lackawaxen, at Hawley (call Philadelphia), should be about 5.0 feet.

Section 2. SR3028 to mouth					
Gradient	Difficulty	Distance	Time	Scenery	Map
56	1 to 3	2.4	1.0	Good to Poor	40

TRIP DESCRIPTION: Middle Creek changes personality instantly, as it begins to crash down long rock gardens, steep boulder patches, and sets of ledges. Approaching Hawley, two six-foot rubble dams form short pools and require carries. More good rapids follow until you reach the brink of an awesome, gently sloping, 20-foot concrete dam, located at the head of a flood channel. At moderate levels, it is runnable. In fact, it is worth a trip to Hawley just to play on this Corps of Engineers-built waterslide. Be sure to bring a camera.

HAZARDS: Three dams.

WATER CONDITIONS: Same as Section 1.

GAUGE: Same as Section 1.

Dyberry Creek

INTRODUCTION: Dyberry Creek is a dwarf canoe route, feeding the Lackawaxen River at Honesdale. It offers a short beginner's run of variable merit way back in the chilly and hilly wilds of Wayne County.

Section 1. Tanners Falls to mouth					
Gradient	Difficulty	Distance	Time	Scenery	Map
6	1	7.2	2.5	Good to Poor	40

TRIP DESCRIPTION: Tanners Falls is just a name where once stood a tannery and houses. Put in at the state game lands parking area, at the confluence of the East and West branches. The first three miles are pleasant. Up there, Dyberry is a clear brook that meanders through a narrow, grassy valley lined by low, wooded hills. The valley floor is uninhabited, as at times of flood, this becomes the upper pool behind a Corps of Engineers flood control dam. The water flows smoothly over its gravel bottom, frequently quickening in succinct riffles. A few strainers may require carries. Unfortunately, if you venture into the fourth mile, you confront the 100-foot-high Jadwin Dam—a flood control structure with no regular pool behind it. Carry the dam by ascending a road on the left and descending straight down the dam face or via the emergency spillway. This dam, two sand and gravel works, and a riprap-bound passage into Honesdale limit the appeal of the lower creek. For those who paddle it anyway, there is an easy take-out at the mouth, on the right, where a short footpath leads up to the YWCA parking lot on Park Street.

HAZARDS: Strainers and heart attack carrying Jadwin Dam.

WATER CONDITIONS: Canoeable in spring throughout snowmelt and within four days of hard rain.

GAUGE: USGS gauge on right bank, 0.3 miles below Jadwin Dam, along T556, should read at least 2.2 feet. USGS gauge at Hawley, on the Lackawaxen (call Philadelphia), must be above 3.1 feet.

West Branch Lackawaxen River

INTRODUCTION: The tiny West Branch is the source of the Lackawaxen, becoming the Lackawaxen at Prompton. It is a pretty stream that offers a little fun for both the whitewater and flatwater paddler. But unfortunately, just a little bit for each.

Section 1. Creamton (Pa. Rte. 247) to mouth					
Gradient	Difficulty	Distance	Time	Scenery	Map
29	A to 2+	7.7	3.0	Good	40

TRIP DESCRIPTION: The whitewater paddler will enjoy the first four miles of this creek. The crystal clear waters rush down a delightful course of small boulders and cobbles, separated only by short pools. The surrounding valley is pastoral and pretty. If you advance past the fourth Pa. Rte. 170 bridge, you should be on guard for strainers. But, if you are purely a whitewater paddler, you probably will stop at that bridge, as the lake begins shortly below.

Prompton Reservoir is about three miles long. Though plugged by a grotesque, 140-foot-high dam, this is a pretty lake that is surrounded by low, wooded hills and is protected by a state park. For those purely interested in lake paddling, there is a boat launch area near the south end of the lake. For the rare individual planning to portage the dam, either side will do.

There remains just a short bit of smooth to riffly, clear water below the dam. Take out at U.S. Rte. 6, unless you plan to continue down the Lackawaxen.

HAZARDS: Strainers, especially below the fourth Rte. 170 bridge.

WATER CONDITIONS: Canoeable in spring during snowmelt and within three days of hard rain.

GAUGE: Staff gauge on left abutment of Pa. Rte. 247 should read at least 2.4 feet. Roughly, USGS gauge on right bank, 1,500 feet above U.S. Rte. 6, should read over 2.0 feet. Even more roughly, USGS gauge at Hawley, on Lackawaxen (call Philadelphia), should read over 3.3 feet.

Equinunk Creek

INTRODUCTION: There is probably no prettier collection of hills than those of upper Wayne County. Barely over a hundred miles from the "Big Apple," this is a surprisingly remote neighborhood whose image would be right at home on a traditional calendar picture. If you would like to see it from a canoe, try traveling Equinunk Creek (Indian for "where cloth is distributed").

Section 1. SR4024 to mouth					
Gradient	Difficulty	Distance	Time	Scenery	Map
52	2 +	8.0	2.0	Good	42

TRIP DESCRIPTION: Equinunk is a fast track to the Delaware River. Tilting down a cobble bed that is spiced with boulders and small ledges, the creek offers easy but almost continuous whitewater, slowing down only in the last mile. Although it is a tiny stream, obstructions are surprisingly few. High, cobble banks often border Equinunk Creek's clear waters, but they are not high enough to block the paddler's view of the silver-sided, wooded hills that sandwich the narrow valley. Only the shabby state of some of the local farms and dwellings flaw this picturesque scene. Take out at the last bridge, by the town of Equinunk.

HAZARDS: Maybe a few strainers and possibly a fence.

WATER CONDITIONS: Canoeable in spring during snowmelt and within three days of hard rain.

GAUGE: Staff gauge on right abutment of SR1023 Bridge. Level of 3.6 feet is minimum for boating. Roughly, USGS gauge at Archibald, on the Lackawanna River (call Central PA), should read over 3.0 feet.

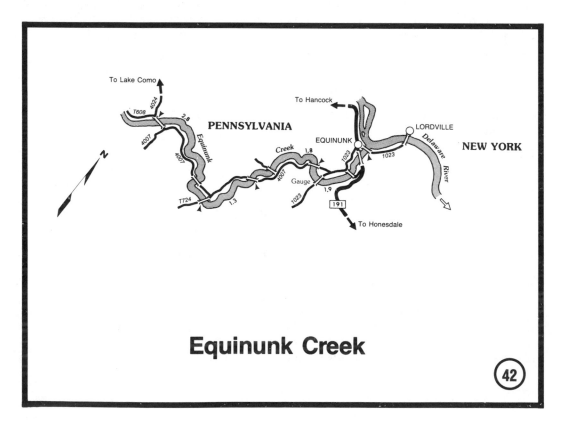

Equinunk Creek

42

West Branch Delaware River

INTRODUCTION: The West Branch Delaware starts way back in upstate New York, not far from the source of the Susquehanna River. Much of its canoeable length lies buried beneath huge Cannonsville Reservoir, and only the last few miles of what is left runs along the Pennsylvania border.

Section 1. Hale Eddy, N.Y. to mouth					
Gradient	Difficulty	Distance	Time	Scenery	Map
6	1	9.6	3.0	Good	1

TRIP DESCRIPTION: The West Branch resembles a scaled down upper Delaware River. It flows through a scenic and narrow farm valley that is marred only by the presence of the busy N.Y. Rte. 17 freeway. The most provocative development on this river's mostly undeveloped banks is a forlorn, long-abandoned oil well, about two miles upstream of Balls Eddy. Beginners can easily handle this stream, as nothing more difficult than gentle gravel riffles break its smooth surface. Take out at Hancock, or continue another seven miles (5.7 miles on the Delaware) to Buckingham PFC Access, near Equinunk.

HAZARDS: None.

WATER CONDITIONS: Levels subject to vagaries of New York City reservoir manipulation. One day Cannonsville Dam is releasing and Pepacton is not. The next day it is the opposite. You can usually count on good levels in April and early May. Sustained canoeable release levels usually appear again in mid-July or August.

GAUGE: USGS gauge at Hale Eddy (call Philadelphia). Minimum is around 3.2 feet.

The Canals

While Pennsylvania's canals may have passed into commercial obsolescence and disuse a century ago, those bits and pieces that remain are today enjoying a recreational renaissance. Joggers, hikers, and bicyclers have replaced the mules on the towpaths, while canoeists and, in winter, ice skaters have replaced the barges on the water. We paddlers are fortunate to be able to enjoy several rewatered segments scattered along the Schuylkill, Delaware, and Lehigh rivers.

One word of caution though. These rewatered stretches are sometimes dewatered. Flood damage, leaks, maintenance work, and seasonal drawdowns can leave you with only a muddy ditch where you had contemplated aimlessly drifting. So if you plan to paddle a canal, be sure to come with an alternate itinerary.

Delaware & Raritan Canal

A 27-mile segment of this canal follows the Jersey side of the Delaware, from Raven Rock (opposite Lumberville) to Trenton. The entire canal once linked Raven Rock, on the Delaware River, with Somerville, on the Raritan River. But the stretch from downtown Trenton to Princeton is now mostly filled in. Paddlers will find all but the last few miles in Trenton pleasant, if not always pretty. The first few miles, above Stanton, are the nicest, as the canal distances itself from busy N.J. Rte. 29. Three locks (at Bulls Island, Stanton, and Lambertville) and four low bridges require carries. While you can paddle either up or down the canal, an extremely swift current will encourage most boaters to direct their trip downcanal.

Lehigh Canal

The Lehigh Canal once ran from White Haven to Easton, linking to the Pennsylvania Canal. It now only remains in bits and pieces, as do its rewatered segments. Those segments include about two miles between Weissport and Pohopoco Creek, about three miles through Walnutport, about seven miles from Hamilton Street, Allentown, to Lock 44, Freemansburg, and about three miles between Guard Lock 8, above Glendon, to the Delaware River, at Easton.

Manayunk Canal

This short canal branches off the Schuylkill at Flat Rock Dam and is rewatered for about two miles, down to Lock Street, Philadelphia (off Main Street, Manayunk). It runs entirely through an industrialized area dominated by the stale smell of a huge cardboard factory.

Pennsylvania Canal

This canal connected Easton, and the Lehigh Canal, to tidewater at Bristol. Most of it remains in good to at least recognizable shape, protected since 1940 by Roosevelt State Park. Paddlers should consider the 35-mile stretch from Easton to New Hope. Below New Hope there is some water for a while, but hardly enough for boating. Though often followed closely by busy roadways, this is a pretty route that takes you past sturdy, old houses, mills, cliffs, and views of the beautiful Delaware River. Like the Delaware and Raritan Canal, this one has a stiff current. So once again it is most enjoyable to paddle downcanal (southeast). Locks, low bridges, and culverts require periodic portages.

Schuylkill Canal

About two miles are rewatered through Mont Clare, across the river from Phoenixville.

Susquehanna River Tributaries

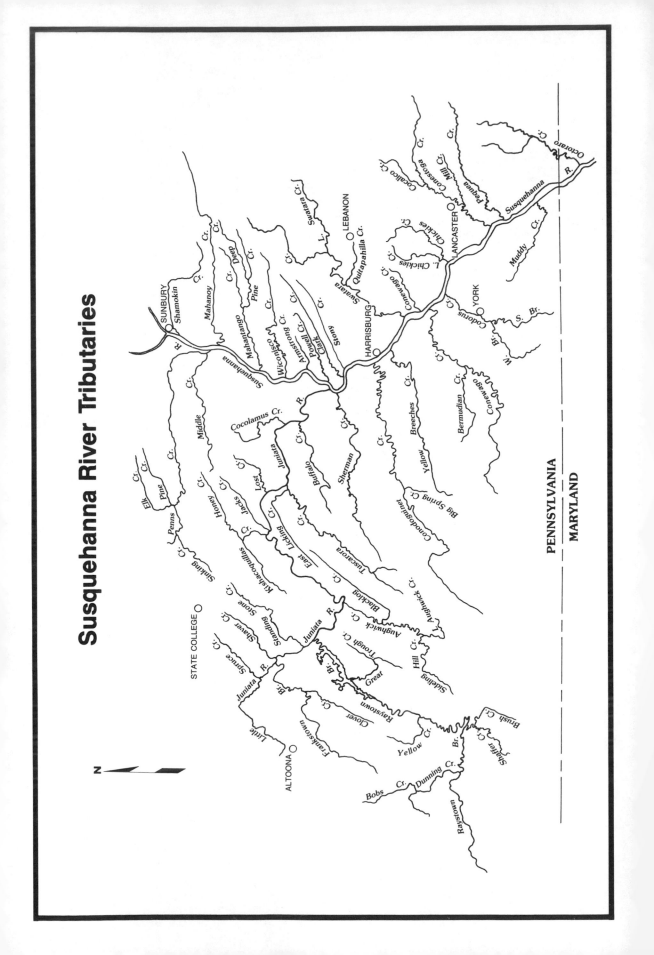

Chapter 3
The Lower Susquehanna Basin

About 8791 square miles of the heart of Pennsylvania drain directly to the Susquehanna mainstem. There is no prettier chunk of real estate in the Keystone. It ranges from a washboard of narrow mountain ridges separated by rural valleys, on the north, to a rolling and intensely agricultural Piedmont, near the Maryland Line. It includes scores of beautiful towns whose closely packed rows of brick and stone houses date back to the 18th century. These are towns that, like fine wines, only improve with age. The basin is a major corridor of travel for cars, trucks, trains, planes, and even flocks of migrating ducks and geese. And it is a place to stop too, for Harrisburg, the state capital, is set right in the middle.

This basin suffers no shortage of streams on which to paddle. Try a few and you may conclude that there is no finer way to tour this area.

The following streams are described in this chapter:

Susquehanna River
Octoraro Creek
Muddy Creek
Pequea Creek
Conestoga Creek
Mill Creek
Cocalico Creek
Chickies Creek
Little Chickies Creek
Codorus Creek
South Branch Codorus Creek
West Branch Codorus Creek
Conewago Creek
Bermudian Creek
Conewago Creek (east)
Swatara Creek
Quittapahilla Creek
Little Swatara Creek
Yellow Breeches Creek
Conodoguinet Creek
Big Spring Creek
Clark Creek
Sherman Creek

Juniata River
Buffalo Creek
Cocolamus Creek
Tuscarora Creek
East Licking Creek
Lost Creek
Jacks Creek
Kishacoquillas Creek
Honey Creek
Aughwick Creek
Blacklog Creek
Little Aughwick Creek
Sideling Hill Creek
Raystown Branch Juniata River
Great Trough Creek
Yellow Creek
Brush Creek
Shaffer Creek
Dunning Creek
Bobs Creek
Standing Stone Creek
Shaver Creek
Little Juniata River

Spruce Creek
Frankstown Branch Juniata River
Clover Creek
Powell Creek
Armstrong Creek
Wiconisco Creek
Mahantango Creek
Pine Creek
Deep Creek
Mahanoy Creek
Penns Creek
Middle Creek
Pine Creek
Elk Creek
Sinking Creek
Shamokin Creek

Susquehanna River

INTRODUCTION: The Susquehanna River, its mainstem and North Branch combined, is the longest and largest river on the east coast of the United States. Collecting its water from almost 28,000 square miles of New York, Pennsylvania, and Maryland, this beautiful river flows over 440 miles from Cooperstown, New York to Havre de Grace, Maryland. Then in addition, the Susquehanna's estuary, the Chesapeake Bay, extends another 180 miles through Maryland and Virginia before mixing with the Atlantic near Virginia Beach. The Susquehanna's path wanders down the heart of eastern Pennsylvania, draining nearly 21,000 square miles, or almost half the state. The upper portion of this river, above Sunbury, is also known as the North Branch and is described in another chapter. This description deals entirely with the main stem, which begins at the confluence of the North and West branches, at Northumberland.

It is difficult to mistake the Susquehanna for any other river in the United States, or even for either of its impressive branches. For few rivers in the east can match the majesty of this river. Wide as a river of several times its flow, studded with islands and rocks, and framed by a series of abrupt but symmetrical mountain gaps, the Susquehanna is unique. It inspires artists to paint it, photographers to photograph it, and canoeists to canoe it.

Ironically though, the Susquehanna makes a poor canoe stream, for a river rat at least. It is so wide that you can spend a half hour just paddling to the other side. With straightaways of three to five miles, the floater sees the Susquehanna scenery change at an excruciatingly slow rate. Even with a good current, the experience is too much like paddling a lake, complete with contrary winds, chop, and, on the lower river, motorboats. Finally, the low perspective of the floater hides many of the river's scenic attributes. So you are better off touring the Susquehanna by land, concentrating on nearby high points where you can best appreciate the river's size, the number and shape of its islands, and the real height of its abutting mountains and palisades.

If you take this advice, there are many impressive overlooks of this grand river. The first is right at the beginning, on the right, from the bluffs of Shikellamy State Park. A few others are from the Appalachian Trail, above and west of Duncannon, from Chickies Rock, in a county park along Pa. Rte. 441 north of Columbia, and from Pinnacles Overlook, on river left, above Holtwood Dam. Just the views from Pa. Rte. 147 or U.S. Rte. 11-15 can be breathtaking.

The water quality in the Susquehanna is all right, but not great. While certainly safe for canoeing, swimming, and consumption of its fish, this water still suffers subtle effects of upstream pollution. One of the big culprits, upstream coal mining, has long degraded its waters. The anthracite industry once discharged tons of coal fines from its processing plants into headwater tributaries. So much coal washed downstream and settled in the Susquehanna's pools that a fleet of floating dredges, the "Pennsylvania Navy," once plied these pools to profitably recover the black sediment for resale. While coal dust is no longer a major problem, acid mine drainage from both the hard and soft coal regions continues to devastate many miles of the Susquehanna's tributaries. While diluted by the time it reaches the big river, the resultant concentrations of sulfates and other dissolved minerals has driven many Susquehanna towns to seek other streams for their water supply. The water is adequate, however, for cooling condensers and spinning turbines. As a result, the Susquehanna is a major source of electric power, generated by ten plants (three fossil, two nuclear, four hydro, and one pumped storage) between Northumberland and Havre de Grace.

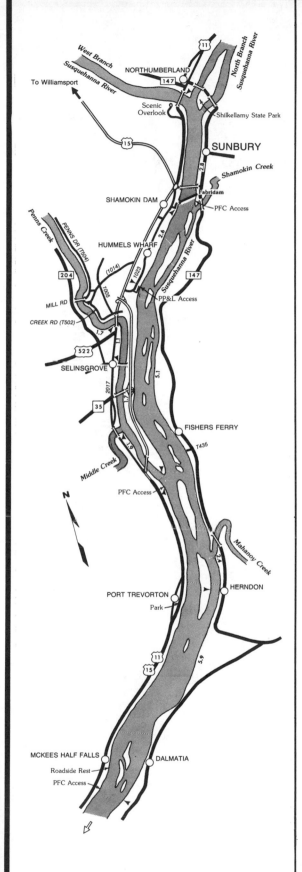

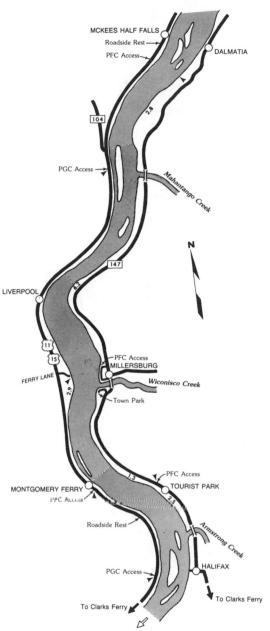

Susquehanna River
Penns Creek

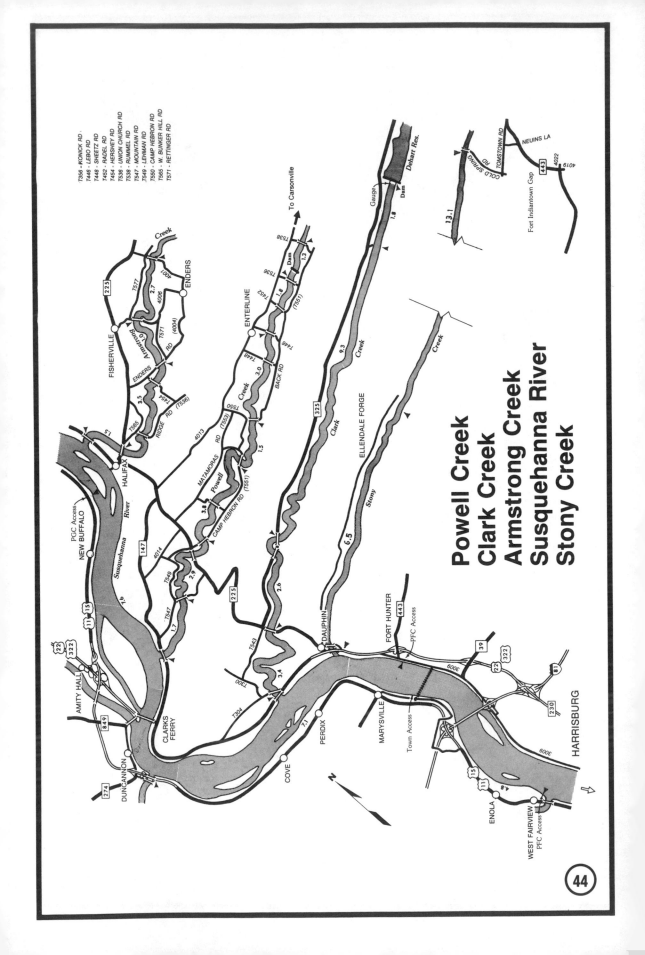

Powell Creek
Clark Creek
Armstrong Creek
Susquehanna River
Stony Creek

T356 - KONICK RD
T446 - LEBO RD
T448 - SHEETZ RD
T452 - RADEL RD
T454 - HERSHEY RD
T536 - UNION CHURCH RD
T538 - RUMMEL RD
T547 - MOUNTAIN RD
T549 - LEHMAN RD
T550 - CAMP HEBRON RD
T565 - W. BUNKER HILL RD
T571 - RETINGER RD

To Carsonville

Dehart Res.

Gauge

Dam

1.8

13.1

443 4022
4019

COLD SPRING RD
TOMSTOWN RD
NEUINS LA

Fort Indiantown Gap

Creek

ENDERS

225

T577

2.7

4006

4001

T571

RD (4004)

FISHERVILLE

Armstrong 0.1

ENDERS RD (T536)

2.5

RIDGE RD

T597

T565

1.5

HALIFAX

225

ENTERLINE

T452

T446

T448

BACK RD

3.0

T550

4013

MATAMORAS RD (T553)

1.5

Powell Creek

3.8

CAMP HEBRON RD (T551)

T538

Dam 1.3

T536

1.8

(T551)

325

9.3

Clark Creek

ELLENDALE FORGE

Stony Creek

6.5

Susquehanna River

PGC Access

NEW BUFFALO

147

4014

T549

2.9

T547

1.7

225

2.6

2.6

DAUPHIN

3.4

T543

T304

T300

AMITY HALL

849

11 15

0.9

CLARKS FERRY

DUNCANNON

274

23 323

7.1

PERDIX

COVE

N

MARYSVILLE

Town Access

FORT HUNTER

443

PFC Access

600E

300G

23 322

39

81

230

15

111

4.8

ENOLA

WEST FAIRVIEW
PFC Access

HARRISBURG

44

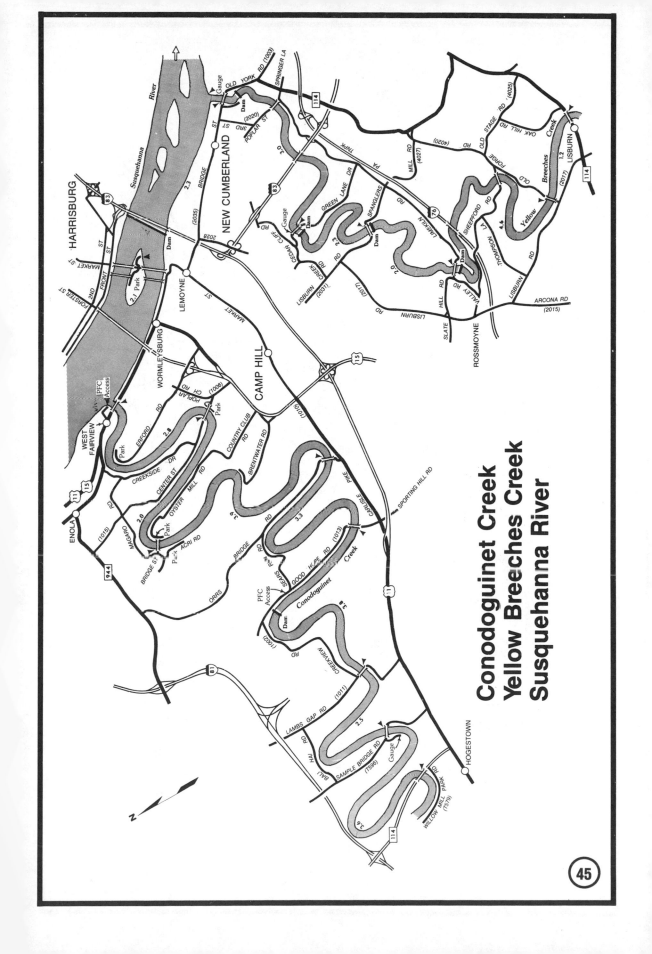

Conodoguinet Creek
Yellow Breeches Creek
Susquehanna River

45

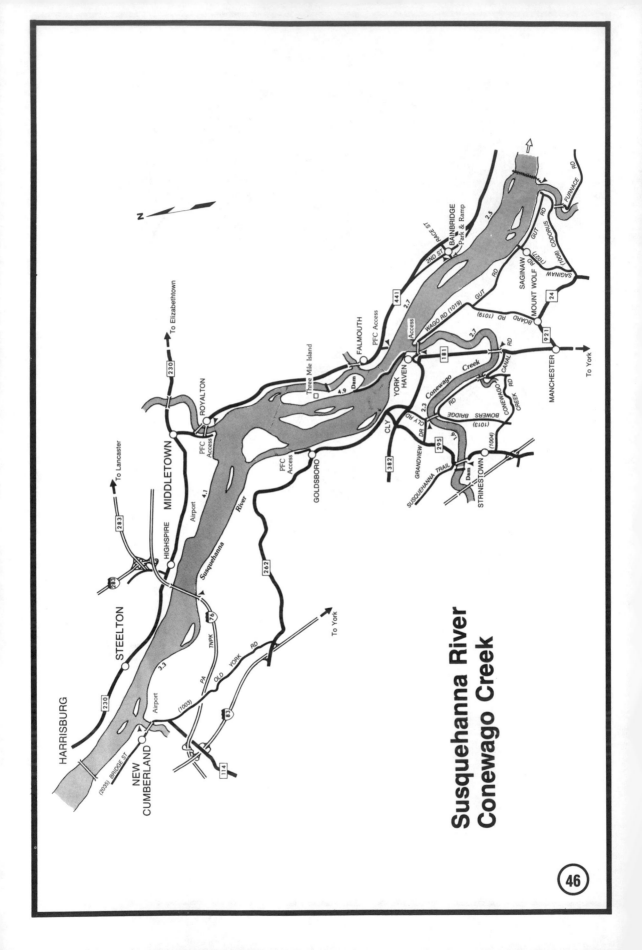

Susquehanna River
Conewago Creek

HARRISBURG

STEELTON

NEW CUMBERLAND

MIDDLETOWN

HIGHSPIRE

To Lancaster

To Elizabethtown

ROYALTON

Three Mile Island

FALMOUTH

GOLDSBORO

PFC Access

PFC Access

PFC Access

Dam

4.9

YORK HAVEN

CLY

BAINBRIDGE
Park & Ramp

SAGINAW

MOUNT WOLF

MANCHESTER

STRINESTOWN

Dam

Conewago Creek

Susquehanna River

Airport

Airport

PA TNPK

OLD YORK RD

(1003)

(2035) BRIDGE ST

To York

4.1

3.3

2.5

2.7

2.3

2.7

1.4

114

83

262

76

283

230

230

441

181

382

295

24

921

(1019)

(1019)

(1013)

(1004)

(1008)

(1021)

CODORUS RD

FURNACE RD

GUT RD

GUT RD

BOARD RD

WAGO RD (1019)

CANAL RD

BOWERS BRIDGE RD

CONEWAGO CREEK RD

GRANVIEW DR

SUSQUEHANNA TRAIL

CLY RD

RACE ST

2ND ST

Access

N

46

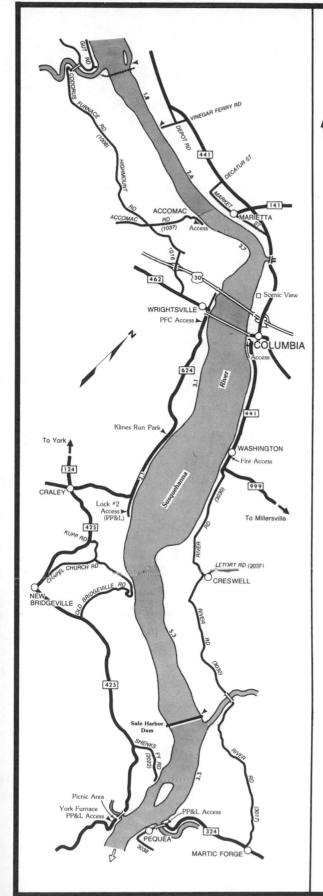

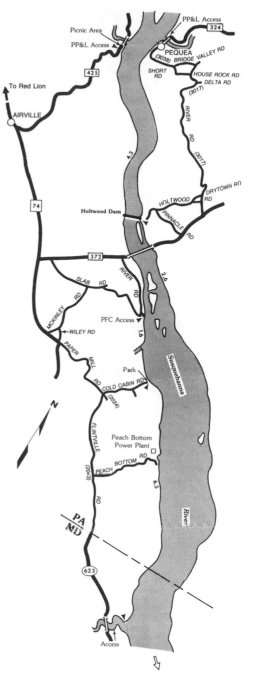

Susquehanna River

47

Finally, there are various explanations of the Indian origins of the name Susquehanna. Two popular translations are "mud river" and "river that rubs upon the shore." Come here during an early spring high water, and you will find both versions descriptive as you watch the swollen, turbid, and ice-filled Susquehanna gnaw away at its banks, bridges, and towns. Come here in the summer when the old river is lazy, and you will conclude that the linguists had been drinking too much river water.

Section 1. Northumberland to Clarks Ferry (U.S. Rte. 22)					
Gradient	Difficulty	Distance	Time	Scenery	Map
2	A to 1	40.7	13.5	Good	43,44

TRIP DESCRIPTION: You can begin this section right at the confluence of the two branches, in Northumberland or on the island in Shikellamy State Park. But a better idea is to start 2.8 miles downstream, below the Fabridam (either side), and thus avoid a lot of deadwater paddling.

This is a pretty section often decorated by rocky bluffs, ends of mountains, and mountain gaps. The river is filled with islands and, in between, with a million rocks. The riverside suffers only moderate summer home development while the riverside towns are usually attractive, especially Liverpool. This would be a nice stream for canoe camping if you could only escape the noise of busy Rte. 11-15 and the railroad.

The river is gentle, but there are many riffles, especially below Liverpool. The most interesting spot is a chain of rocks and chutes near Dalmatia, called McKees Half Falls—a good place to play. There are some particularly rocky reaches of river below Liverpool and near Millerstown. In spite of this condition, an ancient car ferry at Millersburg finds a route through the shallows, and, even more amazing, motor boats buzz all about the river. The motor boats have adapted by using raised airplane-type propellers, like the airboats of the Everglades, instead of outboards. But how these noisy boats dart about the shallows so fast without crashing into a boulder is a mystery.

HAZARDS: Fabridam, an eight-foot-high inflatable (no kidding) dam, below Sunbury, must be carried, even in winter when it is deflated. The deceptively harmless-looking foundation forms a small but sharp drop that can severely damage your boat.

WATER CONDITIONS: Always canoeable except when frozen or flooding.

GAUGE: Respectively, USGS gauges at Sunbury and Harrisburg (call Central PA) typically drop to around 5.7 and 3.5 feet in late summer low water. This is still adequate.

Section 2. Clarks Ferry (U.S. Rte. 22) to Wrightsville					
Gradient	Difficulty	Distance	Time	Scenery	Map
3	A to 2 –	43.3	15.0	Fair to Good	44,45,46,47

TRIP DESCRIPTION: The Susquehanna now passes through the heavily populated zone surrounding Harrisburg. There are strings of towns, highways, railroads, steel mills, airports, and power plants (including the infamous Three Mile Island) on this section. But there are also mountain gaps, bluffs, islands, the pretty skyline of Harrisburg, and the graceful 48 stone arches of the railroad bridge at Rockville. It is still, overall, an attractive stretch.

This section has riffles and occasional easy rapids, most often found where the river cuts through a mountain ridge. It also has some long pools, some of which are formed by dams. There is a two-foot weir beneath the I-83 Bridge at Harrisburg, run through the breach on the left end. You must carry (left) a sloping four-foot dam that arcs diagonally across the river at York Haven. Just below this dam is Conewago Falls, a rapid, that is long and heavy enough, even at moderate levels, to swamp an ineptly managed open canoe. Take out at the PFC access in Wrightsville or the town access in Columbia.

HAZARDS: Weirs at I-83 and York Haven.

WATER CONDITIONS: Always canoeable except when flooding or frozen.

GAUGE: USGS gauge at Harrisburg (call Central PA) typically drops to around 3.5 feet in late summer low water. This is still adequate.

Section 3. Wrightsville to Broad Creek Access, Md.					
Gradient	Difficulty	Distance	Time	Scenery	Map
0	A to 1	29.0	15.0	Fair	47

TRIP DESCRIPTION: Most of this section is consumed by the dreary flatwaters behind three hydroelectric dams. This is lake paddling, not floating, and it is hard work. If you are taking an extended trip and plan on having to portage the dams, save yourself some more work by calling the dams in advance. The power companies are good enough to provide a portage service, though they can be slow in getting someone to you. At Holtwood Dam you will find a phone at the take-out (above the dam on left) to call for service. Though this section is purely a beginner route, during spring high water some advanced big water playing materializes on the half-mile rocky reach below the right side of Holtwood Dam. The adventuresome can reach this spot by paddling upriver from the Muddy Creek PFC Access.

This section is inherently pretty thanks to long stretches of high, wooded bluffs and a relatively narrow reach called the Holtwood Narrows. But all this is often spoiled by extensive shoreline development with summer homes. If you want to go someplace pretty and unspoiled, skip the river and take a hike up the cool, hemlock glen of the Susquehanna's sidestream, Otter Creek, upstream of Holtwood.

HAZARDS: High dams at Safe Harbor and Holtwood.

WATER CONDITIONS: Always canoeable except when frozen.

GAUGE: USGS gauge at Harrisburg (call Central PA) drops to around 3.5 feet in low water. This is irrelevant on this impounded stretch.

Octoraro Creek

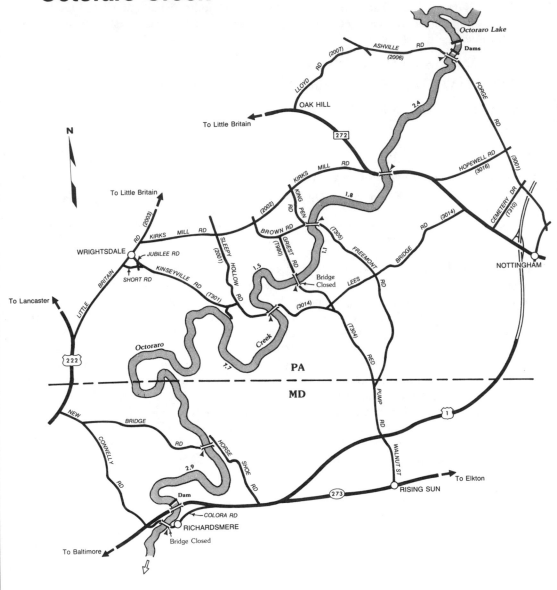

Octoraro Lake

Dams

ASHVILLE RD (2006)

LLOYD RD (2007)

FORGE RD

OAK HILL

To Little Britain

272

2.4

HOPEWELL RD (3016)

(3001)

KIRKS MILL RD

1.8

KING PEN RD

CEMETERY DR (T310)

(2002)

BROWN RD

RD (3014)

NOTTINGHAM

To Little Britain

KIRKS MILL RD

RD (2003)

WRIGHTSDALE

JUBILEE RD

SLEEPY HOLLOW RD (2001)

(T980)

GRIEST RD

(T305)

FREEMONT BRIDGE RD

1.1

SHORT RD

KINSEYVILLE RD (T301)

1.5

Bridge Closed

LEES RD

To Lancaster

LITTLE BRITAIN

(3014)

(T304)

222

Octoraro

1.7

Creek

PA

RED RUN RD

MD

1

NEW BRIDGE RD

2.9

HORSE SHOE RD

PUMP RD

WALNUT ST

Dam

273

RISING SUN

To Elkton

COLORA RD

RICHARDSMERE

CONNELLY RD

Bridge Closed

To Baltimore

N

48

Octoraro Creek

INTRODUCTION: Octoraro Creek drains the rolling and prosperous farm country of southern Lancaster and Chester counties. Formed by the confluence of the East and West branches, deep beneath the waters of Octoraro Lake, the creek rushes (Octoraro is Indian for "rushing waters") on into Maryland, for an eventual rendezvous with the Susquehanna River.

Section 1. Forge Road to Richardsmere, Md. (Colora Road)					
Gradient	Difficulty	Distance	Time	Scenery	Map
9	1 to 1+	17.4	6.0	Good	48

TRIP DESCRIPTION: The put-in is at the covered bridge just below the little dam, below the big dam that backs the reservoir. The creek follows a mellow course of long and slow pools separated by enjoyable gravel bar riffles, all the time wandering through attractive, rolling fields and woodlands. If you are fortunate enough to catch this stream up in late May, the air will be laced with the fragrance of the flowering Russian olive trees that seem to grow everywhere in this valley.

The creek then enters a shallow and wooded gorge, which is pretty, except for the eyesore of one huge gravel pit. After passing this pit and the beginning of a boy scout camp, Octoraro begins a long and delightful descent through a series of rock gardens that ends in the pool behind a four-foot rubble dam, just above U.S. Rte. 1. The dam is runnable, but is usually scratchy. Because of limited parking space on Rte. 1, take out just downstream at the abandoned Colora Road Bridge at Richardsmere.

HAZARDS: Rubble dam just above U.S. Rte. 1.

WATER CONDITIONS: Canoeable winter and spring within three days of hard rain (providing that Octoraro Lake is full).

GAUGE: Count grooves on downstream end of pier of U.S. Rte. 1 Bridge. Six grooves down from top is zero. Also you can judge by the riffle beneath the covered bridge at Forge Road. Roughly, USGS gauge at Chadds Ford, on Brandywine Creek (call Philadelphia), should read at least 2.4 feet.

Muddy Creek

INTRODUCTION: York County's Muddy Creek is a canoeist's delight. Forget its bland name. This vivacious, little trout stream can charm both the novice and advanced paddler. And to top things off, it is only an easy hour's drive from Harrisburg and Baltimore and an hour and a half from Philadelphia.

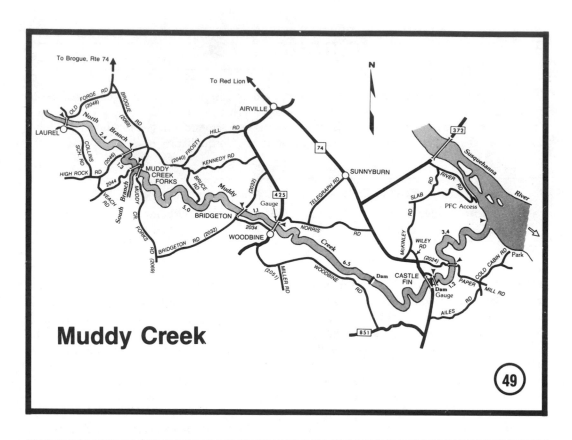

Muddy Creek

(49)

Section 1. Muddy Creek Forks to mouth					
Gradient	Difficulty	Distance	Time	Scenery	Map
15	1 to 2 +	17.2	5.0	Good to Excellent	49

TRIP DESCRIPTION: With moderately high water, one can start another 3.7 miles upstream at Laurel, on the North Branch Muddy Creek. The North Branch is a scaled down Muddy Creek, flowing within a shallow, isolated gorge and rushing over countless easy rapids and riffles. Then with the addition of the South Branch's waters, one gains more elbow room. The creek continues dropping over short, easy, but sometimes fairly blind rapids, often formed by patches of big boulders. As far as Bridgeton the gorge is mostly undeveloped. From Bridgeton to Woodbine, where many paddlers begin their trip, and for a few miles beyond, the surroundings are somewhat cluttered by summer homes. But it is all primitive below here. A few interesting boulder and ledge drops spice this reach, while lots of riffles and fast current tie it all together. One must carry a four-foot milldam a few miles below Woodbine. But, at moderate levels, one can run the six-foot dam that hides just below Pa. Rte. 74.

The long-favored access via the abandoned, old concrete arch bridge, just below Pa. Rte. 74, is no longer open to the public. Most paddlers now enter or leave at Paper Mill Road, right end of the bridge. Novices should venture no farther downstream.

Below here, Muddy begins seriously cutting to the level of the Susquehanna. While mostly an easy run, several spots require skill to manage. The most notable of such spots is a marked, sharp, four-foot ledge, runnable on the extreme right corner. Stay away from this drop at high water, as the hole to the left is a lethal keeper. The Muddy mellows for another half mile until

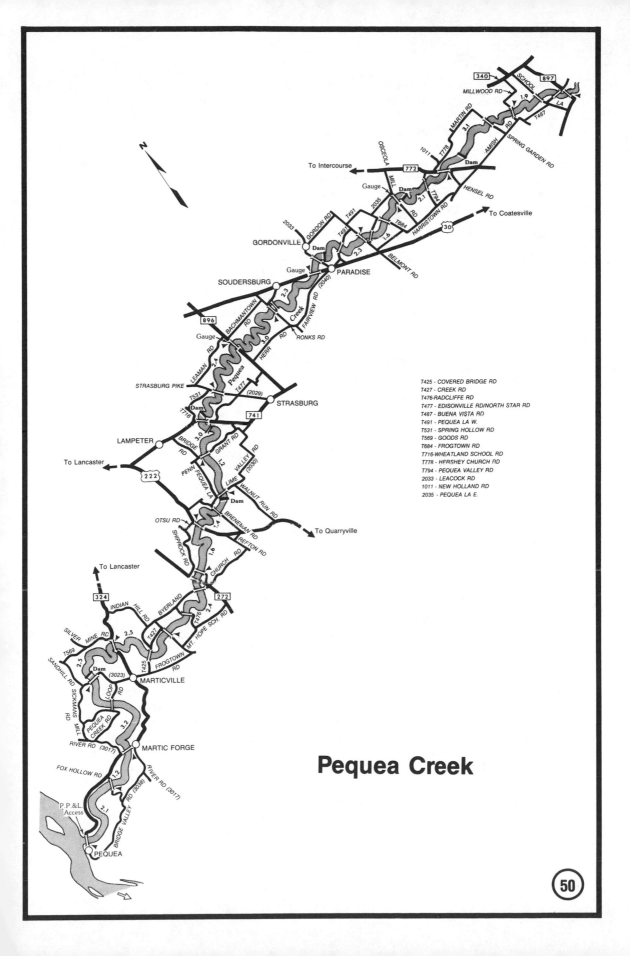

Pequea Creek

T425 - COVERED BRIDGE RD
T427 - CREEK RD
T476 - RADCLIFFE RD
T477 - EDISONVILLE RD/NORTH STAR RD
T487 - BUENA VISTA RD
T491 - PEQUEA LA W.
T531 - SPRING HOLLOW RD
T569 - GOODS RD
T684 - FROGTOWN RD
T716 - WHEATLAND SCHOOL RD
T778 - HERSHEY CHURCH RD
T794 - PEQUEA VALLEY RD
2033 - LEACOCK RD
1011 - NEW HOLLAND RD
2035 - PEQUEA LA E.

50

a jagged cliff and great tilting ledges suddenly squeeze the water, and the creek disappears from sight. Get out well above, on the right, and carry. This tortuous seven-foot flume is a potential deathtrap. You may curse the slippery and steep portage, but the next mile makes it all worthwhile. The creek tumbles over short, steep rapids formed by the same great fins and buttresses of sparkly schist that hem the channel. A sidestream waterfall, shady hemlocks, and smothering remoteness complete the superb setting. But all too soon the current dies in the backwater of Lake Conowingo, and summer homes inherit the banks. A short, painful paddle up the Susquehanna delivers you to a PFC access area or an easier downstream paddle reaches the park (free) at the foot of Cold Cabin Road.

HAZARDS: Two small dams, and, below Rte. 74, a dangerous ledge.

WATER CONDITIONS: For optimal conditions, the section below Muddy Creek Forks is canoeable late fall, winter, and spring within three days of hard rain. But you can get down the lower creek (below Rte. 74) almost anytime, from ice-out to July, except during prolonged drought.

GAUGE: Painted canoe gauge on pier of Woodbine bridge. Minimum level is about three inches below zero. Dim, homemade staff gauge on old concrete arch bridge, below Rte. 74 (Castle Fin). Zero is canoeing zero. Roughly, USGS gauges at Chadds Ford, on Brandywine Creek (call Philadelphia), and at York, on Codorus Creek (call Central PA), should be over 2.5 feet and 3.7 feet respectively to start at Muddy Creek Forks.

Pequea Creek

INTRODUCTION: Pequea Creek (pronounced Peck'·way) arcs across southern Lancaster County by the crookedest possible route. But the more miles of Pequea, the better, for this is by far the prettiest canoe trail in the county. It provides a simple way to glimpse a bit of the plain people culture, rural Pennsylvania today, and the mills, houses, and bridges of Pennsylvania past.

Section 1. Pa. Rte. 897 to Paradise (U.S. Rte. 30)					
Gradient	Difficulty	Distance	Time	Scenery	Map
6	1 –	11.0	4.0	Good	50

TRIP DESCRIPTION: Up here the creek is tiny—a cowpasture brook that rises and falls fast. Too fast to catch it very often. Its low banks are an open window to view the most intensively farmed acres of what is said to be some of the most fertile soil in the nation. Many of the nearby farms belong to the Amish. These farms are conspicuous for their absence of power lines, automobiles, and tractors. You observe, instead, the use of hydropower (from the little weirs on the creek), windmills, and horses to fill the slack left by the taboo electricity and internal combustion.

The creek flows as serenely as the countryside about it. Water tends to be pooled behind numerous foot-high weirs (for water power), fords, and three old dams, each about four feet high and each of which should be carried. This being cow country, plan on finding many fences strung across the path.

126

HAZARDS: Three dams and possible fences.

WATER CONDITIONS: Canoeable winter and spring within 24 hours of hard rain.

GAUGE: Staff gauge on left abutment of Osceola Mill Road, T766. A half inch below zero is minimal. Staff gauge on right pier of U.S. Rte. 30. About 1.3 feet is minimal. Roughly, USGS gauge at Chadds Ford, on the Brandywine (call Philadelphia), should read over 4.3 feet.

Section 2. Paradise (U.S. Rte. 30) to Martic Forge (Pa. Rte. 324)					
Gradient	Difficulty	Distance	Time	Scenery	Map
5	1	25.5	8.5	Good	50

TRIP DESCRIPTION: The creek now meanders through a changing landscape, evolving from open, tidy farmlands at first, to a more rolling terrain that is more wooded in spots, and where weedy, abandoned fields mix with those that are cultivated. Towards the end of this section, the creek works down into a shallow, wooded gorge. All along, the banks are higher now and often lined by a screen of box elder, sycamore, and silver maple. Though the path is still simple, there are now many riffles to speed the miles along. You must carry a three-foot dam, above Pa. Rte. 741, and a five-foot dam, below SR2030, Lime Valley Road. However, you can safely zoom down the left side of the sloping seven-foot milldam, above SR3023, Frogtown Road.

HAZARDS: Three dams and two low-water bridges.

WATER CONDITIONS: Canoeable winter and spring within four days of hard rain.

GAUGE: Staff gauge on right pier of U.S. Rte. 30 should read over 0.3 feet. Staff gauge on right pier of Pa. Rte. 896 should read over negative 1.0 foot. Roughly, USGS gauge at Chadds Ford, on Brandywine, should read over 2.4 feet.

Section 3. Martic Forge (Pa. Rte. 324) to mouth					
Gradient	Difficulty	Distance	Time	Scenery	Map
11	1, 3 –	3.4	1.0	Good to Very Good	50

TRIP DESCRIPTION: Below Martic Forge, the Pequea bends to the right, and the walls of a rock-ribbed, hemlock-lined gorge envelope the stream. At its heart roars an exciting, twisting flume wrought by two narrow, three-foot drops, squeezed very closely together. A bunch of riffles and easy rapids round out this tiny whitewater delight. Take out at the power company recreation area, as the last mile is backwater from the Susquehanna and is lined by summer homes.

HAZARDS: Rapid below Martic Forge is narrow enough to cause serious broach.

WATER CONDITIONS: Same as Section 2.

GAUGE: Same as Section 2.

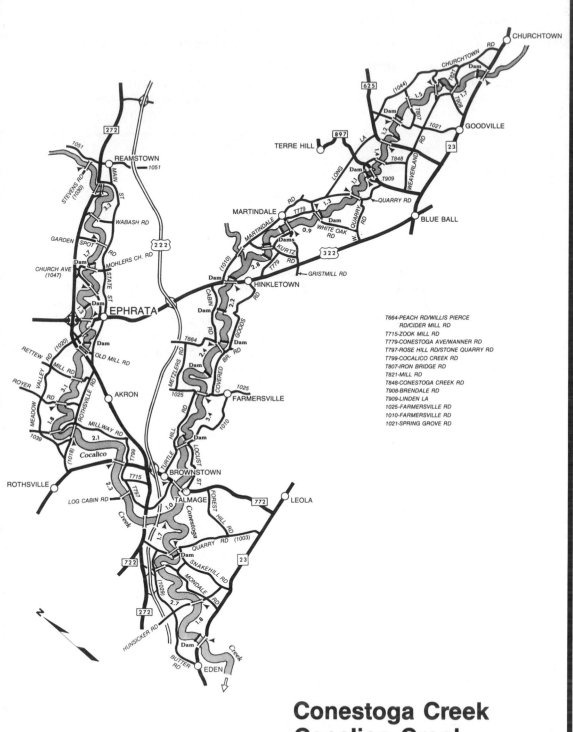

CHURCHTOWN

CHURCHTOWN RD

625

(1044)

1.5

T807

Dam

1.2

897

TERRE HILL

LONG LA

1.4

T848

Dam

1.1

T909

QUARRY RD

T821

Dam

1.7

T908

GOODVILLE

23

WEAVERLAND RD

1021

SPRING GROVE RD

MARTINDALE

T779

1.3

W. QUARRY RD

WHITE OAK RD

BLUE BALL

MARTINDALE RD

Dam

0.9

KURTZ RD

322

1051

REAMSTOWN

1051

272

STEVENS RD (1030)

MAIN ST

3.3

WABASH RD

222

GARDEN SPOT RD

1.7

CHURCH AVE (1047)

Dam

MOHLERS CH. RD

STATE ST

Dam

Dams

2.8

T779

GRISTMILL RD

Dam

HINKLETOWN

1.3

EPHRATA

CABIN RD

2.1

Dam

RETTEW RD (1020)

Dam

OLD MILL RD

T664

VALLEY RD

MILL RD

ROYER RD

2.1

ROTHSVILLE RD

AKRON

METZLERS RD

2.4

Dam

GOODS BR. RD

COVERED BR. RD

1025

FARMERSVILLE

MEADOW RD

1.8

1039

MILLWAY RD

1025

3.4

1010

Dam

2.1

(1018)

Cocalico

T799

LOCUST ST

ROTHSVILLE

2.3

T715

T797

BROWNSTOWN

1.0

TALMAGE

772

LEOLA

LOG CABIN RD

Creek

1.7

Conestoga

FOREST HILL RD

QUARRY RD (1003)

23

Dam

722

SNAKEHILL RD

272

(1029)

MONDALE RD

2.7

HUNSICKER RD

1.8

BUTTER RD

Dam

Creek

EDEN

T664-PEACH RD/WILLIS PIERCE
    RD/CIDER MILL RD
T715-ZOOK MILL RD
T779-CONESTOGA AVE/WANNER RD
T797-ROSE HILL RD/STONE QUARRY RD
T799-COCALICO CREEK RD
T807-IRON BRIDGE RD
T821-MILL RD
T848-CONESTOGA CREEK RD
T908-BRENDALE RD
T909-LINDEN LA
1025-FARMERSVILLE RD
1010-FARMERSVILLE RD
1021-SPRING GROVE RD

N

Conestoga Creek
Cocalico Creek

51

Conestoga Creek

INTRODUCTION: Conestoga Creek is a lazy, muddy ribbon that meanders across the middle of pretty, agrarian Lancaster County. It was named after a small local Indian tribe. But in the 19th century, the name became famous throughout our nation as the ubiquitous Conestoga wagon, first built in this valley, served to settle the western frontier.

If you boat on Conestoga Creek, you will be carrying forth an old tradition. In addition to the undocumented passage of Indian canoes and pioneer rafts, these waters floated the first steamboat built in America, back in 1763. And during the early 19th century, the Conestoga Navigation Company constructed nine dams and locks, between Lancaster and the Susquehanna, so that canal boats could ply its smooth waters.

Section 1. Churchtown (Pa. Rte. 23) to Lancaster (Pa. Rte. 462)					
Gradient	Difficulty	Distance	Time	Scenery	Map
6	A to 1	30.8	11.5	Good	51,52

TRIP DESCRIPTION: This section of the Conestoga grows from a rippling country brook to a wide and placid creek. Its most notable characteristic is its incredible collection of dams and weirs, about 16 worthy of a boater's attention. Too numerous to describe here, they are all located on the shuttle map. In addition, there are countless other foot-high weirs, fords, and ruins of weirs that can be safely negotiated.

Unlike weirs on most streams about the state, many of those on Conestoga and other Lancaster County streams are still functional; for the Plain People of the county are not ones to waste valuable, free water power. Thus, you often find a concrete sluice box at one end of the weir. Inside that box is a paddle wheel or turbine that turns a crank that pushes a lever that pulls a cable that runs back to some distant well-water pump, butter churn, etc. Rube Goldberg surely must have visited rural Lancaster County.

These weirs are a mixed blessing for the paddler. For some people they mean too much flatwater paddling and a maddening number of portages. But, on the other hand, so much of the creek is pooled behind these barriers, that the section from Hinkletown to Pa. Rte. 462 can float a canoe even into the dry midsummer, with only a minimum of dragging.

This is an attractive section, in spite of the occasional crushed-stone plant, trash pile, or power line. Above Hinkletown the banks are often low, allowing good views of the picturesque and prosperous farmlands. Below there, on down to Cocalico Creek, high, tree-lined banks and wooded bluffs prevail, while down to Lancaster some horse farms and attractive residential neighborhoods rise above the creek.

HAZARDS: Dams and weirs. Fences on first several miles.

WATER CONDITIONS: Above Hinkletown, canoeable winter and spring within two days of hard rain. From Hinkletown to Rte. 462, usually canoeable by virtue of all the dam pools. However, for a scrape-free trip, catch within four days of hard rain.

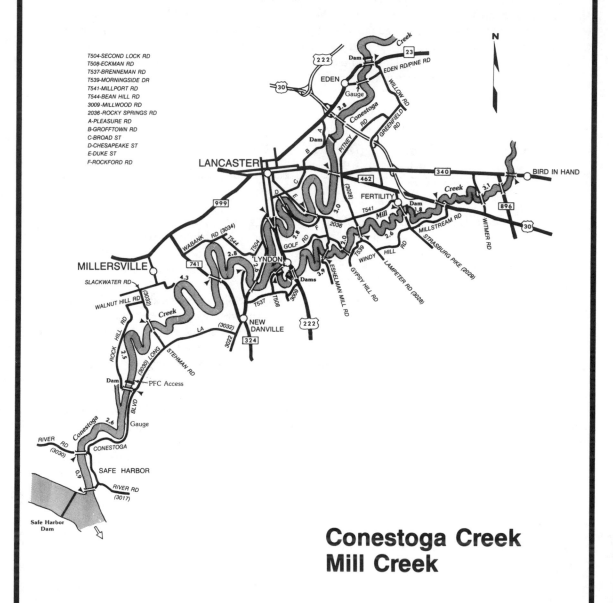

T504-SECOND LOCK RD
T508-ECKMAN RD
T537-BRENNEMAN RD
T539-MORNINGSIDE DR
T541-MILLPORT RD
T544-BEAN HILL RD
3009-MILLWOOD RD
2036-ROCKY SPRINGS RD
A-PLEASURE RD
B-GROFFTOWN RD
C-BROAD ST
D-CHESAPEAKE ST
E-DUKE ST
F-ROCKFORD RD

Conestoga Creek
Mill Creek

52

GAUGE: Staff gauge on pier of U.S. Rte. 322—1.55 feet is enough to start at Rte. 23. Staff gauge on left abutment of Pa. Rte. 772—1.3 feet is minimum to clear shallows. Staff gauge on left abutment of Bridge Road, T620—0.2 feet is minimum in shallows. Staff gauge on left abutment of SR1029, Hunsicker Road—negative 1.5 feet is minimum. Staff gauge on left pier of Eden Road—negative 0.1 foot is minimum. Roughly, USGS gauge at Chadds Ford, on Brandywine Creek (call Philadelphia), should read over 3.2 feet to start at Rte. 23 and over 1.7 feet to start below Cocalico Creek.

Section 2. Lancaster (Pa. Rte. 462) to mouth					
Gradient	Difficulty	Distance	Time	Scenery	Map
4	A to 1	21.5	7.0	Good	52

TRIP DESCRIPTION: Conestoga flows past Lancaster through mostly undeveloped woodlands and well-groomed parks. Only the short stretch between U.S. Rte. 222 and Pa. Rte. 324 is drab. From there to the mouth, the creek flows through a rolling landscape clothed in fields and woods. Much of the countryside is visible to the paddler, in spite of high, cutaway, mud banks. The current is fair, riffles are frequent, and there are occasional gentle, rocky rapids formed by the ruins of old dams. Some ruins of old canal locks remain by these rapids. The only intact dam on this section is a five-footer at Rockhill, to be carried on the left.

HAZARDS: Dam at Rockhill.

WATER CONDITIONS: Canoeable winter, spring, and into July, except in dry years. During such periods, catch within a week of rain.

GAUGE: USGS gauge (call Central PA or inspect on site) located along Conestoga Boulevard, SR3030, 0.2 miles below confluence of Little Conestoga Creek. This should read at least 1.9 feet for above Mill Creek, 1.5 feet for below. Roughly, USGS gauge at Chadds Ford, on Brandywine Creek, should read over 1.6 feet for above Mill Creek, 1.4 feet for below.

Mill Creek

INTRODUCTION: Mill Creek is a teensy and radically twisting tributary to the Conestoga, entering just downstream of Lancaster. It makes an enjoyable and scenic beginner's cruise—a great alternative to plodding down some big, dull river or lake.

Section 1. Bird-in-Hand (Pa. Rte. 340) to mouth					
Gradient	Difficulty	Distance	Time	Scenery	Map
6	A to 1	13.7	5.0	Good	52

TRIP DESCRIPTION: This quiet creek snakes through pretty farm country and an attractive suburban fringe of Lancaster. It is initially a placid path, but the last half is spiced with lots of simple riffles formed by gravel, little ledges, and rubble of past dams. As far as present dams are concerned, you must carry a four-foot dam just above Strasburg Pike, near Fertility, a ten-foot dam just below U.S. Rte. 222, and a six-foot dam about 70 yards above Eckman Road (last convenient take-out on Mill Creek). Beginners would also want to carry the rubble dam below Dutch Wonderland.

Dutch Wonderland? Yes, a trip down Mill Creek also includes a pass through this colorful amusement park, complete with such attractions as miniture Eiffel Tower, Big Ben, and Leaning Tower of Pisa. Your friends will never believe your trip report. Finally, if you paddle through the Wonderland in season, be careful not to get run over by the miniture tug boat or sternwheeler.

HAZARDS: Four dams.

WATER CONDITIONS: Canoeable winter and spring within three days of hard rain.

GAUGE: Staff gauge on left abutment of Pa. Rte. 340. Zero is the minimum level.

Cocalico Creek

INTRODUCTION: Cocalico is Indian for "serpent's den." But the only thing serpentine about this creek is its direction. Regretably, Conestoga Creek's biggest tributary wanders in muddy mediocrity down agrarian Lancaster County's busiest, most crowded corridor. Beginners can find better streams to paddle.

Section 1. Reamstown (SR1030) to mouth					
Gradient	Difficulty	Distance	Time	Scenery	Map
6	A to 1	15.6	6.0	Fair to Poor	51

TRIP DESCRIPTION: Cocalico can be pretty at times, especially in its last few miles. Some great, white barns with decorative trim, sleek cows in pasture, a covered bridge, and some limestone outcrops all remind you that this is Lancaster County. But in contrast, all through Ephrata and Akron, you find yourself paddling through people's backyards. There are noisy and busy roads nearby, and you peer over steep, mud banks at power lines, trash heaps, and shopping centers, for too many miles.

The water is mostly sluggish. A four-foot dam above Mohlers Church Road, T668, a six-foot dam (deadly) around the bend and upstream of U.S. Rte. 322, a six-foot dam above Old Mill Road, SR1045, and two low-water bridges below Akron all force short carries. Occasional riffles are poor compensation for all of this effort. Take out a mile down the Conestoga at Quarry Road, SR1003.

HAZARDS: Three dams and two low-water bridges. Fences are also a possibility.

WATER CONDITIONS: Canoeable winter and spring within two days of hard rain, above Ephrata, within four days, below.

Little Chickies Creek
Chickies Creek

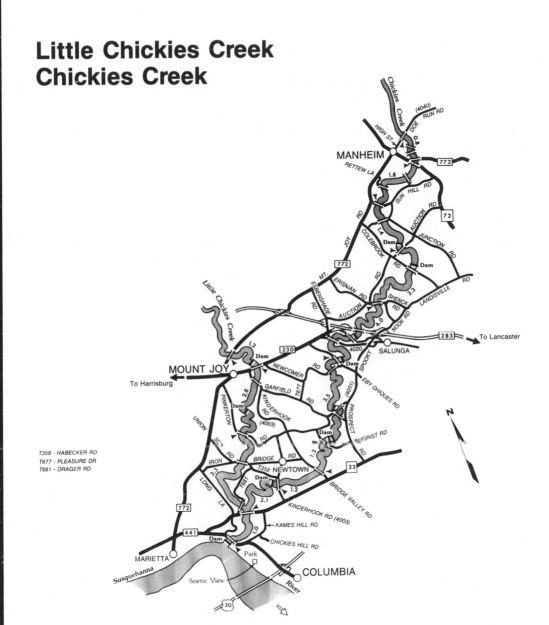

T358 - HABECKER RD
T677 - PLEASURE DR
T681 - DRAGER RD

53

Chickies Creek

INTRODUCTION: Chickies is a small creek that drains the northwest corner of Lancaster County. Its name is probably a shortening of Chickieswalungo, which translates to "place of the crawfish." There are probably no more crawfish in Chickies than the next creek. But this makes a great excuse to call attention to one of the more interesting, but often overlooked, attractions of the streams we paddle.

As far as the lay person is concerned, crawfish are just miniature aquatic lobsters. Also known as crayfish and crawdads, these little creatures possess such talents as looking funny, swimming backwards, and painfully pinching budding amateur naturalists who try to handle them. Crawfish are always fun to feed, and these comical little carnivores and scavangers will gratefully accept a tasty snack of chicken, baloney, small children, etc. Crawfish are also rather shy, which is why you see as few as you do. But they are almost everywhere. In fact, there are probably several of these voracious, little clowns creeping up behind you right now.

Section 1. Manheim (High Street, SR4040) to Pa. Rte. 441					
Gradient	Difficulty	Distance	Time	Scenery	Map
7	A to 1	20.4	8.0	Poor to Good	53

TRIP DESCRIPTION: Chickies is at least inherently nice. It follows a twisting route through a gently rolling landscape that becomes more rugged as it nears the Susquehanna. This is rich, attractive farm country, but as the creek cuts deeper into the steep hills, it spends more and more time hiding back in the woods. The creek is small, intimate, and adorned by limestone outcrops, bubbling springs, covered bridges, and old mills. But Chickies is far from perfect. Manheim and Salunga show their ugliest sides to the creek, with a clutter of old factories, commercial structures, and copious streambank trash. The countryside in between also suffers from too much indiscriminate trash dumping.

Chickies Creek's smooth-flowing waters are broken only by simple riffles that sluice over fine gravel. It runs fastest in its final few miles into the Susquehanna. But navigation is complicated by some logjams, deadfalls, sharp concrete fords, and last, but not least, nine dams (located on shuttle map). A pair of two and three-foot weirs, on the loop above the Seigrist Road, T360, covered bridge, are runnable. Carry all the other dams. You only must deal with the last dam if you continue past Pa. Rte. 441 to the Susquehanna.

HAZARDS: Nine dams and weirs, some fords, strainers, and possibly fences.

WATER CONDITIONS: Canoeable winter and spring within two days of hard rain.

GAUGE: Staff gauge on Auction Road, T875—negative 0.5 feet is minimum for floating. If you can cleanly run the easy rapid just above Pa. Rte. 23, then level is also adequate.

Codorus Creek
West Branch Codorus Creek
South Branch Codorus Creek

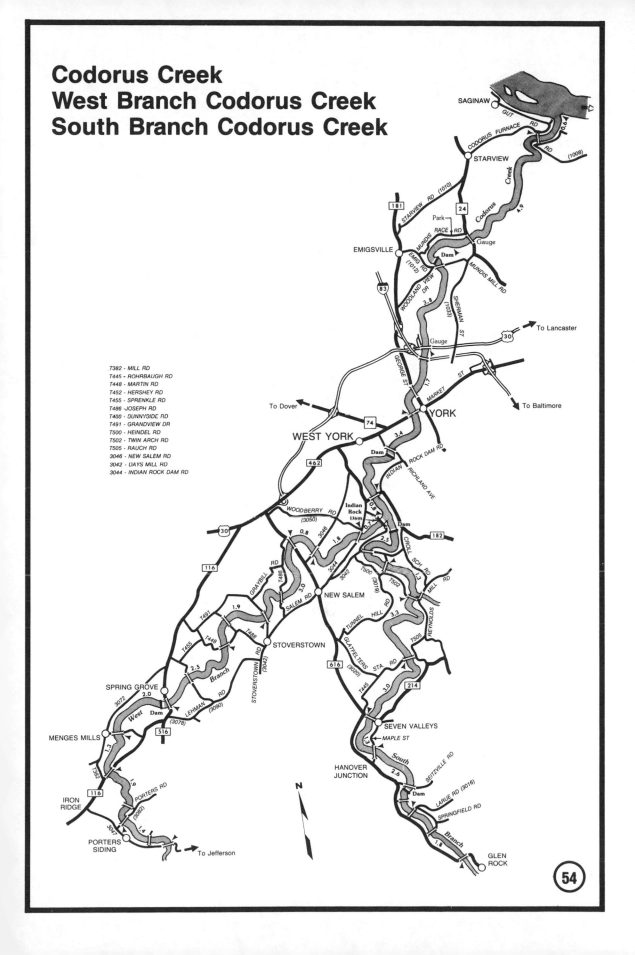

T382 - MILL RD
T445 - ROHRBAUGH RD
T448 - MARTIN RD
T452 - HERSHEY RD
T455 - SPRENKLE RD
T486 - JOSEPH RD
T400 - SUNNYSIDE RD
T491 - GRANDVIEW DR
T500 - HEINDEL RD
T502 - TWIN ARCH RD
T505 - RAUCH RD
3046 - NEW SALEM RD
3042 - DAYS MILL RD
3044 - INDIAN ROCK DAM RD

54

Little Chickies Creek

INTRODUCTION: Little Chickies Creek offers a short and scenic beginner's trip through the hilly countryside of western Lancaster County. Although it is floatable with surprisingly little water, Little Chickies is also a fine place to take refuge when larger streams are dangerously high.

Section 1. Mount Joy (Manheim Road, Pa. Rte. 772) to mouth					
Gradient	Difficulty	Distance	Time	Scenery	Map
9	A to 1	7.3	2.5	Good	53

TRIP DESCRIPTION: The muddy little ditch that you see at Manheim Road, Pa. Rte. 772, hardly looks inviting. But do not be fooled. The creek starts with a pleasant passage through a town park (although the sign says "No Boating"). It then carries you on a twisting journey past steep, wooded hillsides, countless rock cliffs and outcrops, and rolling farmland. Though the scenery is often closed in by high banks, that just adds to the air of isolation. Another attribute is that there is surprisingly little litter or development along the banks of Little Chickies Creek.

This creek is easy to manage. Smooth water and numerous gravel bar riffles typify the run. Two dams, a seven-footer just above Pa. Rte. 230 and a four-footer about a mile downstream require carries. And you might find a few deadfalls in your way. Finally, the ruins of an old dam, about five miles into the trip, form a swift chute that constitutes your whitewater ration for the day.

HAZARDS: Two dams and possible strainers.

WATER CONDITIONS: Canoeable winter and spring within two days of hard rain.

GAUGE: None. If rock weir beneath Drager Road, T356, is runnable, then the level is acceptable.

Codorus Creek

INTRODUCTION: Draining the heart of York County, Codorus Creek is a scenic, whitewater wonder, only surpassed in this corner of the state by the utterly beautiful Muddy Creek. Appropriately, the name Codorus is from the Indian term for "rapid water." Although suffering the slings and arrows of outrageous pollution from York's sewage treatment plant and paper mills, it is well worth a trip to visit. Envy York area paddlers who are only 15 minutes away.

Section 1. Pa. Rte. 182 to John Rudy Co. Park					
Gradient	Difficulty	Distance	Time	Scenery	Map
5	A to 1	8.9	3.0	Poor to Good	54

TRIP DESCRIPTION: This is not the part of Codorus Creek that has made it so beloved. Formed by the confluence of the West and South branches, about three quarters of a mile above Pa. Rte. 182, the creek soon files into the sterile, leveed flood channel that whisks it through York. To add insult to injury, you must carry a four-foot concrete and rubble dam for the privilege of running this ugly corridor. The most impressive whitewater here is the billowing foam below the municipal sewage treatment plant outfall.

After leaving York and its flood channel, the creek courses smoothly past pretty farm country, wooded hillsides, old houses, and mills. A sloping four-foot dam, around the bend from SR1012, Mundis Mill Road, can be run anywhere. It is the only excitement on this section. Take out at the county park canoe dock on left, a half mile above Rte. 24.

HAZARDS: Two weirs.

WATER CONDITIONS: Canoeable winter and spring within four days of hard rain. In a wet year it can stay up continuously from early March to late May.

GAUGE: Canoe gauge on left side of center pier, U.S. Rte. 30, Arsenal Road. Six inches is about minimal. Canoe gauge on left pier of PA. Rte. 24. Zero is minimal. A reading of 2.5 feet on the USGS gauge at York (call Central PA) is about minimum.

Section 2. John Rudy Co. Park to Codorus Furnace Road, SR1008					
Gradient	Difficulty	Distance	Time	Scenery	Map
16	1 to 2 +	4.9	2.0	Excellent	54

TRIP DESCRIPTION: Not far below the put-in, Codorus burrows into a remote, wooded gorge. The gorge is filled with numerous rapids, both long and short, of up to intermediate difficulty. They are rocky rapids, often ledge-formed, and the rocks are sharp. Flanking the rapids are equally rocky hillsides, decorated at times by low, jagged cliffs. A sparkling sidestream waterfall, tumbling in from the right, completes the pretty package.

The finish is at the SR1008, Codorus Furnace Road Bridge, below the well-preserved old Codorus Iron Furnace. There is still a half mile of creek below, but the only access to the mouth is via a mudhole of a road that branches off of Gut Road. This last stretch is not worth the trouble to explore.

HAZARDS: None.

WATER CONDITIONS: Same as Section 1. Often stays ice-free through winter.

GAUGE: Same as Section 1.

West Branch Codorus Creek

INTRODUCTION: With over 80,000 inhabitants and all sorts of major industry, you would think that York's presence would be unavoidably felt for miles around. Yet only a half dozen miles from the town center, little West Branch Codorus Creek displays to the traveler of its waters hardly a hint of the nearby urban sprawl.

Gradient	Difficulty	Distance	Time	Scenery	Map
7	A to 1	16.6	5.5	Good	54

TRIP DESCRIPTION: The muddy dribble at SR3047 is indeed a canoeable-size stream, barely. But it grows and carries you past a variety of pleasant scenery: farms, fine old houses, mills, open pasture, confining woodlands, and rocky outcrops, all often framed by an arbor of nodding river birch and box elder. The banks are a bit high for good views, but the surrounding landscape often tilts toward the creek, revealing its features like a display case in a shop. The immense and odoriferous Glatfelter Paper Mill dominates the skyline of Spring Grove, while its treated wastewaters still discolor the creek water below to coffee. But the mill is soon forgotten as the creek resumes winding past hills girdled by green and brown bands of winter wheat and corn stubble, and then moves back into more woodland. A curiosity of these last few miles are the numerous snowy white calcite outcrops and boulders along the banks.

As for difficulty, the creek ranges from smooth and swift, to sluggish in the pool behind the unrunnable paper mill dam, to riffly over gravel bars, and to briefly thrilling, where it plunges over a sloping and easily shot, four-foot dam, back in the woods above Pa. Rte. 616. While the West Branch is not steep, a frequently tortuous channel around islands and snags can keep you as busy as whitewater would. Unfortunately, an abundance of deadfalls is likely to plague your progress.

Indian Rock Dam, a Corps of Engineers flood control monolith, blocks the last mile of this creek, below the recommended take-out. The steep portage around the dam, on the left, is just too much work to justify paddling that last mile. If, however, you should be so lucky as to find the control gate in the dam's discharge tube raised (it is usually maintained a few inches off of the water), the tube is easily and safely runnable. The Corps, of course, would frown on such activity.

HAZARDS: Dam at paper mill.

WATER CONDITIONS: Canoeable winter and spring within three days of hard rain.

GAUGE: None currently. If USGS ever replaces the outside staff on its gauge at Hershey Road, T452, a level of 2.6 feet is adequate. USGS gauge at York, on Codorus Creek (call Central PA), should read at least 3.0 feet.

South Branch Codorus Creek

INTRODUCTION: The South Branch is not as nice a canoe stream as the West Branch. But it is all right. Like the West Branch, it is small, twisty, and variable; so if you do not like what you see on one bend, you just have to paddle a few strokes, and you will be looking at something new. Give it a try if you live nearby.

Conewago Creek

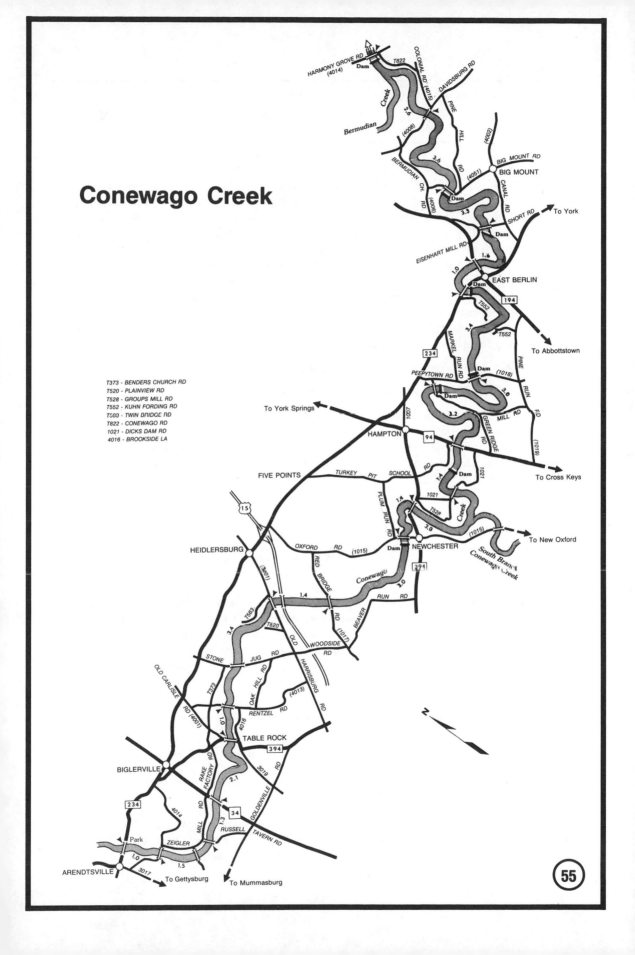

T373 - BENDERS CHURCH RD
T520 - PLAINVIEW RD
T528 - GROUPS MILL RD
T552 - KUHN FORDING RD
T500 - TWIN BRIDGE RD
T822 - CONEWAGO RD
1021 - DICKS DAM RD
4016 - BROOKSIDE LA

55

Section 1. Glen Rock (Pa. Rte. 616) to mouth					
Gradient	Difficulty	Distance	Time	Scenery	Map
9	1	15.8	6.0	Fair to Good	54

TRIP DESCRIPTION: The South Branch flows northward through an attractive, narrow, and sometimes even gorge-like valley. Quite tiny at the beginning, it twists between scrubby trees and moderately high, eroded mud banks, which tend to limit one's view of the immediate scenery. The upper valley is cluttered by houses and buildings with forgettable architecture. This is offset by a much prettier stretch, between Seven Valleys and the East Branch, which runs away from most roads and is set in nicely proportioned sylvan and rural surroundings.

Navigation includes dealing with occasional fallen trees, logjams, two crumbling low-water bridges, fences, and an unrunnable six-foot dam at T525, Seitzville Road. On the other hand, lots of gravel riffles and a final, fun plunge over a gently sloping, five-foot dam, at the waterworks, makes the floating in between easy and enjoyable. There is no access at the mouth, so continue on three quarters of a mile to Pa. Rte. 182.

HAZARDS: Two dams, low-water bridges, fences, and strainers.

WATER CONDITIONS: Canoeable winter and spring within four days of hard rain.

GAUGE: If there is enough water to float over the riffles at Pa. Rte. 616, then the level is adequate. There is a USGS gauge just above the railroad bridge at the York Waterworks, but you must hike a half mile up the railroad tracks to reach it (waterworks property closed to visitors). You want 1.6 feet to do the whole creek. USGS gauge at York, on Codorus Creek (call Central PA), should read at least 3.0 feet.

Conewago Creek

INTRODUCTION: Conewago is a dull creek. It flows 69 canoeable but lackluster miles from the Blue Ridge, across Adams and York counties, to the Susquehanna at York Haven. For most of its length, if you have seen one mile of Conewago, you have seen it all. The name Conewago is Indian for "at the rapids." But the rapids are not at the Conewago. It is a sluggish stream, often a chain of pools behind old milldams. But it is, nevertheless, a good destination for beginners who are content just to be out on the water.

Section 1. Arendtsville (Pa. Rte. 234) to SR3001					
Gradient	Difficulty	Distance	Time	Scenery	Map
13	1	10.3	3.5	Good	55

TRIP DESCRIPTION: Before starting your cruise, drive west from Arendtsville, up Pa. Rte. 234, and see a sparkling, frothing Conewago tumble down through big, gray boulders and ledges in a hemlock-shaded gorge. When other nearby streams are flooding, it might even be runnable.

Conewago Creek
Bermudian Creek

NEWBERRYTOWN

GRANDVIEW DR

Creek

SUSQUEHANNA TRAIL

SHEEP BDR RD

295

BOWERS BR. RD

1.6

STRINESTOWN

KISE MILL RD (4016)

(4016)

2.6

Dam

83

(1004)

CONEWAGO CR. RD

YORK RD (4009)

Conewago

4.0

T827

T930   T929

To York

T931

BULL RD

2.4

LEWISBERRY RD (4009)

BORING BR. RD

BULL RD

3.0

ANDERSONTOWN RD

(4018)

T912

(7893)

Access

ALPINE RD (4019)

ROHLERS CH. RD

CONEWAGO RD

Gifford
Pinchot
State
Park

4.0

74

MOUNT ROYAL

To Dover

T627 - BERMUDIAN CH. RD
T628 - BATEMAN RD
T629 - LEATHERY RD
T808 - BLUE HILL SCH. RD
T822 - CONEWAGO RD
T827 - BREMER RD
T843 - PINE RIDGE RD
T912 - KUNKLE MILL RD
T929 - CLOVERLEAF RD
T930 - SHEEP BRIDGE RD
T931 - COPENHAFFER RD
1007 - BRAGGTOWN RD
1005 - LATIMORE VALLEY RD

DETTERS

RD

4.0

MILL

CONEWAGO RD

(4014)

HARMONY GROVE RD

DETTERS MILL

Dam

T822

To Rte 74

1.1

COLONIAL RD

2.6

DOE RUN RD (4017)

MYERS RD

T808

1.9

(4008)

KRALLTOWN

KRALLTOWN RD

(4012)

2.1

Bermudian

HULL RD

T843

DAVIDSBURG RD

BERMUDIAN

1006

T629

1.8

(1012)

194

(4044)

Creek

RD

BERMUDIAN CH. RD

PONDTOWN RD

T627

1007

CREEK RD

1.3

LAKE MEAD RD

1005

RIDGE RD

1005

1.0

BALTIMORE RD

T628

1.5

(1009)

QUAKER CH. RD

N

YORK SPRINGS

15

94

To Hanover

56

Upper Conewago is the nicest section of this creek. Flanked by very low banks, the tiny brook presents sumptious views of beautiful farms, forest, and the receding Blue Ridge. It waters, actually clear until farm country tributaries cloud it, rush over plenty of riffles, until slowing down at SR3001, Old Harrisburg Road. Too bad this is only a wet weather stream.

HAZARDS: Possible fences and deadfalls.

WATER CONDITIONS: Canoeable winter and spring during fast snowmelt or within two days of hard rain.

GAUGE: None on this section. Roughly, USGS gauges at Frederick, Md., on the Monocacy River (call Washington), should be over 4.0 feet, and Camp Hill, on Yellow Breeches Creek (call Central PA), should be over 3.0 feet.

Section 2. SR3001 to mouth					
Gradient	Difficulty	Distance	Time	Scenery	Map
4	A to 1+	58.6	22.0	Fair to Good	55,56,46

TRIP DESCRIPTION: There is nothing inherently wrong with this section. The basic scenery of farms, woodlands, and bluffs is attractive. But too many miles of riverbank are cluttered by lines of monotonous summer homes and trailer camps, where people escape to the great outdoors by cramming together, side by side, in little aluminum pods, furnished with TVs, stereos, motorbikes, and all the other necessities of primitive survival. Long, slow pools behind the dams can make paddling into hard work. With about 22 bridges spanning this section, you can choose the run that suits you. Best choices are the wooded gorge beneath I-83 and a short, boulder-studded section below New Chester, formed by some hard diabase rock.

Because of its width, this section of Conewago is free of tree or fence problems. But there are ten dams on Conewago, many of which are runnable at certain levels. The first is a sloping seven-footer just above SR1015, Oxford Road, runnable on the right half. Next comes an eight-footer below SR1021, Dicks Dam Road, that is runnable on its sloping left side, at high water. A sloping four-footer at Mill Road, T546, is runnable at low water when its hydraulic is weak. A two-footer at SR1018, Peepytown Road, is runnable anywhere. Carry the vertical six-footer above Pa. Rte. 234, East Berlin. A diagonal, vertical four-footer just above T388, has a sloping, runnable chute on the extreme right. At SR4051, Big Mount Road, where the creek forks around an island at the trailer camp, take the left, where a four-footer can be run on the extreme left. Carry the vertical three-footer at SR4008, Davidsburg Road, because of the strong reversal, and carry the vertical six-footer at SR4014, Detters Mill. Finally, a crumbling three-footer above Pa. Rte. 295 is runnable on the right.

HAZARDS: Ten dams.

WATER CONDITIONS: Canoeable winter and spring until June 1, unless it is a dry year.

GAUGE: Staff gauge on left pier of Harmony Grove Road—0.7 feet is just enough to go from Bermudian Creek on down and 1.5 feet is needed to start at Bus. Rte. 15. Count joints on downstream right pier of SR4009, Lewisberry Road—13 joints down is enough for below Bermudian Creek. Roughly, USGS gauges at Frederick, Md., on the Monocacy River, should be over 3.0 feet and Camp Hill, on Yellow Breeches Creek, should be over 2.2 feet for whole section.

Bermudian Creek

INTRODUCTION: Little Bermudian Creek trickles out of the orchards and tidy farms of the Blue Ridge foothills of Adams County to an eventual, placid rendezvous with Conewago Creek, northwest of York. Its finest feature is a short, sweet stretch of excellent novice whitewater, best enjoyed by local paddlers during those all-too-brief and infrequent periods of high water.

Section 1. Pa. Rte. 94 to mouth					
Gradient	Difficulty	Distance	Time	Scenery	Map
11	A to 2	13.1	4.0	Good	56

TRIP DESCRIPTION: There is enough creek on which to float a canoe by Pa. Rte. 94. The hazy waters rush off over gentle, gravel bars and through scrubby, tangled woodlands. Some dead-falls and logjams are an annoyance until the creek bloats itself on a few tributaries, to become relatively wide and sluggish. But at Hull Road, T848, the creek begins cutting through a series of diabase reefs, the debris of which forms a delightful series of boulder patch rapids that extend for about two miles. The terrain through here is comparably rugged and mostly undeveloped. When the whitewater ends, it unfortunately really ends, the last miles being lost in the sluggish backwater from the Detters Mill Dam on the Conewago. The first take-out below the mouth is at this dam.

HAZARDS: Strainers in the first few miles.

WATER CONDITIONS: Canoeable winter and spring within two days of hard rain.

GAUGE: None. If water half covers the drainholes on the left abutment of Bermudian Creek Road, T627, Bridge, then the level is sufficient to start at Rte. 94. Roughly, USGS gauge at Camp Hill, on Yellow Breeches Creek (call Central PA), should read over 4.0 feet.

Conewago Creek

INTRODUCTION: Not to be confused with that big slug to the west, this Conewago Creek flows westward to the Susquehanna, forming the Lancaster-Dauphin County Line. It is a fascinating little creek that is alternately either very easy or very exciting. Nearby whitewater paddlers should plan to investigate this wonder after the next hard rain.

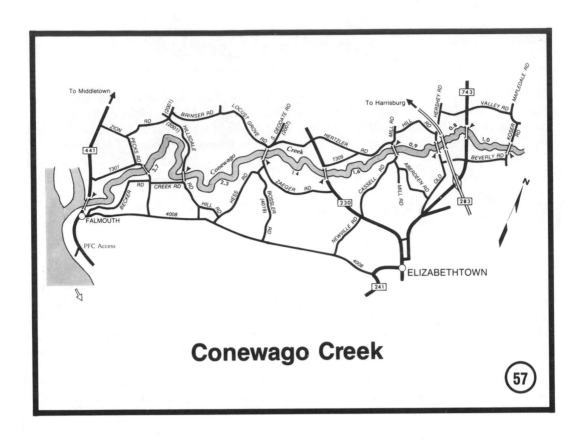

Conewago Creek

57

Section 1. Kosers Road, T871, to Pa. Rte. 441					
Gradient	**Difficulty**	**Distance**	**Time**	**Scenery**	**Map**
12	1 to 3	11.6	4.0	Good	57
0.7 @ 40					

TRIP DESCRIPTION: The little brook at the start, winding about meadows and then through quiet woodlands, clearly suggests that this is a beginner's trip. But then, about a quarter mile above Aberdeen Mills (Aberdeen Road), the creek enters a wooded ravine whose slopes are a chaos of gray, broken diabase boulders and ledges. The creek responds to this geological trauma by tumbling steeply down a blind maze of boulders and standing, living trees to the smooth water below the bridge. All is calm again until the creek approaches South Deodate Road, SR2007-SR4019, where a few ledges appear. Then around the bend, once again, the creek enters a ravine and does another quarter-mile dash down through the boulders. Slowly leveling off below the high Conrail bridge, the creek flows calm once again until a final mile of brisk riffles delivers its waters to the Susquehanna. Watch for several fences and a low-water bridge on the easy stretches.

HAZARDS: Fences, low-water bridge, and trees that grow in the rapids.

WATER CONDITIONS: Canoeable winter and spring within two days of hard rain.

GAUGE: Judge at South Deodate Road. If you think you can clear the ledges just upstream of that bridge, then the level is adequate.

Swatara Creek

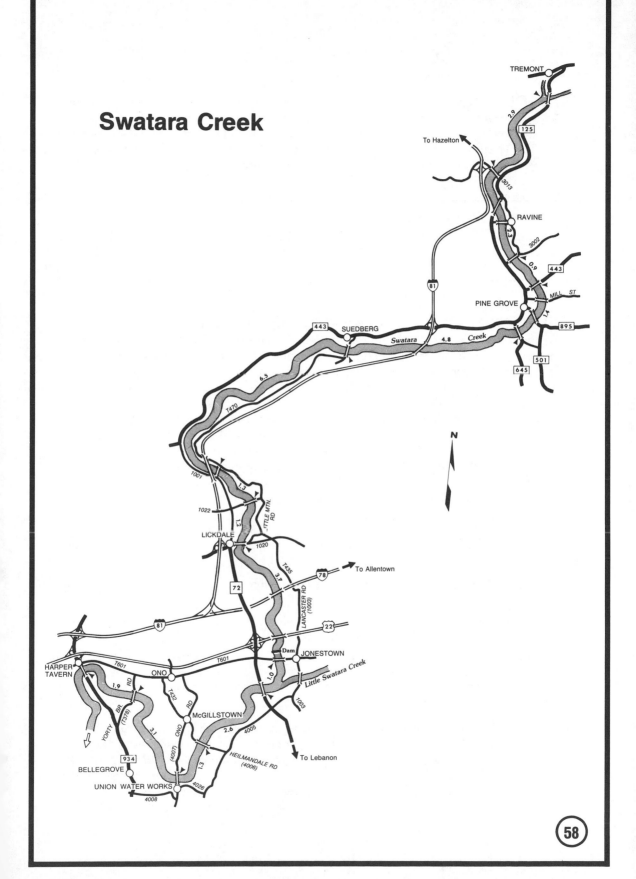

Swatara Creek

INTRODUCTION: Swatara Creek flows from the edge of the coal fields, near Pottstown, to the Susquehanna at Middletown. Mostly a long and lazy path through mountain gaps and scenic farm country, Swatara is runnable late into the season and is relatively free of dangers or difficulties. This is a good stream on which to put down the paddle, pick up the fishing pole, and float away the miles as your body submits to spring fever.

Section 1. Tremont (Pa. Rte. 125) to Jonestown (Market Street)					
Gradient	Difficulty	Distance	Time	Scenery	Map
14	1 to 2 +	25.0	7.5	Poor to Good	58
5 @ 43					

TRIP DESCRIPTION: There is actually some sporting whitewater on the far upper Swatara. Put in about a mile south of beautiful, downtown Tremont at the Pa. Rte. 125 Bridge, where Good Spring Run boosts the flow. For the next three miles the foaming waters dash down a rock-studded, hemlock- and rhododendron-bound corridor. Except for one complex, little boulder patch, it is just a fun time through closely packed, Class 2 rapids. After a few splashy drops near Ravine, the water gradually mellows while the scenery degenerates.

By Pine Grove, Swatara has moderated to smooth water and riffles—a pleasant novice run. The aesthetics are variable. A forested passage between the two I-81 bridges is pretty, in spite of some nasty logging scars. Unfortunately, the noise from that nearby freeway hints of something other than wilderness. The stretch around Lickdale is developed with vacation homes while it is less so below. Watch out for a low dam with a dangerous roller, at the waterworks a half mile below U.S. Rte. 22 and for occasional fallen trees all along.

HAZARDS: Weir at Jonestown and possible trees.

WATER CONDITIONS: Canoeable winter and spring during fast melt and within two days of hard rain.

GAUGE: USGS gauge at Harpers (call Central PA) should read over 2.7 feet to start at Tremont.

Section 2. Jonestown (Market Street) to mouth					
Gradient	Difficulty	Distance	Time	Scenery	Map
3	A to 1	38.2	13.0	Fair to Good	58,59

TRIP DESCRIPTION: This section is perfect for beginners. With the input from Little Swatara Creek, this is now a fairly large stream—too big for strainers. The only regular hazard is a five-foot dam, with an absolutely lethal hydraulic, located about a hundred yards below Pa. Rte. 39, Union Deposit. Carry on either side. There are a few strong rocky riffles, formed by old dam debris, with the best being below the Pennsylvania Turnpike (watch for iron bars). But generally this is a stretch of smooth water, broken only by riffles that are little more than ripples.

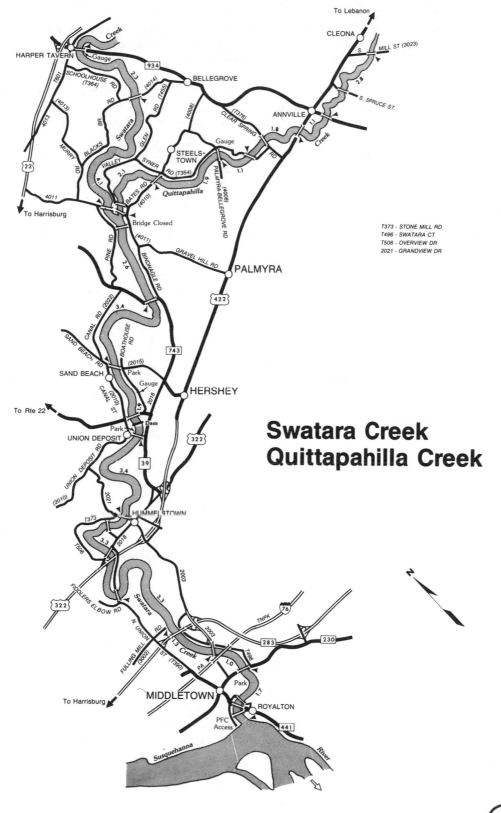

Swatara Creek
Quittapahilla Creek

To Lebanon

CLEONA

S. MILL ST (3023)

S. SPRUCE ST.

2.8

HARPER TAVERN

Creek

Gauge

SCHOOLHOUSE (T364)

934

BELLEGROVE

2.3

(4014)

RD (T455)

T801

(4013)

BR. RD

BLACKS

Swatara

GLEN RD

(4009)

CLEAR SPRING (T376)

RD

ANNVILLE

1.1

Creek

1.8

4013

22

MURRY RD

VALLEY

SYNER

STEELS-TOWN

Gauge

RD (T354)

4.1

2.1

PALMYRA-BELLEGROVE RD (4008)

1.1

6.1

4011

BATES RD (4010)

Quittapahilla

Bridge Closed

T373 - STONE MILL RD
T496 - SWATARA CT
T506 - OVERVIEW DR
2021 - GRANDVIEW DR

To Harrisburg

PINE RD

(4011)

GRAVEL HILL RD

PALMYRA

2.6

BINOMAGLE RD

422

CANAL RD (2022)

3.4

BOATHOUSE RD

SAND BEACH RD

743

(2015)

Park

SAND BEACH

Gauge

2016

HERSHEY

To Rte 22

CANAL ST (2010)

2.9

Park

Dam

322

UNION DEPOSIT

UNION DEPOSIT RD

39

3.4

2021

(2010)

HUMMELSTOWN

T373

3.3

2018

T506

2003

322

FIDDLERS ELBOW RD

Swatara

3.3

N. UNION RD

TNPK

76

FULLING MILL (3002)

1.3

Creek

2003

283

230

ST (T360)

PA

1.0

T496

To Harrisburg

MIDDLETOWN

Park

1.7

ROYALTON

PFC Access

441

Susquehanna

River

59

As far as Hummelstown, your view is confined to the creek's high, tree-topped mud banks, a few bluffs, and little cliffs. There are a few pockets of summer homes around Harpers Tavern and Valley Glen, but otherwise this is a pleasant, woodsy, and lonely journey. Periodically you see old, crumbling, stone embankments, and if you investigate further, you are likely to find an old, tree-filled ditch just beyond. These are the remains of the old Union Canal, which linked the Susquehanna at Middletown to the Schuylkill at Reading. Finally, if the sun is shining, but the serenity is disturbed by the sound of distant thunder, do not worry. You are just hearing the sound of artillery fire from nearby Fort Indiantown Gap.

The remaining miles from Hummelstown to the mouth are fairly built-up, but contain some pretty limestone outcrops. If you go all the way to the mouth, a Fish and Boat Commission access on the right makes an easy take-out.

HAZARDS: Dangerous dam below Pa. Rte. 39, Union Deposit.

WATER CONDITIONS: Canoeable winter and spring until mid-June, except in dry years. Often up after summer rains.

GAUGE: USGS gauge at Harpers (call Central PA) should read over 2.1 feet. USGS gauge along Boathouse Road, near Hershey (call Central PA), about a half mile above Rte. 39—minimum is about 2.0 feet.

Quittapahilla Creek

INTRODUCTION: The locals just call it the "Quitty." But the whole mouthful is Indian for "spring which flows from among the pines." Actually the Quitty is the product of several such limestone springs that gush forth from the hillsides south of Lebanon and Annville to end up in the Swatara. Though terribly small, it is clearly canoeable and is suitable for a delightful beginner's trip.

Section 1. Cleona (S. Mill Street) to mouth					
Gradient	Difficulty	Distance	Time	Scenery	Map
6	1	10.9	3.5	Fair to Good	59

TRIP DESCRIPTION: Put in below the old mill, where the millrace rejoins the main channel. These first few miles down to U.S. Rte. 422 are swift, rocky, and extremely tiny. The partly suburbanized scenery is only fair, but the numerous springs and the strange, striated patterns on the limestone outcrops make it all worthwhile.

Beginners should start below U.S. Rte. 422. The Quitty returns to the country, but only after starting with an odd journey down a long concrete box channel, back in the middle of the woods. This is all that remains from a portion of the huge Bethlehem Steel Millard Limestone Quarry, much of which is still active a short distance to the west. All of the rest of the creek flows down a narrow and remote valley, through woodlands, past a few farms, under some stone arch bridges, by pastures, and by fields gone to scrub. The water is mostly smooth and swift, but there may be some trees and fences to avoid. In summer, dense growths of water weeds make this a viscous medium through which to paddle. Take out a quarter mile down the Swatara at the abandoned bridge at Valley Glen.

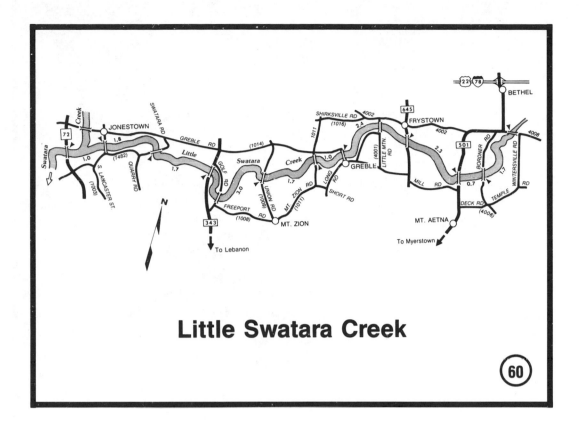

Little Swatara Creek

⑥⓪

HAZARDS: Some fallen trees and fences.

WATER CONDITIONS: Canoeable above Rte. 422 winter and spring within two days of hard rain. Below Rte. 422, canoeable most of the year, except in severe drought.

GAUGE: USGS gauge on right bank below SR4008, Palmyra-Bellegrove Road. You need about 3.95 feet to start at S. Mill Street and 3.5 feet to start at Rte. 422.

Little Swatara Creek

INTRODUCTION: Little Swatara Creek is indeed little, quietly flowing through the rich farm lands of Lebanon and Berks counties. A wet weather canoe stream only, it offers many winding miles of pleasant novice paddling.

Section 1. Bethel (SR4008) to mouth					
Gradient	Difficulty	Distance	Time	Scenery	Map
5	1	17.0	6.0	Good	60

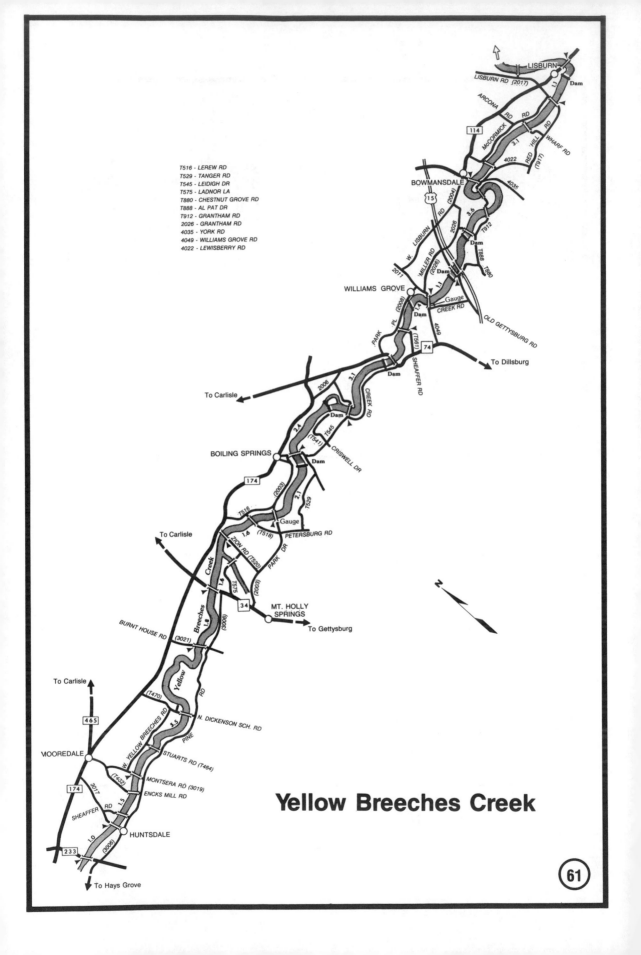

T516 - LEREW RD
T529 - TANGER RD
T545 - LEIDIGH DR
T575 - LADNOR LA
T880 - CHESTNUT GROVE RD
T888 - AL PAT DR
T912 - GRANTHAM RD
2026 - GRANTHAM RD
4035 - YORK RD
4049 - WILLIAMS GROVE RD
4022 - LEWISBERRY RD

Yellow Breeches Creek

61

TRIP DESCRIPTION: If Little Swatara is high enough to float, then it will be fairly swift and there will be many tiny riffles. The best riffles are formed by the debris from old dams. The worst problems are formed by a few downed trees, fences, and one low-water bridge. The creek winds through gently rolling farm country, with the almost level ridge of Blue Mountain dominating the distant skyline. The passage alternates between confining woods, dense briar patches, and wide open fields and pastures. Generally, you will have no trouble seeing over the banks. Only a few trash heaps, one junkyard, and a few summer homes detract from the beauty of this trip. Take out down the Swatara at Pa. Rte. 72.

HAZARDS: Trees, fences, and a low-water bridge.

WATER CONDITIONS: Canoeable winter and spring within five days of hard rain.

GAUGE: None on creek, but you can judge by the riffle at the put-in. Roughly, USGS gauge at Harpers, on Swatara Creek (call Central PA), should read about 2.5 feet.

Yellow Breeches Creek

INTRODUCTION: Yellow Breeches Creek is a high quality canoe stream that is conveniently situated right in the backyard of Harrisburg and York. Flowing through a limestone valley, Yellow Breeches is endowed with numerous, gushing tributary springs, whose constant contributions sustain this creek at floatable levels for far longer than would rainfall runoff. In addition, this is often a good early season run, as all that relatively warm spring water impedes ice formation during the deep winter freeze.

Section 1. Pa. Rte. 233 to Pa. Rte. 34					
Gradient	Difficulty	Distance	Time	Scenery	Map
11	1	9.9	5.0	Good	61

TRIP DESCRIPTION: You can start paddling Yellow Breeches all the way up at Pa. Rte. 233. But the journey down through these first ten miles is not for everybody. For it is an aquatic obstacle course. Waiting there to torment you are numerous barbed wire and electric fences, low cables, fallen trees, logjams, carries through dense vegetation, low road and foot bridges, splitting channels with woefully wrong choices, lush poison ivy, and a three-foot dam. So why would anybody, besides the author, be stupid enough to want to paddle this?

Because it is a nice place to hide from the world. After a pastoral start, followed by a healthy injection (25 cfs average) of clear, cold water from the Huntsdale Fish Hatchery Springs, the Yellow Breeches loses itself in a dense, gloomy, but beautiful swamp forest. Such forests are rare in Pennsylvania. In this sodden environment, trees seem to grow bigger and taller. Great flocks of misanthropic waterfowl are bound to be shocked and surprised by your presence. This is one stretch of Pennsylvania streamscape that you are unlikely to have to share with other paddlers or fishermen. And then when the creek wanders beyond the swamp, it often flows by pretty farms, fine old houses, and attractive contemporary structures. In between all the annoying carries, a strong current and many riffles make for easy floating. So as you can see, this fluvial cloud has a silver lining.

HAZARDS: Strainers and a weir.

WATER CONDITIONS: To start at Rte. 233, catch within three days of hard rain in winter or spring. Below Montsera Road, canoeable all through March and April, and in a wet year, until early July.

GAUGE: USGS gauge at Camp Hill (call Central PA) should read at least 2.4 feet to start at Rte. 233. For below Montsera Road, 1.5 feet is adequate.

Section 2. Pa. Rte. 34 to New Cumberland (Bridge Street)					
Gradient	Difficulty	Distance	Time	Scenery	Map
6	A to 1	34.2	12.0	Good	61,45

TRIP DESCRIPTION: With the addition of Mountain Creek's waters, Yellow Breeches widens a bit and becomes much less an obstacle course. But some fallen trees, fences, and logjams may still trouble you for a few more miles. One thing is certain. You cannot travel far on Yellow Breeches Creek without encountering a few old milldams to carry. But the pools are short and, in between, you always have the assistance of a swift current and the pleasure of lots of riffles. The riffles are often formed by trout weirs and crumbled remnants of old milldams. Numerous roads allow you to divide this section into any number of trips.

From Pa. Rte. 34 to Williams Grove, the creek flows through a combination of farmland and residential areas. Low banks allow long views across the pretty valley, especially to the south where the Blue Ridge forms the skyline. This reach of the Yellow Breeches is a very popular trout stream, particularly around Boiling Springs, where the State only allows fishing with barbless hooks, but maintains a year-long season. Please respect the rights of the many fishermen (even the few grumpy ones) who no doubt will be right out there in the riffles with you.

Now about these dams. The first, a low rubble weir at Park Drive, SR2003, is runnable. The next, a four-foot dam about a quarter mile above Boiling Springs, is not, with a lousy, tangled portage to boot. Carry (right) a sharp, three-foot weir at the Boiling Springs Sewage Treatment Plant. Next comes a five-footer above Pa. Rte.74, also unrunnable. You can shoot a crumbling, diagonal, three-foot weir at the Williams Grove amusement park via a chute on the far left. But first scout carefully for sharp debris in the chute. Finally, carry the four-foot dam just above Old Gettysburg Road.

Much of the area along the stream, below U.S. Rte. 15, is wooded and seems amazingly remote, considering its proximity to Harrisburg. The creek wanders at the base of bluffs and even rock cliffs, interrupted by more open reaches of farms and rolling fields. Development along this section, which includes an attractive college campus, is usually spotty. Those houses that are present are usually pretty. Some are absolutely beautiful, surrounded by acres of carefully tended grounds. Only on approaching New Cumberland does the scenery turn offensively urban.

The dams, unfortunately, do not quit. A crumbling dam, above the railroad bridge near Grantham, has a narrow, runnable chute in the middle. Another crumbling dam, diagonally spanning the creek above Bowmansdale, is best through the middle breech. But the four-foot dam above Lisburn (carry either side), a six-foot dam at the graceful stone arch Rossmoyne Bridge (carry left), a five-foot dam at the big mill at SR2031, Spanglers Mill Road (carry right), a dam above Greenlane Drive (carry left), and the seven-footer at the park in New Cumberland (carry left) are all unrunnable.

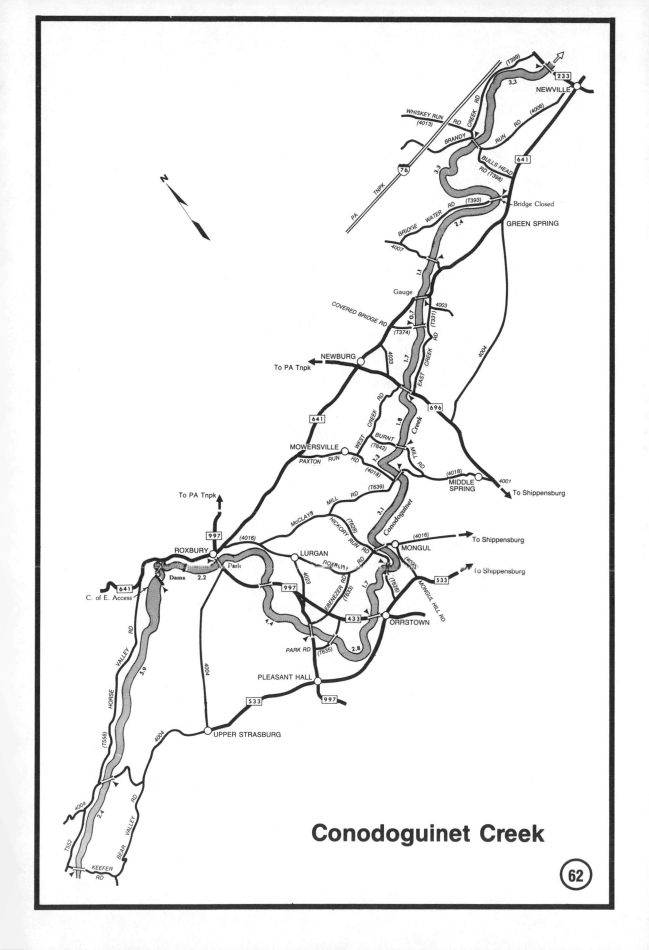

Conodoguinet Creek

HAZARDS: Dams and weirs. Some strainers in first few miles.

WATER CONDITIONS: Canoeable all through March, April, and, in a wet year, up until early July.

GAUGE: USGS gauge at Camp Hill (call Central PA) should read at least 1.4 feet. Staff gauge on right abutment of Park Drive, SR2003, above Boiling Springs, should read at least 1.5 feet. Staff gauge on right abutment of Williams Grove Road, SR2011, should read at least 1.25 feet. Staff gauge on Bridge Street, SR2035, New Cumberland, should be at least 1.7 feet.

Conodoguinet Creek

INTRODUCTION: Anybody can canoe this creek, but not everybody can pronounce its name — not even some of the locals. So say Con'·o·do·gui'·net. It flows by such far-apart towns as Shippensburg, Carlisle, and Harrisburg, for like its name, the creek is a long one. Winding, sometimes most excessively, through a broad, fertile, and limestone-ribbed, agricultural valley, this is an excellent and frequently floatable stream for beginners.

Section 1. Bear Valley Road to Roxbury (Pa. Rte. 997)					
Gradient	**Difficulty**	**Distance**	**Time**	**Scenery**	**Map**
30	A to 2	10.5	4.0	Good	62

TRIP DESCRIPTION: This is the prettiest and most remote section of the Conodoguinet — a high water run only, suitable for experienced novices. Only a canoe-length wide at the put-in, the shallow ribbon of clear water glides over a sand and cobble bottom, through hemlock groves and past lonely farms, in a narrow mountain valley. While the water is generally easy, fallen trees, especially in a few braided sections, are troublesome. Following a short and lively tumble through some rock gardens and over some small ledges, the creek pauses in an attractive, mile-long reservoir. This pool is the water supply for Letterkenny Army Depot. A steep but easy carry around the right side of the dam delivers you back to free-flowing waters. The remaining run, through a gap in Blue Mountain, is a delightful, very busy, and often bouncy Class 2 flush. Watch out for two low-water bridges and a sharp concrete ford (all carries), a half mile below the dam, some nasty strainers a little farther downstream, and a sloping four-foot dam, about a mile above Roxbury (runnable). The creek splits around an island above Pa. Rte. 997, and both choices are grim.

HAZARDS: Two dams, low-water bridges, a sharp ford, and some strainers.

WATER CONDITIONS: Canoeable winter and spring within two days of hard rain.

GAUGE: Roughly, USGS gauge at Hogestown (call Central PA or inspect on spot) should read about 3.9 feet. It takes about 20 hours for water on Section 1 to reach this gauge.

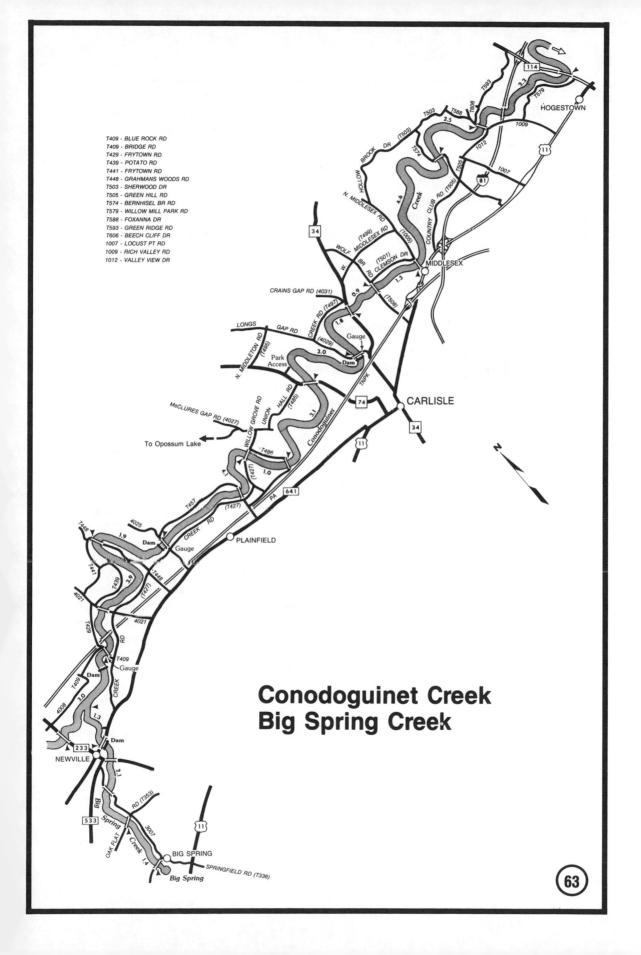

Conodoguinet Creek
Big Spring Creek

T409 - BLUE ROCK RD
T409 - BRIDGE RD
T429 - FRYTOWN RD
T439 - POTATO RD
T441 - FRYTOWN RD
T448 - GRAHMANS WOODS RD
T503 - SHERWOOD DR
T505 - GREEN HILL RD
T574 - BERNHISEL BR RD
T579 - WILLOW MILL PARK RD
T588 - FOXANNA DR
T593 - GREEN RIDGE RD
T606 - BEECH CLIFF DR
1007 - LOCUST PT RD
1009 - RICH VALLEY RD
1012 - VALLEY VIEW DR

HOGESTOWN

MIDDLESEX

CARLISLE

PLAINFIELD

NEWVILLE

BIG SPRING
Big Spring

To Opossum Lake

Section 2. Roxbury (Pa. Rte. 997) to Pa. Rte. 696					
Gradient	Difficulty	Distance	Time	Scenery	Map
13	A to 1 +	15.1	5.0	Fair to Good	62
2.3 @ 33					

TRIP DESCRIPTION: Put in at the Lions Club Park south of Roxbury. For a few miles the creek hurries over almost continuous, cobbly riffles, while splitting around numerous islands. If you choose correctly, it is often possible to avoid having to portage around any strainers. Below Pa. Rte. 433, Conodoguinet loses its steam and, hence, becomes suitable for beginners. This whole passage runs through either scrubby woods or farmlands. It is pleasant and peaceful, but hardly outstanding.

HAZARDS: Strainers.

WATER CONDITIONS: Canoeable winter and spring within three days of hard rain.

GAUGE: Staff gauge on right abutment of Pa. Rte. 641 (on Section 3) should read at least 4.9 feet. USGS gauge at Hogestown should read over 3.3 feet.

Section 3. Pa. Rte. 696 to Pa. Rte. 74					
Gradient	Difficulty	Distance	Time	Scenery	Map
4	A to 1	29.5	10.0	Good to Fair	62,63

TRIP DESCRIPTION: The Conodoguinet now settles down into a seemingly torpid state—a river of long pools, both natural and dam-formed, separated by gentle riffles. You must portage a five-foot dam, located about two miles below Pa. Rte. 233 (carry left) and a five-footer (also carried left) above SR4025, at the beautiful, old, red mill. Take out at the public boat ramp and township park, on the left, about .75 miles below Pa. Rte. 74.

On the average, this is an attractive section. Medium-high banks are usually tree-lined, partially screening the beautiful agricultural lands beyond. But you still see an ample number of big and well-kept barns and roomy, old, red brick and white stone farm houses nearby. Several clear and voluminous springs gush into the south bank, some of which may be floated. Unfortunately, you also see an occasional trash heap, some of the Pennsylvania Turnpike, and on the creek's lower reaches, usually along pools behind dams, some ugly strings of houses and camps, vulnerably sitting on the floodplain.

The banks of the Conodoguinet are also home to an unusually large population of osage orange trees. The osage orange's green, convoluted, and grapefruit-sized fruit are great conversation pieces and, when hurled at someone, lethal weapons. So stop and collect a few souvenirs to show your botanically ignorant friends.

HAZARDS: Two dams.

WATER CONDITIONS: Canoeable winter and spring within two weeks of hard rain.

GAUGE: USGS gauge at Hogestown should read about 2.5 feet to start at Rte. 696 and over 2.0 feet to start below Newville. Staff gauge on right abutment of Rte. 641 should read 4.2 feet to clear the shallowest spots. Staff gauge on right pier of Bridge Road, T409, should read over 4.5 feet. Staff gauge on right abutment of SR4025 should read over 2.4 feet. Staff gauge on SR4029, Longs Gap Road (on Section 4), should be over 1.1 feet.

Section 4. Pa. Rte. 74 to mouth					
Gradient	Difficulty	Distance	Time	Scenery	Map
3	A to 1	39.3	13.0	Good to Fair	63,45

TRIP DESCRIPTION: This serpentine section of the Conodoguinet flows in and out of some intensively residential areas that really crowd the creek, especially near Carlisle, Hogestown, and Camp Hill. While some of those neighborhoods are quite attractive, did you really take up canoeing to paddle through suburbia? Of particular interest on this section is a grotesque, tower-like edifice, below I-81, and the plastic, polka-dotted hippos at the amusement park near Hogestown. In between these distractions, wooded bluffs and bottoms, pastures, fields, and farms maintain an attractive riverscape.

The wide creek flows over a ledgy or gravelly bottom which can be tedious to negotiate at low water. Long pools lie behind the six-foot dam above Long Gap Road (long carry on right to avoid tramping through the front yards on the left) and a five-foot dam at Good Hope Mill (carry left). Take out at the mouth at the West Fairview Fish and Boat Commission Access, on the left.

HAZARDS: Two dams.

WATER CONDITIONS: Canoeable usually throughout March and April and into mid-May. In a wet year, it may stay up until July.

GAUGE: USGS gauge at Hogestown should read over 1.7 feet.

Big Spring Creek

INTRODUCTION: There is water, water everywhere, but not necessarily a drop on which to canoe. That unavailable water is called ground water. Ground water is that portion of the rainfall, or snowmelt, that does not run off, evaporate, or get consumed by plants, but rather trickles into and collects in the voids between soil particles and in the cracks in the bedrock.

But ground water is not forever lost to paddlers. Much of this water returns to our streams — very slowly. It oozes into the stream beds, drop by drop, ounce by ounce, steadily, day by day, providing the base flow in our streams that prevails through the worst of droughts. In limestone regions, such as the Cumberland Valley, the hydraulics are a bit more dramatic. Here the ground water first collects in caves and fissures which are dissolved out of the limestone by this same water. Then, rather than oozing from the soil, lime country ground water gushes from cracks and holes in the rock, in the form of springs.

In Cumberland County, many of the springs that feed Conodoguinet Creek surface three to seven miles to the south to form instant creeks. Some of these springs are voluminous enough, combined with a mild enough gradient, to be canoeable. The biggest and most reliable of these is Big Spring.

Big Spring emerges near U.S. Rte. 11, about eight miles northeast of Shippensburg, and feeds Conodoguinet Creek near Newville. It is the fifth largest spring in Pennsylvania, with a median flow of 18 million gallons a day (27cfs). And that is enough water, in this instance, to make an honest canoe route.

Section 1. Springfield Road to mouth					
Gradient	Difficulty	Distance	Time	Scenery	Map
8	1	4.8	2.0	Good	63

TRIP DESCRIPTION: You can start your trip just below the springhead. For the following miles Big Spring Creek meanders lazily past cedar-studded hillsides, farm houses, and Newtown. Cattail marshes often bracket the creek, whose waters filter through thick, waving mats of water weeds. You will need to lift over some fish barriers and maybe over the sharp rubble of some dam ruins. A five-foot dam still stands just upstream of Pa. Rte. 641, by a restored mill that dates back to 1763. The dam requires a carry. Since there is no access at the mouth, you must continue down the Conodoguinet about two miles to Bridge Road. If you run Big Spring during the summer, you will probably have to wade the shallows on Conodoguinet.

HAZARDS: A dam at Newville.

WATER CONDITIONS: Canoeable winter, spring, and summer, except in dry years.

GAUGE: None.

Clark Creek

INTRODUCTION: Clark Creek is not the sort of stream that you can run just any time you want. Flowing straight down a stringbean of a valley that averages less than two miles wide from one ridge top to the other, Clark normally picks up little runoff from those ridges' wooded slopes. And then, to make matters worse, DeHart Reservoir, Harrisburg's water supply, bottles up the upper third of the valley. So, if you are a lover of tiny and remote woodland torrents, and if it has been raining enough lately to fill that old reservoir, and in addition, if one heavy rain is falling on eastern Pennsylvania at this moment, drop tomorrow's plans, hurry up to Dauphin County, and check out this beauty.

Section 1. DeHart Dam to mouth					
Gradient	Difficulty	Distance	Time	Scenery	Map
13	1 +	17.2	5.0	Good	44

Sherman Creek

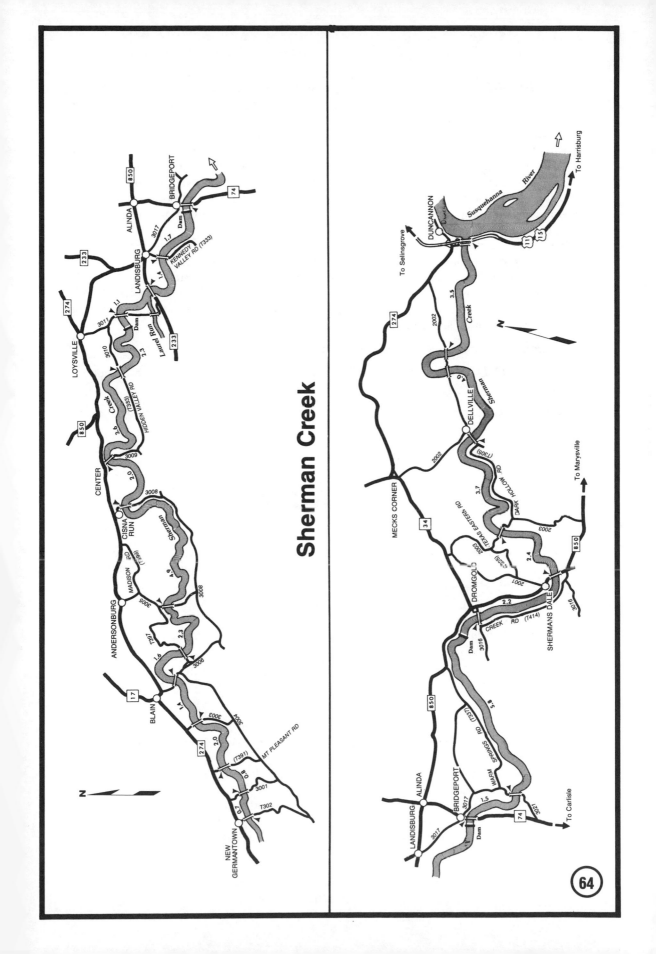

TRIP DESCRIPTION: Put in at the bottom of the long spillway of DeHart Dam. But first pause for a moment and fantasize what a wild experience it would be to shoot that flume in your little boat. A few strokes downstream of your real put-in is a USGS gauging station on the right. This marks a two-foot weir that possesses an ugly, churning hydraulic that the wise will portage. Mostly insulated by state game lands for the next several miles, the creek seems far from civilization as its clear waters rush through a corridor, sometimes even a tunnel, of hemlock and rhododendron. Expect to carry a few low bridges, fallen trees, and one low-water bridge (runnable at very high water). All through here the water runs swiftly, but is mostly smooth, ruffled periodically by stretches of easy rapids. An old iron furnace marks the end of state game lands and the best of Clark Creek.

The lower creek widens a bit, as does the valley. Farms appear, but so do numerous and sometimes shoddy summer homes. The parallel highway becomes more apparent now. Compensating for the drabber scenery, the gradient picks up in the last few miles to Pa. Rte. 125, and two little weirs form exciting drops with strong holes lurking when the water is high. Below Rte. 125 the aesthetics improve as the stream twists through quiet woods and by small bluffs to its meeting with the Susquehanna, above the village of Dauphin.

HAZARDS: Strainers, low bridges, and the gauging station weir.

WATER CONDITIONS: Rarely canoeable. Catch in winter or spring within 24 hours of hard rain.

GAUGE: USGS gauge on right bank, a quarter mile below DeHart Dam, should read at least 3.0 feet.

Sherman Creek

INTRODUCTION: Sherman Creek arcs across the heart of pretty Perry County, northwest of Harrisburg. It is a particularly pleasant path for the novice paddler to tour the central Pennsylvania ridge and farm country at its finest.

Section 1. New Germantown (Buck Ridge Road, T302) to mouth					
Gradient	Difficulty	Distance	Time	Scenery	Map
8	1	49.0	16.0	Good to Fair	64

TRIP DESCRIPTION: While there is plentiful access to Sherman Creek, it divides most nicely into three runs: New Germantown to Pa. Rte. 233, Pa. Rte. 233 to Dromgold, and Dromgold to the mouth.

At New Germantown, Sherman Creek is a mere rivulet. If it looks scratchy here, start 1.5 miles below, at Mt. Pleasant Road, T391, or five miles below, near Blaine, where tributaries add the precious gallons necessary to float you. Though still narrow, the creek is usually blocked by only a few fallen trees. Little cobbly or ledgy riffles are plentiful, and there is even somewhat of a rapid through the old dam ruins near Bixler. Carry a six-foot dam south of Loysville.

The banks along this creek are usually low, so you can view a lot of the surrounding well-kept farms and deep groves of bottomland hardwoods. At times there are some nice exposures of rock, particularly a few miles below Blaine, where an unusual, smooth, and sloping rock cliff, capped with cedars, rises above the creek. In spite of the agricultural surroundings, Sherman's waters are often remarkably clear, even at canoeable levels. Several lovely covered bridges span these relatively narrow waters.

With the addition of Laurel Run at Pa. Rte. 233, the creek widens, but remains fairly remote and undeveloped to Dromgold. This section flows more through the woods and nearer to the mountains than the upper creek. A three-foot dam, just above Pa. Rte. 74, is runnable, while a sharp three-footer, several miles below, is best carried.

The remaining miles below Dromgold are inherently nice, but are continually cluttered by residential and second home development. The creek still rushes along nicely, especially where it splashes through a chute in a crumbling three-foot dam, above the covered bridge in Dellville.

HAZARDS: Three weirs, two of which require carries. Some deadfalls above Rte. 233.

WATER CONDITIONS: Canoeable winter and spring. Above Rte. 233, catch within four days of hard rain. Below Rte. 233, canoeable within ten days of rain and usually up until late May.

GAUGE: Roughly, USGS gauge at Hogestown, on Conodoguinet Creek (call Central PA), should read over 3.1 feet to canoe above Rte. 233 and over 2.3 feet to canoe below. USGS gauge at PA. Rte. 34, Shermans Dale (call Central PA), should read a minimum of 1.5 feet to canoe lower creek.

Juniata River

INTRODUCTION: An imposing and sinuous sweep of tangled ridges, representing a possibly traumatic geologic past, arcs across central Pennsylvania. Mountains and ridges merge and diverge chaotically, while right alongside, in contrast, the next couple of ridges lie peacefully beside each other, so even and parallel that they resemble furrows in a cornfield. There are places where the ends of these ridges almost explode out of the valley, looking like great, green ships in a sea of cornfields and pastures. Beneath these mountains' smooth, green exterior, their rocky strata is twisted, tilted, creased, and sometimes even flipped upside down. When one observes this landscape from the air, or on a map, one can only marvel at how a drop of rain, falling on the east slope of the Allegheny Front, the highest and westernmost of these ridges, could ever find its way eastward through this maze to the Atlantic.

Possibly the most dramatic example of the imaginative drainage pattern resulting from this topography is that of the Juniata River and its tributaries. Looking at the start, the asymmetric Allegheny Front slopes steeply on its eastern face, like a roof on a Cape Cod house. The rainfall runs off this slope quickly, by only the tiniest of brooks. All of this water then collects in long streams, running parallel to the base of the Front, like rain gutters on that roof. Such is the upper Frankstown Branch and Little Juniata. And finally, to complete the allusion, these rivers and the Juniata, the downspouts, carry this water southeastward, northeastward, and any way you can imagine, snaking and zigzagging through the mountains, and more often around mountains, in a great arc that ends at the Susquehanna above Harrisburg.

Back before they invented airplanes, even an indirect route such as the Juniata Valley was the keystone to east-west commerce. After all, anything beat climbing over mountains, especially with

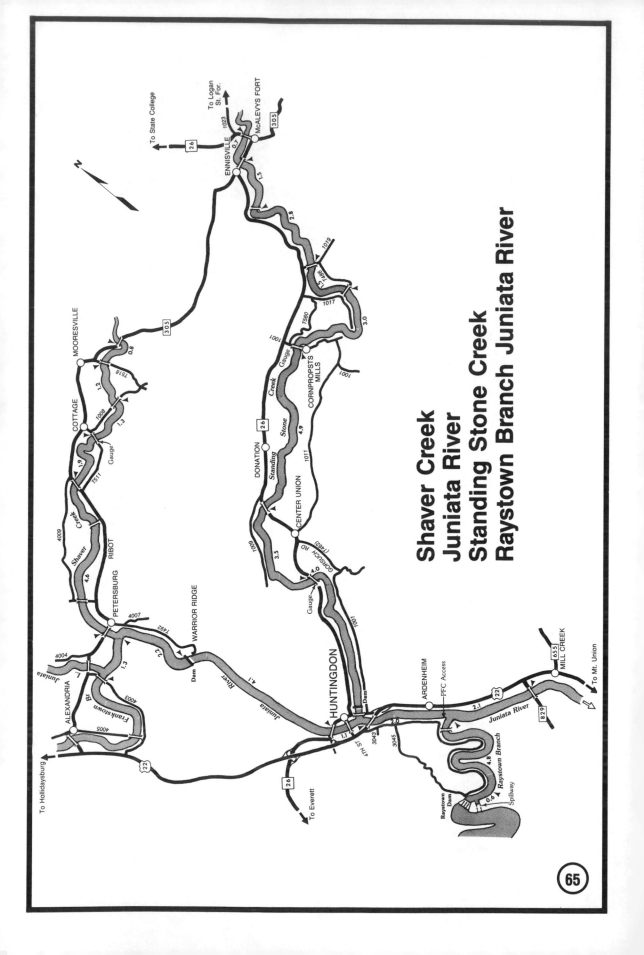

Shaver Creek
Juniata River
Standing Stone Creek
Raystown Branch Juniata River

Juniata River

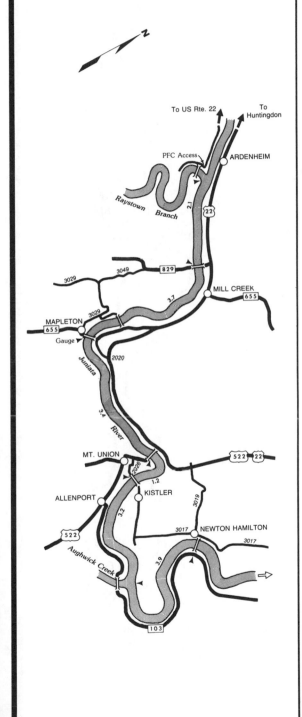

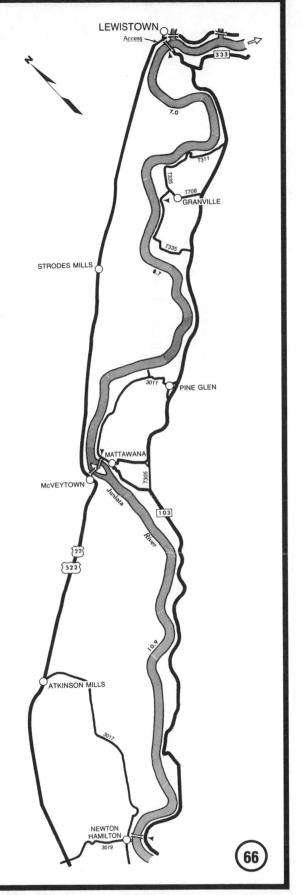

To US Rte. 22

To Huntingdon

PFC Access

ARDENHEIM

Raystown Branch

2.1

22

829

3029   3049

3029

3.7

MILL CREEK

655

MAPLETON

655

Gauge

2020

Juniata

River

3.4

MT. UNION

2026

1.2

KISTLER

ALLENPORT

3.2

3019

522

NEWTON HAMILTON

3017

3017

Aughwick Creek

3.9

103

LEWISTOWN

Access

333

7.0

T311

T335

T708

GRANVILLE

T335

STRODES MILLS

8.7

3011   PINE GLEN

MATTAWANA

T305

McVEYTOWN

Juniata

103

22

522

River

10.9

ATKINSON MILLS

3017

NEWTON HAMILTON

3019

66

East Licking Creek
Tuscarora Creek
Juniata River
Lost Creek

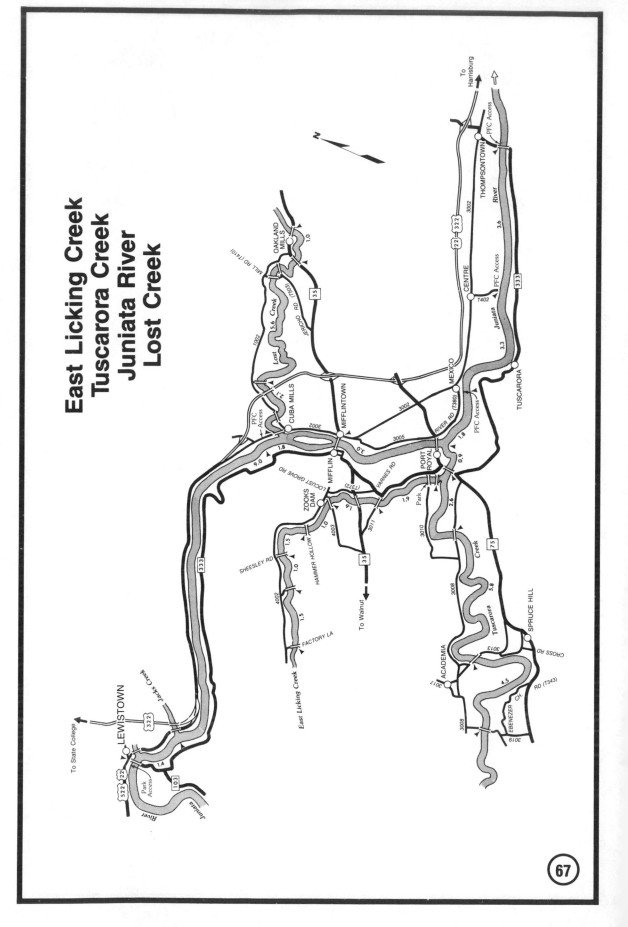

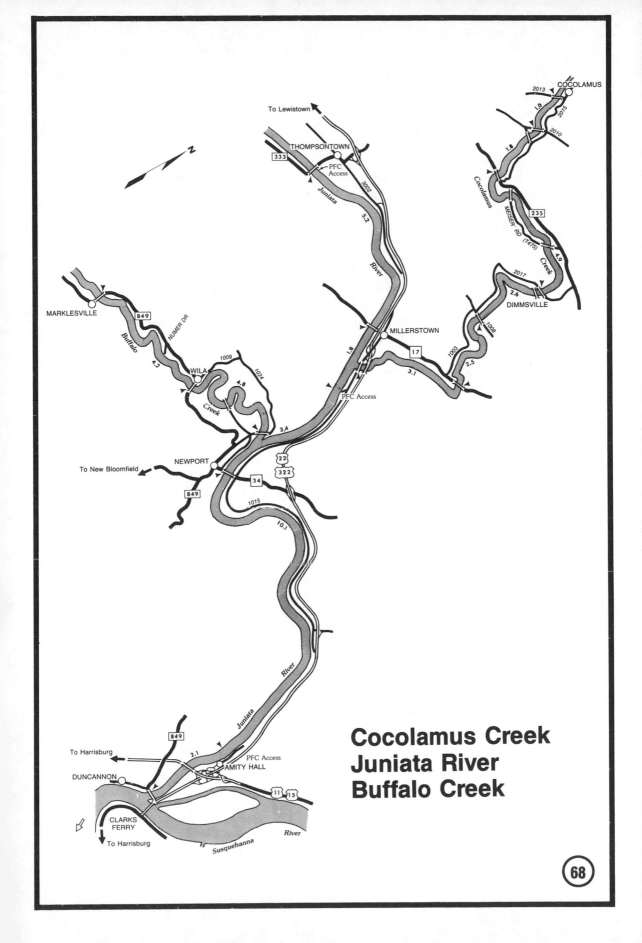

**Cocolamus Creek
Juniata River
Buffalo Creek**

COCOLAMUS
2013
1.0
2015
2010
1.4
Cocolamus
MEISER RD (T479)
235
4.9
Creek
2017
2.6
DIMMSVILLE
1008
2.5
1003
3.1
17
MILLERSTOWN
1.8
PFC Access
To Lewistown
THOMPSONTOWN
333
PFC Access
Juniata
3002
5.2
River
MARKLESVILLE
849
NUMER DR
Buffalo
4.2
WILA
1009
1024
4.8
Creek
3.4
NEWPORT
To New Bloomfield
849
34
22
322
1015
10.1
Juniata
River
849
To Harrisburg
2.1
PFC Access
AMITY HALL
DUNCANNON
11 15
CLARKS
FERRY
Susquehanna River
To Harrisburg

68

a load of grain or coal. Indians followed the Juniata for ages. When the canal era of the 19th century arrived, the Juniata and its Frankstown Branch were chosen as the middle part of the route of the Cross-Pennsylvania Canal. Construction of the Juniata portion of the canal commenced in 1827 and was completed to Hollidaysburg by 1832. Alas, the canal never really flourished, and by 1890 the experiment was turned over to the frogs and cattails.

The most noteworthy reason that the canal failed was the concurrent emergence of the railroad. The Pennsylvania Railroad (later Penn-Central, later Conrail) also followed the banks and bends of the Juniata and both of its forks too. Any paddler quickly appreciates just how important this route remains, as they observe train after train after train rumble by.

The Juniata begins at the confluence of the Frankstown Branch and the Little Juniata, above Huntingdon. Its 101 lazy and peaceful miles are encumbered by only one dam and are free of fences, strainers, and difficult rapids. It is floatable for much of the year, and all of it is easy to reach via speedy Routes 322 and 22. Needless to say, this stream was made for beginners.

There are, surprisingly, no cities and only a few large towns along the Juniata. Civilization has relegated this as a place through which to pass, not stop and stay. With so little population, the stream remains fairly clean, with good fishing. If it were not for the highway and train noise and a frequent presence of summer homes, this would be a classic canoe camping stream.

Section 1. Confluence Frankstown Branch and Little Juniata to Raystown Branch					
Gradient	Difficulty	Distance	Time	Scenery	Map
7	A to 1	10.6	4.0	Fair to Good	65

TRIP DESCRIPTION: This is the only part of the Juniata that is relatively small. It gets off to a poor start, with a dead pool bottled behind a 20-foot power dam. Carry on the left by following a fishermen's path along the outside of a high chain-link fence. The ensuing passage through the narrow cut in Warrior Ridge serves as a fair apology for this drudgery. But the remainder of the run is unnoteworthy, either for excitement or for scenery. Take out at the PFC access, on the right, at the confluence with the Raystown Branch.

HAZARDS: High dam 3.5 miles below start.

WATER CONDITIONS: Canoeable in spring, normally until late May and, in wet years, until early July.

GAUGE: USGS gauges at Huntingdon and Mapleton (call Central PA) should read at least 4.0 feet and 2.6 feet respectively.

Section 2. Raystown Branch to mouth					
Gradient	Difficulty	Distance	Time	Scenery	Map
3	A to 1	90.6	30.0	Fair to Good	66,67,68

TRIP DESCRIPTION: The Juniata is now a mature river. It is a broad stream that carries itself in a grand and serene manner, as it slowly and deliberately advances through a mountainous maze. The initial miles down to Mount Union sheer the last few of several parallel ridges, with the talus slopes of Jacks Narrows being the most impressive and at least momentarily beautiful.

Past Mount Union the river generally parallels the high ridges for many miles at a time, as it seeks a way around them. The water, usually clear if it has not rained recently, flows quite peacefully. Little riffles lie far apart. In summertime the shallows of the upper river can be even slower than usual, as dense shrouds of waterweeds reduce it to a viscous medium. At the other end of the river, down below Newport, a few ledges, up to two feet high, create the only whitewater on the Juniata.

While the surrounding hills are grand, the immediate riverbanks get mixed reviews. Up on the left bank, you can frequently still discover the ruins of stone locks and the overgrown ditch of the old canal. On either bank, far too often, summer camps, often materializing as shanties, old trailers, and rusting (but lived in) hulks of old school buses, fill the bottomlands.

But all civilization along the Juniata is not ugly. Many of the little towns along the river, such as Mifflintown or Newport, complement the trip. Their tranquil personalities often belie the importance, hustle, and bustle that brought some of them into being. For example, sleepy Millerstown, back in the boom times of canal construction, flourished with no fewer than 17 inns, making it a virtual 19th-century Breezewood.

You can easily divide this river into many short segments, thanks to plentiful access via bridges and public and private launch areas. Or just load your canoe with a week's worth of gear, and do the whole thing at once.

HAZARDS: None.

WATER CONDITIONS: Canoeable in spring and summer until mid-August and often again in November and early December.

GAUGE: USGS gauge at Mapleton (call Central PA) should read at least 2.6 feet to canoe above Mount Union. USGS gauge at Newport (call Central PA) should read at least 3.5 feet for the river below Mount Union.

Buffalo Creek

INTRODUCTION: This Buffalo Creek (there are many in Pennsylvania) steals into the broad lower Juniata at Newport. It is small and is prone to the common small stream problems of strainers and dearth of adequate water. But its tiny size draws you closer to the pretty farm and ridge country through which it winds. And that is good. And in addition, it is only 30 short miles from downtown Harrisburg.

Section 1. Pa. Rte. 17 to mouth					
Gradient	Difficulty	Distance	Time	Scenery	Map
14	1 to 2 –	23.6	7.5	Good to Very Good	69,68

TRIP DESCRIPTION: Unquestionably, the section of Buffalo from Pa. Rte. 17 to Pa. Rte. 74 is the prettiest. As it rounds the end of Bilman Ridge, the creek cuts a wild, wooded gorge that is studded with rock outcrops and lush with hemlock. But also, unquestionably, anybody who tries these first miles will have their hands full. For since this section is only passable at very high water, be assured that the muddy torrent will push you through a lot of nasty braiding and into ill-placed strainers, including overhanging alder bushes.

167

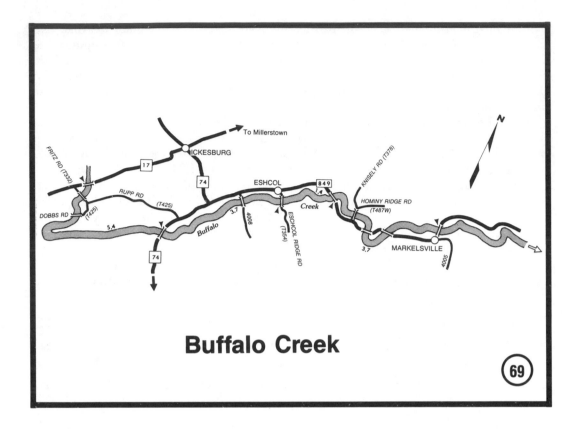

Buffalo Creek

(69)

Those seeking a more reasonable pace should start at Pa. Rte. 74. Strainers still hinder you at least as far down as Markelsville, but not enough to make this a masochistic run. At the same time, fast current and simple riffles hurry you to the Juniata. There are good views, over the low banks, of the thinly populated surrounding valley, while little shale cliffs and a covered bridge add extra interest. Take out above the mouth at the right downstream end of the first railroad bridge.

HAZARDS: Strainers and possibly fences.

WATER CONDITIONS: Canoeable late winter and spring within two days of hard rain.

GAUGE: None. Roughly, USGS gauges at Hogestown, on Conodoguinet Creek, and Shermans Dale, on Sherman Creek (call Central PA), should read over 4.0 feet and 3.1 feet respectively.

Cocolamus Creek

INTRODUCTION: Cocolamus Creek is a tiny mimic of the broad Juniata, to which it feeds. It wiggles and winds through the ridgy obstacles of Juniata and Perry counties by the most indirect route. This is a scenic but rigorous, novice canoe trail, opened up only by exceptionally wet weather.

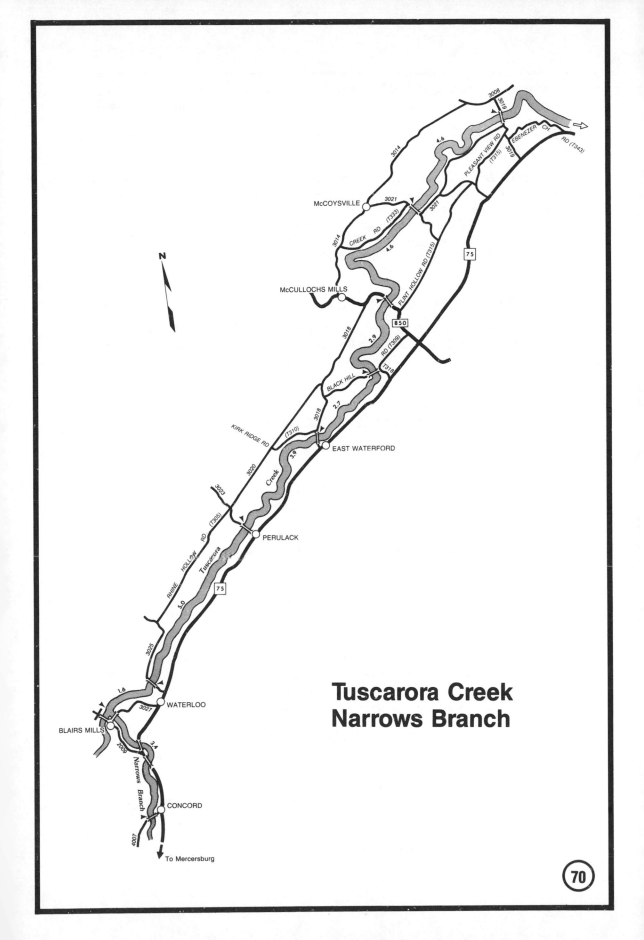

Tuscarora Creek
Narrows Branch

70

TRIP DESCRIPTION: Cocolamus Creek provides a pleasant trip through a series of mountain gaps and thinly populated rural valleys. It passes in and out of farm and forest and bumps up against numerous crumbling shale outcrops. With nearby roads being only lightly traveled, it is a quiet journey. The water moves quickly, and riffles are plentiful. The narrow bed, unfortunately, is repeatedly complicated by fallen trees, snags, logjams, and sharp, undercut bends. An inexperienced or out-of-shape paddler is likely to be victimized. Everything has its price.

HAZARDS: Numerous strainers.

WATER CONDITIONS: Canoeable in late winter and spring within two days of hard rain.

GAUGE: None. Roughly, USGS gauges at Hogestown, on Conodoguinet Creek, and Shermans Dale, on Sherman Creek (call Central PA), should read over 4.0 feet and 3.1 feet respectively.

Tuscarora Creek

INTRODUCTION: Juniata County's Tuscarora Creek is your basic nice canoe stream. Spend a day on it, or maybe even three. You will find it easy to get to, easy to paddle, and easy to grow fond of.

Section 1. Blairs Mills (SR2009) to Port Royal (Pa. Rte. 75)					
Gradient	Difficulty	Distance	Time	Scenery	Map
8*	1	38.2	12.0	Good	70,67
*Narrows Branch drops at 42					

TRIP DESCRIPTION: If the water is high, you can tack on a zesty little whitewater run by putting in 3.4 miles above Blairs Mills on Narrows Branch, at SR4007 in Concord. Hurrying over a cobbly and sometimes bouldery bed, this tiny stream carries you past the pretty talus slopes of a gap through Tuscarora Mountain. The continuous but easy whitewater is suitable for experienced novices.

Tuscarora, in contrast, meanders placidly down its valley, though there are many simple riffles along the way. Here is a rare creek that is free of dams. Deadfalls and fences are unlikely. Only a few concrete fords may trouble the beginner, while some island passages can be annoyingly shallow at lower levels. Small streams are seldom this friendly.

This is a pretty route past old farms and through wooded bottoms — bottoms that support some graceful, silvery beech groves. Views of Tuscarora Mountain and lesser ridges are frequent and uncluttered, as this is a lightly populated valley. Posted land signs are still few up here. This, coupled with the lack of portages, hints that Tuscarora would make a fine springtime, small stream, canoe camping trip. As for day tripping, several bridges, including a graceful covered bridge at Academia, and several fords easily divide this long stream. Pa. Rte. 75, the last take-out on Tuscarora Creek, is 0.9 miles above the mouth.

HAZARDS: Possible strainers.

WATER CONDITIONS: Narrows Branch is only canoeable within 24 hours of hard rain. Tuscarora is canoeable late winter and spring within three to seven days of hard rain.

GAUGE: None. Roughly, USGS gauges at Hogestown, on Conodoguinet Creek, and Shermans Dale, on Sherman Creek (call Central PA), should read over 2.2 feet and 2.5 feet respectively.

East Licking Creek

INTRODUCTION: East Licking Creek slips into Tuscarora Creek behind Port Royal. Draining just a sliver of a valley, it forms a subcompact canoe trail that should please the lucky novice who manages to catch it flowing with enough water.

Section 1. Factory Lane, T359 to mouth					
Gradient	Difficulty	Distance	Time	Scenery	Map
20	1	8.6	2.0	Good	67

TRIP DESCRIPTION: This is a swift and riffly passage. Though it braids often, strainer problems are surprisingly infrequent. The run begins in thick stands of hemlock and hardwood, but soon transforms into a tour of farms and pastures. Low banks provide an excellent opportunity to peruse the thinly populated valley and the mountain ridges that define it. The trip ends all too soon above the mouth and beneath the graceful span of an old covered bridge.

HAZARDS: Occasional strainers.

WATER CONDITIONS: Canoeable late winter and spring within two days of hard rain.

GAUGE: None.

Lost Creek

INTRODUCTION: Lost Creek is worth finding. It is a lovely and lively novice run that creeps into the Juniata River near Mifflintown. A heavy rainfall is the price of admission.

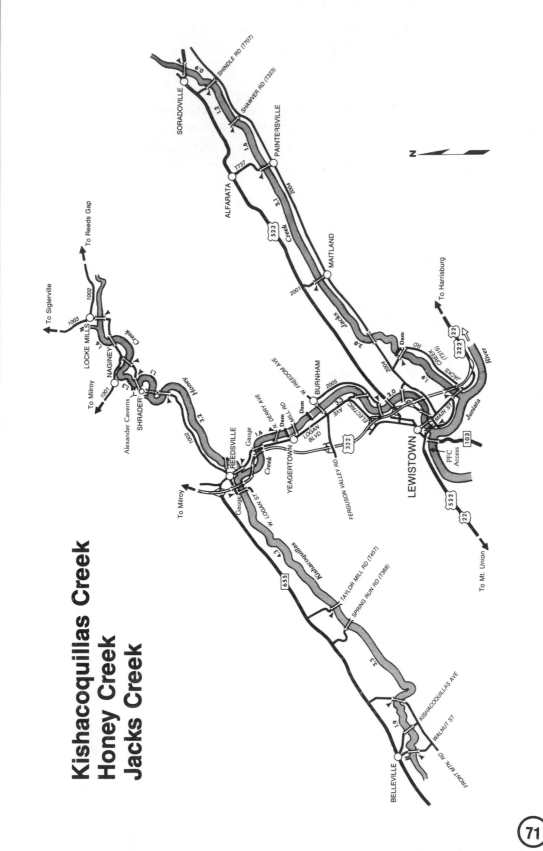

Kishacoquillas Creek
Honey Creek
Jacks Creek

N

To Reeds Gap

To Siglerville

1002

1003

LOCKE MILLS

1004

NAGINEY

Creek

1.4

1001

To Milroy

Alexander Caverns

SHRADER

1.3

1.1

Honey

1007

3.2

SORADOVILLE

0.9

SHINDLE RD (T707)

1.2

SHAWVER RD (T323)

T737

1.6

PAINTERSVILLE

ALFARATA

3.1

2004

522

Creek

MAITLAND

2001

Jacks

3.0

2004

Dam

REEDSVILLE

Gauge

Creek

1.6

N. DERRY AVE

W. FREEDOM AVE

Dam

MILL RD

BURNHAM

2005

3.3

W. LOGAN ST

Gauge

YEAGERTOWN

LOGAN BLVD

ELECTRIC AVE

322

2.0

FERGUSON VALLEY RD

2002

1.9

JACKS CREEK RD (315)

MAIN ST

LEWISTOWN

Juniata

322

To Harrisburg

22

322

River

PFC Access

103

522

22

To Mt. Union

To Milroy

655

4.1

Kishacoquillas

TAYLOR MILL RD (T457)

SPRING RUN RD (T368)

3.3

1.9

KISHACOQUILLAS AVE

WALNUT ST

FRONT MTN. RD

BELLEVILLE

(71)

Section 1. Oakland Mills (Pa. Rte. 35) to mouth					
Gradient	Difficulty	Distance	Time	Scenery	Map
16	1	8.8	3.0	Very Good	67

TRIP DESCRIPTION: Lost Creek provides a surprisingly remote trip through beautiful woodlands, intimate ravines, and past occasional forgotten farms. Though you would most likely explore this creek only in winter or spring, dense growths of hemlock and rhododendron often impart a summertime greenness to the surroundings. The creek rushes over lots of riffles, which are unevenly distributed. There are surprisingly few strainers or fences to trouble you, and you can avoid most of them by starting a mile downstream at the next Rte. 35 bridge. What more could you want?

HAZARDS: Strainers, fences, and a low log footbridge by Oakland Mills.

WATER CONDITIONS: Canoeable late winter and spring within day of hard rain.

GAUGE: Count stones on downstream edge of center pier of second Rte. 35 bridge. A fine level is 6.5 stones down from the top.

Jacks Creek

INTRODUCTION: Jacks Creek flows in the shadow of Shade Mountain, to a meeting with the Juniata River at Lewistown. Many of its good neighbors have maintained this waterway as a living and classic example of America's traditional approach to refuse disposal—dump it over the bank and let the sucker downstream worry about it. You will find few streams in eastern Pennsylvania more plastered in limp cardboard, tattered plastic, and twisted and rusting metal. With so many beautiful streams around Lewistown, why waste your time here?

Section 1. Soradoville (U.S. Rte. 522) to mouth					
Gradient	Difficulty	Distance	Time	Scenery	Map
12	1	11.8	4.0	Good to Poor	71

TRIP DESCRIPTION: This is generally an easy stream to navigate when the water is up. But as far as Paintersville, fallen trees, tortuous and brush-clogged channels, and splits around debris-jammed islands might be a bit much for the beginner. Otherwise, long series of riffles, broken by long pools, typify this run. The only certain portage is around the five-foot dam beneath Jacks Creek Road, T315.

Short woodland interludes, some handsome farms, the wooded and rockbound flank of Jacks Creek Ridge, and the undulating skyline of Shade Mountain remind one of how pretty a cruise this might be. But the valley is heavily populated, crowded with many dwellings and some unsightly and noisy industry, often located right beside the creek. It is many of the residents of the streamside dwellings who pour their rubbish over the bank, right from their backyards, to be carried away in high water and then lodged in their neighbors' yards and in the tangled flood-plain shrubbery for miles below. A compact neighborhood park at U.S. Rte. 22 makes a good take-out (escape).

HAZARDS: Dam at T315 and strainers on the upper miles.

WATER CONDITIONS: Canoeable late winter and spring within two days of hard rain.

GAUGE: None.

Kishacoquillas Creek

INTRODUCTION: Kishacoquillas Creek drains a wide, gently rolling, and intensively culti-vated valley, sandwiched between Stone and Jacks mountains, in Mifflin County. The creek was named for a friendly Indian inhabitant of many moons past. The Indians, of course, friendly or otherwise, are long gone, now replaced by numerous Amish people. Their well-kept farms flourish atop a valley floor of limestone.

Because rainwater is slightly acidic (even without man's alterations), it dissolves limestone, so that beneath this solid-looking landscape hides an incredible system of caves. For this reason, many a brook tumbles off of Stone Mountain straight into yawning pits, called sinkholes, to trav-el many dark, uncharted, stygian miles before emerging as springs that nurture the Kish.

Section 1. Belleville (Walnut Street, T350) to Reedsville (W. Logan Street)					
Gradient	Difficulty	Distance	Time	Scenery	Map
21	1 +	9.4	3.0	Very Good	71

TRIP DESCRIPTION: This is an exceptionally beautiful cruise. After a slow start, past a fac-tory and some big farms, the creek entrenches in an inner gorge of this expansive valley. The wooded flank of Jacks Mountain rises on the right, with the feathery boughs of hemlock trees often shading that bank. On the left lies mostly pasture, broken by groves of cedar and jumbles of wild rose. Few houses intrude on this serene setting. The wildflowers on this southern exposure are outstanding in the spring.

The Kish hurries over an almost continuous chain of easy rock garden rapids formed by a bed of cobbles and boulders. Since the creek can spread fairly wide at times, you want lots of water on this section. Count on being surprised by at least a few fences, in fast spots of course.

HAZARDS: Fences and fallen trees.

WATER CONDITIONS: Canoeable in spring during snowmelt and within two days of hard rain.

GAUGE: Staff gauge on W. Logan Street Bridge (Railroad Street), just upstream of U.S. Rte. 322, Reedsville. Minimal level is 0.5 feet. Abandoned USGS gauge a mile below Reedsville, be-low old U.S. Rte. 322 crossing, on left, should read about 4.7 feet.

Section 2. Reedsville (West Logan Street) to mouth					
Gradient	Difficulty	Distance	Time	Scenery	Map
22	1 to 3 −	7.0	2.5	Poor	71

TRIP DESCRIPTION: If you paddle this section, you trade aesthetics for excitement. The creek turns 90 degrees and cuts a great gap through Jacks Mountain. But it must share this gap, unfortunately, with the busy four lanes of U.S. Rte. 322, a railroad, and the old highway. Then below there, the streambanks are crowded by the homes, industry, and trash of Burnham, Yeagerstown, and Lewistown.

The stream tumbles down technically challenging, bouldery, and sometimes steep rapids, separated by short pools. The best whitewater runs through Burnham and Yeagerstown. Two small dams interrupt this section—a three-footer above Mill Road, in Yeagerstown, runnable on the right (but a carry is still advisable) and an unrunnable six-footer, by the Standard Steel Mill, with a short but rough carry on the right. Below Burnham the rapids begin moderating until the last mile becomes flat. Take out 200 yards below Main Street, Lewistown, on the left by the electrical substation.

HAZARDS: Two dams.

WATER CONDITIONS: Canoeable in spring during snowmelt and within four days of hard rain.

GAUGE: Staff gauge on W. Logan Street Bridge, Reedsville, should read at least 0.4 feet. USGS gauge should read at least 4.4 feet.

Honey Creek

INTRODUCTION: Honey Creek drains the north half of tongue twisting Kishacoquillas Valley, joining the "Kish" at Reedsville. While, at best, a mediocre canoe stream, Honey Creek is a geological conversation piece owing to its leaky limestone foundation. At low flow this creek takes an underground detour through Alexander Caverns, near Shrader. At boatable water levels a flood channel, fortunately, provides a much more well-lit route for paddlers.

Section 1. Locke Mills (SR1002) to mouth					
Gradient	Difficulty	Distance	Time	Scenery	Map
14	1	7.2	2.0	Fair	71

TRIP DESCRIPTION: Locke Mills is a good starting point, as Treaster Run doubles the flow just downstream. Although Honey Creek flows through a pretty and mostly agricultural valley, most of the neighborhood population and minor industry is clustered closely along its banks. At one such industry, a ghostly, old lime plant at Shrader, you find a debris-choked channel on the right—the route to the dark world below. You go left of course, down the flood channel,

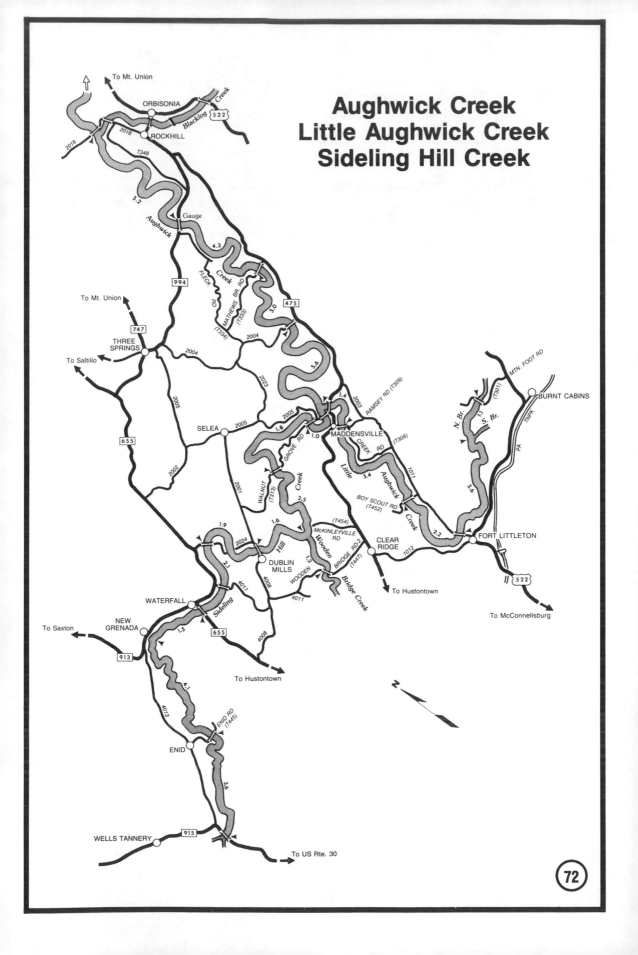

Aughwick Creek
Little Aughwick Creek
Sideling Hill Creek

To Mt. Union

ORBISONIA
ROCKHILL
Blacklog Creek
522
2016
2016
T348
5.2
Aughwick Creek
Gauge
4.3
994
FLECK CREEK RD
MATHEWS BR. RD.
(T334)
(T333)
2004
3.0
475
5.6
To Mt. Union
747
THREE SPRINGS
To Saltillo
2004
2023
2005
1.4
2003
RAMSEY RD (T309)
MTN. FOOT RD
(T301)
BURNT CABINS
N. Br.
1.7
S. Br.
PA TNPK
2005
1.8
GROVE RD
MADDENSVILLE
1.0
CREEK RD
(T308)
3.6
SELEA
2005
Walnut Creek
(T313)
Little
3.4
Aughwick Creek
1011
655
2002
2001
2.5
BOY SCOUT RD
(T452)
2.2
FORT LITTLETON
1.9
2024
1.6
Hill
McKINLEYVILLE RD
(T454)
Wooden
BRIDGE RD-2
CLEAR RIDGE
1012
522
2.1
4011
4008
1.3
WOODEN
BRIDGE RD
(T447)
Bridge Creek
To Hustontown
DUBLIN MILLS
4011
WATERFALL
Sideling
To McConnellsburg
NEW GRENADA
1.5
655
4008
To Saxton
913
To Hustontown
4.1
4013
ENID RD
(T445)
ENID
3.6
N
WELLS TANNERY
915
To US Rte. 30

72

beneath the highway bridge. The flood channel is easy and only slightly complicated by brush. However, just past the next road bridge, where the main creek rejoins, watch out for a dangerously situated woven wire fence in the swift riffle below. About a quarter mile beyond is another woven fence. Except for these fences, a mix of smooth water and easy, rocky riffles make Honey Creek a suitable novice run. Take out at either of two town parks in Reedsville. Also, a fishermen's path at the mouth, on the right, leads back to good parking by the sewage treatment plant.

HAZARDS: Strainers, including two woven wire fences.

WATER CONDITIONS: Canoeable in spring during snowmelt and within three days of hard rain.

GAUGE: Abandoned USGS gauge on Kish, one mile below Reedsville, on the left, below old Rte. 322, should read about 4.5 feet.

Aughwick Creek

INTRODUCTION: Aughwick Creek is a relatively large fork of the Juniata, subtly merging a few miles below Mount Union. Beginners will find this creek an easy path by which to explore the hills and hollows of Huntingdon County's rugged terrain.

Section 1. Maddensville (SR2005) to Pa. Rte. 103					
Gradient	Difficulty	Distance	Time	Scenery	Map
6	1	30.4	10.0	Good	72,73

TRIP DESCRIPTION: The put-in is on Sideling Hill Creek, just above its confluence with Little Aughwick Creek. Aughwick works its way north by a lazy and serpentine path. Though it is generally a smooth route, there are plenty of short and insignificant riffles. In summertime, these riffles turn into fields of flowering waterweeds, with the channel carving only a narrow corridor to the pool below. The surrounding agricultural valley is remarkably unpopulated, especially near the creek where the land is often forested. Good views of surrounding hills and ridges are commonplace. And where the creek bumps up against these hills, there are rows of rock shelves and even a few cliffs with sharply tilting strata. Remember this stream when you are searching for a springtime overnight cruise.

HAZARDS: None.

WATER CONDITIONS: Canoeable in late winter and spring during snowmelt and within five days of hard rain, above Orbisonia, and within ten days below.

GAUGE: Staff gauge on right abutment of Pa. Rte. 997 Bridge should read over 0.0 feet for upper creek and at least minus 0.5 feet for below Orbisonia. Roughly, USGS gauge at Saxton, on Raystown Branch (call Central PA), should read over 3.0 feet to do the entire creek.

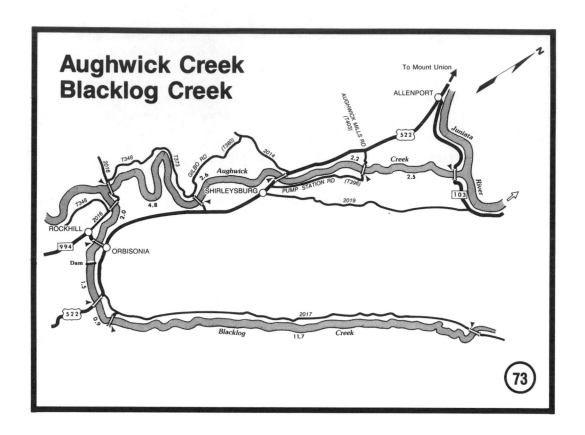

Blacklog Creek

INTRODUCTION: Blacklog Creek rushes out of a long and skinny valley, sandwiched between Shade and Blacklog mountains, to find its way to Aughwick Creek at Orbisonia. It is a pleasant, but mediocre, novice run that one might consider after a period of wet weather in central Pennsylvania.

	Section 1. SR2017 to mouth				
Gradient	**Difficulty**	**Distance**	**Time**	**Scenery**	**Map**
17	1 to 2 –	16.1	5.0	Fair to Good	73

TRIP DESCRIPTION: The put-in is located 9.5 miles up SR2017 from U.S. Rte. 522. Blacklog Creek flows for miles down a straight, gently v-shaped, and pastoral valley—a valley only moderately populated, with most people living up along the road, high above the stream. The paddler sees little of either people or the valley, as the creek is nicely hidden away, first in a tangled and shrubby jungle, then in woodlands. Though the gradient is moderate, it seems as if this creek spends at least half of its time flowing over gravelly riffles. Many fallen trees and a few fences are an annoyance.

At U.S. Rte. 522 the Blacklog gains extra volume and cuts a gap through Blacklog Mountain. The creek assumes a pleasant pool and drop nature, with rapids of up to Class 2 difficulty. You must carry a five-foot dam below the gap. The scenery below the gap is fair, at best, so you might consider ending your trip at Orbisonia. If it is summer or early fall, you can then round off your day with a ride on the East Broad Top Railroad.

HAZARDS: Fences, deadfalls, and a dam.

WATER CONDITIONS: Canoeable late winter and spring during snowmelt or within three days of hard rain.

GAUGE: None on creek. Roughly, USGS gauges at Saxton, on Raystown Branch, and Hogestown, on Conodoguinet Creek (call Central PA for both), should each read about 3.5 feet.

Little Aughwick Creek

INTRODUCTION: Little Aughwick Creek joins with Sideling Hill Creek to form the Aughwick proper. It is a pleasant, perfectly typical ridge and valley stream. But if you must choose between the two forks, Sideling Hill Creek is nicer.

Section 1. Mountain Foot Road, T301 to Maddensville (Pa. Rte. 475)					
Gradient	Difficulty	Distance	Time	Scenery	Map
11	1	11.5	4.0	Good	72

TRIP DESCRIPTION: The put-in is a bit extreme, located on the tiny North Branch of Little Aughwick Creek. But that head start entitles you to a few attractive, remote, woodsy, and unlittered miles down to Fort Littleton, the next access point. From here on down, the scenery varies from forest to farms, from low banks to small rock cliffs, and from empty miles to occasional houses and trailers. The whitewater materializes only as a lot of riffles, but you must still plan on dodging two low-water bridges and maybe some fences.

HAZARDS: Fallen trees, fences, and low-water bridges.

WATER CONDITIONS: Canoeable late winter and spring within three days of hard rain.

GAUGE: None on creek. Roughly, USGS gauges at Hogestown, on Conodoguinet Creek, and Saxton, on Raystown Branch (call Central PA for both), should each read about 3.5 feet.

Sideling Hill Creek

INTRODUCTION: Do not confuse this beauty with the popular Sideling Hill Creek that flows into Maryland, 30 miles to the southwest. Even though it is just as pretty, this tiny tributary to Aughwick Creek is yet a relatively unknown run. Be sure to put it near the top of your scenic, micro-stream hit list.

Section 1. Pa. Rte. 915 to Waterfall (Pa. Rte. 655)					
Gradient	Difficulty	Distance	Time	Scenery	Map
24	1 to 2 +	9.2	3.0	Excellent	72

TRIP DESCRIPTION: As you drive down Pa. Rte. 915 looking for the put-in, be sure not to blink, or you might miss it. That insignificant brook is what you have just driven all this distance to canoe on. Though narrow, it runs deep and quickly disappears between steep and sandy banks into a pine, oak, and hickory forest. A few fallen trees and some fences complicate this otherwise smooth start. The hills then close in to form a shallow gorge decorated by eroded cliffs and outcrops of sandstone. The creek, in turn, commences a busy descent over cobbles, boulders, and little ledges. One rapid is even endowed with several good playing holes. The fun ends too soon at New Granada, with the reappearance of civilization and the passage through a disappointing gap through Sideling Hill. The take-out, Waterfall, is a village, not an obstacle.

HAZARDS: Some deadfalls and fences.

WATER CONDITIONS: Canoeable late winter and spring within three days of hard rain or during snowmelt.

GAUGE: None on creek. Staff gauge on right abutment of Pa. Rte. 994, over Aughwick Creek, should read over 0.7 feet. Roughly, USGS gauge at Saxton, on Raystown Branch (call Central PA), should read about 4.7 feet.

Section 2. Pa. Rte. 655 to SR2005					
Gradient	Difficulty	Distance	Time	Scenery	Map
13	1	10.8	3.5	Very Good	72

TRIP DESCRIPTION: The creek now wanders through an attractive and lonely farm valley, as it weaves through a series of low, pine-covered ridges. For some unknown reason, an unfortunately disproportionate amount of trash fouls the streambanks here. But this is about the only aesthetic flaw that you should find. The gradient on this section remains healthy, but is expressed only as riffles. The take-out is a few yards above the confluence with Little Aughwick Creek.

HAZARDS: Possible trees or fences.

WATER CONDITIONS: Canoeable late winter and spring within four days of hard rain or during snowmelt.

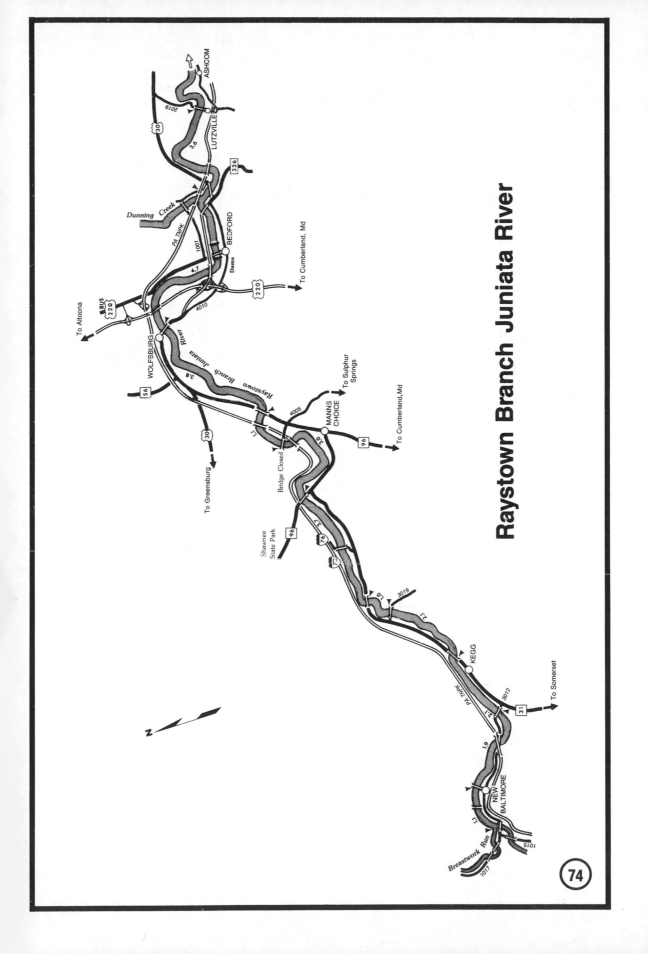

Raystown Branch Juniata River

74

GAUGE: None on creek. Staff gauge on right abutment of Pa. Rte. 994, on Aughwick Creek, should read over 0.5 feet. Roughly, USGS gauge at Saxton, on Raystown Branch, should read about 4.5 feet.

⌐── Raystown Branch Juniata River ──⌐

INTRODUCTION: The Raystown Branch is by far the largest and longest tributary of the Juniata River, draining almost a thousand square miles of south central Pennsylvania and flowing about 118 canoeable and often serpentine miles, from its head in the Allegheny Mountains of Somerset County to the confluence with the Juniata, near Huntingdon. It also has some other significant qualities that people have recognized and exploited. Trailblazers, and later, engineers recognized that the upper river had carved a convenient east-west path through several Appalachian ridges, ultimately just the perfect right-of-way for U.S. Rte. 30 and the Pennsylvania Turnpike to follow. Cooped-up city dwellers and real estate developers recognized the value of the scenic riverfronts and empty bottomlands as a place to fill with strings of second homes. Finally, vote-hungry politicians, smelling pork, recognized what a great place this would be to send the Corps of Engineers to build a major dam. So it is now, for the most part, a flawed river. But maybe you might still like some parts of it, so this is how it goes.

Section 1. SR1015 to second Pa. Rte. 31					
Gradient	Difficulty	Distance	Time	Scenery	Map
40	1 to 2 +	8.2	2.0	Good	74
1.1 @ 76					

TRIP DESCRIPTION: When the water is really high, you can start all the way up 1.5 miles above New Baltimore, where SR1015 crosses at the confluence with Breastwork Run. The first five miles down to Pa. Rte. 31 will delight the competent connoisseurs of tiny whitewater torrents. While rating only a strong Class 2 from a technical standpoint, the initially steep flush over cobbles and little ledges is significantly complicated by numerous fences. Electric, barbed wire, and woven wire—they are all out there waiting to snag you. Then add to this puzzle some fallen trees and a few spots where the channel splits into a twisting array of small passages, and you have a challenging run before you. The gradient then slowly moderates below the first Pa. Rte. 31 bridge, becoming mostly placid by Pa. Rte. 96. As for scenery, the narrow and cultivated valley is mostly attractive, when you get a chance to look at it.

HAZARDS: Strainers and fences.

WATER CONDITIONS: Canoeable in late winter and spring during hard snowmelt or within two days of heavy rain.

GAUGE: None. Judge level by riffles at upper Rte. 31 bridge. USGS gauge at Saxton is too far down to reflect this flashy section.

Raystown Branch
Juniata River
Yellow Creek

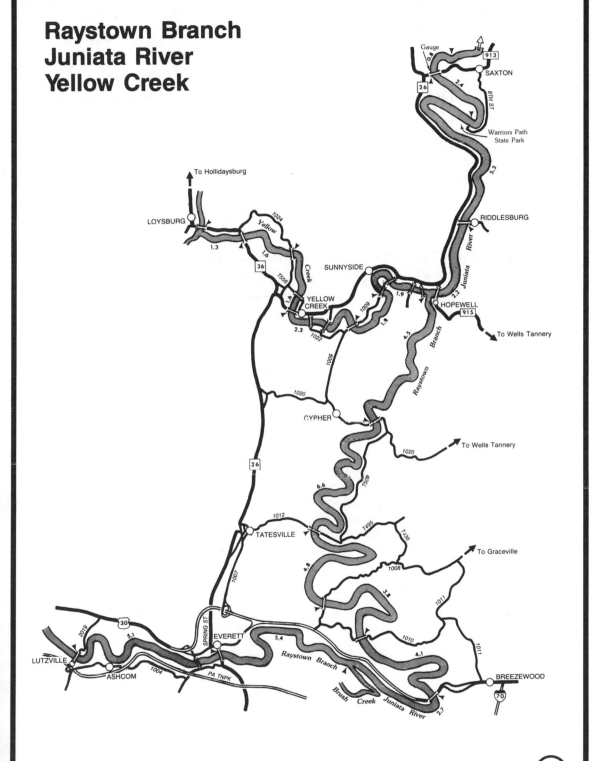

To Hollidaysburg

LOYSBURG

1.3

1024

Yellow

1.6

36

T556

Creek

SUNNYSIDE

1.9

1009

YELLOW
CREEK

1.2

2.3

1022

1.8

1009

1020

CYPHER

26

6.6

1012

TATESVILLE

4.8

1007

LUTZVILLE

2019

30

5.1

ASHCOM

1004

SPRING ST

EVERETT

PA TNPK

5.4

Raystown Branch

Brush Creek

Juniata River

2.7

4.1

1010

3.8

1008

T436

To Graceville

1011

T495

T500

1020

To Wells Tannery

4.5

Raystown Branch

2.2

Juniata River

HOPEWELL

915

To Wells Tannery

RIDDLESBURG

5.3

Warriors Path
State Park

2.4

8TH ST

Gauge

0.6

26

913

SAXTON

BREEZEWOOD

70

75

Section 2. Pa. Rte. 31 to Breezewood (U.S. Rte. 30)					
Gradient	Difficulty	Distance	Time	Scenery	Map
5	1	33.1	11.0	Good to Poor	74,75

TRIP DESCRIPTION: This section offers few rewards. Shortly below the put-in is a sprawling trailer park, the first of many, along with many scattered houses in between. It is difficult to escape the noise from, not to mention the view of, several busy nearby highways. The now flat water is only occasionally broken by a riffle or two, and fallen trees may still complicate things as far down as Bedford. As for dams, there are two: both in Bedford. You can run the right side of the three-footer, just above Bus. Rte. 220, while a quarter mile downstream, the next three-foot dam has a roller that would justify a carry. The best part of this section, a still relatively unspoiled stretch, runs below Bedford, between U.S. Rte. 30 and Everett.

HAZARDS: Some deadfalls and two dams in Bedford.

WATER CONDITIONS: Canoeable in late winter and spring during snowmelt and within week of rain, above Bedford, and anytime until late May, below Bedford.

GAUGE: USGS gauge at Saxton (call Central PA) should read over 2.0 feet.

Section 3. U.S. Rte. 30 to Warriors Path State Park					
Gradient	Difficulty	Distance	Time	Scenery	Map
5	1	31.3	10.5	Fair to Good	75

TRIP DESCRIPTION: The Raystown Branch passes under Rte. 30 for the last time just west of busy Breezewood, fast food capital of the world, and from there heads in a generally northeastward direction, as streams in this part of Appalachia are supposed to do. But it is a most indirect path, as the river forms great bends and loops, reaching almost harmonic motion as it bounces back and forth between parallel and shale-covered ridges. It is a river of long placid pools, separated by long series of riffles that are formed by tiny ledges and gravel bars. This is a pretty section that would be beautiful, were it not so often interrupted by monstrous strings of summer cottages. Take out at the launching ramp just inside the entrance of the state park or at a town park west of Saxton.

HAZARDS: None.

WATER CONDITIONS: Canoeable from late winter until late June and again in late fall, except in dry years.

GAUGE: USGS gauge at Saxton should read over 1.7 feet.

Raystown Branch Juniata River
Great Trough Creek

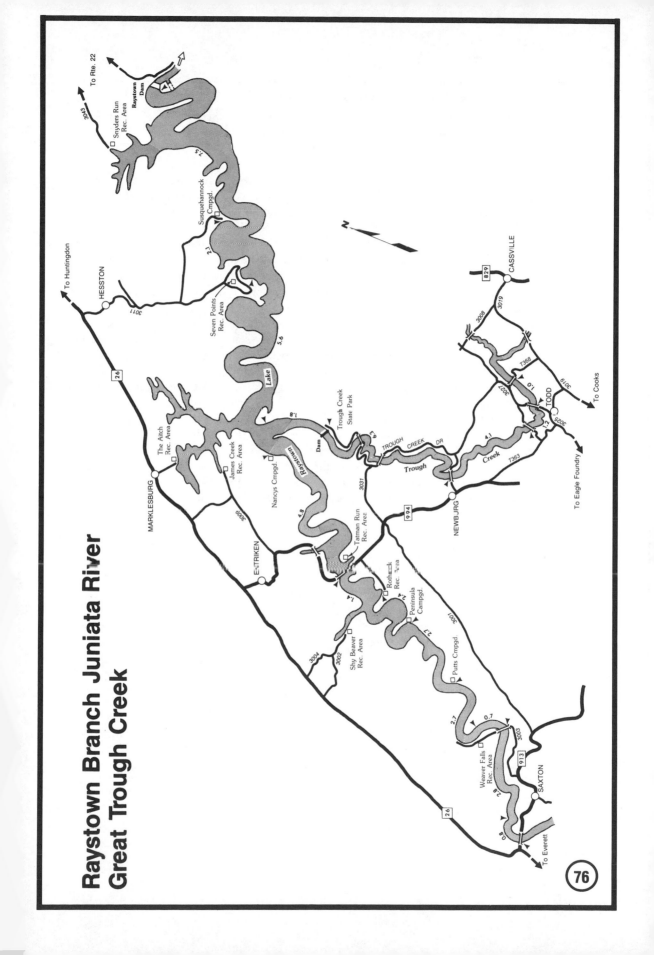

Section 4. *Warriors Path State Park to Raystown Dam*					
Gradient	Difficulty	Distance	Time	Scenery	Map
0	A to 1	36.0	17.5	Good	75,76

TRIP DESCRIPTION: Just below some rebar-studded dam remains at Saxton, the free-flowing Raystown Branch sputters to a dead halt—a victim of big-time dam building. What did we lose?

Like the river above, the Raystown Branch used to meander back and forth between a great mountain and some lesser ridges. It might have been an outstanding float stream if so many miles of its banks had not been lined by endless and drab summer camps and the roads that served them. Privacy and quiet were at a premium. The water was often sluggish and there was even a three-mile-long pool backed behind a medium-size dam (to carry of course).

What did we gain? Thirty miles of water that goes nowhere, filled with water skiers, motorboats, and their vile internal combustion exhaust fumes. On the other hand, the shores are now all government owned and undeveloped, except for a handful of well-designed campgrounds and recreation areas. There are even three boat-in camping areas. And if you visit in the off season, the crowds and the speedboat jockeys will be gone, and peace and quiet will be yours. For a man-made lake, it is surprisingly attractive.

Access to Raystown Lake is generally good. There are eight official boat launch ramps, in addition to the more typical access that paddlers are accustomed to, that is, numerous roadsides, roadheads, overlooks, and bridges. If you are taking an extended trip, and you must portage the dam, it is tough going. This dam is a big one—rising 285 feet above the riverbed. The best and shortest portage route is up the right edge of the dam (which is officially trespassing on U.S. Government property) to the visitors' center overlook, then down the access road (legal) which runs diagonally down and across the face of the dam, and onward to the tailrace pool. There may be a potential and more secluded route over the narrow ridge, east of the dam and emergency spillway.

HAZARDS: None.

WATER CONDITIONS: Above lake, same as Section 3. The lake is open from March thaw until December freeze-up.

GAUGE: Above lake, same as Section 3.

Section 5. *Raystown Dam to mouth*					
Gradient	Difficulty	Distance	Time	Scenery	Map
3	1 –	5.4	1.5	Good	65

TRIP DESCRIPTION: A final short and free-flowing run is possible from the dam, or more conveniently, a half mile downstream at Corbins Island Picnic Area, to the Fish and Boat Commission access area at the mouth. This section gives a taste of the original serene mountain river, minus any development blight.

HAZARDS: None.

WATER CONDITIONS: Usually canoeable, except in dry fall.

GAUGE: None.

Great Trough Creek

INTRODUCTION: Great Trough Creek feeds Raystown Lake with waters gathered from the rugged ridges and plateau of south central Huntingdon County. To get from ridge to lake, it cuts a long and rugged gorge (you might say a trough) through the plateau-like Terrace Mountain. Flowing mostly within Rothrock State Forest and Trough Creek State Park, this is one of the wilder and woodsier runs in this part of the state. And to add iceing to the cake, Trough Creek is also a fine whitewater run.

Section 1. T368 to Trough Creek State Park (Ice Mine)					
Gradient	Difficulty	Distance	Time	Scenery	Map
26	1 to 3 –	12.6	4.0	Good to Very Good	76

TRIP DESCRIPTION: The put-in at T368 is the first available access below the confluence of Great and Little Trough creeks. You can also begin your trip on either fork, but numerous fences and downed trees would discourage the effort.

The quiet creek wanders, for the most part, way back in the forest, past steep hillsides, in the shadows of which grow dense and green groves of hemlock. Only a few houses are visible from the water, while a few logged areas are the only blemishes. Eventually some riffles appear, and then, almost suddenly, the creek tilts downhill to rush over long and mild rapids punctuated by short pools. If the water is high, this becomes a busy, bouncy, and uncomplicated ride, while at lower levels one must work hard to pick through rock gardens of cobbles, little ledges, and small boulders. The creek rushes down through the pretty state park, but past ugly gabion retaining walls, to a climactic plunge over a four-foot dam. The dam has a thrilling and runnable sluice on the left. Take out immediately below on the right, as a hundred yards downstream the creek drowns in the backwaters of Raystown Lake. If you have time to be a tourist while you are down there, inspect the Ice Mine, a strange natural refrigerator, and hike the trail up to Balanced Rock.

HAZARDS: Dam at end.

WATER CONDITIONS: Canoeable in late winter and spring during snowmelt and within three days of hard rain.

GAUGE: None. Judge by scouting from road in state park.

Yellow Creek

INTRODUCTION: Yellow Creek is a tiny tributary to the placid Raystown Branch Juniata, entering the big one at Hopewell. It spills from one mountain valley to another to form a zesty, little whitewater path through scenic Bedford County.

Section 1. Loysburg (Pa. Rte. 36) to mouth					
Gradient	Difficulty	Distance	Time	Scenery	Map
24	1 to 3 –	10.5	3.0	Good	75
2 @ 43					

TRIP DESCRIPTION: Put in at the Pa. Rte. 36 Bridge at Loysburg, where Beaver Creek injects the critical flow to help you clear the shallows below. Smooth water allows you to enjoy the rocky scenery of Loysburg Gap through Tussey Mountain until, quite suddenly, the creek tilts downhill. The muddy waters begin by dashing through patches of small boulders, but then settle to a steady and continuous descent over gravel bars and rock gardens. Be alert for low-slung cables. The action ends near Pa. Rte. 26, and the remaining miles revert to a mostly smooth passage. An old steel truss at the mouth offers an easy exit.

Yellow Creek offers miles of your basic, no-frills, central Pennsylvania mountain scenery. Attractive farms cover much of the bottomland and rolling valley, while steep and wooded ridges rise all around. Peculiar to this creek is the great number of black walnut trees that dot its banks. If you paddle by in late fall, grab one of these trees' blackened fruits off of the ground, and try to beat, battle, and break you way through its formidable armor to its sweet meat. You will then understand why you never see any fat squirrels in black walnut country.

HAZARDS: Several fences, low cables, and some low bridges.

WATER CONDITIONS: Canoeable late winter and spring during fast snowmelt or within three days of hard rain.

GAUGE: None on creek. Roughly, USGS gauge at Saxton (call Central PA) should read over 6.0 feet.

Brush Creek

INTRODUCTION: You usually do not associate scenic canoe tours with interstate highways and hamburger joints. Yet, just four miles south of busy Breezewood, on I-70 (two exits to be exact), wedged between the Interstate and the Pennsylvania Turnpike, is the exception to the rule. Here you will find little Brush Creek. Hidden from the hurry, noise, and clutter, it quietly flows in great, eccentric loops through a trough cut in the rolling and high valley between Polish Mountain and Rays Hill. Only of novice difficulty, Brush Creek can be enjoyed by all who are quick enough to catch it after a rain.

Section 1. Pa. Rte. 915 to mouth					
Gradient	Difficulty	Distance	Time	Scenery	Map
12	1	14.2	4.5	Good to Very Good	77

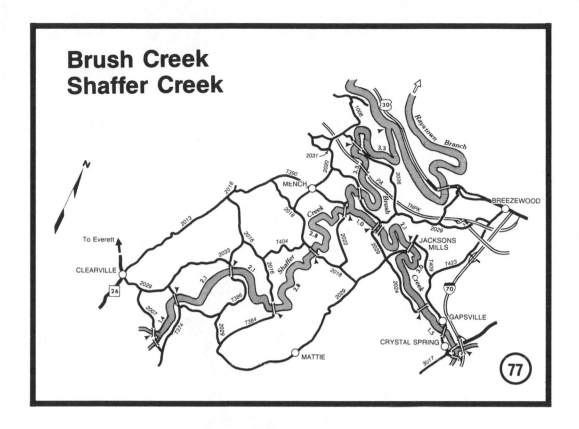

**Brush Creek
Shaffer Creek**

TRIP DESCRIPTION: The best put-in spot is directly beneath the I-70 Bridge that spans both Pa. Rte. 915 and Little Brush Creek. Following a lackluster pass through the gap in Rays Hill with I-70, the creek disappears into a land of little farms and big woods. Frequent north exposures are usually crowded with stands of hemlock and rhododendron. Lichen-mottled, red rock outcrops protrude from many a steep hillside, and there are even some high cliffs towering above the rustic old Jackson Mill. Speaking of rustic, do you like covered bridges? There are three of them, all beauties, on Brush Creek.

This is an easy stream, with swift current and many brief riffles. As for "big" drops, a little weir at the USGS gauging station at SR2024 will have to do. You can run it over the center. Only a sporting riffle remains of the dam at Jackson Mill. Beware though of several barbed wire and electric fences and a few fallen trees.

The best take-out is at the miniature golf course on the left, about 50 yards down the Raystown Branch. This is private, so get permission first. Otherwise, it is an additional 2.7-mile paddle down to the U.S. Rte. 30 Bridge.

HAZARDS: Fallen trees and fences.

WATER CONDITIONS: Canoeable late winter and spring within three days of hard rain.

GAUGE: None. Roughly, USGS gauge at Saxton, on Raystown Branch (call Central PA), should read about 4.0 feet.

189

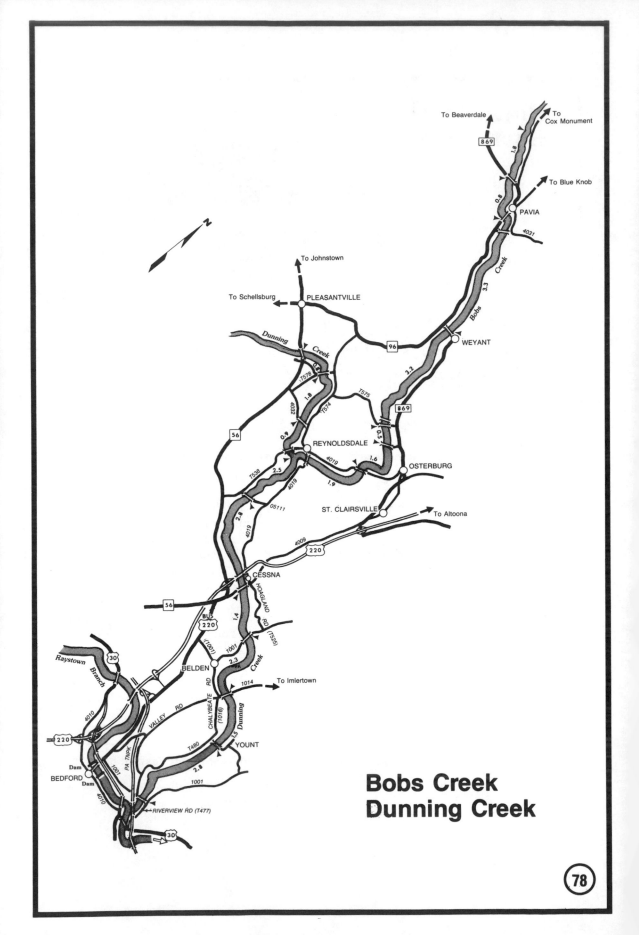

Bobs Creek
Dunning Creek

78

Shaffer Creek

INTRODUCTION: Shaffer Creek is a micro-stream that feeds Bedford County's Brush Creek. Interestingly, this creek is formed by the confluence of Chapman Run and another Brush Creek. Though the names may be plain, the creeks are fancy.

Section 1. SR2007 to mouth					
Gradient	Difficulty	Distance	Time	Scenery	Map
18	1	11.2	4.0	Good	77

TRIP DESCRIPTION: SR2007 crosses both Brush Creek and Chapman Run just above their confluence. Put in on the Brush Creek fork. The creek works a crooked route through an even mix of woodland and rolling, rural valley, all of which is often visible to the paddler, thanks to the creek's low banks. This is a thinly populated valley where most people reside on ridges far away from the water. As on Brush Creek, little cliffs of reddish shale and sandstone often decorate the streamside.

Contrary to what one might expect, this creek is not an obstacle course. There are relatively few fallen trees and fences across the way, but count on carrying a low wooden bridge, shortly after the start. Slightly steeper but no more difficult than Brush Creek, this run is spiced by lots of riffles, swift little chutes, and broken ledges. Then to top things off, there is even easy egress, thanks to a convenient ford just below the mouth.

HAZARDS: Low bridge, fences, and trees.

WATER CONDITIONS: Canoeable late winter and spring within three days of hard rain.

GAUGE: None. Roughly, USGS gauge at Saxton, on Raystown Branch (call Central PA) should read about 4.0 feet.

Dunning Creek

INTRODUCTION: Dunning Creek is a major feeder to the Raystown Branch, joining just downstream of Bedford. It is a dull and easily forgettable stream, mostly suitable for beginners and most likely to please only the easily pleased.

Section 1. Pa. Rte. 56 to mouth					
Gradient	Difficulty	Distance	Time	Scenery	Map
6	1	17.1	5.0	Poor to Good	78

TRIP DESCRIPTION: The first short bit of Dunning Creek, down to Reynoldsdale, is just a tiny run—a highwater cruise only. It is swift and full of riffles, including a fun little chute through a weir. Flowing through woods and past crumbly shale cliffs, it is fairly scenic. But this does not last long. If you do not like the strings of summer cottages at the start and through Reynoldsdale, then proceed no farther than Reynoldsdale.

With the addition of Bobs Creek, Dunning settles into an insignificant gradient. Most of the path is now flat and swift. Being unusually narrow and deep, this creek is passable at slightly lower levels than you might expect. The scenery alternates between banks that are intensively developed with long lines of summer homes, and quiet stretches of farms and woodlands. But high eroded banks often impede your view into this pretty valley. Take out beneath the noisy Pennsylvania Turnpike on Riverview Drive.

HAZARDS: Strainers above Reynoldsdale.

WATER CONDITIONS: Canoeable late winter and spring during snowmelt or within three days of hard rain, above Reynoldsdale, and within ten days below.

GAUGE: None. Roughly, USGS gauges at Saxton, on Raystown Branch, and Williamsburg, on Frankstown Branch (call Central PA for both), should read over 4.0 feet and 5.0 feet respectively to canoe above Reynoldsdale, and over 3.0 feet and 4.0 feet to canoe below. If USGS ever restores the outside staff on their gauge by SR1014, near Belden, 2.3 feet is adequate for paddling below Reynoldsdale.

Bobs Creek

INTRODUCTION: When the relentless spring sun beats down on the snow-laden slopes of Blue Knob Ski Area, skiers may sorrow, but paddlers rejoice. Part of that meltwater will be filling Bobs Creek, a splashy and exhilarating downhill run in its own right.

Section 1. 1.7 miles above Pa. Rte. 869 to mouth					
Gradient	Difficulty	Distance	Time	Scenery	Map
37	1 to 3 –	13.1	3.5	Fair to Good	78
2.6 @ 74					

TRIP DESCRIPTION: It is the first half dozen miles that make this creek worth visiting. To reach the put-in, turn off of Pa. Rte. 869, west of Pavia, onto the road to the Cox Monument. Follow 1.7 miles to where the road hits the tiny torrent, and jump in. The clear and fast whitewater is almost uninterrupted as far as Pavia. It is relatively untechnical, but very pushy, short on eddys, and bristles with ill-placed strainers. You may be too busy to notice the beautiful surrounding woodland scenery. The gradient gradually decreases below Pavia, but remains healthy. Watch out for a few trees and fences. Then, below Weyant, the water starts to turn flat, and by Osterburg Bobs Creek becomes clearly a beginner's run. Though the open farm valley is pretty, the perspective from the creek is often disappointing. Whitewater paddlers would probably choose to exit at Weyant, while novices will start there and perhaps continue onto Dunning Creek.

HAZARDS: Strainers located on fast water.

WATER CONDITIONS: Canoeable late winter and spring during hard snowmelt or within two days of hard rain, above Weyant, and three days below.

GAUGE: None. Roughly, USGS gauges at Saxton, on Raystown Branch, and Williamsburg, on Frankstown Branch (call Central PA for both), should each be about 6.5 to 7.0 feet to start at the top. Levels of 4.0 feet and 5.0 feet respectively are adequate for paddling below Weyant.

Standing Stone Creek

INTRODUCTION: Standing Stone Creek is a scenic Juniata tributary that drains the north end of Huntingdon County. When the first visitors arrived here, at the creek's mouth, they found an Indian camp whose lodges were arranged in a circle, centered by a 14-foot-high, six-inch-square stone pillar, marked with petroglyphs. When the Indians left, they took the stone with them. But the creek's name remains in memory of that odd monument.

Section 1. McAlevys Fort (Pa. Rte. 26) to mouth

Gradient	Difficulty	Distance	Time	Scenery	Map
6	1	22.0	7.0	Good	65

TRIP DESCRIPTION: You can begin paddling Standing Stone Creek at Pa. Rte. 26 in McAlevys Fort. But first take a drive up to its headwaters in Logan State Forest, up in a jumble of ridges that form the county line. There you will find Alan Seeger Natural Area, where a footpath leads down through a magnificent grove of huge virgin hemlocks. At the base of these giants a clear Standing Stone Creek braids through the roots and rhododendron to the valley below.

At McAlevys Fort, in the valley below, a murky Standing Stone Creek flows past the put-in, carrying precious topsoil from the farms that now flank it. Soil conservation problems aside, this is an exceptionally beautiful farm valley, and the creek is a splendid way to tour it. For most of its length, the creek avoids Rte. 26, along which much of the valley's population clusters. The pretty farms are balanced by an abundance of floodplain forest and steep, wooded mountainsides.

For all of this section, Standing Stone Creek provides a mostly smoothwater cruise, broken by wide-open gravel riffles. Though fences are rare here, be alert for some anyway. Because the creek is relatively wide for its volume, avoid a low water cruise, as it can be tedious. The best take-out in Huntingdon is on the right, in the town park, at the waterworks. This saves you a carry around a dangerous five-foot dam.

HAZARDS: A dam at the end and possible fences.

WATER CONDITIONS: Canoeable late winter and spring during snowmelt or within three days of hard rain.

GAUGE: Black-painted staff gauge on left abutment of Rte. 26, south of Center Union, should read over 1.6 feet. Staff gauge on right abutment of SR1001, at Cornpropsts Mill, should read over 2.2 feet. Roughly, USGS gauge at Huntingdon, on Juniata (call Central PA), should read 4.5 to 5.0 feet.

Shaver Creek

INTRODUCTION: Shaver Creek is a small tributary to the far upper Juniata, in Huntingdon County. Although only runnable after lots of rain, this is a fairly safe stream for novices to tackle in the spring.

Section 1. Mooresville (Pa. Rte. 305) to mouth					
Gradient	Difficulty	Distance	Time	Scenery	Map
8	1	10.2	3.5	Good	65

TRIP DESCRIPTION: Shaver Creek follows a usually twisting route across wide bottomlands at the base of a rolling and rural valley. The paddler can see plenty of the attractive countryside this way, with a minimum of distraction. The water is mostly flat, but swift, being only broken by the simplest of gravel bar riffles. Take the left channel to avoid the ruins of an old dam about two miles above Petersburg. You can expect a few fallen trees with which to wrestle, spread out all along the way, but fences are usually absent from this stream. The town park behind the fire hall in Petersburg makes a good take-out.

HAZARDS: Fallen trees and fences.

WATER CONDITIONS: Canoeable late winter and spring during snowmelt and within three days of hard rain.

GAUGE: Staff gauge on right abutment of T511 ends at 1.7 feet. About 0.5 feet would be minimal level. Roughly, USGS gauge at Huntingdon, on Juniata (call Central PA), should be reading 4.5 to 5.0 feet.

Little Juniata River

INTRODUCTION: The Little Juniata was once the stinky, black sewer for a stinky, black paper mill in Tyrone. But the mill is now gone, the water now sparkles, fish now abound, and one of the most enjoyable novice whitewater cruises in central Pennsylvania remains. Like the Juniata, this is also a good trip for train buffs and admirers of railroad bridge architecture. In just the 16 miles between Tyrone and the mouth, there are 17 railroad bridges, many of these being ancient, stone arch masterpieces. Perhaps we should rename this Conrail Creek.

Little Juniata River
Spruce Creek

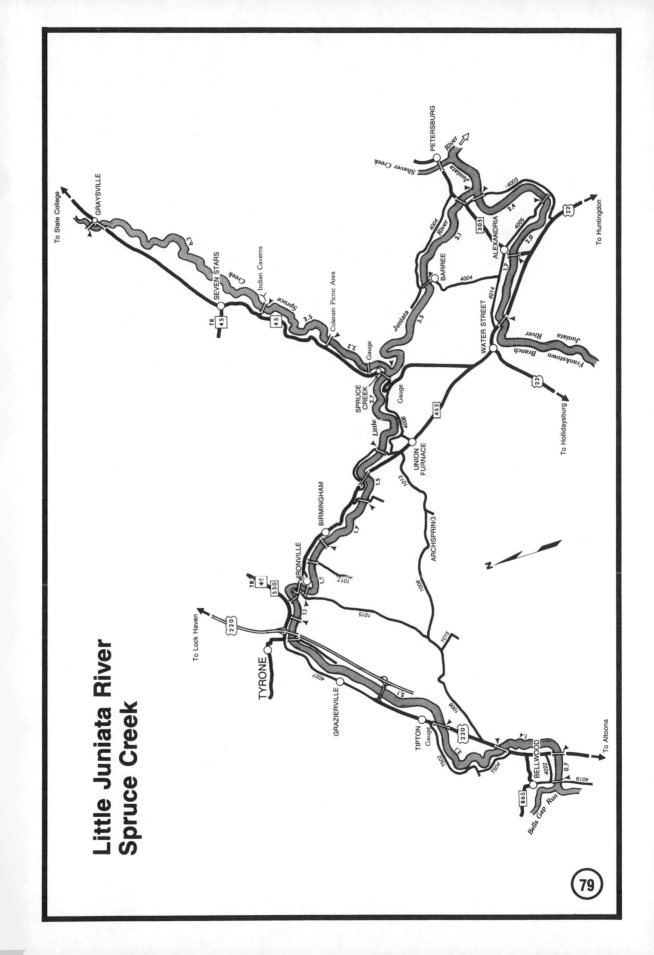

79

Section 1. Bellwood (SR4019) to mouth					
Gradient	Difficulty	Distance	Time	Scenery	Map
14	1 to 2	25.4	8.0	Poor to Excellent	79

TRIP DESCRIPTION: Bells Gap Run promotes the Little Juniata to navigable size at Bellwood. The river here is just a creek—a swift and riffly passage that would be fairly scenic were it not decorated by such copious quantities of trash. But most paddlers choose to start about a half mile below Tyrone, below a reach of wide shallows. The stream now begins cutting a gorge through a handful of ridges and the valleys in between. Although the gorge is cluttered with roads, railroads, towns, quarries, and junkyards, it is still a remarkably pleasant setting. And if you still yearn for the wild and unspoiled, one beautiful loop in the gap through Tussey Mountain, below Spruce Creek, shakes free of even the tenacious railroad.

Little ledges and cobble bars form countless rapids and riffles. Some are fairly long and some are fairly bouncy, but all are within reach of novices with moderate whitewater experience. Watch out for a strong hydraulic at a ford at Ironville. Also, be aware that with all the good access, this is a popular fishing stream. So please take care to give the anglers a wide berth.

Most paddlers choose to take out at Barree. The remaining miles, through a wide valley, are not quite as interesting or as fast as above. Those who follow the Little Juniata to the very end can easily exit on the right, at the mouth, at SR4003.

HAZARDS: Bridge piers in fast current and possible strainers.

WATER CONDITIONS: Canoeable late winter, spring, and often again in November and December, during snowmelt and within week of rain. In average year this creek is usually floatable through most of March, April, and May and often rises to good levels after summer rains.

GAUGE: Old USGS gauge downstream left of U.S. Rte. 220, Tipton, should be at least 2.5 feet for section above Tyrone. USGS gauge on right bank of Little Juniata River, a half mile upstream of Pa. Rte. 45 Bridge, Spruce Creek (call Central PA or inspect on site), should be at least 2.9 feet to start at Bellwood and 2.5 feet to start at Ironville. Roughly, USGS gauge at Huntingdon, on Juniata (call Central PA), should be about 2.8 feet to start at Bellwood and 2.0 feet to start at Ironville.

Spruce Creek

INTRODUCTION: Spruce Creek is a swift little trout stream that rushes into the Little Juniata several miles below Tyrone. The upper part of this creek, unfortunately, has at least one adjacent landowner who objects to paddlers floating through his property. So paddlers wishing to avoid confrontations should only consider attempting the last few miles of Spruce Creek, below Indian Caverns.

Section 1. *Indian Caverns to mouth*					
Gradient	Difficulty	Distance	Time	Scenery	Map
30	1 to 2	4.7	1.5	Fair to Good	79

TRIP DESCRIPTION: By far, the nicest part of this stream lies in the 6.3 miles between Graysville and Indian Caverns. Here Spruce Creek rushes through an isolated, velvety, and pastoral landscape, backed by high mountainsides and fronted by groves of hemlock and a few pretty farm houses. But an abundance of barbed wire fences, low bridges, and trees force you to sooner or later set foot (trespass) on the surrounding land.

Below Indian Caverns the creek still provides a pretty journey, as it bumps against mountains and hills. But the immediate floodplain is heavily developed with summer homes. The water is fun, being comprised of a busy sequence of riffles and rapids and numerous sharp, little drops over fish weirs. Two two-foot weirs, located near the end, form strong hydraulics. Take out at the mouth on the left.

HAZARDS: Trees and fences.

WATER CONDITIONS: Canoeable late winter and spring during hard snowmelt and within two days of hard rain.

GAUGE: Painted canoe gauge on right abutment of T515 (half mile above mouth) — zero is zero canoeing level. Roughly, USGS gauge at Huntingdon, on Juniata (call Central PA), should read over 5.0 feet.

Frankstown Branch Juniata River

INTRODUCTION: The Frankstown Branch starts on the slopes of the Allegheny Front, south of Altoona. It forges a sometimes scenic, novice to beginner path across Blair County to join the Little Juniata near Alexandria. It also once provided the path for the Pennsylvania Canal's westward journey.

Building canals up and down river valleys was no relatively big deal, even back in the 1820s. But nature, unfortunately, never cut a valley through the formidable Allegheny Front. Passing a canal through or over that barrier was a big deal. So the engineers resorted to a new and exciting technology. They built a 37-mile long "portage" railroad that included a series of ten inclined planes, to surmount the 1,400-foot rise from Hollidaysburg to the summit and the nearly 1,200-foot descent down to Johnstown. But this was not your typical unload, carry, and reload style portage. The railroad carried the entire canal boat, its cargo within, over the mountain. Almost. For canal boats used on this section of the canal were segmented. Thus, upon reaching either terminus, a boat would be disassembled into a few large segments, each to be loaded on a separate railcar. Thus began one of the earliest experiments in containerized freight. An endless hemp cable, using descending boats as counterbalances, tugged the load upward. Horses and mules and, later, steam locomotives pulled the boats across the level stretches. Too bad nobody skied back in those days. What a great lift system this would have made.

Frankstown Branch
Juniata River
Clover Creek

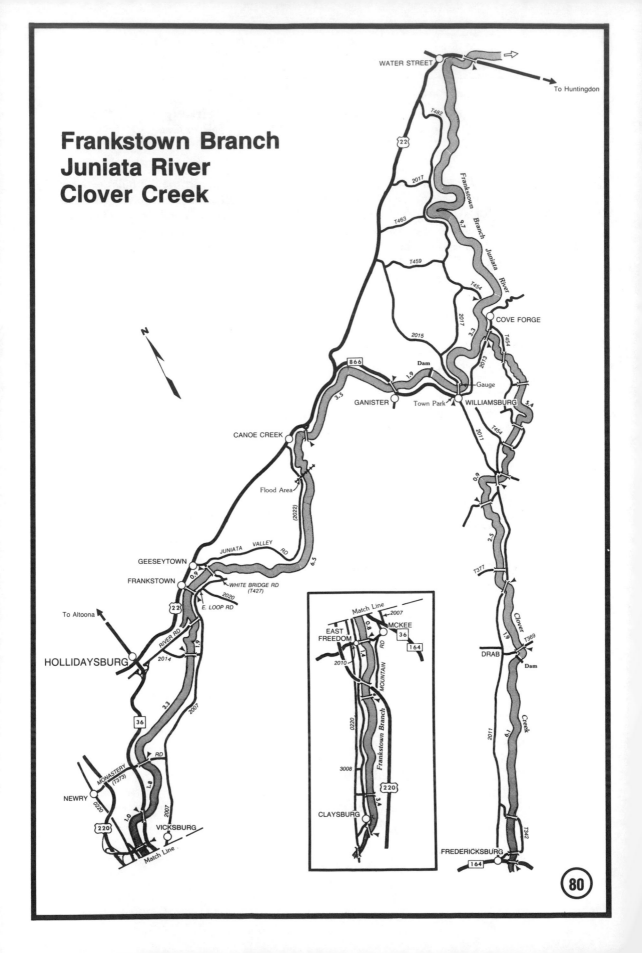

WATER STREET

To Huntingdon

T482

22

2017

T463

Frankstown Branch Juniata River

9.7

T459

T454

2017

COVE FORGE

2015

3.3

T454

866

Dam

2013

1.9

5.4

GANISTER

Town Park

Gauge

WILLIAMSBURG

3.5

CANOE CREEK

2011

Flood Area

0.9

(2022)

2.5

JUNIATA VALLEY RD

6.5

T377

GEESEYTOWN

0.9

FRANKSTOWN

WHITE BRIDGE RD (T427)

Clover

1.9

T369

2020

DRAB

E. LOOP RD

Dam

To Altoona

22

RIVER RD

1.9

2014

HOLLIDAYSBURG

3.3

2007

36

MONASTERY (T373)

RD

1.8

NEWRY

0220

1.9

2011

Creek

2007

1.0

220

VICKSBURG

Match Line

Match Line

2007

EAST FREEDOM

0.8

MCKEE

36

164

2010

MOUNTAIN RD

0220

FRANKSTOWN BRANCH

3008

220

3.4

CLAYSBURG

FREDERICKSBURG

164

T342

80

Section 1. Claysburg (Old Bedford Road) to Frankstown (SR2007)					
Gradient	Difficulty	Distance	Time	Scenery	Map
17	1 to 1 +	13.6	4.0	Poor to Good	80
3.4 @ 29					

TRIP DESCRIPTION: These are the formative miles for the Frankstown Branch. At Claysburg, an appropriate name for a town built around a brick factory, it is just a brook. But the Frankstown Branch quickly gobbles up tributaries and swells. Its first five miles are swift and riffly, making this a pleasant novice whitewater run. But watch out for the sharp concrete chunks of a pair of old bridge piers, behind the brickworks, and some barbed wire fences farther below. As the stream grows, it mellows. Be prepared, however, for strainers to menace you on a brief braided section down past Hollidaysburg.

You are unlikely to mistake the upper Frankstown Branch for the Garden of Eden. Claysburg, regretably, seems to have unofficially designated the Frankstown Branch as its municipal dump, and its tattered, multicolored effects are seen for many miles downstream. Nearby old Rte. 220 and its adjacent dwellings also do little to enhance the scenery. Once past East Freedom though, the creek escapes the roads and houses and heads into farmlands and woods.

HAZARDS: Possible trees and fences. Old bridge piers in Claysburg.

WATER CONDITIONS: Canoeable late winter and spring during snowmelt and within a week of rain.

GAUGE: USGS gauge at Williamsburg (call Central PA) should be 5.0 feet to start at Claysburg.

Section 2. Frankstown (SR2007) to mouth					
Gradient	Difficulty	Distance	Time	Scenery	Map
8	1	31.9	10.0	Good	80,79

TRIP DESCRIPTION: This is all a pleasant section. To Williamsburg, roads and summer homes are often present, but the impressive mountain scenery overshadows these flaws. But nothing overshadows the steep and slippery portage (on left) around an unrunnable eight-foot dam at the power plant above Williamsburg. Navigation is otherwise a simple matter.

Below Williamsburg the creek seeks a more remote route, often away from any roads. It can be a quiet and somber passage at times, hidden away in the dark forest. But count on lots of riffles and easy rapids to brighten up the run. You can take out right at the mouth at SR4003.

HAZARDS: Dam at power plant above Williamsburg.

WATER CONDITIONS: Canoeable late winter, spring, and again in November or December, during snowmelt or within ten days of rain. In average year, it is usually canoeable from mid-March to mid-May.

GAUGE: USGS gauge at Williamsburg (call Central PA) should be over 3.3 feet.

Clover Creek

INTRODUCTION: Clover Creek is a siren-like stream that can easily lure the unsuspecting paddler to grief in its ubiquitous strainers or on its underwatered and cheesegrater stream bed. Flowing down a beautiful and bucolic valley in eastern Blair County, this tributary to the Frankstown Branch Juniata is custom designed for the masochistic paddler.

Section 1. Fredericksburg (Pa. Rte. 164) to mouth					
Gradient	Difficulty	Distance	Time	Scenery	Map
28	1 to 2 −	16.9	6.5	Very Good	80

TRIP DESCRIPTION: Only ten feet wide at Pa. Rte. 164, Clover Creek can still look very tempting in wet weather as it gushes off across the pasture. Do not be fooled. Downstream it widens considerably and, possibly because of its dolomitic underpinnings, it does not seem to gain any significant flow from tributaries. So as the creek widens, it turns shallow. But too little water, bad on any stream, is worse here, as the stream bed is paved in hull-ripping sharp rocks. Even if you are fortunate enough to have sufficient water, dozens of fences, low bridges, low-water bridges, fallen trees, and a four-foot weir (above T369) will put more stop and go into this cruise than a drive across Philadelphia at rush hour. In general though, the creek rumbles down a bed of cobbles, angular rocks, and a few ledges, with short pools and long and frequent riffles. Watch for a set of sharp limestone ledges at the rod and gun club, in the last few miles.

The bright side of this adventure is the surrounding scenery. Clover Creek flows through a narrow, out-of-the-way valley, through lovely farms and pasture. It twists a lot, so you get to see everything at different angles, including the high and forested slopes of Tussey Mountain. It might even make you glad that you are there.

HAZARDS: A weir, low bridges, and frequent strainers.

WATER CONDITIONS: Only canoeable within a day of hard rain, in late winter or spring.

GAUGE: None on creek, so check out riffles from T454 along the last few miles. Roughly, USGS gauge at Williamsburg, on Frankstown Branch (call Central PA), should read over 7.0 feet.

Powell Creek

INTRODUCTION: Like nearby Armstrong Creek, Powell Creek is a relatively safe place for the novice paddler to retreat when everything else in Dauphin County is in flood. Powell is just a thread of canoeable water fed by a most limited drainage. You can only find it up a few times a year, but when you do, you will appreciate what you find.

Section 1. Rummel Road to mouth					
Gradient	Difficulty	Distance	Time	Scenery	Map
16	1	16.0	5.5	Good	44

TRIP DESCRIPTION: Powell Creek flows down a beautiful and v-shaped farm valley. For most of its length, low banks allow great views of alternating woods and croplands. In its final miles, rocky and hemlock clad bluffs rise all around. The water is fast and smooth for one stretch, riffly for another, but nowhere difficult. The liveliest going, though still easy, is below Pa. Rte. 225. A four-foot weir, above Union Church Road, T536, requires a carry, while some fallen trees, overhanging limbs, and a low bridge at T448 may also slow you down. Take out at Pa. Rte. 147, below the tank farm.

HAZARDS: A weir, low bridge, and strainers.

WATER CONDITIONS: Canoeable late winter and spring within two days of hard rain.

GAUGE: None.

Armstrong Creek

INTRODUCTION: Armstrong Creek sneaks into the Susquehanna River on the north side of Halifax. It is a nice and easy place to paddle near Harrisburg when everything else in the area is too high and too scary. In fact, these are the only conditions under which you are likely to find canoeable water in this obscure brook.

Section 1. SR4001 to mouth					
Gradient	Difficulty	Distance	Time	Scenery	Map
19	1	8.8	3.0	Good	44

TRIP DESCRIPTION: This is a pleasant run through a rolling, agricultural valley where a few suburbs are beginning to rear their ugly heads. The tiny creek meanders a lot, usually through hardwood bottoms. Many of these fine trees, unfortunately, have fallen across the channel. The water is mostly smooth and fast, while the final two miles liven up with riffles and a runnable two-foot weir (carry if you are inexperienced).

HAZARDS: Little weir with strong hydraulic. Strainers.

WATER CONDITIONS: Canoeable late winter and spring within day of hard rain.

GAUGE: None.

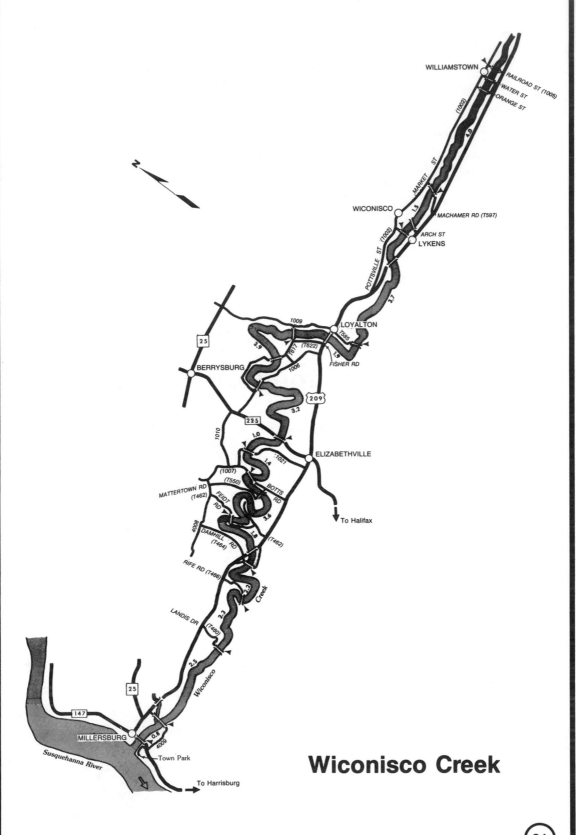

Wiconisco Creek

WILLIAMSTOWN

RAILROAD ST (1005)
WATER ST
ORANGE ST

(1002)

4.0

MARKET ST

WICONISCO

1.5

MACHAMER RD (T597)

ARCH ST
LYKENS

POTTSVILLE ST (1002)

3.7

1009

LOYALTON

T585

25

3.9

1617 (T622)

1.9

FISHER RD

BERRYSBURG

1006

1010

209

3.2

225

1.0

ELIZABETHVILLE

1.4

T621

(1007)

(T550)

MATTERTOWN RD
(T462)

FEIDT
RD

BOTTS
RD

3.9

To Halifax

4008

DAMHILL RD
(T464)

1.8

(T462)

RIFE RD (T466)

2.2

LANDIS DR

2.3

Creek

(T480)

2.5

Wiconisco

25

147

MILLERSBURG

0.5

4009

Town Park

Susquehanna River

To Harrisburg

81

Wiconisco Creek

INTRODUCTION: Wiconisco, Indian for "wet and dirty camp," carves a crooked course across northern Dauphin County to the Susquehanna at Millersburg. In its 34 navigable miles, it presents a variety of canoeing conditions—some good, some poor, but all suitable for the novice paddler.

Section 1. Williamstown (Railroad Street, SR1005) to mouth					
Gradient	Difficulty	Distance	Time	Scenery	Map
9	1 to 2	34.0	10.0	Poor to Good	81
3.7 @ 27					

TRIP DESCRIPTION: Wiconisco Creek starts in coal country, as is evident by the murky, black water and blackened sand banks at the put-in. The creek here is tiny—a smooth and fast ribbon that winds through swampy bottomland, in the shade of overhanging alders. It stays that way until Lykens.

A road bridge with insufficient clearance marks the approach to Lykens. So does discoloration from some mine-polluted tributaries. Surprisingly, locals boast that they still pull some healthy trout from Wiconisco's troubled waters. From the boater's point of view, Lykens is ugly—just a lot of shabby dwellings and trashy banks. But the creek, luckily, now commences distracting you with a chain of Class 1 and 2 rapids. When the creek leaves Lykens, it speeds toward some pretty hemlock groves. But because of a braiding channel, the combination of fast current and fallen hemlocks create some dangerous strainers. Novices must approach this braided section with caution.

Wiconisco Creek becomes much more conservative below Loyalton. Calming down to a mellow mix of riffles and smooth water, it winds past forested bluffs and bottoms and some pastures, while offering occasional glimpses of distant mountains. Alas, this picturesque setting is too often marred by piles of trash on the banks and hillsides. All of this section is unobstructed, except maybe for an occasional fallen tree. The washout channel around an old dam, below U.S. Rte. 209 below Elizabethville, is particularly likely to be choked with debris.

In its last few miles, Wiconisco hurries through a shallow gorge, rushing over a delightful series of riffles that climaxes in the ruins of an old dam. If you take out at SR4009, you spare yourself the letdown of paddling past Millersburg's ugly creekfront. If you float the whole way anyhow, take out at the town park at the mouth, on the left.

HAZARDS: Strainers, especially in the braided section between Lykens and Loyalton.

WATER CONDITIONS: Canoeable late winter and spring during snowmelt or within three days of hard rain, above Loyalton, five days below.

GAUGE: None, but the riffles below U.S. Rte. 209, at Lykens, are a good indicator. Roughly, USGS gauge at Harpers, on Swatara Creek (call Central PA), should read over 4.3 feet for paddling above Loyalton, 4.0 feet for below.

Mahantango Creek

INTRODUCTION: Mahantango Creek slips into the Susquehanna from the east, about thirty miles upriver of Harrisburg. It is gutturally pronounced Ma·ha·tun·ga and is Indian for "where

203

Mahantango Creek
Pine Creek
Deep Creek

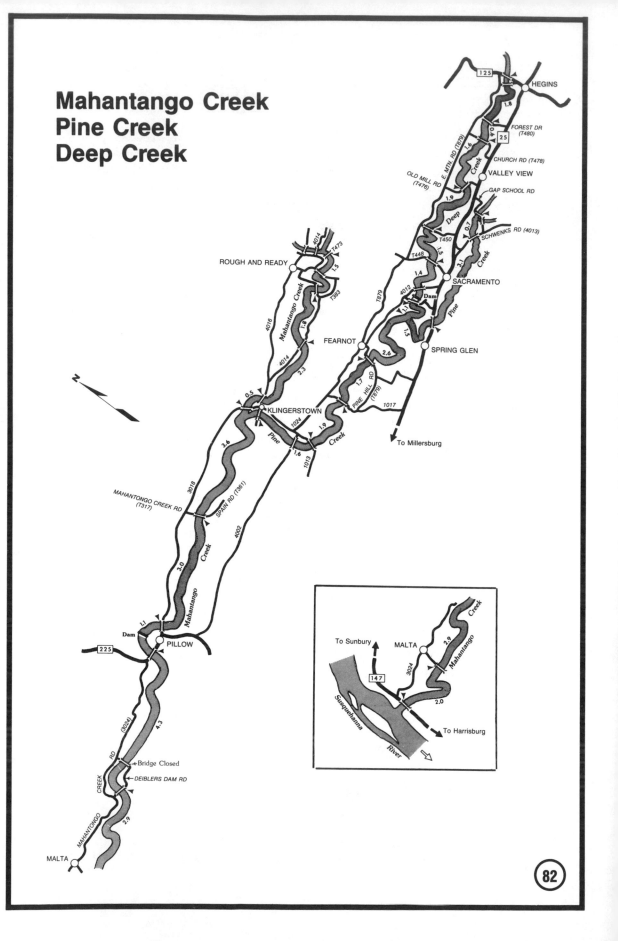

HEGINS

125

1.2

1.8

FOREST DR (T480)

4.0

25

CHURCH RD (T478)

E. MTN RD (T879)

1.6

Creek

VALLEY VIEW

OLD MILL RD (T479)

GAP SCHOOL RD

1.9

Deep

0.7

SCHWENKS RD (4013)

T450

T448

1.5

Creek

ROUGH AND READY

4014

T473

1.5

1.4

3.1

SACRAMENTO

T383

4012

Dam

1.9

Creek

4016

Mahantango Creek

1.8

7879

1.1

Pine

4014

1.5

SPRING GLEN

2.3

FEARNOT

2.6

0.5

1.7

KLINGERSTOWN

PINE HILL RD (T879)

1017

3.6

1024

Pine

1.9

Creek

To Millersburg

1.6

3018

1013

MAHANTONGO CREEK RD (T317)

SPAIN RD (T361)

4002

3.0

Creek

Mahantango

1.1

Dam

225

PILLOW

Mahantango

4.3

(3024)

CREEK RD

Bridge Closed

DEIBLERS DAM RD

MAHANTONGO

2.9

MALTA

Creek

To Sunbury

MALTA

2.9

Mahantango

147

3024

2.0

To Harrisburg

Susquehanna

River

82

we kill deer." Canoeists generally fare better than deer, for this is a tranquil beginners' spring-time run.

Section 1. T473 to mouth					
Gradient	Difficulty	Distance	Time	Scenery	Map
10	1	23.2	7.5	Good	82

TRIP DESCRIPTION: The put-in is at the confluence with the Little Mahantango Creek, about a mile southeast of the village of Rough And Ready and three miles northeast of Fearnot. What a siege mentality the founding fathers must have had. From there the puny creek ripples past woods, farms, and slanting, fern-covered rock outcrops. Challenge is limited to lots of easy riffles and a few downed trees.

If the upper creek is too low, conditions improve at Klingerstown with the inflow of Pine Creek. Mahantango now flows through a beautiful and very rolling farm valley, presided over by the great, wooded wall of Mahantango Mountain, to the south. Much of the good scenery is visible from the creek, though eclipsed by fairly high streambanks. There is surprisingly little recreational development along these banks, but sadly, many heaps of local refuse.

It is easy to navigate Mahantango Creek, as the pools are long and the riffles short and uncomplicated. An easy rapid through the break in a deteriorating dam, about 200 yards upstream of Pa. Rte. 147, offers some final splash to the trip. You should portage the diagonal three-foot weir at Pillow to avoid misfortune in its roller. The last take-out on the creek is at Pa. Rte. 147.

HAZARDS: A few strainers above Klingerstown and nasty weir at Pillow.

WATER CONDITIONS: Canoeable late winter and spring during snowmelt and within three days of hard rain, above Klingerstown, and a week below.

GAUGE: None for upper creek. If water level is up to the bottom of the drain pipe hole on the lower end of the north abutment of SR1013, over Pine Creek (south of Klingerstown), there is enough water for a clean run from Klingerstown to the mouth. Roughly, USGS gauge at Harpers, on Swatara Creek (call Central PA), should be over 3.6 feet for the upper creek and over 3.2 feet for the creek below Pine Creek.

Pine Creek

INTRODUCTION: This Pine Creek, located in eastern Schuylkill County, is an extra pleasant way to start a Mahantango Creek trip. It would more appropriately be called "Hemlock" Creek, as it is now hemlocks, not pines, that shade much of this diminutive novice run.

Section 1. Valley View (Gap School Road) to mouth					
Gradient	Difficulty	Distance	Time	Scenery	Map
11	1	13.5	4.0	Good	82

TRIP DESCRIPTION: The put-in is located just above the welcome addition of rushing Rausch Run. The shallow Pine Creek speeds off over a sandy or rocky bottom, usually through deep groves of hemlock. Some of these trees have been around for a long time, reaching diameters in excess of three feet. This is an intimate and shut-in run, as one sees little of the countryside for the trees. Some coal waste piles and a coal processing plant interrupt the serenity between Valley View and Spring Glen, but on the other hand, there is amazingly little litter on this stream.

Pine Creek handles its gradient by an orderly succession of riffles and pools. Watch out for a few electric fences just below Spring Glen and occasional fallen trees throughout. A shallow and rocky rapid at the waste piles below Valley View may require some dragging.

HAZARDS: Electric fences and deadfalls.

WATER CONDITIONS: Canoeable winter and spring during snowmelt or within three days of hard rain.

GAUGE: None on creek. If level is up to the bottom of the drain pipe hole on the lower end of the north abutment of SR1013 (south of Klingerstown), the level is adequate from Spring Glen on down. Roughly, USGS gauge at Harpers, on Swatara Creek (call Central PA), should read over 3.6 feet to start at Valley View and 3.2 feet to start at Spring Glen.

Deep Creek

INTRODUCTION: Deep Creek starts in the hills of Schuylkill County, northeast of Hegins. It offers the energetic paddler one more pleasant way to begin an extended Mahantango Creek trip.

Section 1. Pa. Rte. 125 to mouth					
Gradient	Difficulty	Distance	Time	Scenery	Map
12	1	9.9	3.5	Good	82

TRIP DESCRIPTION: Deep Creek offers a smorgasboard of rural Pennsylvania streamscapes. There are shady hemlock groves, sunny pastures, farmhouses, old mills, wretched junkheaps, and clean bends that sweep beneath rocky outcrops. Though the stream is usually bound in a woodland setting, one catches frequent glimpses of the countryside beyond. The surrounding valley tilts steadily from the narrow bottomlands to the foot of wooded ridges. About the only undesirable aspect of this place is the persistent drone of a distant mine vent fan on a mountain to the south.

This is a shallow stream (in spite of its name), divided between pools and broad riffles, all running over a cobble bottom. There is a three-foot weir above T605, runnable in the middle with great care (beware of a strong roller). Expect to tangle with several fallen trees, but fences are rarely present. Take out at T605, or continue on down Pine Creek to the bridge of your choice.

HAZARDS: Occasional strainers and a weir (with nasty hydraulic) above T605.

WATER CONDITIONS: Canoeable late winter and spring during snowmelt and within three days of hard rain.

GAUGE: None. Roughly, USGS gauge at Harpers, on Swatara Creek (call Central PA), should read over 3.6 feet.

Mahanoy Creek

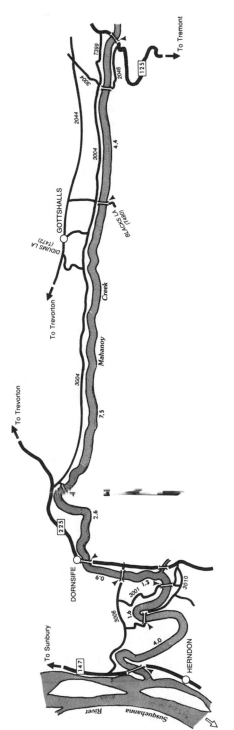

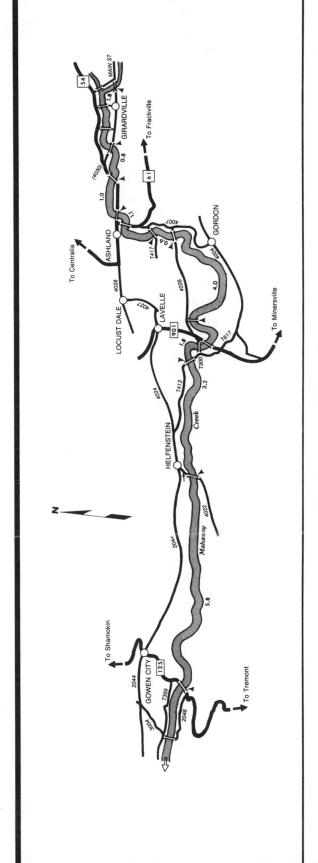

Mahanoy Creek

INTRODUCTION: Mahanoy Creek rises deep in the heart of the anthracite coal fields of Schuylkill County. Remember the depressing wasteland of abandoned stripmine gouges, waste piles, crumbling tipples, and burned over mountainsides that you have observed while traveling I-81 between Harrisburg and Hazelton? That is where this stream, known locally as "Coal Creek," starts. It does not finsh there, fortunately. Part way down its 43-mile journey to the Susquehanna, it shakes free of this tortured land and evolves into a first-class canoeing stream. This is certainly a living monument to Mother Nature's resilience to man's abuse. One should come and explore the entire length of Mahanoy Creek to most appreciate this renewal.

Section 1. Girardville (Main Street) to T300					
Gradient	Difficulty	Distance	Time	Scenery	Map
22	1 to 2 +	10.5	3.0	Poor to Worse	83
1.2 @ 43					

TRIP DESCRIPTION: At high water, you can put in at Main Street, at the upstream end of Girardville, or maybe even higher if being raked by alders is tolerable to you. The coal dust-darkened water rushes through backyards, past barking dogs, beneath mounds of streambank trash, and by assorted crumbling structures. Just below the start Shenandoah Creek almost doubles the flow, and as you continue, injections of gray sewage on the left and gushing orange mine discharges on the right swell the flood.

Outside of morbid curiosity, the best reason for paddling up at this end of the creek is to enjoy its whitewater. The rapids through Girardville and on to Ashfield are almost continous and fairly pushy, but neither very complex nor very heavy—a good open boat run. There are no tree problems on this small stream, as most of the riparian trees are puny birch saplings. Beware, however, of some menacing debris jams perched on bridge piers and at the heads of islands. The rapids climax in a relatively complex and powerful stretch where the creek gushes through a gap below Ashfield.

Below the gap through Ashfield Mountain, the stream flattens out and meanders about an open valley rimmed by pretty, blue mountain ridges, but also dotted by great man-made mountains of coal mine waste. In places the floodplain is dead, blackened, and gouged—the remains of old coal washing and storage operations. Even past the areas of scarred landscape, dense streambank shrubbery displays a sparkling and colorful bounty of plastic, metal, and other trash that the floods have carried down from upstream communities. But this is a transition zone, and blemishes become fewer with the miles.

HAZARDS: Debris jams in fast water.

WATER CONDITIONS: Canoeable late winter and spring during fast snowmelt or within two days of hard rain.

GAUGE: None. Judge riffles at put-in. Roughly, USGS gauge at Harpers, on Swatara Creek (call Central PA), should read over 6.0 feet.

Section 2. T300 to mouth					
Gradient	Difficulty	Distance	Time	Scenery	Map
7	1 to 2	32.4	11.0	Good	83
1.3 @ 40					

TRIP DESCRIPTION: If you start near Pa. Rte. 901, near Lavelle, you will think that you are on another creek. While the water remains discolored, upstream saplings have by now filtered out most of the trash, and except for one old mine portal, the surroundings appear mostly wild. Much of the southern view is protected by state game lands. Hemlock and tall pines line the mostly smooth waters, allowing only occasional views of nearby mountainsides. The mountains come together and squeeze the creek below Helfenstein, resulting in a long stretch of bouncy and boulder-pocked rapids.

The creek changes again, after passing beneath the arch of Pa. Rte. 125. A nearby road brings occasional houses to the streambank. But fairly high banks and dense stands of hemlock, river-birch, alder, and even patches of reed grass maintain a mostly remote sense to the place. The smooth stream is now only broken by many easy riffles and a few runnable rubble weirs. These weirs were constructed here as sediment traps for a few streamside dredging operations that recover coal dust that has washed down from upstream mines. At Dornsife, Mahanoy cuts through a gap and rushes over broad and rocky riffles. In its final several miles, great bends of this creek carry you past hardwood-covered hillsides, rock outcrops, and fields. A short and steep carry up to Pa. Rte. 147 marks the end of the trip. If you continue to the mouth, the next take-out is a mile down the Susquehanna at Herndon.

HAZARDS: None.

WATER CONDITIONS: Canoeable late winter and spring during snowmelt and within three days of hard rain, above Pa. Rte. 125, and within a week below.

GAUGE: None. Riffles in the gap at Dornsife are a good indicator for from Rte. 125 on down. Roughly, USGS gauge at Harpers, on Swatara Creek (call Central PA), should be over 5.0 feet for above Rte. 125 and over 2.8 feet for below.

Penns Creek

INTRODUCTION: Penns Creek is a medium-sized, medium-length, mediocre tributary to the Susquehanna River, flowing from near State College to Selinsgrove. For Pennsylvania paddlers, the relatively remote Coburn to Weikert stretch has long been a springtime whitewater favorite. For retreat-seeking urbanites, its miles of subdivided bottomlands have made it one of the most popular streams in the state on which to build that rustic vacation hideaway, next to Mr. Smith's hideaway, next to Mr. Jones' hideaway, next to Mr. Brown's hideaway, ad nauseum. See for yourself. There may still even be some lots left for sale.

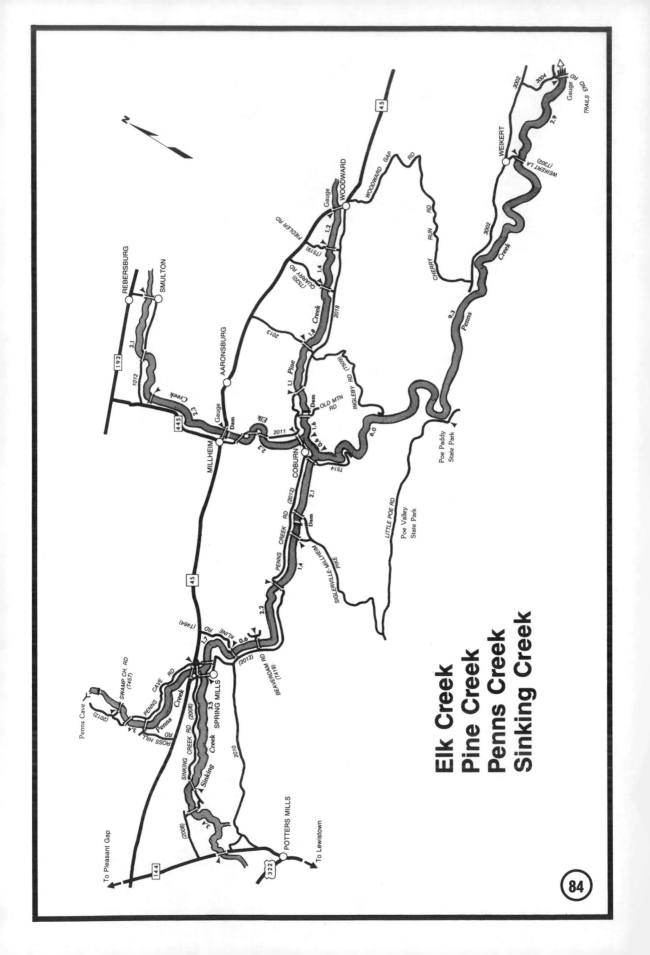

Elk Creek
Pine Creek
Penns Creek
Sinking Creek

84

Section 1. Swamp Church Road to Coburn (T514)					
Gradient	Difficulty	Distance	Time	Scenery	Map
10	1	11.4	3.0	Good	84

TRIP DESCRIPTION: This creek is unusual in that it is born a canoeable stream, gushing from a spring whose origin is the black labyrinth of Penns Cave. In fact, they even guide you on tours of this beautiful commercial cave by boat. But unless you can secure special permission from the cave owners to cross their land, the first access to Penns Creek is about a half mile below the cave at the end of Swamp Church Road.

The tiny brook rushes off through rugged and lightly populated farm country. The creek is easy, but look for a few fences and trees to block the smooth to riffly waters. Of even more concern should be the narrow and twisting shuttle road. Take your time.

Some voluminous springs and Sinking Creek swell the stream at Spring Mills. A now mostly smooth creek winds through an attractive farm valley, slightly more populated than above. A six-foot dam, about two miles above Coburn, requires a carry.

HAZARDS: Possible fallen trees or fences. Carry the dam above Coburn.

WATER CONDITIONS: Canoeable late winter and spring during snowmelt or within two days of hard rain, above Spring Mills, within a week of rain below.

GAUGE: Staff gauge on SR2012 Bridge in Spring Mills should read over 3.0 feet to start at Swamp Church Road and 2.5 feet to start at Spring Mills.

Section 2. Coburn (T514) to Weikert (Weikert Lane)					
Gradient	Difficulty	Distance	Time	Scenery	Map
19	1 to 2	15.3	5.0	Good to Very Good	84

TRIP DESCRIPTION: By far, this is Penns Creek's most popular run. The creek has carved a pretty canyon as it cuts through several high ridges. It maintains a consistent and healthy gradient for several miles, expended as an ideal series of rapids and pools. At moderate levels, the average rapid is fairly long and rocky, formed by a cobble bottom. About the only significant hazards are strainers, encountered where the stream splits around islands. In general, this is a good run for experienced novices. With part of the gorge within state forest lands, this is a good section for canoe camping. Even in this rugged canyon, unfortunately, it is hard to go for more than a mile or two without encountering a summer home. As the floodplain widens, a few miles above Weikert, the left bank becomes totally developed.

HAZARDS: Strainers on some side channels.

WATER CONDITIONS: Canoeable late winter and spring during snowmelt and within a week of hard rain.

GAUGE: Staff gauge on Trails End Road (below Weikert), should read at least 2.5 feet. USGS gauge at Penns Creek, Rte. 104 (call Central PA), should be over 3.5 feet. Very roughly, a reading of 8.5 to 9.0 feet on Beech Creek Station USGS gauge, on Bald Eagle Creek, or over 7.0 feet on USGS gauge at Newport, on Juniata River (call Central PA for both), indicates that there is probably enough water to do Penns Creek.

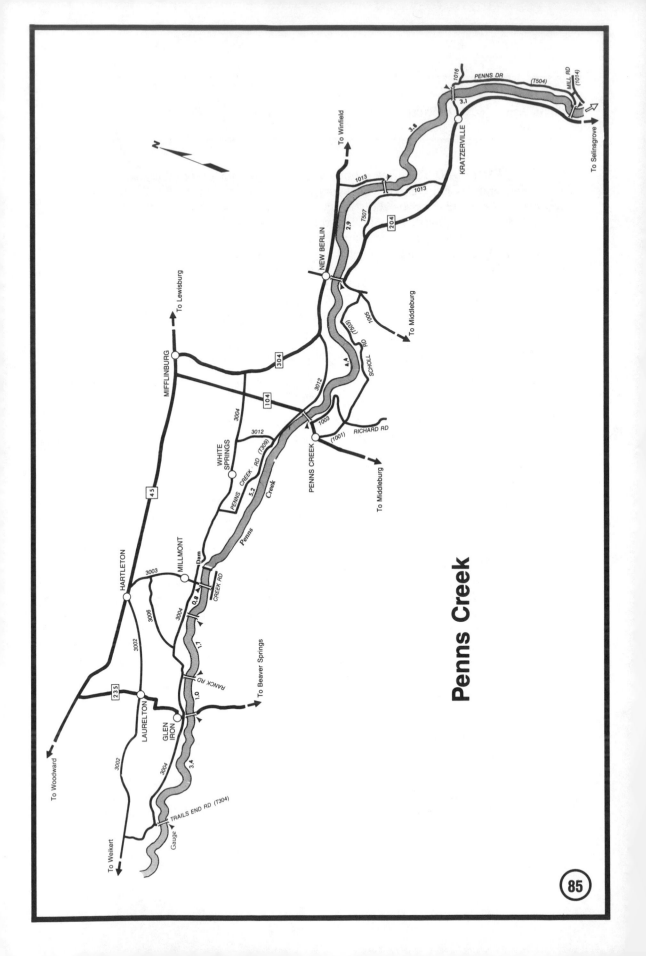

Penns Creek

85

Gradient	Difficulty	Distance	Time	Scenery	Map
10	1	35.6	12.0	Poor to Good	84,85,43
3 @ 24					

TRIP DESCRIPTION: Between Weikert and Glen Iron, both banks are crowded with houses, trailers, and campgrounds. Amid this clutter, an old iron furnace stands on the right bank below the bridge at Glen Iron—a hint at how that village got its name. With the decreasing gradient, the paddler has more time to pay attention to the scenery, and if so disposed, to maybe even shop for real estate. A few, but not many, acres of floodplain have still not been developed.

Relatively wide now, the creek splits around many islands. A riffly section above New Berlin breaks what is otherwise now a smooth water run. The lower creek's only obstacle is a two-foot weir below Creek Road, T322, Millmont. The weir blocks both sides of an island. Take the chute just to the right of the island because, although the left channel carries more water at low levels, there are strainer problems on that route.

Penns Creek should end just north of Selinsgrove. But instead, it procrastinates for five miles, flowing parallel to the Susquehanna, separated by a strip of prime alluvial farmland named the Isle of Que (French for "tail"). Those floating the whole distance can find a convenient take-out just below the mouth at the Hoover Island PFC Access.

HAZARDS: Weir at Millmont.

WATER CONDITIONS: Canoeable late winter and spring during snowmelt and within a week of hard rain, above Glen Iron. Below Glen Iron, it is usually passable until mid-May and often again reaches canoeable levels after summer showers.

GAUGE: Staff gauge on Trails End Road Bridge should be at least 2.5 feet to canoe from Weikert to Glen Iron. The USGS gauge at Penns Creek, Rte. 104 (call Central PA), should be over 2.6 feet.

Middle Creek

INTRODUCTION: Middle Creek flows down the middle (where else?) of beautiful, rolling, and ridgy Snyder County, to join the very end of Penns Creek, below Selinsgrove. This small beginners' stream reflects the character of its surroundings—pleasant, but not spectacular. Perhaps that is why it has been spared the insult of harboring endless strings of river slums such as those that sully its parallel neighbor to the north, Penns Creek.

Section 1. Pa. Rte. 235 to mouth

Gradient	Difficulty	Distance	Time	Scenery	Map
6	1	24.5	8.0	Fair to Good	86

TRIP DESCRIPTION: Middle Creek is plainly navigable as far upstream as SR4008, northwest of Beaver Springs. But just below that road the creek spreads out into a lake backed up by a large earthen dam, located just upstream of Pa. Rte. 235. A simple but tiring portage over

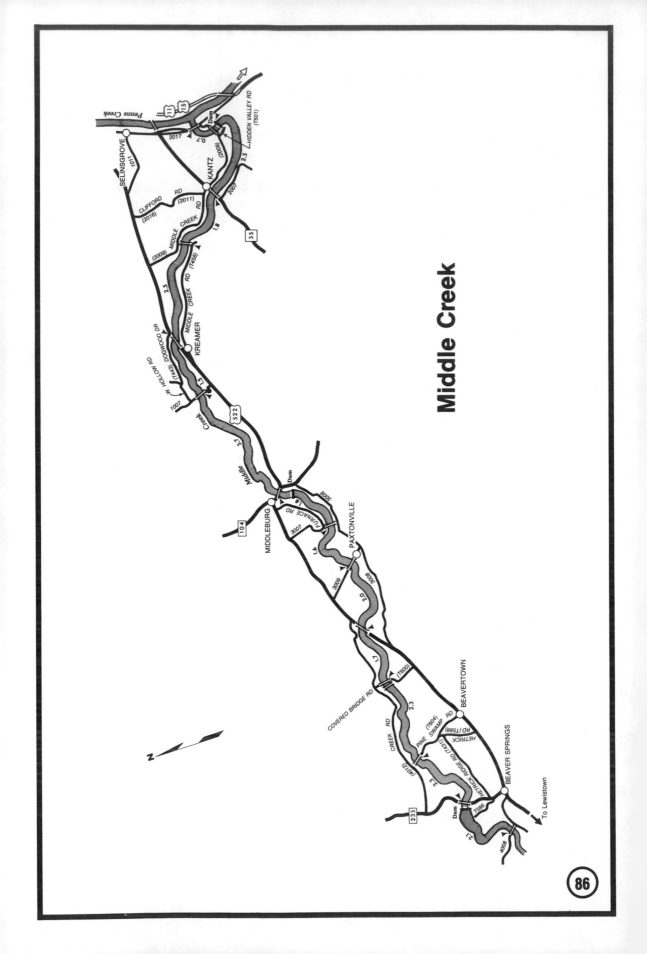

Middle Creek

the middle of this structure is the reason why most paddlers would choose to put in below.

The creek is most pleasant in its first several miles below Rte. 235, as it spends much of its time wandering through deep woods—woods that are often comprised of shady young hemlocks. On below, the scenery rounds out to a mix of rolling farms, bottomland woods, and wooded bluffs. The only exception is Middleburg, a pretty community from any other angle, which blights the creek banks and hillsides with cascades of trash.

Cruising Middle Creek is easy. It is mostly smooth, riffles are easy, and strainers are only likely to threaten if you take the wrong side of an island. A four-foot dam at Middleburg requires a carry. But a growing washout on the right promises a bypass, if the huge debris jam that now plugs it ever washes away. You can avoid a portage around a high dam at the end of a long and pretty pool, below Kantz, by taking out at the Fish and Boat Commission ramp, on the left, at the dam. You only miss the final half mile of Middle Creek if you stop here.

HAZARDS: Dams at Middleburg and below Kantz.

WATER CONDITIONS: Canoeable late winter and spring during snowmelt and within a week of hard rain.

GAUGE: Staff gauge on right pier of U.S. Rte. 522, between Beavertown and Middleburg. You need about 2.3 feet to start at Rte. 235 and 2.0 feet to float below this gauge. There is also a painted canoe gauge on the right abutment of this bridge. Level of eight inches is minimal to start at Rte. 235 and four inches is minimal for below this point. Very roughly, USGS gauges at Beech Creek Station, on Bald Eagle Creek, and at Penns Creek, on Penns Creek (call Central PA), should read over 9.0 feet and 3.8 feet respectively.

Pine Creek

INTRODUCTION: Do not confuse this Pine Creek with the famous Grand Canyon of Pennsylvania run in Tioga County. This one is just an obscure country brook that feeds Penns Creek at Coburn. It is a perfect means by which to tour the lonely, limestone landscape of Penns Valley.

Section 1. Woodward (Pa. Rte. 45) to mouth					
Gradient	Difficulty	Distance	Time	Scenery	Map
13	1	7.7	2.5	Good	84

TRIP DESCRIPTION: If you think that the stream that gurgles beneath the Pa. Rte. 45 Bridge is insignificant, you should see it a short way downstream, at low water, when the entire flow disappears temporarily into a limestone honeycomb of subterranean channels that no canoeist will ever navigate. That is why brush chokes portions of the creek above Fiedler Road, T519.

Pine Creek is easy, but not simple. The swift and tortuous channel through that brushy section quickly weeds out all clumsy paddlers. Below there the creek hurries through a pleasant riffly section before finishing up smooth. A four-foot milldam, located a half mile above Elk Creek, has a potentially runnable flume on the right, providing that there is no debris jammed in that narrow slot.

The creek wanders through a perfect mix of rolling and empty farmland and wooded bottom-lands and mountainsides, all easily observed over Pine Creek's low banks. Few people live up along this creek, and nobody has fouled the view with summer homes. The best spot to finish is at the town park in Coburn.

HAZARDS: Strainers and an old milldam.

WATER CONDITIONS: Canoeable late winter and spring during snowmelt and within three days of hard rain.

GAUGE: Staff gauge on the right abutment of Pa. Rte. 45. A level of 1.6 feet is about minimum.

Elk Creek

INTRODUCTION: Elk Creek is a highwater run, tributary to Penns Creek, that possesses the choicest whitewater in the watershed. When heavy rains convert Penns Creek's Coburn to Weikert run into a muddy and washed-out flush, switch to the rocky challenge of this intimate torrent.

Section 1. Smulton (SR1012) to mouth					
Gradient	**Difficulty**	**Distance**	**Time**	**Scenery**	**Map**
26	1 to 3 –	7.8	2.5	Good	84
2.3 @ 48					

TRIP DESCRIPTION: You can start on Elk Creek as far up as the hamlet of Smulton. Up here Elk Creek is just a smooth to riffly brook, hurrying down a lovely and intensively farmed limestone valley. Since most of the farms are owned by the Amish, this is one stream along which you should not see junked cars or old washing machines sullying the banks. While this rural scenery should please you, several low bridges and some fences will also vie for your attention.

Hardcore whitewater paddlers usually start at a little bridge at the head of the narrow gap through Brush Mountain and finish two and a half miles downstream at Pa. Rte. 45 in Millheim. The creek maintains a fairly even gradient through the gap, running over continuous rock gardens and small ledges. Then, surprisingly, when it hits the flat country below, the creek starts tumbling down steeper rapids of cobbles and boulders, pushing the difficulty up a step. The best of the whitewater climaxes with a plunge over a runnable (you will crunch your stern though) four-foot dam beneath the Rte. 45 Bridge.

The still busy creek gradually decelerates below Millheim, as it once again returns to farm country. Watch for hard-to-spot fences in this stretch. Either take out at the last bridge, or continue down Pine Creek to the park in Coburn.

HAZARDS: Strainers, fences, and the dam beneath Rte. 45 in Millheim.

WATER CONDITIONS: Canoeable late winter and spring during snowmelt and within two days of hard rain.

GAUGE: Staff gauge on left abutment of Rte. 45 in Millheim. Level of 1.8 feet is minimal, but adequate.

Sinking Creek

INTRODUCTION: Sinking Creek is an alternate start for a Penns Creek cruise. Its interesting name is found commonly throughout the limestone regions of the U.S. While nothing dramatic happens on this particular stream, other such streams literally sink into their beds, sometimes not resurfacing for many miles. Imagine canoeing down a creek and having it disappear on you. It has happened to the author. If you doubt such phenomena, go over to Mifflin County and try following Laurel Creek from Milroy to Naginey, along SR1001. You will find that about a mile east of Milroy a big sinkhole swallows this canoeable-sized trout stream. So leave your boat on your car.

Section 1. Pa. Rte. 144 to mouth					
Gradient	Difficulty	Distance	Time	Scenery	Map
8	1	6.9	2.5	Good	84

TRIP DESCRIPTION: One can start paddling at Pa. Rte. 144, or maybe even three miles upstream at U.S. Rte. 322. Until Potter Run joins, Sinking Creek is a tiny and twisting passage crowded by much overhanging vegetation. It is blocked by more than a few fences and some fallen trees. The creek carries you past woodlands, old abandoned pastures dotted with little trees and clumps of multiflora, and active farms. The water is mostly smooth, and if you stay out of the strainers, it should deliver you to Spring Mills in one piece.

HAZARDS: Strainers, including trees, brush, and fences.

WATER CONDITIONS: Canoeable late winter and spring during snowmelt and within week of hard rain.

GAUGE: Staff gauge on SR2012 Bridge over Penns Creek, in Spring Mills, should read over 2.5 feet.

Shamokin Creek

INTRODUCTION: If there is ever a "March of Dimes" campaign for crippled and deformed creeks, then Shamokin will be chosen as the poster stream. For the business of coal extraction has not been kind to this Northumberland County waterway. One should find little incentive to paddle here.

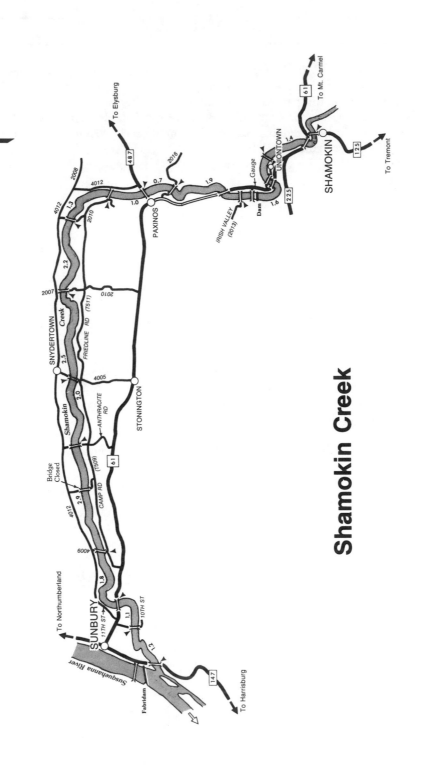

Shamokin Creek

Section 1. Shamokin (Pa. Rte. 125) to Sunbury (Pa. Rte. 147)					
Gradient	Difficulty	Distance	Time	Scenery	Map
14	1 to 3	21.6	7.0	Poor to Fair	87

TRIP DESCRIPTION: You are not likely to mistake the put-in, at Shamokin, for Shangri-La. About 12,000 souls inhabit Shamokin, a classic eastern Pennsylvanian coal town. The town is surrounded by old mines, breaker stations, high ridges, and on its very fringes, incredibly high, black culm heaps. That these piles have not slid down and buried Shamokin seems a miracle.

The creek at Pa. Rte. 125, in downtown Shamokin, is confined by high stone walls. But they are not too high for you to descend over, under the watchful eyes of curious locals. The rapids, down which these polluted waters rush, run almost continuously for the first two miles. They are rocky, wide, and relatively easy, except for one long, powerful, complex, and boulder-formed rapid below the Glen Burn Colliery. But the whitewater gradually subsides until, by Paxinos, the creek runs smooth, with only occasional cobble-formed sluices. Watch for a two-foot weir at the gauging station, two miles below Shamokin. It is nasty enough to carry.

Much of the first few miles of this run flows through a commercial and industrial wasteland, past banks strewn with tons of trash. As the creek heads north and then west, it swings through a wide and low floodplain, seemingly devastated by floods, fires, and past development. Trees here are stunted, and deposits of culm pave the cobble bars. Finally, by Snyderstown, Shamokin Creek has mostly escaped the coal country blues and rolls the remainder of its way past wooded banks and through farm country, in a mostly mediocre fashion.

HAZARDS: Gauging station weir below Shamokin.

WATER CONDITIONS: Canoeable late winter and spring during snowmelt or within two days of hard rain.

GAUGE: USGS gauge, on right just upstream of unsigned bridge that is a quarter-mile upstream of the SR2013 Bridge, should read at least 3.2 feet to start at Shamokin. Roughly, USGS gauge at Harpers, on Swatara Creek (call Central PA), should read over 6.0 feet.

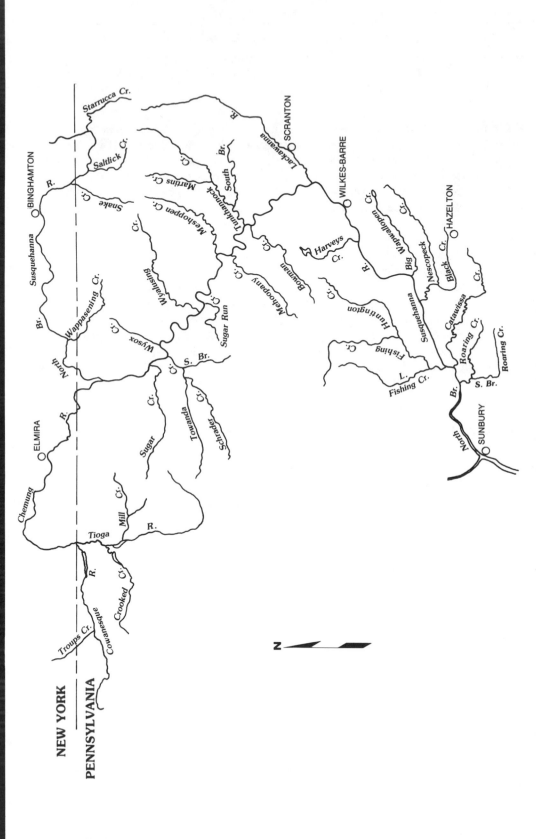

North Branch Susquehanna Tributaries

Chapter 4
The North Branch Susquehanna Basin

Pennsylvania's portion of the North Branch Susquehanna River Valley covers a funnel-shaped 4,944 square miles. This is up and down country—a rolling and dissected plateau where the only flat land is down along the rivers. Much of the countryside is a patchwork of dairy farms and forest, speckled by tidy little New Englandesque villages of white frame houses and maple-shaded streets. In stark contrast, this valley possess an industrial heart in the Scranton and Wilkes-Barre area and its neighboring anthracite fields to the southeast.

For all of its beauty and remoteness, this valley has been spared much of the recreational development that has overwhelmed the Poconos, just to the east. Though still relatively near to New York and Philadelphia, it is still common to find streambanks devoid of posted signs, to find places to camp along a stream, and to avoid endless strings of river slums lining the banks.

Except for the North Branch proper, streams in this basin are small and their levels rise and fall quickly. You will find that most of these streams are scenic and that many are steep. So you must be quick and opportunistic to paddle here, but you will be rewarded for the effort.

The following streams are described in this chapter:

North Branch Susquehanna River
Roaring Creek
South Branch Roaring Creek
Catawissa Creek
Fishing Creek
Little Fishing Creek
Huntington Creek
Nescopeck Creek
Black Creek
Big Wapwallopen Creek
Harveys Creek
Lackawanna River
Bowman Creek
Tunkhannock Creek
South Branch Tunkhannock Creek
Martins Creek
Mehoopany Creek
Meshoppen Creek
Sugar Run Creek
Wyalusing Creek
Wysox Creek

Towanda Creek
South Branch Towanda Creek
Schrader Creek
Sugar Creek
Chemung River
Tioga River
Cowanesque River
Troups Creek
Crooked Creek
Mill Creek
Wappasening Creek
Snake Creek
Saltlick Creek
Starrucca Creek

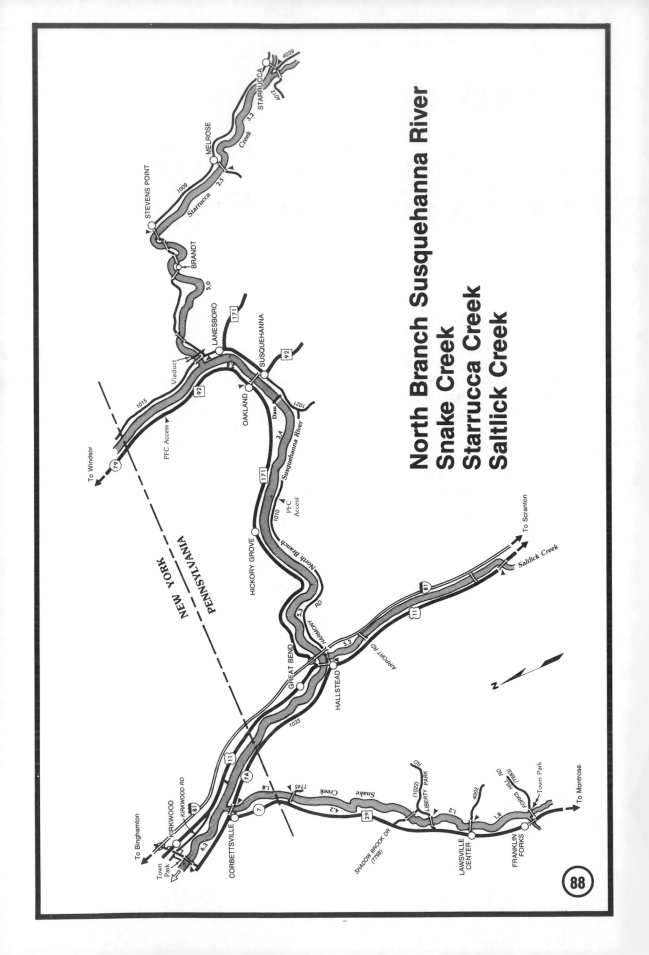

North Branch Susquehanna River
Snake Creek
Starrucca Creek
Saltlick Creek

88

North Branch Susquehanna River

INTRODUCTION: The North Branch Susquehanna is really just another name for the upper Susquehanna River. It is born in the heart of New York State, at the outlet of beautiful Lake Otsego, by the home of the Baseball Hall of Fame, Cooperstown. From Cooperstown the river takes no shortcuts to the sea. Its course is a great zig-zag that brings it into Pennsylvania and then out. Pennsylvania reclaims the North Branch for good near the town of Sayre, in Bradford County, and puts up with more zig-zagging until the river combines with the West Branch to officially become the Susquehanna, at Northumberland.

Through the Great Bend, and from the New York Line to Pittston, this is a beautiful river—a good place to go canoeing. Much of it follows a great serpentine course through a rolling plateau that the local chambers of commerce have embellished as the "Endless Mountains."

Beauty yields to mild blight as the river rolls by Pittston, Wilkes-Barre, Kingston, and Nanticoke—an area compositely known as the Wyoming Valley. But while civilization here has not been kind to the North Branch, the North Branch has not been kind to civilization either. For in 1972 the North Branch rolled over, not through, these towns. On June 23 of that year Hurricane Agnes' floodwaters began topping the extensive dike system that supposedly protected the Wyoming Valley towns, ultimately driving 100,000 people from their homes. When the river crested the next day, it swirled at more than 18 feet above flood stage. The late summer floater, who glides by just inches off the bottom of this wide and shallow river, will find such a record incomprehensible.

The remainder of the North Branch leaves the plateau region to cut through and run along side of high mountain ridges. It settles in a spacious valley that is filled with farms and medium-sized towns. Less restrained by topography, the river begins to fill out now to the wide dimensions that make the Susquehanna so unique. It can be a picture of fluvial serenity and a good place to canoe, if you are in no hurry.

Section 1. Great Bend PFC Access to Kirkland, N.Y.					
Gradient	Difficulty	Distance	Time	Scenery	Map
3	A to 1	17.8	6.0	Fair to Good to	88

TRIP DESCRIPTION: The PFC access is located on Pa. Rte. 92, 2.8 miles north of the Susquehanna bridge in Oakland, and 1.5 miles south of the State Line. If you want to see every inch of Pennsylvania's portion of the river, start at Chapel Street in Windsor, N.Y. for a pretty cruise through a narrow, mountain-fringed farm valley.

This section of the North Branch spans the bottom of a great, roughly U-shaped turn in the river called The Great Bend. The river cuts a deep and narrow valley in this area of remote, rolling hills. Prettiest and least developed between the towns of Susquehanna and Hallstead, this is the only reach of Pennsylvania's Susquehanna that can be described as a small river.

This still small Susquehanna looms big in the hearts of members of the Mormon Church. Back in the 1820's, Joseph Smith, the founder of that church, roamed the surrounding hills, translating the *Book Of Mormon,* gathering his first converts, and tasting the beginning of a long trail of persecution.

The paddling on this stretch is easy. Riffles are few and far between, but the current is swift. Be alert for an eight-foot power dam at the lower end of Susquehanna (carry on right side). If

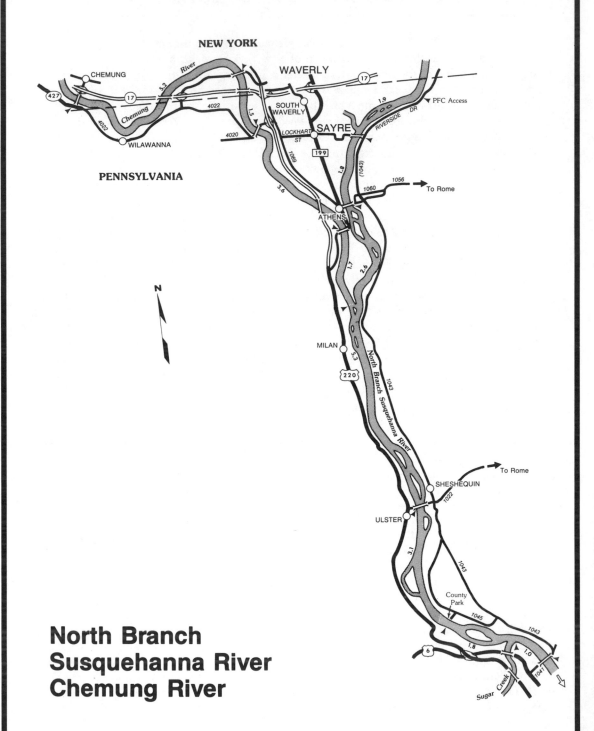

**North Branch
Susquehanna River
Chemung River**

NEW YORK

CHEMUNG

WAVERLY

17

River

Chemung

5.2

SOUTH WAVERLY

SAYRE

427

17

4022

1.5

1.9

PFC Access

RIVERSIDE DR

WILAWANNA

4022

4020

LOCKHART ST

199

(1043)

PENNSYLVANIA

1069

1.8

1056

To Rome

N

3.6

1060

ATHENS

1.7

2.6

MILAN

5.3

North Branch Susquehanna River

220

1043

To Rome

SHESHEQUIN

1022

ULSTER

3.1

1043

County Park

1045

1.8

1043

6

1.0

Sugar Creek

1041

89

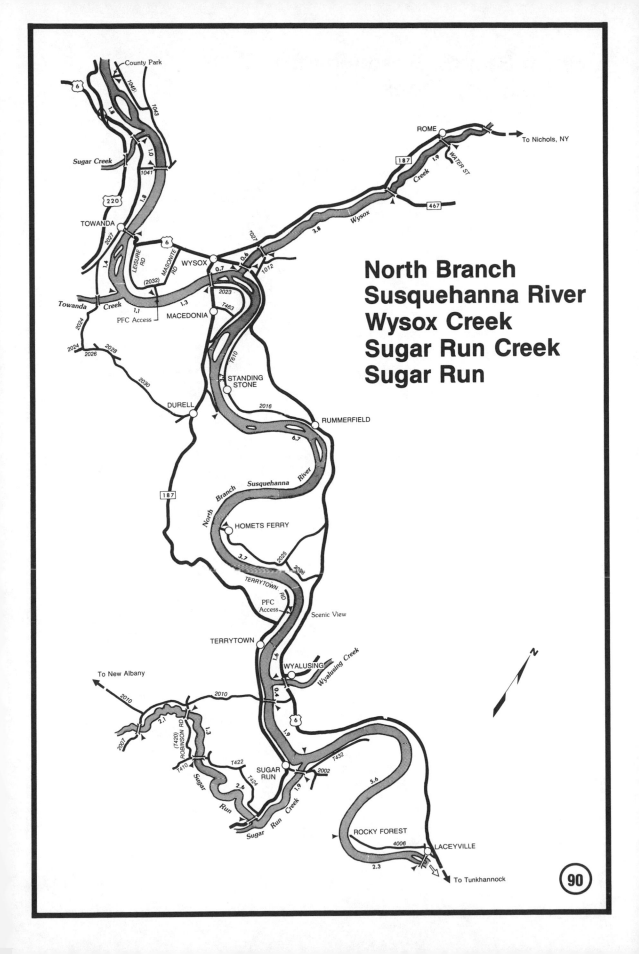

North Branch
Susquehanna River
Wysox Creek
Sugar Run Creek
Sugar Run

County Park

6

1045

1043

1.3

Sugar Creek

1.0

1041

220

1.8

TOWANDA

2027

ROME

187

1.9

WATER ST

To Nichols, NY

Creek

467

Wysox

3.8

1027

6

LEISURE RD

MASONITE RD

WYSOX

0.7

0.5

1012

2023

1.3

(2032)

1.4

Towanda

Creek

1.1

PFC Access

MACEDONIA

T463

T610

STANDING STONE

2016

2024

2026

2028

2030

DURELL

187

RUMMERFIELD

6.7

North   Branch   Susquehanna   River

HOMETS FERRY

3.7

2025

304?

TERRYTOWN RD

PFC Access

Scenic View

TERRYTOWN

1.6

WYALUSING

Wyalusing Creek

0.4

To New Albany

2010

2010

6

1.9

2.1

ROBINSON RD (T420)

1.3

T410

T422

SUGAR RUN

2002

T432

5.6

Sugar

Run

2.6

T424

1.9

Sugar Run Creek

ROCKY FOREST

4006

LACEYVILLE

2.3

To Tunkhannock

N

90

North Branch Susquehanna River
Mehoopany Creek
Bowman Creek

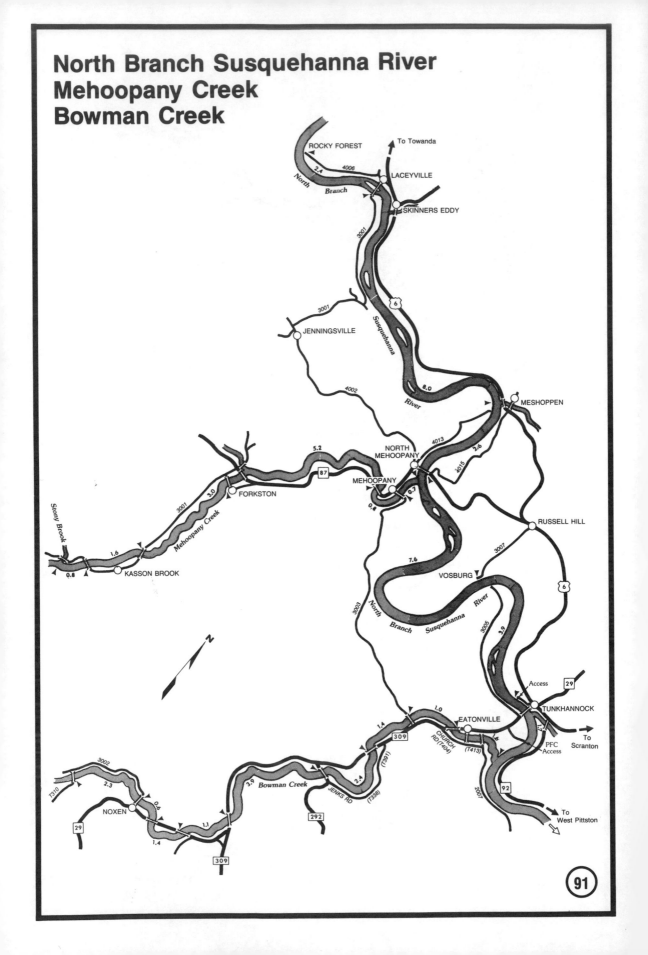

ROCKY FOREST

To Towanda

2.4   4006

LACEYVILLE

North   Branch

SKINNERS EDDY

3001

3001

6

JENNINGSVILLE

Susquehanna

4002

8.0   MESHOPPEN

River

5.2   4013   2.6

NORTH
MEHOOPANY   4015

FORKSTON   3001   3.0   MEHOOPANY

0.7

0.4

Stony Brook   Mehoopany Creek   RUSSELL HILL

1.6   7.6   3007

0.8   KASSON BROOK   VOSBURG   6

3003   North   Branch   Susquehanna   River   3005   3.9

Access   29

TUNKHANNOCK

1.0   EATONVILLE

1.4

309   CHURCH   To Scranton
RD (T404)   1.5

(T391)   (1413)   PFC
Access

3002   2.4   (T338)   2007   92

T310   2.3   3.9   Bowman Creek   JENKS RD   To
West Pittston

0.6   292

NOXEN

29   1.1

1.4

309

91

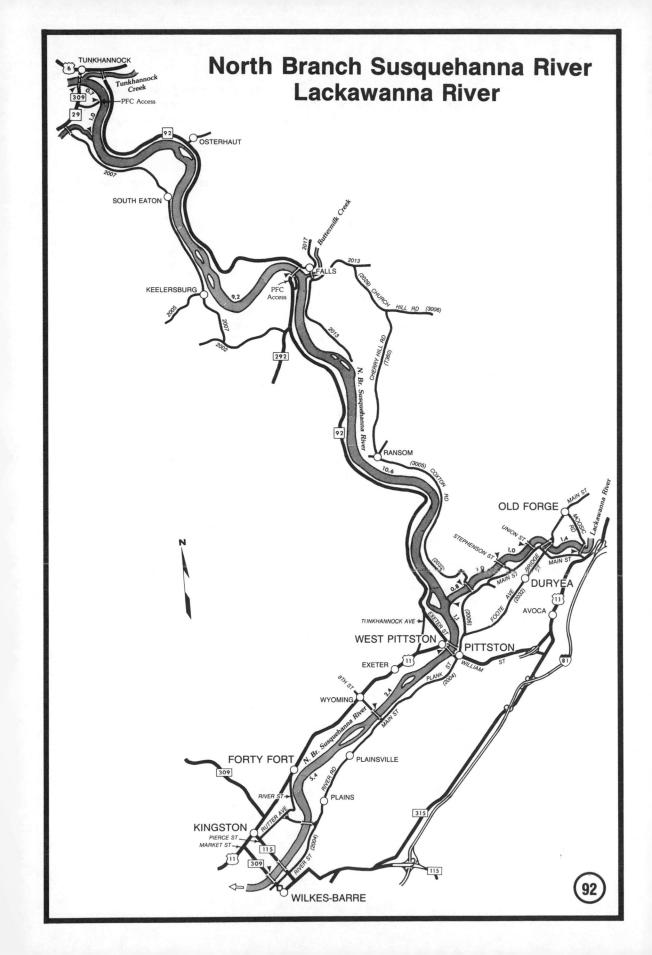

North Branch Susquehanna River
Lackawanna River

TUNKHANNOCK

Tunkhannock Creek

PFC Access

OSTERHAUT

SOUTH EATON

Buttermilk Creek

FALLS

PFC Access

KEELERSBURG

9.2

CHURCH HILL RD

CHERRY HILL RD

292

N. Br. Susquehanna River

92

RANSOM

10.6

COXTON RD

OLD FORGE

MAIN ST

MOOSIC RD

Lackawanna River

UNION ST

STEPHENSON ST

MAIN ST

BRIDGE ST

MAIN ST

DURYEA

0.8

FOOTE AVE

AVOCA

TUNKHANNOCK AVE

EXETER ST

WEST PITTSTON

PITTSTON

EXETER

WILLIAM ST

8TH ST

PLANK ST

WYOMING

MAIN ST

FORTY FORT

N. Br. Susquehanna River

Plainsville

RIVER RD

5.4

RIVER ST

PLAINS

KINGSTON

PIERCE ST

MARKET ST

RUTTER AVE

RIVER ST

WILKES-BARRE

92

you continue into New York State, take out at the first bridge (connecting Conklin and Kirkwood) on the right, at the Kirkwood Town Park. If you decide to continue paddling on through New York to Section 2, beware of a low but lethal dam that blocks the river in Binghamton.

HAZARDS: Power dam just below Oakland and Susquehanna. Carry on right.

WATER CONDITIONS: Canoeable from ice-out (usually late March) to winter freeze-up (December), though you often need to drag through the shallow spots during August through October.

GAUGE: USGS gauge at Conklin, N.Y. (call Central PA) drops to about 2.0 feet during the late summer dry period.

Section 2. Sayre PFC Access to Pittston (U.S. Rte. 11)					
Gradient	Difficulty	Distance	Time	Scenery	Map
2	1	94.6	31.0	Good to Very Good	89,90,91,92

TRIP DESCRIPTION: With the inflow of the Chenango River in Binghamton and the Chemung River below Sayre, the North Branch now becomes a true river and a handsome one. This section starts within a mile-wide valley, with farms covering the bottomlands and low mountains along its edge. But the mountains rise as the river progresses southward, and below Towanda the narrowing and deepening valley assumes a canyon-like stature. Long and tiered cliffs of reddish sandstone begin to alternately cap the mountain walls that form the outsides of the river's great bends. Clearly the highlight of this journey, these cliffs are particularly striking above and below Wyalusing.

Civilization has been relatively forgiving to this section of river. Only the ubiquitous presence of summer homes mar the grandeur of these miles. There are several towns along this section, all of which would be right at home in backwoods New England. Industry is scattered, but that which is there is big, such as the sprawling paper mill at Mehoopany or the Masonite Plant at Wysox. A busy railroad follows the river, but busy U.S. Rte. 6 generally stays up and away. So combining all these characteristics with a river that is smooth, swift, and only occasionally ruffled by the simplest of riffles, this reach makes a fine extended canoe trip, providing that you can find a campsite between all the summer homes.

There was once one additional town along this section, and it was unlike any other. Located between Towanda and Wyalusing, this settlement, known as Asylum, became an instant home in 1793 for aristocratic French refugees who had escaped the horrors of the French Revolution. Fueled by ample reserves of wealth, these settlers established a genteel frontier culture, where buckskin mixed with lace, and where one might live in a log cabin, but beneath it would lie a cellar filled with the finest of wines. The good times lasted for nine years, until 1802, when Napoleon granted these people amnesty, and they responded most gratefully by returning to their homeland.

HAZARDS: None.

WATER CONDITIONS: Canoeable from ice-out in spring to winter freeze-up.

GAUGE: USGS gauges at Towanda and Meshoppen (call Central PA) can respectively drop to around minus 0.3 feet and 7.5 feet in late summer. Both are passable levels.

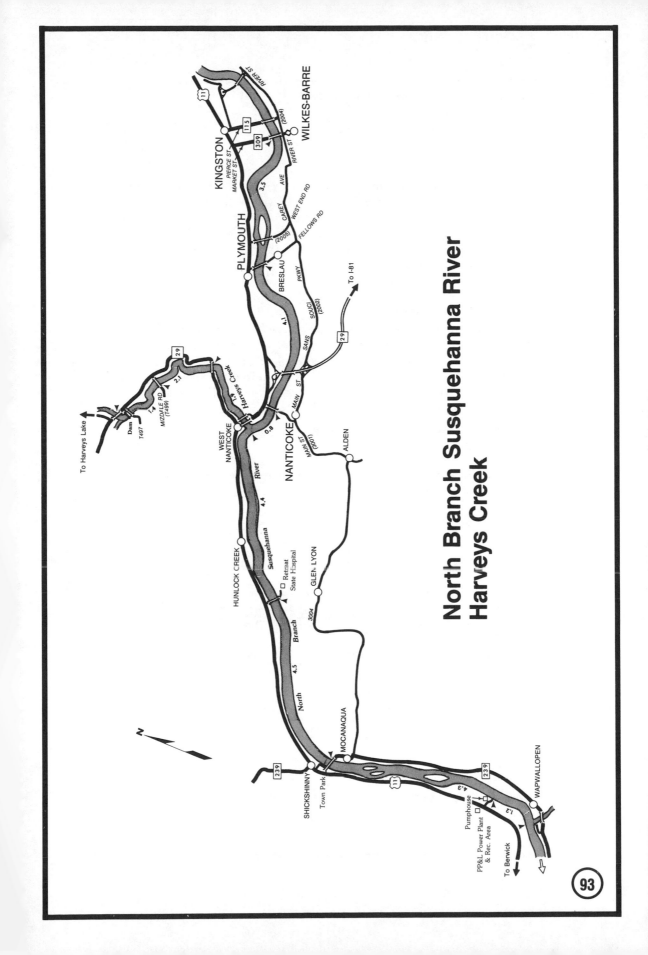

North Branch Susquehanna River
Harveys Creek

WILKES-BARRE

KINGSTON

PLYMOUTH

RIVER ST

RIVER ST (2004)

115

309

PIERCE ST.

MARKET ST.

3.5

CAREY AVE

WEST END RD

FELLOWS RD

BRESLAU

(2005)

SANS SOUCI PKWY

(2002)

To I-81

29

11

4.1

MAIN ST

2.9

2.1

MIZDALE RD (T499)

Harveys Creek

1.7

1.9

Dam T497

To Harveys Lake

WEST NANTICOKE

River

0.8

NANTICOKE

MAIN ST (3001)

ALDEN

HUNLOCK CREEK

4.4

Susquehanna

Retreat State Hospital

GLEN LYON

3004

4.5

Branch

North

MOCANAQUA

N

239

SHICKSHINNY

Town Park

11

4.3

239

WAPWALLOPEN

Pumphouse

PP&L Power Plant & Rec. Area

1.2

To Berwick

93

Section 3. Pittston (U.S. Rte. 11) to Nanticoke					
Gradient	Difficulty	Distance	Time	Scenery	Map
2	1	15.4	5.0	Fair	92,93

TRIP DESCRIPTION: The Wyoming Valley is not exactly Pennsylvania's garden spot. So with that in mind, you should appreciate just how relatively well the riverside has fared, with only modest damage. The paddler views little of the surrounding, unbroken, urban sprawl, thanks to a screen of high and wooded banks. In contrast, the passage through Wilkes-Barre and Kingston is all leveed, which while bland, provides a clear and impressive panorama of the best of Wilkes-Barre's skyline. This is most striking at Christmas, after dark, when the downtown skyline is accented by an outstanding light display.

The match box houses on the hillsides, the coal mines, industry, and ugliness seem as if they have been there forever. But in the mid-1700s, the Wyoming Valley was the wildest of frontiers—a few log cabin settlements and bottomland cornfields breaking the endless wilderness. Just who owned this territory was bitterly disputed.

New Englanders vied with Pennsylvanians for control, while the Indians insisted that the land was theirs. Over 35 years of bickering exploded in 1778, when Indians allied with Tories, swooped down on the outnumbered settlers near Forty Fort and commenced a massacre that may have removed as many as 300 men, women, and children from the census.

HAZARDS: None. Indians and Tories have all moved away.

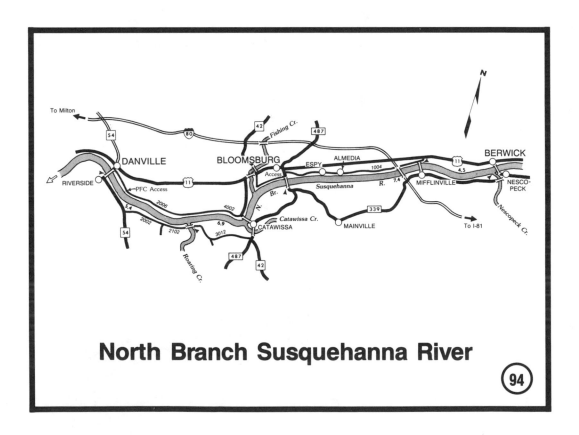

North Branch Susquehanna River

(94)

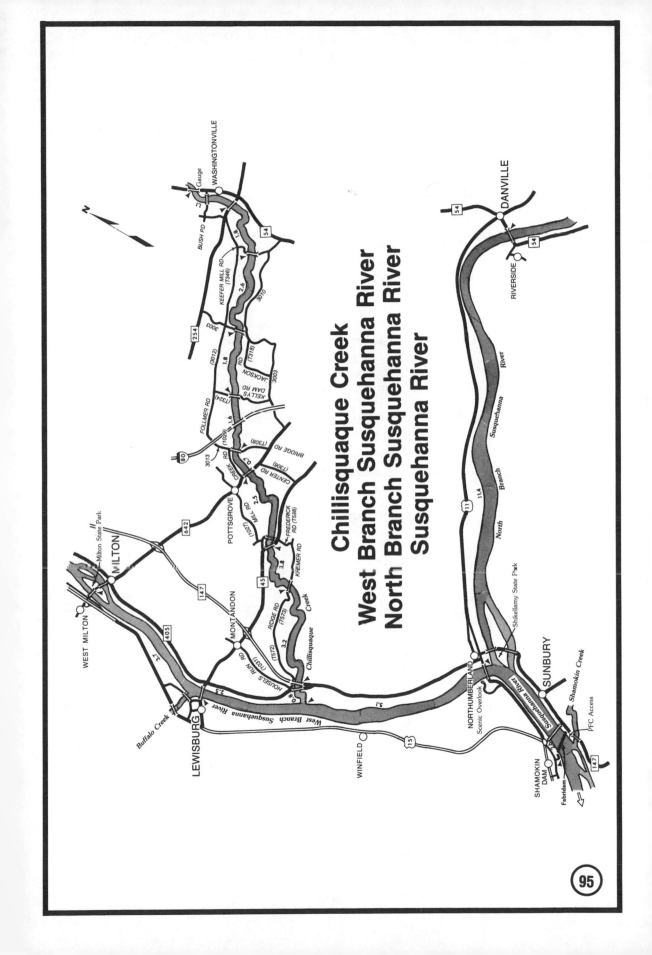

Chillisquaque Creek
West Branch Susquehanna River
North Branch Susquehanna River
Susquehanna River

95

WATER CONDITIONS: Canoeable from spring ice-out (usually March) until winter freeze (December).

GAUGE: USGS gauge at Wilkes-Barre (call Central PA) gets down to around 0.0 feet in late summer. This level is still floatable.

Section 4. Nanticoke to mouth					
Gradient	Difficulty	Distance	Time	Scenery	Map
2	A to 1	56.1	12.0	Good	93,94,95,100

TRIP DESCRIPTION: This section starts off in style, with the brownstone ramparts of Tilsbury Knob on the right, a bouncy chain of wavelets, called Nanticoke Falls, straight ahead, and many ensuing miles of steep and forested mountain palisades guiding the river southwestward. The great, white cooling towers of the new power plant near Wapwallopen then mark the transition to a wide farm valley and wider river. There are three large towns on this section: Berwick, Bloomsburg, and then Danville. The first has found a hallowed place in American history as the birthplace of the potato chip. As far as Berwick, the riverbanks are lined with summer homes. But below Berwick, development is surprisingly spotty. A giant, smelly industrial plant below Danville is the only real eyesore (and nosesore) on this reach.

Most of the river is glass smooth, with only short riffles. The riffles include, at low water levels, the v-shaped form of old fishtrap weirs. The smooth water is at least accompanied by a strong current, though even this dies in the wide, miserable, and motorboat-infested pool formed by the Fabridam. Take out on the lower left side of the island at Shikellamy State Park or at the ramp in Northumberland, at the confluence of the North and West branches.

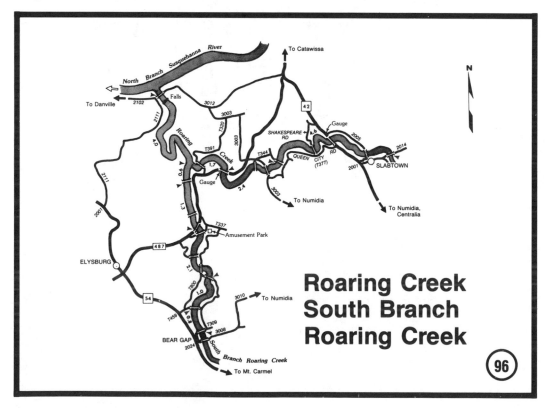

**Roaring Creek
South Branch
Roaring Creek**

(96)

HAZARDS: None.

WATER CONDITIONS: Canoeable from spring ice-out to winter freeze.

GAUGE: USGS gauge in Danville (call Central PA) gets down to around 2.5 feet in late summer. This is an adequate level.

Roaring Creek

INTRODUCTION: Roaring Creek is a small and easy-to-overlook wet weather stream that enters the other side of the Susquehanna, between Bloomsburg and Danville. The name Roaring Creek is a bit of an overstatement. But it does rush. Thus, the main creek makes a pleasant novice to intermediate open boat run, while its strainer-infested South Branch can be a real terror.

Section 1. Slabtown (SR2014) to mouth					
Gradient	Difficulty	Distance	Time	Scenery	Map
25	1 to 2 +	13.0	4.0	Fair to Good	96

TRIP DESCRIPTION: After a warm-up flush through the backyards and frontyards of downtown Slabtown, Roaring Creek heads for the hills. As far as the confluence with the South Branch, the creek flows through a narrow and seemingly remote farm valley, lined by hardwood-covered hillsides that are mottled by the deep green of hemlocks. This is an outstanding creek for viewing covered bridges, as is its South Branch. The water initially rumbles down almost continuous cobbly and rocky rapids, but the pace gradually slows.

Below the South Branch, the now wider creek winds through a secluded and shadowy hemlock gorge, decorated in spots by pretty cliffs and not-so-pretty power lines. The water is relatively smooth until some ledges appear. These quickly increase in height and interest until a real whopper, a falls, demands a carry. A few strokes through the chasm below, usually calmed by the back-up from the high Susquehanna, takes you around the bend to an easy take-out at SR3012. If Roaring Creek is high, but the Susquehanna is not, there are a few more interesting ledges below the falls.

HAZARDS: Strainers and waterfalls above SR3012.

WATER CONDITIONS: Canoeable in spring during fast snowmelt or within three days of hard rain.

GAUGE: Painted canoe gauge on right abutment of Pa. Rte. 42, 0.5 feet being minimum canoeable level. Painted canoe gauge on Pa. Rte. 487, 1.5 feet being minimum.

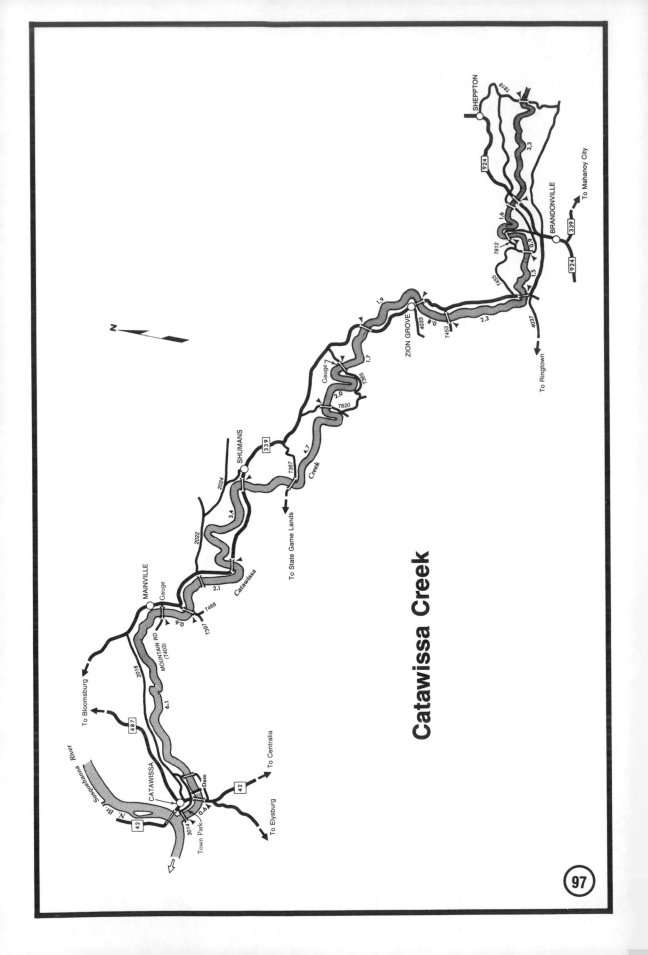

Catawissa Creek

Gradient	Difficulty	Distance	Time	Scenery	Map
35	1 to 3 –	5.8	2.0	Poor to Very Good	96

TRIP DESCRIPTION: The clear waters of this tiny trout stream rush down an almost continuous rocky rapid, past hemlock-lined banks, in a narrow and often gorge-like valley. The whitewater is pushy but not inherently that difficult. However, you can count on a few fallen trees lying in the most inconvenient of spots, to make the run a challenge. The pretty scenery ends at an amusement park and string of summer homes above Pa. Rte. 487. The gradient also eases here to just simple and steady riffles. Take out at the covered bridge (T369) where Rte. 487 veers east to leave the creek, unless you desire to continue down Roaring Creek.

HAZARDS: Strainers in fast water.

WATER CONDITIONS: Same as Section 1.

GAUGE: None. Judge conditions at T309.

Catawissa Creek

INTRODUCTION: It would be difficult to dislike a trip on Catawissa Creek. This medium small tributary of the North Branch Susquehanna follows a scenic and fast-moving path from the Schuylkill County coal fields to its mouth near Bloomsburg. Its name is Indian for "growing fat." The exact relevance of this name escapes the author, who has never gained so much as a pound since last running this creek.

Section 1. T818 to mouth

Gradient	Difficulty	Distance	Time	Scenery	Map
17	1 to 2	33.7	10.5	Good to Very Good	97

TRIP DESCRIPTION: The put-in is about four miles northeast of Brandonville, just a ridge away from heavy-duty coal country. The influence is only evident by the fine black coating of coal dust on the bottom of the brook. The creek hurries off down a crooked valley, where great mountainsides loom above the water on almost every turn. Catawissa files down a cozy green corridor of rhododendron and hemlock, often broken by finely tiered cliffs and shelves of reddish shale. County roads and a few summer homes are only sporadic intrusions.

This is a rocky stream that can keep novices scurrying, but hardly threatened. Rapids are continuous at first, but then mellow into an endless line of riffles, punctuated by occasional easy rock gardens and boulder patch rapids. The only hazard is a sharp three and a half-foot dam above Pa. Rte. 42. Carry on the left when the creek is high and on the right at low water.

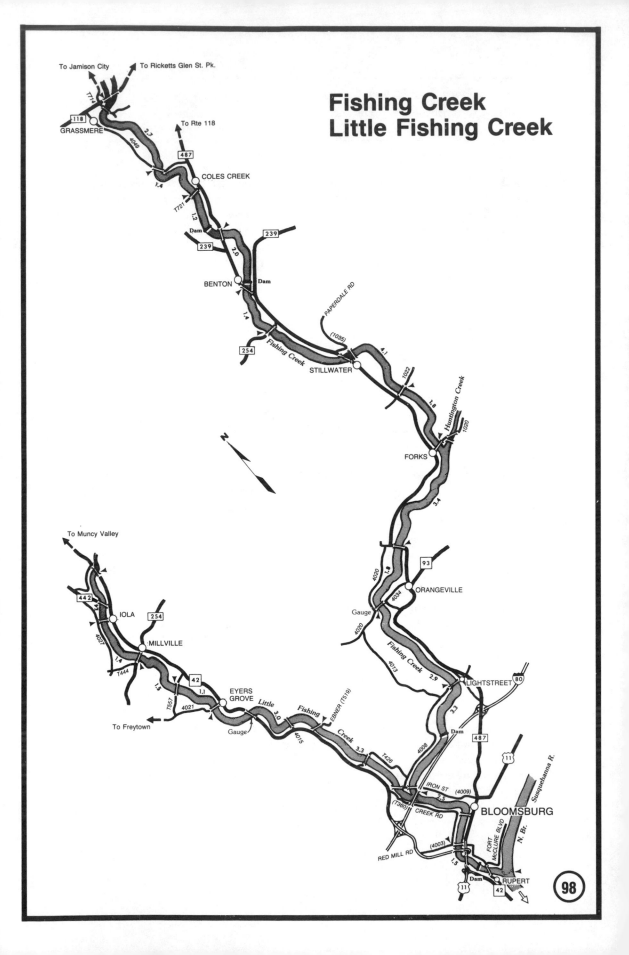

Fishing Creek
Little Fishing Creek

To Jamison City

To Ricketts Glen St. Pk.

T714

118
GRASSMERE

4049

2.7

To Rte 118

487

1.4

COLES CREEK

T721

1.2

Dam

239

2.0

239

BENTON

Dam

1.4

254

Fishing Creek

PAPERDALE RD

(1035)

STILLWATER

4.1

1022

1.8

Huntington Creek

1020

FORKS

3.4

N

4020

1.4

93

ORANGEVILLE

4034

Gauge

4020

Fishing Creek

4013

2.9

LIGHTSTREET

80

To Muncy Valley

442

IOLA

254

4027

MILLVILLE

T444

1.4

42

1.5

T557

4021

EYERS GROVE

1.1

Little

3.0

Fishing

EBNER (T519)

Creek

3.3

To Freytown

Gauge

4015

T426

4008

3.3

Dam

487

11

IRON ST

(4009)

2.5

(7360)

CREEK RD

BLOOMSBURG

Susquehanna R.

FORT McCLURE BLVD

N. Br.

RED MILL RD

(4003)

1.5

Dam

11

RUPERT

42

98

HAZARDS: Weir above Rte. 42, Catawissa. Strainers in first several miles.

WATER CONDITIONS: Canoeable in spring during snowmelt or within two days of hard rain, above Brandonville, and four days below.

GAUGE: Painted gauges on right abutment of T365 and on Mountain Road (T403). Respectively, they should read at least 2.0 feet and 1.5 feet to start at T818 and over 1.5 feet and 0.8 feet to start near Zion Grove. Roughly, USGS gauge at Berne, on Schuylkill River (call Philadelphia), should be at least 7.0 feet to start at top, and 5.9 feet for below Zion Grove.

Fishing Creek

INTRODUCTION: Fishing Creek picks a path down through the rugged terrain of northern Columbia County, to mix with the Susquehanna at Bloomsburg. This is a generally scenic path which, in spite of its rugged surroundings, is quite suitable for novice travelers.

Section 1. Pa. Rte. 118 to mouth					
Gradient	Difficulty	Distance	Time	Scenery	Map
16	1 to 1 +	30.0	10.0	Fair to Good	98

TRIP DESCRIPTION: The Rte. 118 put-in starts you out on about 300 yards of the tiny West Branch Fishing Creek. If the West Branch looks too small, low, or snaggy, start a quarter mile downstream at T714.

For the most part, Fishing Creek presents a pleasing atmosphere, set in a narrow valley that is bordered by a line of generally low hills, clothed in woods or pasture. At moderate levels, especially in its upper reaches, the creek runs surprisingly clear. As far as Benton, development is scarce. Below Benton, periodic strings of seasonal homes interrupt the otherwise wooded, riparian facade. Except for a brush with I-80, Fishing Creek remains mostly rustic even as it swings around Bloomsburg.

In its first several miles, Fishing Creek is fairly busy, but not inherently difficult. Then for the remainder of the way, easy rapids and riffles come and go at a more gradual pace. A predominately gravel stream bed means that undercut bends and split channels blocked by strainers may periodically inconvenience you. You must also deal with four small dams, all unrunnable, located on the shuttle map. Particularly interesting among these dams is a three-foot-high and curving barrier constructed of sheet piling, located below Light Street. Just think of it—an iron dam. Doesn't that sound intimidating?

Take out at the covered bridge at Rupert. If you still insist on floating every last inch, a short path leads up from the left bank, at the mouth, to Fort McClure Boulevard.

HAZARDS: Strainers and four small dams.

WATER CONDITIONS: Canoeable in spring during snowmelt or within five days of hard rain.

GAUGE: USGS gauge (call Central PA or visit) at county bridge connecting SR4024 and SR4020, near Orangeville, must read at least 3.1 feet to start at Rte. 118. Also, there is a painted gauge on the left abutment of that county bridge. A level of 1.1 feet is minimum at start at Rte. 118. Staff gauge on right pier of Creek Road, T360, Bloomsburg, should read 0.8 feet to do entire creek and 0.5 feet to do the last dozen miles.

Little Fishing Creek

INTRODUCTION: Little Fishing Creek is a disappointing little feeder to Fishing Creek, joining the mainstem on the west side of Bloomsburg. This creek just does not do justice to the beautiful countryside through which it flows. So go paddle elsewhere, on some stream that does.

Section 1. Pa. Rte. 42 (N. of Iola) to mouth					
Gradient	Difficulty	Distance	Time	Scenery	Map
18	1	11.8	3.5	Good to Poor	98

TRIP DESCRIPTION: The creek starts out with promise, rushing over lots of riffles and heading away from the highway (be alert here for fences and low-sweeping limbs). But this promise proves to be an illusion, as the gradient gradually lessens and the creek returns to the highway. This highway, Pa. Rte. 42, is the bain of Little Fishing Creek. Rte. 42 is fairly busy and noisy, and the many houses and buildings that line it range from ugly to uninteresting. The immediate streambanks offer little relief, for they are often littered with rubbish. Only one short attractive stretch remains, where the creek parts from the road, between Millville and Eyers Grove. Take out at the mouth, carrying up the steep hill to Creek Road, T360, beneath the high I-80 Bridge.

HAZARDS: Strainers, mostly in the first few miles.

WATER CONDITIONS: Canoeable in spring during snowmelt or within two days of hard rain.

GAUGE: Abandoned USGS gauge, upstream right of Rte. 42 below Eyers Grove, should read 0.9 feet to start at top and 0.8 feet to start at gauge.

Huntington Creek

INTRODUCTION: Gathering its waters from the south face of Luzerne County's North Mountain Plateau, Huntington Creek doubles the size of Fishing Creek, which it joins at the village of Forks. Its varied headwaters include Kitchen Creek, whose waterfall wonderland, back in Ricketts Glen State Park, more than justifies a trip to this part of the state. Unlike its wild origins though, the canoeable Huntington Creek follows a quiet path that is particularly suitable for novices.

Section 1. Pleasant Valley (SR4024) to mouth					
Gradient	Difficulty	Distance	Time	Scenery	Map
12	A to 1	17.1	5.0	Good	99

TRIP DESCRIPTION: For most of its length, Huntington Creek flows through rugged and thinly populated country. The creek meanders about flat bottoms backed by pine-covered hills. Except for a string of summer homes above Jonestown and a few villages, the paddler usually views only quiet forest, the flank of Huntington Mountain, and some farms. Even better, there are no busy highways to disturb the piece along this stream.

The relatively clear waters are usually smooth and swift. But deadfalls, a problem when the creek periodically braids, demand some reasonable boat-handling or stopping ability. There are three dams across this creek: a two-footer at the mouth of Marsh Run in Huntington Mills, runnable at center, a three-footer above the old gray covered bridge a half mile below Huntington Mills, to be carried on either side, and a six-footer just above Jonestown, carried on the right.

HAZARDS: Strainers on split channels and three small dams.

WATER CONDITIONS: Canoeable in spring during snowmelt or within four days of hard rain.

GAUGE: Staff gauge on left abutment of SR1020, upstream of the twin covered bridge above Forks, should read at least 1.0 feet.

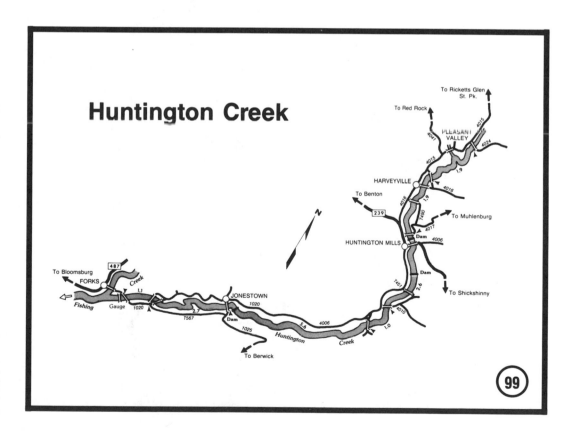

Huntington Creek

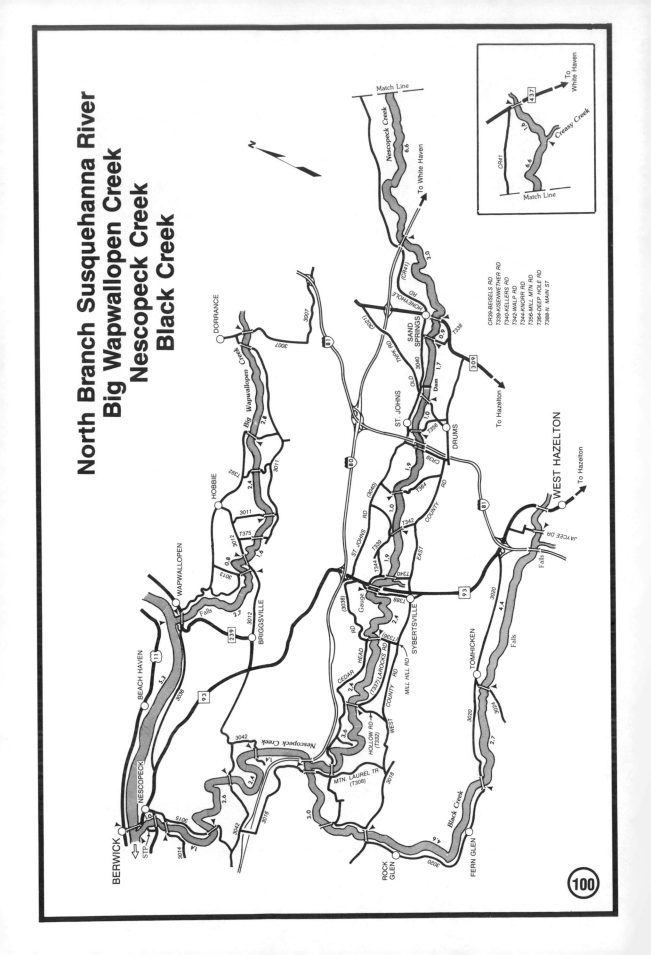

North Branch Susquehanna River
Big Wapwallopen Creek
Nescopeck Creek
Black Creek

CR39-BEISELS RD
T339-KISENWETHER RD
T340-KELLERS RD
T342-WALP RD
T344-KNORR RD
T356-MILL MTN RD
T364-DEEP HOLE RD
T388-N. MAIN ST

100

Nescopeck Creek

INTRODUCTION: Nescopeck Creek is one of the traditional whitewater favorites of Pennsylvania paddlers, and rightfully so. It offers consistent miles of beautiful scenery, some excellent intermediate whitewater, and lots of fast and easy miles of novice water also. While, thanks to I-80 and I-81, it is close to millions, once on the water, the floater of Nescopeck will feel a million miles from anywhere.

Section 1. Pa. Rte. 437 to Pa. Rte. 309					
Gradient	Difficulty	Distance	Time	Scenery	Map
19	A to 3 –	11.3	4.0	Fair to Excellent	100
1.5 @ 86					

TRIP DESCRIPTION: This is an offbeat run that will only appeal to a few. The clear upper Nescopeck flows mostly through an utterly beautiful wilderness valley. But getting into there is not easy. While most of this section flows silky smooth, the first few miles are anything but that. For the ten-foot-wide brook at Pa. Rte. 437 screams downhill, over a rocky bed, through tight chutes, and with little opportunity to eddy out if strainers appear. Another problem is that the first mile flows through a private club where your right to be on the creek might be challenged, especially after trout season begins. If you survive the man-made and natural problems of the first mile and a half, Creasy Creek's flow adds some elbow room, and the gradient substantially decreases. But another mile of nastily braiding channels prolongs the challenge of this run. After that, except for an isolated and short stretch of bouldery rapids, the creek meanders peacefully through hardwood forests, glades, scores of white birch, and alder swamps until it reaches the amusement park at Pa. Rte. 309.

HAZARDS: Strainers in fast water and possible encounter with hostile landowner in first mile.

WATER CONDITIONS: Canoeable in spring during snowmelt or within three days of hard rain.

GAUGE: None. Judge at Rte. 437. Roughly, USGS gauge at White Haven, on Lehigh River (call Philadelphia), should be over 4.4 feet.

Section 2. Pa. Rte. 309 to Pa. Rte. 93					
Gradient	Difficulty	Distance	Time	Scenery	Map
20	1 to 1 +	8.4	3.0	Fair to Good	100

TRIP DESCRIPTION: This is the least desirable segment of Nescopeck Creek. To I-81, the creek winds past scores of summer homes, while below there, it retreats to the seclusion of a beautiful, shady, shut in, and hemlock-bound corridor. But the channel through this pretty stretch, unfortunately, repeatedly divides (or multiplies, depending on how you look at it) into narrow and inevitably tree-choked channels. Most of this passage runs fast and smooth, but there are some easy rapids around St. Johns, a runnable two-foot weir at St. Johns, and an old two-foot wooden weir at Kellers Road, T340 (run left).

HAZARDS: Strainers are a real hazard on this stretch. Two weirs are both runnable.

WATER CONDITIONS: Canoeable in spring during snowmelt or within four days of hard rain.

GAUGE: Canoe gauge at Pa. Rte. 93 and pole gauge at T388 should each read about eight inches. Roughly, USGS gauge at White Haven, on Lehigh River (call Philadelphia), should be over 3.8 feet.

Section 3. Pa. Rte. 93 to Black Creek					
Gradient	Difficulty	Distance	Time	Scenery	Map
27	1 to 3 –	8.4	2.5	Excellent	100

TRIP DESCRIPTION: Now begins a most delightful piece of whitewater. Not only is this section fun to paddle down, but its numerous eddys, surfing waves, and holes make it an exceptional playing stream. Rapids are formed by ledges and patches of unusually convoluted sandstone boulders, including one spectacular sharkfin-like monolith that splits the current of a strong chute. Pin a boat here and they will be talking about you for years to come. All of this whitewater is confined to a hemlock-filled gorge that, so far, has been spared much development. Many paddlers take out at Hollow Road, T332, if they seek only the cream of the whitewater. But the extension of this trip to Black Creek treats one to some beautiful cliffs and miles of busy Class 1 and 2 rapids.

HAZARDS: None.

WATER CONDITIONS: Canoeable in spring during snowmelt and within ten days of hard rain. In average year, it is usually up all during late March and April.

GAUGE: Painted gauge on left abutment of Rte. 93 and striped red and white pole gauge by left abutment of T388. About one inch on the former and minus one inch on the latter is minimal level. Roughly, USGS gauge at White Haven, on the Lehigh River (call Philadelphia), should be over 3.6 feet.

Section 4. Black Creek to mouth					
Gradient	Difficulty	Distance	Time	Scenery	Map
16	1	8.8	2.5	Fair to Very Good	100

TRIP DESCRIPTION: The remaining miles of Nescopeck are ideal for the novice. Except where I-80 crowds the creek, the scenery is about as nice as that above. The gradient subsides to form easy rapids between quiet pools, with no permanent hazards. Take out on the left, behind Nescopeck's sewage treatment plant.

HAZARDS: None.

WATER CONDITIONS: Canoeable in spring during snowmelt and within seven days of hard rain.

GAUGE: Gauges at Rte. 93 and T388 should read about four inches. Roughly, USGS gauge at White Haven should read over 3.7 feet.

Black Creek

INTRODUCTION: Black Creek is a little-known whitewater wonder, tributary to the popular Nescopeck Creek. Gushing from the bowels of Hazelton, this creek demands a paddler who is not only skilled, but able to stare dysentery, hepatitis, and typhoid in the eye without even blinking. So if you have had your shots, check this one out after the next downpour.

Section 1. Hazelton (Jaycee Drive) to mouth					
Gradient	Difficulty	Distance	Time	Scenery	Map
56	1 to 4 – , 6	14.6	5.0	Very Good to Poor	100

TRIP DESCRIPTION: Pitifully little watershed contributes to Black Creek's flow at the put-in on Jaycee Road in Valmont Industrial Park. So you must catch this immediately after a hard rain. Under such conditions, brown and oil streaked runoff from the streets of Hazelton mixes with black, coal dust-laden mine runoff, which is then diluted with stinking gray sewage bypassing (why?) Hazelton's shiny and modern sewage treatment plant.

But one has only a few minutes to contemplate this soup before confronting the brink of an incredible cataract of sandstone boulders, railroad ties, and logs. A short, savage drag on the right, through dense birch and laurel thickets, delivers you to the safety of the pool below, while oblivious motorists whiz by, high above, on I-81. A few miles of smooth water, boulder patch rapids, and ledges carry you through remote and pleasant woodlands, marred only by the ribbons of dried toilet paper caked on every overhanging branch and fluttering in the breeze. Then, where a big rock outcrop rises above the right bank, the creek splits about an island and cascades over another long and unnegotiable pile of big boulders. One should notice by now that the boulders on this creek are of a rough, flesh and boat-ripping sandstone conglomerate, so paddle with care.

Below Tomhickon, the gradient steepens and a busy stream begins careening for mile after delightful mile down bars of boulders and cobbles. The surrounding scenery degrades to houses, backyard trash heaps, and coal tailings piles, but the whitewater should mostly distract you. Eventually though, the run mellows.

Then, just when the fun appears to be over, Black Creek comes back for an encore. Passing the village of Rock Glen, the creek rushes off into a remote, cool, and hemlock-shaded rock glen. Sporting some steep and technical rapids and finally having escaped from the coal country blight, poor and abused Black Creek finishes in style.

HAZARDS: Cataract beneath I-81 and a Class 6 (or higher) rapid a few miles below. Also, watch for strainers.

WATER CONDITIONS: Canoeable in spring within 24 hours of hard rain.

GAUGE: None.

Big Wapwallopen Creek

INTRODUCTION: The only thing big about "Big Wap" is its name, which was taken from that of an Indian village that was situated nearby, along the Susquehanna. This clear brook spills off the southwest edge of the Pocono Plateau to join the Susquehanna above Berwick. It offers a little bit of nice whitewater canoeing for the novice to intermediate paddler and some outstanding hiking for anybody.

Section 1. SR3007 to mouth					
Gradient	Difficulty	Distance	Time	Scenery	Map
45	1 to 2 +	10.3	4.5	Good to Excellent	100
2.8 @ 86					

TRIP DESCRIPTION: Big Wapwallopen Creek offers a short and scenic run through an open and rural valley that slopes steeply up from the stream. The creek is small—so small that at times the hemlock forms a solid, cool, green canopy over its waters. The first few miles rush down almost continuous rapids formed by small ledges and boulders. The remainder of the way is fairly slow. It is best to end your canoe trip at SR3013.

It is possible to paddle and portage the remaining miles to the mouth, but it is much easier and more rewarding to hike it. This has the additional advantage of not requiring highwater to accomplish. If you elect to hike this section, it is best to start your walk at Pa. Rte. 239. You soon discover that the primary reason for hoofing this section is that it is graced with three big and beautiful waterfalls. The uppermost cuts a jagged profile formed by brick-like tiers of reddish sandstone. It is a masterpiece. Then adding to the interest are the scattered ruins of an extensive powder mill complex that utilized Wapwallopen's steep gradient for hydropower. Bring your camera and fast film too, as it is cool and shady down there.

HAZARDS: Three waterfalls below SR3013. Occasional strainers.

WATER CONDITIONS: Canoeable in spring during snowmelt and within two days of hard rain.

GAUGE: None. Roughly, USGS gauge at White Haven, on Lehigh River (call Philadelphia), should read over 4.4 feet.

Harveys Creek

INTRODUCTION: Harveys Creek is an obscure torrent that gushes into the North Branch Susquehanna across from Nanticoke. It is an outstanding whitewater run that advanced paddlers will surely enjoy, if they are lucky enough to corner its brief periods of high water.

Section 1. Pa. Rte. 29 to mouth					
Gradient	Difficulty	Distance	Time	Scenery	Map
82	2 to 4	5.4	1.5	Good to Very Good	93

TRIP DESCRIPTION: The put-in is at the second Pa. Rte. 29 bridge above West Nanticoke, exactly five road miles above U.S. Rte. 11. For its first two miles, Harveys' clear but dark waters are hidden from the road. In classic form, that is where the creek displays its most troublesome side. You will hardly be warmed up before you have to follow a steep and tangled portage around a deteriorating old dam. And just a bit farther downstream, the creek squeezes through a rocky notch to plunge over a small falls (or big ledge), worth carrying. Then, immediately below Mizdale Road, T499, on a blind bend, the creek accelerates down a long and nasty slide, also worth carrying. Finally Harveys Creek settles down into a wonderful and steadily steepening descent over a bouldery and ledgy bed. All this climaxes just above West Nanticoke in a plunge through a narrow and nasty cleft in a wide ledge. The well-aerated pool below is long enough for a roll attempt or two.

The entire creek lies within a pretty and forested gorge, but the adjacent highway dominates the scenery on the second half of the run. The rusty, columnar cliffs of Tilsbury Knob preside over the finish, before the creek files through West Nanticoke, between its stone retaining walls. Because of these walls there is no good take-out in town. So count on shortcutting through some backyards or bushwacking to get back to U.S. Rte. 11.

HAZARDS: A dam, two big ledges, and possible strainers.

WATER CONDITIONS: Canoeable in spring during fast snowmelt or within two days of hard rain.

GAUGE: None. Judge from road. Roughly, USGS gauge at White Haven, on Lehigh River (call Philadelphia), should read over 4.5 feet

Lackawanna River

INTRODUCTION: What paddlers in their right mind would canoe the Lackawanna River? Do you know just where and what the Lackawanna Valley is? This is the valley of Scranton, Pittston, Carbondale, and little towns with funny names like Throop, Moosic, and Olyphant. It is one big and sprawling strip city; the capital of Pennsylvania's crumbling anthracite empire. It is a place where towns were built on coal, literally. For it is here that, when old mines far below cave in, building foundations and city streets, up top, subside. It is a place where the mountain that you see in the distance is really, on closer inspection, not a mountain, but rather a huge pile of mine refuse. In summary, it is a place that most of us associate with ugliness, with a capital U.

But the Lackawanna River, the stream that drains this valley, is not entirely a lost cause. It is not all ugly. And it most definitely is not all flat. Whitewater boaters will find the extreme upper and lower Lackawanna to be a real, first class, whitewater playground. As for in between, who in their right mind would travel from anywhere beyond this valley to canoe there?

Section 1. Stillwater Lake to Carbondale (SR1033)					
Gradient	Difficulty	Distance	Time	Scenery	Map
56	1 to 3	9.8	3.5	Good to Poor	101

TRIP DESCRIPTION: Put in north of Forest City at the dead-ending old highway, off Pa. Rte. 171, 0.6 miles above the Rte. 171 Bridge over the Lackawanna. The whitewater starts abruptly at the outlet of Stillwater Lake, as the Lackawanna breaks through the runnable ruins of the old Stillwater Dam. From here the clear water dashes over cobbles and small boulders and then a few ledges, before pausing in a short pool behind a four-foot dam (carry) at Forest City. The Lackawanna reveals that it is an unusually rocky stream whose whitewater is almost continuous. Since this is a small stream, strainers are an occasional problem.

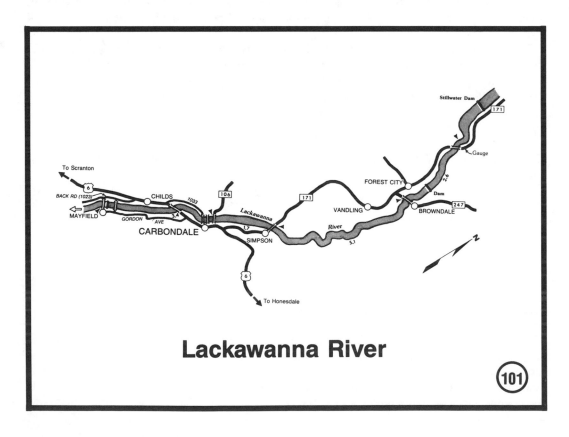

Lackawanna River

101

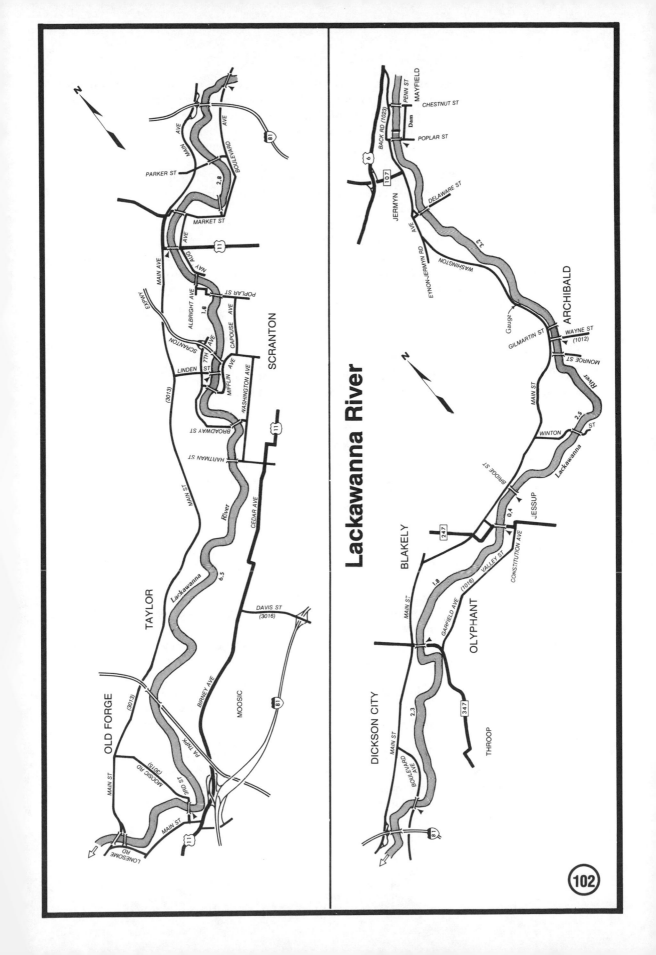

Lackawanna River

102

Below Forest City the bed assumes an increasingly ledgy nature. This characteristic is most outstanding approaching Simpson. When the houses of Simpson appear high above on the right, there is a blind bend, around which the friendly Lackawanna plunges over a distinctly high and nasty ledge, split by a craggy rock islet. You can choose between a narrow, blind, and curving flume on the left, or a vertical plunge through a notch on the right, where you flirt with undercut rocks.

From Simpson to Carbondale the stream remains as busy as above. But it is unusually well-endowed with lots of small, smooth, and sloping ledges that form wonderful surfing holes. This is no stretch through which to hurry.

The scenery is briefly beautiful below Stillwater Lake, as the stream rushes by stands of rhododendron and birchy woods. But the forest eventually deteriorates to predominately scrubby growth that struggles to survive on old mine refuse piles and other disturbed areas. On the other hand, with few structures visible from the river, an atmosphere of remoteness prevails as far as Simpson. Below Simpson the banks are totally urbanized or industrialized.

HAZARDS: Dam at Forest City, strainers, and difficult ledge above Simpson.

WATER CONDITIONS: Canoeable in spring during rapid snowmelt or within three days of hard rain.

GAUGE: USGS gauge on left, just below the put-in, should read at least 2.6 feet. USGS gauge at Archibald (call Central PA or inspect on site) should read at least 2.9 feet.

Section 2. Carbondale (SR1033) to mouth					
Gradient	Difficulty	Distance	Time	Scenery	Map
17	1, 4	28.6	9.5	Fair to Poor	101,102,92

TRIP DESCRIPTION: The Lackawanna gradually slows down below Carbondale, but remains lively as far as I-81. Occasional ledges still spice the trip. Potential hazards are limited to a five-foot dam (between Chestnut and Poplar streets) in a channelized stretch through Mayfield (run on left or right at moderate levels) and a combination broken dam and natural ledge below Jermyn, which demands scouting. From I-81 to Moosic the river runs fairly smooth, though there are still some long sets of riffles scattered along the way. The Lackawanna temporarily shifts personality at Moosic, as it suddenly roars down a long and curving Class 4 rapid formed by a complex staircase of ledges. This is a good place to stop and play. But this is a bad place to run in the late afternoon on a sunny spring day, as the sun and glare will blind you. As quickly as it started, the whitewater fizzles, and the remaining few miles to the mouth are smooth again. If you go the whole way, take out down the Susquehanna at the U.S. Rte. 11 Bridge in West Pittston.

This is seldom a pretty run. Trash and junk cover the banks. Even if they were clean, the banks are still ugly and unnatural. In Scranton the river flows through a canyon of stone and concrete retaining walls and high slag banks.

On the bright side, the urbanity can be interesting. Many a beautiful church dominates the skylines of the several towns above Scranton. There are still patches of woods here and there. And finally, there are the many sewage treatment plants that you will see. While not particularly pretty, they are comforting reminders of how much progress has been made in cleaning up what was once a stinking, open sewer.

HAZARDS: Dam at Mayfield and broken dam below Jermyn.

WATER CONDITIONS: Above I-81, it is canoeable during snowmelt and within five days of hard rain. Below I-81, canoeable in spring during snowmelt and within a week of hard rain. Also often up again in November and early December.

GAUGE: USGS gauge in Archibald, on right bank along Washington Avenue, 0.5 miles above Gilmartin Street (call Harrisburg or inspect on site), should read at least 2.7 feet for above I-81 and 2.4 feet for below. Also, USGS gauge at Old Forge (call Central PA) should read at least 3.1 feet for above I-81 and 2.9 feet for below.

Bowman Creek

INTRODUCTION: Bowman Creek drops off of the wild North Mountain Plateau, east of Ricketts Glen, to meet the Susquehanna across the river and just downstream of Tunkhannock. It offers an easily accessible and easy to shuttle, springtime novice whitewater cruise.

Section 1. Pa. Rte. 309 to mouth					
Gradient	Difficulty	Distance	Time	Scenery	Map
26	1 to 2	10.3	3.5	Fair to Good	91

TRIP DESCRIPTION: This is a fairly pretty stream that hurries down a deep and almost gorge-like mountain valley. It unfortunately falls short of its scenic potential because of an abundance of houses, rip-rapped banks, and proximity of the highway.

The put-in at Pa. Rte. 309, near its junction with Pa. Rte. 29, is not the head of navigation. You can squeeze in a few more action-packed miles by starting up above Noxon. If you do, watch for strainers.

From Rte. 309 the stream provides a pleasant and gravelly array of Class 1 and 2 rapids, and pools that are seldom too long. Be alert though, for about two miles below the start is Evans Falls—a beautiful eight-foot ledge that twists and squeezes Bowman's waters through a nasty notch into the emerald pool below. Carry on the left. The best finish is at SR2007, 0.7 miles above the Susquehanna, as there is no easy access at the mouth.

HAZARDS: Evans Falls, about two miles below the start.

WATER CONDITIONS: Canoeable in spring during snowmelt and within four days of hard rain.

GAUGE: None on creek. Judge conditions at put-in.

South Branch Tunkhannock Creek
Tunkhannock Creek
Martins Creek

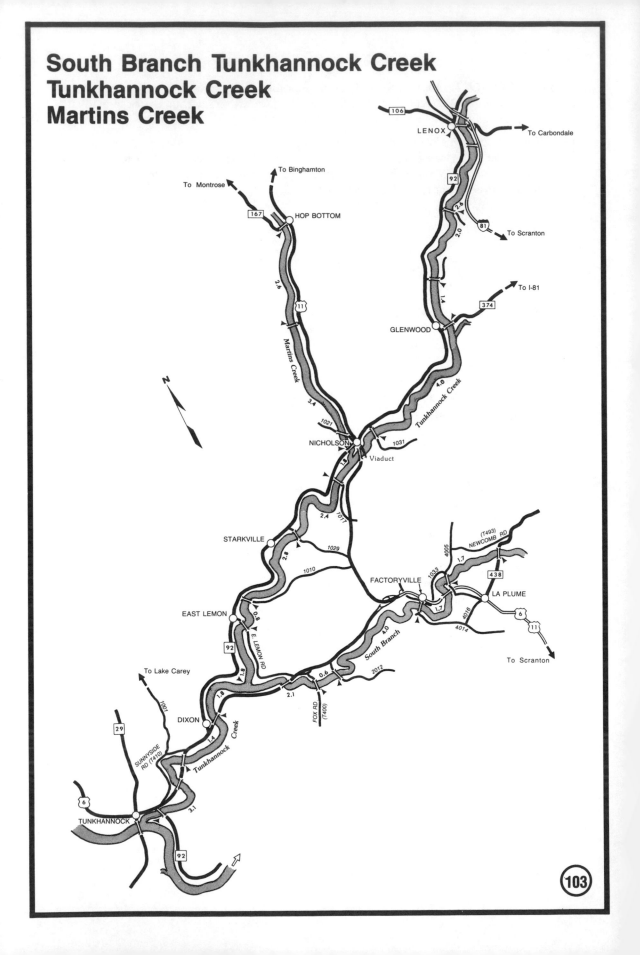

To Carbondale

106

LENOX

92

2.6

2.0

81

To Scranton

To Binghamton

To Montrose

167

HOP BOTTOM

11

2.6

Martins Creek

3.4

To I-81

374

1.4

GLENWOOD

4.0

Tunkhannock Creek

1021

1031

NICHOLSON

Viaduct

1.8

2.4

1077

STARKVILLE

2.8

1029

1010

(T493)

NEWCOMB RD

4005

1.7

1033

FACTORYVILLE

438

LA PLUME

EAST LEMON

0.8

92

E. LEMON RD

1.8

1.7

4016

4014

6

11

South Branch

4.0

To Scranton

0.6

2012

To Lake Carey

1.8

2.1

FOX RD

(T400)

DIXON

1001

29

1.4

SUNNYSIDE

RD (T410)

Tunkhannock Creek

6

3.1

TUNKHANNOCK

92

103

Tunkhannock Creek

INTRODUCTION: Tunkhannock Creek is a pleasing little beginner to novice canoe route located just a short and convenient drive over the mountain from the ugly and crowded Wyoming Valley. It drains enough of a roomy and fan-shaped piece of Wyoming, Lackawanna, and Susquehanna counties to sustain frequently canoeable water levels.

There is no consensus on the meaning of Tunkhannock's guttural name. Translations include "meeting of the waters," "small stream," "wilderness stream," and " full of timber." If named today, it would probably be dubbed "creek of the long bridge." For the most notable feature of this creek is the old, 2,400-foot-long Erie And Lackawanna Railroad Viaduct, whose high, multiple concrete arches add an almost Old World dignity to this rural valley.

Section 1. Lenox (Pa. Rte. 106) to mouth					
Gradient	Difficulty	Distance	Time	Scenery	Map
11	1	26.0	8.5	Good	103

TRIP DESCRIPTION: Tunkhannock Creek resides in a narrow and pastoral valley hemmed by pine-mottled hillsides that slowly rise to the dimensions of mountainsides. The streambanks are usually lined by a facade of hemlock and rhododendron. When they are not, it is easy for the paddler to see that this is an only sparsely populated valley. The most scenic section lies above East Lemon, and this includes the passage beneath the great and stately viaduct. Below East Lemon the topography is about the same, but more development and trash mar the view. If you float the whole way, there is an easy take-out right at the mouth, on the right, where a steep dirt road drops down from the Rte. 309-29 Bridge over the Susquehanna.

The canoeing is easy on the relatively roomy Tunkhannock. Amazingly, there are no dams in all these miles of creek. You may encounter a few electric fences in the first few miles, and fallen trees are rare, but always a possibility. It is otherwise just a simple float down easy gravel and ledge-formed rapids and swift and shallow pools in between.

HAZARDS: Possibly a few strainers.

WATER CONDITIONS: Canoeable in spring during snowmelt and within four days of hard rain, above Nicholson, within a week of rain, below, and often up again in November and December.

GAUGE: None. At USGS gauge, 100 yards upstream left of U.S. Rte. 6, Dixon (call Central PA), a level of 2.9 feet is minimal to start at Lenox and 2.5 feet will suffice for below Nicholson. Roughly, USGS gauges at Archibald and Old Forge, on Lackawanna River (call Central PA), should respectively be about 2.9 feet and 3.2 feet to start at Lenox.

251

South Branch Tunkhannock Creek

INTRODUCTION: The South Branch gathers its waters just north of Scranton, and feeds them to the Tunkhannock a few miles east of the town of Tunkhannock. It offers a delightful whitewater run of intermediate difficulty in a pleasant setting.

Section 1. Pa. Rte. 438 to mouth					
Gradient	Difficulty	Distance	Time	Scenery	Map
28	1 to 2 − , 3	10.0	3.5	Good	103

TRIP DESCRIPTION: Except where it passes through Factoryville, the South Branch takes you through sparsely populated and woodsy surroundings, with nice views of the high and close-by mountains. Such aesthetic quality is a surprise when you consider this creek's proximity to busy U.S. Rte. 6.

And the South Branch is busy too. It scrambles down through rock gardens, over cobble riffles, and over a few sharp scattered ledges. But the best comes at the end.

Just below SR2012 (silver plate girder bridge), the creek gushes through a tight and ledgy Class 3 rapid, in a red-walled chasm. That is just the warm-up. Following a few more little ledges and the Rte. 6 Bridge, the creek enters another short chasm that contains a frighteningly big, sloping, and runnable ledge. Before your pulse returns to normal, the South Branch delivers you to its mouth, where an easy walk puts you on the shoulder of Rte. 6.

HAZARDS: Possible strainers and a big ledge below U.S. Rte. 6.

WATER CONDITIONS: Canoeable in spring during snowmelt and within three days of hard rain.

GAUGE: None.

Martins Creek

INTRODUCTION: This Martins Creek offers a short and pleasant run into the Tunkhannock at Nicholson. Just add water, and enjoy.

Section 1. Hop Bottom (Pa. Rte. 167) to mouth					
Gradient	Difficulty	Distance	Time	Scenery	Map
21	1 +	6.5	2.0	Good	103

TRIP DESCRIPTION: Martins Creek rushes down an evenly distributed gradient, over frequent and often continuous cobble and rock garden riffles. The whitewater is thus easy, but watch out for a few electric and barbed wire fences and maybe a fallen tree. Though U.S. Rte. 11 closely follows it, the creek provides the paddler mostly with views of wooded banks and hillsides. You can finish in Nicholson, or take out three quarters of a mile down Tunkhannock Creek at SR1017.

HAZARDS: Fences and possibly fallen trees.

WATER CONDITIONS: Canoeable in spring during snowmelt or within two days of hard rain.

GAUGE: None. The USGS gauge on Tunkhannock Creek at Dixon (call Central PA) should, roughly, be over 3.0 feet.

Mehoopany Creek

INTRODUCTION: Up on the wild North Mountain Plateau, in Sullivan and Wyoming counties, an untold number of little woodland ponds and bogs, swamps, and glades that once were ponds ooze clear and clean water that flows and gathers together to form the creek with the funny name. That creek leaps and gushes off the plateau to a point where you can reach its last ten miles by automobile and then enjoy some delightful paddling on intermediate and novice grade whitewater.

Section 1. Stony Brook to Forkston (Pa. Rte. 87)					
Gradient	Difficulty	Distance	Time	Scenery	Map
55	2 to 3 +	5.8	1.5	Good	91

TRIP DESCRIPTION: Stony Brook is a tributary that joins Mehoopany Creek where the valley road finally leaves the river for good. It is there that Mehoopany emerges from its remote canyon into a narrow but slowly widening, flat-bottomed, and steep-walled valley. The creek roars over a substantially tilting bed of cobbles, small boulders, and even a few ledges, gradually levelling off and getting easier with each mile. The most exciting spot is at the top, at a memorable ledge-formed flume that plunges several feet. Later on, after the gradient has decreased, the stream begins to meander and braid. So be prepared for some surprise strainers, across fast spots of course.

HAZARDS: Dangerously situated strainers.

WATER CONDITIONS: Canoeable in spring during snowmelt and within three days of hard rain.

GAUGE: None. Judge riffles at SR3003 in Mehoopany, as this is as shallow as any spot on the creek.

Section 2. Forkston (Pa. Rte. 87) to mouth					
Gradient	Difficulty	Distance	Time	Scenery	Map
25	1 to 2	6.3	2.0	Very Good	91

TRIP DESCRIPTION: The creek is now suitable for novices. The rapids are frequent and sometimes even continuous, but flowing over cobble bars, they do not exceed Class 2. This reach of Mehoopany flows down a steep-sided and narrow valley with little bottomland. The wooded banks and the hillside farms are all very nice, but two high, cascading waterfalls that shower in from the right, shortly above the village of Mehoopany, are reason enough for anybody to explore this section. The last take-out on the creek is SR3003, in Mehoopany, 0.7 miles above the mouth.

HAZARDS: None.

WATER CONDITIONS: Canoeable in spring during snowmelt and within four days of hard rain.

GAUGE: None. Judge riffle at SR3003 in Mehoopany.

Meshoppen Creek

INTRODUCTION: Meshoppen is an awfully pretty little creek. But who will paddle it? Easy here, difficult there, and then in some spots absolutely impossible, it takes a boater of diverse tastes to tackle its entire modest length.

Section 1. SR3004 to Meshoppen (U.S. Rte. 6)					
Gradient	Difficulty	Distance	Time	Scenery	Map
23	1 to 3 –	17.0	6.5	Good to Excellent	104

TRIP DESCRIPTION: Down at the foot of a long hill east of the crossroads of Springville, Susquehanna County, a narrow bridge crosses just a little bit of clear green water oozing between weedy mud banks. What you see is what you get, for the first phase of Meshoppen is gentle. Smooth water seeks a crooked path through a dense forest that bristles with many ghostly, dead, but still standing trees. The going through here is fairly easy, blocked by few deadfalls.

A few houses interupt the wild where SR3017 crosses. But below there, the creekscape reverts to a remote mix of hemlock groves, hardwood forest, and some pasture. There is some gradient here, but it is just expressed as wide and shallow riffles.

After Meshoppen passes under Pa. Rte. 29, the gradient steepens and the riffle action becomes almost unbroken. Unbroken by pools, that is. There is a sudden set of sharp ledges beneath SR4019 that climaxes with a plunge into a surprisingly strong hole, on the right. And shortly downstream, a less problematic staircase of sharp ledges further suggest a capricious nature to this stream. And if you are still not convinced, about two miles above Meshoppen, just below a trailer park, the

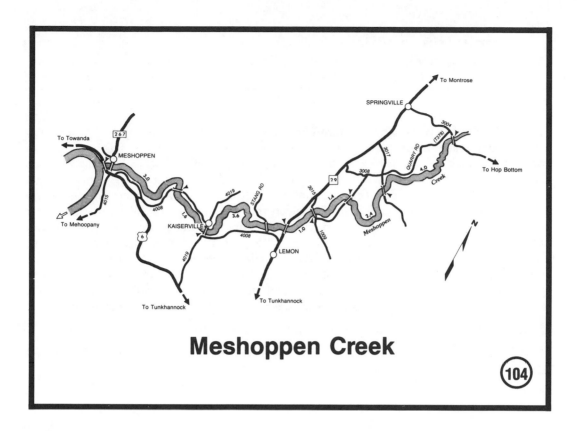

Meshoppen Creek

(104)

creek plunges over a 20-foot falls. The beauty of this cataract and the rock chasm below may convince you to forgive the 200-yard carry on the right. Not far below, unfortunately, is another chasm, plugged with a Class 6 rapid that forces you to a strenuous portage on the left. Once again, it is painful, but pretty. Finally, a sloping falls in Meshoppen requires a short lift over on the left. A few hundred yards of easy riffles then gets you down to an easy take-out at the ballfield, on the right, above U.S. Rte. 6.

HAZARDS: Two falls and a Class 6 rapid are always a problem. At high water some of the ledges upstream can create dangerous hydraulics.

WATER CONDITIONS: Canoeable in spring during snowmelt and within three days of hard rain.

GAUGE: None. If riffles in Meshoppen are passable, level is adequate. Roughly, USGS gauge at Archibald, on Lackawanna River (call Central PA), should be about 3.1 feet.

Sugar Run and Sugar Run Creek

INTRODUCTION: The Sugars offer an interesting whitewater descent into the North Branch Susquehanna River below Wyalusing. Strictly a highwater venture, they are well worth your time to explore.

Gradient	Difficulty	Distance	Time	Scenery	Map
41	1 to 3	7.9	3.0	Good to Excellent	90

TRIP DESCRIPTION: The trip begins on Sugar Run, which starts off by winding aimlessly about meadows and woods, its channel entrenched between high mud banks. This is just smooth water, but it is pretty, and it makes a nice warm-up. Riffles and easy rapids begin at Robinson Road, T420, and by T410 the creek displays some downhill momentum. Sugar Run eases into a shallow and hemlock-filled gorge, which unfortunately is marred by some logging activity and a few houses. But very long rapids of small boulders and ledges weave a complex path that should divert your attention. After passing through a fairly primitive stretch, the creek passes a farm on the right. Here you will encounter a large rock ledge with a tempting chute on the right. Scout first, as a hidden log that may be lodged in that chute could spell entrapment. Shortly below, a giant sloping ledge will probably encourage a portage on the right. There are no more problems below, other than possible trees. The bed turns to a simpler cobble descent below Pa. Rte. 187, with the confluence of Sugar Run Creek, but remains exhilarating to the end.

HAZARDS: Large sloping ledge and assorted strainers.

WATER CONDITIONS: Canoeable in spring during snowmelt or within three days of hard rain.

GAUGE: None.

Wyalusing Creek

INTRODUCTION: Wyalusing Creek carves a gentle canoe path through the rugged plateau of Susquehanna and Bradford counties. This is primarily dairy country, for you cannot grow many crops on such steep slopes and narrow bottoms. The creek runs from Montrose to Wyalusing, past Lawton and Camptown. These are all neat and whitewashed New Englandesque towns, possibly so because 200 years ago the pioneers of this remote corner of Pennsylvania were migrants from New England.

Speaking of Camptown, you have no doubt heard the song "Camptown Races," by Stephen Foster. Most people assume, because Foster has been long associated with the South, that Camptown was somewhere down south. But most people have been wrong. For Stephen Foster, a Pennsylvanian, was actually "doo-dah"ing about this tiny Bradford County village.

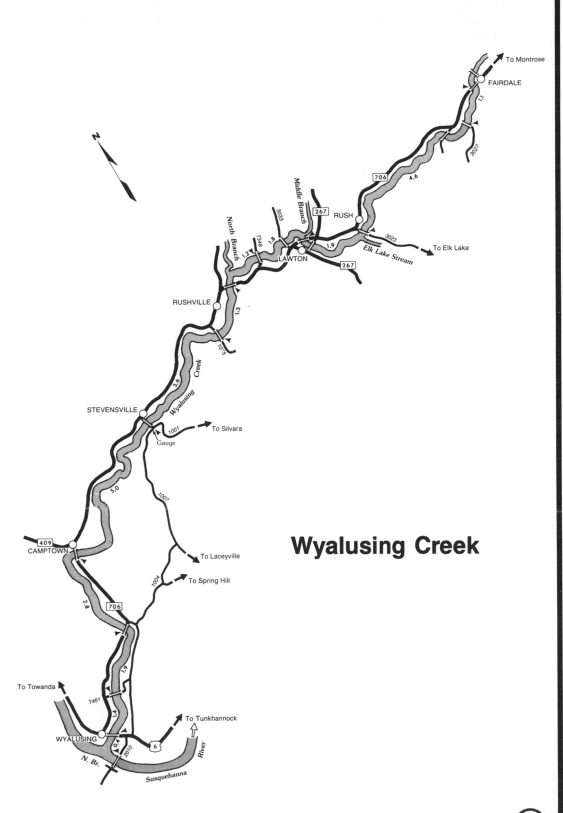

Wyalusing Creek

To Montrose

FAIRDALE

1.1

3027

706

4.6

Middle Branch

3033

267

RUSH

To Elk Lake

3023

Elk Lake Stream

North Branch

T348

1.8

1.2

LAWTON

1.9

267

RUSHVILLE

1.3

10.5

Wyalusing Creek

3.6

STEVENSVILLE

1001

To Silvara

Gauge

5.0

1007

409

CAMPTOWN

To Laceyville

1004

To Spring Hill

2.8

706

1.9

To Towanda

T461

1.4

To Tunkhannock

WYALUSING

0.4

2070

6

N. Br.

Susquehanna

River

Section 1. Fairdale (Pa. Rte. 706) to mouth					
Gradient	Difficulty	Distance	Time	Scenery	Map
16	1	27.0	9.0	Good	105

TRIP DESCRIPTION: The confluence of the East and South branches and Forest Lake Creek form a more than canoeable-size stream at Fairdale. But a couple of braided sections that are clogged by horrendous logjams would encourage most paddlers to start at Rush. The whole run affords good views of this sparsely populated, narrow, and pastoral valley. Where the creek bumps up against the bordering wooded hillsides, the high bank often solidifies into pretty rock shelves. Although a state highway runs up the valley, it is lightly traveled and seldom near the creek. Perhaps that is why so little trash fouls the banks of Wyalusing Creek.

A fast current and easy riffles and rapids that flow over a cobble bed assure easy and interesting progress. A relatively broad stream for its length, Wyalusing is uninterrupted by deadfalls or fences below Rush. It is by no means a demanding stream. For a finish that is as easy as the creek, take out at U.S. Rte. 6, a quarter mile above the mouth.

HAZARDS: Strainers above Rush.

WATER CONDITIONS: Canoeable in spring during snowmelt and within four days of hard rain, above Lawton, and within a week below.

GAUGE: Painted gauge on right pier of Pa. Rte. 706, Lawton, should read over 1.5 feet to start at Fairdale and about 1.0 feet to start at Lawton. Painted gauge on left abutment of SR1007, Stevensville, should read about 2.0 feet for above Lawton and 1.2 feet for below.

Wysox Creek

INTRODUCTION: Wysox Creek offers a short and fairly attractive novice cruise that ends in the Susquehanna just below Towanda. But it is not really worth a special trip from anywhere far to explore.

Section 1. Rome (Water Street) to U.S. Rte. 6					
Gradient	Difficulty	Distance	Time	Scenery	Map
21	1 +	6.3	1.5	Good	90

TRIP DESCRIPTION: Wysox Creek flows down a flat and narrow valley, bordered by wooded hillsides. The creek usually finds a route back in floodplain forest, a maximum distance from Pa. Rte. 187, the valley road. Wysox sometimes wanders about the very movable gravel floor of the valley, carving out undercut banks and braided channels. Such spots, of course, can breed strainers. Otherwise, this is an easy stream to navigate, with whitewater appearing only as frequent and simple, gravel bar type riffles. Finish with a steep and tangled climb up the embankment to busy U.S. Rte. 6, a third of a mile above the Susquehanna, taking care not to get run over by a truck.

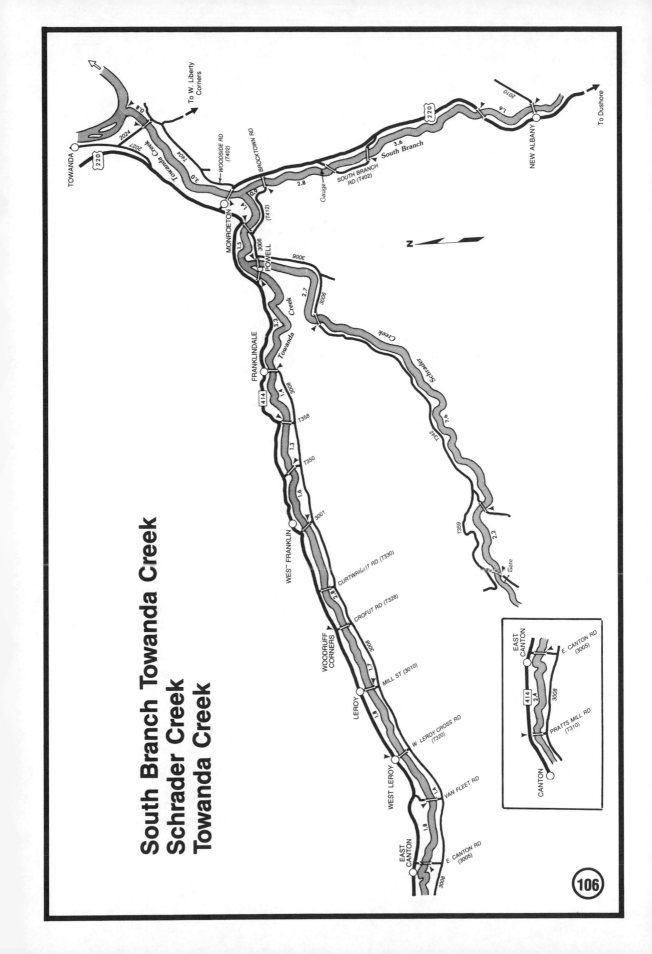

South Branch Towanda Creek
Schrader Creek
Towanda Creek

TOWANDA

220

To W. Liberty Corners

To Dushore

220

New Albany

1.6

2010

3.6 South Branch

South Branch

3.0

2024

2021

Towanda Creek

T404

Woodside Rd (T402)

Brocktown Rd

0.8

2.8

Gauge

South Branch Rd (T402)

0.5

1.4

(T412)

Monroeton

1.5

3006

Powell

3006

2.7

3006

Schrader

Creek

7.6

T342

1.3

3.3

Towanda Creek

Franklindale

414

1.4

3008

T358

T350

1.6

3001

T359

2.2

Gate

West Franklin

Curtwright Rd (T330)

2.8

Crofut Rd (T328)

Woodruff Corners

3009

1.7

Mill St (3010)

Leroy

1.8

W. Leroy Cross Rd (T320)

West Leroy

1.4

Van Fleet Rd

1.8

East Canton

E. Canton Rd (3005)

3008

East Canton

E. Canton Rd (3005)

414

2.4

3008

Canton

Pratts Mill Rd (T310)

106

HAZARDS: Strainers.

WATER CONDITIONS: Canoeable in spring during snowmelt and within four days of hard rain.

GAUGE: None.

Towanda Creek

INTRODUCTION: Towanda Creek offers a long and enjoyable cruise across the pastoral setting of Bradford County to the Susquehanna near (where else?) Towanda. Towanda is Indian for "burial ground," but do not let that intimidate you, as this is purely a novice run. If you are a whitewater paddler, you will find satisfaction in its delightful tributaries, Schrader Creek and the South Branch. Off the river, if you are a fan of grand Victorian architecture, you will want to spend some time exploring Canton, above the put-in, and Towanda, near the end. It is an interesting neighborhood, far from most of us, but well worth the long trip to visit.

Section 1. T310 to mouth					
Gradient	Difficulty	Distance	Time	Scenery	Map
16	1	26.2	8.5	Good	106

TRIP DESCRIPTION: This long run can be easily dissected, inspected, and selectively rejected by using numerous, evenly-spaced secondary road bridges. The initially clear and tiny creek rattles down between often high and cutaway mud banks, as it slowly gains tributaries and widens. In spite of its banks, one has little trouble viewing the great wooded escarpment on the right and the pretty dairy farms clinging to the hillsides of the valley to the left. Parallel Pa. Rte. 414 generally stays pleasantly away from and out of sight of the creek until Franklindale.

After the substantial inflow of Schrader Creek and the South Branch, Towanda Creek doubles in size. The valley widens and flattens, but rimmed by a bold mountain skyline, it is still attractive. The last take out on Towanda is SR2024, 0.8 miles above the mouth.

This is a beginner run, though beginners might want to skip the first few miles, where fallen trees are a possibility. The creek eases over gravel riffles between long and smooth stretches. There are some longer and rockier rapids around Franklindale, even some little ledges, but they are all straightforward. The remains of an old dam just above U.S. Rte.220 form a nice surfing wave.

HAZARDS: Occasional strainers, mostly in the first few miles.

WATER CONDITIONS: Canoeable in spring during snowmelt and within week of hard rain.

GAUGE: Concrete footing of right abutment of T350, below West Franklin, is your gauge. Minimal level to float from T310 is three inches below the top of the footing. USGS gauge above Monroeton (call Central PA) probably should be over 7.5 feet to start at T310. Very roughly, USGS gauge at Mansfield, on Tioga River (call Central PA), should read about 9.8 feet to start at T310.

South Branch Towanda Creek

INTRODUCTION: The South Branch Towanda Creek is a steeply dropping mountain brook that can easily distract your attention from the road when driving up U.S. Rte. 220, between New Albany and Towanda. It provides about nine miles of intermediate whitewater fun and games for those who are quick enough to catch the emphemeral runoff that feeds it.

Section 1. New Albany (SR2010) to mouth					
Gradient	Difficulty	Distance	Time	Scenery	Map
50	1 to 3	8.6	2.5	Fair to Good	106

TRIP DESCRIPTION: You must be lucky to find this creek with adequate water, much less with lots of water. So look forward to a seemingly endless slalom through rock gardens formed by boulders, cobbles, and ledges. Of particular interest is a tight mini-chasm located about two miles into the trip (below the old piers of a former railroad bridge), and a little farther downstream, a pushy and complex staircase of ledges. While the South Branch cuts down a deep and canyonlike valley, an often dense riparian population, often sheltered in mobile homes and run-down houses, renders the scenery only sporadically pretty. But it is the whitewater that justifies your presence. Take out 0.3 miles down Towanda Creek at the U.S. Rte. 220 Bridge, Monroeton.

HAZARDS: Occasional strainers.

WATER CONDITIONS: Canoeable in spring during snowmelt and within three days of hard rain.

GAUGE: None. Judge from highway.

Schrader Creek

INTRODUCTION: Schrader Creek is an outstanding and little known, whitewater wonder that feeds sleepy Towanda Creek. Cutting down the heart of a wild and wooded sandstone plateau, this exciting brook is every bit the peer of nearby and popular Loyalsock Creek.

Section 1. T359 to mouth					
Gradient	Difficulty	Distance	Time	Scenery	Map
45	2 – to 4	12.7	3.5	Good to Excellent	106

TRIP DESCRIPTION: For most of its length, Schrader Creek rumbles down a canyon-like valley, whose steep slopes are at times crowned with gray standstone rimrock cliffs. With only a few camps scattered at the start and along the last few miles, and with the shuttle road usually

Sugar Creek

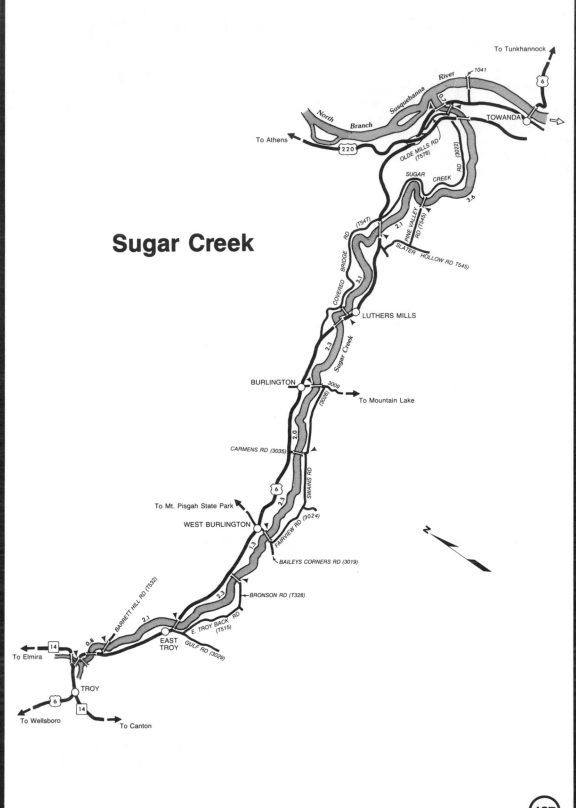

To Tunkhannock

To Towanda

Susquehanna River

North Branch

1041

6

TOWANDA

To Athens

220

OLDE MILLS RD (T578)

SUGAR CREEK

RD (3022)

0.7

3.6

COVERED BRIDGE RD (T547)

PINE VALLEY RD (T545)

2.1

SLATER HOLLOW RD T545)

3.1

LUTHERS MILLS

2.3

Sugar Creek

BURLINGTON

3009

(3026)

To Mountain Lake

2.0

CARMENS RD (3035)

6

SWAINS RD

2.5

To Mt. Pisgah State Park

WEST BURLINGTON

FAIRVIEW RD (3024)

1.3

BAILEYS CORNERS RD (3019)

BARRETT HILL RD (T532)

2.3

BRONSON RD (T328)

2.1

E. TROY BACK RD (T515)

0.8

EAST TROY

GULF RD (3029)

14

To Elmira

TROY

6

14

To Wellsboro

To Canton

107

up and away, this seems like a wilderness excursion.

Rapids are almost nonstop, rushing over cobbles, boulder patches, and ledges. About five miles below the put-in, approaching a footbridge, the creek zig zags down a long and complex ledge rapid that climaxes in a sharp and tricky three-foot ledge. Scout this. Otherwise there are no major problems. Even fallen trees are uncommon.

On the final two miles, a wider and easier creek flows down a more open, but still wooded valley, providing an nice cool-down. Take out in Powell at town bridge by SR3006, unless you want to continue on Towanda Creek.

HAZARDS: Possible strainers and a mean hydraulic at the bottom of a long ledge rapid.

WATER CONDITIONS: Canoeable in spring during snowmelt and within four days of hard rain.

GAUGE: None. Scout from road. Roughly, USGS gauge at Mansfield, on Tioga River (call Central PA), should read over 10.6 feet.

Sugar Creek

INTRODUCTION: Sugar Creek is a long and pleasant novice run through the hilly dairy country of western Bradford County. Although U.S. Rte. 6 and 220 provide easy access from Scranton, Binghamton, and the rest of the outside world, once in your canoe, Sugar Creek will seem far off the beaten path.

Section 1. Troy (U.S. Rte. 6) to Towanda (SR3022)					
Gradient	Difficulty	Distance	Time	Scenery	Map
16	1 to 2	22.1	7.0	Good	107
0.7 @ 37					

TRIP DESCRIPTION: Whitewater boaters can put in at the U.S. Rte. 6 Bridge over the North Branch, on the east end of Troy, to enjoy a cliff-lined narrows where the creek tumbles down a long, ledgy, and rocky Class 2 rapid. Novices and beginners can start just below this, or two miles downstream at East Troy.

Though often bracketed by high banks, Sugar Creek offers the paddler ample opportunity to survey the fields, dairy farms, and forests of this quiet valley. U.S. Rte. 6 maintains a comfortable distance from the creek and totally abandons it below Luthers Mills. This final section is the prettiest, with many dark cliffs framing tall mountainsides. Finish your tour 0.7 miles above the mouth at Sugar Creek Road, SR3022, as the remaining distance is flat, slow, and uninteresting, and that is the last reasonable place to exit.

Most of Sugar Creek runs fast but flat, broken only by easy gravel riffles. There are a few rapids formed by ledges or chunks of ledges, but they also are easy. Surprisingly, for a cattle country stream, there are no fences and deadfalls are unlikely.

HAZARDS: Fences are a possible problem.

WATER CONDITIONS: Canoeable in spring during snowmelt and within six days of hard rain.

GAUGE: Use drainholes on left abutment of the U.S. Rte. 6 Bridge below Luthers Mills. Zero canoeing level is two inches below the bottom of the holes. Roughly, USGS gauge at Mansfield, on Tioga River (call Central PA), should be 10.0 feet to start at Troy and 9.8 feet to start at West Burlington.

Chemung River

INTRODUCTION: The Chemung (Indian for "big horn") is born at the confluence of the Cohocton and Tioga rivers, at Corning, New York. It is a relatively big river, draining over 2,500 square miles by the time it reaches the suggested put-in at N.Y. Rte. 427. Most of the river lies in New York, but the last 13 miles meander back and forth across the border, finally merging with the Susquehanna below Athens, Pennsylvania.

Section 1. N.Y. Rte. 427 to mouth					
Gradient	Difficulty	Distance	Time	Scenery	Map
4	1	12.0	4.0	Fair to Good	89

TRIP DESCRIPTION: The only special recreational value of the Chemung is its size. When all the better small stream selections in the neighborhood have dropped below runnable levels, you can still float the good, old Chemung. The river is basically attractive, flowing through a wide farm valley that is bordered by low, wooded mountains. But houses, summer shacks, scattered miscellaneous development, and noise from busy N.Y. Rte. 17 neutralize that quality. The river is relatively wide and flat, but possesses a strong current, even at low flows. It expends its modest gradient over well-spaced and gentle gravel riffles. So this is a safe stream for beginners.

There is no access at the mouth of the Chemung, so either stop at Pa. Rte. 199, two miles upstream, or continue an extra 5.3 miles below the mouth to the bridge at Ulster, on the Susquehanna. If you decide to start above Rte. 427, the scenery, difficulty, and necessary water levels are about the same. But watch out for a rebar-studded three-foot dam if you are passing through Elmira.

HAZARDS: None.

WATER CONDITIONS: Canoeable in spring from when the ice clears until mid to late June and again often in November.

GAUGE: USGS gauge at N.Y. Rte. 427, Chemung (call Central PA), should be about 4.0 feet, though if you do not mind some scraping, you can probably get by with less.

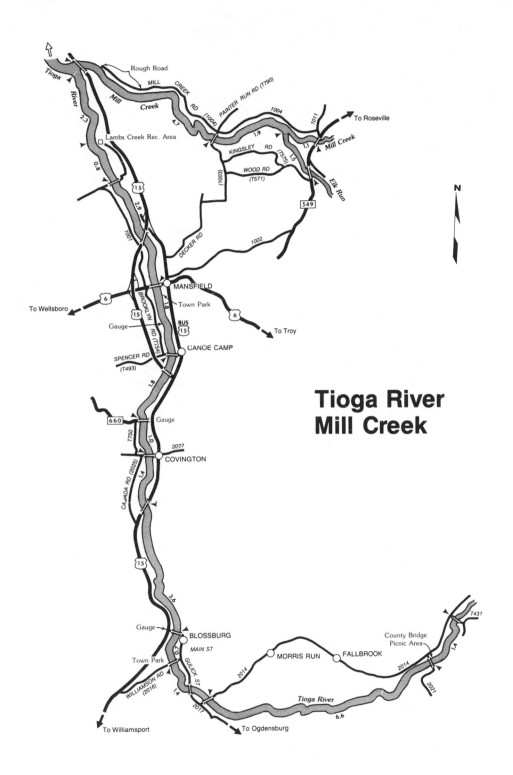

Tioga River
Mill Creek

Rough Road

Tioga

MILL CREEK RD (1004)

PAINTER RUN RD (T790)

Mill

Creek

1004

1011

To Roseville

2.3

4.7

Lambs Creek Rec. Area

1.9

KINGSLEY RD (T575)

1.1

Mill Creek

0.8

(1003)

WOOD RD (T571)

1.5

Elk Run

15

2.9

549

1001

DECKER RD

1002

N

MANSFIELD

To Wellsboro

6

BROOKLYN RD (T754)

1.8

Town Park

15

6

Gauge

BUS 15

To Troy

SPENCER RD (T493)

CANOE CAMP

1.8

660

Gauge

T750

1.9

COVINGTON

2022

CAJADA RD (2025)

1.4

15

3.6

Gauge

BLOSSBURG

T431

MAIN ST

County Bridge
Picnic Area

1.4

Town Park

GULICK ST

1.0

2014

MORRIS RUN

FALLBROOK

2014

2021

WILLIAMSON RD (2016)

1.4

2017

Tioga River

6.6

To Williamsport

To Ogdensburg

108

Tioga River

INTRODUCTION: The Tioga River rises in the remote uplands astride the Tioga-Bradford County Line, west of Canton and Troy. It takes a northward journey into New York State, there joining with the Cohocton River to form the Chemung River. The Chemung then arcs past Corning and Elmira, only to return to Pennsylvania, to join the Susquehanna at Athens. Thus you might say that the Tioga is Pennsylvania's recycled river.

Section 1. T431 to Blossburg (Main Street)					
Gradient	Difficulty	Distance	Time	Scenery	Map
49	2 to 3 +	10.1	2.5	Good to Excellent	108

TRIP DESCRIPTION: The upper Tioga presents a superb little whitewater run of intermediate to advanced difficulty. Start at remote T431, or if the water level at this point appears marginal, retreat to County Bridge Picnic Area for a few extra gallons and a few less strainers.

The clear creek dashes off into the sylvan wilderness of a gently sloped gorge. Though strip mining of coal has ravaged parts of the surrounding plateau, the only evidence that you will observe from the river is the eventual addition of sidestreams yellowed by acid mine drainage. The Tioga drops at an uneven gradient, but nevertheless its rapids run almost without interruption over bars of cobbles, boulder patches, and a few small ledges. It is rocky enough to keep you scrambling, but bouncy enough to get at least a decked boater drenched. The route is unfortunately prone to nasty and frequent strainer problems, though some highwaters can flush the stream conveniently clean. Finally, approaching Blossburg, the Tioga is channelized. But it remains fast and lively right to the finish.

HAZARDS: Strainers in fast water.

WATER CONDITIONS: Canoeable in spring during snowmelt and within three days of hard rain.

GAUGE: Staff gauge on right abutment of Main Street Bridge, Blossburg, should read over 2.0 feet, while 2.5 feet is excellent. USGS gauge at Mansfield (call Central PA) should read at least 9.9 feet.

Section 2. Blossburg (Main Street) to Lambs Creek Rec. Area					
Gradient	Difficulty	Distance	Time	Scenery	Map
16	1 to 2	13.4	4.0	Fair to Good	108,109

TRIP DESCRIPTION: This is an aesthetically forgettable section of the Tioga, but in partial compensation, it offers miles of almost continuous novice whitewater. Though the surrounding valley is attractive, it usually lies hidden behind high gravel banks and, in Mansfield, behind levees. A majority of the stream bed seems to have suffered, at one time or another, rearrangement by busy bulldozers. Take out at the head of Tioga Lake, at the Corps of Engineers recreation area.

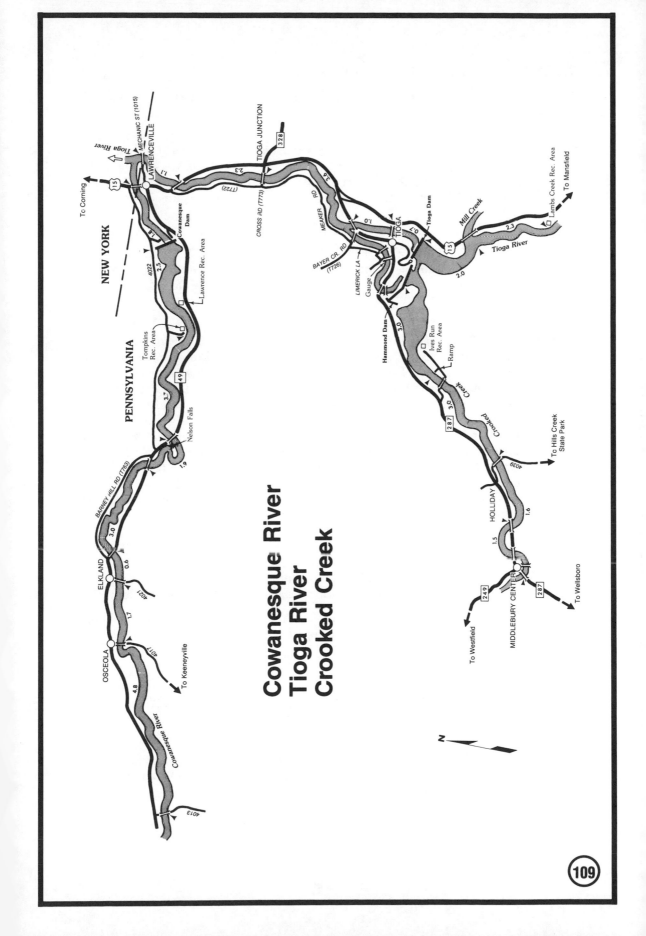

Cowanesque River
Tioga River
Crooked Creek

109

HAZARDS: Occasional strainers above Covington.

WATER CONDITIONS: Canoeable in spring during snowmelt and within five days of hard rain.

GAUGE: Staff gauge on right abutment of Main Street Bridge, Blossburg, should read about 2.0 feet to start at Blossburg. Painted gauge on right abutment of Pa. Rte. 660, Covington, should read at least 2.4 feet to start at Blossburg and 2.0 feet to start at Rte. 660. USGS gauge at Mansfield, located a mile south of U.S. Rte. 6 on Brooklyn Road (inspect on site or call Central PA), should read about 9.8 feet to start at Blossburg and 9.5 feet to start at Rte. 660.

Section 3. Lambs Creek Rec. Area to Lawrenceville (Mechanic Street)					
Gradient	Difficulty	Distance	Time	Scenery	Map
6	A, 1	13.0	5.5	Fair to Good	109

TRIP DESCRIPTION: The first part of this section is lake. The lakeshore is attractive and undeveloped, as it should be, for the lake drowned the prettiest and most remote miles of the lower Tioga. An unusual facet of this Corps of Engineers-built flood control reservoir is that it is connected to a similar reservoir, Hammond Lake, on neighboring Crooked Creek. Thus, when the larger and more flood-prone Tioga exhausts Tioga Lake's capacity, it can then overflow into Hammond Lake, which usually contains excess storage capacity.

Most river cruisers will choose to start below the dam, while lake lovers can splash around above. For those oddballs who are passing through and thus need a portage route over the 140-foot obstacle, land at the left upstream corner of the dam, follow the road up the face of the dam to the crest, and then head downhill to the tailrace. Hopefully the damkeeper will not see you.

The lower river is larger and much smoother than above. Hidden behind high wooded banks, it is a pleasant but hardly awe inspiring beginners' cruise. If you find that you like this, you can continue on into New York and enjoy many more miles of the same.

HAZARDS: None.

WATER CONDITIONS: Canoeable in spring during snowmelt and within a week to ten days of hard rain. Usually up until early May. Tioga Lake is canoeable from ice-out to freeze-up.

GAUGE: USGS gauge at Tioga Junction (call Central PA) should be over 7.4 feet. Roughly, USGS gauge at Mansfield (call Central PA or inspect on site) should read over 8.9 feet.

Cowanesque River

INTRODUCTION: Thank goodness the Cowanesque does not live up to its name, which is Indian for "overrun with briars." On the contrary, this is a very well-behaved and generally docile creek that flows into the Tioga River at the New York State Line.

Section 1. Elmer (Pa. Rte. 49) to Westfield (Pa. Rte. 49)					
Gradient	Difficulty	Distance	Time	Scenery	Map
32	1 to 2	4.7	1.5	Good	110

TRIP DESCRIPTION: The upper Cowanesque is relatively steep, but forgiving, as the gradient is distributed evenly over cobble bars and through rock gardens. Only a few sharp bends can be troublesome. But since this is dairy country, always be alert for wire fences. This is the only section of the Cowanesque that might challenge the novice boater.

HAZARDS: Fences and fallen trees.

WATER CONDITIONS: Canoeable in spring during snowmelt and within two days of hard rain.

GAUGE: Staff gauge on right abutment of Water Street Bridge, in Knoxville (Section 2), should read at least 3.1 feet. Roughly, USGS gauge at Tioga Junction, on Tioga River (call Central PA), should be over 11.0 feet.

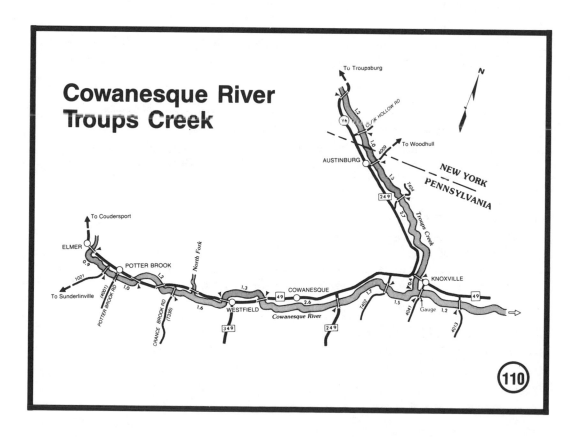

Section 2. Westfield (Pa. Rte. 49) to Tompkins Rec. Area					
Gradient	Difficulty	Distance	Time	Scenery	Map
14	A to 1	23.2	8.0	Good	110,109

TRIP DESCRIPTION: This stretch takes you on a pleasant journey through a pastoral valley which, between towns, is thinly populated. Medium-high banks hide much of the valley floor from view, but only to draw your attention to the gray hardwood-covered mountainsides, dappled green by clusters of pines. Bottomland forests and brush-filled fields provide a rich habitat for wildlife, especially below Elkland, where all bottomland is kept vacant to accomodate occasional inundation by the flood pool of Cowanesque Lake. In springtime the waterfowl population includes an unusual number of mergansers, and there may even be a great blue heron rookery above Knoxville.

The whitewater mellows to gravel riffles, with a continually declining gradient. You might want to carry a small dam (or pipe crossing) just downstream of the first Pa. Rte. 49 bridge at Westfield. You definitely want to carry Nelson Falls, a sharp eight-foot drop onto a flat ledge. This is located a few miles below Elkland, where the river takes a shortcut through the base of a hairpin loop, with most of the flow gushing through the gap and over the falls. At highwater you can probably follow the loop around and avoid a carry (this adds 0.8 miles to the trip). The summer pool of Cowanesque Lake begins shortly above the take-out.

HAZARDS: Possible strainers, sharp drop in Westfield, and Nelson Falls.

WATER CONDITIONS: Canoeable in spring during snowmelt and within four days of hard rain.

GAUGE: Staff gauge on right abutment of Water Street Bridge, in Knoxville, should read at least 2.0 feet. Roughly, USGS gauge at Tioga Junction, on Tioga River (call Central PA), should read over 9.4 feet.

Section 3. Tompkins Rec. Area to Lawrenceville (U.S. Rte. 15)					
Gradient	Difficulty	Distance	Time	Scenery	Map
0,9	A, 1	4.4	2.5	Good to Fair	109

TRIP DESCRIPTION: A 150-foot-high earth-fill barrage plugs the Cowanesque, to form a short, wide, and often windy lake. The Corps provides access to both sides of the upper end of the lake and both sides of the dam's tailrace. If for some reason you need to portage the dam (why?), it is easiest to climb straight up and down the right side, after landing at the intake structure. Only about two miles of quiet and uninteresting river remains to Rte. 15.

HAZARDS: None.

WATER CONDITIONS: Lake is canoeable from spring thaw (April) until winter freeze (December). The lower river is canoeable in spring during snowmelt and within a week of hard rain.

GAUGE: USGS gauge on left, a half mile below the dam, should be over 3.7 feet. Roughly, USGS gauge at Tioga Junction, on Tioga River (call Central PA), should be over 8.0 feet.

Troups Creek

INTRODUCTION: Troups Creek flows out of the Empire State to join the Cowanesque River at Knoxville. It is an ephemeral stream that offers a short tour of the type of hilly dairy country so typical of the upper tier counties.

Section 1. N.Y. Rte. 36 to mouth					
Gradient	Difficulty	Distance	Time	Scenery	Map
30	2	6.8	2.0	Good	110

TRIP DESCRIPTION: This is a pretty path through a narrow and pastoral valley. The banks are low, allowing good views of farms, hills, and sycamore-studded floodplain groves. The frequent practice of riprapping of the banks is the only significant blemish.

Troups Creek meanders and braids about thick cobble deposits, dropping busily over gravel bars and rock gardens. At lower levels one really must work to pick a path through the rocks. But there are, surprisingly, few strainers on this creek. Take out a few yards down below the mouth, on the Cowanesque, at Knoxville.

HAZARDS: Occasional strainers.

WATER CONDITIONS: Canoeable in spring during rapid snowmelt or within two days of hard rain.

GAUGE: Staff gauge on Pa. Rte. 49, right abutment, should be over 1.6 feet to clear the shallowest spots. Roughly, USGS gauge at Tioga Junction, on Tioga River (call Central PA), should be over 11.0 feet.

Crooked Creek

INTRODUCTION: Crooked Creek is a small and quiet branch of the Tioga, joining at the village of Tioga. Like the Tioga River, Crooked Creek has been partially sacrificed to provide the illusion of flood protection for downstream communities, and more importantly, to make political hay (or pork) for the local politicians. Gaze upon structures such as these, of which there are hundreds about the country, and you will better understand why the federal budget is in the red.

Section 1. Middlebury Center (Pa. Rte. 287) to Ives Run Boat Launch					
Gradient	Difficulty	Distance	Time	Scenery	Map
10	A to 1	6.1	2.0	Good	109

TRIP DESCRIPTION: This is a good springtime cruise for novices or beginners. The creek lives up to its name as it wiggles down an attractive and relatively empty valley, much of whose floor is now dedicated to occasional innundation by the Hammond Lake flood pool. So you pass through lots of abandoned farm lands, bordered by rounded and wooded hills, all of which are partially eclipsed by moderately high streambanks. There are many brief and simple riffles to speed you along, but even they become scarce toward the end. The end, of course, is the head of Hammond Lake.

There is little reason to proceed farther. Hammond Lake is a short and fat impoundment that is no place for a river rat. It is not even a particularly attractive lake for lake lovers. Only a little over two anemic, drab, and piddly miles of Crooked Creek survives below the dam—hardly worth the effort to explore.

HAZARDS: None.

WATER CONDITIONS: Canoeable in spring during snowmelt and within four days of hard rain.

GAUGE: Painted gauge on the right abutment of Pa. Rte. 287, Middlebury Center is faded below the 3.0 foot mark. The concrete footing is 0.0 feet, and 1.0 foot is about the minimum level for floating.

Mill Creek

INTRODUCTION: Mill Creek is a beautiful little Tioga tributary that drowns in the depths of Tioga Lake. It offers an absolutely delightful novice whitewater trip through a hidden and hilly corner of northern Tioga County.

Section 1. Pa. Rte. 549 (over Elk Creek) to U.S. Rte. 15

Gradient	Difficulty	Distance	Time	Scenery	Map
29	1 to 2	8.2	2.5	Very Good	108

TRIP DESCRIPTION: You can start on either Mill Creek or Elk Creek, the latter being the most preferable. Either way, it is a narrow, winding, and smooth to riffly start in an open farm valley.

Below the confluence, the hills draw closer as Mill Creek hurries down a remote and thinly inhabited valley. Though nearby, the valley road is seldom visible and only lightly used. What you mostly see are wooded mountainsides, a few cliffs, bottomland woods and thickets, an odd cornfield, and many pastures that are reverting to the domain of goldenrod and teasle.

The whitewater is a joy. The creek is just full of riffles and rapids that sometimes run continuously for long stretches. Ledges up to two feet high and cobbles form the rapids. There are even a number of nice surfing holes on Mill Creek. Trees should only present an occasional problem. The run finishes quietly, as the last half mile is an arm of Tioga Lake.

To get out, a fishermen's path descends from U.S. Rte. 15 to the lakeshore, about a hundred yards south of the high highway bridge. Or you can avoid the deadwater paddle by shuttling down Mill Creek Road, on hard surface, to within a mile of the regular head of the lake. From there the road continues on Corps of Engineers' property—a periodic flood zone. Its unmaintained, potholed, muddy mile is open to all who are adventurous enough to follow it.

HAZARDS: Occasional strainers.

WATER CONDITIONS: Canoeable in spring during snowmelt or within four days of hard rain.

GAUGE: Use footing on right abutment of Pa. Rte. 549 over Elk Creek. Seven inches below the top of the footing is minimum. Roughly, USGS gauge at Mansfield, on Tioga River (call Harrisburg or inspect on spot), should be about 10.0 feet.

Wappasening Creek

INTRODUCTION: Wappasening Creek is an obscure brook flowing out of northern Bradford County into New York State, to join the North Branch Susquehanna River about nine miles above Sayre. It offers a fairly pleasant, off-the-beaten-track novice cruise for spring highwater.

Section 1. West Warren (SR1049) to Pa. Rte. 187					
Gradient	Difficulty	Distance	Time	Scenery	Map
28	1	8.7	2.5	Fair to Good	111

TRIP DESCRIPTION: Wappasening Creek flows northward through a lightly populated and rolling dairy farming valley, fringed by low and wooded hills. Though generally high banks tend to border the creek, there is still ample opportunity to look out upon this lovely landscape. The immediate riparian scenery is not quite so idyllic, often suffering from logging scars, eroded banks and bluffs, some riprapping, and channel dredging. Except for nasty debris jams on some braided portions, the going is generally easy. Swift current and lots of easy riffles are the rule, with a pleasing increase of gradient towards the end of the trip. Take out at the old highway approach on the left, a few hundred feet downstream of Pa. Rte. 187.

HAZARDS: Strainers.

WATER CONDITIONS: Canoeable in spring during snowmelt and within four days of hard rain.

GAUGE: None. Roughly, USGS gauge at Archibald, on Lackawanna River (call Central PA), should be over 4.2 feet.

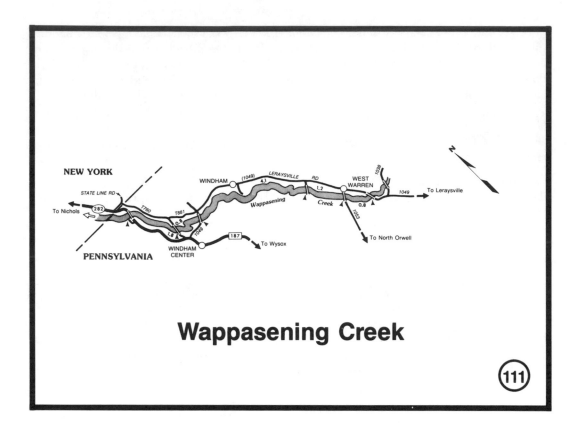

Wappasening Creek

(111)

Snake Creek

INTRODUCTION: Snake Creek is a tiny tributary to the Great Bend of the North Branch Susquehanna, up in Susquehanna County. In its rare periods of high water it offers the novice paddler a short and delightful cruise through this attractive hill country.

Section 1. Franklin Forks (Fork Hill Road, T683) to Corbettsville, N.Y.					
Gradient	Difficulty	Distance	Time	Scenery	Map
26	1	9.0	3.0	Good	88

TRIP DESCRIPTON: Put in at the town park in Franklin Forks, where Silver Lake Creek contributes welcome flow. Snake Creek follows a moderately crooked course down a moderately straight valley. A wooded mountainside follows faithfully on the right, while pastures, cornfields, and woodlots cover the flat bottomlands on the left. Pa. Rte. 29, to which most of the valley's population clings, usually keeps its distance from the creek, leaving only a mobile home park to interrupt the rural serenity.

Swift water separates easy cobble-formed rapids and riffles, making this an easy float. Jammed

274

debris on two braided sections, below Lawsville Center, keep it from being too easy. Take out one third of a mile above the mouth, by the post office in Corbettsville. If you decide that this creek is figuratively worth writing home about, you can literally do so here.

HAZARDS: Strainers on braided sections.

WATER CONDITIONS: Canoeable in spring during snowmelt or within four days of hard rain.

GAUGE: None. Roughly, USGS gauge at Archibald, on Lackawanna River (call Central PA), should be over 4.1 feet.

Saltlick Creek

INTRODUCTION: Any true river rat cannot drive down a highway without looking over every bridge and scouting every roadside river, creek, and ditch, at 55 mph of course. Such a paddler driving southbound on I-81 in Susquehanna County would certainly notice the little stream, usually just a rocky dribble, between Hallstead and New Milford. That is Saltlick Creek. And when the weather has been very wet, there lies a delightful open boat whitewater run.

Section 1. New Milford (U.S. Rte. 11) to mouth					
Gradient	Difficulty	Distance	Time	Scenery	Map
34	1 to 2	5.3	1.5	Fair	88

TRIP DESCRIPTION: The put-in is about a quarter mile north of the New Milford town line. Saltlick yields a busy run over a cobbly, rocky, and shallow bed. This is small water canoeing with lots of maneuvering around rocks and lining up for little chutes. A few strainers further complicate matters. Whitewater boaters would be happiest finishing at the roadside park, just above Hallstead. The final mile to the mouth is smooth, fast, and extremely twisting.

Sandwiched between I-81 and U.S. Rte. 11, this creek wins no beauty contests. But development and trash are minimal, and besides, most of your attention will be on the rocks.

HAZARDS: A few strainers in fast water.

WATER CONDITIONS: Canoeable in spring during rapid snowmelt and within 24 hours of hard rain.

GAUGE: None. The road runs right alongside. The creek will be down before any nearby big river gauges indicate highwater.

Starrucca Creek

INTRODUCTION: Beneath the tall and stately arches of the old Erie and Lackawanna Railroad Viaduct, near Lanesboro, a trivial mountain brook dashes its last few yards to its meeting with the Great Bend of the great Susquehanna. Ten delightful miles of this brook, called Starrucca, occasionally carry enough water to float a canoe down into the shadow of those tall arches. It is a trip worthy of your time.

Section 1. Starrucca to Lanesboro (SR1015)					
Gradient	Difficulty	Distance	Time	Scenery	Map
39	1 to 2	10.3	3.5	Good to Excellent	88

TRIP DESCRIPTION: This is a pretty run down through a narrow and sparsely populated farm valley that could easily pass for somewhere in the beautiful Berkshires of Massachusetts. Start your trip in the village of Starrucca, at the bridge over Shadigee Creek. Little Starrucca commences an almost unbroken race over cobble-formed, shallow riffles. One place that *is* broken is at a surprise, sharp, four-foot ledge, above T765. Carry this natural dam. You enter the nicest reach of Starrucca below Brandt, where the creek curves through a beautiful and hemlock-lined glen. Not only is the scenery better in there, but so is the whitewater, now a slalom through patches of little boulders and ledges. Since there is no convenient access to the mouth of Starrucca, take out a third of a mile upstream at SR1015.

HAZARDS: Sharp ledge above T765 and possible strainers.

WATER CONDITIONS: Canoeable in spring during snowmelt and within three days of hard rain.

GAUGE: None. Roughly, USGS gauge at Archibald, on Lackawanna River (call Central PA), should be over 3.2 feet.

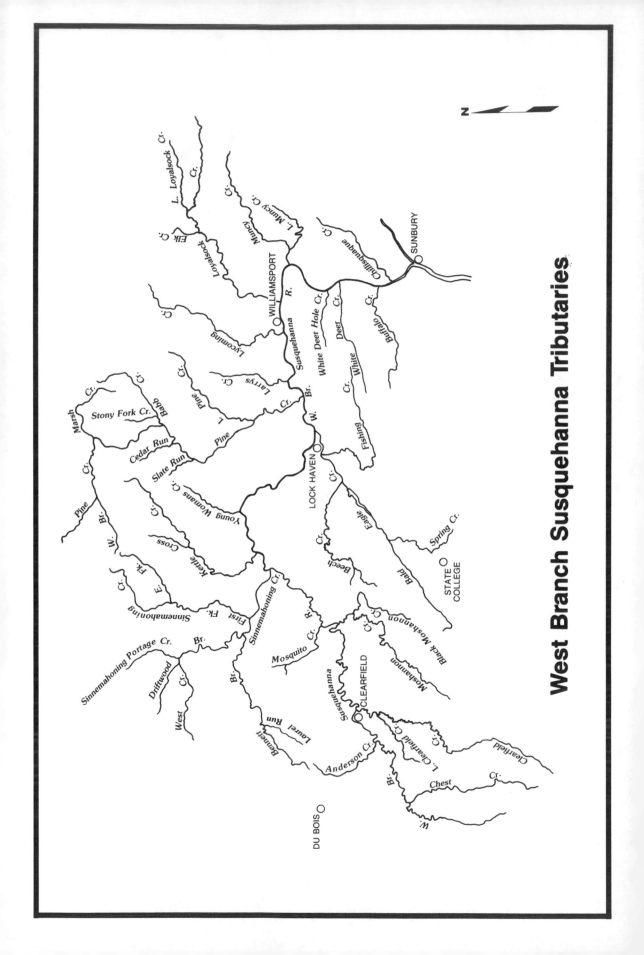

West Branch Susquehanna Tributaries

Chapter 5
The West Branch Susquehanna Basin

The valley of the West Branch Susquehanna River covers 6,990 square miles of north central Pennsylvania. Much of this area can truly be described as "Penn's Woods." Here you will find vast roadless tracts of trees and more trees, thousands of acres of which are now protected within state forest and game lands. Needless to say, this is prime vacation land for people who seek their fun in the outdoors, canoeing, hiking, cross-country skiing, snowmobiling, hunting, fishing, and camping. This is also coal country in the headwaters area and rich farm country down at the lower end. But wherever you go in the West Branch Basin, you will never feel crowded.

The following streams are described in this chapter:

West Branch Susquehanna River
Chillisquaque Creek
Buffalo Creek
White Deer Creek
White Deer Hole Creek
Muncy Creek
Little Muncy Creek
Loyalsock Creek
Elk Creek
Little Loyalsock Creek
Lycoming Creek
Larrys Creek
Pine Creek
Little Pine Creek
Slate Run
Cedar Run
Babb Creek
Stony Fork Creek
Marsh Creek
West Branch Pine Creek
Bald Eagle Creek
Fishing Creek
Beech Creek
Spring Creek
Young Womans Creek
Kettle Creek
Cross Fork

Sinnemahoning Creek
First Fork Sinnemahoning Creek
East Fork Sinnemahoning Creek
Driftwood Branch Sinnemahoning Creek
Sinnemahoning Portage Creek
West Creek
Bennett Branch Sinnemahoning Creek
Laurel Run
Mosquito Creek
Moshannon Creek
Black Moshannon Creek
Clearfield Creek
Little Clearfield Creek
Anderson Creek
Chest Creek

West Branch Susquehanna River

INTRODUCTION: The West Branch Susquehanna describes a great, jagged arc across the heart of the state, from its headwaters in the pastures, woods, and strip mines of Cambria County to the wide pool of the Susquehanna, at Northumberland. Just look at a state map and you will see that it is almost perfectly centered. So it is within easy reach of most Pennsylvania paddlers. And that is good news.

Much of the West Branch is an outstanding canoeing river. It flows through an incredibly empty tract of plateau and forest, and the river reflects this. No other big river in the state is so undeveloped for so many miles. Though popular, it has so far escaped the invasions that have ruined the Delaware. You can still load up your canoe with provisions and freely camp on many miles of this river. And when you do, your campsite will not have to be by a busy highway, power plant, or mile-long string of river slums. While it is not a pristine wilderness, the West Branch is as good as big rivers get in Pennsylvania.

Man has never been content to simply canoe the state's big rivers. The Allegheny, Ohio, and Monongahela, having been modified by dams and locks, carry a thriving barge traffic. The tidal Delaware carries ocean-going ships. The upper Delaware, Susquehanna, Schuylkill, and Juniata once carried springtime traffic of rafts and barges and, more importantly, served as routes and water supplies for parallel canals. They thrived, or at least survived, mostly in the 19th century. But the West Branch was somewhat different. The canals only advanced as far up the West Branch as Lock Haven, and they were never that important. Instead, in the mid-19th century, the West Branch itself was the important medium, distributing north Pennsylvania's great timber treasure to the rest of the world.

The lumberjacks swept across the unbroken forests of northern Pennsylvania like locusts. Getting their harvest to sawmills and market, back in the days before railroads and logging trucks, required ingenuity and water. The task started back on the hilltops and in the remote hollows, far from the West Branch. Beasts of burden might get the logs the first few yards (remember Paul Bunyan's ox Babe). Then the water went to work. One technique used in winter was to build a slide. Logs were split in half and positioned to form a V-shaped channel, and these were joined together to snake along the hillsides and down to navigable water. The channel was then doused with water, which froze, thus forming an ice-coated flume. Logs were then loaded, and gravity did the rest. Then, springtime technique was to impound the waters of small West Branch feeder streams behind log dams. The ponds were filled with logs and then, when the water was high, the lumbermen would blow up the dam, sending a wave of tumbling, thrashing logs down this flood to the big river. The dams were, appropriately, called splashdams. When the logs reached the river, they were lashed together as rafts or sent downriver loose. The next stop was at the mills, mostly at Williamsport. At one time in the mid-19th century, Williamsport had 30 sawmills. In one year they turned out 318,000,000 board feet of lumber. To catch the logs, booms were built. They ran diagonally across the river, funneling the logs to the mills. They were anchored by a chain of rock-filled log cribs, the remains of which you can still see as a mysterious chain of rocky islets spread across the river near Linden. Finally the finished lumber left Williamsport, at first by canal boat, later by railroad.

Extraction of wood in the 19th century gave way to extraction of coal in the 20th. Past coal mining practices were as sloppy as the logging, and thus left a legacy of ravaged hills and, more importantly to paddlers, a polluted river. Coal mining pollution takes the form of siltation and acid drainage. Silt and mine acid will not hurt your health, but it turns the streams tan, the rocks orange, and the fish belly up. Between Clearfield and Lock Haven most of the West Branch is dead. You can still bring along your fly rod, but you will only use it in the clean side streams.

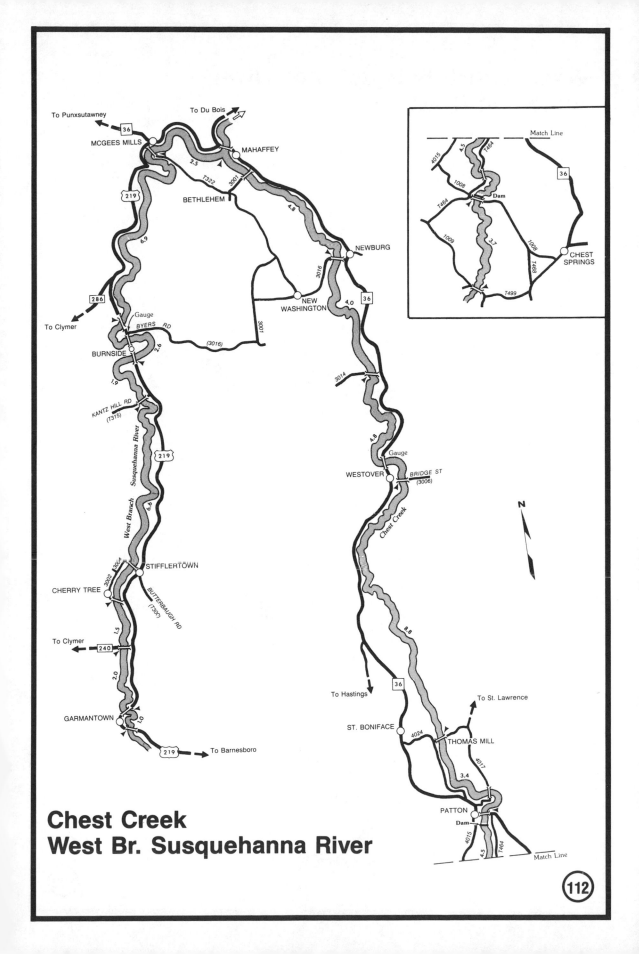

Chest Creek
West Br. Susquehanna River

112

West Branch Susquehanna River
Anderson Creek

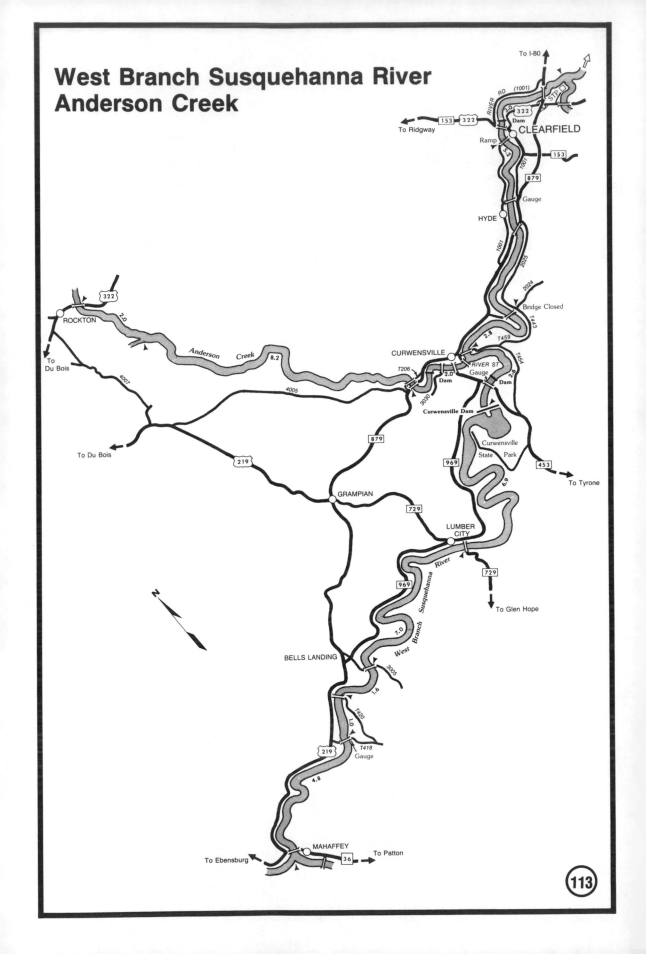

To I-80

RIVER RD (1001)
To Ridgway
153 322
3.0
Dam
CLEARFIELD
322
STP
Ramp
5.2
153
1001
879
Gauge
HYDE
1001
2025
2024
Bridge Closed
T443
2.8 T459
T454

322
ROCKTON
2.0
To Du Bois
Anderson Creek 8.2
4007
4005
To Du Bois
879
219
GRAMPIAN
729
LUMBER CITY
CURWENSVILLE
T206
2.0 Dam
RIVER ST Gauge
2.0 Dam
3030
Curwensville Dam
Curwensville State Park
969
6.9
453
To Tyrone
729
To Glen Hope
969
West Branch Susquehanna River
7.0
BELLS LANDING
3005
1.6
T420
1.0
219
T418 Gauge
4.8
MAHAFFEY
To Ebensburg
36
To Patton

N

This problem, ironically, can at times beautify the river. The acid and minerals kill all the algae that often clouds the healthy rivers in the summer, and it even helps pull the silt out of suspension. So if you visit the West Branch after a few consecutive dry weeks, the water will be unbelievably clear. So clear that you can see the corroded beer cans on the bottom, 15 feet below.

Section 1. Garmantown (lower U.S. Rte. 219) to Mahaffey (Pa. Rte. 36)					
Gradient	Difficulty	Distance	Time	Scenery	Map
6	1	24.0	8.0	Fair to Good	112

TRIP DESCRIPTION: This upper section of the West Branch, only a creek at this point, not a river, is a pleasant canoe route considering the impoverished countryside through which it winds. The start, at the lower U.S. Rte. 219 Bridge in Garmantown, is discouraging. There is essence of sewage in the air, trash on the banks, and the water is murky. But once past Cherry Tree the stream, cradled in a narrow valley, withdraws back into attractive hardwood forest backed by wooded mountainsides. Medium high mud banks usually fringe the creek. You seldom see nearby Rte. 219 but, unfortunately, you often hear its roaring coal trucks. Below Burnside the valley widens and the woods become noticeably scragglier.

These are gentle waters with lots of simple cobble- and boulder-formed riffles. The most interesting riffles are between McGees Mills and Mahaffey. Beginners should watch for a sharp 18-inch drop over a pipe crossing, about a quarter mile below Pa. Rte. 240.

HAZARDS: Hole formed by the pipe crossing above Cherry Tree could be troublesome to the inexperienced.

WATER CONDITIONS: Canoeable in spring during snowmelt and within week of hard rain. Often up continuously from thaw until mid-May, and again in late November.

GAUGE: Judge riffle below U.S. Rte. 219 put-in. Staff gauge on the second (heading downstream) bridge at Burnside ends at 2.0 feet. Level of 1.0 foot is about minimum. USGS gauges at Curwensville and Hyde (call Central PA) should be running about 4.4 feet and 3.9 feet respectively.

Section 2. Mahaffey (Pa. Rte. 36) to Clearfield (Market Street)					
Gradient	Difficulty	Distance	Time	Scenery	Map
5	A to 2 −	31.9	10.5	Fair to Good	113

TRIP DESCRIPTION: Once again, the start is discouraging, for Mahaffey is clearly a town that has seen better days. But the West Branch quickly leaves that behind for a pretty passage past silvery forested mountainsides studded with evergreens. Rhododendron chokes the bottomlands while grassy benches, that suggest good campsites, line the river. The current is always swift, there are many riffles, and there are even some boulder patch rapids reminiscent of far more difficult rivers. The good times end near the Pa. Rte. 729 Bridge, with the head of Curwensville Reservoir. If you do not like lakes, an old road loops from the northeast approach to the bridge down to within easy walking of the streambank.

Curwensville Reservoir is fairly attractive for a Corps of Engineers creation. It is about seven

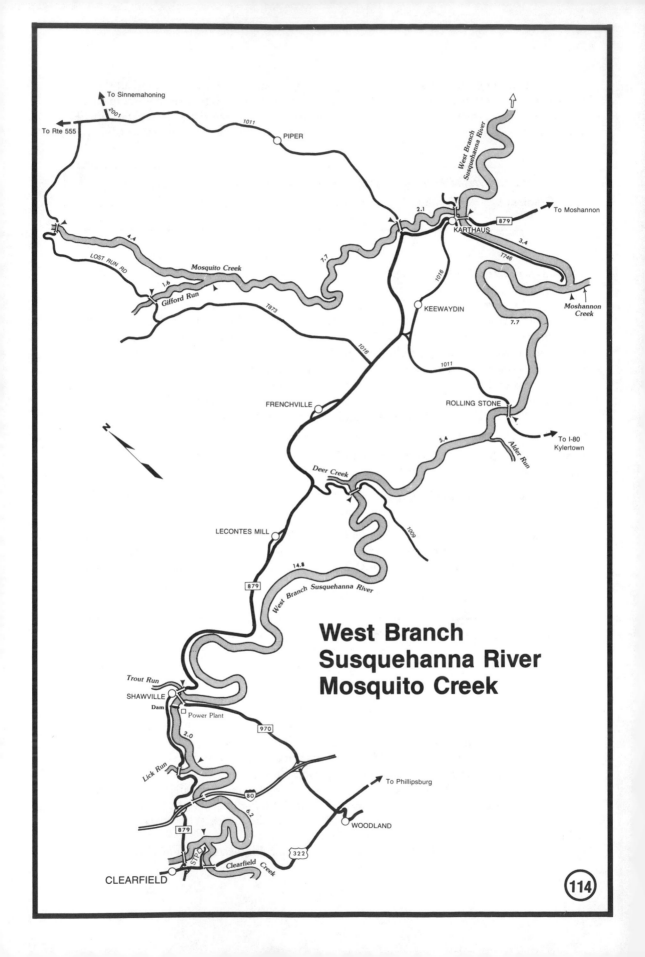

West Branch
Susquehanna River
Mosquito Creek

To Sinnemahoning

To Rte 555

2001

1011

PIPER

West Branch Susquehanna River

To Moshannon

879

2.1

KARTHAUS

3.4

T748

4.4

LOST RUN RD

Mosquito Creek

7.7

1016

1.6

Gifford Run

T873

KEEWAYDIN

Moshannon Creek

7.7

1016

1011

FRENCHVILLE

ROLLING STONE

To I-80
Kylertown

5.4

Alder Run

Deer Creek

1009

LECONTES MILL

14.8

879

West Branch Susquehanna River

Trout Run

SHAWVILLE

Dam

Power Plant

970

2.0

Lick Run

80

To Phillipsburg

6.2

879

WOODLAND

STP

322

CLEARFIELD

Clearfield Creek

114

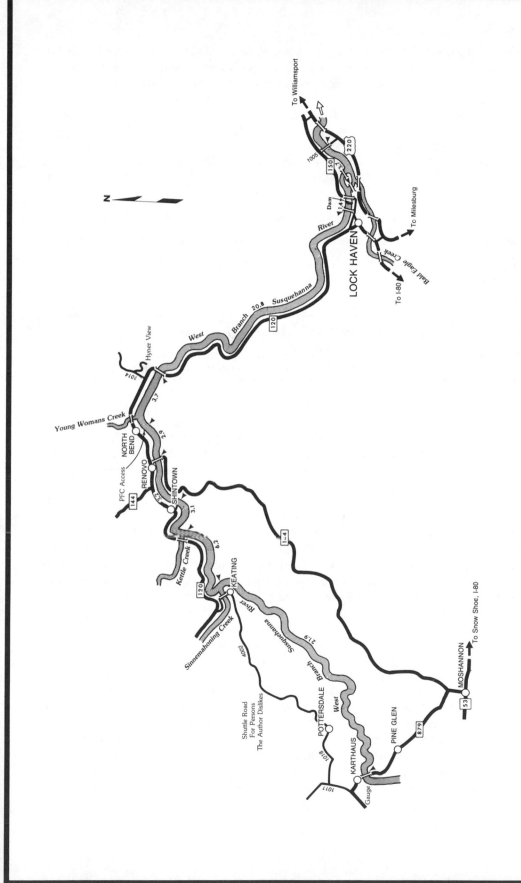

West Branch Susquehanna River

115

miles long at regular pool. A state park on the lower right end provides easy access for the lake paddler. If you need to portage the dam (needlessly masochistic thing to do), a long trek starting at the intake tower, and climbing up and down the left half of the 131-foot dam, delivers you to the tailrace and moving water.

The stretch from Curwensville to Clearfield makes a dull trip. Most of the river is flat and the current is only fair. There is a three-foot dam below Pa. Rte 453. It is runnable in a variety of spots, but beginners should carry, because if you miss the slots, you end up in some nasty holes. Oddly, the prettiest part of this final segment is the entry into Clearfield, where a string of big, beautiful old houses preside over the right bank. Take out at the boat ramp about a hundred yards below Market Street (first bridge in town) on the right.

HAZARDS: Weir below Rte. 453, Curwensville. Dangerous weir below Market Street, Clearfield.

WATER CONDITIONS: Canoeable in spring until end of May and often again in November.

GAUGE: USGS gauges at Curwensville and Hyde (call Central PA) should be over 3.5 and 3.1 feet respectively.

Section 3. *Clearfield (Market Street) to Lock Haven (Jay Street)*					
Gradient	Difficulty	Distance	Time	Scenery	Map
5	A to 1, 2 –	104.3	34.0	Good to Very Good	114,115

TRIP DESCRIPTION: This is the reach that makes the West Branch such a treasure. The trip starts with a portage, on left, around a deceptively dangerous five-foot weir, below Pa. Rte. 153. There is a small memorial by the dam paying respects to your predecessors, the raftsmen of the 19th century. After a brush with industry and I-80, the river heads off into the pretty beginnings of a canyon, scarred in spots by mining activity. Long pools and easy riffles mark the miles until a power plant and dangerous dam beside it indicate that you have reached Shawville. Carry the dam on the left, via Rte. 879.

Now begins a 53-mile section where roads may cross the river but seldom follow. A railroad line does snake up the deep canyon, but it is lightly travelled. Clusters of camps appear only here an there, and are usually far apart. There are still a few mining scars, particularly near Karthaus. But as big rivers go, this ranks as a wild one. Recognizing this quality, many paddlers take along their gear and camp out along the way. Numerous grassy benches and, at the mouths of side canyons, hemlock groves make fine campsites. Carrying your gear is seldom risky as most of this section is easy. Only long, gentle riffles over a uniform cobble bottom speed you from pool to pool. There is only one significant rapid, a long boulder patch above the Red Mo, that beginners with boats full of gear must treat with caution.

The highway returns at Keating, at the mouth of the Sinnemahoning, but the canyon remains sparsely developed and only lightly populated until Renovo. Renovo (Latin for "I renew") is the first big town since Clearfield. It was once a major railroad repair center, hence its name. At Renovo the West Branch's canyon widens to a narrow valley. It is still most impressive, and you can really appreciate it if you take a side trip up to Hyner View State Park and see it from the top. The river continues almost as it was, only a bit wider, slower, and lined by a few more camps. Mining scars are left upstream. The fun ends at Lock Haven where the steep mountain walls diverge, and the river slows in a pool. Take out at a boat ramp on right, below the Jay Street Bridge (first bridge in town).

HAZARDS: Dam below Rte. 153 in Clearfield. Carry.

WATER CONDITIONS: Usually continuously canoeable from spring thaw until mid-July. It also often comes up for three or four days after summer rains and consistant water often again appears in November. If you do not mind some dragging, the river below Keating is usually passable all summer and fall.

GAUGE: USGS gauge at Karthaus (call Central PA) should be at least 2.0 feet for the river above Keating. This is about 850 cfs, which on a river this wide, gets stretched out pretty thin.

Section 4. Lock Haven (Jay Street) to mouth					
Gradient	Difficulty	Distance	Time	Scenery	Map
2	A to 1 –	70.0	23.0	Fair to Good	128,116,117,95

TRIP DESCRIPTION: The quality of the remainder of the West Branch, as a canoe stream, is compromised by civilization. Now there are big towns, busy highways, railroads, industry, noise, and strings of summer homes. But all is not ruined, and parts are still nice. With the inflow of Bald Eagle Creek and the escape from the coal fields, the water quality in the river actually improves, and fish return.

This is all beginner water with even the riffles now far apart. But a strong current still helps out. A five-foot dam in Lock Haven, below Jay Street, is dangerous, and you should carry on

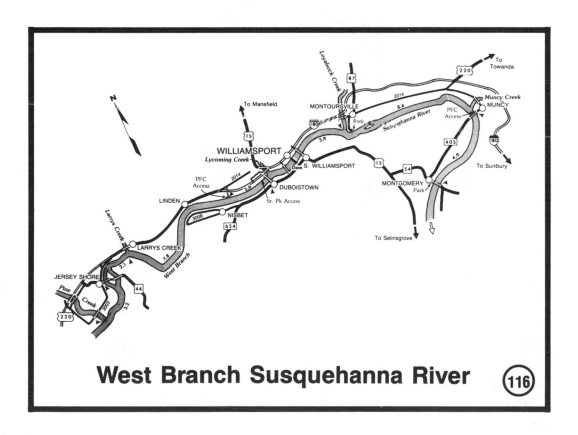

West Branch Susquehanna River (116)

White Deer Creek
White Deer Hole Creek
West Branch Susquehanna River

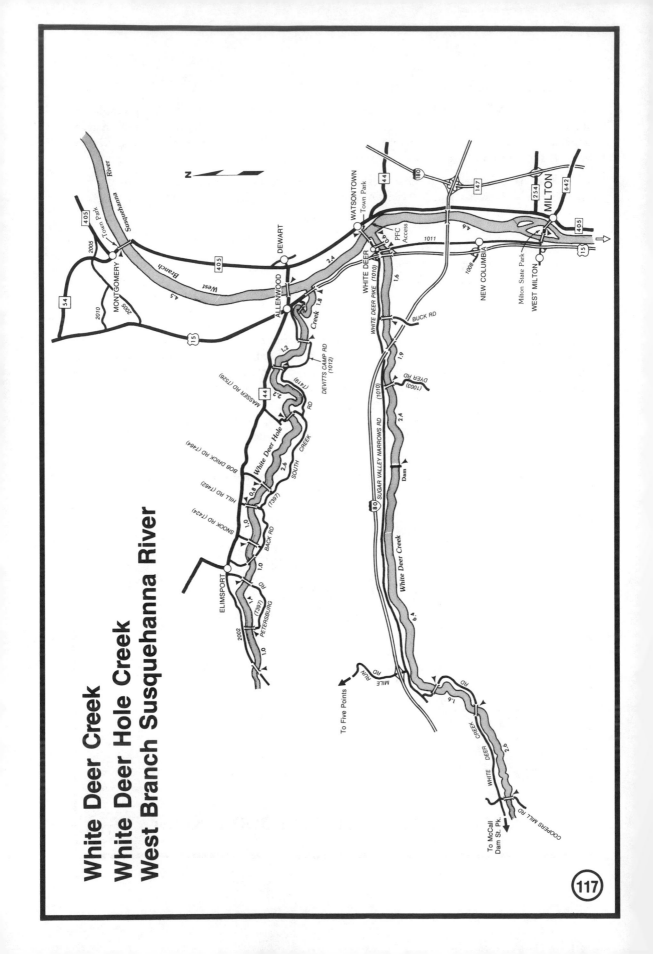

the right. There is a seven-foot dam in Williamsport, above U.S. Rte. 15. It has an absolutely lethal reversal at its base. So steer clear of this dangerous obstacle.

From Lock Haven to Jersey Shore the floater sees high banks, big farms, and Bald Eagle Mountain. From Jersey Shore to Williamsport, summer homes clutter the waterfront, and highway noise can be distracting. Look for old canal ruins on the left and, at Linden, the remains of an old logging boom. A high levee hides most of Williamsport. Below Williamsport, the river is once again undeveloped, particularly between the mouths of Loyalsock and Muncy creeks. Below here development comes and goes. Steep hemlock-covered bluffs below Muncy, mountain views, and the bluffs at Shikellamy State Park add some final color to this otherwise plain section.

HAZARDS: Dams at Lock Haven and Williamsport.

WATER CONDITIONS: Always passable, except when frozen or flooding.

GAUGE: USGS gauges at Williamsport and Lewisburg (call Central PA) drop down to 0.0 and 1.2 feet respectively in late summer low flow. This is still adequate.

Chillisquaque Creek

INTRODUCTION: Chillisquaque Creek feeds the West Branch Susquehanna just east of Lewisburg. Its name is Indian for "snowbird's place." It is hard to imagine such a mystical creature still residing in such a plain and down-to-earth, rural neighborhood. But then again, it is hard for many to imagine taking a canoe down such a tiny creek. So who knows?

Section 1. Washingtonville (Pa. Rte. 54) to mouth					
Gradient	Difficulty	Distance	Time	Scenery	Map
3	1	17.9	6.0	Good	95

TRIP DESCRIPTION: This is a placid stream, broken only by murmuring riffles that speed over bars of gravel. Tree and fence obstructions, surprisingly, are generally absent here. So at moderate levels, Chillisquaque is fit for a beginner.

The creek passes through a wooded floodplain, backed by rolling farmlands. And though high mud banks often hog the view, you still get to see a lot of the pretty countryside. If you catch this up in April, you may be additionally treated to an outstanding display of bluebells and other woodland wildflowers. Take out at Pa. Rte. 405, 0.8 miles above the mouth, as there is no access at the mouth.

HAZARDS: Occasional strainers.

WATER CONDITIONS: Except in dry years, Chillisquaque is canoeable most of March, April, and May. It takes only a little bit of water to run this gentle brook, and this is partly sustained by an average of 10 cfs kicked in from the PP & L power plant upstream and a spring just below Rte. 54.

GAUGE: Staff gauge on left abutment of Pa. Rte. 54 should read at least 1.5 feet.

Buffalo Creek

INTRODUCTION: There is no shortage of Buffalo Creeks in Pennsylvania. This one is in Union County, blending into the West Branch Susquehanna at Lewisburg. Offering pleasant and tame, springtime cruising through a fairly remote setting, it is but a short and convenient hop off of busy U.S. Rte. 15 or I-80.

Section 1. Mifflinburg (4th Street) to mouth					
Gradient	Difficulty	Distance	Time	Scenery	Map
7	1	14.8	4.5	Good	118

TRIP DESCRIPTION: The old and very typically central Pennsylvanian town of Mifflinburg, with a covered bridge at the put-in, is a fitting place to begin this scenic trip. But Buffalo Creek is quite tiny and twisting up there, with some fences and logs to further complicate things. So if you are a beginner, you should start no higher than Buffalo Road, SR3007, where the additional waters of the North Branch provide a little more elbow room. The entire creek is often uniformly shallow, even in the pools. It does its dropping over the gentlest of riffles. Below Mazeppa a runnable foot-high weir, with a strong backwash, presents the only potential hydraulic hazard on this creek.

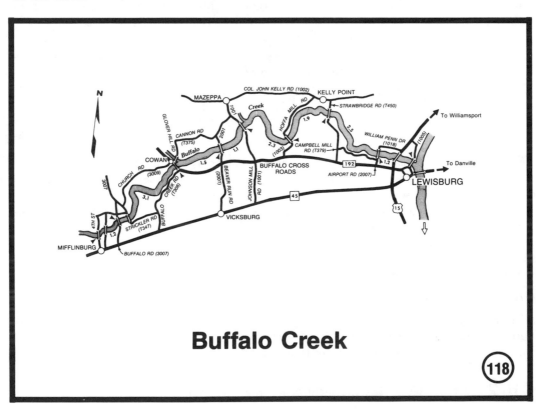

Buffalo Creek

(118)

With its wide surrounding valley and negligible banks, Buffalo Creek provides a nice way to see a lot of Union County. Though a fair number of houses occupy the area, there are more than enough unspoiled views of farms, fields, and far distant ridges to compensate. Even the federal penitentiary at Lewisburg looks attractive (from the outside of course). Take out in Lewisburg at St. Anthony Street, SR1005, just above the mouth.

HAZARDS: Some strainers, mostly found above Buffalo Road.

WATER CONDITIONS: Canoeable in spring during snowmelt and within four days of hard rain.

GAUGE: Staff gauge on center pier of Airport Road, SR2007, should be at least 3.2 feet and staff gauge on right abutment of Strawbridge Road, T450, should be at least 1.8 feet.

White Deer Creek

INTRODUCTION: White Deer Creek is a superior trout stream and highwater run that parallels I-80 in northern Union County. Its only flaw, and a big one, is that it is one of the most tree-infested and strainer-struck streams in the state. If one could paddle tandem with a beaver in the bow, they would be properly prepared for White Deer Creek.

Section 1. Coopers Mill Road to mouth					
Gradient	Difficulty	Distance	Time	Scenery	Map
48	1 to 3 −	17.1	6.0	Good	117
1.5 @ 77					

TRIP DESCRIPTION: White Deer Creek is certainly an attractive place to paddle. At least half of this run lies within state forest lands, so most of the surrounding, narrow valley is filled with woods or dense patches of mountain laurel. Though I-80 is nearby, one seldom sees or hears the highway. There are occasional camps alongside the creek, but no dense development until the last few miles.

Tiny White Deer starts out easy and as innocent-looking as a fawn, but as it enters a gap through Nittany Mountain, it tears down a series of long and rocky rapids of intermediate difficulty. The difficulty slowly diminishes, but the whitewater never stops until the very end. As little tributaries enter, they boost the volume and add noticeably extra pushiness. Strainers, unfortunately, also increase with each mile, especially aggrevated by sometimes excessive braiding of the channel. Other hazards include a low bridge on the upper creek and a four-foot water supply dam a few miles above I-80 Bridge. Only attempt this creek if you can reliably make your canoe stop where and when you so desire.

HAZARDS: A small dam, a low bridge, and strainer after strainer after strainer.

WATER CONDITIONS: Canoeable in spring during rapid snow melt or within five days of hard rain.

GAUGE: None. If rapid above covered bridge at Buck Road, T516, is runnable anywhere, the level is adequate.

White Deer Hole Creek

INTRODUCTION: Do not confuse this brook with nearby White Deer Creek. The only things that they have in common is the difficulty of finding canoeable water in them and that they both flow by prisons.

Section 1. Elimsport (Back Road, T397) to Allenwood (U.S. Rte. 15)					
Gradient	Difficulty	Distance	Time	Scenery	Map
9	1	10.6	3.5	Good	117

TRIP DESCRIPTION: White Deer Hole Creek offers a good springtime beginner cruise through a pretty, agricultural valley. The creek's low banks provide many satisfying views of the countryside, while its waters spoil you with a good current and many easy riffles. Some fallen trees are the only hardship on this run.

You can start on White Deer Hole even farther upstream, at SR2002. The first two miles possess a busy Class 2 character, dropping 57 feet in the first mile, which includes a frothy plunge over a sloping three-foot wooden dam. But for this little bit of fun it is just not worth dealing with the mess that follows — a nightmarish tangle of trees and debris caused by logging activity just above Elimsport. If you want some whitewater, find it elsewhere. Finally, the steep take-out, on the left, at Rte. 15, also stinks, but you should be able to cope with that with only a minimum of discomfort.

HAZARDS: Strainers, especially if you start above the recommended put-in.

WATER CONDITIONS: Canoeable in spring during snowmelt and within four days of hard rain.

GAUGE: Water should be within two inches of the top of the concrete footing on the right abutment of SR2002, above Elimsport, to start at that point.

Muncy Creek

INTRODUCTION: Most paddlers enjoy Muncy Creek at 50 mph, from their automobiles, while driving to the more popular and nearby Loyalsock Creek. But probably only local paddlers will care to slow down for this sometimes pleasing but generally mediocre mountain stream.

Muncy Creek
Little Muncy Creek

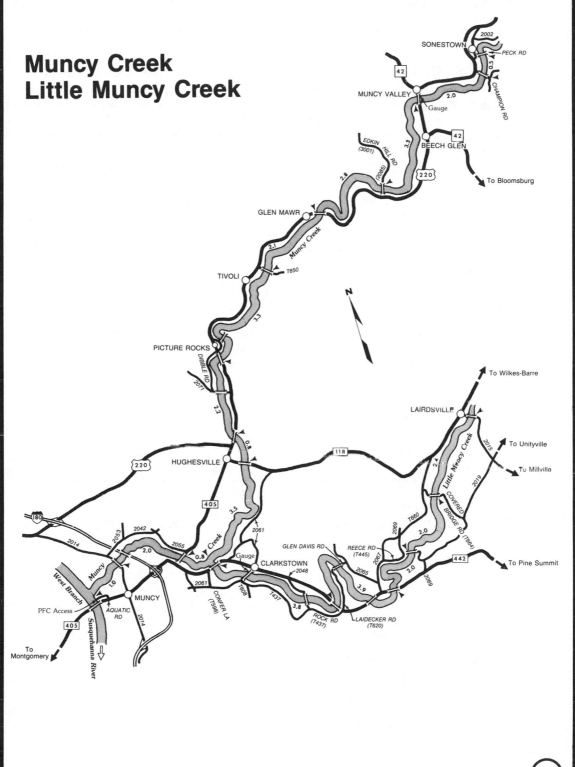

SONESTOWN
2002
PECK RD
MUNCY VALLEY
42
Gauge
2.0
0.5
CHAMPION RD
EDKIN (3001)
3.3
BEECH GLEN
42
220
HILL RD (2085)
2.8
To Bloomsburg
GLEN MAWR
2.1
Muncy Creek
TIVOLI
T650
3.3
PICTURE ROCKS
DIBBLE RD 2071
2.2
N
To Wilkes-Barre
LAIRDSVILLE
0.8
2015
To Unityville
220
118
2.4
To Millville
HUGHESVILLE
Little Muncy Creek
2019
180
405
3.5
COVERED BRIDGE RD (T664)
To Pine Summit
2014
2053
2042
Creek
2061
T660
2069
2.0
442
2.0
2055
0.8
Gauge
GLEN DAVIS RD
REECE RD (T445)
2067
Muncy
2.0
CLARKSTOWN
2048
2061
2065
2069
West Branch
1.0
2061
CONFER LA (T598)
T608
T437
3.9
PFC Access
MUNCY
AQUATIC RD
2014
3.8
ROCK RD (T437)
LAIDECKER RD (T620)
405
Susquehanna River
To Montgomery

119

Section 1. Sonestown (Peck Road, T309) to Hughesville (U.S. Rte. 220)					
Gradient	Difficulty	Distance	Time	Scenery	Map
23	1 + to 2	16.2	5.0	Fair to Good	119

TRIP DESCRIPTION: Upper Muncy Creek is a tiny stream that becomes canoeable after it completes its plunge off of the western edge of the North Mountain Plateau. Twisting through a pretty farm valley that is flanked by high wooded slopes, this could be an above average canoe tour. But, except at very high water, Muncy's high banks seldom permit the paddler to see anything more than those hillsides. This is too bad, as there is little development to ugly the valley floor, not even many summer camps. Towards the end of this section, the creek offers a bonus, as it sweeps against the base of Picture Rock, an attractive cliff that once bore a display of Indian paintings (hence the name).

As for difficulty, this is a pleasant novice run. The little creek seems always to be rushing over little cobble or gravel bars. And for spice, just above the village of Muncy Valley, a patch of slab-like boulders form a relatively complex, Class 2 rapid. Strainer problems on Muncy Creek are usually few, further increasing its attractiveness for novices.

HAZARDS: Possible strainers.

WATER CONDITIONS: Canoeable in spring during snowmelt and within three days of hard rain.

GAUGE: Staff gauge on center pier of U.S. Rte. 220, Muncy Valley, should be at least 1.1 feet. Level at Pa. Rte. 405, north of Muncy, should be no less than four grooves down from the top of either pier (not abutments) of that bridge. USGS gauge above Sonestown (call Central PA) should be over 2.6 feet.

Section 2. Hughesville (U.S. Rte. 220) to mouth					
Gradient	Difficulty	Distance	Time	Scenery	Map
14	1	8.1	2.5	Fair	119

TRIP DESCRIPTION: The surrounding mountains now diverge and, except for a levee-bound trip through Hughesville, so does the creek. Striking out into a open valley, unrestrained, Muncy Creek braids and meanders about the soft alluvium, choking on debris jams and lesser strainers. The scenery is a nice, but dull, combination of floodplain woods and high gravel banks, unsullied by development. The creek broadly bypasses the town of Muncy, keeping between high and tree-topped, mud banks. A crude Fish Commission boat ramp, beneath the east end of the Pa. Rte. 405 Bridge over the West Branch, a third of a mile below the mouth of Muncy, makes an easy take-out. To reach this ramp, turn off Rte. 405 at Aquatic Road, T813, and follow to river.

HAZARDS: Strainers between put-in and confluence with Little Muncy Creek.

WATER CONDITIONS: Canoeable in spring during snowmelt and within four days of hard rain.

GAUGE: Same as Section 1, but this section can be managed at levels of about an inch lower on either gauge.

Little Muncy Creek

INTRODUCTION: If the water is up, do not waste your time on Muncy Creek. Try the Little Muncy instead. Nestled among the hills of southeast Lycoming County, this tiny novice stream offers a picture-perfect run through an off-the-beaten-path rural valley.

Section 1. Lairdsville (SR2015) to mouth					
Gradient	Difficulty	Distance	Time	Scenery	Map
16	1	14.2	4.5	Fair to Excellent	119

TRIP DESCRIPTION: By far, the best of this creek lies between Lairdsville and the third Pa. Rte. 422 bridge, southeast of Clarkstown. The creek quickly wanders off beneath a covered bridge, past wooded hillsides, and by pleasantly proportioned hillside farms. But the real glory of this segment is in the frequent siltstone and shale cliffs that tower above the outsides of bends. The creek rushes over frequent cobble bar riffles at first, but the gradient gradually decreases. Fallen and overhanging trees are the only problems encountered on this narrow creek.

The lower few miles to Muncy Creek are lackluster. The valley opens up, highways and trash depreciate the scenery, and, with the exception of an interesting series of ledges just below Clarksville (Class 2), the water is mostly slow. After the wonderful start, these last few miles are a letdown.

HAZARDS: Strainers in first several miles.

WATER CONDITIONS: Canoeable in spring during snowmelt and within four days of hard rain.

GAUGE: Staff gauge on right abutment of SR2061, Clarkstown, should read about 1.8 feet.

Loyalsock Creek

INTRODUCTION: Loyalsock Creek is a relatively large West Branch Susquehanna tributary that drains most of the ruggedly beautiful backwoods of Sullivan County. Sullivan is one of the emptiest counties in the state, with less than 6,000 residents. In fact, Laporte, the county seat, is home to only 200 souls. It is only natural then that with thousands of acres of state park, forest, and game lands, both here and in neighboring Lycoming County, this area is renown for not only canoeing, but also for its hunting, fishing, hiking, camping, and cross-country skiing. This is an outdoors lover's paradise, and Loyalsock Creek is your path to enjoy it by canoe.

Loyalsock can please a wide range of paddling interests. Its exciting whitewater, above Forksville, has long been a favorite of paddlers who are quick and tolerant enough to endure its fickle water levels and weather. Likewise, an annual early spring slalom race held at Worlds End State Park has attracted similarly hardy contestants since the 1960's. But the greatest portion of the Loyalsock remains to please the novice paddler and canoe tripper. It is a long creek and you should be able to find a section for you.

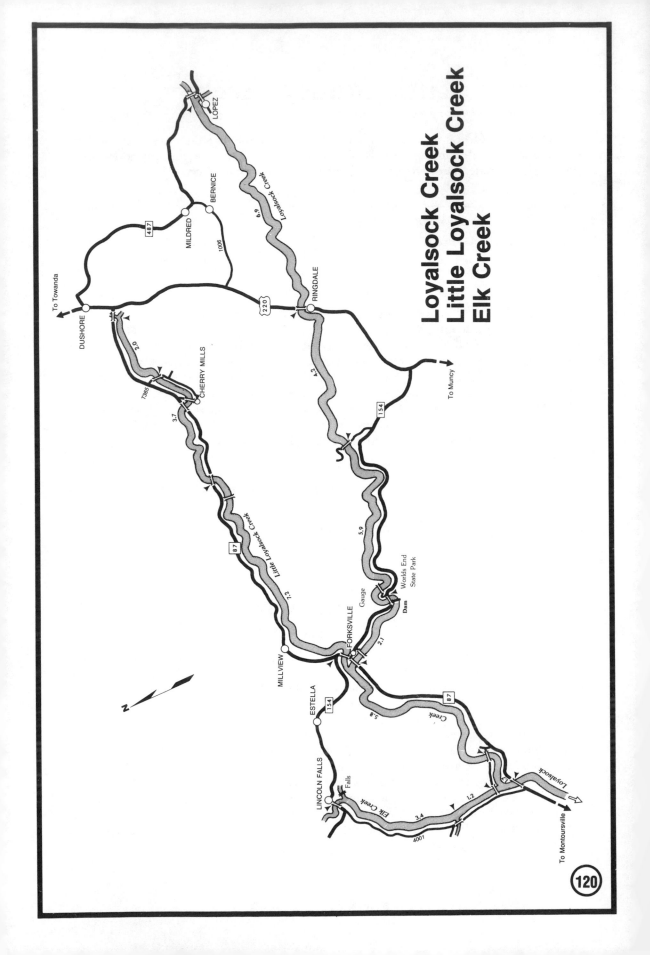

Loyalsock Creek
Little Loyalsock Creek
Elk Creek

LOPEZ

BERNICE

MILDRED

487

1006

6.9

Loyalsock Creek

To Towanda

DUSHORE

220

RINGDALE

2.0

T385

CHERRY MILLS

3.7

4.2

154

To Muncy

5.9

87

Little Loyalsock Creek

7.2

MILLVIEW

Worlds End
State Park

Gauge

FORKSVILLE

Dam

2.1

N

ESTELLA

154

5.8

87

Creek

LINCOLN FALLS

Falls

Elk Creek

3.4

4001

1.2

Loyalsock

To Montoursville

120

Section 1. Lopez to U.S. Rte. 220					
Gradient	Difficulty	Distance	Time	Scenery	Map
30	1 to 2 +	6.9	2.0	Excellent	120

TRIP DESCRIPTION: Lopez is a surprise. A former mining town in the heart of an isolated pocket of bituminous coal, it could easily be mistaken for any neat, typical, New England village, were it not for the onions of its Eastern Orthodox churches. It is here that tiny Pigeon and Lopez creeks pool their clear yellow swamp waters with Loyalsock's to form a canoeable stream.

Upper Loyalsock is a novice whitewater run. Short, rocky, and cobbly rapids link clear pools, until a long and complex rock garden rapid signals the approach of U.S. Rte. 220. The creek flows past low, grassy, and mossy banks backed by a few pastures at first, then only deep woods. Hills do not appear until the end. The surroundings up here are free of litter, and except for the numerous "no trespassing" signs, it would be a nice stretch for a short overnighter.

HAZARDS: None.

WATER CONDITIONS: Canoeable in spring during snowmelt and within three days of hard rain.

GAUGE: Staff gauge on right abutment of low-water bridge near the park office in Worlds End State Park should read at least 3.9 feet. Very roughly, USGS gauge at Mansfield, on Tioga River (call Central PA), should read about 9.7 feet.

Section 2. U.S. Rte. 220 to Forksville (Pa. Rte. 87)					
Gradient	Difficulty	Distance	Time	Scenery	Map
41	2 to 3 + , 4	12.2	4.0	Excellent	120

TRIP DESCRIPTION: It is now obvious that the creek is cutting a canyon. From U.S. Rte. 220 to the cabins at the confluence of Mill Run (T346 crossing), only one upstream view of a hillside farm challenges the illusion that you are in a remote wilderness. Rapids become fairly continuous, but still not very difficult, except for about three miles below the start, where the creek thunders over an irregular sandstone reef. Experts can run this drop, while others should carry on the left.

Below Mill Run, Pa. Rte. 154 joins the creek. But long, steepening, and complex boulder patch and ledgy rapids demand your attention. In a classic pattern, the best whitewater is usually on bends away from the road. A boaters' chute through the middle of the swimming area dam at Worlds End State Park climaxes this run. It marks the end of the best whitewater, after which a rocky two-mile cool-down run to Forksville rounds out the journey.

HAZARDS: High and difficult ledge located about three miles below U.S. Rte. 220.

WATER CONDITIONS: Canoeable in spring during snowmelt and within four days of hard rain.

GAUGE: Staff gauge on right abutment of low-water bridge near park office in Worlds End State Park should read at least 3.6 feet. Very roughly, USGS gauge at Mansfield, on Tioga River (call Central PA), should read about 9.6 feet.

297

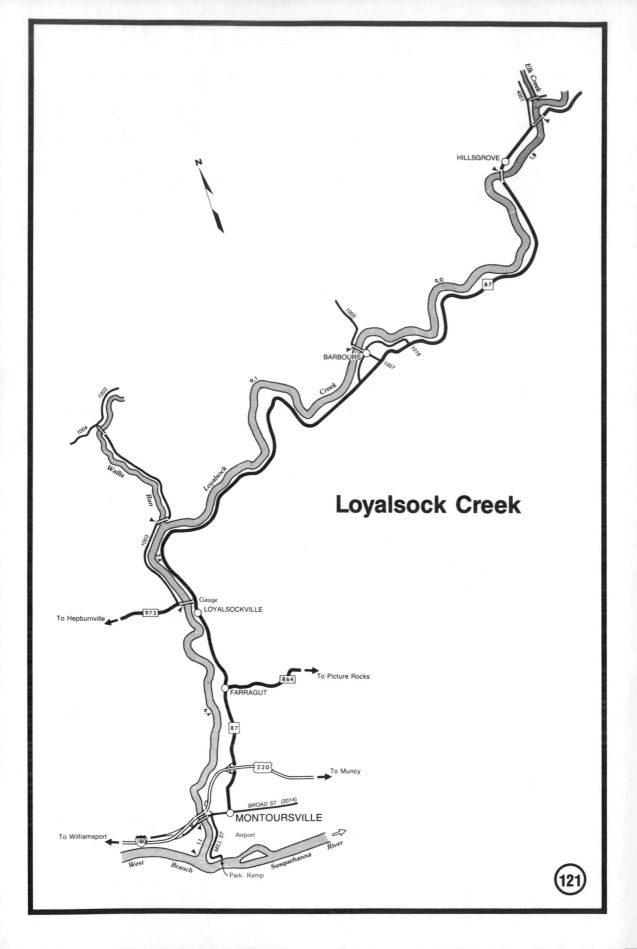

Loyalsock Creek

N

Elk Creek
4001

HILLSGROVE

1.8

9.0

87

1005

BARBOURS

1016

1007

Creek

9.1

1003

1004

Wallis

Loyalsock

Run

1003

2.7

Gauge
LOYALSOCKVILLE

To Hepburnville

973

864 → To Picture Rocks

FARRAGUT

6.4

87

220 → To Muncy

BROAD ST (2014)

MONTOURSVILLE

To Williamsport

180

1.1

MILL ST

Airport

Park. Ramp

West Branch

Susquehanna River

(121)

Section 3. Forksville (Pa. Rte. 87) to mouth					
Gradient	Difficulty	Distance	Time	Scenery	Map
14	1 +	37.4	11.0	Good	120,121

TRIP DESCRIPTION: All of this section is suitable for novice paddlers. Rapids and riffles can sometimes be fairly long and even heavy, but are always straightforward and drop gently over bars of gravel and cobbles. The whitewater is most frequent between Forksville and Hillsgrove. The long emerald pools in between can be deep and make great swim stops during those rare periods of warm weather highwater.

The creek runs down a beautiful and canyon-like valley that is steep walled and flat bottomed. As far as Barbours, recreational development is spotty, although almost every inch of streambank is heavily posted. But with proper permission from landowners, this makes an excellent canoe camping trip. Below Barbours, summer camps become unpleasantly frequent. The valley widens and graceful pine-covered hillsides rise beyond. One can take out at Montoursville or go the final mile and a half across the West Branch floodplain to a local park, just below the mouth.

HAZARDS: None.

WATER CONDITIONS: Canoeable in spring during snowmelt and within a week of hard rain.

GAUGE: Staff gauge at USGS gauging station, on left old bridge abutment, at Loyalsockville. Minimum level is not known, but is roughly about 1.0 feet. Very roughly, USGS gauge at Mansfield, on Tioga River (call Harrisburg), should read over 9.4 feet.

Elk Creek

INTRODUCTION: Elk Creek is a tiny and picturesque branch of the Loyalsock, joining several miles downstream of Forksville. It offers about five miles of easy-paced novice grade whitewater in a typical woodsy Sullivan County setting.

Section 1. Lincoln Falls (Pa. Rte. 154) to mouth					
Gradient	Difficulty	Distance	Time	Scenery	Map
43	1 to 2	4.7	1.5	Good	120

TRIP DESCRIPTION: There really is a Lincoln Falls. But this beautiful cascade down red sandstone ledges is located on tributary Kings Creek, about a quarter mile east of the put-in, off Pa. Rte. 154.

Elk Creek hurries down a slender mountain valley, through wooded bottomlands that harbor groves of hemlock, spruce, and tall straight sycamores. The creek steadily descends over a series of cobble bars and a few boulder patches, which are only difficult where fallen trees or overhanging vegetation make them so. An infestation of mobile homes, that crowd a bulldozed channel near the confluence with Hoadland Run, is the only blemish on this run.

HAZARDS: Possible strainers.

WATER CONDITIONS: Canoeable in spring during snowmelt and within three days of hard rain.

GAUGE: None.

── Little Loyalsock Creek ──

INTRODUCTION: Little Loyalsock Creek is the other fork at Forksville. It is a tiny and difficult to catch whitewater run, suitable for experienced novices.

Section 1. Dushore (Pa. Rte. 87) to Forksville (Pa. Rte. 87)					
Gradient	Difficulty	Distance	Time	Scenery	Map
31	1 to 2	12.9	4.0	Good	120

TRIP DESCRIPTION: The name Dushore is a backwoods Pennsylvanian attempt, ala Ellis Island, to Americanize the name and memory of Aristide Aubert Dupetit Thouars, a refugee from the French Revolution and an early resident of this neighborhood. Just south of this hamlet, a five-foot-wide unrunnable Payne Run adds to a ten-foot-wide unrunnable Little Loyalsock to form a ten-foot-wide canoeable brook (fluvial algebra). You can start right there.

Little Loyalsock flows down a lovely, narrow, and steep-walled, farm valley, blemished only by a fair frequency of summer homes. Though initially tiny, it is surprisingly free of fence problems, and there are few fallen trees. In time, numerous small tributaries add some elbow room, but the Little Loyalsock never grows very big.

Its whitewater is a delight. This is a run graced mostly by cobble bar rapids that run into short pools, speckled with flat boulders. There are also many little sets of ledges, individually up to two feet high, requiring some tight boat control to properly manage. At lower levels it can be a natural slalom. The most exciting spot on Little Loyalsock is an intimidatingly blind, ledgy, mini-chasm, encountered early in the trip at Cherry Mills. It is formed by the same pretty rock as all the other ledges. Finally, if you continue onto the final half mile of this creek, down to the Loyalsock, and past Pa. Rte. 87, at Forksville, watch out for strainers.

HAZARDS: Occasional strainers.

WATER CONDITIONS: Canoeable in spring during snowmelt and within three days of hard rain.

GAUGE: None. Judge riffles at township road bridge two miles below start.

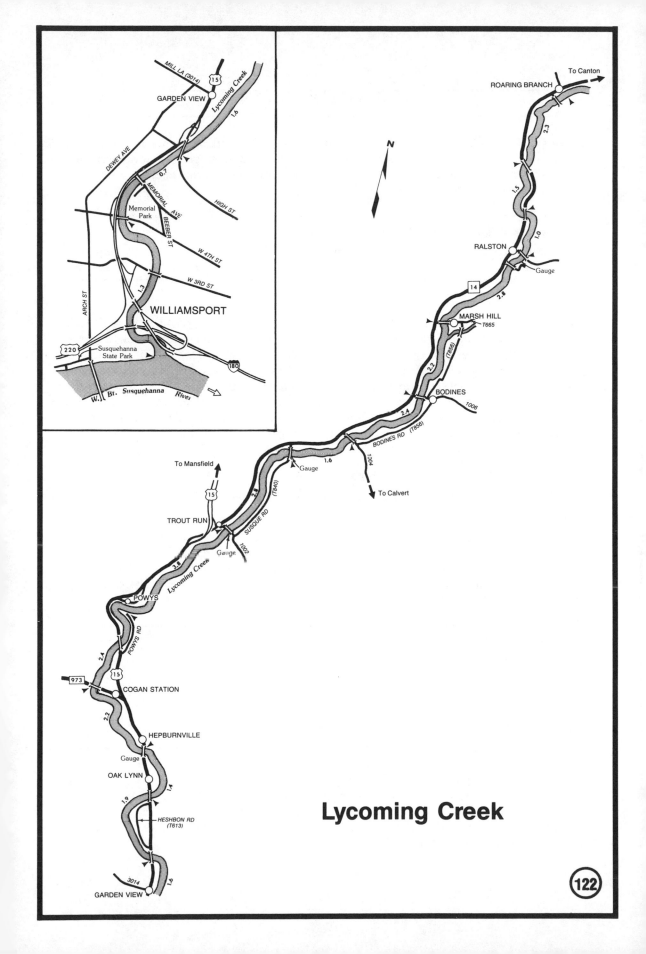

Lycoming Creek

To Canton
ROARING BRANCH
2.3
1.5
1.0
RALSTON
Gauge
14
2.8
MARSH HILL · T665
(T856)
2.2
BODINES
2.4 · 1006
BODINES RD (T856)
1304
To Calvert
Gauge · 1.6
2.8 (T840)
SUSQUE RD
To Mansfield
15
TROUT RUN
Gauge · 1002
3.8
Lycoming Creek
POWYS
POWYS RD
2.4
973 · 15
COGAN STATION
2.2
HEPBURNVILLE
Gauge
OAK LYNN · 1.4
1.9
HESHBON RD (T613)
3014 · 1.6
GARDEN VIEW

Inset map (Williamsport):

MILL LA (3014)
15
Lycoming Creek
GARDEN VIEW
1.6
DEWEY AVE
0.7
HIGH ST
MEMORIAL AVE
Memorial Park
BEEBER ST
W 4TH ST
W 3RD ST
ARCH ST
1.3
WILLIAMSPORT
220
Susquehanna State Park
180
W. Br. Susquehanna River

122

Lycoming Creek

INTRODUCTION: Lycoming Creek flows down out of the northeast corner of its namesake county, to join the West Branch Susquehanna in the heart of Williamsport. It provides a novice run, of only mediocre quality for a stream draining this scenic corner of the state, that will mostly be of interest only to local boaters.

Section 1. Roaring Branch to Trout Run (SR1002)					
Gradient	Difficulty	Distance	Time	Scenery	Map
18	1 to 1+	16.6	5.0	Good	122

TRIP DESCRIPTION: This is the best part of Lycoming Creek. Put in right at the confluence of Mill Creek, at the upper end of the town of Roaring Branch. Lycoming Creek follows a narrow and steep-walled valley where lots of people reside. But high banks hide much of their impact from the paddler, revealing mostly towering, wooded mountainsides. The clear creek initially dashes about a wide gravel floodplain. The resulting unstable banks tend toward undercutting, shifting, and, after some highwaters, littering the stream with toppled trees. While these initial miles sport a busy gradient, the pace gradually calms to a sequence of Class 1 rapids separated by roomy pools. In those years when the creek has purged itself of its woody obstacles, novices should be able to easily handle all of this swiftly paced run.

HAZARDS: Sometimes strainers are a problem in the first several miles.

WATER CONDITIONS: Canoeable in spring during snowmelt and within three days of hard rain.

GAUGE: Staff gauge on old pier (left) downstream of an old railroad bridge (now a footbridge) in Ralston should read 1.5 feet. Staff gauge on right abutment of Susque Road, T840, should be 3.9 feet to start at Roaring Branch. Staff gauge on SR1002, Trout Run, should be 2.0 feet to start at Roaring Branch. Roughly, USGS gauge at Mansfield, on Tioga River (call Central PA), should be over 10.2 feet.

Section 2. Trout Run (SR1002) to mouth					
Gradient	Difficulty	Distance	Time	Scenery	Map
10	1	15.3	3.0	Fair	122

TRIP DESCRIPTION: This is the lousy section of Lycoming Creek. Busy U.S. Rte. 15 descends into the valley, with plenty of population then clinging to its shoulders. From here on down to Williamsport, at least one bank is usually developed, and this is clearly visible from the river. There are still some pretty stretches, but they get farther and farther apart. The valley widens, the creek flattens, and as a final disgrace, Williamsport hides Lycoming's last mile and a half behind high, sterile levees. Take out at Memorial Park, at 4th Street, or if you insist on sticking it out to the bitter end, when you reach the mouth, paddle up the West Branch a half mile to the boat ramp at Susquehanna Park, by the Arch Street Bridge.

HAZARDS: None.

WATER CONDITIONS: Canoeable in spring during snowmelt and within a week of hard rain.

GAUGE: Staff gauge at SR1002, Trout Run, should be over 1.0 foot. Staff gauge on right abutment of the U.S. Rte. 15 Bridge, Hepburnville, should read over 1.2 feet. Roughly, USGS gauge at Mansfield, on Tioga River (call Central PA), should be over 9.6 feet.

Larrys Creek

INTRODUCTION: Remember Larrys Creek the next time the heavens break open. This small West Branch feeder, located near Jersey Shore, has an exceptionally scenic, ultra-highwater, whitewater run that is really worthy of your attention.

Section 1. T786 to Pa. Rte. 973					
Gradient	Difficulty	Distance	Time	Scenery	Map
65	3	8.0	3.0	Good to Excellent	123

TRIP DESCRIPTION: Flowing through a remote chunk of state game lands, this is a true wilderness venture. After passing beneath an old covered bridge, the tiny torrent cuts a narrow, v-shaped canyon, often characterized by steep, rocky, and even talus slopes. The water maintains a fast and steady pace down continuous rapids, formed by sharp rocks and little ledges, all complicated by far too many strainers. You are likely to be pushed enough here that you must catch eddies to snatch time to enjoy the scenery. A six-foot water supply dam (carry), some houses, and diverging canyonsides mark the end of the best of Larrys Creek.

HAZARDS: Strainers and a six-foot dam.

WATER CONDITIONS: Canoeable in spring during rapid snowmelt and within a day of hard rain.

GAUGE: None.

Section 2. Pa. Rte. 973 to mouth					
Gradient	Difficulty	Distance	Time	Scenery	Map
31	1 to 2	7.5	2.0	Good	123

TRIP DESCRIPTION: Larrys Creek continues, usually at a busy pace, over cobbles, rock gardens, and broken ledges, on past Salladasburg (pronounced Sal'·la·days'·burg). With the addition of some big tributaries, the gradient then slows and the valley, now fringed by a line of low, piney hills, widens. Though the valley is fairly populated, the trees and streambanks screen

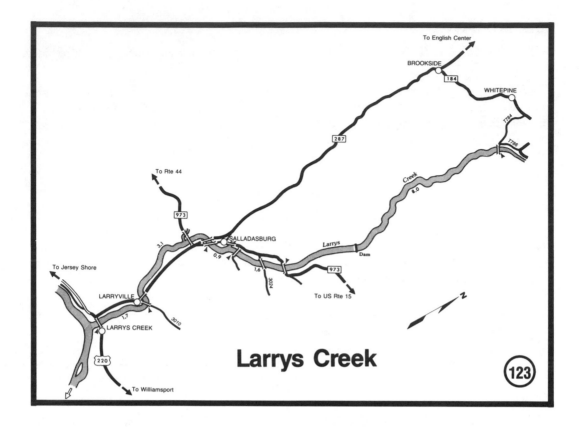

Larrys Creek

(123)

a lot, but not enough, of the blight. Take out at the downstream left side of the U.S. Rte. 220 crossing, a few yards above the mouth.

HAZARDS: Possible strainers.

WATER CONDITIONS: Canoeable in spring during snowmelt and within three to four days of hard rain.

GAUGE: None.

Pine Creek

INTRODUCTION: Pine Creek, the one up in Tioga and Lycoming counties, and the one that carved out Pennsylvania's "Grand Canyon," is possibly Pennsylvania's most famous canoe stream. Tell a person that you paddle in Pennsylvania and they will inevitably inquire as to whether you have run Pine Creek.

Several factors have contributed to Pine Creek's notoriety. For although it is certainly a worthwhile and wonderful float stream, Pine is not really as extraordinary as its reputation and popularity would would lead one to believe. First of all, this is an unusually visible stream. Each year, tens of thousands of tourists peer into Pine Creek's spectacular abyss from the overlooks of Leonard Harrison and Colton Point state parks, and naturally a fraction of them are inspired to go see

West Branch Pine Creek
Pine Creek

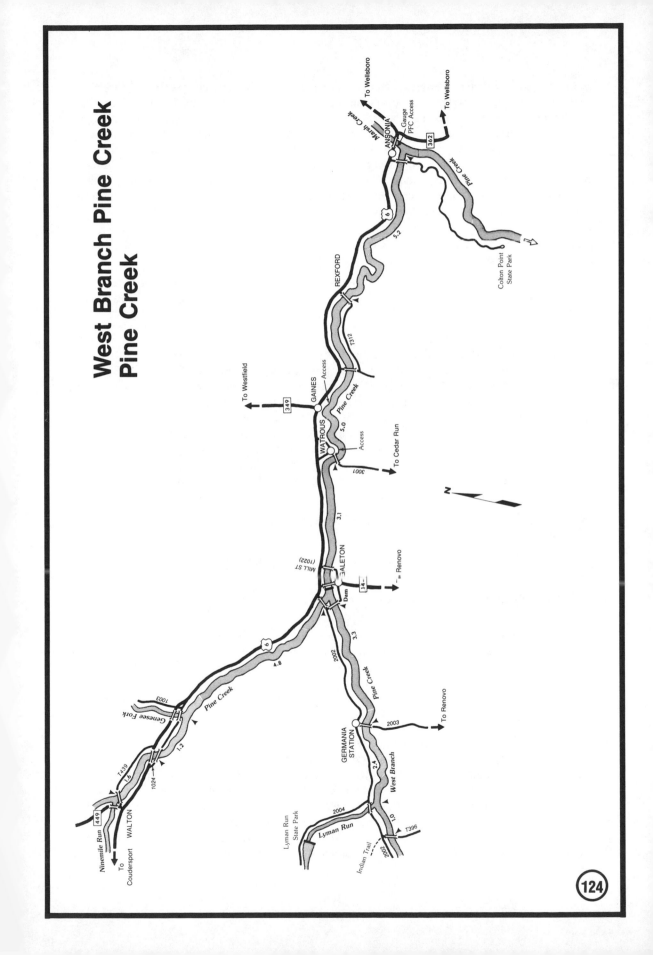

To Wellsboro

To Wellsboro

Marsh Creek

ANSONIA

Gauge
PFC Access

362

Pine Creek

Colton Point
State Park

6

5.2

REXFORD

T312

To Westfield

349

GAINES

Access

WATROUS

Pine Creek

5.0

Access

To Cedar Run

3001

N

3.1

GALETON

MILL ST (1022)

14

Renovo

Dam

6

4.8

2002

3.3

Pine Creek

1003

Genesee Fork

Pine Creek

1.2

T439

1.6

1024

To Renovo

2003

449

WALTON

Ninemile Run

To
Coudersport

GERMANIA
STATION

2.4

West Branch

Lyman Run
State Park

2004

Lyman Run

Indian Trail

1.0

T396

2002

more of it from a different angle. Second, because the creek is relatively gentle and forgiving, most beginners who converge on Pine will manage to blunder down and survive. Next, this stream usually tends to be reliably up in the late spring, when most normal people's hearts turn to thoughts of paddling. And if you are of a conservative bent, commercial raft tours are on hand to safely introduce you to the canyon's beauty. And then, a trip down Pine Creek's canyon is in many cases an annual tradition with scout troops and canoe clubs—a practice that permits even more newcomers to be introduced. Finally, the canyon is beautiful. Who could dislike it?

So why fight it? Go there at least once. After all, you have not paddled Pennsylvania until you have paddled Pine Creek.

Section 1. Walton (T439) to Galeton (Pa. Rte. 144)					
Gradient	Difficulty	Distance	Time	Scenery	Map
33	2	8.0	2.5	Good	124

TRIP DESCRIPTION: If the water is high, if you can get permission to cross private property, and if you like to live dangerously, you can put in at the confluence of Ninemile Run and Pine Creek, at Walton. If there is enough water to float this far up, the creek will be a terror. A powerful current that surges around tight bends, through braided channels, and under fallen trees can make this Class 2 water a risk of life. So approach with caution.

The waters of the Genessee Fork expand Pine Creek to a reasonable and more well-behaved canoe stream. Long rapids, running over cobbles and a few sloping ledges, speed you along. Though U.S. Rte. 6 runs nearby, the scenery is still pretty and you view little development. Take out at the town park at the confluence with West Branch Pine Creek, and thus avoid a paddle across the pool formed by the dam at Rte. 144.

HAZARDS: Strainers in fast water, especially above the Genessee Fork. Eight-foot dam at take-out.

WATER CONDITIONS: Canoeable in spring during snowmelt and within three days of hard rain.

GAUGE: Roughly, USGS gauge at Cedar Run (call Central PA) should be about 4.5 feet.

Section 2. Galeton (Pa. Rte. 144) to Ansonia (confluence Marsh Creek)					
Gradient	Difficulty	Distance	Time	Scenery	Map
14	1 to 1+	12.9	4.0	Good	124

TRIP DESCRIPTION: A big dam lurks just above the Pa. Rte. 144 Bridge, so be sure to put in below. Pine Creek rambles down a scenic mountain valley whose moderately sloping walls are thickly forested. The valley leaves enough room for the creek to usually stay out of sight and sound of U.S. Rte. 6, as Pine plays hide and seek behind small shaly cliffs and bluffs, over which cascade little side-stream waterfalls. Straightforward, choppy rapids sluice regularly down the cobble bottom. With highwater, some sharp bends spawn big waves and turbulence. But under moderate flows, this is gentle whitewater. You can take out at the road bridge to Colton Point, or you can paddle up Marsh Creek to the public launch area below the Rte. 6 Bridge.

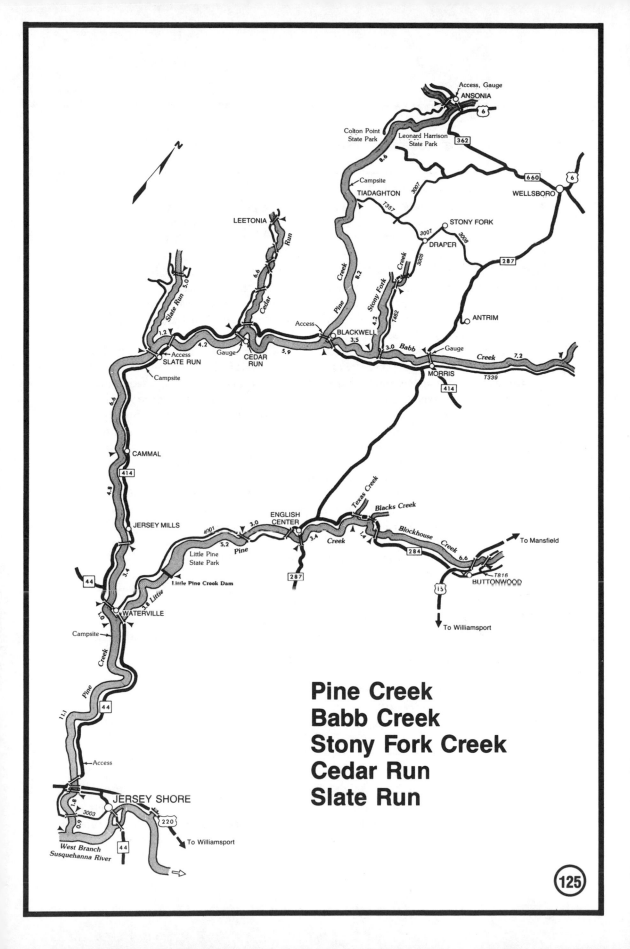

Pine Creek
Babb Creek
Stony Fork Creek
Cedar Run
Slate Run

HAZARDS: None.

WATER CONDITIONS: Canoeable in spring during snowmelt and within a week of hard rain.

GAUGE: USGS gauge at Cedar Run (call Central PA) should be about 3.0 feet.

Section 3. Ansonia to Blackwell					
Gradient	Difficulty	Distance	Time	Scenery	Map
16	1, 2 –	16.8	5.5	Excellent	125

TRIP DESCRIPTION: This, of course, is the prime section, the filet, the heart of Pine. This is the most remote, most impressive, and most popular piece of the creek.

Put in at the public access area at U.S. Rte. 6, on Marsh Creek. The valley walls quickly close in, but all remains calm for about a mile and a half, whereupon you stare down the maw of Owassee Rapid, the scourge of Pine Creek. By general standards, this is a nothing rapid—a strong Class 2 at best. But so many inept boaters travel Pine Creek and blunder needlessly down the right side of this rip, where all the rocks lie exposed at low water and all the big waves and holes wait at highwater, that Owassee probably has a more fearsome and bloodier reputation than most of the real rapids of the Grand Canyon of the Colorado. Simply keep to the left to avoid trouble.

Most of this section is simple, consisting of fast water and wide, gently dropping rapids over a cobble bottom. The wooded canyon walls and rock cliffs tower straight above one side, while a bit of sandy or rocky floodplain on the other side suggests good camping opportunities. Also, the State maintains a primitive campsite on the left, nine miles south of Ansonia, near Tiadaghton. A permit for camping on state lands (here and Section 4) is required. Write Bureau of Forestry, Box 94, Rte. 287 South, Wellsboro, PA. 16901 (for Tioga Co.) and 423 E. Central Ave., So. Williamsport, PA 17701 (for Lycoming Co.). In spite of a railroad track, a few summer camps, and hoards of boaters, this all makes a pretty fair wilderness experience.

You can abbreviate the trip by exiting at Tiadaghton, via a primitive and precipitous forest road, to be avoided in foul weather. Most people choose to finish at Blackwell, where a public access area sits below the left end of the road bridge.

HAZARDS: None.

WATER CONDITIONS: Canoeable in spring during snowmelt and, except in dry years, it usually holds a runnable level until mid-June and often again in November and early December.

GAUGE: USGS gauge at Cedar Run (call Central PA) should be over 2.1 feet.

Section 4. Blackwell to mouth					
Gradient	Difficulty	Distance	Time	Scenery	Map
8	1	40.8	13.0	Good	125

TRIP DESCRIPTION: Officially, the canyon extends almost to the West Branch, but from here on down, it is really more of a narrow valley. But this just allows one a better angle from which to appreciate the great, forested slopes that rise so high above. There are strings of summer camps along here, but also many long stretches that are still undeveloped. Camping potential along here still looks good. In addition to informal sites (ask permission), there are state camp-sites two miles south of Slate Run, on the left, and three miles below Waterville, on the right, just below the railroad bridge. The creek gets even easier now, regularly speeding over long and uniform gravel riffles, but nothing worse. Below Waterville, the high hardwood-covered slopes shrink to piney foothills and then yield to the West Branch Valley. If you paddle these last bland few miles across the valley, there is no access to the mouth. So continue on down the West Branch to Jersey Shore.

HAZARDS: None.

WATER CONDITIONS: Canoeable in spring during snowmelt and, except in dry years, usually until the end of May and again in late fall.

GAUGE: USGS gauge at Cedar Run (call Central PA) should read over 2.4 feet. Painted gauge on Pa. Rte. 414, below Jersey Mills. Minimum is unknown, but is probably about 1.0 feet.

Little Pine Creek and Blockhouse Creek

INTRODUCTION: Little Pine Creek is just that. Cutting into the deepest part of the Pine Creek Gorge, at Waterville, it resembles a scaled-down Pine Creek, but with much faster water. Blockhouse Creek is essentially upper Little Pine Creek, and it offers an even faster run.

Section 1. Blockhouse Creek: Buttonwood (T816) to Texas Creek					
Gradient	Difficulty	Distance	Time	Scenery	Map
37	1 to 2 +	8.0	2.5	Good	125

TRIP DESCRIPTION: It takes lots of water to start beneath the gray covered bridge at Buttonwood, for this is but a pint-sized torrent up here. With U.S. Rte. 15 as its initial neighbor, it is not terribly scenic, but high velocity, surprise bends, and bouncy chutes will distract you. When the creek leaves Rte. 15, it enters a beautiful and almost empty valley, marred only by an ugly power line. The creek moves through here at a fast pace, with many easy rapids, some fallen trees, and a few runnable two-foot weirs. The only drawback to this section is that a private club, which locals report to be aggressively territorial, owns the surrounding lands along the last two miles. So avoid this stream during trout season and minimize the chance of confrontation. The first available take-out is about a half mile below Texas Creek, where Pa. Rte. 287 hits Little Pine Creek.

HAZARDS: Strainers and hostile landowner.

WATER CONDITIONS: Canoeable in spring during rapid snowmelt and within two days of hard rain.

GAUGE: Painted gauge on left abutment of Pa. Rte. 287, English Center (Section 2), should read over 1.7 feet.

Section 2. Little Pine Creek: Texas Creek to mouth					
Gradient	Difficulty	Distance	Time	Scenery	Map
25	A to 2 –	15.6	5.0	Good	125

TRIP DESCRIPTION: Little Pine Creek actually starts at the confluence of Blockhouse Creek and Blacks Creek, but the first practical access point is along the side of Pa. Rte. 287, below Texas Creek. From here Little Pine flows down a beautiful, narrow valley that becomes almost a canyon by the end. The bottomlands are occupied by groves of sycamore and a few too many summer camps. The creek rolls along quickly, bouncing down lots of cobble and gravel rapids, before stalling in a short lake, at Little Pine Creek State Park. The short lake, unfortunately, is plugged by a tall dam, approximately 120 feet high. The portage up and down the center, via an endless staircase, is not all that unreasonable if you think positively, if your boat is light, if you have been training marathon, etc. The remaining miles below the dam continue with more of the same pleasantness that prevailed above the reservoir.

HAZARDS: None.

WATER CONDITIONS: Canoeable in spring during snowmelt and within four days of hard rain.

GAUGE: Painted gauge on left abutment of Pa. Rte. 287, English Center, should be over 0.9 feet. Roughly, USGS gauges at Mansfield, on Tioga River, and Cedar Run, on Pine Creek (call Central PA for either), should respectively read over 9.9 feet and 3.6 feet.

Slate Run

INTRODUCTION: The clear waters of Slate Run tumble out of the near-wilderness of northeast Lycoming County's Black Forest to join Pine Creek at (where else?) Slate Run. It is just about as wonderful a canoe stream as Cedar Run, and being only five miles down Pine Creek from Cedar, it can easily fit on the same day's itinerary.

Section 1. Morris Run to mouth					
Gradient	Difficulty	Distance	Time	Scenery	Map
55	2 to 3	5.0	1.5	Excellent	125

TRIP DESCRIPTION: To reach the put-in, head northwest from the village of Slate Run up the hard surface forest road about three and a half miles, until it turns to gravel. Shortly beyond, the road forks, and you take the right. Follow this about a mile and a half until another gravel road, on the right, cuts back downhill to the creek and then on to Morris Run.

Except for the presence of a few camps, this seems like a wilderness run. Snug at the bottom of a deep and narrow canyon, with the shuttle road far above and away, Slate Run rushes over its steep and rocky bed, past cascading sidestreams and beneath groves of shady hemlock. The whitewater is continuous, over cobbles, gravel, ledges, and small boulders. About a mile below the start, the creek pours through a rocky notch over a seven-foot double drop. The left side is fine, but scout this before attempting. A sharp drop over a ford, at the mouth, adds a final bounce to this run before entering the relatively enormous Pine Creek.

HAZARDS: Strainers.

WATER CONDITIONS: Canoeable in spring during snowmelt and within two days of hard rain.

GAUGE: None. Roughly, Pine Creek at Cedar Run (call Central PA) should be running 3.8 feet to 4.0 feet.

Cedar Run

INTRODUCTION: Cedar Run is the type of stream that one might expect would flow through heaven. It is a teensy whitewater gem that dashes down a steep-walled and shadowy side canyon to join the famous Pine Creek at (where else?) Cedar Run. Do not pass up an opportunity to run this stream.

Section 1. Leetonia to mouth					
Gradient	Difficulty	Distance	Time	Scenery	Map
61	3	6.6	2.0	Excellent	125

TRIP DESCRIPTION: Only for a creek this fine should one risk driving their precious vehicle up to Leetonia via the narrow and tortuous shuttle road which, when this creek is up, will be treacherously muddy or icy. Leetonia is just a name on the map, beside a blue line that represents only a ten-foot-wide brook. But do not worry. Put in. That really is ample water on which to float a boat. For unlike most streams, Cedar Run accepts the additional flow of its many tributaries without growing considerably wider. So each additional inflow just means more push.

For the next six and a half miles the sparkling clear water carries you over a twisting staircase of gently sloping ledges, boulder patches, and gravel bars. It is fast, exhilarating, and fascinating. Obstructions are surprisingly few: some beaver dams near the start and maybe a fallen tree. The action is almost nonstop, with only a few welcome interludes on deep green pools, and they are mostly near the end. Several sidestream waterfalls and cascades, and in early spring, ice curtains on the cliffs, grace the sides of the beautiful, v-shaped, and forested canyon. Everyone should have a Cedar Run to call their own.

HAZARDS: Possible strainers.

WATER CONDITIONS: Canoeable in spring during snowmelt and within two days of hard rain.

GAUGE: None. Roughly, USGS gauge on Pine Creek at Cedar Run (call Central PA) should be about 4.2 feet.

Babb Creek

INTRODUCTION: Babb Creek is a crystaline and sparkling tributary to Pine Creek, joining at Blackwell. Plenty of paddlers glance at Babb's dashing waters as they ride up Pa. Rte. 414 to shuttle the Pine Creek Grand Canyon, but few ever stop and wet their paddles there. Look what they have missed.

Section 1. Middle of nowhere to Morris (Pa. Rte. 287)					
Gradient	Difficulty	Distance	Time	Scenery	Map
45	2	7.2	2.0	Excellent	125

TRIP DESCRIPTION: To get to the head of navigation, drive up the valley out of Morris, via T339 (a sorry suggestion of a road), that patient and brave drivers can manage in a conventional vehicle. Follow this trail for 6.7 miles, stop, unload, and portage down into the howling wilderness for about a hundred yards until you find a creek. If you navigate correctly, you will arrive below the confluence with Lick Run on the banks of a canoeable-sized stream.

These upper several miles of Babb Creek are the finest. The scenery up here is excellent. It is a near wilderness setting, with only the remains of an old logging railroad grade to suggest man's presence. Steep and forested slopes rise up above just a narrow bit of tangled bottomlands. The clear brook rushes over scores of gravel bars and one interesting ledge that you run by a tight slot in the center. Babb bumps against the tiered sandstone faces of some little rock cliffs, hurries around sharp and sometimes undercut bends, and slides under a few troublesome fallen trees. All together, this section is well worth the slow shuttle.

HAZARDS: Moderate number of strainers.

WATER CONDITIONS: Canoeable in spring during snowmelt and within two days of hard rain.

GAUGE: Painted gauge on Pa. Rte. 287, upstream edge of center pier, should read at least six inches.

Section 2. Morris (Pa. Rte. 287) to mouth					
Gradient	Difficulty	Distance	Time	Scenery	Map
27	1 to 2	6.5	2.0	Very Good	125

TRIP DESCRIPTION: Below Morris a moderate amount of civilization encroaches upon the creek in the form of bulldozed channels and some summer camps. But it is otherwise still a pleasant cruise. The valley remains narrow, and its wooded hillsides just reach higher and higher. Occasional cliffs rise above the waters—waters which continue to rush over long, frequent, but mild rapids, set in a relatively broad cobble bed. When you reach the end, paddle a hundred yards up Pine Creek to the public access area.

HAZARDS: None.

WATER CONDITIONS: Canoeable in spring during snowmelt and within four days of hard rain.

GAUGE: Painted gauge on Rte. 287 should read over zero. Roughly, USGS gauge at Cedar Run, on Pine Creek (call Central PA), should read over 4.0 feet.

Stony Fork Creek

INTRODUCTION: Stony Fork Creek is an obscure but absolutely delightful whitewater tributary to Babb Creek. If you are ever fortunate enough to find adequate water in Stony, drop all other plans, and immediately put your boat and body on this rocky route.

Section 1. State Forest Picnic Area to mouth					
Gradient	Difficulty	Distance	Time	Scenery	Map
66	2 to 4 –	4.2	1.5	Excellent	125

TRIP DESCRIPTION: What makes this run so great is sandstone. Cliffs and shelves of the material decorate the banks, while sandstone ledges, boulders, and gravel fill the stream bed. The ledges are often sloping and smooth, but there are exceptions. Be alert in particular where, about two miles into the trip, a mine drainage-tainted sidestream that stains the Stony Fork's rocks orange enters on the left. This spot is at the head of a blind curve. Get out immediately, and carry before you are committed to flushing into a short and rocky mini-chasm that harbors two ugly and jagged ledges that drop a total of ten feet. Quickly following this hazard are several delightful drops, including a memorable flume that terminates with a sharp, vertical, six-foot plunge into a deep, green pool. There is no access at the mouth, so either carry up the bank of Babb Creek about a hundred yards to T462 Bridge, or continue down Babb Creek to Blackwell.

HAZARDS: Nasty double drop two miles below put in. Carry.

WATER CONDITIONS: Canoeable in spring during snowmelt and within two days of hard rain.

GAUGE: None on creek. Scout from shuttle road, keeping in mind that the creek's clear water and rocky bed can deceive you into mistaking a perfectly adequate level for being too low. Roughly, the painted gauge on Rte. 287 over Babb Creek at Morris should be at least six inches.

Marsh Creek

INTRODUCTION: Since the public access area for the renown Grand Canyon of Pine Creek run is on Marsh Creek, this technically makes the lower 1% of Marsh Creek one of the most popular canoe streams in Pennsylvania. The other 99% of Marsh Creek is a neglected highwater run, suitable for beginners with low expectations of what they should find on a nice canoe stream.

Section 1. Webster Road to mouth					
Gradient	**Difficulty**	**Distance**	**Time**	**Scenery**	**Map**
4	1	6.5	2.5	Good	126

TRIP DESCRIPTION: This is a fairly pretty cruise through a wide and often marshy valley. The narrow, winding creek flows between grassy banks which, although often blocking out your view of the adjacent scenery, still allow clear views of the surrounding mountains, which rise like walls above the flat valley. The hazy water is mostly flat and sluggish down to Asaph Run, but below, gentle gravel riffles quicken the pace. You get most of your exercise on Marsh portaging one low bridge and several logjams that unfortunately clog the creek. The last take-out on Marsh Creek is at the public access below the U.S. Rte. 6 Bridge, Ansonia.

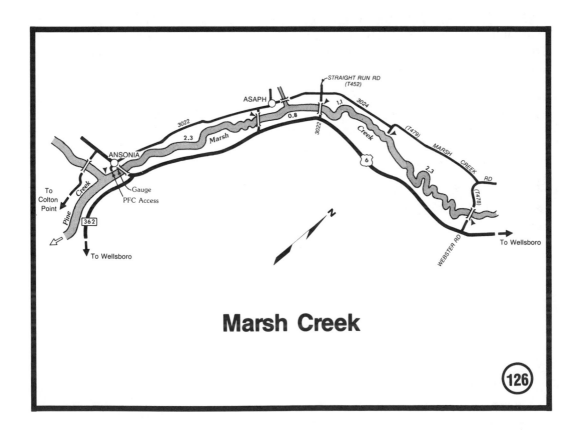

Marsh Creek

126

314

HAZARDS: Low bridge and logjams.

WATER CONDITIONS: Canoeable in spring during snowmelt and within a week of hard rain.

GAUGE: Staff gauge on right pier of U.S. Rte. 6 should be over 0.0 feet. You can also use the riffle below Webster Road as an indicator.

West Branch Pine Creek

INTRODUCTION: The West Branch offers a short and fairly scenic novice cruise down to Pine Creek at Galeton. It is remarkably similar to the upper Pine Creek (Section 1), including the cellulose slalom that will plague those who try to start too far upstream.

Section 1. Burrows (T396) to mouth					
Gradient	Difficulty	Distance	Time	Scenery	Map
33	2	6.9	2.5	Good	124

TRIP DESCRIPTION: Just because you can put in as far up as Burrows does not mean that you should. Save yourself the aggravation of a mile and a half of nasty encounters with fallen trees and sharp, undercut bends by putting in from the roadside, about a half mile below Lyman Run.

The West Branch flows through a reasonably narrow valley shared by woods, pastures, and overgrown, abandoned farms. The width of the valley is nice in that it gives one a good view of the rolling and rounded profile of the high, surrounding plateau. Though some clusters of houses and camps occasionally foul the vista, they are soon forgotten. The creek rushes through this setting down long, almost continuous, cobbly rapids, while several sets of gently sloping ledges add some variety to the whitewater. A town park at Galeton allows easy egress at the mouth.

HAZARDS: Strainers and a possibility of fences.

WATER CONDITIONS: Canoeable in spring during snowmelt and within four days of hard rain.

GAUGE: None. Roughly, USGS gauge at Cedar Run (call Central PA) should be about 4.5 feet.

Bald Eagle Creek

INTRODUCTION: Bald Eagle Creek flows up the center of centrally located Centre County. Novices have long sought out this long and straight-flowing tributary of the West Branch Susquehanna because of its miles of smooth water, forgiving swiftwaters, and relatively long canoeable season.

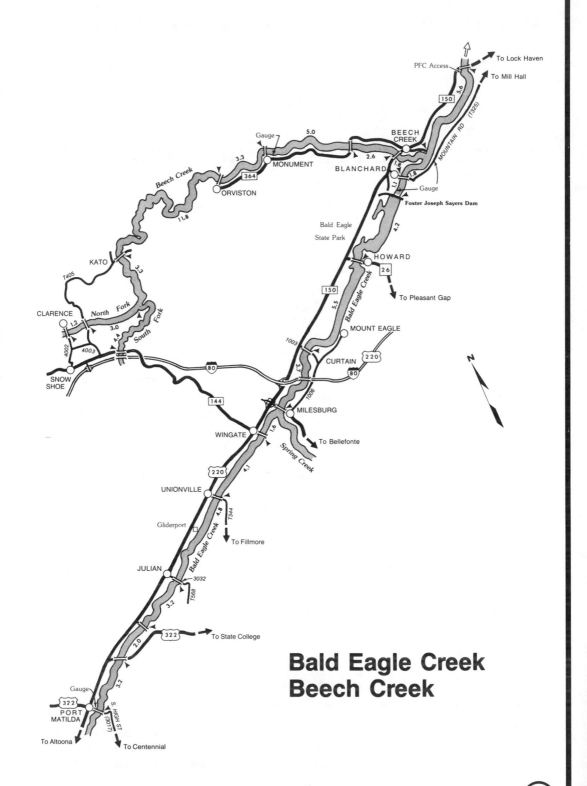

**Bald Eagle Creek
Beech Creek**

To Lock Haven
To Mill Hall
PFC Access
150
5.6
MOUNTAIN RD (T325)

Gauge
5.0
BEECH CREEK
Monument
3.3
2.6
Blanchard
1.6
1.8
364
Beech Creek
Orviston
1.1
Gauge
11.8
Foster Joseph Sayers Dam
4.2
Bald Eagle State Park
KATO
3.3
HOWARD
26
T405
To Pleasant Gap
150
North Fork
CLARENCE
1.2
3.0
5.5
South Fork
4.4
4002
4003
MOUNT EAGLE
1003
220
SNOW SHOE
80
CURTAIN
80
3.7
144
1006
MILESBURG
WINGATE
1.6
To Bellefonte
Spring Creek
220
4.1
UNIONVILLE
4.8
T344
Gliderport
To Fillmore
Bald Eagle Creek
JULIAN
3032
3.2
T568
2.0
322
To State College
3.2
Gauge
322
PORT MATILDA
S. HIGH ST (3017)
To Altoona
To Centennial

N

127

Section 1. Port Matilda (S. High Street) to Curtin (SR1003)					
Gradient	Difficulty	Distance	Time	Scenery	Map
15	1	22.6	7.5	Fair to Good	127

TRIP DESCRIPTION: Canoe navigation on Bald Eagle Creek starts, appropriately, at a port — Port Matilda. The first 23 miles, to Curtin, are suitable for paddlers possessing novice whitewater skills. The tiny creek hurries over numerous short gravel bars that sometimes prove exciting when they sweep into undercut bends. Though not common here, fallen trees are always a possibility. Staying small all the way to Milesburg, the creek is generally closed in by medium-high banks and dense vegetation. There are, nevertheless, still frequent views of the gracefully undulating rim of Allegheny Front, running parallel on the west. Unfortunately, there are also too many views of, and too much noise from, too close U.S. Rte. 220. If natural features begin to bore you, the graceful aerial display put on by glider planes out of an airstrip between Julian and Unionville makes a most pleasant diversion. It seems that the updraft on the west face of parallel Bald Eagle Mountain, from here on up to Williamsport, create exceptional gliding conditions no doubt once enjoyed by its feathered namesake. The volume swells at Milesburg with the addition of Spring Creek, but Bald Eagle Creek gets no more difficult, just a little bouncier and more powerful. The take-out for this segment, Curtin, is a tiny village that, along with an old ironworks, is currently being restored. Several bridges in between Port Matilda and Curtin allow you to shorten this run to your taste.

HAZARDS: Undercut banks and occasional strainers.

WATER CONDITIONS: Canoeable in spring during snowmelt and within five days of hard rain, above Milesburg. Except in dry years, the section below Milesburg is passable until late June.

GAUGE: Staff gauge on left abutment of South High Street, Port Matilda, should read at least 0.6 feet to paddle between here and Milesburg. No gauge is currently available for below Milesburg. But if USGS ever replaces the outside staff on its gauging station at Milesburg, on right, 100 yards below Spring Creek, a level of about 0.1 foot would be minimum. USGS gauge at Beech Creek Station is frequently useless because of influence of reservoir in between.

Section 2. Curtin (SR1003) to Sayers Dam					
Gradient	Difficulty	Distance	Time	Scenery	Map
10,0	1,A	9.7	5.0	Good	127

TRIP DESCRIPTION: The creek quickly widens out into Foster Joseph Sayers Reservoir just below Curtin. At summer pool the lake is about eight miles long. Being a wide lake in a wide valley, it affords excellent and unobstructed vistas of pretty mountains, in all directions. Fall drawdown, unfortunately, does mar the scene with a "bathtub ring" of mudflats. The shores of the lake belong to Bald Eagle State Park. The park offers campgrounds, picnic areas, beaches, etc. It is ideal for the casual paddler with no special itinerary. If you do have an itinerary, and if it includes continuing past the dam, you can make the long but easy carry around the left side of the dike-like structure faster than you can say Foster Joseph Sayers.

HAZARDS: Power boats and water skiers during summer.

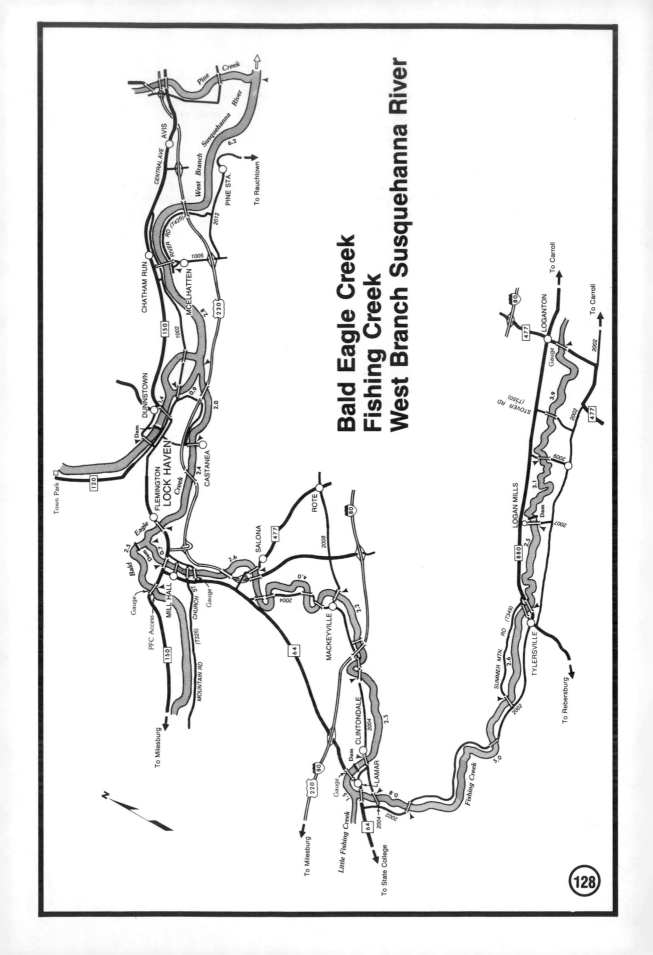

Bald Eagle Creek
Fishing Creek
West Branch Susquehanna River

128

WATER CONDITIONS: The lake is canoeable from spring thaw until winter freeze. The mile and a half from Curtin to the summer pool may get too low after the end of July.

GAUGE: None necessary.

Section 3. *Sayers Dam to mouth*					
Gradient	Difficulty	Distance	Time	Scenery	Map
3	A to 1 –	15.4	5.0	Fair to Good	127,128

TRIP DESCRIPTION: Up at runnable levels into the warm parts of the year, the remaining miles of Bald Eagle Creek offer a mostly smooth and unobstructed cruise that, at moderate levels, is most suitable for beginners. Unless you like long carries, put in at the bridge at Eagleville, 1.1 miles below the dam. The best section of this section runs down to Mill Hall. It offers a winding passage through a pretty floodplain forest. There are many little islands here, including a curious chain of equidistant islets that are probably a vestige of an ancient logging boom. If you continue past the first U.S. Rte. 220 bridge at Mill Hall, there is a sloping six-foot dam that experienced paddlers may run. But scout first as some iron spikes protrude from its otherwise smooth face. Just below the dam a short maze of divergent channels will test your sense of direction. This short stretch can be hazardous at high levels because of numerous strainers. The final miles of Bald Eagle, near Lock Haven, inherit some industry, trash, and the company of busy highways, but this will still provide pleasant canoeing for some. Since there is no access at the mouth, take out a mile upstream by the roadside or continue down the West Branch to McElhatten.

HAZARDS: Six-foot dam near Mill Hall (watch for spikes) and strainers downstream.

WATER CONDITIONS: Canoeable from spring thaw until late July. Also comes up often in November and December. The two final weeks of November are usually flowing because of drawdown of Sayers Reservoir.

GAUGE: USGS gauge below Sayers Dam tailrace, on left (entails quarter mile walk to get there), should read over 3.6 feet. New (1985) USGS gauge at Beech Creek Station (call Central PA) will probably read about 6.8 feet at minimal level. This corresponds to about 2.0 feet on the staff gauge still attached to the abandoned USGS Beech Creek Station Gauge, on an old bridge pier opposite the mouth of Beech Creek (approach via Mountain Road and look for white guardrail). Staff gauge on left abutment of Pa. Rte. 150. Minimum is unknown, but probably around 3.0 feet.

Fishing Creek

INTRODUCTION: This Fishing Creek blends with Bald Eagle Creek just above Lock Haven. It is strikingly similar to nearby and better known Penns Creek and worthy of far more attention than it receives.

Section 1. Loganton (Pa. Rte. 477) to Tylersville (Pa. Rte. 880)					
Gradient	Difficulty	Distance	Time	Scenery	Map
13	1	9.5	3.0	Good	128

TRIP DESCRIPTION: Up here Fishing Creek flows through what is called Karst topography—a lumpy limestone landscape whose shape and drainage are determined by a subterranean labyrinth of caves. The evidence is all around. Look at the valley about Loganton, and you will observe side valleys that dead end into ridges. You will find streams that sink into holes in the ground. In fact, at low water the entire flow of Fishing Creek sinks into its bed below Loganton, Logan Mills, and again below Tylersville. That is why you will find Fishing Creek's bed so brushy in those sections. Finally, you may spot depressions, called sinkholes, that mark caved-in caves beneath the seemingly sturdy landscape.

This upper section is tiny, mellow, and scenic. Low banks permit the paddler to enjoy sumptious views of this pretty farm valley. The water is mostly smooth, but it periodically breaks into long series of riffles. At times living brush and trees that grow in the streambed can be inconvenient. Bristle as they do, they seldom block the channel. Frequent fences, unfortunately, do block the way. Also you must carry a five-foot dam just above SR2007, Logan Mills.

HAZARDS: A five-foot dam at Logan Mills, fences, and patches of brush.

WATER CONDITIONS: Canoeable in spring during snowmelt and within two days of hard rain.

GAUGE: Staff gauge on center pier of Pa. Rte. 477 should be over minus four inches.

Section 2. Tylersville (Pa. Rte. 880) to Clintondale (SR2004)					
Gradient	Difficulty	Distance	Time	Scenery	Map
34	2 to 3 –	9.9	3.0	Fair to Good	128

TRIP DESCRIPTION: Fishing Creek now switches valleys and does a 180-degree change in direction by cutting a pair of long and beautiful mountain gaps. This is most reminiscent of the Coburn to Weikert section of Penns Creek, including being sullied by the annoying presence of summer homes. The gradient steepens through here, and the rapids become pushy and exciting. But be aware of several braided spots that end in nasty strainers. There are also two little weirs on this section, both runnable, but with the first having a strong roller.

HAZARDS: Strainers in fast water.

WATER CONDITIONS: Canoeable in spring during snowmelt and within two days of hard rain.

GAUGE: Staff gauge on right abutment of Pa. Rte. 64, below Lamar, should be at least 2.2 feet.

Section 3. Clintondale (SR2004) to mouth					
Gradient	Difficulty	Distance	Time	Scenery	Map
17	1 to 2	12.0	4.0	Poor to Good	128

TRIP DESCRIPTION: The whitewater slowly mellows, although at least riffles are frequent as far as Mill Hall. The valley and creeksides are fairly well inhabited now, but appealing views of mountains and farms still prevail. In contrast, Mill Hall, with its dredged and leveed channel, is an eyesore. The final passage across the Bald Eagle Valley is again pleasant, presenting a smooth path through a floodplain forest. Take out down Bald Eagle Creek at Pa. Rte. 120.

HAZARDS: None.

WATER CONDITIONS: Canoeable in spring during snowmelt and within four days of hard rain.

GAUGE: Staff gauge on Pa. Rte. 64, below Lamar, should be about 2.0 feet. Staff gauge on uppermost bridge in Mill Hall. Minimum is unknown, but is probably about 4.0 feet.

Beech Creek

INTRODUCTION: Beech Creek offers some fair to good springtime canoeing in its long descent off the Allegheny Front into Bald Eagle Creek. It drains a relatively remote area of woodlands and coal mines north of I-80 and a frosty village called Snowshoe. Remoteness has a price though, for this creek has an unusually long and roundabout shuttle. So allow for a long day.

Section 1. T405 to Monument					
Gradient	Difficulty	Distance	Time	Scenery	Map
28	1 to 2 +	21.4	6.5	Fair to Good	127

TRIP DESCRIPTION: Most of this section is remote from any place a conventional vehicle will get you, though its condition varies from wild to ravaged. The put-in is on the North Fork Beech Creek. Tiny as this creek is at T405, you can start even farther upstream at Clarence. But a refractory plant's refuse heaps and everybody's everyday trash dumped into the stream makes this piece unrewarding. So start at T405.

The North Fork is fast and busy, but not inherently complex. What can make it a real challenge are a few fallen trees, overhanging alder bushes, and a haul road culvert (carry). From the creek, the surroundings appear undeveloped. Progressing onward, upstream trash begins to disperse, and a shallow and forested gorge begins to take shape.

The confluence with the South Fork creates welcome elbow room, but Beech Creek is still small enough that some trees and logjams will force a few carries. Strainer problems vary greatly from year to year. But whatever the year, they usually diminish as a few more tributaries expand the creek. Also watch out for a low footbridge in fast water about two miles below the forks. The creek moves along at a lively pace, rushing over fairly continuous rapids of cobbles and little boulders. They are bouncy but seldom complex. Well-tutored novices can handle this run, if they can stop for strainers.

Set in a remote, wooded, and ever-deepening gorge, Beech Creek provides generally attractive scenery. There are, ironically, relatively few beech trees in these woods. Mine scars, acid seeps, camps, or railroad bridges (railroad abandoned) occasionally disrupt the harmony. But taking advantage of the acid condition, cranberry vines thrive on many of the sandbars. And then civilization returns to stay, at Orviston.

If the water level on the North Fork is marginal, you can still start below the forks at Kato. You reach Kato via T710, a wretched but passable excuse for a road. It is possible to shuttle directly between Kato and Orviston, but those of us with conventional, low-clearance, two-wheel-drive vehicles should not even consider this. Take the interstate.

HAZARDS: Strainers, low bridge, and culvert.

WATER CONDITIONS: Canoeable in spring during snowmelt and within three days of hard rain, to start on North Fork, and five days to start at Kato.

GAUGE: USGS gauge at Pa. Rte. 144, over the South Fork Beech Creek, should read over 2.2 feet to start at T405. USGS gauge at Monument, on right bank 800 feet below the bridge, should be over 7.1 feet to start at Kato and over 7.5 feet to start on North Fork. Also, the canoe gauge on the bridge pier at Monument should be over 0.7 feet to start on North Fork and 0.2 feet to start at Kato.

Section 2. Monument to mouth					
Gradient	Difficulty	Distance	Time	Scenery	Map
19	1	9.4	3.0	Fair	127

TRIP DESCRIPTION: Beech Creek begins leveling off below Monument. Watch out for one braided section between there and Rte. 150. Otherwise this is an easy piece, with the whitewater consisting of riffles only, and all smooth water below Pa. Rte. 150. Though there are still some attractive spots, houses and trash increasingly become a fixture of the riverscape. The final few miles revert to woods with towering Bald Eagle Mountain as the backdrop. Take out at the mouth, on the left, at the end of Maple Street.

HAZARDS: Possible strainers on braided sections.

WATER CONDITIONS: Canoeable in spring during snowmelt and within a week of hard rain.

GAUGE: USGS gauge at Monument should be over 6.9 feet and canoe gauge on bridge in Monument must be over zero.

Spring Creek

INTRODUCTION: Draining the leaky limestone of the scenic Nittany Valley near State College, well-watered Spring Creek lives up to its name. Yet, only after a good rain is there enough water for one to really enjoy all of its many miles of pleasant cruising. If the rains come on the first week of trout season, find another place to go canoeing. With hatcheries along its banks and feeder springs, and with its waters just boiling with trout, you will not be able to see the stream for all the fishermen.

Section 1. Houserville (community park) to SR3001					
Gradient	Difficulty	Distance	Time	Scenery	Map
16	1 to 2 –	10.6	3.5	Good to Very Good	129

TRIP DESCRIPTION: If the whole world is in flood, adventuresome sorts can start a few strainer-infested miles upstream, on tributary Slab Cabin Run. More reasonable sorts will start downstream at Spring Creek Park, Houserville, regardless of whether the water is extra high.

The creek quickly shakes loose from its suburban start to wander about a rolling and rural landscape. The cruising would be easy if it were not for such an abundance of fences and downed trees. After a few miles Spring Creek crosses into the grounds of Rockview State Prison and be-

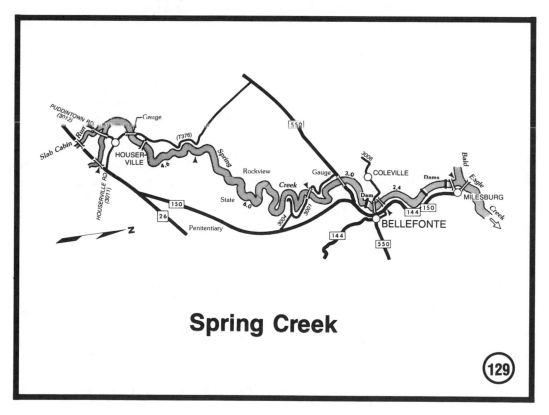

Spring Creek

comes incarcerated in a beautiful, shallow gorge. This is Spring Creek's finest reach. It is almost like a park in there. But since the surrounding land is not a park, but a prison, it is best to confine your activities strictly to the creek. Try not to look suspicious and remember that files and hacksaws would be considered contraband. Three two-foot weirs in this stretch are runnable, though the last two have rollers that merit respect. There are plenty of wide and rocky riffles in between. If the creek is low, you will find that the riffles have some very sharp rocks.

HAZARDS: Trees, logjams, fences, and three weirs.

WATER CONDITIONS: Canoeable in spring during snowmelt and within three days of hard rain.

GAUGE: Staff gauge on right abutment of Houserville Road, T376/SR3011, should be over 1.6 feet. Staff gauge on pier of Pa. Rte. 550 (Section 2) should be over 2.6 feet.

Section 2. SR3001 to mouth					
Gradient	Difficulty	Distance	Time	Scenery	Map
19	A to 1	5.4	2.0	Fair	129

TRIP DESCRIPTION: The lower creek is easier to paddle and to catch up than the creek above. But it is scenically inferior. The surrounding valley becomes instantly populated below the prison and hatchery and stays that way on past Bellefonte. While this town appears uninteresting from the creek, it is worth a side trip. The name Bellefonte is from French for "beautiful fountain," but Bellefonte's claim to fame is its amazing collection of beautiful and ornate old mansions.

This section consists of flatwater and riffles, the flatwater partly the fault of some dams. To paddle through Bellefonte, you must carry a five-foot dam. Luckily a set of big steps on the retaining wall, on the left, keep the carry short and easy. Then there is a fifteen-foot, stepped dam by an old abandoned power plant. Believe it or not, it is runnable. Most would be wise to portage it on the left. Finally you must carry a four-foot dam at the big power plant in Milesburg. Take out on Bald Eagle Creek at Rte. 144.

HAZARDS: Three dams.

WATER CONDITIONS: Canoeable below dam in Bellefonte most of year because of voluminous springs around Bellefonte (hence its name). The flow seldom drops below 120 cfs through Bellefonte, even in September and October. The paddleable season also includes much of winter because the relatively warm spring water retards ice formation.

Young Womans Creek

INTRODUCTION: Young Womans Creek is a short and delightful whitewater excursion that rushes into the canyon of the West Branch Susquehanna River, just downstream from Renovo. Its name is currently irrelevant. In exploring this sparkling mountain brook, the author encountered seven ugly fishermen, a spotted dog (male), and a rather torpid frog (gender unknown), but no young women.

Section 1. SR4005 to Pa. Rte. 120					
Gradient	Difficulty	Distance	Time	Scenery	Map
47	3 – to 3 +	7.4	2.5	Good to Very Good	130

TRIP DESCRIPTION: The clear creek is set in a deep and narrow canyon, civilized only by the presence of the shuttle road and numerous camps. The creek, nevertheless, will seem quite remote at times.

You can start as far up the creek as its confluence with Bull Run. Driving upstream from Gleasonton, this is at the third bridge of SR4005 over Young Womans Creek. The first mile is plagued with downed trees, especially where it braids (often) through pretty hemlock groves. But the remainder of the run stays fairly open. This is just fine because the rapids are almost continuous and can be pushy. Rock gardens and cobble bars shape the rapids and combine to create an excellent intermediate run. There is still another 0.4 miles of fastwater below Pa. Rte. 120, but there is no access to the mouth.

HAZARDS: Strainers.

WATER CONDITIONS: Canoeable in spring during snowmelt and within four days of hard rain.

GAUGE: USGS gauge 1.5 miles above the confluence with the Left Fork, on left, with the outside staff on the abutment of the weir. Level of 1.4 feet is minimal.

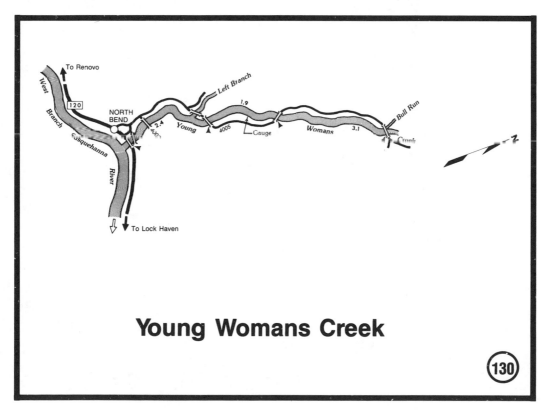

Young Womans Creek

130

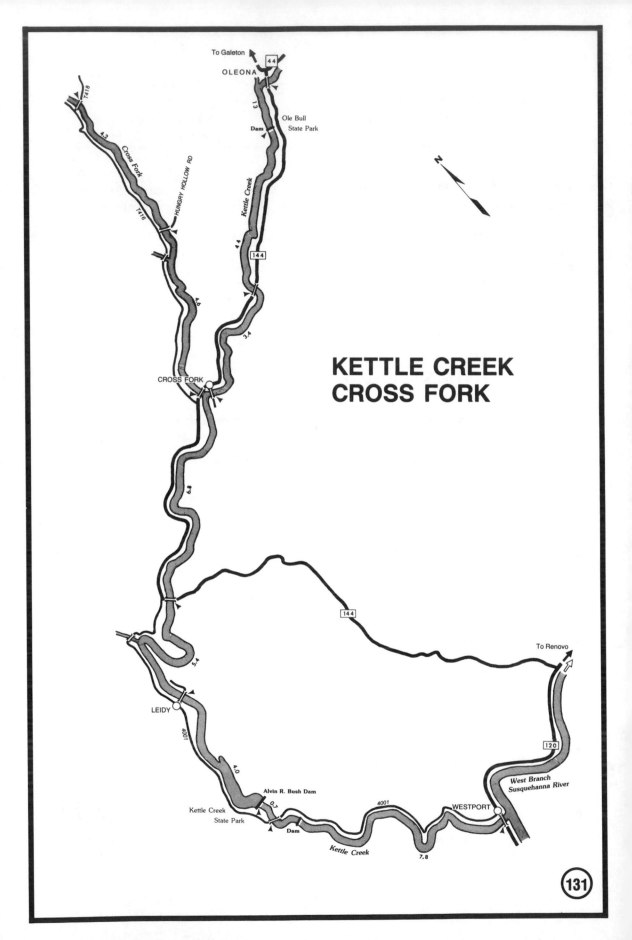

KETTLE CREEK
CROSS FORK

To Galeton

44

OLEONA

1.3

Ole Bull
State Park

Dam

T418

4.2

Cross Fork

HUNGRY HOLLOW RD

Kettle Creek

4.4

144

T416

4.6

3.4

CROSS FORK

6.8

144

To Renovo

5.4

LEIDY

4001

120

4.0

West Branch
Susquehanna River

Alvin R. Bush Dam

0.7

Kettle Creek
State Park

4001

WESTPORT

Dam

Kettle Creek

7.8

131

Kettle Creek

INTRODUCTION: Kettle Creek is a beautiful child of Pennsylvania's great north woods. It begins in Potter County, "Gods Country" according to all the billboards, and ends up in the wide West Branch Susquehanna above Renovo. In its upper section it is a cherished trout stream, and in its entirety, it is a superb place to paddle.

Section 1. Oleona (Pa. Rte. 144) to Cross Fork					
Gradient	Difficulty	Distance	Time	Scenery	Map
22	1 to 2	9.0	3.0	Very Good	131

TRIP DESCRIPTION: This is a beautiful section, as it should be, for the little creek is really out in the sticks. The valley here is narrow and flat-bottomed, with those bottoms populated by pines, hemlock, beech, birch, and sycamore, with little glades in between. One can seldom see any houses from the water, nor see sleepy Rte. 144. The creek meanders a lot and braids too much. The resulting overhanging and fallen vegetation often constricts but seldom totally blocks the channel. The water hurries busily over series of cobble bars while pausing in between in short, clear pools. One such pool, at Ole Bull State Park, forms behind a five-foot dam. Carry the dam and the low-water bridge below.

HAZARDS: A dam and low-water bridge at Ole Bull State Park and strainers.

WATER CONDITIONS: Canoeable in spring during snowmelt and within three days of hard rain.

GAUGE: None presently on creek. If USGS ever replaces outside staff on their gauging station at Cross Fork, located on right bank 0.7 miles downstream of Cross Fork (at old bridge abutment), level of 3.0 feet would be adequate. Roughly, USGS gauge at Cedar Run, on Pine Creek (call Central PA), should be over 4.5 feet.

Section 2. Cross Fork to Hammersley Fork (Pa. Rte. 144)					
Gradient	Difficulty	Distance	Time	Scenery	Map
16	1 +	6.8	2.0	Fair to Good	131

TRIP DESCRIPTION: With the addition of the Cross Fork, below the hamlet of that name, the creek substantially widens, slows down, and gets easier. But the biggest change is the overdose of summer camps that crowd the otherwise beautiful valley. Skip this section if your time is limited.

HAZARDS: None.

WATER CONDITIONS: Canoeable in spring during snowmelt and within a week of hard rain.

GAUGE: None currently. If USGS ever replaces the outside staff on its gauge below Cross Fork, 1.9 feet would be acceptable. Roughly, USGS gauge at Cedar Run, on Pine Creek (call Central PA), should be over 3.0 feet.

Section 3. Hammersley Fork (Pa. Rte. 144) to Westport (Pa. Rte. 120)					
Gradient	Difficulty	Distance	Time	Scenery	Map
15	1	17.9	6.0	Good to Very Good	131

TRIP DESCRIPTION. Pa. Rte. 144 now abandons Kettle Creek for the mountains, leaving only a narrow and lightly travelled secondary road (until fishing season that is) to follow the valley. The valley is sparsely populated, mainly by a few farms, with great gray mountains looming steeply, just beyond. The creek is broad, shallow, and riffly until it stalls out in a Corps of Engineers puddle, called Alvin Bush Lake. There is an access area near the head of this fortunately short reservoir. If you must portage the dam, go from the bottom right to the top left and then down to the bottom right. The dam rises 165 feet above the natural riverbed.

Below Bush Dam the valley narrows to a deep canyon. Except for a small clot of summer homes, just below the dam, this is a pretty and rustic stretch. A little bit farther down, you will have to carry the six-foot dam that forms the state park swimming area. Below here acid mine drainage slightly clouds the water and ruins the fishing, but paddling remains just fine to the very end.

HAZARDS: Dam at state park swimming area.

WATER CONDITIONS: Canoeable in spring during snowmelt and within week of hard rain.

GAUGE: USGS gauge on left bank, 3.5 miles above Westport, should read at least 2.8 feet. Roughly, USGS gauge at Cedar Run, on Pine Creek (call Central PA), should be over 2.7 feet.

Cross Fork

INTRODUCTION: Those who delight in navigating tiny mountain torrents will love the Cross Fork. You can find it flowing into Kettle Creek at the village called Cross Fork, and you will most likely only find it up on some wet, cold, and miserable spring day. But it is worth suffering for.

Section 1. T418, Short Run, to Pa. Rte. 144					
Gradient	Difficulty	Distance	Time	Scenery	Map
40	3 –	8.8	2.5	Very Good	131

TRIP DESCRIPTION: The ten-foot-wide flume of clear and cold water swirling through the alders at T418 does not look like much. But it grows quickly. Cross Fork hurries down through the heavily wooded bottom of a narrow valley, darting in and out of state forest land. Though a gravel road (your shuttle road) and numerous camps share the valley, the paddler seldom notices either. For dense stands of hemlock screen out the world beyond and make this a shadowy passage even at midday. The impression is of being in a wilderness.

The creek drops almost continuously over its gravel bed. Though not that technically difficult,

First Fork Sinnemahoning Creek
East Fork Sinnemahoning Creek
Sinnemahoning Creek

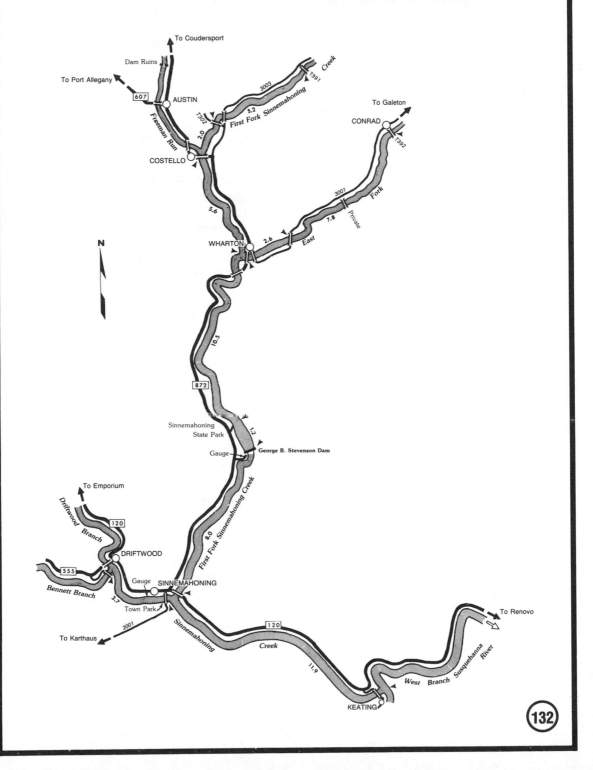

To Coudersport

Dam Ruins

To Port Allegany

607

AUSTIN

Creek

3003

T391

5.2

First Fork Sinnemahoning

T302

2.0

Freeman Run

To Galeton

CONRAD

T392

COSTELLO

5.6

3001

Fork

Private

7.8

WHARTON

2.6

East

N

10.5

872

Sinnemahoning
State Park

1.2

Gauge

George B. Stevenson Dam

To Emporium

Driftwood

120

First Fork Sinnemahoning Creek

8.0

Branch

DRIFTWOOD

555

Gauge

SINNEMAHONING

Bennett Branch

3.7

Town Park

To Karthaus

2001

Sinnemahoning

120

To Renovo

Creek

11.9

West

Branch

Susquehanna

River

KEATING

132

it is fast, pushy, and when it braids, you can count on trees trying to ambush you. If you do well on Cross Fork, you get a bonus. It comes as a splashy plunge over a set of sharp ledges just above the take-out.

HAZARDS: Strainers.

WATER CONDITIONS: Canoeable in spring during snowmelt and within three days of hard rain.

GAUGE: None. Roughly, USGS gauge at Cedar Run, on Pine Creek (call Central PA), should be about 4.5 feet.

Sinnemahoning Creek

INTRODUCTION: Sinnemahoning Creek is a large and impressive fork of the even more impressive West Branch Susquehanna, entering the big river 12 miles above Renovo at a place called Keating. The name is Indian for "stony lick." The Indians used the crooked canyon of the Sinnemahoning as a trade route, via the Driftwood Branch and Portage Creek, to the Allegheny River and points northwest. When white man started logging the vast surrounding forests in the 1840's, the river became the highway, a one-way street, as spring freshets were put to work carrying logs to sawmills down on the West Branch. Today the Sinnemahoning is mainly a route for tourists—a way for droves of fishermen, hunters, and campers to get to Pennsylvania's emptiest areas.

Section 1. Driftwood to Keating					
Gradient	Difficulty	Distance	Time	Scenery	Map
6	1	15.6	5.0	Good to Very Good	132

TRIP DESCRIPTION: This is a fine beginners' run. The river is wide, mostly smooth, and consistently fast, while its simple rapids are always well-spaced. It flows through a deep canyon that bears only light development. Parallel Pa. Rte. 120 carries little traffic and railroad business is also slow. So this is a quiet place. Avoid this stream at marginal levels as this broad waterway becomes relentlessly shallow, and you may thus find yourself taking a canoe hike.

HAZARDS: None.

WATER CONDITIONS: Canoeable in spring during snowmelt and within a week of hard rain. In average year, it is passable until the end of May and often again in late November.

GAUGE: USGS gauge at Sinnemahoning (call Central PA or inspect on site), located a quarter mile above town and reached by a dirt road that parallels the railroad, should be over 3.3 feet. Painted staff gauge on right pier of road bridge to Keating should read over 1.5 feet.

First Fork Sinnemahoning Creek

INTRODUCTION: The First Fork gushes out of the wilds of Potter and Cameron counties. These are the home of the great north woods of Pennsylvania—an area that has long been the domain of the traditional outdoorsman. It is a place where they ask you how many trout you caught, not how many eddies. It is a place where real men shoot deer, not rapids. But do not be intimidated. During the few good weeks of spring highwater, even wimpy paddlers have a place up here. Just stay away during the first week of trout season.

Section 1. T391 to Pa. Rte. 120					
Gradient	Difficulty	Distance	Time	Scenery	Map
20	A to 2	32.4	11.0	Good to Very Good	132
5 @ 35					

TRIP DESCRIPTION: This is but a diminutive bit of sparkling water for its first six miles down to Costello. The First Fork passes through a narrow and most beautiful valley, bordered by steep, forested slopes or old pasture that groves of hawthorn and crabapple are slowly reclaiming. Though the valley floor is cluttered by summer camps, an ample facade of trees and rhododendron screen much of this from the paddler. When the creek hugs the hillside, pretty rock ledges often line that bank. These first miles of the First Fork hurry busily, but not steeply, over gravel bars around tight bends, and often through strainers, including a few barbed wire fences. The creek can be pushy and mean at times.

If you have the time, take a ride up Pa. Rte. 872 from Costello, up along Freeman Run, to Austin and then two miles beyond. There, down in the woods, you will spot several great white chunks of masonry, clearly once a high dam, strewn about like a child's play blocks. Back in 1911, only two years after it was completed, torrential rains burst the dam. The subsequent deluge performed instant urban renewal on the paper mill town of Austin while floating 87 of its citizens to the promised land. When you look at 15-foot-wide Freeman Run, this is indeed difficult to imagine.

Freeman Run and then the East Fork swell the First Fork. There is much less development in the valley below Costello. With bottomlands now only occupied by empty and grassy or weedy meadows and with the decreasing gradient and widening bed, there is much more opportunity to just enjoy the aesthetics. The creek now hurries over long sets of shallow, gravel-bottomed riffles. Normally there are about ten scenic miles of free-flowing stream between Wharton and the head of the lake backed by George B. Stevenson Dam. But in rare flood conditions, this lake can back up almost to Wharton. The normal pool is only about a mile and a half long. You can take out at the state park recreation area or, if you are continuing on down, portage the 166-foot dam on the left.

The valley seems canyon-like below the dam with only occasional summer camps detracting from its beauty. And the banks are so low that you see about everything. The creek remains as easy as above, but sometimes getting critically shallow in wide spots. It is then that you will clearly recognize this as a fork of the Sinnemahoning.

HAZARDS: Strainers above Costello.

WATER CONDITIONS: Canoeable in spring during snowmelt and within four days of hard rain above Costello and a week below. Below Wharton the creek is often continuously runnable, except in dry years, until mid-May and often again in late November.

GAUGE: USGS gauge on right bank along road to Stevenson Dam tailrace (T357). Outside staff should be at least 0.8 feet to start at T391 and 0.7 feet to start at Wharton. Note that the readings taken inside the gauging station are two feet higher than those outside. So some day the USGS may replace the outside staff so that minimum levels will then read 2.8 and 2.7 feet. Roughly, USGS gauge at Sinnemahoning, on Sinnemahoning Creek (call Central PA), should be running about 3.8 feet to start at T391 and 3.6 feet to start at Wharton.

East Fork Sinnemahoning Creek

INTRODUCTION: The East Fork joins with the First Fork at Wharton. Disguised as a typical trout stream, this is a fine springtime cruise that resembles the best of the upper First Fork. Like the First Fork, this is another run to forego during the first week of trout season.

Section 1. Conrad (T392) to Wharton (Pa. Rte. 872)					
Gradient	Difficulty	Distance	Time	Scenery	Map
37	2 –	10.4	3.5	Very Good	132

TRIP DESCRIPTION: The East Fork is a clear-flowing and tiny brook that crookedly works down a deep, narrow, and flat-bottomed valley. In spite of numerous camps, this is a pretty trip. The creek usually hugs steep and wooded mountain slopes, while wooded bottomland broken by little glades characterize the other side. The banks are low and grassy. An almost continuous procession of short cobble riffles provides easy entertainment. Periodic strainers remind you that small intimate streams have their drawbacks.

HAZARDS: Strainers.

WATER CONDITIONS: Canoeable in spring during snowmelt and within four days of hard rain.

GAUGE: None on creek. USGS gauge below Stevenson Dam, along T357, should read at least 1.0 foot. Roughly, USGS gauge at Sinnemahoning, on Sinnemahoning Creek (call Central PA), should read about 3.9 feet.

Driftwood Branch Sinnemahoning Creek

INTRODUCTION: The Driftwood Branch is an excellent way to extend a Sinnemahoning trip into a pleasant overnighter. Except in its swifter upper reaches, it is an especially suitable route for the novice and even the beginner paddler.

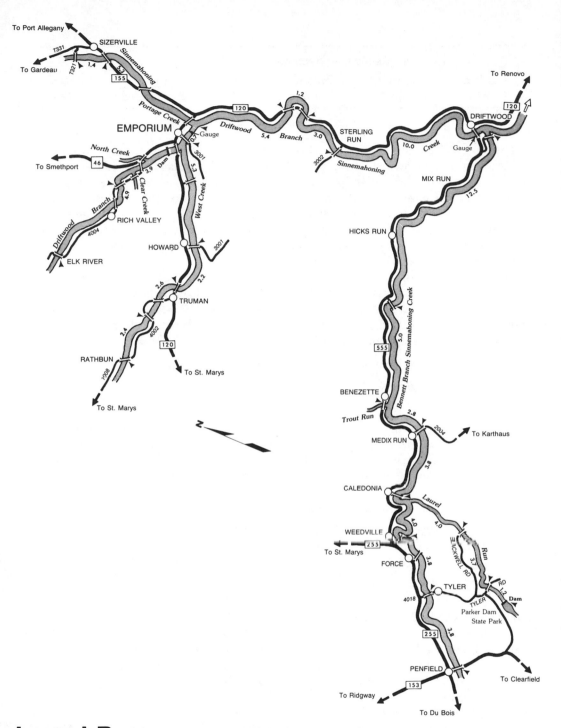

Laurel Run
Sinnemahoning Portage Creek
Driftwood Branch Sinnemahoning Creek
Bennett Branch Sinnemahoning Creek
West Creek

133

Section 1. Elk River (SR4004) to Emporium (SR3001)					
Gradient	Difficulty	Distance	Time	Scenery	Map
27	1 to 2	8.8	3.0	Fair to Good	133

TRIP DESCRIPTION: Up here the Driftwood Branch is just a tiny stream that does some rapid growing. After a hurried start in pretty hemlock woods, it draws closer to the valley road and more out into the open. High banks and vegetation, however, generally screen the paddler from view of all the development that fills the valley. A special quality of the Driftwood Valley, though shared with many of the northern tier counties, is the presence of tamarack groves about the forest. While just another tree for most of the year, in late autumn, long after all the hardwoods have lost their leaves, the tamarack's needles turn gold, adding a striking and lacy splash of cheeriness to the otherwise somber hillsides.

The creek is quite busy at the start and pushy enough to make hazards out of dead trees and the debris that dangles on sharp bends. The pace gradually slows, although a series of ledges lurk above Clear Creek to shake you out of any complacency. A five-foot dam at the upper end of Emporium requires a carry. Also, be alert for some dangerously poised old sheet piling at the end of a rapid about a mile below North Creek.

HAZARDS: Strainers, dam above Emporium, and sheet piling in stream bed.

WATER CONDITIONS: Canoeable in spring during snowmelt and within three days of hard rain.

GAUGE: There is a painted gauge on the left concrete abutment of a sewer crossing (opposite the sewage treatment plant) in Emporium, above Portage Creek and behind and downstream of a yellow brick building on a side street. This should read about 3.5 feet. Roughly, USGS gauge at Sinnemahoning, on Sinnemahoning Creek (call Central PA), must be over 5.0 feet.

Section 2. Emporium (Broad Street, SR3001) to Driftwood (Pa. Rte. 555)					
Gradient	Difficulty	Distance	Time	Scenery	Map
11	1	20.2	6.5	Very Good	133

TRIP DESCRIPTION: Emporium, with less than 4,000 souls, seems like a metropolis out there in the wilds of Cameron County. To the casual observer it is not all that apparent why it is there. But such a diverse sequence of activities as manufacturing of explosives, vacuum tubes, and wood products have kept it prospering over the years. It is at Emporium that West Creek and Sinnemahoning Portage Creek mature the Driftwood Branch into a moderate-sized and even-paced canoe stream.

Driftwood Branch wanders off into a deep and canyon-like valley, inhabited by few people. Acres and acres of beautiful, forested slopes dominate the scenery along here. So it is easy to forget that this entire area was once logged over, and in a most brutal fashion too. Remember when you gaze upon a solitary hemlock that there were once whole forests of these giants, sometimes felled simply to harvest their bark for local tanneries. Today only the sight of lightly traveled Pa. Rte. 120 and a railroad track interfere with the serenity.

The creek generally runs smooth, but it is graced by many uncomplicated rapids and riffles that demand little skill to negotiate. Beginners should beware, however, of a short braided section above Sterling Run, which may include some menacing strainers.

HAZARDS: Maybe a few strainers above Sterling Run.

WATER CONDITIONS: Canoeable in spring during snowmelt and within a week of hard rain. Except in dry years, this section is usually passable until mid-May and often again in late November.

GAUGE: Painted gauge at sewer crossing in Emporium should be 2.5 feet. Painted gauge on right abutment of Pa. Rte. 555, Driftwood, should be over 1.7 feet. Roughly, USGS gauge at Sinnemahoning, on Sinnemahoning Creek (call Central PA), should be over 3.3 feet.

Sinnemahoning Portage Creek

INTRODUCTION: Sinnemahoning Portage Creek feeds the Driftwood Branch at Emporium. The creek earned its name because its valley was the vital link (along with Allegheny Portage Creek) in the Indian trade route between the Susquehanna Valley and the Allegheny Valley. Occasionally there is enough water in this creek for the contemporary voyageur, free of the burdens of a cargo of furs, corn, and trinkets, to paddle, not portage many of its swift-flowing miles.

Section 1. Sizerville (T321) to Emporium (Pa. Rte. 120)					
Gradient	Difficulty	Distance	Time	Scenery	Map
28	2	6.5	2.0	Good	133

TRIP DESCRIPTION: This is an enjoyable novice ride marked by almost nonstop, but easy, whitewater. Though it flows through a heavily populated valley, this is seldom evident from the water. For banks hide a lot. While you may occasionally peer into someone's backyard or at a junkheap, the atmosphere is generally pleasant. The hemlock-lined hillsides and fine mountain views are more likely to command your attention. There is no road access at the mouth, so either take out at Rte. 120 or a few blocks upstream at a little local park.

HAZARDS: Potential for strainers, especially in first half mile.

WATER CONDITIONS: Canoeable in spring during snowmelt and within three days of hard rain.

GAUGE: None on creek. Roughly, USGS gauge at Sinnemahoning, on Sinnemahoning Creek (call Central PA), should be over 5.0 feet.

West Creek

INTRODUCTION: When the water is high, it is a hard choice of where to start a cruise on the Driftwood Branch. Those seeking the prettiest route should try West Creek.

Section 1. Rathbun (SR1008) to mouth					
Gradient	Difficulty	Distance	Time	Scenery	Map
24	1 to 2	12.4	3.0	Good	133

TRIP DESCRIPTION: West Creek, above Truman, twists through a narrow and sparsely settled valley. Only a few cabins and a junkyard spoil the solitude of the surrounding groves of pine and hemlock and alder-lined banks. The creek hurries through numerous rapids that drop over cobbles and a few small sloping ledges. Bends with overhanging trees or limbs sometimes add extra challenge to this otherwise easy whitewater.

Pa. Rte. 120 joins the valley at the drab little hamlet of Truman. In spite of the highway and the increased population that clings to it, the creek remains attractive. It keeps to itself, hugging the steep mountainside and hiding behind a screen of trees. West Creek continues to move along nicely, now over a bottom of evenly distributed cobbles. One very long and relatively rocky rapid pushes you into Emporium, adding a final kick to the run. Take out below the confluence with the Driftwood Branch, at Broad Street, SR3001.

HAZARDS: Possible strainers, mostly above Truman.

WATER CONDITIONS: Canoeable in spring during snowmelt and within three days of hard rain.

GAUGE: None on creek. Painted gauge at sewer crossing in Emporium should be about 3.5 feet. Roughly, USGS gauge at Sinnemahoning, on Sinnemahoning Creek (call Central PA), should be over 5.0 feet.

Bennett Branch Sinnemahoning Creek

INTRODUCTION: The Bennett Branch is generally overlooked as a canoe stream, partly because of its association with the coal fields and partly because it is so far from population centers. Such a shame, as this is a really scenic stream. And its mine drainage problems can prove a blessing, for this is a good place to take refuge on the first week of trout season.

Section 1. Penfield (Pa. Rte. 153) to mouth					
Gradient	Difficulty	Distance	Time	Scenery	Map
13	1	35.8	11.0	Poor to Very Good	133

TRIP DESCRIPTION: The Bennett Branch gets off to a poor start. The surrounding hills of this narrow valley are scarred by mining, logging, and fires. Coal slag heaps and trash piles abound, the coal trucks roar down the nearby highway, and the creek is yellowed by acid mine pollution. But you can bypass most of this blight by starting at Caledonia.

From Caledonia on, the scenery just gets prettier and prettier. The valley narrows and deepens almost to a canyon, whose hillsides are usually a velvet of unbroken second growth forest. Gone are most of the scars. Parallel Pa. Rte. 555 and the railroad are unobtrusive and little used. There are few people living up this way, and the many camps of the part-time residents are adequately spaced. And the creek, while still acidic, makes the best of its condition by nurturing a luxuriant growth of wild cranberries. Through all of this the current rolls along nicely, often rippling over long and easy riffles. There are no special hazards on this beginner stream. The last take-out is at T343, 0.2 miles above the mouth.

HAZARDS: Possible strainers on upper reaches or island passages.

WATER CONDITIONS: Canoeable in spring during snowmelt and within week of hard rain. In average year most of this section is passable until mid-May.

GAUGE: Count stones on upstream end of pier, Pa. Rte. 153, Penfield. Six stones and 14 inches down is approximately zero. Roughly, USGS gauge at Sinnemahoning, on Sinnemahoning Creek (call Central PA), should be over 3.5 feet for upper reaches and 3.3 feet for below Benezette.

Laurel Run

INTRODUCTION: Bennett Branch has several tiny tributaries that offer a few miles of occasional canoeing. None are so accessible as Laurel Run. And we are fortunate, as this is a gem worth travelling for.

Section 1. Parker Dam to mouth					
Gradient	Difficulty	Distance	Time	Scenery	Map
58	3 –	8.2	2.0	Excellent	133

TRIP DESCRIPTION: The put-in is right at the foot of the dam in Parker Dam State Park. The little stream hurries off into a near-wilderness canyon as it cuts down to the level of the Bennett Branch. A few camps, some rusty gas pipes, and two bridges are the only reminders of civilization. The rest of the setting is attractive second-growth forest, including a dismal patch at the top that was devastated by wind storms.

Laurel's rapids are fairly steep and continuous, dropping over small boulders, ledges, and cobbles. Clear water makes seeing the stones easy. There are surprisingly few tree problems, even where it passes through the wind storm area. Such a fun run, unfortunately, gets you to the mouth all too quickly. Continue another three quarters of a mile on Bennett Branch to a good take-out at the bridge at Caledonia.

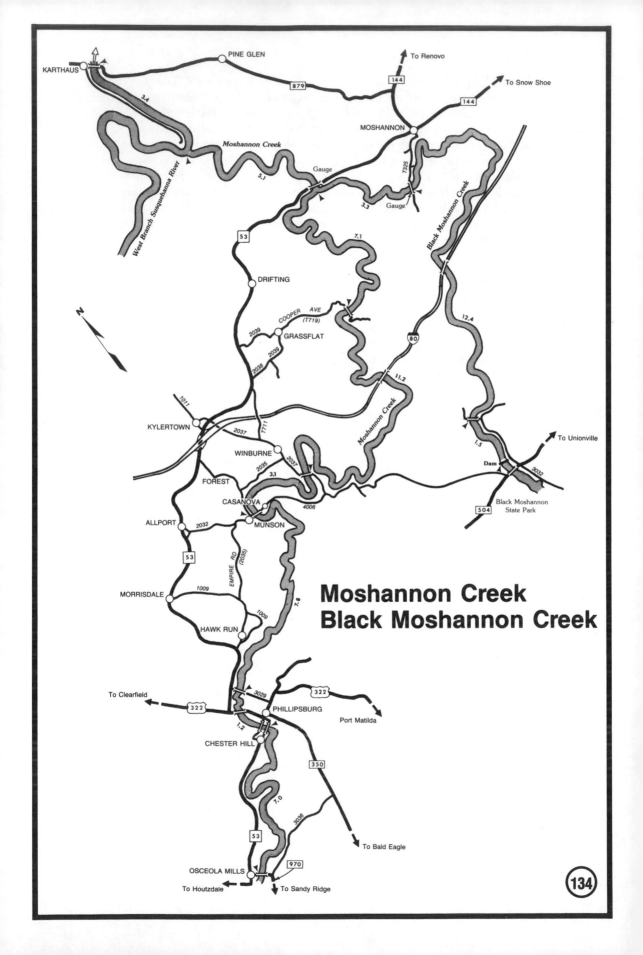

Moshannon Creek
Black Moshannon Creek

134

HAZARDS: Some strainers, inevitably in fast water.

WATER CONDITIONS: Catch in late fall and spring during rapid snowmelt of within two days of hard rain.

GAUGE: None. Judge riffles at put-in or at first bridge. Roughly, the USGS gauge at Sinnemahoning, on Sinnemahoning Creek (call Central PA), should be over 4.0 feet.

Mosquito Creek

INTRODUCTION: Mosquito Creek is a tiny, back country jewel that for most of the year trickles into the West Branch Susquehanna at Karthaus. On those rare days when it gushes, it offers a splendid intermediate whitewater run in the middle of the nicest of nowheres.

Section 1. Gifford Run to mouth					
Gradient	Difficulty	Distance	Time	Scenery	Map
47	2 to 3 −	9.8	3.0	Excellent	114

TRIP DESCRIPTION: You cannot reach the mouth of Gifford Run by road. Either you start four and a half miles farther up Mosquito Creek, or one and a half miles up Gifford Run, where Lost Run Road (a state forest road) crosses each creek respectively. But this may be easier said than done. Usually when Mosquito Creek is high, then there is still ice or snow on Lost Run Road. If this is the case, start on Gifford Run, as T873 should be passable and get you as far as the Lost Run Road turnoff. From there it is still three quarters of a mile to the creek, but if there is snow on the steep road, this makes an easy downhill drag.

Upper Mosquito Creek consists of a succession of easy rapids and pools. Because acres of forest above and just below the put-in were flattened in May of 1985 by a band of tornados (the place looks like it was nuked), look forward to starting out with about a half-mile fight through nasty strainers. Gifford Run is steeper, rockier, and busier. Only a few camps intrude on this otherwise wilderness setting.

Below the confluence, Mosquito Creek is set in a deep canyon whose wilderness is unbroken until the bridge above Karthaus. Only a few power lines intrude on the view. The clear, dark waters rush over a roomy bed of cobbles and small boulders. They form rapids that are continuous, but not particularly complex. But be on guard for a few low-slung cables here and on Gifford Run. A few trees may also be a problem on either upper section. Finish your run right at the mouth, beneath the railroad bridge.

HAZARDS: Strainers and low cables.

WATER CONDITIONS: Canoeable in spring during snowmelt and within two days of hard rain.

GAUGE: None on creek. Very roughly, USGS gauges at Sinnemahoning, on Sinnemahoning Creek, and Karthaus, on West Branch Susquehanna (call Central PA for both), will probably be running over 5.0 feet and 6.0 feet respectively.

Moshannon Creek

INTRODUCTION: Conveniently situated near State College, Moshannon Creek is a prime canoe stream whose miles of fine scenery, smooth water, and novice to intermediate whitewater will delight a wide range of paddlers. It is commonly called the Red Moshannon, or Red Mo for short. A glance at its reddish orange rocks, banks, and water, and you will call it the Red Mo also. The red is an iron compound that precipitates out of the acidic waters that seep into the stream from numerous old coal and clay mines in the basin. While very colorful, this type of pollution does nothing for the poor fish. But this has good side. The Red Mo is one of the few creeks in Eastern Pennsylvania on which one can paddle on the first week of trout season without perturbing anybody.

The acid environment of the Red Mo is not entirely a sterile environment. One plant that seems to thrive on this acidity is the wild cranberry. If you keep an eye on the low banks and bars, especially below Phillipsburg, you will notice long mats of low and feathery vines. If it is autumn or very early spring, these mats will be dappled with the bright red of tart little cranberries. Taste them and see. You can find similar growths on Clearfield Creek, West Branch Susquehanna, and other acidic streams in central Pennsylvania.

Finally, the name Moshannon is Indian for "elk stream." You will find even fewer elk than trout, but you probably cannot blame the mine drainage for that.

Section 1. Osceola Mills (Pa. Rte. 970) to Munson (SR4006/2032)					
Gradient	Difficulty	Distance	Time	Scenery	Map
3	1– to 1	16.0	5.0	Poor to Good	134

TRIP DESCRIPTION: Like many plateau rivers, the upper Moshannon wanders about in a mellow fashion before involving itself in the task of cutting canyons and creating rapids. Generally the creek is smooth, swift, and deep—a good place for novices. Between Osceola Mills and Phillipsburg it creeps through a bottomland forest of silvery barked trees. Only a few buildings interrupt the sylvan setting, while one low-water bridge interrupts navigation. Already living up to its nickname, the creek's banks, rocks, and nearby tree trunks are all stained orange and rusty red.

Phillipsburg has no use for the Moshannon. That is why it hustles the stream through town via a drab, dredged, and leveed flood channel. But below town the creek loses itself for a few beautiful and twisting miles in an almost swamp-like forest. Then a slow transition takes place. The still-wooded bottomlands begin to rise, and then bluffs appear on one side or the other. Finally a few riffles announce an increasing gradient. The presence of a few strip mines, buildings, and a railroad only slightly mar the scenery.

HAZARDS: A low-water bridge and maybe a few strainers.

WATER CONDITIONS: Canoeable in spring during snowmelt and within week of hard rain, which in average years means that this section is passable most of April and early May.

GAUGE: Enamelled staff gauge on right abutment of Pa. Rte. 53 should read over zero. USGS gauge in Osceola Mills, on left bank a quarter mile above Rte. 940, by railroad bridge (you get there by walking up tracks), should be over 2.7 feet. Roughly, USGS gauge at Karthaus, on West Branch Susquehanna, and Dimeling, on Clearfield Creek (call Central PA for both), should be at least 3.8 feet and 4.5 feet respectively.

Gradient	Difficulty	Distance	Time	Scenery	Map
20	1 to 2 +	26.5	8.0	Excellent	134
4 @ 33					

TRIP DESCRIPTION: Below Munson a gorge begins to form. Except for an occasional strip mine, the gorge is wild, even losing the company of the railroad below I-80. Pretty little rock cliffs periodically enhance the profile of the pretty wooded hillsides. Riffles become more and more frequent, eventually maturing into long and easy rapids formed by a cobble stream bed. As the miles pass, the gradient continues to increase. Although little maneuvering is required, the continuity of the whitewater demands more than a beginner's skill and stamina.

The best whitewater peaks above Pa. Rte. 53, but the scenery keeps improving below. The river now rushes down a corridor of tall, green hemlocks and pines, at the bottom of a remote canyon. Additional volume and easy, bouncy rapids allow you more time now to enjoy the scenery.

Upon reaching the mouth, the little Moshannon does not so much join with, but rather collides with, the big West Branch. The change is almost shocking. You can take out a short way down on the left (private) or continue three miles to Karthaus.

HAZARDS: None.

WATER CONDITIONS: Same as Section 1.

GAUGE: Same as Section 1.

Black Moshannon Creek

INTRODUCTION: Black Moshannon Creek (Black Mo for short) offers about the best whitewater run in the upper West Branch Susquehanna Watershed. Starting atop the high Allegheny Plateau, less than 20 miles northwest of State College, the creek takes a no-nonsense approach to relieving itself of that elevation.

Section 1. Black Moshannon State Park to Moshannon (above T325)

Gradient	Difficulty	Distance	Time	Scenery	Map
46	2 +	13.4	3.5	Poor to Excellent	134

TRIP DESCRIPTION: Put in just below the dam at Black Moshannon State Park. The Black Mo is only a tiny trout stream up here, as it should be, for this spot is only a few miles from its source. For most of its first 13 miles, the Black Mo's clear, clean, and amber-stained water dashes over a rocky bed at a fairly even gradient to form almost continuous, straightforward, Class 2 rapids. Though exhilarating, the uniformity and continuity eventually becomes almost hypnotizing. However, stay alert. Many deadfalls, usually negotiable without a carry, complicate the

Clearfield Creek

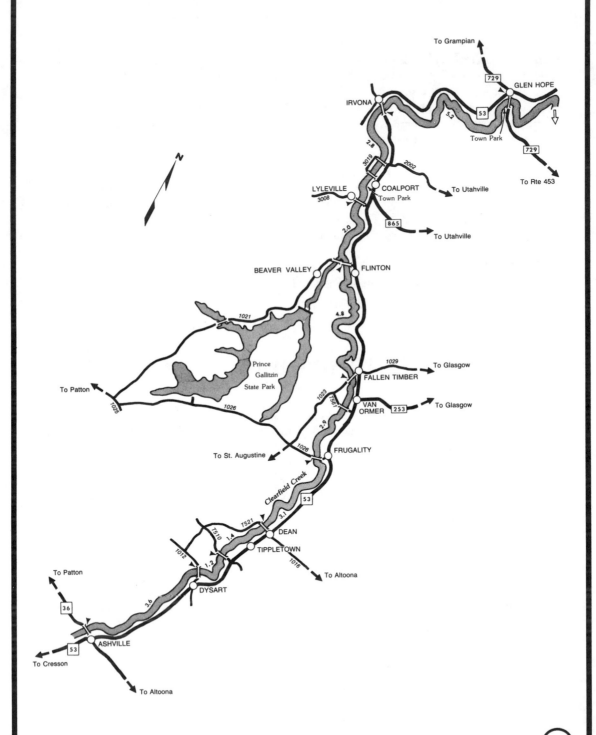

To Grampian

729
GLEN HOPE

IRVONA

53

5.2

Town Park

729

To Rte 453

2.8

3019

2002

LYLEVILLE

COALPORT

To Utahville

3008

Town Park

2.0

865

To Utahville

BEAVER VALLEY

FLINTON

1021

4.8

1029

To Glasgow

FALLEN TIMBER

To Patton

Prince
Gallitzin
State Park

1023

1591

VAN
ORMER

253

To Glasgow

1026

2.9

1025

1026

FRUGALITY

To St. Augustine

Clearfield Creek

53

T521

3.1

T510

1.4

DEAN

1072

1.2

TIPPLETOWN

1016

To Altoona

To Patton

DYSART

36

3.6

53

ASHVILLE

To Cresson

To Altoona

135

passage. While the surroundings of almost park-like rolling forests are visually a wilderness, the drone of highway noise, through a five-mile stretch that parallels I-80, unfortunately mars the experience. So does a huge swath of clear cut forest, also surrounding the interstate.

HAZARDS: Strainers in fast water.

WATER CONDITIONS: Canoeable in spring during snowmelt and within three days of hard rain.

GAUGE: Staff gauge on left abutment of T325 Bridge must be at least 0.6 feet. Or look at rapids above mouth and figure that you need at least six inches of runnable water. Roughly, USGS gauge at Karthaus, on West Branch Susquehanna (call Central PA), should be running over 6.0 feet.

Section 2. Moshannon (above T325) to mouth					
Gradient	Difficulty	Distance	Time	Scenery	Map
70	2 + to 4 −	3.8	1.0	Excellent	134

TRIP DESCRIPTION: Just south of the village of Moshannon, near a point accessible by T325, the Black Mo becomes much more difficult. Put in at a turn-off logging road 0.5 miles upstream of the T325 bridge over the Black Mo. In this final 3.8-mile plunge to the Red Mo, piles of sandstone boulders fill the Black Mo's bed, forming long and often steep rapids. If the water is high enough to start at the dam, then this section will be really pushy. Pa. Rte. 53, right at the confluence with the Red Mo., makes a convenient take-out.

HAZARDS: Possible strainers in fast water.

WATER CONDITIONS: Canoeable in spring during snowmelt and within two days of hard rain.

GAUGE: Staff gauge at T325 Bridge must be over zero. Or scouting the take-out, enough water to clean the rapids above the mouth is enough to do this section.

Clearfield Creek

INTRODUCTION: Clearfield Creek carves a long and crooked path through the coal-laden plateau of Cambria and Clearfield counties to join the West Branch Susquehanna near (where else?) Clearfield. It was so named because long ago buffalo are said to have had the peculiar habit of tearing up long stretches of undergrowth along the creek. The resulting destruction apparently resembled fields that were cleared by man. The buffalo are a memory now, and most likely many of the cleared fields that you will observe will now be strip mines. But the creek does an admirable job of dodging most of the ugliness of this mine-scarred countryside and thus offers long segments that would be well worth your time to explore.

Little Clearfield Creek
Clearfield Creek

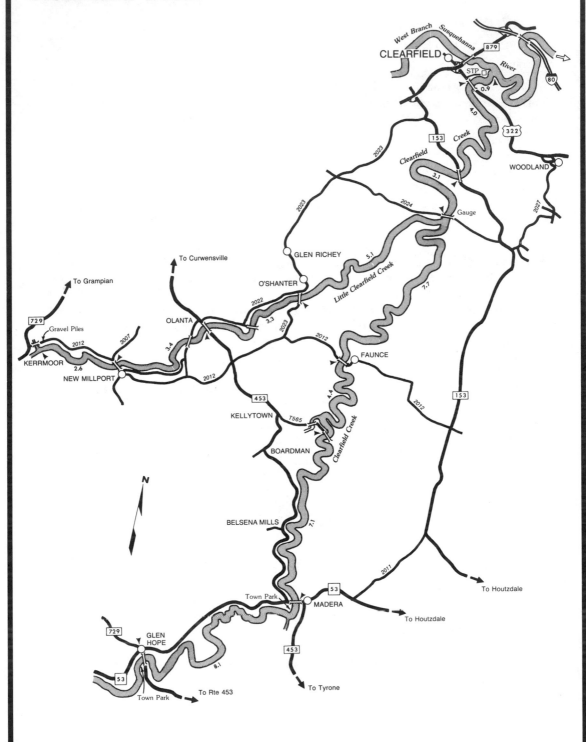

West Branch Susquehanna River

CLEARFIELD

879

STP

0.9

4.0

153

Creek

Clearfield

3.1

2023

2024

Gauge

WOODLAND

322

80

2027

To Curwensville

GLEN RICHEY

5.1

To Grampian

O'SHANTER

Little Clearfield Creek

7.7

729

Gravel Piles

2022

2012

OLANTA

3.3

2023

2012

KERRMOOR

2012

3007

3.4

FAUNCE

153

2.6

NEW MILLPORT

2012

2012

453

4.4

KELLYTOWN

T565

BOARDMAN

Clearfield Creek

N

BELSENA MILLS

7.1

2011

To Houtzdale

Town Park

53

MADERA

To Houtzdale

729

GLEN HOPE

453

8.1

To Tyrone

53

Town Park

To Rte 453

(136)

Section 1. Ashville (Pa. Rte. 36) to Frugality (SR1026)					
Gradient	Difficulty	Distance	Time	Scenery	Map
18	1,2 +	9.3	30	Good	135
1.2 @ 35					

TRIP DESCRIPTION: This is a fine section. The narrow creek beneath the Pa. Rte. 36 Bridge quickly widens and speeds over a continuous chain of shallow, cobble-formed riffles. Occasional overhanging trees are (or someday will be) your only complications, assuming you can handle whitewater. If not, a surprise half-mile stretch of relatively steep, boulder-strewn riverbed, located between Dysart and T510, may cause all kinds of problems. Often enveloped by state gamelands, this is a pretty section whose frequently low banks allow a good view of rhododendron groves and hardwood forest. Though it is nearby, Pa. Rte. 53 usually stays out of sight, if not out of hearing.

HAZARDS: Possible strainers.

WATER CONDITIONS: Canoeable in spring during snowmelt or within ten days of hard rain. In average year, it is usually up until mid-May.

GAUGE: Count red tiles on right abutment of Pa. Rte. 36. Seven full tiles down from top is zero. Roughly, USGS gauges at Curwensville, Hyde, and Karthaus, on West Branch Susquehanna, and Dimeling, on Clearfield (call Central PA), should respectively be running over 4.3, 4.0, 2.9, and 4.0 feet.

Section 2. Frugality (SR1026) to Madera (Pa. Rte. 53)					
Gradient	Difficulty	Distance	Time	Scenery	Map
5	1 –	25.8	8.5	Poor to Good	135,136

TRIP DESCRIPTION: Much of this section is easy to pass up. The gradient subsides, and swift flatwater replaces the riffles. The creek is often hemmed in by high banks of mud and sand, which can make getting around that occasional tree or logjam treacherous. More buildings are in sight now, often forlorn cinder block structures with broken windows or tired, sagging houses with peeling paint. From the perspective of the floater, towns such as Coalport are just concentrations of such ugliness. The creek suffers channelization through Irvona and pollution throughout. Amazingly, the murky waters, fouled by acid mine drainage and some sewage, actually supports fish (tough ones).

On the bright side, the worst of this section is confined between Flinton and Irvona. Above and below there the stream still flows mostly through a more natural and remote setting. These stretches are still worth your time to explore.

HAZARDS: Occasional strainers as far as Coalport.

WATER CONDITIONS: Canoeable in spring during snowmelt or within ten days of hard rain. In an average year it is usually up until late May.

GAUGE: Count stones on center (right) pier of Pa. Rte. 53, Madera. Eleven stones and one foot down from top is about minimum.

Section 3. Madera (Pa. Rte. 53) to mouth					
Gradient	Difficulty	Distance	Time	Scenery	Map
9	1	27.2	8.5	Fair to Very Good	136

TRIP DESCRIPTION: Try this section, at least from Madera down to Little Clearfield Creek. A few miles below Madera the state highway climbs away to the plateau, leaving the creek alone to twist its way down a shallow and secluded gorge. Filled with the soothing greenness of pine, hemlock, and rhododendron, it is a cheery place to be even on a gray winter's day. Only a few mining and logging scars interrupt the mood of this wilderness-like run. The water, still yellow from mine drainage, can be relatively sluggish, although frequently broken by easy gravel bar riffles.

Below Little Clearfield Creek the valley opens up, and more houses and mining activity alter the scenery. Take out just above the sewage treatment plant on the left, above the mouth, or continue down the West Branch to where it hits Pa. Rte. 879 above Shawville.

HAZARDS: None.

WATER CONDITIONS: Canoeable in spring during snowmelt and within 12 days of hard rain. In average year this section often stays up until mid-June.

GAUGE: It only takes about 300 cfs (at SR2024) to float this section. Painted gauge on left abutment of SR2024, Dimeling, should read over 0.3 feet and USGS gauge at Dimeling (call Central PA) should read at least 3.7 feet. Roughly, USGS gauges at Curwensville and Karthaus, on West Branch (call Central PA), respectively should be running over 3.9 and 2.5 feet.

Little Clearfield Creek

INTRODUCTION: Little Clearfield Creek is not exactly the sort of stream on which you should expect to run into crowds. Small and obscure, it is hard to find on most maps. It has no whitewater of any consequence, it seldom carries enough water to float a canoe, and much of its scenery is plain. But are you a hermit looking for a stream to have all to yourself? Maybe this creek is for you.

Section 1. Kerrmoor to mouth					
Gradient	Difficulty	Distance	Time	Scenery	Map
14	1 to 1 +	14.4	4.5	Fair to Good	136

TRIP DESCRIPTION: Put in by the gravel piles along SR2012, just east of Kerrmoor. Gazam Run, just above the put-in, pumps the creek up to canoeable size, barely. But a creek this small is easily blocked by a fallen tree, and sure enough, there are many in its first few miles. Compensating for the carries around trees are a fast current and many long riffles. As the creek takes its twisting route down this thinly populated valley, it reveals an often cut-over and scrubby landscape. Only in its last few miles does Little Clearfield Creek assume the wild beauty of nearby Clearfield Creek.

HAZARDS: Strainers.

WATER CONDITIONS: Canoeable in spring during snowmelt and within two days of hard rain.

GAUGE: None. Rougly, USGS gauge at Dimeling, on Clearfield Creek, should be over 6.2 feet. Roughly, USGS gauge at Curwensville, on West Branch Susquehanna (call Central PA for both), should be running at least 5.2 feet, but probably it will be about 5.5 feet.

Anderson Creek

INTRODUCTION: Outdone only by the wild Black Moshannon, Clearfield County's Anderson Creek is a first class whitewater run that should be on every Central Pennsylvania paddler's list of must-dos. Like all the other whitewater wonders of the West Branch Susquehanna, this is a high water run only. But unlike so many of these, it has easy access at both ends.

Section 1. U.S. Rte. 322 to mouth					
Gradient	Difficulty	Distance	Time	Scenery	Map
39	2 to 3 +	12.2	3.5	Poor to Excellent	113

TRIP DESCRIPTION: The busy brook rushing under U.S. Rte. 322 stays busy for miles as it cuts an ever-deepening canyon. A few camps and, after a mile and a half, a railroad track are your only company. The water, muddied from mining operations up on tributary Little Anderson Creek, rushes through alder thickets and past evergreens in an uncomplicated manner until about halfway between Rte. 322 and Rte. 879. There the creek begins churning down long, fairly steep, and moderately complex rapids formed by a boulder-cluttered stream bed. And it stays that way almost to Rte. 879.

The remaining two miles from Pa. Rte. 879 to the West Branch are not worth doing. Mild, cobble-formed rapids speed you past high banks, debris piles, and industry. If you do run this, at the lower end of the refractory plant be alert for a two-foot drop with a nasty roller. Sneak this on the right. The best take-out is at the Bloomington Street Bridge over the West Branch, where there is a park on the right.

HAZARDS: Possible strainers and a dangerous weir by the factory in Curwensville.

WATER CONDITIONS: Canoeable in spring during snowmelt and within two days of hard rain.

GAUGE: None on creek. Roughly, USGS gauge at Curwensville, on West Branch (call Central PA), should be running over 5.0 feet.

Chest Creek

INTRODUCTION: Chest Creek is the first major canoeable tributary to the West Branch Susquehanna. Starting just north of Ebensburg, this little stream drains and cuts a canyon through the cold, windswept, and rugged plateau country of Cambria and Clearfield counties. In spite of some human incursions, this is a generally attractive waterway. As for difficulty, novices and intermediates will find long sections of Chest Creek to their liking.

Section 1. SR1009 to Thomas Mill (SR40 24)					
Gradient	Difficulty	Distance	Time	Scenery	Map
7	1	11.6	4.0	Poor to Good	112

TRIP DESCRIPTION: You can start floating Chest Creek way up near its headwaters, putting in at SR1009. This first section is suitable for novices. It is just a tiny creek, usually placid, that winds, often excessively, past rolling farmlands and through pretty beech-filled woods. What grows up, unfortunately, must fall down, in this case often across the creek. In addition, there is a three-foot dam under the bridge at Eckenrode Mill, which one can run at center, and an impressive and sloping eight-foot dam about 200 yards above the first bridge in Patton, runnable via a seemingly made-for-boating chute in the center. But novices should carry both. Except for a drab passage through Patton, the beauty of this section is worth the occasional inconveniences.

HAZARDS: Strainers and two dams.

WATER CONDITIONS: Canoeable in spring during snowmelt and within two days of hard rain.

GAUGE: None on this section. Staff gauge at Pa. Rte. 36, Westover, should be about 1.9 feet. Roughly, USGS gauges at Curwensville, on West Branch Susquehanna, and Dimeling, on Clearfield Creek (call Central PA), should be running about 5.5 feet and 6.4 feet respectively.

Section 2. Thomas Mill (SR4024) to Westover (SR3006, Bridge Street)					
Gradient	Difficulty	Distance	Time	Scenery	Map
40	1 to 3	8.8	2.5	Good	112
4.5 @ 60					

TRIP DESCRIPTION: At Thomas Mill Chest Creek is suddenly endowed with gradient and begins its descent through a narrow canyon. For the next five miles it rushes down through an almost nonstop series of rock gardens and patches of sandstone boulders, reaching intermediate difficulty. While much of the canyon rim is crowned by almost continuous coal stripping operations, the stream banks and lower canyon slopes are wooded and attractive. The river then calms down almost suddenly, the surroundings, from top to bottom, return to quiet woodlands, and all stays that way to the next take-out, at Westover.

HAZARDS: Possible strainers, especially where the creek braids following the end of the whitewater.

WATER CONDITIONS: Same as Section 1.

GAUGE: Staff gauge on right abutment of Pa. Rte. 36, Westover, should be at least 1.9 feet (bottom of staff is 2.0 feet). Roughly, USGS gauges at Curwensville, on West Branch, and Dimeling, on Clearfield Creek (call Central PA for both), should be about 5.5 feet and 6.4 feet respectively.

Section 3. Westover (SR3006, Bridge Street) to mouth					
Gradient	Difficulty	Distance	Time	Scenery	Map
6	1	13.6	4.0	Good	112

TRIP DESCRIPTION: After a raunchy start, thanks to Westover's smelly tannery and an unhealthy injection of the town's raw sewage, the rest of Chest Creek flowers as a very nice piece of novice cruising. Bracketed by medium-high eroded mud banks, the creek twists down a narrow valley filled by hardwood forest. With the presence of some houses, the railroad, strip mines, and noise from coal trucks rumbling down Pa. Rte. 36, this falls short of being wilderness. But its woodsy attributes far outweigh its blemishes. The water is simple—occasional cobble bar and boulder riffles, most numerous approaching Mahaffey, separated by smooth water with a good current. Even on this section, you will probably find a few trees to carry.

HAZARDS: Occasional strainers.

WATER CONDITIONS: Canoeable in spring during snowmelt and within a week of hard rain.

GAUGE: Staff gauge on Rte. 36 at Westover should be at least 1.3 feet. Roughly, USGS gauges at Curwensville and Dimeling should be about 4.4 feet and 4.0 feet respectively.

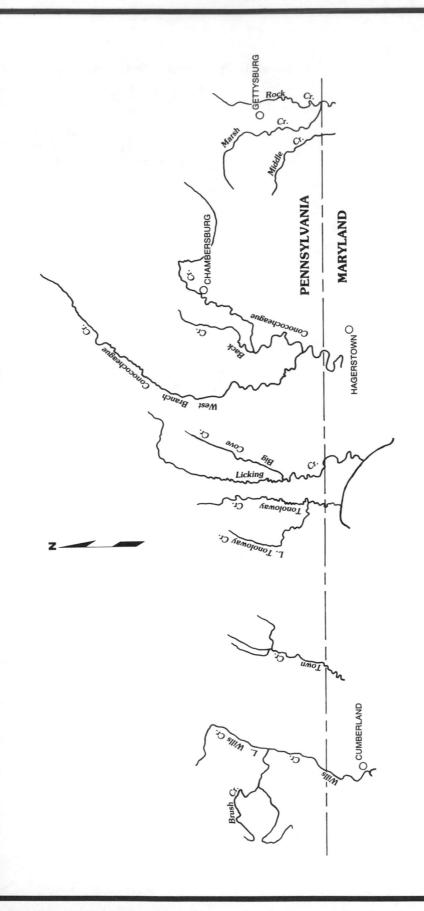

Potomac River Tributaries

Chapter 6
The Potomac Basin

The Potomac River draws the drainage from a 1,540-square mile slice of five southern tier counties, reaching from Somerset, on the west, to Adams, on the east. This is entirely a Maryland River, though it swings within three miles of the Pennsylvania Line at Hancock, Maryland.

The Potomac's Pennsylvania tributaries are all small, most are easy to paddle, and all are difficult to catch with enough water on which to float. They drain a varied landscape, that includes the cold and coal-rich plateau, on the west, an up and down belt of ridges and valleys, in the middle, and the rich and rolling farmlands of the Great Valley and Piedmont, on the east. Much of this territory is only lightly populated, and the streams are often remote. Yet a good highway system brackets the area, making access easy for all. If you love small streams, follow those highways to the Potomac Basin when the next hard rains come.

The following streams are described in this chapter:

Rock Creek
Marsh Creek
Middle Creek
Conococheague Creek
West Branch Conococheague Creek
Back Creek
Licking Creek
Big Cove Creek
Tonoloway Creek
Little Tonoloway Creek
Town Creek
Wills Creek
Little Wills Creek
Brush Creek

Marsh Creek
Rock Creek

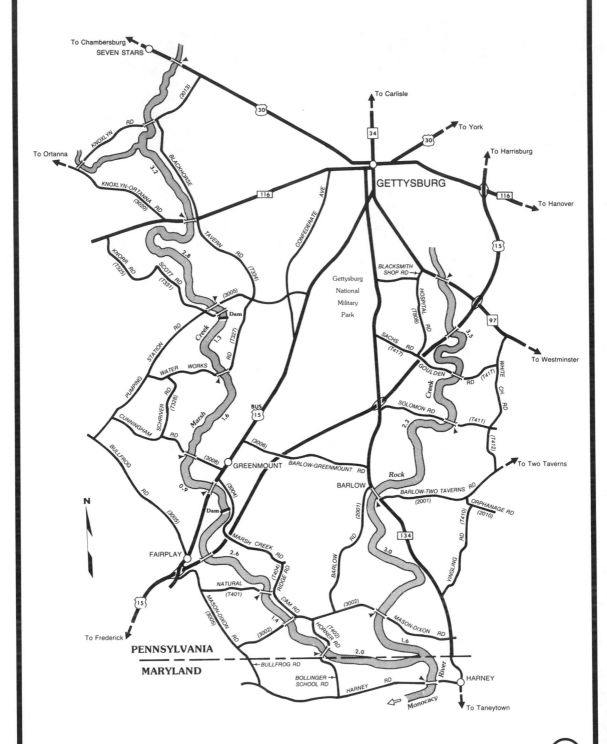

Marsh Creek

INTRODUCTION: Marsh Creek drains the Blue Ridge foothills west of Gettysburg, pooling its waters with those of Rock Creek's, to form Maryland's Monocacy River. It flows through an attractive valley occupied by dairy farms and orchards — a picture of timeless tranquility. But this valley is best known for three days in July of 1863, when it was anything but tranquil. On those three days, the forces of the Civil War pitted 84,000 Union soldiers against 75,000 Confederate soldiers on the height of land between Marsh and Rock creeks. When the dust had cleared, over 50,000 casualties had earned the Battle of Gettysburg the distinction of being the bloodiest engagement of the Civil War. A trip on Marsh Creek gives you a perfect excuse to visit the nearby national military park and relive this important moment in our history.

Section 1. Seven Stars (U.S. Rte. 30) to Bus. Rte. 15					
Gradient	Difficulty	Distance	Time	Scenery	Map
9	A to 1,2 –	9.8	3.5	Very Good	137

TRIP DESCRIPTION: What a fine way to tour beautiful, rural Adams County. When not winding through deep woods, Marsh Creek glides past lovely, well-kept dairy farms, marked by herds of sleek cattle, sturdy old farm houses, and big, brightly painted barns decorated with hex signs. Because its banks are low, the paddler enjoys liberal views of all that is worth seeing.

Complicated only by a few downed trees early in the trip and one rocky rapid at the ruins of an old mill dam, this section is suitable for novices. Generally smooth and straightforward riffles typify the run. One carry will be necessary to avoid a sharp, two-foot weir below the covered bridge downstream of SR3005.

HAZARDS: A weir at the Gettysburg Water Works and fallen trees.

WATER CONDITIONS: Canoeable winter and spring within two or three days of hard rain.

GAUGE: None on creek. USGS gauge at Frederick, Md., on the Monocacy (call Washington), should read at least 4.0 feet.

Section 2. Bus. Rt. 15 to Harney Road					
Gradient	Difficulty	Distance	Time	Scenery	Map
12	A to 3	6.0	2.0	Fair	137
1 @ 40					

TRIP DESCRIPTION: This section starts off with mostly flat water and another weir to carry (durable boats can clunk over), while flowing through fair scenery marred by summer homes. But after passing beneath U.S. Rte. 15, the creek cuts a short wooded gorge through the hard diabase of Harpers Hill, to create some interesting whitewater that climaxes with three exciting, complex, and boulder-choked rapids. Looking more like the Yough than Marsh Creek, this is by far the best piece of whitewater in the Monocacy Basin, short as it may be. The action concludes about a half mile below these rapids, with a nasty plunge over a masonry-capped, four-foot ledge. You can run this via a tight slot to the right of center, or you can easily carry it. Below here Marsh Creek quickly reverts to its original tranquil pace and, excepting an easy rapid through a washed out dam below Rock Creek, stays that way to the Harney Road take-out, a half mile down the Monocacy.

HAZARDS: A thinly watered three-foot weir a half mile below Bus. Rte. 15, possible debris jams in rapids, and a sharp four-foot ledge below Harpers Hill Gorge.

WATER CONDITIONS: Same as Section 1.

GAUGE: Same as Section 1.

Rock Creek

INTRODUCTION: Rock Creek is a generally mediocre stream that winds mostly through farm land, southeast of Gettysburg. Its waters are typically flat, and the scenery contains nothing particularly memorable. It is really not worth driving a long way for to paddle.

Section 1. Gettysburg (Pa. Rte. 97) to Harney Road					
Gradient	Difficulty	Distance	Time	Scenery	Map
7	A to 1	10.4	3.5	Fair	137

TRIP DESCRIPTION: One can start on the southeast side of Gettysburg at Rte. 97, or if the water level is marginal, three and a half miles downstream at T411, below the welcome in-flow of Littles Run. This first section, above T411, is drab and noisy, as it flows past a rock quarry and busy Rte. 15. Below here it is quieter. You occasionally see some pretty, fern-fringed, shale outcrops and some attractive farm structures, but high mud banks tend to block any real views across the picturesque countryside. The only thing resembling whitewater on this trip is a curving rapid that dances through the ruins of an old dam above the take-out. The take-out is on the Monocacy, about a half mile below Marsh Creek. Best parking is at the east approach of Harney Road Bridge.

HAZARDS: None.

WATER CONDITIONS: Canoeable in winter and spring within two days of hard rain.

GAUGE: None on creek. USGS gauge at Frederick, Md., on the Monocacy (call Washington), should read at least 4.5 feet.

Middle Creek

INTRODUCTION: Middle Creek is born on the eastern slope of the Blue Ridge Mountains, and from there it flows through a lightly populated valley in Adams County, Pa. and Frederick County, Md., to join Toms Creek near Emmitsburg. Although both the creek and its watershed are tiny, its forested mountain headwater drainage seems to sustain floatable water levels long enough for the lucky paddler to exploit it. The finest quality of this stream is the presence of a delightful mile and a half of whitewater in a little gorge above Harney Road. It is well worth a visit when all the streams in the neighborhood are brimming.

Section 1. T318 to Harney Road					
Gradient	**Difficulty**	**Distance**	**Time**	**Scenery**	**Map**
18	A to 3 –	6.5	2.0	Good	138
1 @ 40					

TRIP DESCRIPTION: The stream that you find at the put-in is not for the claustrophobic paddler, for it is only about 15 feet wide, and it squeezes even tighter downstream. Middle Creek starts off flowing over a bed that is peppered with fairly large, rounded boulders. But since the gradient is only modest, there is no great danger or difficulty here, just some interesting natural

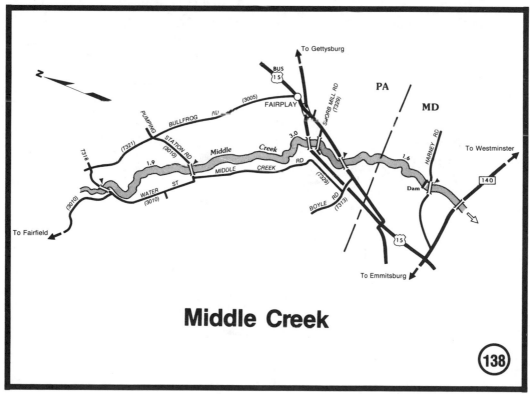

Middle Creek

Conococheague Creek
Back Creek

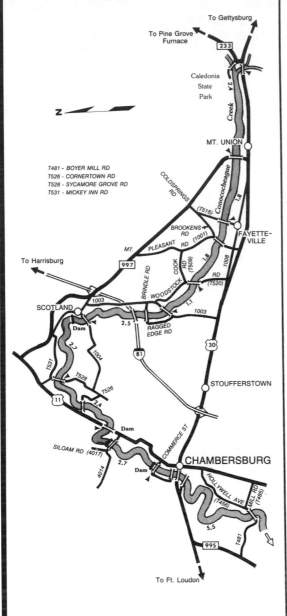

To Gettysburg

To Pine Grove Furnace

233

Caledonia State Park

2.4

Creek

MT. UNION

T481 - BOYER MILL RD
T526 - CORNERTOWN RD
T528 - SYCAMORE GROVE RD
T531 - MICKEY INN RD

N

COLDSPRINGS RD

Conococheague

1.8

(T516)

BROOKENS RD

FAYETTE-VILLE

MT. PLEASANT RD (1001)

To Harrisburg

997

COOK RD (T509)

1.8

1008

WOODSTOCK RD (T520)

BRINDLE RD

1.1

1003

SCOTLAND

Dam

2.5

RAGGED EDGE RD

1003

30

81

STOUFFERSTOWN

2.7

1004

T531

T528

T526

11

2.4

Dam

SILOAM RD (4017)

4014

2.7

Dam

COMMERCE ST

CHAMBERSBURG

HOLLYWELL AVE (T456)

MILL RD (T485)

5.5

995

T481

To Ft. Loudon

30

T481

T467

Mill Rd (T485)

LEAFMORE RD

TALLOW HILL RD

LOOP RD (T486)

HADE RD (3012)

Creek

2.4

ETTER RD (T456)

TURKEYFOOT RD (T469)

SOCIAL IS. RD (3012)

3.1

JACK RD

JACK RD

(3012)

To St. Thomas

ROLLING RD (3028)

3013

GRAPEVINE RD

4.5

JACK MILL RD (T458)

LEHMAN RD (T455)

(T665)

MILLER RD

MARION

Back

995

GOMER RD

3015

3.3

11

2.1

BULLITT RD

COLDSMITH RD (3013)

KAUFFMAN RD (2016)

WILLIAMSON

Dam

4.0

STONE BRIDGE RD

WILLIAMSON RD (3002)

3015

PATTON BRIDGE RD (T459)

3.4

SPORTSMAN RD

RD

(3013)

(3002)

3.4

Conococheague

GREENCASTLE

KUHN RD (T340)

N. RABBIT RD

UPTON

16

HILL RD (3005)

GRANT SHOOK RD (T348)

4.9

3001

WORLEYTOWN RD

WEAVER RD (T341)

Creek

FILER RD (T341)

(3004)

(3005)

WORLEYTOWN

6.0

BINO RD (T325)

YOUNG RD

416

PA

MD

63

LOCUST LEVEL RD (3003)

Gauge

WISHARD RD

58

CEARFOSS

494

To Hagerstown

N

139

slaloming in a woodland setting. An occasional fallen tree and three stout cattle fences will require carries. The remaining miles to Bus. Rte. 15 wind in and out of fields and woods, through what appears to be thinly settled countryside, which the paddler can easily view over the creek's low banks. The current through here is relatively sluggish, with only occasional riffles and easy rapids.

Below Bus. Rte. 15, Middle Creek begins an enjoyable descent, of low intermediate difficulty, over a rocky bed, through a gently sloped, wooded gorge that cuts through the same mass of diabase rock that forms the exciting Harpers Hill Gorge on nearby Marsh Creek. The rapids are formed by small boulders and ledges. Although the rapids are neither as exciting nor as intense as those on Marsh Creek, the unusually sharp stream bed rocks will keep you scrambling. The rapids end in the short pool of an eight-foot dam just upstream of Harney Road.

HAZARDS: Trees and fences on the upper creek. An old milldam above Harney Road requires an easy carry on left.

WATER CONDITIONS: Canoeable within two days of hard rain, in winter and spring. Snowmelt can sustain water even longer.

GAUGE: None on creek. Judge conditions along the road near the put-in or at Harney Road, where the riffle below the dam should be clearly passable. USGS gauge at Frederick, Md., on the Monocacy (call Washington), should probably read over 5.0 feet.

Conococheague Creek

INTRODUCTION: Conococheague is an Indian phrase for "it is a long way." And indeed it is. Draining the prosperous Cumberland Valley of Franklin County, Pa. and Washington County, Md., Conococheague winds 71 canoeable miles from Caledonia State Park to its confluence with the Potomac River at Williamsport, Md. And if the main stem is not enough to satiate you, it is fed by two navigable tributaries, the West Branch and Back Creek, also described in this guide.

The valley of the Conococheague, which is the northern extention of the Shenandoah Valley, is dedicated to agriculture. It is a sea of corn, cattle, and orchards, from South Mountain on the east to Tuscarora Mountain on the west. Since this is obviously civilized territory, you will probably best remember the Conococheague for its fine cultural features, such as well-built barns, farm houses of native limestone, covered and stone arch bridges, and the nearby beautiful old towns, such as Mercersburg, Williamsport, and Greencastle. Most of this tour is suitable for beginners.

Section 1. Caledonia State Park (U.S. Rte. 30) to Chambersburg (U.S. Rte. 30)					
Gradient	Difficulty	Distance	Time	Scenery	Map
22	1 to 2 +	17.8	5.5	Fair to Good	139

TRIP DESCRIPTION: The main stem of Conococheague Creek starts on South Mountain, growing to canoeable size at the confluence with Carbaugh Run and Rocky Mountain Creek. Put in at the Rte. 30 Bridge over Rocky Mountain Creek, or at the picnic area in Caledonia Park. The Conococheague drops steeply and continuously over gravel bars and rock gardens, and soon rushes off into a beautiful grove of giant hemlocks. Unfortunately, after a short pleasant inter-lude in this shady corridor, the channel braids, putting you face to face with many of these fallen giants. The going gets easier below Caledonia, but fallen trees and split channels still cause occa-sional problems as far down as Scotland. Meanwhile, the creek remains fast and riffly to Cham-bersburg. There are three dams on this section: a two-footer at Scotland, which may be run on right, a seven-footer (Siloam Dam) four miles below Scotland, which should be carried on left, and a seven-footer above Commerce Street in Chambersburg, carried on right.

Although this segment passes through some thick woods and by some pretty rural areas, the scenery also includes too many mobile homes, gravel pits, logged over hillsides, and stretches of dredged creek bed. So, if whitewater is not your priority, start your tour below Chambersburg.

HAZARDS: Fallen trees, especially in Caledonia Park, and three dams.

WATER CONDITIONS: Canoeable winter and spring within a day of hard rain.

GAUGE: If rapids at the put-in look passable, then level is fine. USGS gauge at Fairview, Md. (call Washington or inspect on site), located a half mile upstream of Rte. 494, on Wishard Road, should read about 3.5 feet to start at top. With 3.2 feet you can start as far up as Woodstock Road. For rough guess, USGS gauge at Hogestown, on Conodoguinet Creek (call Central PA), should be over 3.5 feet.

Section 2. Chambersburg (U.S. Rte. 30) to Md. Rte. 58					
Gradient	Difficulty	Distance	Time	Scenery	Map
6	A to 1 –	32.9	10.5	Good to Very Good	139

TRIP DESCRIPTION: Below Chambersburg the Conococheague winds through a remarka-bly beautiful, predominately rural setting. Its banks are usually low, affording a panorama of what appears, from the boater's viewpoint, to be sparsely settled territory. Complementing this picturesque passage are three graceful stone arch bridges and an exceptionally long covered bridge.

These are peaceful miles, with the creek expending its small gradient over occasional riffles. However, stay alert for a few fences (electric fences are popular around here) and, below the Cham-bersburg sewage treatment plant, a sharp-crested two-foot weir that beginners and paddlers of delicate boats should carry. Thirteen bridges allow you to break this section down into comforta-ble cruises.

HAZARDS: One weir and some fences.

CONDITIONS: Canoeable winter and spring within three days of hard rain, above Back Creek, and for week to two weeks after hard rain below.

GAUGE: USGS gauge at Fairview, Md. (call Washington or inspect on site) should read at least 2.5 feet to put in at Chambersburg, and 2.0 feet to put in below the West Branch. For rough guess, USGS gauge at Hogestown, on Conodoguinet creek (call Central PA), should read over 3.0 feet to start at Chambersburg.

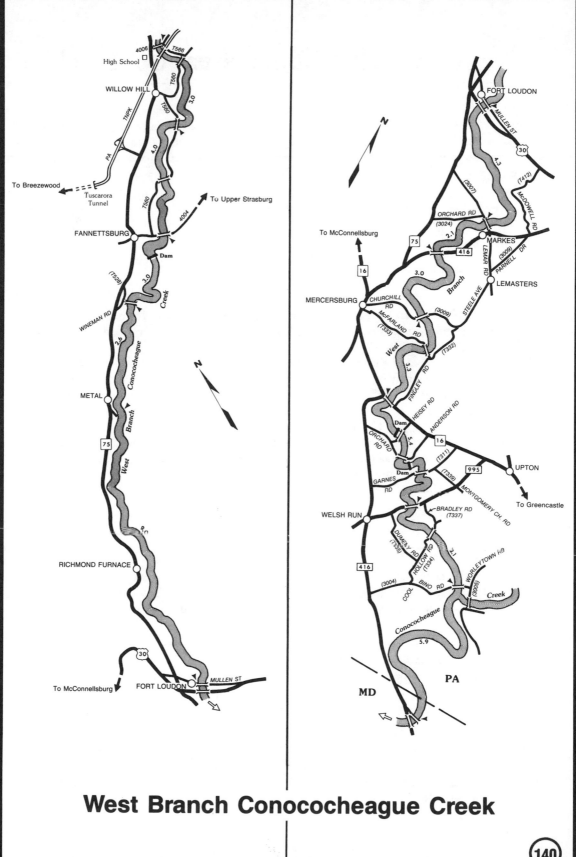

West Branch Conococheague Creek

West Branch Conococheague Creek

INTRODUCTION: The West Branch flows for almost the entire length of western Franklin County, before finally joining the main stem near Greencastle. In its early stages it is confined by high mountain ridges, but for the rest of the way it is free to wander about a wide rural valley where it grows to resemble the main Conococheague. All of this creek makes a suitable run for novices.

Section 1. Pennsylvania Turnpike to Fort Loudon (U.S. Rte. 30)					
Gradient	Difficulty	Distance	Time	Scenery	Map
9	A to 1 +	21.7	8.0	Fair	140

TRIP DESCRIPTION: To reach the put-in, drive north on Pa. Rte. 75, past the Pa. Turnpike. A quarter mile past Fannett-Metal High School, turn right onto a secondary road and follow to a concrete arch bridge over the tiny West Branch.

Most of this run down to Richmond Furnace is bland. The water is often flat, shallow, and fairly slow, while the scenery of fields, farms, and scrubby woods is not particularly striking. An old 12-foot dam backs a small lake at Fannettsburg, but there is an easy portage to the left of the spillway. The lake water once powered a small hydroelectric plant, now crumbling away, that was unusual in that the generators were driven by a water wheel, rather than by a turbine.

Below Richmond Furnace the scenery turns woodsy, featuring pretty views of nearby mountains. The gradient and volume pick up, so that pleasant riffles abound. So skip the upper reaches, start at Fannettsburg, and enjoy the final 16 miles of this section. Take out in Fort Loudon, at the town park by Mullen Street.

HAZARDS: Trees and fences, a dam at Fannettsburg, and an unusual doubledecker low-water bridge below Fannettsburg.

WATER CONDITIONS: Canoeable winter and spring within two days of hard rain.

GAUGE: Riffle at put-in must be passable, as a bare minimum. Because the stream gathers many small tributaries, enough water at the start will be plenty by Richmond Furnace. USGS gauge at Fairview, Md. (call Washington or inspect on site) should read at least 3.2 feet.

Section 2. Fort Loudon (U.S. Rte. 30) to mouth					
Gradient	Difficulty	Distance	Time	Scenery	Map
7	A to 2 –	21.4	7.0	Good	140

TRIP DESCRIPTION: At Fort Loudon the West Branch leaves the mountains behind, and spends its last miles winding about a wide valley. The scenery is predominately agricultural, with high banks partially obscuring visibility above Pa. Rte. 16, but with lower banks and improved visibilty below Rte. 16.

The stream hurries over plenty of riffles in its first few miles, but then slows to only fast flat water, occasional riffles, and easy rapids. You can run the two-foot weir at the fish hatchery below Fort Loudon, but you must carry a five-foot milldam at Heisey Road (on left, across private property) and another five-footer a half mile below Licking Creek (also on left). Take out at SR3004, a quarter mile above the mouth. A recommended run is from Pa. Rte. 16, on the West Branch, to Md. Rte.58, on the main stem, a total distance of 15 miles.

HAZARDS: Three small dams, and possible fences.

WATER CONDITIONS: Canoeable winter and spring within week of hard rain.

GAUGE: Judge riffles at Fort Loudon. Fairview USGS gauge (call Washington or inspect on site) should be at least 2.6 feet. As a rough correlation, USGS gauge at Hogestown, on the Conodoguinet (call Central PA), should be at least 3.0 feet.

Back Creek

INTRODUCTION: Back Creek feeds into the Conococheague at the village of Williamson. It offers a mediocre run through uninspiring scenery, via mostly slow flat water. The best part of your day may be running the shuttle, which is much more scenic and no less an exciting way to enjoy this beautiful countryside.

Section 1. U.S. Rte. 30 to Williamson (SR3002)					
Gradient	Difficulty	Distance	Time	Scenery	Map
3	A to 1	9.4	3.0	Fair	139

TRIP DESCRIPTION: After a dismal start as a channelized ditch running through a suburban housing development, Back Creek winds through fields and woods. Although the creek only murmurs through an occasional riffle, you must be alert for many electric fences and a four-foot milldam behind Williamson. Carry the dam on the right. Back Creek joins the Conococheague about a third of a mile below town.

HAZARDS: A dam at Williamson, and fences.

WATER CONDITIONS: Canoeable winter and spring within two days of hard rain.

GAUGE: Judge shallows at put-in. USGS gauge at Fairview, Md. should be over 3.2 feet.

Licking Creek

INTRODUCTION: Licking Creek starts on the west slope of Tuscarora Mountain, near Cowans Gap State Park, twists and turns through eastern Fulton County, a corner of Franklin County, and finally enters Maryland, to join the Potomac below Hancock. It cuts through a beautiful

Licking Creek
Big Cove Creek

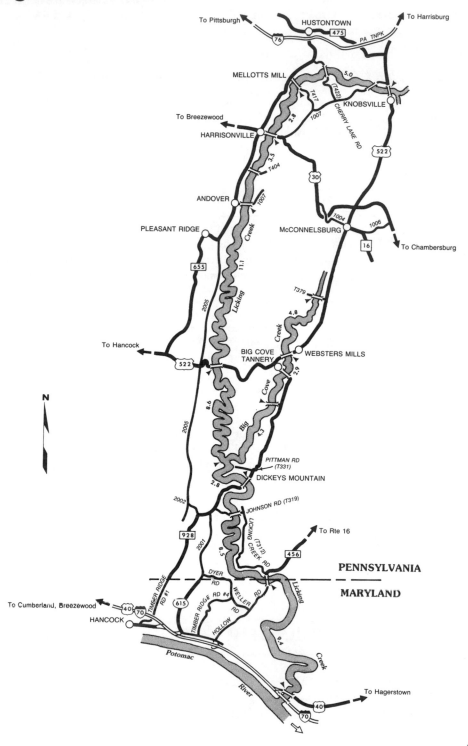

landscape of low, parallel ridges, covered with orchards, forests, and pastures. Many of the roads in the area follow the ridgetops, which afford enough good views to make the shuttling for this stream almost as pleasant as the paddling.

Section 1. Knobsville (U.S. Rte. 522) to U.S. Rte. 30					
Gradient	Difficulty	Distance	Time	Scenery	Map
20	1 to 2 –	7.8	3.0	Good to Very Good	141

TRIP DESCRIPTION: Only the real hardcore purist will want to put in at Rte. 522. Here the stream is no more than ten feet wide, shallow even at high water, and bristles with obstacles. After leaving Rte. 522, it immediately rushes through a long tunnel of arching alder bushes, best negotiated on your belly. You can avoid this masochism by starting three quarters of a mile downstream, at SR1007 Bridge, leaving you with only fallen trees, barbed wire, footbridges, and sharp turns for interest. Actually, the only reason for putting up with all of this nonsense is that it is the only way to gain access to the full length of the beautiful wooded gorge above Mellotts Mill. Here you will find the going easy, riffles frequent, and the solitude almost complete.

HAZARDS: Multitude of strainers, both natural and man-made.

WATER CONDITIONS: Up only within 24 hours of hard rain, in winter or spring.

GAUGE: Judge riffles at Rte. 522. For rough correlation, USGS gauge at Saxton, on the Raystown Branch (call Central PA), should read about 5.0 feet.

Section 2. U.S. Rte. 30 to Pa. Rte. 456					
Gradient	Difficulty	Distance	Time	Scenery	Map
10	A to 1	34.5	10.0	Very Good	141

TRIP DESCRIPTION: The creek now settles into a course suitable for nonmasochistic novices in search of beauty and solitude. Like other rivers in these parts, Licking twists unbelievably, bumps up against a lot of pretty shale cliffs, flows mostly through woods, and passes an occasional farm. Below Andover there are few roads or structures. The water is mostly flat, but there are enough riffles and strong current to make you feel that the stream is doing the work.

HAZARDS: Some fallen trees and fences in the first ten miles. Low-water bridge several miles below Rte. 522.

WATER CONDITIONS: Canoeable winter and spring. Above Pa. Rte. 928, catch within three days of hard rain, and below, within a week of hard rain.

GAUGE: For rough correlation, USGS gauge at Saxton should read at least 3.0 feet. If you are approaching from the south, use the concrete footing on the west pier of the U.S. Rte. 40 bridge in Maryland as a gauge. The top upstream corner should be covered with about four inches of water to start at Rte. 30, and about one inch to start at Rte. 928.

Big Cove Creek

INTRODUCTION: Big Cove Creek, which is anything but big, starts up by McConnellsburg and drains the eastern edge of Fulton County to feed Licking Creek. Like Licking Creek, it twists a lot and possesses copious quantities of peace, solitude, and beauty. Unlike Licking Creek, it has some real live whitewater on it.

Section 1. T379, Rock Hill Road to mouth					
Gradient	Difficulty	Distance	Time	Scenery	Map
21*	1 to 3 –	12.0	3.5	Very Good	141
*Reaches 80					

TRIP DESCRIPTION: To reach the put-in, drive 2.3 miles north of Webster Mill on U.S. Rte. 522, and turn left onto a paved side road, making sure not to blink, so that you will not miss the creek. Big Cove Creek is extremely tiny at T379, flows across private property (open cow pastures), and access is across someone's front lawn. Accordingly, please ask permission to put in, and do not invade with a large party. For at least the first mile, count on finding lots of fences, some deadfalls, logjams, and herds of curious cattle on the banks, trotting downstream with you. The stream then leaves the cowpastures and burrows into a beautiful, wooded gorge. The gradient increases, and soon its waters are rushing over continuous gravel bars and some broken ledges. The pace does not abate until Big Cove Tannery, about five miles below the start. The novice might consider putting in here, where Pa. Rte. 928 parallels the creek, as the water is much slower from here on. One can take out at a ford, just below the mouth, or continue about three miles down Licking Creek to Pa. Rte. 928.

HAZARDS: Deteriorating 18-inch wooden weir at Big Cove Tannery, visible from Rte. 928. It has a strong roller at high water, but can be run. Strainers spread throughout this creek.

WATER CONDITIONS: Canoeable winter and spring within a day of downpour.

GAUGE: If everything that you cross on the way looks really high, then this might be up.

Tonoloway Creek

INTRODUCTION: Tonoloway Creek drains an area of rolling hills and low ridges east of Sideling Hill Creek, to join the Potomac River at Hancock, Md. This is apple country, and many a hillside is decorated by the orderly patterns of orchards. Yet, little of this activity is apparent to the Tonoloway paddler, who sees and enjoys what seems to be the remotest of streams.

Little Tonoloway Creek
Tonoloway Creek

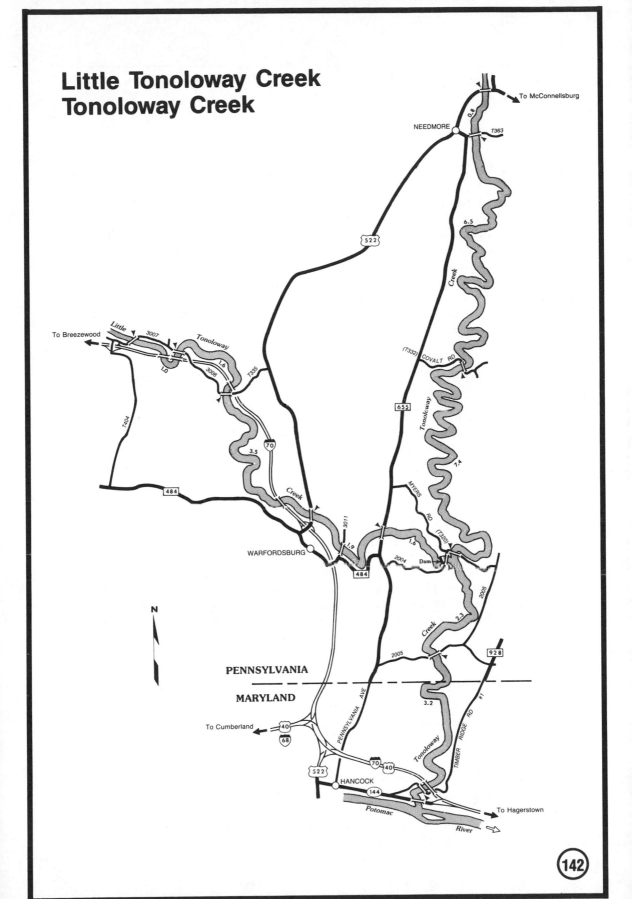

To McConnellsburg

NEEDMORE
0.8
T363

522

6.5

Creek

To Breezewood
Little
3007
Tonoloway
1.6
T335
3006
1.0
T404

(T332) COVALT RD

655

Tonoloway

7.4

3.5

70

MYERS RD

484

Creek

3011

WARFORDSBURG
1.9
1.6
(T320)
2004
Dam

484

2005

Creek
2.3

928

PENNSYLVANIA

N

MARYLAND

2005

PENNSYLVANIA AVE

3.2

Tonoloway

TIMBER RIDGE RD #1

To Cumberland
40
68

522
70 40

HANCOCK
144

Potomac

To Hagerstown

River

142

Section 1. Needmore (U.S. Rte. 522) to Hancock, Md. (Md. Rte. 144)					
Gradient	Difficulty	Distance	Time	Scenery	Map
10	A to 1	20.5	6.5	Good to Excellent	142

TRIP DESCRIPTION: Put in at U.S. Rte. 522, or one mile downstream at the tiny concrete arch bridge of T363, east of Needmore. The following miles to the confluence with Little Tonoloway Creek describe an incredibly serpentine course that advances you about one mile down the valley for every two miles paddled. While there are occasional farms and fields, most of the way is through woodlands, easily viewed over low banks. Almost every bend exposes pretty shale cliffs, and almost every northern exposure has a cool green hemlock grove clinging to it. Most of the surrounding hills are close by and steep, the combined effect being one of intimacy and remoteness. There are many easy riffles, but beginners can still make this trip. However, since the stream is narrow, look for fallen trees to be an occasional problem.

Below the Little Tonoloway Creek confluence, Tonoloway is slightly larger and slower than above, while the surroundings are more settled and open. Nevertheless, it is still a pretty stretch to paddle.

HAZARDS: Occasional deadfalls.

WATER CONDITIONS: Canoeable winter and spring within a day or two of hard rain. Below Little Tonoloway, it lasts a day longer.

GAUGE: If you can run the riffle at T363, then there is just enough water. For a rough correlation, USGS gauge at Saxton, on Raystown Branch (call Central PA), should be at least 3.2 feet for upper creek and 3.0 feet for below Little Tonoloway.

──── Little Tonoloway Creek ────

INTRODUCTION: Considering that Interstate 70 follows over half of this course, it is amazing what a pleasant run Little Tonoloway is. It accomplishes this seemingly impossible feat by twisting behind little hills and cliffs, which not only block the view, but screen out the sound of the busy highway. Little Tonoloway does not have much of a watershed, so you have to rush to catch it up, and that is where the Interstate can be very useful.

Section 1. Deneen Gap to Johnsons Mill (SR2004)					
Gradient	Difficulty	Distance	Time	Scenery	Map
21	1 to 2	9.6	3.5	Good	142

TRIP DESCRIPTION: To reach the put-in, get off I-70 (heading north) at Exit 32, turn right, then left, and park. The stream is about a hundred feet across the grassy field, down a steep bank. Little Tonoloway gets off to a lively start as it tumbles out of a gap in Sideling Hill and heads eastward, cutting across the geological grain of the land. Almost continuous rapids are formed by small ledges and gravel bars, and there are many tricky spots caused by swift water sweeping under trees and roots on bends. The scenery alternates between rural and woodsy, while shale cliffs abound all the way. Around Warfordsburg, the pace slows, while the scenery degrades to sumptious views of the Interstate and a large gravel quarry. There is a two-foot-high rock dam at the quarry, best run on the left. Below here the good scenery returns, but the water is mostly slow. However, one gets a final splash at a crumbling dam above Johnsons Mill. If not clogged with debris, there is a passable breach on the far left that drops three feet into a juicy hole. The take-out is a tenth mile above the mouth.

HAZARDS: Trees and roots on bends on upper creek. Broken dam above Johnsons Mill.

WATER CONDITIONS: Canoeable winter and spring within day of hard rain.

GAUGE: If little ledges at the put-in are clearly passable, or if rock dam at Mellott Quarry, near Warfordsburg, has a clean chute on the left, then level is adequate. For rough estimate, USGS gauge at Saxton, on Raystown Branch (call Central PA), should be over 4.0 feet.

Town Creek

INTRODUCTION: Town Creek flows out of the heart of Bedford County into Maryland, for an eventual rendezvous with the Potomac River. Its course runs through rugged mountain country where numerous, level-topped ridges fringe valleys filled with steeply rolling hills. This is the sort of topography that supports few residents but beckons outdoor-oriented visitors. Canoeists should be pleased with Town Creek or any other stream that drains this scenic corner of Pennsylvania.

Section 1. Chaneysville to U.S. Rte. 40					
Gradient	Difficulty	Distance	Time	Scenery	Map
15	A to 1+	15.6	5.0	Good to Very Good	143

TRIP DESCRIPTION: Town Creek is formed by the confluence of Sweet Root Creek, Elklick Creek, and Wilson Run. Put in a half mile southeast of Chaneysville, on Elklick Creek (watch out for fences), or a half mile south of town where Pa. Rte. 326 swings close to Town Creek (be sure to get permission from landowners first).

Town Creek meanders through a sparsely inhabited valley. The stream bumps up against countless little shale cliffs while winding through woodlands and by attractive farms. There is one lovely, white covered bridge near Hewitt. The fairly clear water rushes over numerous, short and easy riffles, formed by gravel and some broken ledges. The only complications are three low-water bridges and maybe a fallen tree or new fence. Finish your cruise in Maryland at the Old Rte. 40 Bridge, just downstream of the main highway.

HAZARDS: Low-water bridges, trees, or fences.

WATER CONDITIONS: Canoeable in winter or spring within three days of hard rain.

GAUGE: None on creek. Roughly, USGS gauge at Saxton, on Raystown Branch (call Central PA), should be over 3.2 feet.

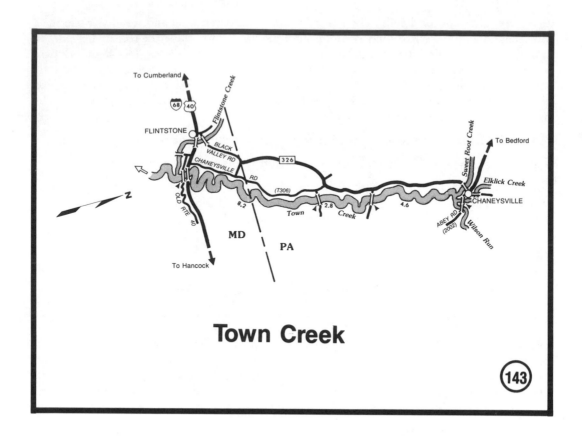

Town Creek

(143)

── Wills Creek ──

INTRODUCTION: Wills Creek drops off of the Allegheny Plateau of southeastern Somerset County, to eventually feed the North Branch Potomac River at Cumberland, Maryland. That drop creates some of the most challenging and most enjoyable whitewater in Pennsylvania.

During July of 1984 one of those once-in-a-lifetime storms zeroed in on the basin of Wills Creek, dumped five inches of rain in two hours on already rain-soaked ground, and generated a flood that devastated the towns of Fairhope and Hyndman, the river road, and the railroad. But the towns, the railroad, road, and stream have been rebuilt, with busy bulldozers pushing up riprapped banks, channelizing the bed, and relocating buolders. It is a mess from the boater's point of view. But take comfort in that time heals all wounds. Experience on other flood-devastated streams has demonstrated that vegetation will reclaim the banks, and future high water will move the boulders and gravel back to cxactly where the river pleases. Future paddlers will never suspect what Wills Creek looked like back in 1984.

Section 1. Glencoe (SR2015) to Fairhope (SR2019)

Gradient	Difficulty	Distance	Time	Scenery	Map
61	2 + to 3 +	4.3	1.5	Fair	144

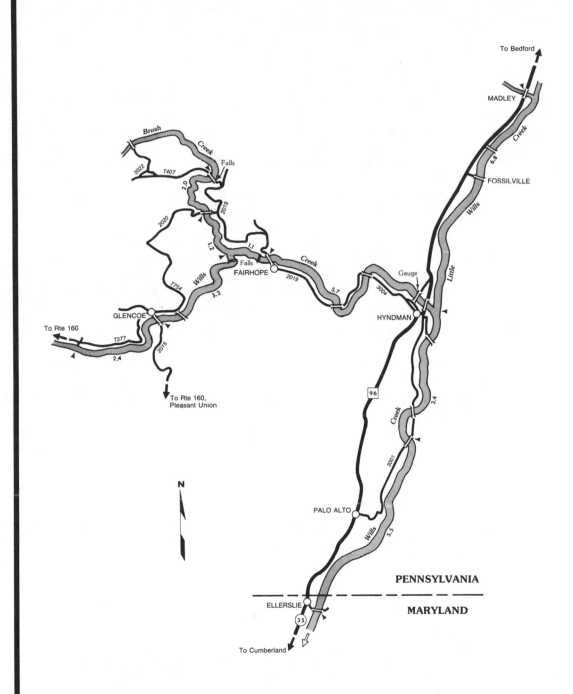

To Bedford

MADLEY

Creek

6.8

FOSSILVILLE

Brush

Creek

2022

T407

Falls

2.0

2019

2020

1.2

1.1

Creek

FAIRHOPE

2019

5.7

Falls

Gauge

3004

Wills

Little

HYNDMAN

T754

Wills

3.2

GLENCOE

To Rte 160

T377

2015

2.4

3.4

To Rte 160,
Pleasant Union

96

Creek

3001

N

PALO ALTO

Wills

5.5

PENNSYLVANIA

MARYLAND

ELLERSLIE

35

To Cumberland

Little Wills Creek
Brush Creek
Wills Creek

TRIP DESCRIPTION: Upper Wills Creek provides a zesty rush down continuous and boun-cy little rapids, punctuated by sets of exciting ledges with individual drops of up to three feet. Although this run is mostly of intermediate difficulty and is considerably easier than Section 2, you should be overqualified to attempt it, as you will need to avoid two dangerously situated waterfalls; one which could destroy your boat and one which could destroy your health.

You can start at the highway bridge in Glencoe, or better yet, 2.5 fun-filled miles upstream. To reach this upper access point from Fairhope, take the first right in the center of Glencoe and then, a tenth mile beyond, turn left. Follow this rough dirt road 2.5 miles upstream to a house, a road to the right, a small creek, and then a trail on the left that leads a hundred yards down to the water.

To Glencoe, the tiny stream rushes over gravel bars and a few ledges in a mostly uncomplicated manner, which is fine since alder- and brush-choked banks make escape or rescue difficult. When you reach Glencoe, begin counting railroad bridges. For directly beneath the fifth bridge is the first falls. If you lose count, this bridge has a tunnel at its downstream end, labelled Falls Cut Tunnel. The falls has a six-foot vertical drop that goes splat onto a rock. Scout this and carry left, or if the level permits and you want to live dangerously, eddy out on the right brink and lift over the slippery and sloping rocks to the pool below. A half mile below the confluence with Brush Creek is the Railroad Cut Falls. This is a man-made cataract, blasted out of rock by the railroad to bypass a hairpin loop of the creek and thus eliminate the need for two bridges. Paddle down as far as your good sense or nerves allow you, and carry on the left.

HAZARDS: Trees above Glencoe and the two falls. Before setting up shuttle the paddler should hike up the railroad grade from Fairhope to establish some landmarks (most notably a black cliff on river right and a concrete retaining wall on the left) so as not to miss that last very important eddy.

WATER CONDITIONS: Canoeable in the winter and spring during snowmelt or within two days of hard rain.

GAUGE: None. See Section 2. You need about six inches to a foot more water than the mini-mum for Section 2.

Section 2. Fairhope (SR2019) to Hyndman (Pa. Rte. 96)					
Gradient	Difficulty	Distance	Time	Scenery	Map
73	2+ to 4+	5.5	1.5	Fair	144

TRIP DESCRIPTION: These are five miles of probably the most enjoyable and challenging whitewater in the Potomac Basin. The first few miles, which cut through Big Savage Mountain, are a memorable tumble over a mostly bouldery bed. At low levels it is an often tedious and incredibly rocky natural slalom suitable for both open and decked boats. At medium levels it becomes powerful and pushy, with complexity that includes not only dodging boulders but also powerful holes. At higher levels the rocks are all covered, eddies gone, and there is just one long rapid of big waves and huge holes.

The initiation rites occur about 150 yards below the Fairhope put-in. There is a sloping four-foot diagonal ledge with a powerful stopper which, if entered in the middle, will grab you and violently thrust you to the right before maybe releasing you. This can be traumatic to right-sided canoeists. The timid should sneak on either side. About a mile downstream is a short, boulder-choked rapid called Yo Yo (a preflood name given for the tenacity of one hole) that you can see from the shuttle road where it dips fairly near to the river. With menacingly undercut boulders and jammed debris, your only route choice here is to sneak down the extreme right (if it is free of debris). After the second bridge the stream widens and conditions begin to gradually mellow. At low levels this wide stretch becomes impassable before that above, especially since the bulldozers have changed it.

Set in a deep canyon, this was once a pretty run. But the flood damage has, for the time being, messed all that up. So you might as well keep your eyes on the rapids.

HAZARDS: The whitewater, if your skills are insufficient.

WATER CONDITIONS: Canoeable in winter and spring during snowmelt and within three days of hard rain.

GAUGE: There is a barely visible painted gauge on the retaining wall, downstream right, by the silver truss in Hyndman. But with flood-induced channel changes, its meaning is currently unknown. Prior to the flood, 1.5 feet was minimum, 2.0 feet was suitable for good open boaters, 2.0 to 3.0 feet was reasonable for decked boats, and above 3.0 was only for the best. USGS gauge at intersection of U.S. Rte. 40 and Md. Rte. 36, Eckhart Junction, in Maryland (call Washington or inspect on site), should be at least 3.4 feet. Roughly, USGS gauge at Kitzmiller, on North Branch Potomac (call Washington), should be 5.0 feet and USGS gauge at Markleton, on Casselman (call Pittsburgh), should be over 3.0 feet.

Section 3. Hyndman (Pa. Rte. 96) to Ellersie, Md.					
Gradient	Difficulty	Distance	Time	Scenery	Map
22	A to 2 +	8.9	3.0	Fair	144

TRIP DESCRIPTION: Wills Creek has now broken out of the Allegheny Plateau and settles into a more gentle pace through a trough nestled between the Allegheny Front and Wills Mountain. The run is initially busy, dropping over cobble bars in a bouncy and uncomplicated manner. One particularly steep rapid, about a mile below the start, can throw up waves that are big enough to swamp an open canoe. But the rapids gradually shorten and the pools grow longer.

The scenery through here is disappointing. While the valley is pretty, the view of it from the river is poor, obscured by high banks and dense vegetation.

HAZARDS: None.

WATER CONDITIONS: Canoeable in winter and spring during snowmelt and within a week of hard rain.

GAUGE: Minimum is roughly a little less than that for Section 2, whatever that is. USGS gauge at Eckhart Junction, Maryland (right bank) should be 3.2 feet. Roughly, USGS gauge at Kitzmiller, on North Branch Potomac (call Washington), should be 4.5 feet.

Little Wills Creek

INTRODUCTION: Little Wills Creek flows down a narrow valley between the Allegheny Front and Wills Mountain to enter Wills Creek just below Hyndman. It draws most of its flow off of the well-watered Allegheny Plateau, and it is generally canoeable if upper Wills Creek has water. Pa. Rte. 96 accompanies this run and is never more than a half mile away.

Section 1. Madley (Pa. Rte. 96) to mouth					
Gradient	Difficulty	Distance	Time	Scenery	Map
39	1 to 2 +	6.8	2.0	Good	144

TRIP DESCRIPTION: Fans of small, shallow, and busy streams will delight in Little Wills Creek. It provides a descent down almost continuous easy rapids over gravel bars and rock gardens. Swift flatwater provides periodic pauses. The proximity of the highway has resulted in some trash and other eyesores, but most of the time the view is only of farmlands and mountainsides.

Put in on Wolf Camp Run, at the village of Madley. The take-out at the junction with Wills Creek is poor. So continue on down Wills Creek for a half mile to a road bridge accessible from Hyndman.

HAZARDS: Fallen trees where the stream occasionally braids (not visible from the highway).

WATER CONDITIONS: Canoeable in winter and spring during snowmelt and within two days of hard rain.

GAUGE: If Wolf Camp Run looks passable at the Rte. 96 Bridge, then there is plenty of water on Little Wills. USGS gauge at Eckhart Junction, Maryland, on Wills Creek (call Washington or inspect on site), should probably be close to 4.5 feet. Roughly, USGS gauge at Saxton, on Raystown Branch (call Central PA), will be running about 3.5 feet.

Brush Creek

INTRODUCTION: Brush Creek drains an isolated piece of plateau northwest of Fairhope, in Somerset County. This seldom-run torrent makes an ideal introduction to a Wills Creek run when the water is up and, if water is really high, makes a reasonable alternative to an overly pushy Fairhope to Hyndman flush.

Section 1. Covered Bridge (T407) to mouth					
Gradient	Difficulty	Distance	Time	Scenery	Map
75	2 to 4 –	3.2	1.0	Excellent	144

TRIP DESCRIPTION: Brush Creek is a beautiful mini-wilderness run that enters Wills Creek just above the Railroad Cut Falls at Fairhope. It flows through a wild and wooded gorge that is decorated by falls, rock cliffs, hemlock, and rhododendron, and is only civilized by one road-bridge and a cluster of rustic log structures. Rapids formed by boulders, gravel, and ledges are almost continuous, separated only by short pools. There is an unrunnable ten-foot falls beneath the covered bridge at the put-in, and, about a mile downstream, there is a steep tier of ledges that form a chute dropping about ten feet. Take out above Railroad Cut Falls on Wills Creek, about a half mile below the confluence.

The purist can add on about three miles to this run, if water is extra high, by starting at SR2017, a half mile northwest of Johnsburg. Although the aesthetics are fine, an alder jungle and numerous dangerously placed fallen trees will make this an expedition.

HAZARDS: Steep ledge rapid about a mile below the start. If you decide to carry, look for an old logging railroad grade on the left.

WATER CONDITIONS: Canoeable winter and spring during snowmelt and within two days of hard rain.

GAUGE: None on creek, but you can judge conditions at put-in. USGS gauge at Eckhart Junction, on Wills Creek (call Washington), should probably be close to 4.5 feet.

The Best of the West
(Ohio River and Lake Erie Tributaries)

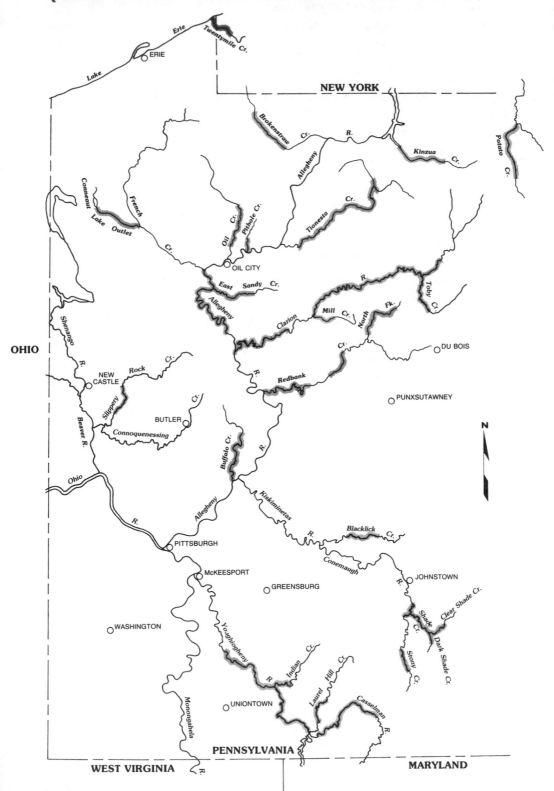

Chapter 7
The Best Of The West

The western third of Pennsylvania is a rolling and sometimes rugged plateau that is markedly sculpted by the streams that drain it. At its southeastern edge is the Allegheny Front—a high point from which emanate a series of long, gentle, and parallel ridges, like great ocean swells. Rivers of this corner of the state cut deep and narrow canyons through the hard sandstone that lies below, to form the rapids and falls that will so delight the whitewater boater. To the north lies an equally high but flat-topped plateau that is deeply dissected by its rivers. Every stream carves a gorge, but the underlying rock has yielded easily, and most of the streams are, as a result, relatively peaceful. To the south and west the hills are more rounded, and the rivers flow in valleys. All but the smallest headwaters are slow and gentle. Finally, to the northwest the land is even more rolling, having been scraped down to size during the last ice age. The resultant landscape features natural lakes, moraines, swamps, and other handiwork of glacial force. With the exception of Slippery Rock Creek, the creeks of this area are mostly tame.

The impact of civilization is difficult to escape when paddling western Pennsylvania. Except for the northeastern plateau and the Allegheny ridges, most of this area is well populated. While industry concentrates down in the major river valleys, extraction of coal, oil, and natural gas reaches into almost every valley and hollow. Sometimes you will spot a rusty gas pipe running through otherwise untrammelled forest. Sometimes you will spot, along the stream, orange rocks that were stained that way by a mine acid seep. Reminders are all around.

So after one totals up what nature has given western Pennsylvania and subtracted what man has taken away, one finds a few handfuls of streams, both exciting and calm, that are outstanding. If you are visiting or living in this area, with no time to waste on second-class waterways, there are 26 either outstanding or representative creeks and rivers that you should make a special effort to explore.

Segments of the following streams are described in this chapter:

Slippery Rock Creek	North Fork
Youghiogheny River	Clarion River
Indian Creek	Mill Creek
Casselman River	Toby Creek
Laurel Hill Creek	Easy Sandy Creek
Allegheny River	Conneaut Lake Outlet
Buffalo Creek	Oil Creek
Blacklick Creek	Pithole Creek
Stony Creek	Tionesta Creek
Shade Creek	Brokenstraw Creek
Dark Shade Creek	Kinzua Creek
Clear Shade Creek	Potato Creek
Redbank Creek	Twentymile Creek

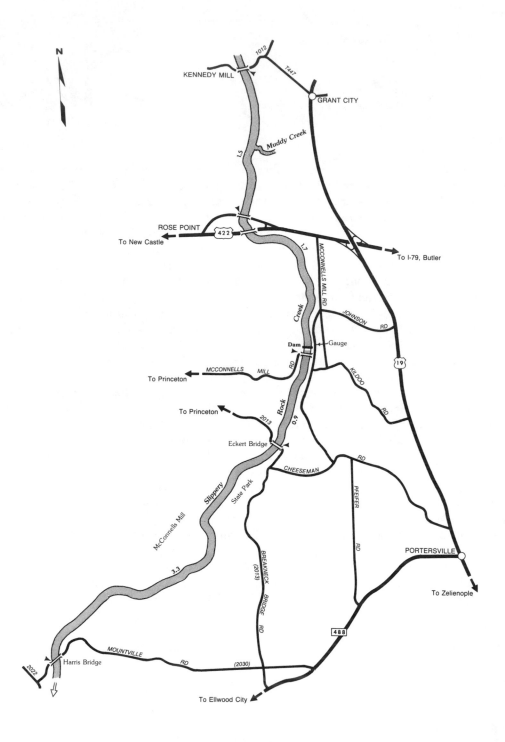

Slippery Rock Creek

145

Slippery Rock Creek

INTRODUCTION: West of Chestnut Ridge (or U.S. Rte. 119, if you do not know your mountains), Pennsylvania has little to offer the whitewater boater. That is why any such boaters that live in Pittsburgh, Erie, Cleveland, Columbus, or any points in between can lead you with their eyes closed to Slippery Rock Creek. For Slippery Rock is the only whitewater show in town—an improbably located, prime piece of frequently runnable and boulder-choked rapids tumbling down a wild and beautiful gorge. The name Slippery Rock was given long ago when some early visitor found a streamside rock coated and slippery from a natural oil seep. You will see no oil today, and it will be skill, not oil, that will help you slip through the narrow chutes and rocky channels that grace this popular run.

Section 1. Kennedy Mill (SR1012) to Harris Bridge (Mountville road, SR2030)

Gradient	Difficulty	Distance	Time	Scenery	Map
24	1 to 3	7.4	2.5	Excellent	145
0.9 @ 40					

TRIP DESCRIPTION: Most of the best of Slippery Rock is enveloped by McConnells Mill State Park. That is where most people paddle, particularly between the mill (McConnells) and Harris Bridge. But the rapids and the pretty gorge start a few miles upstream, just below the old, sloping dam at Kennedy Mill. If you float this upper stretch, be sure to stop at Muddy Creek, which trickles in on the left, and hike up to its rockbound falls. While these upper miles are generally easy, the creek twists through the first of its many blind boulder gardens. When you arrive at McConnells Mill, land on the left to portage the milldam. Immediately below this dam the creek commences a mile-long slalom through room-sized sandstone boulders, blind turns, and narrow chutes. Because the creek is so constricted in spots, the rapids assume big river type turbulence with only a few extra feet of water at the gauge. At such times, only advanced paddlers should attempt this normally intermediate run.

Eckert Bridge marks the end of the excitement. Boulders diverge and the remainder of the way rushes through easy and usually straightforward rapids which, at moderate levels, well-coached novices can safely attempt.

Access is a problem on popular Slippery Rock Creek. If you put in at Kennedy Mill or Rose Point (U.S. Rte. 422), be aware that landowner-paddler relations at these spots are delicate, at best. If you want to paddle from Kennedy Mill, please consider starting two miles upstream at U.S. Rte. 19 (and do not do anything to ruin relations there). At the more popular Rose Point put-in, use the downstream left side of U.S. Rte. 422 only. Parking space is limited, and be sure to park off the highway but not on the grass. Also, if you patronize the private campground (nice) on old Rte. 422, up the hill on the east, they will let you put in from their land. Finally, many paddlers park at the state park office, just off Rte. 422 on McConnells Mill Road, and hike down a trail to the river. It means more work but fewer headaches.

HAZARDS: Dams at Kennedy Mill and McConnells Mill. Possible strainers in narrow chutes.

WATER CONDITIONS: Canoeable in late winter and spring during snowmelt and within ten days of hard rain. In average years the creek stays at runnable levels until mid-May, frequently rises after summer showers, and often returns again in November.

⌐ Youghiogheny River ¬

INTRODUCTION: The Youghiogheny River starts on the slopes of Backbone Mountain, in the far southwestern tip of Maryland, and flows about 140 mountain miles to the Monongahela River at McKeesport, Pennsylvania. The name is pronounced Yok'·a·gay'·nee, but most people just call it the "Yok" (Yough). If judged by its popularity, Pennsylvania's portion of the Yough is the premier whitewater playground of the middle Appalachians. Most of this boating activity takes place on a 18-mile segment bracketing a tiny borough called Ohiopyle.

It is easy to see how the Yough soared to this status. First of all, the dam-controlled Yough can guarantee the paddler canoeable levels 24 hours a day, 365 days a year. How many Appalachian whitewater streams can make that claim? Such an assured flow is not only a luxury to independent boaters, but also provides fertile waters for conducting commercial raft tours and raft and canoe liveries. Second, nature neatly organized the Yough into some ideally lengthed segments of novice and intermediate to advanced whitewater. Man has seen to it that these segments are accessible in many of the right places. So the river can efficiently delight a wide range of boater's tastes and skills. Next, the river is centrally located and conveniently accessible to much of populous Ohio, Pennsylvania, Maryland, Virginia, and West Virginia, where plenty of boaters reside. But the Yough typically draws from even farther. For as the hot summer dries up everybody's favorite local streams, it is common to find river-starved boaters arriving from as far away as New York, New Jersey, Michigan, Illinois, and Tennessee. Finally, because the Yough drains a relatively thinly populated valley, with much of its canyon protected within the 19,000 acres of Ohiopyle State Park, this is a clean and beautiful river. It is the type to which any boater would love to retreat on a hot summer day.

With all the above attributes, the Yough receives visitors on a scale equalled by few, rivers in the country. Over 114,000 people ran the exciting Lower Yough in 1985, and most of them came during the peak period from mid-May to mid-September. In 1981, about 44,000 people floated the more gentle Middle Yough. And the numbers are growing. In addition, throngs of tourists converge on Ohiopyle to see the Falls, to sun themselves on the rocks, to fish, bicycle, and to just enjoy the terrestrial portion of this pleasant setting.

With all the above crowds, the State of Pennsylvania just had to step in with some organization and regulation. Thus you will find that boating here is a far cry from that done on your typical country creek. Crowds mean automobiles. To accommodate the tremendous demand for vehicle space, the park provides parking lots for private boaters at the Ohiopyle put-in, for tourists above the Falls in Ohiopyle, and for commercial raft patrons just outside of Ohiopyle off SR2011. Crowds mean access problems. At Ohiopyle, a wide, graded, and asphalted footpath funnels the tide of rubber, plastic, fiberglass, and humanity from cars, buses, and staging areas to a sandy beach and the river. At the Bruner Run take-out, limited space in the gorge has forced a more complicated arrangement. The parking lots are situated at the top of the gorge, with a bus shuttle service plying the 1.6 miles of narrow road in between. There is a small charge for this service ($1.50 per person in 1993), with tokens purchased at the Ohiopyle put-in. Crowds mean limits. The park has established a daily quota system for boating the Lower Yough: 960 commercial spots and 960 private. The private allocation is split between 768 using inflatable craft and 192 using canoes and kayaks. If you choose to travel commercially, reserving a place is easy if you

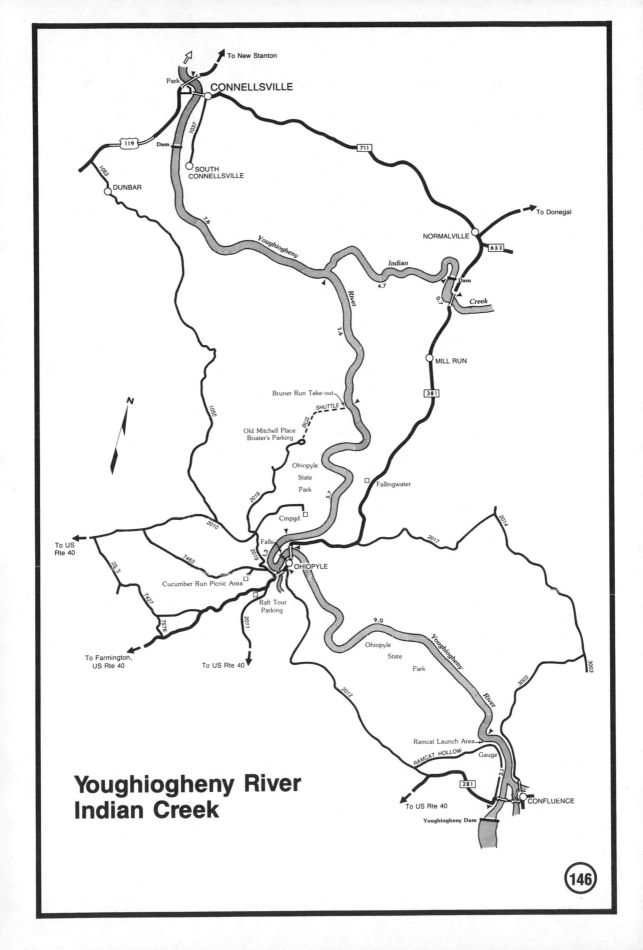

Youghiogheny River
Indian Creek

146

call the outfitter well in advance (the bigger the party, the earlier you must call). If you choose to privately raft the river (for most people this means renting a raft from concessions in Ohiopyle), you must call the park in advance, by phone or in person, and reserve a launch permit. These go fast. For canoes and kayaks, there is now a partial reservation system and a launch fee ($2.50) for all. All boaters must register at the put-in, before launching. These restrictions apply between 8:00 A.M. and 3:00 P.M., from May through October. Finally, crowds mean a need for accomodations. Camping in the park is limited to one exceptionally nice campground, with 223 sites. You can reserve these in advance, but they too go fast. If you paddle year round, the campground is also open year round, and getting a site in the off season is easy. Camping opportunities adjacent to the park include the Corps of Engineers campground at Yough Dam (a slum) and several private campgrounds, which range from pleasant to tasteless.

There is much more to say about the Yough than space allows. If you would like to know more, I highly recommend that you pick up a copy of *Youghiogheny Appalachian River,* by Tim Palmer.

Section 1. Confluence (Tailrace Campground) to Ohiopyle (Pa. Rte. 381)					
Gradient	Difficulty	Distance	Time	Scenery	Map
11	1 +	11.1	3.5	Excellent	146

TRIP DESCRIPTION: This section is commonly called the Middle Yough (the Upper Yough is in Maryland, above Friendsville). It is an increasingly popular reach that is suitable for beginners and novices. The Middle Yough makes not only a pleasant downriver run, but if you exploit its rich assortment of little holes, surfing waves, and sharp eddies, it makes an excellent classroom on which to hone your whitewater skills. The river here is mostly gentle. It rushes down sets of easy boulder patch and ledge rapids below Ramcat Hollow and again as it approaches Ohiopyle. Pools and shallow riffles fill the stretch in between.

The Middle Yough cuts through the southern end of Laurel Hill to form a deep gorge. Most of it is protected by Ohiopyle State Park and state game lands, resulting in a gorge that is totally free of development. Only the busy railroad breaks the harmony. Speaking of railroads, there used to be two. Now the one on the left is abandoned, and the park has converted it to a Confluence to Bruner Run bicycle trail. The river water usually flows clear and cold, coming from the depths of Yough Reservoir. Such fine water supports a healthy trout population that an increasing number of hard-core anglers are pursuing.

You can launch from either the entrance to the Corps of Engineers campground at the tailrace of Yough Dam or 2.1 miles downstream at the Ramcat Hollow Access, maintained by the state park. The park also provides a nice take-out on river left, 150 yards upstream of the Pa. Rte. 381 Bridge.

HAZARDS: Ohiopyle Falls is 0.4 miles below Rte. 381. Not far when the water is up. Do not miss the take-out.

WATER CONDITIONS: Always canoeable, except when frozen or too high.

GAUGE: USGS gauge at Confluence (call Pittsburgh or Washington). The Corps usually maintains levels of between 1.9 and 2.1 feet, but rains on the Casselman can boost it much higher. Staff gauge at put-in for Section 2. Summertime levels usually range from 1.5 to 1.8 feet, except after rains. At levels of over 4.0 feet on either gauge, beginners should avoid the rapids above Ohiopyle as a capsize could easily result in you washing past the take-out and over the Falls.

Section 2. Ohiopyle (below Falls) to Bruner Run					
Gradient	Difficulty	Distance	Time	Scenery	Map
27	1 + to 3 +	7.0	2.5	Excellent	146
1.3 @ 48					

TRIP DESCRIPTION: They call this section the Lower Yough, though for many boaters it is the only Yough they ever know. Here the river cuts a relatively shallow but steep-walled gorge in the bottom of the valley between Laurel Hill and Chestnut Ridge. Beginning with its plunge over the sandstone ledge of Ohiopyle Falls, the Yough first describes a long, U-shaped loop, called The Loop (Youghiogheny is Indian for "river that flows in roundabout course"), in almost pristine surroundings. The railroad rejoins the river below The Loop, but enveloped by the state park, these miles appear otherwise undisturbed. Come here in June to enjoy the mountain laurel in bloom, in July for the rhododendron, and in October to enjoy the fall colors.

The whitewater is composed of an ideal sequence of usually short and moderately steep rapids separated by short pools or wide riffles. The rapids are formed by car to room-sized sandstone boulders and sloping ledges that, at summer levels, provide the boater with tortuous routes, blind turns, countless eddies, and plenty of surfing waves and holes. If you play this river for its potential, you can spend all day on this section without ever putting down your paddle.

HAZARDS: Falls above put-in. Being run over by a rubber raft, being speared by a kayak or C-1, being accidentally hit in the face by a kayak paddle while sitting in line in an eddy, and being intentionally hit in the face by an irate boater waiting for you to stop hogging Swimmer's Hole.

WATER CONDITIONS: Always canoeable, except when frozen or too high.

GAUGE: Same as Section 1. Levels over 3.0 feet at the Ohiopyle put-in gauge can be rough on inexperienced rafters or intermediate hard boaters. Advanced boaters will find this section reasonable at any levels short of floodstage.

Section 3. Bruner Run to Connellsville (U.S. Rte. 119)					
Gradient	Difficulty	Distance	Time	Scenery	Map
12	1 to 3 −	11.2	3.5	Fair to Excellent	146

TRIP DESCRIPTION: This is an infrequently floated section, partly because of its long shuttle and partly because its variable difficulty is acceptable to few boaters. But it is a lovely river. The Yough cuts another deep and steep-walled gorge, this time through Chestnut Ridge. It is mostly undeveloped until South Connellsville, and so far, wonderfully free of all the screaming idiots that plague the Middle and Lower Yough.

This section's whitewater extends for about two miles past Bruner Run. It is filled with boulder and ledge rapids comparable to those on Section 2. The rest consists of a few long pools and miles of long, wide, and shallow riffles over a rocky bottom. Beginners would be overwhelmed by the first portion while intermediates are usually bored with the rest. There is an unrunnable dam in South Connellsville, carried on the right. But it has an incredibly long playing hole below that, at normal summer levels, is far more fun than the bitterly contested Swimmer's Hole. Take out at the town access and beach, on the left, beneath the U.S. Rte. 119 Bridge.

HAZARDS: Dam in South Connellsville.

WATER CONDITIONS: Always runnable though in early summers of dry years you will have to wade the shallows immediately below Indian Creek.

GAUGE: Canoe gauge at Ohiopyle put-in should be at least 1.8 feet to avoid scraping below Indian Creek.

Section 4. Connellsville (U.S. Rte. 119) to Layton (SR4038)					
Gradient	Difficulty	Distance	Time	Scenery	Map
6	A to 1	13.3	4.5	Good	147

TRIP DESCRIPTION: Conveniently close to Pittsburgh and assured of a cool, dependable supply of canoeable water throughout the hottest and stickiest of summers, this section is perfect for the beginner or novice paddler. Somehow all the development that has come and gone, the coal mines, the coking operations, the roads, and the railroads, has not worn out these lonely miles of Yough. From the town park in Connellsville to Dawson, you pass a few houses, an old abandoned distillery, and a private campground, and the everpresent railroad follows along. But the impression is still one of remoteness. From Dawson to Layton, this is not just an impression. The river here is remote. Wooded hillsides form a gorge-like corridor and eventually the river also narrows, with big sandstone boulders littering the banks, hinting of possibly serious whitewater.

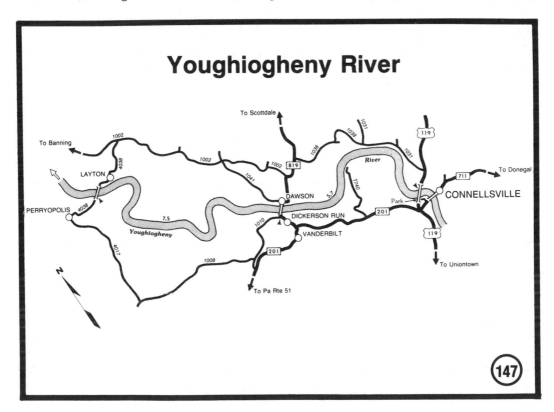

But only the easiest of rapids develop, a few relatively bouncy ones, and then the river returns to its initial placid state with occasional simple riffles. To take out at the high bridge at Layton, look for a dirt road that splits off of SR4038 opposite the canoe livery. This potholed but passable path follows the railroad track and then turns left at the bridge, delivering your vehicle right to the riverbank.

HAZARDS: None.

WATER CONDITIONS: Suitable for floating all year except when frozen or flooding.

GAUGE: USGS gauges at Connellsville and Confluence (call Pittsburgh) seldom dip below 2.4 and 1.9 respectively. These are both perfectly adequate levels.

Indian Creek

INTRODUCTION: Indian Creek drains the west slope of Laurel Hill and uses that water to cut a steep side canyon into the Yough Gorge between Ohiopyle and Connellsville. This is a short, superb, and advanced whitewater run, distinguished as one of the ledgiest series of rapids on the Allegheny Plateau. Few streams can claim such interesting whitewater.

Section 1. Pa. Rte. 381 to mouth					
Gradient	Difficulty	Distance	Time	Scenery	Map
60	3 to 4 + ,6	5.4	2.0	Excellent	146

TRIP DESCRIPTION: The reason that you have probably met few people who have run Indian Creek is because the access stinks. A big dam plugs the creek two thirds of a mile below Pa. Rte. 381 to form a water supply reservoir for Connellsville. Paddling on the reservoir is illegal. But because the road into the dam is gated, you must hike to the start. Then down at the mouth of the creek there is no access either. So you must paddle an additional five miles down the Yough to Connellsville. This is not all that difficult because, if Indian Creek is up, the Yough is usually high and swift. Most whitewater paddlers, nevertheless, grumble at this prospect.

The reward for overcoming the access inconveniences is the enjoyment of 4.5 miles of sloping and vertical sandstone ledges and boulder gardens, all seldom set apart by significant pools. Ledges can be high and complex. Playing holes abound, as do some fearsome boat-eating holes. You will want to scout a short chasm located below the second island, where the creek constricts between jagged, undercut walls to roar through a complex Class 6 rapid. If you have any doubts about trying this dangerous flume, do not hesitate to carry on the right. Should this formidable stream claim any boats or bodies, a dirt road (private) runs parallel to the creek on the left.

HAZARDS: Dangerous rapid lined by undercut rocks, below second island.

WATER CONDITIONS: Canoeable in spring during snowmelt and within three days of hard rain.

GAUGE: Painted canoe gauge on right abutment of Pa. Rte. 653, southeast of Normalville, should read over zero. Up to 1.0 foot is a delight. Above that level conditions gets progressively bigger and meaner. Do not bite off more than you can chew, or the creek may chew you.

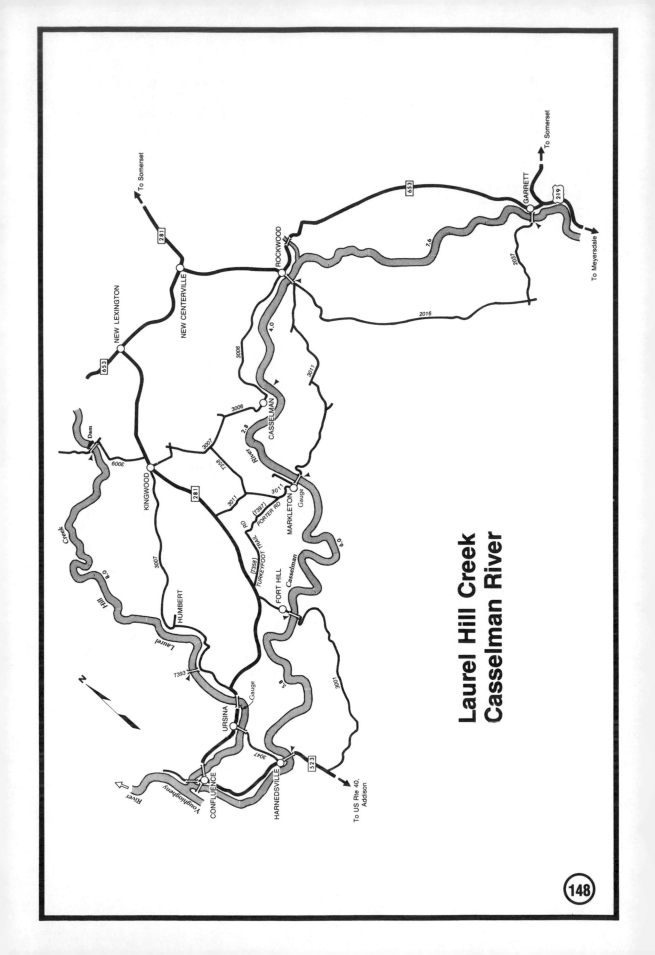

Laurel Hill Creek
Casselman River

148

Casselman River

INTRODUCTION: The Casselman river starts high atop the plateau of western Maryland and then follows a great arc across Somerset County, Pennsylvania to recharge the Yough at Confluence. After it passes Garrett, the Casselman's valley constricts to a gorge and remains that way almost to Harnedsville. All of this gorge offers attractive paddling, available in segments that you can select according to your ability. If you enjoy a river of intermediate difficulty, try the playful six miles between Markleton and Fort Hill. If you enjoy an easy but fast river, try the rest.

Section 1. Garrett to Markleton					
Gradient	Difficulty	Distance	Time	Scenery	Map
17	1 to 2	14.4	4.5	Good	148

TRIP DESCRIPTION: This section flows through a pretty, wooded gorge that suffers some from an overly visible railroad grade and some forest fire damage. After a few warm-up rapids, the river slows to a long reach of mostly smooth water extending to Rockwood. Below Rockwood the river begins accelerating through a long series of riffles and rapids that become progressively more challenging. Be aware that landowner relations at Markleton have been troubled. Avoid the north end of the bridge and be on your best behavior elsewhere.

HAZARDS: None.

WATER CONDITIONS: Canoeable in spring during snowmelt and within four days of hard rain.

GAUGE: USGS gauge at Markleton (call Pittsburgh) should read at least 2.4 feet.

Section 2. Markleton to Fort Hill					
Gradient	Difficulty	Distance	Time	Scenery	Map
30	2 to 3	6.0	2.0	Very Good	148

TRIP DESCRIPTION: This has long been the most popular segment of the Casselman because of its sustained and delightful whitewater. Not only is it fun as a downriver run, but it is also an ideal place to play or to practice your basic whitewater moves. It perfectly fills the niche for someone who is outgrowing novice whitewater, but is not yet ready for the difficulties of the Lower Yough. The rapids are composed of patches of small to car-sized sandstone boulders and small ledges. The rapids are often long and, at moderate levels, quite technical. As the river steepens, the gorge deepens. You will find it pretty through here, especially where the railroad bypasses a long, horseshoe bend by tunnelling through the mountain.

If Markleton's access difficulties ever increase, you should consider starting upstream at Cassel-man or even Rockwood. While this lengthens the trip, it compensates by being a very good warm-up. Also, if you are energetic, you might continue six easy miles on past Fort Hill to Pa. Rte. 523 at Harnedsville. The exciting whitewater continues part way into this stretch,and the scenery is impressive to the end.

HAZARDS: None.

WATER CONDITIONS: Same as Section 1.

GAUGE: Same as Section 1.

Laurel Hill Creek

INTRODUCTION: Draining the east slope of its namesake, Laurel Hill Creek flows to a meeting with the Casselman River just a few yards above that river's meeting with the Yough, at Confluence. While the entire creek is worthy of exploration, one particularly remote and rapid reach of the lower creek, near Kingwood, has long been popular with boaters.

Section 1. SR3009 to T393					
Gradient	Difficulty	Distance	Time	Scenery	Map
45	1+ to 3−	8.0	2.0	Very Good	148

TRIP DESCRIPTION: Put in below Whipkey Dam, a six-foot-high weir that backs up a long, summer home-lined pool. More houses persist for about a mile below the dam, after which deep and empty forest reclaims the creek. This stretch starts with riffles. Then as the miles flow by the pitch steepens, and the creek dashes down long rapids of small boulders and a few low ledges. Though pushy, this section can be managed by tutored novices. As the best of the whitewater concludes, the creek begins to scurry through a confusing stretch of braided channels. Be alert for strainers here. The channels eventually combine, woods yield to farms, and a graceful covered bridge marks the take-out. Just a few steps get you from the water to your vehicle.

HAZARDS: Strainers on braided section.

WATER CONDITIONS: Canoeable in spring during snowmelt and within three days of hard rain.

GAUGE: USGS gauge at Ursina (call Pittsburgh) should be at least 2.0 feet.

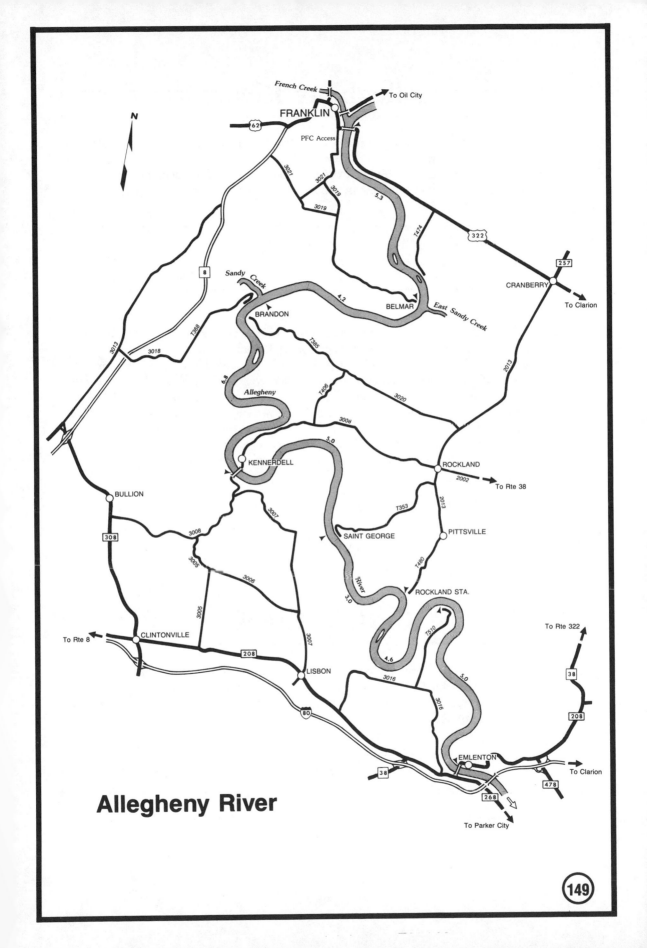

Allegheny River

149

Allegheny River

INTRODUCTION: It is difficult to find a scenic big river in western Pennsylvania. Most are lined by industry, towns, and highways and are developed for commercial navigation. But a 34-mile stretch of the Allegheny, between Franklin and Emlenton, retains much of the elegant flavor that once characterized most of these rivers. Try it if you like your rivers roomy and mellow.

Section 1. Franklin (U.S. Rte. 322) to Emlenton (Pa. Rte. 208)					
Gradient	Difficulty	Distance	Time	Scenery	Map
3	A to 1 –	34.0	11.0	Good	149

TRIP DESCRIPTION: Put in at the PFC access below the U.S. Rte. 322 Bridge, along Elk Street, Franklin. In the following miles, the river valley becomes canyon-like, complete with a fringe of rock cliffs for a rim. The banks are often lined by boulders that would appear much more impressive if they derived their scale from a smaller river. No highways follow this stretch, and even the ubiquitous railroad shortcuts some loops via tunnels. The only fault with this section is the abundance of summer homes that infest almost every bend and view. Their impact, however, like the boulders, is lessened by the size of the river and canyonsides.

This is a beginner run. The river usually flows smooth, only occasionally quickening through wide open riffles. The worst navigation problem on this wide river may be wind.

HAZARDS: None.

WATER CONDITIONS: Always canoeable from spring thaw until winter freeze.

GAUGE: USGS gauges at Franklin and Parker (call Pittsburgh) respectively get down to around 2.8 and 1.8 feet during summer and early fall low flows.

Buffalo Creek

INTRODUCTION: The beauty of Buffalo Creek is its proximity to Pittsburgh, only 23 miles from The Point as the crow flies. Entering the Allegheny River at Freeport, Buffalo follows an attractive course through a so far little developed neighborhood, and in doing so, it affords the urban refugee some pleasant interludes of isolation. A small, wet weather creek, this is a good springtime run on which novices can stretch their wings.

Section 1. Worthington (SR4010) to mouth					
Gradient	Difficulty	Distance	Time	Scenery	Map
12	1 +	20.3	6.0	Fair to Very Good	150

Buffalo Creek

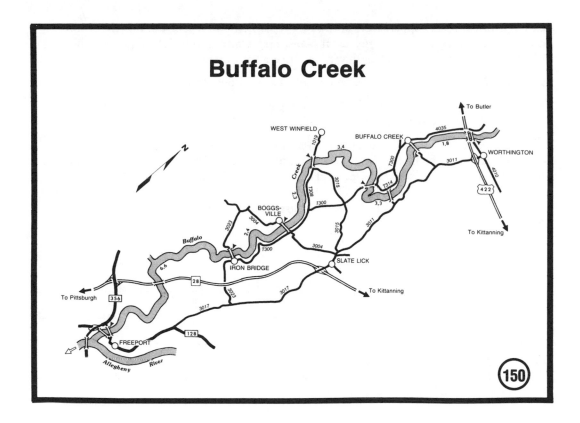

WEST WINFIELD

BUFFALO CREEK

To Butler

4035

1,8

WORTHINGTON

3011

To Kittanning

422

4010

BOGGS-VILLE

Buffalo

IRON BRIDGE

6.6

T300

SLATE LICK

3004

3015

3011

To Kittanning

28

To Pittsburgh

356

3023

3017

3017

FREEPORT

128

Allegheny River

150

TRIP DESCRIPTION: Aesthetically, this is a hot and cold trip. So regard a start as far up as Worthington as a warm-up only. The passage to the village of Buffalo Creek is narrow and swift, and may harbor a few strainers. The surroundings are woodsy and pleasant, but SR4035 follows the right bank and proves to be a source of much litter.

From Buffalo Creek to T300 (Wilson Road), the route is more remote, flowing first through a wooded ravine, then past farmland. Some big, mossy sandstone boulders and rock shelves enhance the scenery while some houses and camps detract. Riffles are easy and frequent.

The first of two particularly choice sections begins at T300 and extends to SR3015, near West Winfield. The creek passes through a seemingly remote wooded gorge. A steeper gradient offers frequent and sometimes long riffles or easy rapids. One spot, where a jumble of boulders clog the creek and form a small, steep chute (about three quarters of a mile below T300) has a troublesome history with the inexperienced.

Between West Winfield and Iron Bridge, the valley opens a bit and things seem not so remote. A soft-surface secondary road follows the left bank while an old, abandoned railroad grade generally blends into the scenery on the right. The valley is fairly populated around Boggsville. As tributaries slowly enlarge the creek, the pools become longer now but there are still plenty of easy rapids.

Below Iron Bridge, Buffalo Creek is prettiest, flowing for much of the way through a deep, wooded gorge. Riffles are frequent, easy, and continue to the backwater of the Allegheny River dam pool, which begins about a mile above the mouth, near the brickworks in Freeport. To completely avoid this slackwater, poke around the west side of Freeport and get permission to take out on private property opposite the brickworks. Your first public take-out is at the foot of High Street, left bank, by the sewage treatment plant. Last choice is to paddle a quarter mile up the Allegheny to a public ramp along Riverside Drive at 4th Street.

HAZARDS: Occasionally strainers plug the narrow upper creek.

WATER CONDITIONS: Canoeable in spring and again in late fall, within five days of hard rain, above West Winfield, and within a week, below.

GAUGE: There is a USGS gauge about two miles below Iron Bridge, on the right. But it is on private property and hard to reach. So look at riffles below SR4010, Worthington, and if they are clearly passable, you should have enough water. Roughly, McConnells Mill gauge, on Slippery Rock Creek (call Pittsburgh), should be over a foot and the USGS gauge at Idaho, on nearby Crooked Creek (call Corps of Engineers, Pittsburgh District), should be over 3.5 feet to start at Worthington.

Blacklick Creek

INTRODUCTION: Blacklick Creek is born upon the high, icebox of a plateau that is Cambria County, to flow many abused and battered miles to meet the Conemaugh River near Blairsville. Its prime section, where it cuts through the northern end of Chestnut Ridge, offers a challenging run for intermediate and advanced paddlers.

Section 1. Heshbon (Pa. Rte. 259) to Josephine (T660)					
Gradient	Difficulty	Distance	Time	Scenery	Map
41	1 to 4 –	6.6	2.0	Poor to Good	151

TRIP DESCRIPTION: The whitewater actually begins just above Heshbon, but pursuing that little bit is not worth paddling the 3.5 extra miles of sluggish and flat water from Pa. Rte. 56, the next put-in upstream. When you gaze upon the scene that greets you at and below Heshbon, you will surely grasp the meaning of the expression "raping the land." The canyon slopes are a collage of past mining abuse: strip mine gashes, slag heaps, rusting equipment, and burnt timber. And at the foot of all this flows a sickly tan Blacklick Creek, dotted with orange boulders, all the result of acid drainage from exposed coal and shale seams. This type of pollution, fortunately, is not a hazard to boaters.

Even more fortunately, the river will quickly distract you with a wonderous display of almost continuous rapids, little ledges, boulder patches, playable holes, and surfable waves. While most of the whitewater weaves a technical course, there is still plenty of room for mistakes. Two exceptions occur where the river constricts. The first spot is a steep ledge and boulder drop, early in the run, shot left of center via a tight slot. The second spot, about two miles farther, requires a tight diagonal left to right power move to avoid feeding yourself to a big and hungry hole at the bottom. This spot is hard to recognize. If this is your first run, you will probably know that you are there by the fact that you are stuck in a big hole at what you though was an innocuous spot.

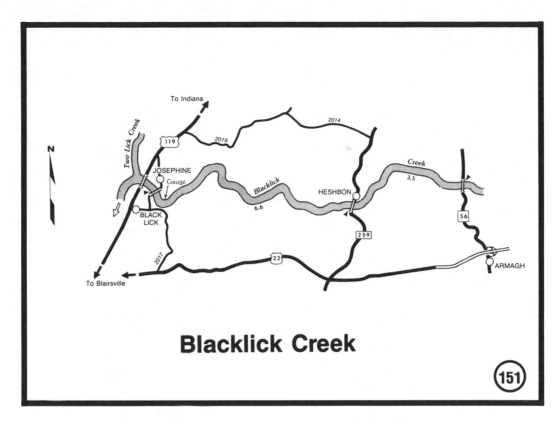

Blacklick Creek

(151)

After the first few miles, Blacklick begins to organize its gradient into distinct rapids and pools, so that you now have time again to observe the scenery. By now the mine-scarred slopes have been replaced by state game lands. Now it is a joy to drift by attractive wooded hillsides, sandstone outcrops, and patches of rhododendron. Only the banks, which have been recently traumatized first by a flood, then by the railroad's rebuilding efforts, remain ugly at times.

HAZARDS: None.

WATER CONDITIONS: Canoeable in spring during snowmelt and within three days of hard rain.

GAUGE: USGS gauge above Josephine (call Pittsburgh) should read over 4.1 feet. Canoe gauge on PA. Rte. 259 should be over 2.5 feet.

Stony Creek

INTRODUCTION: About half of Somerset County drains into Stony Creek and then funnels into Johnstown and the Conemaugh River. Johnstown is a city marked by a history of terrible floods, and Stony has certainly been a contributor. In 1977 Stony carried the entire load, devastating the city and taking lives. But while it has proven a cruel creek to Johnstown, Stony Creek has provided a trove of delights for whitewater boaters. With two fine whitewater sections and a handful of raucous tributaries, your energy will run out before the whitewater does.

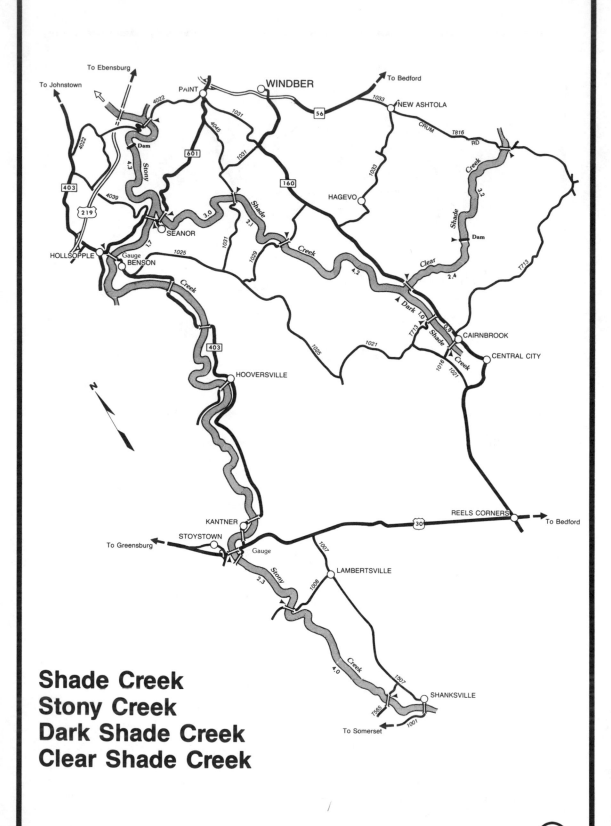

Shade Creek
Stony Creek
Dark Shade Creek
Clear Shade Creek

Section 1. T565 to U.S. Rte. 30					
Gradient	Difficulty	Distance	Time	Scenery	Map
71	3 to 4	6.2	2.0	Good to Very Good	152

TRIP DESCRIPTION: T565 crosses Stony via a covered bridge, and any run that starts at a covered bridge cannot be all bad. This one is all good. Cloudy green water, somewhat tainted by mine drainage, rushes down a bed of small boulders and some shallow, sloping ledges. The ledges form some fine playing holes. Rapids are almost continuous and initially steep. But your biggest concern on this section is a perennial logjam lodged on a right hand bend shortly below the start. It really sneaks up on you, though you can usually sneak it on the extreme right. Finally, although the whitewater is excellent, it is not so fierce that you must ignore the fine scenery, which is usually dominated by a thick facade of hemlock and rhododendron.

HAZARDS: Logjam about half mile below start.

WATER CONDITIONS: Canoeable in spring during snowmelt and within three days of hard rain.

GAUGE: Painted canoe gauge on U.S. Rte. 30 should be over two inches. Roughly, USGS gauge at Markleton, on Casselman River (call Pittsburgh), should be over 3.3 feet.

Section 2. Holsopple (Pa. Rte. 403) to SR4022					
Gradient	Difficulty	Distance	Time	Scenery	Map
35	3 to 4	6.0	2.0	Good to Very Good	152

TRIP DESCRIPTION: First Quemahoning Creek joins, then comes Shade Creek, to swell Stony to a respectable mountain river. It is characterized by tiers of tilting ledges that create some awesome stoppers and waves when the water is high. The best rapids start just above Shade Creek and extend to the end. At moderate levels these long rapids are adequately spaced by pools, and the playing is superb. When you reach an island, about a mile below Shade Creek, take the right side of the island but stick to the left side of that passage to avoid some nasty holes. A little farther, a high dam is easy to spot and easy to portage, on the left. Below this dam, on a right hand bend, a difficult to spot diagonal pipeline drop forms a lethal roller. This is runnable towards the left, via a slot that lines up with a downstream boulder. Scout, and if there is any doubt, carry on the right. The going is then easy to the end.

HAZARDS: High dam and pipeline crossing, both carries. At high water (over 3.0 feet at Holsopple) there are some nasty holes to avoid.

WATER CONDITIONS: Canoeable in spring during snowmelt and within five days of hard rain.

GAUGE: Painted gauge on Pa. Rte. 403, Holsopple (bridge has yellow-tiled piers), should be over 1.5 feet. USGS gauge at Ferndale (call Pittsburgh) should be over 3.5 feet. Roughly, USGS gauge at Markleton, on Casselman River (call Pittsburgh), should be over 2.7 feet.

Shade Creek

INTRODUCTION: Shade Creek is formed by the meeting of Dark Shade and Clear Shade creeks. It flows nine and a half wonderful and exhilarating miles down to Stony Creek near Windber, creating an intermediate to advanced course that would please just about anyone. And if that is not enough to satisfy you, just come here in high water, start on Dark Shade at Cairnbrook, and finish on Stony Creek near Paint. The step by step transition from the pick and choose technicality of Dark Shade to the crashing, rolling, foaming, and stopper-studded mayhem of a high Stony, all in one run, is to be found nowhere else in Pennsylvania. It is unbelievable.

Section 1. Confluence Dark and Clear Shade Creeks to mouth					
Gradient	Difficulty	Distance	Time	Scenery	Map
58	3 to 4	9.6	3.0	Good to Very Good	152

TRIP DESCRIPTION: Shade Creek was once characterized by a fairly even Class 2 to 3 descent over a cobble bed, punctuated by periodic drops over sloping ledges. Then along came the summer flood of 1977, which rammed downstream all the cobbles and boulders in the bed, similar to the kicking and kinking of a rug. The resulting stairstep descent over boulder and cobble piles has made this creek far more challenging, often resembling parts of Maryland's North Branch Potomac River above Kitzmiller. The ledges, of course, did not move, and some strainers have appeared on braided spots, all to round out the challenge.

Though discolored water and some strip mining scars exist, the creek is usually pretty, flowing down a shallow gorge and between banks bound in thickets of rhododendron.

Start this run at Pa. Rte. 160 on Clear Shade, or if that is too low, carry in a hundred yards along the south bank to the confluence with Dark Shade. The last take-out on Shade Creek is Pa. Rte. 601, at Seanor. But it is much more fun to stay in your boat and continue on down Stony.

HAZARDS: Strainers in fast water.

WATER CONDITIONS: Canoeable in spring during snowmelt and within two days of hard rain.

GAUGE: None on creek. Judge riffles from bridge at Seanor. Roughly, USGS gauge at Markleton, on Casselman River (call Pittsburgh), should be over 3.5 feet.

Dark Shade Creek

INTRODUCTION: If the term "natural slalom" were in the dictionary, Dark Shade Creek would be used for the example. This tiny and tortuous tributary of Shade Creek drains just a patch of boggy, woody watershed north of U.S. Rte. 30, near Central City. It is seldom up, so any fan of steep and technical whitewater should drop whatever they are doing and rush up to Dark Shade the next time the monsoons hit Somerset County.

Section 1. Cairnbrook (SR1016) to mouth					
Gradient	Difficulty	Distance	Time	Scenery	Map
1 @ 94	1 to 4 +	1.9	1.5	Good to Excellent	152

TRIP DESCRIPTION: What a shame that this is so short. You get almost a mile of smooth to riffly water on which to warm up, followed by an abruptly starting downhill tumble for a mile. And then it is done. A jumble of small to car-sized boulders and sloping ledges create a mile-long maze down which you must patiently pick your way. At moderate levels, an experienced boater should be able to boat scout and eddy hop through this whole stretch. While the water and rocks are discolored by acid mine drainage, the combination of green walls of rhododendron, hemlock-shaded banks, and the big boulders is beautiful. Of course, if this is your first descent of Dark Shade, there could be unicorns, dancing naked ladies, and palm trees, and you probably would not notice. Such is the nature of good whitewater. Take out by carrying up the south bank of Clear Shade Creek to Pa. Rte. 160. Better yet, keep going down Shade Creek.

HAZARDS: The river, if you are not ready for it.

WATER CONDITIONS: Canoeable in spring during rapid snowmelt or within a day of hard rain.

GAUGE: None. Walk down Clear Shade from Rte. 160 to Dark Shade. Look upstream. If that last wide rapid looks runnable, then the rest is adequate.

Clear Shade Creek

INTRODUCTION: The pursuit of coal has not been kind to the land and streams of Somerset County. So it is truly a wonder that Clear Shade Creek has somehow escaped destruction and still lives up to its name. Rushing out of the high backcountry of Forbes State Forest, east of Windber, this occasionally watered intermediate run will delight anyone lucky enough to catch it.

Section 1. Crum Road, T816 to mouth					
Gradient	Difficulty	Distance	Time	Scenery	Map
43	A to 3 +	5.6	2.0	Very Good to Excellent	152
2.4 @ 71					

TRIP DESCRIPTION: This run may only be 5.6 miles long, but it seems like a wilderness visit. You begin to feel that isolation before you ever set knee into your canoe, as you drive down the endless three miles of the narrow and deserted forest road out of New Ashtola.

For the first half of the trip, Clear Shade is narrow, shallow, clear, and fast. The gradient is mild, and the rapids are straightforward. The halfway point is marked by a little reservoir that could pass for a natural pond. But this is a municipal water supply. You should not really be paddling on it, but chances are that no one will be there to notice. Immediately below the dam (carry right) the creek tilts seriously downhill, dashing over continuous cobble bars, ledges, and boulder patches. The path is rarely blind, as on Dark Shade, but the water is more pushy. In addition, the flood of 1977 devastated many of the banks (even though this is an undisturbed watershed). Besides spoiling the aesthetics, this condition has increased the incidence of strainers on this section. A steep drop just above Pa. Rte. 160, shot at center, climaxes the run. Take out here, unless you plan on continuing down Shade Creek (great idea).

HAZARDS: Dam and strainers.

WATER CONDITIONS: Canoeable in spring during rapid snowmelt and within a day of hard rain.

GAUGE: None. Judge at Rte. 160.

Redbank Creek

INTRODUCTION: Redbank Creek is a long one, running over 50 miles from its channelized birth at the confluence of Sandy Lick Creek and the North Fork in Brookville to its quiet meeting with the Allegheny River near East Brady. It cuts deeply into the rugged landscape of Armstrong, Clarion, and Jefferson counties to form an exceptionally pretty canoe trail that is conveniently close to Pittsburgh. Redbank is a beginner's run that so far has received much less attention than it deserves. Two sections are especially worth floating.

Section 1. Summerville (SR3007) to Mayport (Pa. Rte. 556)					
Gradient	Difficulty	Distance	Time	Scenery	Map
7	A to 1 −	10.6	3.5	Very Good	153

TRIP DESCRIPTION: Below Summerville Redbank burrows into a shallow gorge. This is a remote passage where to the left is a solid green wall of hemlock and to the right is a hardwood forest with rhododendron understory. The riverbanks are all grassy, all of which makes this a tempting stretch on which to camp. The water runs mostly smooth with occasional little riffles.

If you choose to continue through to Section 2, a drab connecting passage, there is one hazard. Be sure to get out before the deadly six-foot dam just above the Pa. Rte. 28 Bridge in New Bethlehem. There is an easy carry on the right.

HAZARDS: None.

WATER CONDITIONS: On the average, runnable levels usually prevail from ice-out until late May. In late fall, this creek usually stays up for a week after a hard rain.

Redbank Creek

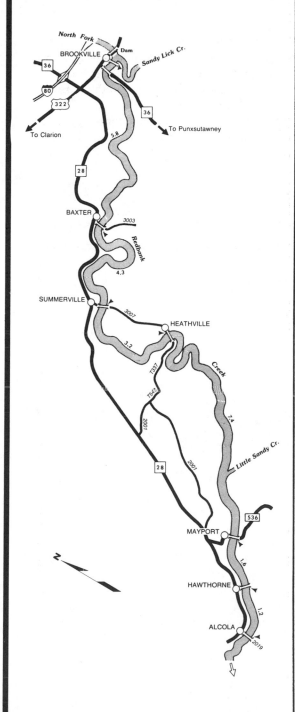

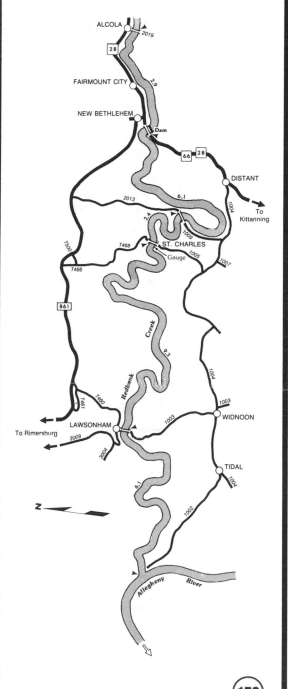

(153)

GAUGE: USGS gauge at St. Charles, left bank about 100 yards below bridge (call Pittsburgh or inspect on site), should read at least 3.6 feet.

Section 2. New Bethlehem (Pa. Rte. 28) to mouth					
Gradient	Difficulty	Distance	Time	Scenery	Map
9	A to 1	23.9	8.0	Very Good	153

TRIP DESCRIPTION: This is a beautiful and remote stretch entrenched in a fairly deep, wooded gorge. A lightly travelled railroad, a few logging scars, some camps (mostly clustered around bridges), and an old brickworks are the only civilized incursions. Again, there is a lot of hemlock on the left and again, the banks are all grassy, but now often dotted with sandstone boulders. And once again, you just might want to spend a night down there.

The water here is faster than on Section 1 with frequent riffles, riffles that are usually broad, rocky, but still easy. The finish is on the backwater of the Allegheny River dam pool. You can take out right at the mouth, at the end of SR1002.

HAZARDS: None.

WATER CONDITIONS: Same as Section 1.

GAUGE: Same gauge as for Section 1, but this stretch may be passable an inch or two lower.

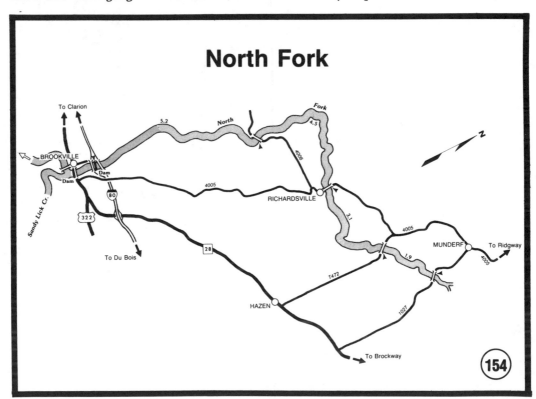

North Fork

INTRODUCTION: You may ask, North Fork of what? Geographically speaking, it is the north fork of Redbank Creek. But North Fork is its whole name. The North Fork, Mill Creek, and Sandy Lick Creek all come together in Brookville to form big Redbank Creek. All are pretty streams. But the North Fork is the most unspoiled. Free of even the ubiquitous railroad, this is a first class remote canoe route that only wet weather can provide.

Section 1. SR1027 to Brookville (I-80)					
Gradient	Difficulty	Distance	Time	Scenery	Map
15	A to 2 –	14.7	3.5	Excellent	154

TRIP DESCRIPTION: Most notably, this is a trip through the woods. From the start, a green fringe of hemlock lines the banks and a mix of hardwood and evergreens cloth the slopes that slowly rise to form a gorge. A few houses cluster about the first roadbridges. And then you see no more until just above Brookville, where a sumptious stone lodge complex lines the right bank. This comes as a shock, but it is quite pretty.

The creek manages a steady gradient down a cobbly bed with a few small ledges thrown in for variety. This creates almost continuous riffles or rapids that, if the water is up a few feet, can provide a bouncy run. Above I-80 a pool begins that ends at a ten-foot dam beneath the highway. Carry on the right and conclude your trip there, at the local park. If you choose to continue into Brookville, an aesthetically unrewarding extension to your trip, BEWARE of a dam with a killer hydraulic, directly beneath the Rte. 322 Bridge. This would be certain death for the unwary.
HAZARDS: Dams at I-80 and Rte. 322. Carry both on right.
WATER CONDITIONS: Runnable in spring during rapid snow melt and with three days of hard rain. GAUGE: None on creek. Very roughly, five feet on the USGS gauge at St. Charles, on Redbank Creek (call Pittsburgh), should provide enough water on the North Fork.

Clarion River

INTRODUCTION: The Clarion River begins up in Elk County, north of Ridgway, and flows well over ninety crooked miles to join the Allegheny River near nowhere important. The name supposedly was given by surveyors who thought the distant sound of the river possessed the "silvery mellowness of a clarion." It is obvious that back then, as now, men could get pretty goofy when they have been back in the woods for too long.

The Clarion is a superb canoeing river that for its entire length is suitable for beginners. It has a long season that runs well into the summer. It is good for both day trips or leisurely canoe camping trips of several days. Needless to say, such qualities make it quite popular, so come prepared to share your river with others.

Clarion River
Toby Creek
Mill Creek

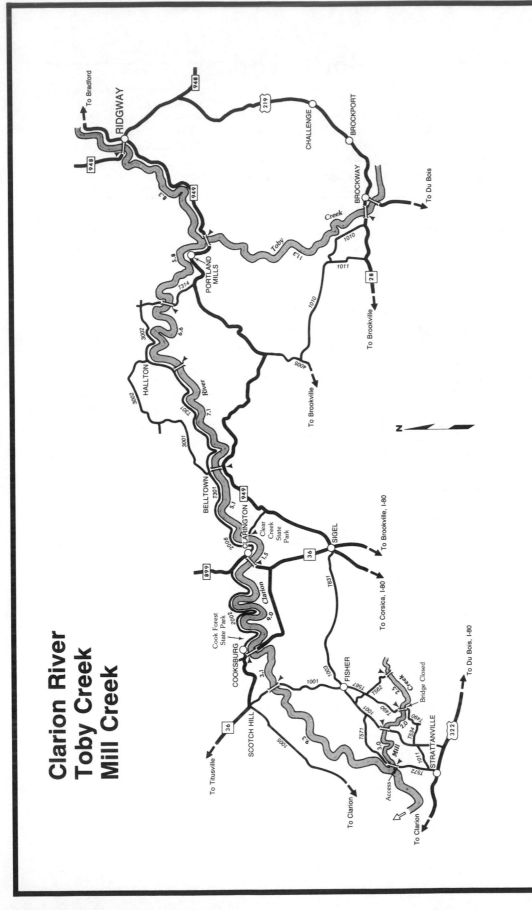

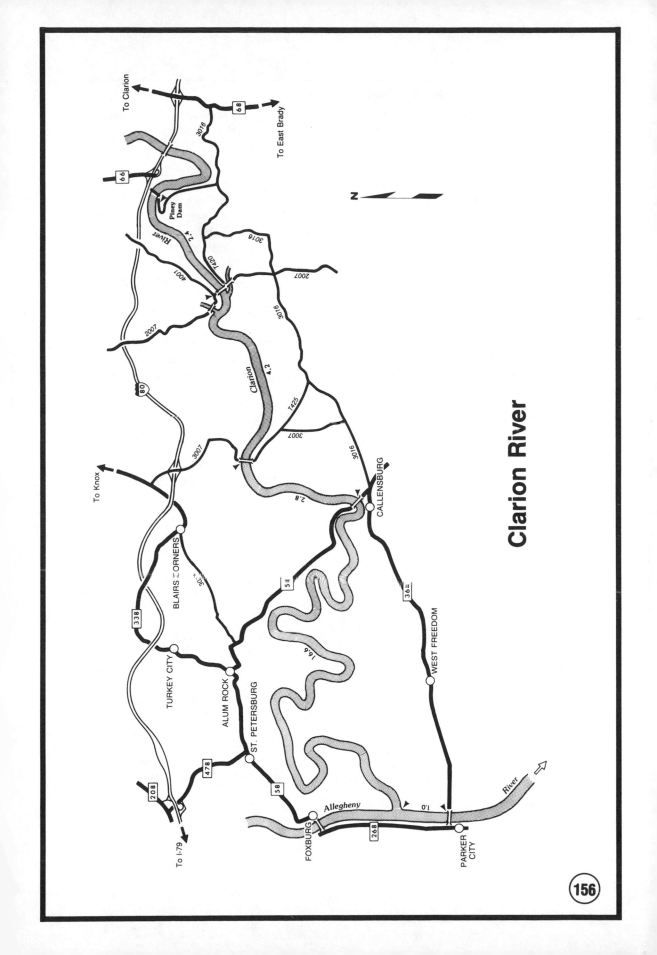

Clarion River

156

Section 1. Ridgway (Pa. Rte. 948) to Mill Creek					
Gradient	Difficulty	Distance	Time	Scenery	Map
5	A to 1	55.8	18.5	Good to Excellent	155

TRIP DESCRIPTION: Cradled in a stately wooded gorge, peace and quiet are the Clarion's trademark. This is generally a smooth but swift river, broken mostly by gentle and straightforward riffles formed by a cobble bottom. Except for one compressor station, there is little unnatural noise, as most nearby roads, where there are any roads at all, are lightly travelled. The railroad forsakes the Clarion also. You will find some strings of summer homes and that one compressor station, but otherwise the banks are undeveloped. Once below SR1001, the gorge is absolutely primitive. With the banks often structured as long and level, grassy benches, camping opportunities are common. The water quality is good (not good enough to drink), though there is a slight essence of paper mill from a point way upstream. This section ends at a PFC boat ramp on the backwaters of Piney Reservoir.

If you visit the Clarion, also set aside some time to visit nearby Cook Forest State Park. Cook Forest preserves a stand of virgin white pine and hemlock. If you cannot journey to the California redwood groves, a stroll through this green cathedral will give you a comparable spiritual high.

HAZARDS: None.

WATER CONDITIONS: Canoeable at Ridgway usually from spring thaw until early June and often again in November. By Cooksburg, adequate levels usually last until early August and rise up for several days following heavy summer showers.

GAUGE: USGS gauge at Cooksburg (call Pittsburgh) should read at least 2.8 feet to start at Ridgway and 2.3 feet to start at Cooksburg.

Section 2. Piney Dam to mouth					
Gradient	Difficulty	Distance	Time	Scenery	Map
6	A to 1	26.0	6.5	Good to Excellent	156

TRIP DESCRIPTION: The lower Clarion is similar to the upper river, but the gorge seems slightly deeper and the water slightly milder. This stretch is mostly roadless and undeveloped. What is peculiar about this section is that almost the entire flow comes from the Piney Reservoir Powerhouse. So the river turns on and off like a faucet, and it either gushes or is dry. The water from the dam is cold and clear. It always flows in a big enough volume to assure a fast run. Campsites this section are scarce, possibly because of the erosional power of such a high volume of clear water.

A carry down a steep slope by the USGS gauging station gets you into the water below the powerhouse. There is no easy access at the mouth of the river, so continue on down the Allegheny another mile, and exit on the river right at the Pa. Rte. 368 Bridge at Parker.

HAZARDS: Fast rising water.

WATER CONDITIONS: For continuous water, it is only up in spring if the weather is wet and the reservoir is full. Otherwise, it is only up when PENELEC is generating power, which is usually between 8 AM and noon and 5 PM to 9 PM on weekdays. Best months for reliable water, both on weekends and weekdays, are November, December, March, April, and May. The generation schedule is erratic and often shortened during drier months.

GAUGE: None. Power releases are usually 4,600 cfs and sometimes 5,400 cfs, which is plenty. Levels of over 5.0 feet at USGS gauge at Cooksburg (call Pittsburgh) combined with a full reservoir means good odds for water on this section, regardless of power demand.

Mill Creek

INTRODUCTION: Almost every tributary to the Clarion makes an exceptionally beautiful run during those brief periods of post-rain canoeability. Mill Creek gets the author's vote as the gem of these gems.

Section 1. T562 to mouth					
Gradient	Difficulty	Distance	Time	Scenery	Map
23	1 to 2	7.5	2.0	Excellent	155

TRIP DESCRIPTION: The truly hard-core can start above Pa. Rte. 949. But if you would prefer to avoid running the gauntlet through a cellulose sieve, you will start at T562. The creek rushes down a shallow, wooded gorge through the middle of a protective strip of state game lands. Only a few bridges interrupt this wilderness-like retreat. The path seems almost a green tunnel as it burrows into the dense hemlock stands that cloth the bottom of the gorge.

Mill Creek is a speedy passage with almost continuous shallow rapids and riffles. The stream bed is uniformly rocky, but spiced with little ledges and patches of small boulders. You only have to work at the end, to cross the short backwater of Piney Reservoir. Take out at the PFC access or by the roadside just upstream.

HAZARDS: Expect some strainers, often nasty ones formed by those fallen hemlocks.

WATER CONDITIONS: Up briefly in late fall or spring, during rapid snowmelt and within three days of hard rain.

GAUGE: None. Judge riffles at T490. Roughly, USGS gauges at Cooksburg, on the Clarion, and St. Charles, on Redbank Creek, should be over 5.0 feet on each (call Pittsburgh).

Toby Creek

INTRODUCTION: Toby Creek is a small and scenic tributary to the Clarion River, joining a few miles below Ridgway. It has an unpromising beginning in the coal country of southern Elk County, where strip mines, acid drainage, and old tires coated with yellowboy comprise much of the streamscape. The damage, nevertheless, proves reparable. The final 11 miles of creek, from

Brockway to the Clarion, burrow into a vast tract of state game lands, providing one of the most remote stream segments in western Pennsylvania. It is a quiet springtime run that is suitable for beginners and hermits.

Section 1. Brockway (Pa. Rte. 28) to mouth					
Gradient	Difficulty	Distance	Time	Scenery	Map
10	1	11.3	3.5	Very Good	155

TRIP DESCRIPTION: You can put in at an athletic field on the right bank below Pa. Rte. 28. After a drab and leveed start, Toby Creek heads off into a wooded, gorge-like valley. A road follows nearby on the right for the first few miles, but there are few houses along this stretch. The remainder of the way is roadless, making this a prime candidate for an overnight canoe camping trip.

The water, which is hazy from upsteam mining activity, runs smooth for much of the way. Riffles, formed by flat cobbles, little ledges, and a smattering of boulders, are well spaced until the end, where they run fairly continuous. Except where a strainer appears (rare), the stream is simple and forgiving.

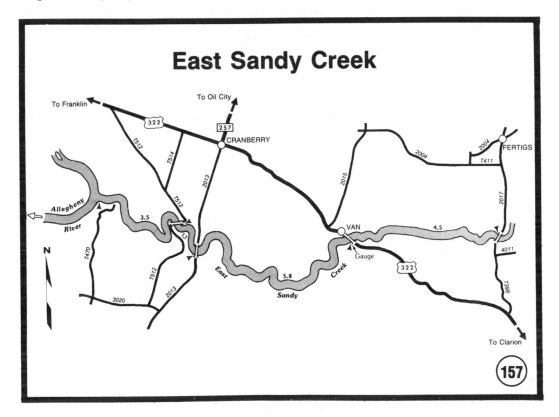

HAZARDS: Possible strainers.

WATER CONDITIONS: Canoeable in spring during snowmelt and within four days of hard rain.

GAUGE: Bottom of second tile from top on right abutment of Pa. Rte. 153, Challenge (seven miles upstream of Brockway), is zero. Roughly, USGS gauge at Cooksburg, on Clarion River (call Pittsburgh), should be over 4.9 feet.

East Sandy Creek

INTRODUCTION: East Sandy Creek is a beautiful little tributary that gushes into the Allegheny about five miles downstream of Franklin. It cuts down into the Allegheny's imposing bluffs and, in doing so, creates miles of easy whitewater. A wet weather delight.

Section 1. SR4011 to mouth					
Gradient	Difficulty	Distance	Time	Scenery	Map
19	A to 2+	14.9	4.0	Very Good to Excellent	157

TRIP DESCRIPTION: The attraction of the first few miles is the woodsy remoteness of Sandy's twisting passage through a chunk of state game lands. The water is not really white up here, just swift. A few fallen trees are the only complication. Whitewater paddlers will want to start at U.S. Rte. 322, Van, where the gradient begins to tilt more steeply. In the following miles a gorge forms. A railroad enters the valley, but it is inconspicuous except where its many bridges span the rushing waters. There are some camps around T512. Otherwise this is a wild setting.

The creek tumbles gently over a bed of large cobbles, some boulders, and a few ledges. The rapids are not continuous, but they are frequent and often long. Take out about 200 yards above the mouth where T470 dips to the floodplain. The final downhill reach of this road, unfortunately, at times of ice or extremely wet weather, may not be passable for two-wheel-drive vehicles.

HAZARDS: A few fallen trees on upper river.

WATER CONDITIONS: Mostly up in spring, during snowmelt or within three days of hard rain.

GAUGE: There is a painted gauge on the downstream side of the pier of the U.S. Rte. 322 Bridge at Van. A level of 5.5 units is excellent and 4.5 units probably represents zero (increments on gauge are neither English nor metric).

Conneaut Lake Outlet

INTRODUCTION: Sizable wetlands are rare in Pennsylvania, and sizable wetlands that are easily paddleable are even rarer. That is why Conneaut Lake Outlet is so special. Flowing out of Pennsylvania's largest natural lake, down the broad bed of an ancient river, the outlet is at times a creek, a swamp, a marsh, and even a shallow lake. It is a wild and often unspoiled stretch of water that, ironically, is partly manmade, the product of manipulation by the State Game Commission. And with much of its surroundings protected by state game lands, this is the place to see a lone bald eagle, great flocks of ducks, geese, and blackbirds, muskrats galore, and anything else that thrives in a wild and wet environment.

Section 1. U.S. Rte. 6 to mouth					
Gradient	Difficulty	Distance	Time	Scenery	Map
2	A	14.2	7.0	Good to Excellent	158

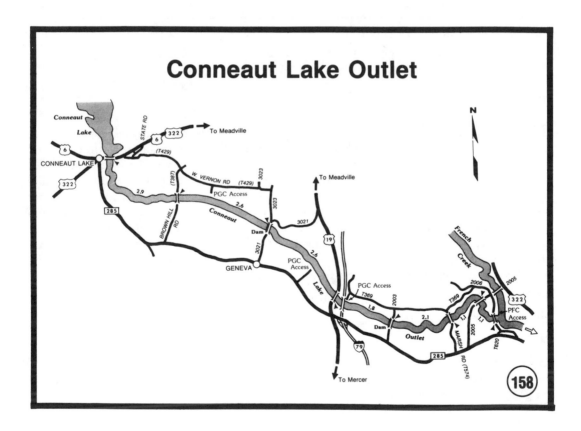

406

TRIP DESCRIPTION: The creek pours out of Conneaut Lake beneath the U.S. Rte. 6 and 322 Bridge, on the edge of the town of Conneaut Lake. The first half mile is the only challenging segment of this run as the channel is narrow, the current swift, and deadfalls are too plentiful. So take along a saw and do yourself and your successor a favor. The reward for this inconvenience is a beautiful, sombre passage through a swamp forest that shuts out most evidence of an outside world.

At Brown Hill Road swamp yields to open marsh. The rambling channel is initially a bit confusing and shallow, but it soon straightens and deepens. Views now are long, out across reeds and alders to a distant line of low, often wooded hills. There is a two-foot weir beneath the SR3021 Bridge. It has sometimes runnable (beginners should carry) chutes at both ends. About three quarters of a mile downmarsh and for about a half mile after, the path flows through a "game propagation area," through which the Game Commission prohibits passage. Law-abiding paddlers can resume the journey at an access area at the lower boundary.

The next few miles become more pond-like but the tranquility is disrupted by the noise and sight of the causeway of I-79. The waterfowl, fortunately, seem unperturbed. Immediately below I-79 vegetation fractures the channel into a puzzling labyrinth. But starting near the right side and slowly working left should deliver you back to open water. There is another weir beneath SR2003. Carry, because its end chutes are blocked by steel grates.

Below SR2003 marsh changes back into swamp and the channel follows a more winding passage. High banks return, ironically, at Marsh Road, and the best is now behind. The scenery of the few remaining miles are still mostly wooded and pleasant. So the creek is worth following to its confluence with French Creek where a Fish Commission access provides an easy take-out.

HAZARDS: Fallen trees at the start and sometimes below Marsh Road.

WATER CONDITIONS: The two weirs mentioned above maintain paddleable pools throughout the year, from just below Brown Hill Road to SR2003. Above or below these points, it is best to come during any normal spring, late fall, or after wet weather.

GAUGE: None. If you can clear the riffle beneath the U.S. Rte. 6 Bridge, you have more than enough in the shallow spots on the upper and lower creek.

Oil Creek

INTRODUCTION: The name is significant. Had you come to the banks of this creek 200 years ago, you might have been repulsed by the scum of oil tainting its surface. The oil had seeped out of the ground. Only Mother Nature was to blame. But this natural pollution was to thrust Oil Creek into every American history book when, along its banks, in 1859, Colonel Edwin Drake drilled for and struck this same oil. Drake's success, coupled with an American market that was searching for a new source of fuel for lighting, triggered this country's first oil boom. And it was this boom that launched this nation into the "petroleum age." The boom, like all booms, subsided. But they still pump oil up in Venango County and refine it too, as you will notice when you drive through Rouseville in your auto, whose engine is probably lubricated with oil refined from Pennsylvania crude.

The creek and its valley has now had over a century to recover from the environmental mayhem wrought by the oil rush. Trees and wildflowers have repossessed the land and it is likely to stay

Oil Creek, Pithole Creek

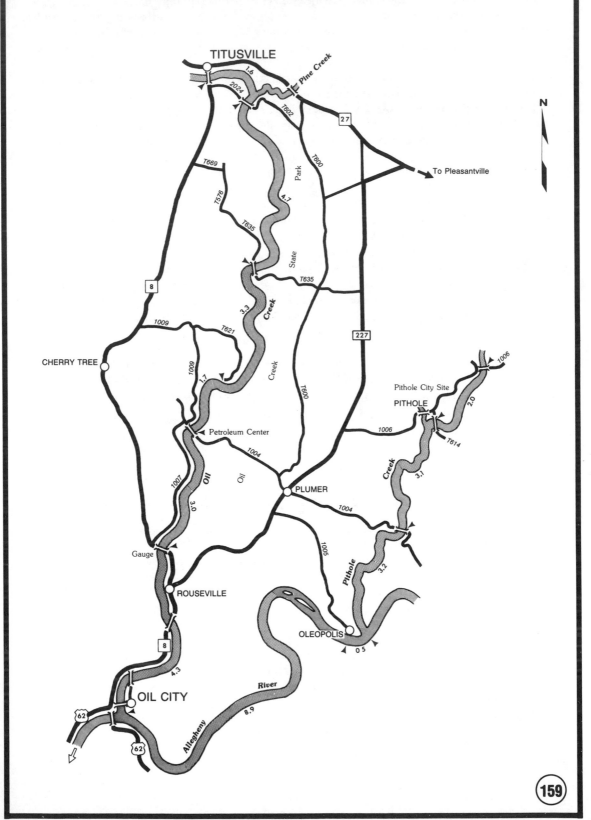

TITUSVILLE

Pine Creek

1.6

2024

T802

27

Park

T669

T576

4.7

To Pleasantville

N

T635

State

T635

8

T600

1009

T621

227

3.3

1006

Creek

Pithole City Site

CHERRY TREE

1009

PITHOLE

1.7

Creek

2.0

1006

Petroleum Center

T614

1004

3.1

1007

Creek

PLUMER

3.0

Oil

Oil

1004

Creek

1005

Gauge

Pithole

3.2

ROUSEVILLE

OLEOPOLIS

0.5

8

4.3

River

OIL CITY

8.9

62

Allegheny

62

159

that way as over 12 miles of Oil Creek's gorge is now within a state park. Here is a good destination for river lovers, whether they are canoeists coming to ride the spring highwater, or hikers and bikers coming to follow the creek by the park's fine system of trails.

Section 1. Titusville (Pa. Rte. 8) to Rouseville (Pa. Rte. 8)					
Gradient	Difficulty	Distance	Time	Scenery	Map
10	A to 1	14.3	4.5	Good	159

TRIP DESCRIPTION: This section starts on the edge of Titusville, out in a wide valley, flowing past high, wooded banks. But the creek soon turns a corner, where Pine Creek joins and boosts the flow, and enters a gorge. The hillsides are now all forested. While your passage will include glimpses of gas pipes and wells, a bicycle trail, a railroad grade, and one power line crossing, you should still enjoy a wonderful sense of remoteness. If the oil-soaked history of the area interests you, stops at Drake Well, Petroleum Centre, and old farm sites will add to the quality of your trip. Launching opportunities within the state park are plentiful.

As for the difficulty, Oil Creek is endowed with frequent, uncomplicated riffles where its waters rush over a gravel bottom. In between, the pools are often swift and shallow, and the channel is relatively broad. At any levels less than high water, this section is suitable for beginners.

HAZARDS: None

WATER CONDITIONS: Usually passable from March through late May in an average year and again in November and December.

GAUGE: None currently usable on site. A level of 2.5 feet on the USGS gauging station at the Rte. 8 Bridge near Rouseville (call Corps of Engineers, Pittsburgh) is about minimum. Also, a call to the state park office might also be productive.

Pithole Creek

INTRODUCTION: Pithole Creek is just a brook. It rises and falls in a flash, and you will be lucky to find it at a runnable level. So if you do catch it at that elusive water level, jump in your boat , paddle down from Pithole to the Allegheny, and enjoy Venango County's whitewater surprise.

Section 1. Pithole (T614) to mouth					
Gradient	Difficulty	Distance	Time	Scenery	Map
46	1 to 3	6.3	1.5	Excellent	159

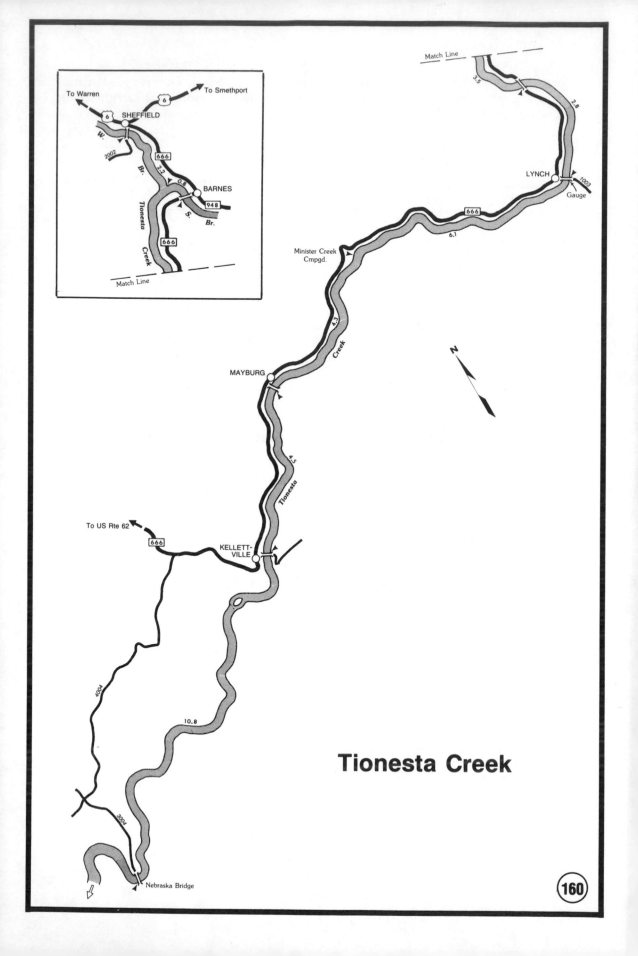

Tionesta Creek

160

TRIP DESCRIPTION: As you drive down SR1006 looking for the village of Pithole, do not blink or you will miss it. But realize that it was not always like that. Back in 1865 this was Pithole City. In that year, over a span of only five months, an isolated farm mushroomed to a town of 15,000. It was the discovery of oil here that lured all that population. And when the oil ran out, so did the citizens of Pithole City, all of them.

You put in on a cowpasture brook. You can start even farther upstream, but trees, pipes, and raking alders will make that a challenging, and possibly dangerous, task. Below Pithole, pastures soon yield to woods and a narrow gorge begins to take shape. Only a bridge interrupts the wild isolation of this hemlock-fringed corridor. The rocky stream slowly steepens and rapids are soon continuous. The last few miles require much maneuvering and are spiced by some boulder cluttered rapids with juicy drops that remind one of the Yough. There is no access to the mouth, so continue a half mile down the Allegheny to Oleopolis. The take-out will be private, so be sure to ask permission first.

HAZARDS: No regular problems, but deadfalls are always a possibility.

WATER CONDITIONS: Most likely caught up in spring, during rapid snowmelt or within two days of hard rain.

GAUGE: None. The first rapid below T614, just around the bend, is a good indicator.

Tionesta Creek

INTRODUCTION: Tionesta Creekdrains the heart of Allegheny National Forest. As one might expect of a creek flowing through such a nice setting, this is a beautiful canoe stream. With many navigable miles and a relatively long season, the Tionesta makes a fine alternative to the nearby Clarion River and is likely to carry less canoe traffic.

Section 1. Confluence West and South branches to SR3004					
Gradient	Difficulty	Distance	Time	Scenery	Map
7	A to 1	32.0	11.0	Good to Very Good	161

TRIP DESCRIPTION: This is a long and scenic stretch that you can easily break into segments of comfortable length. But there is no access to the confluence of the branches. So to start at the beginning of the creek, you must launch either 2.2 miles up the West Branch at SR2002 or 0.7 miles up the South Branch at Pa. Rte. 666. These first few miles of Tionesta are particularly attractive. It is a shallow stream rushing over frequent riffles in a narrow, densely wooded valley, with the nearby highway high above and seldom within view. The branches are roughly similar to the mainstem, just smaller and more twisty. Approaching the first Rte. 666 Bridge and continuing on down to Lynch, a concentration of camps mar the view. Below Lynch the gradient subsides, the creek widens, and long, often deep pools flow swiftly with simple riffles occasionally roughing the surface. Rte. 666 follows closely between Lynch and Kellettville, but is seldom obtrusive and, except during trout season, is lightly travelled. Throughout this stretch, Tionesta flows through a still narrow valley fringed by increasingly high, forested hillsides. On the bottoms, trees grow in park-like density and occasionally they are separated by glades. The banks are usually medium high and grassy. Camps appear sporadically, with concentrations of them around the few villages in this remote valley. Below Kellettville, the state highway leaves the river. You first float by a stretch of utterly devastated hillside forests, the destruction the result of tornados. But from there on a remote, beautiful valley envelops the creek down into Tionesta Reservoir. The backwater of the reservoir starts about two miles above SR3004 Bridge. This low bridge forms a barrier to boats, including motorboats. And if flatwater and motorboats do not bother you, then you can continue on another four and a half miles down this attractive and undeveloped lake to the Corps of Engineers access area near the dam.

HAZARDS: Trees are a possible problem on the two branches and in the first few miles.

WATER CONDITIONS: In an average year, the Tionesta below Lynch is usually passable from March (ice out) through late May and often again in November. To boat above Lynch and for more enjoyable levels below, catch during snowmelt or within five days of hard rain.

GAUGE: Use the USGS gauging station at Lynch (call the Corps of Engineers, Pittsburgh). A level of about 2.5 feet is minimum to start above the forks and 2.0 is minimum below Lynch. Judging from the road also works well. Very roughly, the USGS gauge at Cooksburg, on the Clarion (call Pittsburgh), should read at least 3.0 feet.

Brokenstraw Creek

INTRODUCTION: Brokenstraw Creek is a medium-sized tributary to the Allegheny River, merging from the west several miles below Warren. It is generally a mediocre stream, unworthy of inclusion in this "best of" chapter. But it is endowed with a short, wild stretch near its headwaters that makes a particularly rewarding outing suitable for beginners.

Section 1. Pa. Rte. 426 to Spring Creek					
Gradient	Difficulty	Distance	Time	Scenery	Map
2	A	7.0	3.0	Good	161

TRIP DESCRIPTION: One can start 2.5 miles upstream in downtown Columbus, at the confluence of Coffee Creek, for an attractive float through rolling, pastoral country and past some soothing, green hemlock groves. What makes the passage from Rte. 426 to Spring Creek so special is that it is an almost wild reach of river, lost in a rich and varied floodplain forest. You will see silvery beech, sinewy hornbeam, shaggy hickory, feathery hemlock, red-budding maple, and prickly hawthorne to name a few. Closer to the ground are streamside meadows of tall grass. This natural setting is blemished only by clumps of floating trash that are trapped against deadfalls.

The water is flat and deep. Though narrow, the tortuous channel is blocked by few deadfalls, and where they occur, the carry is usually easy because of low banks. If you start at Columbus, you will have to negotiate a few riffles.

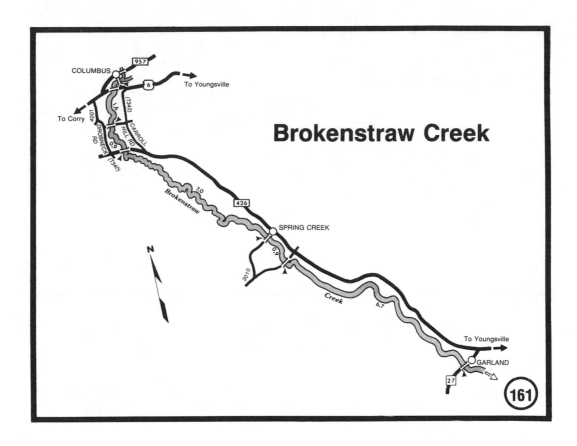

Deserving honorable mention are the succeeding 7.5 miles down to Garland. Regrettably, as the creek emerges from the jungle, it brushes by some houses, highways, and junk. But views of the converging wooded mountainsides and attractive farm valley provide an overall pleasant setting. In contrast with Section 1, this reach is shallow and the water speeds over a cobble bottom to form long, frequent riffles. Though only Class 1, braiding channels that sometimes bristle with strainers, raise the challenge.

HAZARDS: Possible strainers.

WATER CONDITIONS: Runnable almost anytime from late fall to freeze and from thaw to mid-summer. But to clear the riffles in the sections above and below, you need much more water, usually found in late fall and spring within a week of hard rain.

GAUGE: None on this section. Roughly, the USGS gauge at Youngsville (call Corps of Engineers, Pittsburgh) should be over 2.0 feet for Section 1 and over 3.3 feet for above and below. Enough water to clear the riffle just above Rte. 6 also indicates sufficient water in the riffly stretches.

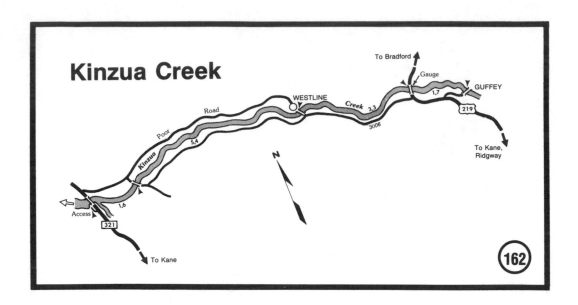

Kinzua Creek

INTRODUCTION: Kinzua Creek (pronounced Kin'zoo, Indian for "turkey") flows into the Allegheny River a few miles above the huge dam of the same name. This creek is probably best know for the high, spindly railroad trestle that spans its upper canyon. It deserves more fame for its merit as a scenic canoe trail.

Section 1. U.S. Rte. 219 to Pa. Rte. 321					
Gradient	Difficulty	Distance	Time	Scenery	Map
22	1	10.4	3.5	Very Good	162

TRIP DESCRIPTION: It is possible to start exploring this creek as far up as Kushequa (near Mt. Jewett), and it is all worthwhile. But the section below Rte. 219, and especially below Westline, is the best. The creek gushes through a gently-sloped, forested gorge. As is typical up here, the banks are often grassy benches, the bottomlands are often crowded by dark groves of hemlock, and the hillsides are dominated by beech, birch, and maple (a glorious combination in autumn). Just a few camps and those ubiquitous gas pipes and wells interrupt the wild setting.

The water, which is likely to be clear, rushes over lots of riffles and easy rapids. Its channel, unfortunately, frequently braids, resulting in many inconvenient strainers. A lot of beaver activity also does not help matters. The finish is on a short backwater of Kinzua Reservoir, with a good take-out on the left.

HAZARDS: Lots of strainers.

WATER CONDITIONS: Most often up in late fall or spring, during rapid snowmelt or within three days of hard rain.

GAUGE: There is a USGS gauge just above Rte. 219 (identified as Guffey, call Corps of Engineers, Pittsburgh). Consider 3.1 feet as minimal.

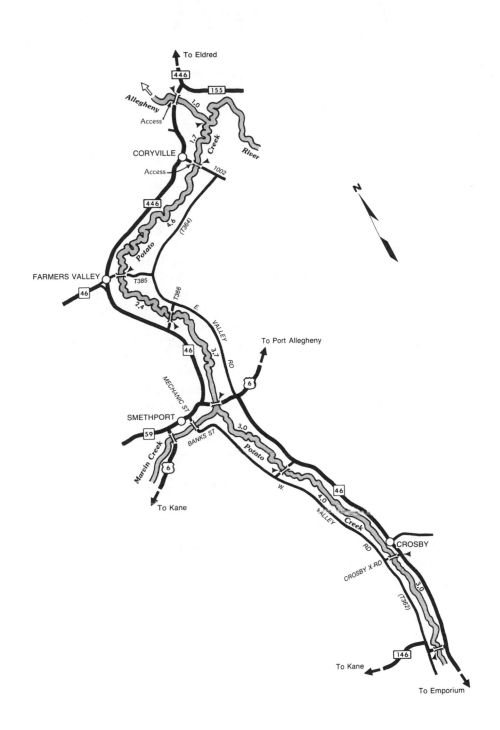

To Eldred

446

155

Allegheny

Access

1.0

CORYVILLE

Access

1.7

Creek

River

1002

446

4.6

Potato

(T364)

FARMERS VALLEY

T385

46

2.4

T366

E. VALLEY RD.

3.7

46

To Port Allegheny

6

MECHANIC ST

SMETHPORT

59

BANKS ST

3.0

Marvin Creek

6

Potato

W.

4.0

VALLEY

Creek

46

RD

To Kane

CROSBY

CROSBY X-RD

3.0

(T362)

146

To Kane

To Emporium

N

Potato Creek

163

Potato Creek

INTRODUCTION: Potato Creek is the first major tributary to the upper Allegheny River, draining the heart of chilly McKean County. It offers many miles of novice to beginner cruising in a peaceful and an amazingly uncluttered setting.

Section 1. Pa. Rte. 146 to mouth					
Gradient	Difficulty	Distance	Time	Scenery	Map
4	A to 1-	22.4	7.0	Good	163

TRIP DESCRIPTION: The first part of this run, to Smethport, meanders down a narrow, pastoral valley. The wooded bottomlands insulate you from most of the scattered dwellings that stick to the valley roads, but not from pleasing views of wooded hillsides. The creek here is narrow and crooked, with a swift current and frequent riffles. Strainers are possible, but rare.

A levee-bound flood channel sneaks the creek through Smethport. You should stop and explore this classic calendar-quality town with its main street lined by big frame houses. At Smethport, Marvin Creek enters from the left and doubles the flow.

If lower Potato twisted any more than it did, it would tie itself in a knot. This is a pretty reach where, even more than above, the creek hides back in a broad swath of rich, floodplain forest. These woods are particularly extensive in the last few miles. Medium to high mud banks confine your view to mostly trees. It is a good place to surprise some game or waterfowl. Flawing the view are a small refinery at Farmers Valley and a few contacts with roads, a railroad grade, and utility lines.

The Potato below Smethport is suitable for beginners. With generally smooth, deep water, it expends its modest two-foot-per-mile gradient over simple gravel-formed riffles. Look for a possible logjam or inconveniently placed overhanging tree to be your only complications. With no roads near the mouth, plan on a mile-long float down the Allegheny to a PGC access at Pa. Rte. 446.

HAZARDS: Possible logjams or fallen trees, even on broad lower reaches.

WATER CONDITIONS: Above Smethport, Potato normally has runnable levels in late fall and spring, during snowmelt or within a week of hard rain. Below Smethport, it has runnable levels almost any time from late October through mid-June and for a week after a hard summer rain.

GAUGE: There is a USGS gauge (call Corps of Engineers, Pittsburgh) at Rte. 6, Smethport. For above Smethport, minimum level is probably about 3.4 feet and for below, it is about 2.5 feet. Also, you can scout the riffle at the end of the flood channel in Smethport. Enough to float there is enough for all shallows below.

Twentymile Creek

INTRODUCTION: Twentymile Creek is just barely a Pennsylvania stream. Most of it flows across Chautauqua County, New York. But this little torrent is so beautiful and so different from any other stream in this book that it would be a sin to omit it.

From east of Erie, Pennsylvania, to Dunkirk, New York, the lands along Lake Erie rise quickly a thousand feet to a rolling plateau. Covered with farms and vineyards, this hardly looks like a landscape that would harbor mini-wildernesses and crashing whitewater. But it does. For the few little streams, like Twentymile, that flow north to the lake must make that thousand- foot plunge off of the plateau and in a short distance too. So in doing so they cut some remarkably beautiful and unspoiled gorges into the shale foundations of this escarpment.

Section 1. Chautauqua Co. Rte. 9 to mouth					
Gradient	Difficulty	Distance	Time	Scenery	Map
49	2 to 3, 4	10.5	4.0	Excellent	164

TRIP DESCRIPTION: As you gaze from the put-in bridge upon the complex pattern of criss-cross hydraulics and waves formed by the tilting rock bottom, the river is trying to tell you something about itself. And you should pay attention. For above all else, this is a ledge stream. Sharp

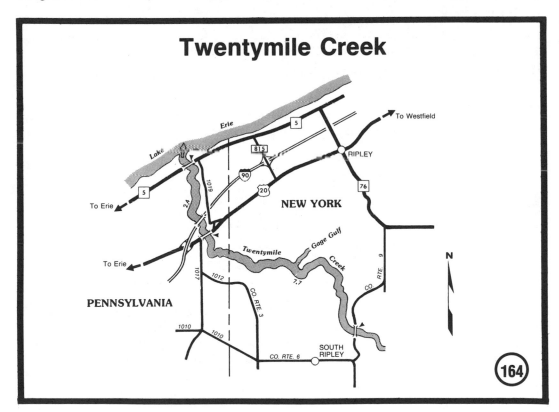

ones, smooth sloping ones, there are scores and scores of them. And it is likely that they will surprise and maybe even embarrass you with their unusual crosscurrents, deceptive routes, and deceptively powerful little hydraulics.

There are two problem spots on this run. The first is where Gage Gulf joins on the right, a few miles into the trip. Stop. Get out right here, above the blind bend, and scout. For the creek narrows to as little as six feet at the bottom of a v-shaped rock chasm as a powerful, twisting flume culminates with a sharp, irregular four-foot drop with a slightly undercut right abutment. A broach here could be a nightmare as slick, sloping rock walls backed by unstable, slippery clay and shale slopes would make rescue most difficult. And a capsize in this drop would be most violent. With a horrendous portage up those unstable slopes (and note that the little shards of shale are as sharp as broken glass), plan on having to run this drop if you run this creek. The other problem spot is at the downstream end of a tunnel underneath the Conrail tracks. Partitioned by a low concrete wall, the watered flume on the left ends with a sharp three-foot drop that at higher levels could have a strong hydraulic. Scout first, and if in doubt, carry down the right.

Most of this journey, until you approach Rte. 20, is a wilderness. It is a forested gorge where 300-foot shale cliffs grace many a bend. Most sidestreams plunge into Twentymile, over tiered cascades and falls. Wet weather multiplies their numbers. These streams are peculiar in the knife-sharp angles at which they intersect the creek.

The last public take-out is at Pa. Rte. 5. It is still another third of a mile down almost continuous whitewater to the mouth, where the almost shocking transition from torrent to what seems like an ocean makes this last bit worthwhile. Private roads reach both sides of the mouth and, with permission, offer you at least a reasonable hike out.

HAZARDS: The flume and drop below Gage Gulf is passable but potentially dangerous. So is the sharp drop beneath Conrail tracks (at U.S. Rte. 20). Strainers are usually few and seldom span the creek, but be ready for them.

WATER CONDITIONS: Best caught in spring during rapid snow melt or within a day of hard rain.

GAUGE: None. If you can negotiate the smooth ledges at the put-in with little or no scraping, water is adequate. Higher water might compound your problems at the above-mentioned trouble spots.

Addendum

Stony Creek

INTRODUCTION: Located less than 15 miles from downtown Harrisburg, Dauphin County's Stony Creek may be the finest wilderness canoe run in eastern Pennsylvania, albeit an ephemeral one. Draining but a sliver of a valley between Second and Stony mountains, most of its watershed is protected within a huge tract of state game lands. It is a wonderful escape.

Section 1. Cold Spring Road to State Game Lands Boundary					
Gradient	Difficulty	Distance	Time	Scenery	Map
24	1 to 2	13.1	5.0	Excellent	44

TRIP DESCRIPTION: A tolerable dirt road crosses over Second Mountain from Fort Indiantown Gap to deliver you to a tiny, rushing stream. For the next 13 miles you can forget civilization. There is no litter. The water is clear and clean. A few duck boxes and some glimpses of an old railroad grade are the only structures. This grade, incidentally, is now a fine hiker/biker trail — an alternate way to enjoy this setting. The scenery ranges from shrubby swamp with sweeping views of wooded mountainsides to deep forest where you see only a hemlock-lined corridor.

The run starts with an uneven gradient, the stream alternating between swamp and rapids. In this reach, you pay the toll for enjoying Stony, as some of the swamp passages are tangled slaloms, including one stretch where the waters thoroughly disperse through the shrubbery. A little sawing would go a long way to improve this run. In the swift pools, the water glides over a sandy bottom, while in the long rapids, the descent is over cobbles and small boulders. Expect some strainers here too. With the miles, the gradient increases, exceeding 40 feet per mile. Though simple, the continuous flush will delight you.

The take-out is ill defined, no place being ideal, and most of the riverside below being private. Scout for yourself.

HAZARDS: Expect some strainers in fast water.

WATER CONDITIONS: Catch in late fall, winter, and spring within two days of hard rain.

GAUGE: None. If riffle at put-in is passable, so is everything else. Roughly, USGS gauge at Harpers, on Swatara Creek (call Central PA) should be between 4.5 and 5.0 feet.

Section 2. State Game Lands Boundary to mouth					
Gradient	Difficulty	Distance	Time	Scenery	Map
19	1 +	6.5	2.0	Fair	44

TRIP DESCRIPTION: After Section 1, this stretch can only disappoint you. The mountainsides recede. The now hazy water is slower, but plenty of riffles remain. The waters float you by a drab collage of power lines, houses, backyards, and roads. It is best to end your trip above Pa. Rte. 225 to avoid a steep carry around a 15-foot dam. If you go to the mouth, continue a mile and a half down the Susquehanna to a PFC access at Fort Hunter.

HAZARDS: Some strainers and a 15-foot dam above Rte. 225 (carry right).

WATER CONDITIONS: Same as Section 1.

GAUGE: None. Scout from road or guess by Harpers USGS gauge.

Backward

So I hope that this gives you a few useful ideas on where to go paddling. Of course there are still some little creeks that this guidebook overlooked. Now it will be your turn to discover.

As if I have not given enough good advice, allow me to finish with one more tidbit. This advice is second hand, given to me one sunny day in May, from the banks of Penns Creek, by a jovial old fisherwoman. I will never forget her hollering, as I drifted off downstream, headed for an eventual rendezvous with the Susquehanna: "Hey! Don't tip your fanny in the Susquehanny." You remember that too.

See You On The River
Ed Gertler

Index